THE CHILD
IN THE WORLD OF TOMORROW
A Window into the Future

THE CHILD
IN THE WORLD
OF TOMORROW

A Window into the Future

GENERAL EDITOR
SPYROS DOXIADIS
Minister of Social Services, Greece

EXECUTIVE EDITOR
JAQUELINE TYRWHITT

ASSOCIATE EDITOR
SHEENA NAKOU

PERGAMON PRESS

OXFORD · NEW YORK · TORONTO · SYDNEY · PARIS · FRANKFURT

U.K.	Pergamon Press Ltd., Headington Hill Hall, Oxford OX3 0BW, England
U.S.A.	Pergamon Press Inc., Maxwell House, Fairview Park, Elmsford, New York 10523, U.S.A.
CANADA	Pergamon of Canada, Suite 104, 150 Consumers Road, Willowdale, Ontario M2J 1P9, Canada
AUSTRALIA	Pergamon Press (Aust.) Pty. Ltd., P.O. Box 544, Potts Point, N.S.W. 2011, Australia
FRANCE	Pergamon Press SARL, 24 rue des Ecoles, 75240 Paris, Cedex 05, France
FEDERAL REPUBLIC OF GERMANY	Pergamon Press GmbH, 6242 Kronberg-Taunus, Pferdstrasse 1, Federal Republic of Germany

First edition 1979

British Library Cataloguing in Publication Data

The child in the world of tomorrow
1. Children—Congresses
I. Doxiadis, Spyros   II. Tyrwhitt, Jaqueline   III. Nakou, Sheena
301.43′14   HQ767.82   78-41219

ISBN 0-08-023685-5

*Printed and bound at William Clowes & Sons Limited
Beccles and London*

CONTENTS

SOCIETY'S ROLE IN EDUCATION   237

SPECIAL SESSIONS   259

4. THE CHILD AND HEALTH   293

MORBIDITY AND MORTALITY TRENDS AND THE NEW ILLNESSES   295

HEALTH CARE: WHOSE RESPONSIBILITY?   325

FOREWORD

THIS book is not a collection of essays and papers, but a reflection of a very lively symposium which took place in Athens the first week of July 1978. Throughout the week more than 500 people were actively engaged in lectures, in discussions, and in a stimulating interchange of opinions. My foreword to this book should therefore reflect as far as possible what were our expectations and what we felt at the end of it. I thought that the best way to give to the reader a picture of what was in our minds and what actually happened would be to include most of my welcoming address and my concluding speech and then to add some thoughts about the book itself.

WELCOMING ADDRESS

In this ancient city, where it was believed and practiced that "man is the measure of all things," we have gathered scientists and professionals from five continents and ten disciplines in the hope that our ideas and our suggestions will help governments, agencies, and individuals to take action so that, in the world of tomorrow, no doors will be closed to any child because of poverty, preventable handicaps, ignorance, or illiteracy.

About 12 years ago I met with two good friends from abroad—Dr. Lourie and Dr. Aldrich—and three friends and associates in Athens—Dr. Valaes, Dr. Lapatsanis, and Dr. Pantelakis. We felt that an attempt should be made to explore the fate of our children in the world of tomorrow. Many things happened, much time was lost, and many obstacles were put in our way. Following the restoration of democracy in Greece, when our Institute of Child Health started working again, we began our efforts to make this plan a reality. At about the same time the first suggestions for an International Year of the Child were being forwarded to the United Nations. In December 1976 this was finally decided upon by the General Assembly of the United Nations and we felt that our old hope for a symposium on "the child in the world of tomorrow" could act as an introduction to the International Year of the Child as a "window into the future."

We approached Mr. George Rallis who was then Minister at the office of the Prime Minister and Minister of Education. He gave us his enthusiastic support, both moral and financial. We also received the support of other ministries, and, finally, we approached the President of the Hellenic Republic, Mr. Constantine Tsatsos, and he very kindly agreed to put this symposium under his auspices. We also asked for and received the cooperation of the following international agencies concerned with children: the World Health Organization, the United Nations International Childrens Fund, the Special Agency for the International Year of the Child, the United Nations Educational, Social, and Cultural Organization, the International Children's Centre, the CIBA Foundation and the World Society for Ekistics. We are grateful to all of them.

To make this symposium a reality we have had the help of very many people. I cannot possibly mention them all, but I consider it not only a duty but also a pleasure to mention specially two people without whose devotion and hard work the symposium could not have become a reality: these are the pediatrician, Dr. Sheena Nakou, and the Executive Director of the Institute, Mrs. Katherine Zachopoulou.

I do not want to give a lecture on any of the many topics that are going to be discussed during the next six days and will be published in the official proceedings of this symposium. I would, however, like to make a few personal observations as to why we are at present not happy with the fate of our children and why many recent well-meaning projects and programs have not been successful, and to draw your attention to some of the mistakes, deficiencies, and weaknesses we should try to avoid in the future. I shall mention four:

1. Our projects, programs, and policies have been too shortsighted

We have been thinking in terms of the needs of yesterday and today and not of the likely needs of our children tomorrow. We have not paid attention to the inevitable time lapse between the conception, planning, and implementation of a program. The various stages of a successful program must be measured in years, not in months. By the time a program conceived today is actually put into practice there may be a gap of five years or more, and by then the needs may be different. So my hope is that our symposium, by its focus on the future, will help remedy this first deficiency.

2. In the past, our outlook, programs, and policies have been formulated and implemented on a much too narrow and rigid basis

I hope that as a result of the discussions at this symposium—hearing participants of so many sciences and disciplines giving evidence of our past narrowness of outlook—our colleagues will be emboldened to take steps to avoid this in the future.

But it is not only our outlook; our policies and programs have also been too rigid. They have lacked the necessary elasticity and ability for adjustment. So that, even if the programs are monitored and even if there is a feedback mechanism, after the information has been collected and the need for change has been established, there are far too many administrative and legal obstacles and far too much inertia. So my hope is that participants in the symposium will advocate pilot schemes before establishing fixed programs.

They will also, I hope, emphasize the need for inbuilt assessment of the progress and success or failure of every project. Only then can we be certain that the money and efforts are well spent. Further, in order to avoid administrative rigidity and inertia, I hope that we shall emphasize the risk of large size projects and programs. The title and the slogan "small is beautiful" is not new. More than two thousand years ago in this country, Aristotle said: "to the size of states there is a limit as there is to other things, plants, animals, implements; for none of these retain their natural power when they are too large or too small."

*3. One of the greatest weaknesses in our work is the gap
between planning and implementation, between theory and practice*

It may be said by outsiders that those of us gathered in this place are an elitist group; that we are interested only in presenting papers; that we are only here for mutual admiration. Let us make sure that this charge is not true. In order to achieve this, we have to study not only the targets and the objectives, but also the cost, the necessary administrative and legal changes, the training and ability of personnel to work on any given project, and, finally, we must pay attention to the likely resistances. To my own personal knowledge many of the participants in this symposium have been able to change theory into practice, to transform banners into tools.

But there is something more. It is not sufficient to produce a very detailed and well-studied program including all that I have said. It is necessary to realize that we cannot influence development nowadays by writing books or papers, having discussions such as these, and then returning to our universities, to our studies, to our ivory towers. All of us here will have to get involved in political activity. Do not misunderstand me. By the term "political activity" I do not mean to stand for election for Parliament or even to become mixed up in party politics. My meaning, as in ancient Greece, is that we should be interested in all things which are of concern to the community, not only to the individual. Again, it is more than 2000 years ago since it was said in this same city that "the heaviest penalty for declining to engage in politics is to be ruled by someone inferior to yourself." Let us try to remember this.

*4. The last and biggest risk, because it is hidden,
is the influence of statistics on our thoughts*

Because of the infiltration, or even the invasion, of statistics into all sciences and professions; because we have to realize the importance of economic factors on health and education; finally, because, quite rightly, we have to be concerned for everybody and not only for favoured minorities, we have been thinking in terms of numbers.

This is a risk: it is a risk when numbers become your masters and not your slaves. So I urge all of us to think not only in terms of large numbers and of quantity, but also of quality. Quality may mean many things, but above all it means the need to foster that most precious gift that makes us what we are: the gift of our uniqueness, or individuality. There is not really a question of quantity versus quality. If we had to choose, there is no doubt that in a democratic country we should give first priority to the extension of health, education, and opportunities to all children. Fortunately, there is no such dilemma. The one does not exclude the other. What I want to emphasize by insisting on quality is that we should no longer be satisfied to provide better health for all children—better education, good opportunities for employment. We should not be satisfied if the children in the world of tomorrow are able to read, to write, to count. Our aim should be to make them able:

— to enjoy learning;
— to be free to choose and to be free to be different;
— to participate in decisions shaping their lives and futures;
— to be spontaneous, to be creative;
— to imagine and to foresee;

— to dream and to be able to work to realize their dreams;
— to be able to give and to take;
— to be able to want and to be wanted;
— to be able to love and to be loved.

Is it asking too much? Of course it is.

However, in this world of greed, hate, violence, and destruction,—but also of concern, of sacrifice, of need to give and need to love—let us show we have not reached our intellectual and (above all) our moral limits. Let us show that there are still ways to ensure that our children in the world of tomorrow will be healthier, better educated, happier, and able to enjoy life more than they do today.

To have among us the Head of the State to address the symposium is an honour, and were the Head of the State somebody else, I would stop here and ask him to declare our symposium open. But with all my respect, Mr. President, let me end on a personal note, because for us you are not only the President of the Republic but also a champion for freedom and democracy, an eminent thinker and a well known author, a philosopher of international reputation, and, for many of us, a teacher in honest and clear thinking. So, I am deeply moved that it is you, Sir, who will address our gathering and open our symposium.

CLOSING ADDRESS

In my above welcoming address, in which I invited the President of the Hellenic Republic to formally open our symposium, I expressed my hopes and my expectations for the symposium, and I described the qualities and abilities which I would like to see our children acquiring in order to be healthier and happier in the world of tomorrow. I do not know how much the symposium was able to contribute to this. It may well be only after a few years, and certainly not before the end of the International Year of the Child, that we may be able to assess how much of our aims and purpose has been attained.

The effects of the participants and organizers of this Athens Symposium will not have been in vain:

— if pediatricians the world over consider that the child is not a collection of cells and of enzymes (impossible to remember and pronounce), but something more;
— if architects and town planners remember that people are not born at the age of fifteen and that there are persons smaller in size and different in their needs;
— if sociologists realize that, behind numbers and percentages, there are individuals with needs, feelings, desires; and that to say that 80% of the population are healthy or educated or have their needs satisfied means that there is another 20% whose needs are not met;
— if economists understand that what in the end matters is not what shows in the statistics and in the curves of economic growth, but what goes into the child, through his mouth as water or food, or through his senses as experiences, as stimulation, as love, as affection;

— if teachers accept that children were not born the day before they entered the
school, nor have they grown in a test tube, but that each brings with him, not
only his unique individuality, but all his previous experiences, which have
taught him more than school is likely to teach him; and that most of his
experiences derive from his parents, who will continue to be his teachers;
— if parents understand that no one loves their children more than they do and
no one can offer them more; and if they therefore express their concern with
a loud voice and a clear vote;
— if all of us remember, every minute, that "the end of all knowledge is action"
and that a little knowledge that acts is infinitely better than much knowledge
that remains idle; and that action is interest and involvement in all activities
and undertakings of the community, from the small informal group to political parties, parliament, and government;
— finally, if politicians make decision as if all children were going to vote at the
next elections; then . . . there is hope that the world of tomorrow will be a
better world for our children.

THIS BOOK

To condense in the few hundred pages of this volume what happened during a
whole week, with over 500 participants in 12 plenary and 20 special sessions is a
nearly impossible task. This task was, however, fulfilled in an admirable way by the
efforts of Professor Jaqueline Tyrwhitt with the close cooperation of Dr. Sheena
Nakou. They had to attend all sessions, to collect manuscripts, to correspond with
participants, to talk with coordinators and chairmen, to work with rapporteurs, and
to edit this final version.

This book has as its main characteristic the contribution of persons from more than
10 scientific disciplines. This is its value, but also its weakness. Persons approaching
many topics from different disciplines have inevitably not only different points of
view regarding the contents of their contributions, but also different ways of expressing and recording their opinions. Some of the contributions were presentations of
original materials, other were reviews of what is known, and many of them include
projections into the future.

This is one of our expectations that was not entirely fulfilled. All of the contributions contain valuable material from the past and the present. But authors have not
always had the courage to go outside what strict scientific discipline allows and to use
their imagination to forecast the future and to suggest means to make this future
better for our children. We "scientists" cannot get away from longstanding habits of
thought, and we are afraid to mix hard data and conclusions based on them with what
might be termed a look into the future. However, projections into the world of
tomorrow, although not expressly stated in many of the lectures and papers, were
implicit in all of the presentations and in all of the discussions. All participants were
concerned with today as a basis for a better world of tomorrow.

So in the end, openly or implicitly, our aim has been achieved, and I feel that this
book does provide a "window into the future": a window that can help governments,
non-governmental agencies, and individuals in planning for the International Year
of the Child.

The presence among the participants from all five continents, including many eminent representatives from the Third World, makes the book useful to countries in all stages of development. The reader, whether he belongs to a highly industrialized country or to a country which has just started on the process of development, will find useful ideas and suggestions for projects and programs for his country and for his own activities. He or she will find descriptions of experiences in other countries, reviews of successful programs, and honest admission of failure. He may not be able to find the exact solution to the problems he is facing in his own area. In view of the multiplicity of the factors influencing children and development in each country, this would be impossible, and it was not our aim. Our hopes, stated in the provisional program, and which we feel have been achieved, were that the descriptions, ideas, and suggestions contained in this book can provide stimulation and result in productive thought, so that all people engaged with children (parents, scientists, politicians) can gain something and be helped in their activities not only during the International Year of the Child, but during the next 20 or more years.

Minister of Social Services, Athens, Greece   SPYROS DOXIADIS
September 1978

EDITORIAL NOTE

THIS book can lay some claim to being a complete record of the Athens Symposium on the Child in the World of Tomorrow since all contributions to the 16 plenary sessions are reported (though obviously some have had to be abbreviated) and all the papers discussed in the 15 special sessions are referred to, together with the comments of a number of the participants of these sessions.

A complete list of all 158 contributors to the book is included as an Appendix with sufficient address for them to be contacted if a complete copy of their contribution is desired. A list of all papers presented to the special sessions is added to the report of each session, and a book of abstracts of these papers is available from the Institute of Child Health, Athens 617, Greece.

The preparation of this present volume, within three months of the date of the symposium, could not have been accomplished without the guidance of Dr. Spyros Doxiadis (general editor), the professional advice of Dr. Shenna Nakou (associate editor), and the expert (and voluntary) assistance of Ingrid Leman, Deanna Trakas, Katia Karas, Judy Triantafyllou, and Anna-Maria Paraskevopoulou. Grateful thanks are also due to the secretarial staff: Ann Makri and Fragiski Goulandri.

Executive Editor   JAQUELINE TYRWHITT
Athens, September 1978

ACKNOWLEDGEMENTS

WE are grateful to Pergamon Press who will produce and circulate the various publications arising from the symposium and donate any profits to the Institute of Child Health as their special contribution for the International Year of the Child. The publications will be made available to participants of the symposium at a reduced price.

COOPERATING AGENCIES

United Nations Children's Fund (UNICEF)
International Year of the Child (IYC)
World Health Organization (WHO)
United Nations Educational, Scientific and Cultural Organization (UNESCO)
International Children's Centre
World Society of Ekistics
The Ciba Foundation

OPENING SESSION

Chairman:
  Spyros Doxiadis
    Ministry of Social Services, Athens, Greece

OPENING ADDRESS

CONSTANTINE TSATSOS
President of the Hellenic Republic

THE CHILD is the man in the initial phase of his development. All of man's problems are the child's problems too; only the angle of vision is narrower. But despite the restricted viewpoint the subject is a vast one, because from the very beginning of a lifetime all the problems confronting man are already posed.

When we are faced with the necessity of discussing a vast subject however, it is no less dangerous than a narrow one; there is the risk that it may dissolve into infinity, just as a narrow topic may crumble into petty detail.

I would say that the questions and issues affecting the child attain coherence, not through any organized rational unity but predominantly because they have a common emotional base: the anxiety we all feel concerning the fate of the children in today's world. We worry about their physical and mental health, about their adjustment to the pace of modern living, about their relationship to both the general environment, and the immediate family environment; and we worry about the best way of forming them into complete human beings.

All these things, nonetheless, merge into one basic question: What kind of man or woman do you want to help the child become? And that question leads to the ultimate one: What should be man's aim? Where should we lead him?

In other words, our answer—except in the matter of health—will depend on this terminal question: What is man's destiny? What is his mission, if indeed he has a mission? Because it is this ultimate point, which lies in infinity, that determines the entire course of a human life from the moment of birth.

To be more precise: if the aim of human life is material well-being, then all of man's problems assume a different light than if his aim is the pursuit of moral and intellectual freedom. Again depending on how we conceive of that freedom—apart from the specific problem of bodily health—our perception of all the other problems of childhood will be illuminated differently. It is not necessary to recall here that there are many ways of apprehending moral and intellectual freedom.

Accordingly, I imagine that many differences of opinion, which will inevitably arise in the course of your debates on particular subjects, and perhaps even some misunderstandings on terminology and meanings, will be due to differences in the terms of reference, pertaining to the *Weltanschauung*—the philosophy of life—of each participant in the debate.

The only area in which unanimity can be achieved is, as I have said, the field of health, because health is a basic premise whatever meaning we ascribe to human life. From there on we enter an area where we must scrutinize our differences of opinion, to see whether they arise over specific and particular instances, or whether they stem from disparate metaphysical terms of reference.

3

Apart from this methodological aspect, there is also a question of priorities in dealing with the problems of children. There are the crying, urgent problems, and there are the chronic problems that can only be resolved with the passage of much time and by gradual stages. This is an exacting and difficult classification, and it is imperative that there should be no inversion of priorities. I attach particular importance to rational order—not only in the debates but also in the solution of the problems, except for those which brook no delay at all in their urgent need of solution.

The task of your congress is a grave and important one. We have not gathered here merely to affirm and demonstrate our loving concern for the children and to raise our voice in a cry of despair at the perils that threaten them in the modern world. The purpose of this congress is much loftier and much more to the point, as is amply demonstrated by the agenda before you.

Announcements will be made by distinguished representatives of many sciences and specialized professions. I hope that despite the difficulties I have not hesitated to mention, a measure of synthesis will be achieved in the opinions to be presented from various scientific viewpoints.

I am certain, in any case, that a shared concern for the child in our times will lead to the formulation of guidelines and injunctions that will help mankind and will help national governments the world over to produce—at least for some of the more critical problems—better solutions than have hitherto been forthcoming.

Mankind, and each individual man and woman, is in a perpetual state of becoming. In this process of becoming, the first—the pre-adolescent years—are particularly critical. Whatever we do to avert the hazards that threaten the child from the natural and social environment is of determinative importance because the early years are the formative years—not only for the body but for the mind and spirit. Words written on the soul of a child during those early years are very difficult to erase later.

Thus, when we make a decision affecting the child we make a decision affecting the roots of the man, affecting the destiny of mankind itself.

I am sure that you, who are all aware of the compound difficulties attending the treatment and rational synthesis of the problems, who are aware of the responsibility weighing upon you—I am sure you will do what is best to protect the child in our turbulent world.

In the face of the enormous problem epitomized by the phrase "the fate of the children" even the smallest contribution is a great good.

Greece is happy to be host to a congress of such importance to the world, and I convey to you my country's best wishes for the success and fruition of your deliberations.

With the highest of hopes, therefore, I now declare the congress open.

GREETINGS

GREETINGS and good wishes for the symposium were expressed on behalf of *UNICEF* by HENRY R. LABOUISSE (Executive Director); *WHO* by ANGELE PETROS-BARVAZIAN (Director, Division of Family Health); *UNESCO* by AKIHIRO CHIBA (Chief, Unit for Cooperation with UNICEF); *International Year of the Child* by JAMES F. MCDOUGALL (Director IYC Europe); *International Children's Center* by MICHEL MANCIAUX (Director-General); *The CIBA Foundation* by SIR GORDON WOLSTENHOLME (Director-General); *World Society for Ekistics* by FELIPE HERRERA (President).

THE PROMISE OF THE YEAR OF THE CHILD

MARGARET MEAD*

American Museum of Natural History, New York, NY, USA

IN A DARKENED world, beset by the fear of nuclear holocaust, degradation of our soil and air, an imbalance of population growth that threatens to strangle our human settlements, the Year of the Child stands like a beacon of hope. We must see that its light guides us and gives us direction for preparing a livable, sustainable, beautiful world for our children, those who have been born, those who have been conceived but not yet born, and those children of the future not yet conceived. By keeping our eyes steadily on the pressing needs of children we can determine what needs to be done now and what must be prepared for but can be accomplished later. For *babies cannot wait:* a few moments without oxygen, a few hours without food or shelter, a few days of desperate emotional deprivation, and, if they survive at all, they carry the marks for life. Within the world initiatives of the last decade for a safer and better-cared-for earth, initiatives to protect the environment, balance population, feed the hungry, design human settlements for human living, this coming year can be the climax as we focus on the needs and well-being of the world's children, and the parents and grandparents of children, the towns within which children live, the food they eat, the water they drink, the education and health care they receive. As we provide children with a fuller life, we will find our reasons for living and protecting the world.

It will be the task of this symposium to sharpen this focus, always remembering that *babies cannot wait.*

---

*Dr. Mead expected to chair the opening session, and deeply regretted that illness prevented her from attending. Sadly, her illness persisted and on Tuesday, 14 November, she died.

The World of Tomorrow

THE ENVIRONMENT OF TOMORROW

CHAIRMAN'S INTRODUCTION

THOMAS STAPLETON

School of Medicine, University of Sydney, NSW, Australia

IF OUR aim is the pursuit of happiness for children in the world of tomorrow, we shall, I feel sure, find that this is not reached merely by providing all the goodies and material needs. Certainly, we must lose the freedom to die of malnutrition and preventable infectious diseases, but youth must have challenges. Youth must have a faith. As somewhat of a humanist, I still feel he may need a religion as a firm set of standards to which he may refer. He must have the opportunity to both receive and give love and to be of service to his fellow beings.

One of the crimes we commit against some of our youth is to tell them to get educated, and then give them no job when they leave school. Oxfam has called unemployment and underemployment the greatest unnatural disasters since the slave trade.

A WORLD OF INEQUALITY

Michel Manciaux

International Children's Center, Paris, France

THIS international and multidisciplinary symposium provides an excellent opportunity for the exchange of opinions and experiences. It will have fulfilled its purpose if, as a result of our meeting here, the life of the child in the world of tomorrow can in some ways be improved.

The world of today is unfortunately a world divided—sick and full of injustice. As an illustration, I present three figures. The first, Fig. 1(a), shows stylized maps of several countries. The small square at the top represents 1 million km²; Figure 1(b) is another graphic representation of the same countries, in which the size of each is based, not on its area but the size of its population in the year 1973. The little square at the top represents 15 million people. You will notice the fantastic difference between these two maps.

Let us now turn to Fig. 1(c) based on the GNP of each country. Without question, the GNP is a crude indicator, open to criticism, but it does reflect fairly well the great inequality of the distribution of wealth around the world.

These three figures give a rough and ready picture of the world of today. What will the world of tomorrow be like? I doubt if the areas of the world will show any marked differences, but let us turn to the population picture. All predictions of the future population are difficult, but even if we take a conservative estimate of population growth over the next century, disparities, noticeable in Fig. 1(b), will have become greatly accentuated.

I am not able to show you a map of the GNP in the world of tomorrow, but we all know that the trends indicate that the gap will continue to increase, not only between the rich and poor countries, but also between the favored classes and the underprivileged within almost all countries if not all of them.

If the world of tomorrow remains, as I have indicated it may, a world of inequality—inequality in the distribution of population and of resources, inequality in access to health care and education, inequality in the amount of money spent on the forces of destruction and the amount invested in the future of children, families and human settlements—then it will be an unlivable world in which the child is menaced and even condemned.

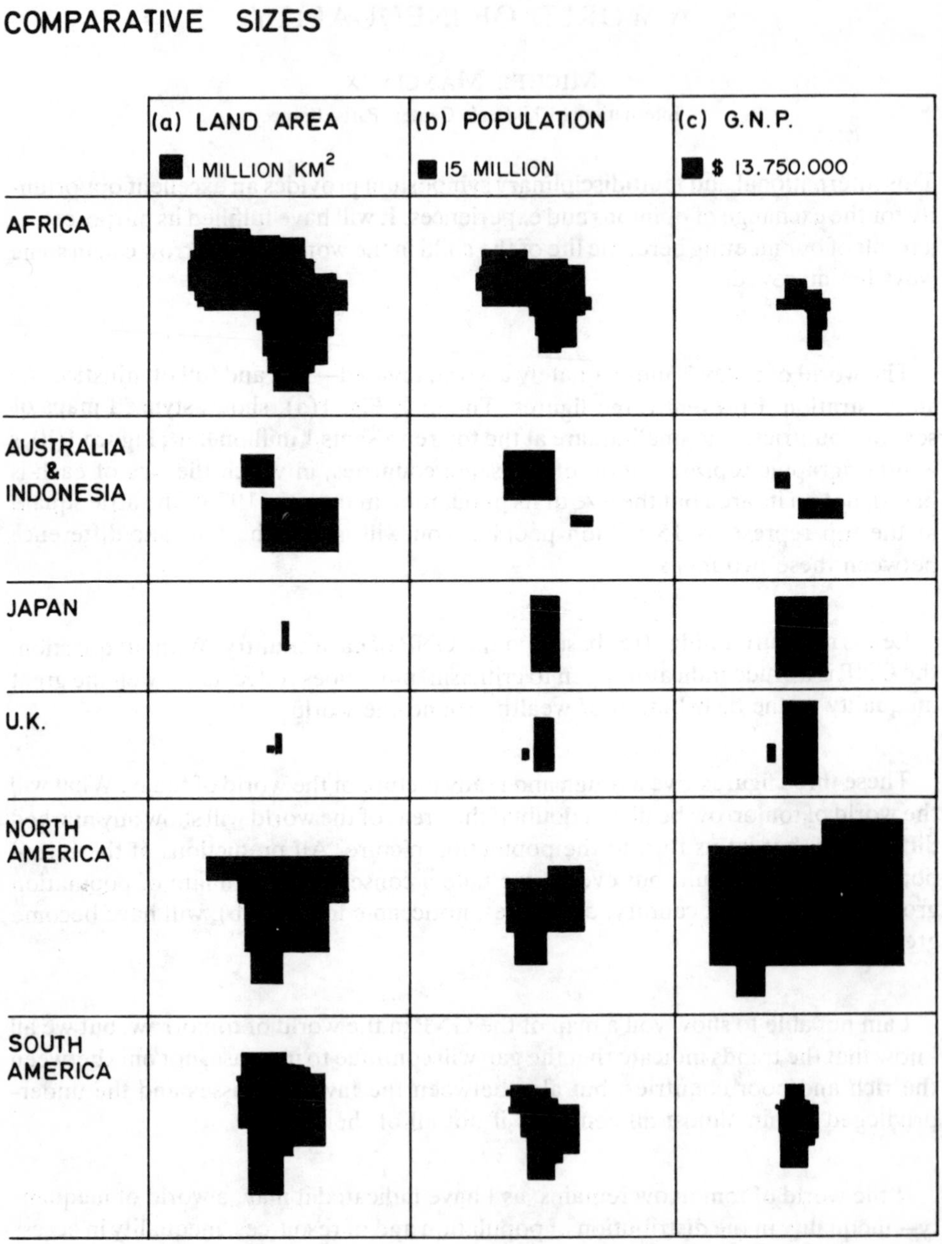

COMPARATIVE SIZES

Fig. 1(a) Land areas; (b) Population; (c) GNP [1973].

We are faced by a veritable challenge to work constantly, even if modestly, to bring about a more viable and humane world.

There is a Chinese proverb which says: "Many little things done in many little places by many little people can change the face of the world."

THE NATURAL AND MANMADE PHYSICAL
ENVIRONMENT OF TOMORROW

P. PSOMOPOULOS

Athens Center of Ekistics, Athens, Greece

THIS paper is based on the findings of the on-going interdisciplinary research project of the Athens Center of Ekistics (ACE), initiated in 1960, "The City of the Future (COF)." Partial project results have been published in ACE's monthly journal *Ekistics* (1965–78), in a series of "internal" monographs and in numerous unpublished studies available in the ACE records as well as in the book *Ecumenopolis, the Inevitable City of the Future,* by C. A. Doxiadis and John G. Papaioannou (Athens, 1975).

Let me first clarify that human settlements:

(a)   are the territorial arrangement made by human beings for their own sake;

(b)   consist of five elements: man, society, shells, networks, and nature;

(c)   are of various kinds ranging from nomadic (whether with animals in the desert or trailers on the highways) to very large "urban" ones from their overbuilt and overcrowded central parts to their farthermost outskirts.

One of the most characteristic scales in any city, the neighborhood scale, is defined by the overlapping "kinetic" fields of the daily movements of the inhabitants to satisfy their needs.

By the end of the next century most of the grandchildren of the young sons and daughters in our homes today will be living in "ecumenopolis", a unified settlement system spanning the entire habitable area of the globe in a totally interconnected network.

THE PRESENT—A CONFUSION

The speed and scale of population growth, the rapid changes in technology, and the corresponding intensive use and abuse of resources—natural and man-made—during the last few decades, have brought the issues of the conservation and/or development of the environment onto the priority list of the world community.

As almost all human life is found in human settlements, and as all activity in human settlements takes place in space, most decisions or actions imply "location" and "connections". Thus spatial consideration within and outside settlements are of utmost importance both in themselves and in their impact on the various other dimensions of human action and well-being.

Many millions of human settlements—small and large, dynamic and static, closely or loosely connected, or enclosed in major systems—are now spread over the surface of our globe.

The average annual population growth rate for large settlements is *ca.* 4·5% and the average annual growth rate for their area is just over 10%. For all settlements the average annual growth rate for their area is *ca.* 5%. In 1960 all human settlements on the globe occupied 0·4 million km²: in 1976 this doubled, becoming 0·8% million km². By the year 2000 it is projected to reach 2·3 million km².

As a result of the expansion of buildings, industry, transportation, etc., expanding cities pollute the soil in and around them to an increasing degree through their sewerage systems, garbage disposal, industrial wastes, the entire layer of topsoil over large areas.

In the past man has always been the dominating factor both in the initial creation of his environment and also in maintaining a desirable balance between the various elements. However, he now finds himself in a complex world of limitless dimensions in which he has to cope with new problems which are increasing at an unprecedented and threatening rate. Studies of human settlements, both in the technologically advanced and in the poor countries, show that: (1) the balance between the five elements of human settlements—man, society, shells (constructions), networks, and, of course, nature—has been dangerously upset and, in some respects, irrevocably damaged during recent years; (2) while this imbalance harms all elements, it is particularly harmful to man who should be able to condition the environment to meet his own needs; (3) despite the facilities provided by modern technology, man seems to have lost control over the tools created by him to form his environment at a human scale; (4) even worse, man now seems to be oblivious as to what his real needs are; what he wants to do; and "where to go from here".

TOWARD THE REMOTE FUTURE—A BALANCE

Over the last 17 years the "city of the future" research project has made intensive efforts to understand the process of the past, present, and future evolution of man's system of life and human settlements, which are the complex physical expression of this system of life in space. The results obtained indicate that long range efforts to forecast the remote future are possible, meaningful, relevant, and also necessary for understanding present-day problems and for planning for the immediate future.

The validity and reliability of the emerging general picture of the future was tested using several independent methods and approaches. Each showed approximately the same features: the evidence of certain trends and limitations shaping a generalized urbanization pattern on the surface of the earth. Three such approaches are sum-marized here:

The "Ultimate Balance" Approach

The total population of the earth, which has been increasing at a constantly accelerating rate, is likely to continue growing well into the 21st century until a level of relative stabilization has been reached.

Complex ecological considerations of balance between man and his environment show that—similar to other animal or plant communities within a limited enclos-ure—man is likely to increase his densities of habitation if these are clearly below saturation level. Once this level is reached, given a sufficient period of time, humans are likely to adapt their genetic mechanisms so as to conquer whatever other habitable space is available on earth.

In spite of the many ever-increasing disadvantages of present urban life, urbanization can be regarded as an inevitable universal trend. Rural dwellers, as well as inhabitants from small and medium size cities, are irresistably attracted into the largest cities by their apparent higher standards of living, the multiple choices offered, the availability of highest order functions, and many other considerations that seem to outweigh by far their disadvantages.

The application of maximum acceptable densities to all habitable areas of the globe (but excluding areas that are essential for production, recreation, resource conservation, etc.), and using relatively conservative projections of income growth and technological progress, shows that, in 100—150 years from now, resources such as food, water, energy, and minerals can be developed to such levels that the earth could sustain a probable maximum population of some 20 billions.

The "Spatial Pattern" Approach

This approach starts from a definite physical pattern of the inhabited planet.

Until around 1940 the evolution of settlements resulted in large, more or less concentrated metropolises surrounded by suburbs. These represented the largest human settlement units at that time. After the Second World War, the phenomenon of urbanization on a regional scale appeared. In areas where centers relatively close to each other exceeded a critical size of some one million inhabitants, bands connecting these centers were progressively urbanized. These bands were not continuously built-up but contained a predominance of urban functions and the process resulted in the formation of a "megalopolis"—a multinuclear band formation with a population of several tens of millions and an area of 10–1000 times larger than the area of a single large metropolis.

At present 12 megalopolises have been identified around the world and six more are already in the stage of formation. Projections show that their number will increase greatly, and over 160 megalopolises are expected to exist around the year 2000.

With the continuing increase of population, the improvement of communication and transportation systems, and greater scarcity of unused habitable space, settlements are expected to become more and more interconnected until:

(a) Towards the end of the first half of the 21st century, megalopolises will gradually be replaced by the next higher unit, the "urbanized region".

(b) Around the middle of the 21st century, or later, the "urbanized region" will in its turn give way to a higher order settlement, the "urbanized continent", as the prevailing settlement pattern.

(c) Probably less than another generation later, all major settlement units will become fully interconnected in a new pattern representing a sort of ultimate equilibrium between human settlements and their wider environment. This highest unit in the hierarchy of settlements has been called "ecumenopolis", meaning a unified settlement system spanning the entire habitable area of the globe, not continuously, but in a totally interconnected network.

Ecumenopolis, like its preceding high order urban formations, will be characterized by a loose and discontinuous internal structure. Figure 1 shows not *built-up areas*, but *areas of intensely urbanized character*. Within these, large open areas will be preserved for recreation, conservation, production, etc. (Fig. 2).

Of the total 70–75 million km² of the surface of the earth that are habitable or semi-habitable, settlements may occupy up to 10 or 15 million km², production 25–30 million, and recreation plus conservation another 30–35 million.

The "System of Interrelated projections" Approach

A third approach made a study of a number of interrelated projections for population, areas and densities, economy, water availability, energy, education, health and nutrition, and several other variables. Its results showed that, as we proceed in the future:

(1) Very high *per capita* incomes and investment figures would be made possible, which means (among other possibilities) that unprecedentedly large scale engineering projects could be undertaken; "difficult" areas (oceans, deserts, underground areas, outer space) could be made more or less habitable; the battle against poverty could be supported; greater funds could be devoted to research and development; and higher order functions such as art and science could be developed.

(2) Water scarcity is quite unlikely, except in local "arid pockets", even without exploiting new sources of supply such as melted polar ice or very deep water reserves. Traditional sources alone could adequately supply a population of 19 billion at the average present-day US level of consumption. Desalinated sea water could be pumped 1000 km inland up to an elevation of some 1000 m at a reasonable cost.

(3) Scarcity of energy could be eliminated and pressure from the high cost of energy could be considerably eased.

(4) Illiteracy is likely to be unknown long before ecumenopolis and even the less-developed areas of today could enjoy higher education levels at least comparable to those now existing in the United States and the United Kingdom.

(5) Nutritional levels in the least-developed parts of the globe could at least be similar to those in advanced countries of today, even as early as the middle of the 21st century.

(6) Present-day known diseases will probably be virtually eradicated, including those attributed to environmental pollution.

(7) Strict controls over environmental pollution and destruction are likely to have been established before the end of this century.

In summary, in addition to several other independent approaches for certain particular aspects, these three approaches converge towards the same future image: that is, some form of ecumenopolis.

If, therefore, ecumenopolis is considered as an inevitable general pattern of future urbanization—but with a large number of alternative interpretations—we need to connect present conditions and trends with such a projected future.

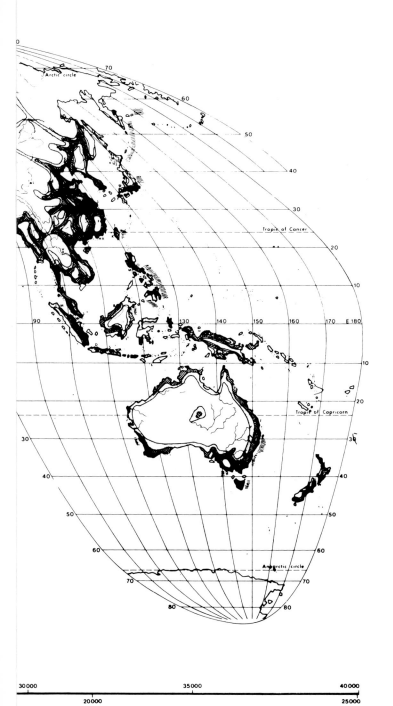

THE NEXT 22 YEARS—CRISIS AND HOPE

There is ample evidence—and the COF study confirms it—that the period between now and the year 2000 is likely to be the most difficult one for humanity. Within
it, a large number of difficult problems are likely to accumulate, many of which
already exist: scarcity of food, water, energy, and other natural resources for a
growing population (reaching alarming proportions in many cases); slow rate of
growth of the economy of most of the poor countries, leading to stagnation and a
dissatisfied awareness of the increasing gap that separates them from rich countries;
environmental deterioration through air, water, and land pollution and widespread
danger to flora and fauna; intensification of dissatisfaction because of higher expectations and lower attainments; increasing tension and stress; violence; the possible
collapse of prevailing social or political systems; insufficient technological and
organizational progress to cope with these problems efficiently.

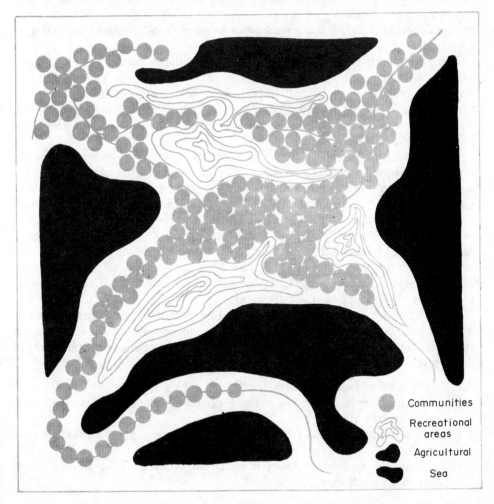

Fig. 2.

All these difficulties may impair the quality and efficient operation of major human settlement units, but they are not expected to stop the formation and growth of megalopolises unless a total failure or catastrophe for humanity occurs. On the contrary, megalopolises attract population with a still greater force than isolated metropolises. Estimates show that the advantages to be gained, such as proximity to two large centers, availability of highest order function, a standard of living considerably higher than areas outside them, etc., will more than compensate for the disadvantages, and that around the year 2000 45% to 50% of the earth's population will be living in megalopolises.

No matter how optimistic the long term prospects may be, there is no certainty that man will find and put into effect the right solutions to some of the very critical problems *in time* to save the situation. And in time means here and now. Because whatever happens now decisively conditions the future. The essence behind any effort in predicting the future is: should we allow the transition to the future to go on by itself following the present trends, or should we try to understand what is happening, conceive clearly what we want our future to be, and then guide the forces in that direction reducing friction as much as possible during this long period of evolution?

There is imperative need for immediate action so that humanity can reach a new balance between man and nature, a balance that will no longer be expressed only at the village scale (this was the goal 10,000 years ago), or even at the city scale (this became the goal later), but at all scales from man to the whole earth. This means that man, nature and all the other elements will have to change direction and move towards the same goal.

This notion of achieving balance is not simple at all, as it depends upon the demands of nature, man, and society, as well as upon the requirements of shells and networks. Such a balance has to be guided by a decrease in the forces derived from man's physical dimensions and personal energy, and an increase in those derived directly from nature itself as a developing and operating system.

Limiting ourselves to the theme of this conference and this paper—the child between 0 and 13 years during the next 22 years—we can define two areas in which urgent action is needed. Action taken now has a good chance of speeding up the establishment of a balance between nature and human settlements as well as between the various elements of human settlements.

(1) The first area is that of organization and location of uses of space (land, water, air). We need land-use planning with proper margins for adjustment within certain ranges that are definable. A first subdivision into four categories can and should be determined at a global, continental, regional, national, and sub-national level.

(a) natural areas (wild life, forests, etc);
(b) cultivation areas, including animal breeding (using various degrees of mechanization);
(c) human settlement areas (which interfere to various degrees with the first two areas);
(d) pollution areas: heavy industry, ports, airports (necessary, because we cannot yet control pollution).

(2) The second area for immediate action is that of small scale communities

within human settlements. This could take the form of sections of the broader built-up areas or of small nodal points within the settlements' web.

These scales are clearly defined by the important share of human energy and human time spent on them, and this emphasis makes them the most crucial scales for improvement of quality of life—at least everyday life—for everybody. This is even truer for children who spend, on the average, 80–100% of their time and energy in the small scale community.

A minimum effort can lead to action related to appropriate spatial organization to fit the needs of pedestrians along with the necessary everyday facilities for shelter, recreation, education, communication and work, free access to the maximum choice and information opportunities, and appropriate connection of these small scale areas with the rest of the human settlement system. Moreover, the residents themselves are more likely to decide, influence, or implement action on a small scale than on the larger scales where higher order facilities, much more complicated decision-making procedures, higher order technological devices and much higher order expenses are involved.

CONCLUSIONS

Throughout human history man has been guided by the same five principles in every attempt he has made to live normally and survive:

1. *The maximization of potential contacts.* Man tries to have the best possible contact with people and other elements such as water, food, houses, facilities, knowledge. This amounts to an operational definition of personal human freedom.

2. *The minimization of effort in terms of energy, time and cost.* In his attempt to maximize his potential contacts, man tries to bring everything close to him. To achieve this in the best possible way he always selects the course requiring the minimum effort.

3. *Optimization of man's protective space* at every moment and in every locality, whether in temporary or permanent situation, whether he is alone or part of a group.

4. *Optimization of man's relationship with the other elements of his system of life,* i.e. with nature, society, shells (buildings and houses of all sorts), and networks (from roads to telecommunications).

5. *Optimization of the synthesis* of the previous four principles. This depends on time and space, actual conditions, and man's ability to create the synthesis. Human settlements have been more successful, made their inhabitants happier, and last longer when the fifth principle of balance between the other four has been applied.

The human settlements of the future will be created by man guided by his own five principles, which should not and cannot be changed.

Ecumenopolis will come inevitably, but it will only come in its most desirable form if mankind guides events toward the forms man most deeply desires. However, experience has also shown that this will take time, leading to many more mistakes and making people suffer over longer periods of time than is necessary.

Our efforts should therefore focus upon reestablishing and maintaining harmony between the five elements that make up human settlements—man, nature, society, shells, and networks. Growth takes place naturally; harmony in the manmade environment can be achieved through man's conscious action.

The development of a rational and scientific approach, making a careful study of the complex system of life in which we live and of the factors which make man happy, is a fundamental pre-requisite for any action.

Immediate action on a global scale requires a lot of courage but it is feasible and desirable. Until we can manage to organize plans on this scale, action should be encouraged on as large a scale as possible.

Action should always be based on the desire to serve man.

Everything we build now lays the foundations for the city of the future.

TOWARD THE ENERGY FUTURE

EARL FINBAR MURPHY
College of Law, Ohio State University, OH, USA

IN HUMAN history, the shift from low to high energy culture has been recent. The movement started in northwestern Europe in the 18th century, but the average member of these societies was probably unaware of what was happening until the second quarter of the 19th century. By that time the steam railroad, the factory steamboiler with its steam-powered machinery, and the telegraph had conveyed to a mass audience the message of a huge recent surge in available power for social purposes.

The increased use of power, and the consciousness of this increase, spread throughout the world from that place and time into the present. Accompanying the steady spread of increased power usage has been the intensification of demand for energy in any society experiencing the movement from low to high levels of energy conversion. There has been only the one social choice opted for so far: the demand for cascades of energy to be used without stint.

Just as high energy demand was not to be confined to northwestern Europe, so also has it proven to be unrestrainable in relation to the young. Long before an infant has the capacity to form a demand, the infant is now the precipitant of high energy usage in a way they were not even as late as 1950. The infant formulas, the disposable diapers, and the inoculations have all been the products of, as well as the contributors to, high energy levels. And those are only harbingers of what will come in the next few years of that infant's life.

While the child of the first part of the century knew film and phonograph and, later, radio, the child of the late 20th century has all these as well as television—and each one has an energy amplitude earlier unknown. If the child learns a musical instrument, he can have the sound enormously expanded with amplifiers. Tapes and records can be used to dominate a city block rather than to fill a room with sound. In affluent segments of high energy societies there are children, not yet in their teens, who can command at the flick of a few switches an awesome spectrum of sight and sound.

But this, too, is only the beginning. Later comes a succession of motorized vehicles from lawn mowers and snow blowers to autos and speedabouts. While it is common not to grant licences to anyone under 16 years of age (and in high energy society 16 has become the age of majority for energy purposes) the image is constantly before the eyes of the young: the motorcycle, the car, the speedboat, the plane.

And what have these objects of aspiration had in common? It has been their dependence on stored energy sources and centrally managed energy supplies. Whatever the talent or the acquired skill of youth to fix the tape deck or the car's engine, what runs them is ultimately—and not very ultimately at that—beyond any youth's

27

control. The electricity and the gasoline both come through the operation of exceedingly complex legal, economic, and technical structures. They can be interdicted at any time from a wide variety of causes.

High energy usage today is marked by centralization of the sources of energy supply and its dependence upon the stored energy of the fossil fuels. There is no accident to this. Centralization offers economy of scale, engineering efficiency, ease of increasing capital formation, and a resulting smoothness for certain kinds of technical innovation, particularly those strengthening centralization. The use of fossil fuels opened up the treasury of paleolithic wealth and freed the economy from the previously experienced limitations of current energy sources. No one can deny the reasons for these two dependencies in high energy society. But none can deny that they are dependencies.

There are those who argue the necessity of soon breaking both dependencies. They say that economies ought not to be mortally reliant upon such fragile complexities as the electric power grid or the world petroleum market. They claim also that nuclear energy cannot prove an available substitute. They argue that high energy societies must move to current energy sources: the sun, the wind, the tides, ocean thermal energy conversion, or some part of the biomass. They claim that many of these sources will require decentralization of the energy converters so that the supply of energy can be restored to the control of the ordinary person. Though these current sources may not supply energy at instants of human command, they are inexhaustible, environmentally suited, decentralized, uninterruptable supplies of energy controllable by the neighborhood, if not by the individual.

What is plainly present here is a conflict of the energy expectations and training of the present young and of children to be born yet in this century. If energy specialists are right and if price alone is not the saviour of the situation, then the brief episode of children and youth's exposure to high energy in the forms experienced since 1950 must change. After all, the more disastrous scenarios of some critics predict the large energy expenditures of all the high energy societies are to come soon to abrupt and total cessation.

Even assuming that the most pessimistic are wrong in their predictions, significant changes loom in the offing. It may be that energy sources can be found to keep everything going as it has been doing. This is improbable, as is a movement in the near future to complete reliance on current energy sources. Nevertheless, a mixture of reliance is quite likely, as evidenced by such countries as Brazil.

Children for the rest of this century—and well into the next one—do not have an energy future easy to predict. The energy cascades have swept over the whole world. They have received a popular welcome everywhere, with only minority opinion preferring low energy usage, whatever the established character of low energy usages. It has meant not only an exchange of human muscle for machinery or of animal fuel for engine fuel. It has also meant a revolution in the effect upon the senses. Humanity has become not only the means of energy release. Human beings have also become the focus of energy to the degree that cultural practices and especially anticipation have been changed to an extent few in 1900 could have prophesied.

The better course in children's expectation for the energy future is flexibility and an encouragement for as much self—or small group—reliance as possible. The bases of the operations of present high energy societies are fragile. Interdictions of months at a time would compel reorganizations of society whose costs in life, health, capital, and public order cannot be calculated in advance.

The social network is probably too tight to make complete self-reliance possible. But the paradoxical freedom/no freedom of present high energy usages ill favors positively coping with the crises that for the moment are dormant in that system.

The surge of the energy cascades has not necessarily meant either peace or democracy. One could argue that the availability of high energy levels has meant an increased availability of material goods and has provided the conduit for larger numbers moving up the social structure simply because so many are needed for maintenance. Perhaps these changes constitute democratization. But the energy cascades, in breaking up the traditional low energy societies, have been powerful forces for destabilization as well.

Just as children did not create either the present energy system, or their place in it, or the expectations about it which culture transmits to children, it is not children who will decide how to behave in relation to energy usage. Immanent in the children is the action of the future, but that action is not yet.

Any generation, of course, can leave its children to "catch as catch can". Sometimes this is inevitable. But the chief claim to greatness of high energy societies has been their asserted control over events, their ability to free humanity from a servitude to traditional energy limitations. If the present managers of high energy systems are to sustain this claim to greatness successfully, then it is not possible to leave events to some sort of helter-skelter passage of time. There is substantial evidence that masses of humanity have benefited from the worldwide inundations from the energy cascades. Nor is there any reason to believe that those same masses—or their related successors—do not want to continue such a profitable relationship. Assuming that events are not serendipitous, the question that prevails is how to deal with the energy problem of the next half century.

In short, today's children must be encouraged to totally avoid rigidity, to swing away from commitment to what immediately previous generations have experienced. High energy demands introduced an uncertainty into social expectations which was unknown to low energy societies. It has been an uncertainty rich in possibilities, many of which have been richly realized. But this has made uncertainty an inescapable part of life, and this means that children inevitably are a part of such a fate.

But fate is not a casting of runes. Choice, election, change are each still available actions, both socially and individually throughout much of the world.

All may turn out automatically for the best. Who would not hope so who had compassion for possible human suffering? Yet, hope aside, one could scarcely anticipate that the energy situation in the ensuing decades would be without grave risk.

It is scarcely too much to ask of educators—and those who support those educators—to prepare children for the possibility of energy crises. To do otherwise is to turn flabby and unprepared contestants into an arena when all opposition would have naked swordpoints drawn and baptized for blood. To design such an array would scarcely be a decent thing to do for any coming generation.

DISCUSSION

Leonard J. Duhl

College of Environmental Design, University of California at Berkeley, CA, USA

To PLAN the external environment via the techniques of ekistics (a study of human settlements) without clearly understanding the personal/social organizing concepts may lead to not fully realizing the potential for optimum development. One must parallel the study of the complex external environment and its interconnected systems with an exploration of the inner environment, for the external and internal environments are interactive aspects of a dialogue which focuses on how we choose to perceive reality.

There are many realities. Physicists have shown that the "particles" of modern physics are "organized" by "consciousness"—the way we perceive matter and organize energy. Similarly, our mind has alternative ways of perceiving the organization of reality, based on a heirarchy of values and of different perceptions. In this heirarchy, private concerns take precedence over social values because, in most parts of the world, people are trained to put self-interests before the collectivity.

Modern settlements deny many of our various perceptions and deny the senses. Analytical statistical thinking may prevent us from recognizing intuitions, feelings, emotions. We spend a lot of time not seeing, not noticing. To open our consciousness to the known senses and the full perception of the mind may be to find new resources to cope with problems we have hitherto dealt with by money, power, or physical reality.

The future of the child is built into the present and past. To look at the child with the eyes of the past is to blind us to what is now happening, yet it is with these perceptions that much of our actions are determined.

One must reduce the noise of past and present to hear that inner voice coming out of the silent actions and processes that, as they occur, will build to that critical mass. What is silent is suddenly heard. One way to reduce the noise is to listen to children; another, to the child in ourselves, free of adult answers already fixed by professionalism and authority.

Still another is to look to those caught in the cracks, belonging nowhere and everywhere at the same time; who, free of the past, can see what is occurring and bearing witness by their behaviour to the solutions of the future. These are not the authorities, but rather those tuned by increased perceptions who are in touch with the elemental truths.

The leader is the teacher who assists us to push aside the blinkers of the present that, through solutions of the past, must be discarded and permit us to draw on our own universal wisdom so that the society as a whole can learn.

To be free of the past does not mean throwing out what exists. It does mean putting together in new forms what has gone into old patterns. It is the patterning, via our organizing concepts, our view of reality, that is critical, not just having available the pieces of the puzzle. That pattern is our "consciousness" and in our consciousness of the child within the whole—its values, its ways of being, and the quality of our dreams. "There is a dream dreaming us!" Let it be the one that holds high the values of the child.

TARZIE VITTACHI
UN Fund for Population Activities, New York, NY, USA

When most people use such terms as "quality of life" what they have in mind is the quantity of life. When they speak of "development" they usually have in mind the supply of food, clothing, shelter, schools, transportation, and employment opportunities. And when they speak of environment they often mean the outer conditions of life. There has been an encouraging change in the measurements used to assess the changes for the better or worse in the conditions in which our children are being born into and raised. Coarse measurements such as *per capita* gross national product are slowly giving way to more sensitive indices such as PQLI (the Physical Quality of Living Index) which takes account of factors that are not included in GNP calculations, such as health and education. But even this new index is concerned with the supply of health and education services, not their content and its impact on the inner environment nor the well-being of the individuals for whom these services are provided.

It is significant that while we concern ourselves, quite rightly, with a new economic order, the younger members of our societies go farther and demand a new world order. The radical changes they seek are not confined to questions of changing the colonial patterns of trade, the indexing of commodities, equitable access to lucrative markets, and the automatic transfer of resources and technology from the rich world to the poor. While they support the demand for these changes, they realize that they constitute only one aspect of new order that has become necessary—the physical or outer aspect—and that such changes cannot be brought about (nor sustained if they could be brought about) unless there is a profound change in the values of society, the values that determine individual and international relationships. This was the meaning behind the youth revolution of the sixties which, in spite of its many aberrent features, was a genuine plea for a saner and more humane world than what was in prospect for the next generation. This was also the motive behind the desire to find guidance from gurus, and in new religions and even cultist movements. As older men and women, we should not take comfort in the possibility of these impulses running down by themselves, or in the fact that many of those young advocates of a different world have yielded to the material blandishments of this one. The demand for a new world order among them is now muted, low key, but it is still widespread and motivated by a genuine desire for changing the values of a society which permits the expenditure of $400 billion a year on armaments while 400 million children go to bed hungry each night.

The evidences of crisis and catastrophe in the outer environment serve as signals for all of us to recognize that the human world is moving from one epoch to another—a transition that seems to occur for no reason I can fathom at the end of every millennium. The problems of population growth, poverty, the exhaustion of resources we once believed were limitless, have gathered and grown in magnitude to the point of critical mass. It would be futile to believe that we can solve those problems of the 21st century—a new epoch—if we set about doing so with the attitudes and values of a moribund epoch.

We were taught in our early lives to believe that competitiveness was the principal key to survival and even human success. This perversion of Darwinism was taken to absurd lengths by a succession of writers from Konrad Lorenz to Robert Ardrey, who claimed that human beings are genetically programmed to be aggressive, and Desmond Morris even saw the human being as no more than a naked ape. The balance has been restored by Richard Leakey, who has shown us in his new book *Origins* that aggression as a way of life began only a few thousand years ago, with settled agriculture, and that homo sapiens was able to evolve and survive, not through aggression and competition but by cooperation and considerateness. Jonas Salk in his *Survival of the Wisest* takes it even farther and suggests that the human evolution in a new epoch would entail the development of the inner being of men and women, their values, the dreams we dream and the wisdom we bring to our relationships with our environment and our global society. Wisdom, according to Dr. Salk, is the ability to see the future retrospectively.

I believe that this is the clue to a better environment for children in the world of tomorrow. If their world is to be a more livable world than ours, a fairer and more rational world than ours, indeed a world in which they can hope to survive, the needed changes are not to new values but to some of the oldest values in the world. Education for the future will need to be a process of discarding the dead and dangerous shibboleths of the recent past and recognizing the truth that W. H. Auden said in a single memorable line: "We must love one another or die."

PRIYANI SOYSA
Faculty of Medicine, University of Sri Lanka, Colombo, Sri Lanka

I think we need to strike a balance between the swings of the pendulum between high and low technology. We have been told that if children are to develop well they need a happy family life. In the third world we have an extended family system, which acts as a support system for the child. There are fewer psychosocial problems and less generation gap problems, for the three generations live together.

On the other hand, we have to bring up our children in a very hostile environment—both in the micro and macro environments. In the micro environment we have the problem of the fact that the child before it is born is deprived of adequate nourishment because the mother herself is undernourished. This gives rise to low birth weight babies, leading to poor and slow development of the child. After birth, the child has to survive in a hostile macro environment, with poor sanitation, poor water, and poor housing.

If we try to look at the child of tomorrow, can we expect that the third world will dispose of the resources of the developed world? But do we need all of them? Perhaps we should halt and look more carefully at the monstrous technology that is so misused in the developed world. It is significant that we already hear of women resenting fetal monitoring and demanding a right to natural child birth, and there are other signs of a revolt against misused technology.

It is true that we in the developing world are seeking innovative approaches to solve our many problems, but we need not imitate and repeat your mistakes. We have to study the values of flexibility and try to find a middle way.

THE SOCIETY OF TOMORROW

FUTURE CHANGES IN SOCIETY

JOHN APLEY

Bristol Royal Hospital for Sick Children, Bristol, UK

I FIND it interesting to speak on a subject I have never studied, and even more to do this at short notice with no time to look it up. But I am encouraged when I remember Socrates, famed for his wisdom—not because he knew everything, but because at the age of nearly 70 he realized he knew nothing (there any resemblance ends). We think of society with the minds of adults, but we should try sometimes to see it through the eyes of a child.

To a child society is like a beehive with its bees. We also have our queens (not many of them), our workers, and our drones; but, unlike the bees, our society is still evolving. So it is instructive to try to predict and ask what—in 20 years—will be changed in the hive, in the bees, and in the honey.

Historians tell us that human society's progress is like the movement of a pendulum. Certainly in the last two or three centuries there have been alternating periods when society was permissive and when it was repressive, e.g. in bringing up children. But there have also been linear and progressive changes: one of these, I am glad to say, is an ever-increasing sensibility and concern for children (and for animals, too).

Whatever truth there may be in the pendulum theory, there is no doubt that society is also influenced by once-and-for-all phenomena particularly by some that became possible only in our own epoch of unprecedented change. One example is "instant communication"; society all over the world can share instantaneously in, say, the recent earthquake in Salonika or, a decade ago, in the so-called "TV war" in Vietnam. This symposium in Athens is an example of almost instant communication with sharing of knowledge from many parts of the world.

Other phenomena unique to this age, and which must increasingly mould society in the future, are mechanization, miniaturization, electronics, computerization; antibiotics, insecticides, and improved nutrition, which can make people's lives longer and better (physically, at least), and birth control. One dramatic consequence is that in the next 20 years the world's population will become larger by many millions and it will also be differently balanced. There will be a much bigger proportion of "oldsters" and much smaller proportion of "youngsters."

AN OUTLINE OF PREDICTED CHANGES

I can mention only briefly a number of the changes in society that I foresee. What I have to say will be an oversimplification, and it will be rather like trying to visit ten Greek islands in one hectic half-day tour. I have to set aside discrepancies between industrialized and developing countries, and the possibility of large scale war.

1. *Family and marriage.* There will be less marriage, and more of what has been called "sequential monogamy." Marriage will tend to be less permanent, a "temporary" provision for the middle third of people's lifetime. Nuclear families will be less widely accepted as the norm, and many different experimental models of family and community life will be tried. An increase in mobility of families and groups will enforce changes in attitudes and values.

"Women's lib" will be firmly established, and I even foresee a counter movement to promote "men's lib."

2. *Children.* Fewer babies will be born in some countries (where parents are already deliberately limiting their children to one or two, or even to none). While these countries will be bribing parents to have more children, others will still be persuading parents to have fewer offspring. The trend for successive generations of children to grow taller than their predecessors will level off.

Children will be given and will demand ever more rights—not only as pre-adults but as individuals. One distasteful right will be that of sueing their own parents for misdeeds or errors; for example, a mother might be sued for having smoked cigarettes or taken drugs during pregnancy, for having had a car accident, or a preventable infection.

3. *Education.* The earlier onset of puberty and the extension of the years of education will lead to increasing conflict. (The "3 Rs", which were traditionally reading, writing, and arithmetic, already seem to be changing to reading, writing, and reproduction.) Children will be paid to stay on longer at school and college; I can only hope that there will be real efforts to give them at the same time a measure of increasing responsibility and independence, and to encourage the concern for people that has become a pleasant characteristic of many young people of today.

4. *Work and recreation.* There will probably be a four-day or three-day week, and a six-hour working day at most. Will working people retire earlier than now?—or will they have to retire later than they do now, because the on-coming generation of working men and women will be so much reduced in number?

Among new and exciting forms of recreation, I hope *not* to see artificial ski slopes on the Acropolis. The creative arts will be taken much more seriously than now, and to a growing proportion of fortunate people work and recreation will mean the same thing.

Youngsters will still need to explore and to seek adventure with some risks. I believe there will be increasing adventure in *outer* space, and work will be done out there, too, for the conversion of solar energy. As regards *inner* space, there will be "spaceships of the mind," exploring social anatomy and physiology, group psychology, ESP, psychedelic drugs, and much more.

5. *Medicine.* Surely there will be less physical disease, and many cancers will be amenable to immunotherapy. But there will be much more psychosocial disease, including such diseases of addiction as alcoholism and drug taking (and attending congresses?). A contrary tendency, the turning to self-treatment by lay people, will grow and be encouraged, perhaps as part of a return to nature. Accidents will always occur and parts of the body will wear out, so repair men and replacement technicians will be needed; but I am tempted to say that if pediatricians learn to do their job well there will be little need for adult physicians—they will become our "follow-up" colleagues.

6. *General.* We cannot, to order, think the unthinkable or take into account the occurrence of vast future movements or calamities; we must be content to extrapolate from existing trends, knowing the only certainty is that events will far outdistance our speculations.

There will be less pollution, more smoke-free and noise-free zones in cities. Relatively traffic-free towns will be bordered by forests of parking meters. Differences between the architecture, fashions, and habits of different countries will be less perceptible. A dull international uniformity will be subject to explosive outbursts of frustrated, picturesque nationalism, and regionalism. I cherish the hope that today's high rise flats will be used as prisons for those planners who built them in our time.

One trend, more than all others, causes me concern. I fear an increasing conflict between different age groups. We know that youngsters, particularly adolescents, are experimenters, revolutionaries, nonconforming free thinkers who live for the day. Increasingly they are rejecting parental, adult values with their traditional, conservative, law-abiding authority-seeking emphasis. Increasingly the young may opt out of our civilization under many-coloured banners. Already they are turning increasingly to violence, such as mugging adults or "grandma-bashing," or breaking into chemist shops to obtain illicit drugs. If the tendency continues, I foresee young people setting up communes from which they may sally forth against the fortresses where the oldsters try to protect themselves. The essential business of running the state could be undermined by continual guerrilla fighting between age groups.

At present this is only a cloud the size of a man's hand, but it might grow with frightening speed. We should be studying now how to guard against and prevent such a schism in society, if only because—for the first time in history—even a small group of people, whether old or young, can destroy those who oppose them, themselves, and the world.

We must enable the young to use their energies and their dreams, creatively and constructively. What is done in the next 20 years may be crucial in the history of mankind. It may even decide whether there is to be a future history for mankind.

POPULATION PERSPECTIVES FOR THE BALANCE OF THE CENTURY

D. V. GLASS*

London School of Economics and Political Science, London, UK

POPULATION projections have a poor reputation and justifiably so. Accurately to forecast a population means, in essence, being able to forecast economic and social changes and the reactions of the population to these changes. This being so, it would be very surprising indeed if, save by sheer accident, a projection of the population of a particular country in, say, the year 2000, proved to agree with reality. Nevertheless, projections can be of considerable value in showing the implications of various assumptions regarding fertility and mortality and providing the basis for considering how those possible developments may influence, or should be taken into account, in formulating economic and social policies. In addition, though it may be impossible to forecast absolute numbers, the age structure of a population has implications for its future growth. Hence some generalizations regarding the future may be both realistic and important. I should like to illustrate this with reference to three recent sets of projections of world population. Two of them were produced by the UN Population Division and the third by the Harvard Center for Population Studies.

All three projections assume a continued decline in mortality and some decline in fertility. But one—the UN medium projection—assumes rather less of a fall in fertility than either the UN low variant or the Harvard projection. In particular, the UN low variant is based upon the assumption of a 40% fall in fertility in less-developed countries by the end of the century as compared with just over 30% for the medium projection. And the Harvard computations assume that the joint declines in mortality and fertility will lead to a replacement rate of 1·0 by 1990—5 for the developed countries and China and by 2000—5 for the rest of the world. How realistic those various assumptions will prove to be, only time will tell, and there is no substitute for waiting. But it would be reasonable to say that there is a more firm foundation for forecasting mortality levels than for forecasting those of fertility. Apart from catastrophes, mortality has tended to move generally in one direction—downwards, without too much of a break with the previous trend. After all, even "miracle drugs", like antibiotics, which have helped to speed that downward trend, have not had an immediate, universal take-up. Death rates have since the Second World War fallen more, and more quickly than earlier studies assumed, especially because—as recent studies have shown—a given reduction in death rates can now be achieved with a lower *per capita* income than was the case 100 or even 50 years ago. It is now far more a matter of political priorities and of the nature and effectiveness of the organization of health care. The new WHO drive for primary health care may help to counter the deficiencies in the third world of low income, provided, that is, that local community involvement in such care can actually be

*Died suddenly 23 September 1978.

achieved and that an appropriate administrative structure can be developed. It is by no means clear that what has been done in China can be easily or directly applied in other countries. That substantial improvements are possible can be seen in India, where in contrast to generally high levels of infant mortality—over 130 per 1000 in 1970—and low expectation of life at birth—below 50 years in 1961–70—Kerala has been able to achieve an infant mortality rate of under 60 per 1000 and an expectation of life at birth of over 60 years. As Professor Panikar[1] has argued recently, Kerala's experience supports the view that economic resources are not the primary constraint on health. But Kerala has had a fairly long tradition, initiated by the maharajahs of Travancore, of health centres located close to the people and thus at a relatively high density, as well as a genuinely widespread educational system covering girls as well as boys, so that the level of literacy (at 66·6% of all males and 54·3% of females in 1971) is the highest of all India's states. It is reported that 10% of infant deaths in India in 1973 and 27% of deaths of children aged 1–4 years were the consequence of digestive disorders.[2] How, unless there are elsewhere in India developments similar to those which have already occurred in Kerala, can a program of rehydration for treating infantile diarrhea be actually carried out? How, even, can neonatal tetanus be avoided unless both mothers and village midwives are much more conversant with health precautions than is the case at present?

The future course of fertility is much more uncertain. In developed countries there has been a rapid shift from the low levels of the 1930s to the marriage and baby booms of the 1950s and 60s and then to sharp declines in the 1970s, some of which occurred in populations which hitherto characteristically produced large families. Part of the change can be accounted for by much wider access to and use of modern contraceptive techniques and by recourse to legalized abortion. But that is only part of the explanation, and still more recently some Western countries have, once again, begun to show a slight upturn in fertility. The future movements of fertility in less-developed countries are also problematic. Many of those countries, containing most of the population of the third world, now have governmental or state-supported birth control programs. But it is not easy to tell how far those programs have helped to bring down fertility. Indeed, in quite a number of cases it is not clear whether the present birth rate is significantly lower than it was, say, 10 years ago. Various, sometimes conflicting, estimates have been produced, not surprisingly, in view of the fact that few developing countries have effective systems of vital registration.

India, with one of the largest populations (some 640 million), derives its estimates from a sample registration system, which yields more reliable results than those for many other third world countries. Even so, there is a fair margin of doubt as to how far the birth rate has fallen since 1960. For China, with an estimated population of over 900 million, no systematic sets of birth rates are available, and a recent estimate by the US Bureau of the Census puts the crude birth rate for 1976 within the range of 18–32 per 1000.[3] There are now ingenious techniques for estimating levels of fertility (and mortality) from census and sample survey data. But those techniques cannot detect with certainty small changes in fertility.

Nevertheless, certain facts are clear. First, unlike developed countries, many of which at present have a somewhat ambivalent attitude to population growth—some are pronatalist—most developing countries are now concerned to lower their growth rates by reducing fertility. Secondly, it is possible to draw profiles of those developing countries in which major reductions in fertility have already taken place. In general, they have fairly small populations; they are relatively high on the ladder of development—not necessarily in *per capita* income but at least in respect of literacy and education; the age at marriage of women has risen significantly—in some cases that change has accounted for up to 50% of the overall fall in fertility; and they have well-organized birth control programs, though the techniques used are not the same in all countries. It is the combination of development and effective birth control programs which appears to account for the sharp fall in fertility in such countries as Taiwan, Singapore, Hong Kong, Sri Lanka, Mauritius, and Costa Rica. But the large land masses seem so far to have shown relatively little change, though it is possible that fertility has fallen more in China than in many other large developing countries.[4] Whether we can expect to see, during the balance of the century, effective combinations of circumstances in the third world as a whole, is a question which cannot easily be answered.

In spite of these various uncertainties, the population projections, which were mentioned earlier in this paper, yield results that, if hypothetical, are unlikely to differ in a radical way from the actual developments during the balance of the century. Even if fertility were to fall very substantially and immediately, absolute numbers would continue to increase, especially in the third world. The reason is that the short-run growth of numbers is affected primarily by the age structure of the population in the initial period. Taking the third world as a whole, almost 41% of the population was under 15 years of age in 1970. As this group moves into the reproductive ages, the resultant births will be very substantial even if fertility falls suddenly and sharply. Hence an increase in the population of the third world by some 60% between 1970 and 2000 may not be an accurate forecast but it is not an unrealistic one, and it has to be taken into account in planning if catastrophes are to be avoided.

Of course, declining fertility has an immediate effect on the age structure of the population. Thus with the fall envisaged by the Harvard Center projection—such that net reproduction rates would be 1·0 by 1995–2005, the under 15 years age group would be only 31% of the total population of developing countries by 2000, and 22% in the developed countries, instead of 41% and 27% respectively in 1970. And the dependancy ratios would improve. That is, the ratio of adults aged 15–64 years to children and old persons would rise from 1·24 to 1·75 in the third world and from 1·75 to 1·93 in the industrialized nations. Part of the theoretical improvement in the third world may prove to be fictitious—the result of transferring children and young persons from the labor force to education. On the other hand, expanded education may well add to the labor force by attracting larger proportions of married women who, in 1970, were not gainfully employed. That, too, would add to the problem of finding employment opportunities, but it would also offer a potential for improving levels of living and for a sharper reduction of fertility.[5]

The reduction in the proportion of children would not necessarily mean a fall in the numbers to be educated. In some Western countries the fall in the birth rate has persuaded governments to reduce the numbers of entrants to teacher-training programs. But this applies to countries in which almost 100% of children are already covered by primary schooling. Even in such countries, secondary education may not always be universal, while the expansion of higher education may add to the numbers

TABLE 1

Estimated and projected populations in millions

	1970	1975	1990			2000			Percentage increase 1975–2000		
			UN(a) medium projection	UN low variant	LK(b) projection	UN(a) medium projection	UN low variant	LK(b) projection	UN(a) medium projection	UN low variant	LK(b) projection
World total	3610	3968	5280	5089	5149	6254	5840	5882	57.6	47.2	48.2
More-developed regions	1084	1132	1277	1250	1260	1360	1308	1324	20.1	15.5	17.0
Less-developed regions	2526	2836	4003	3839	3889	4894	4532	4558	72.6	59.8	60.7

(a) United Nations, *World Population Prospects as Assessed in 1973*, Population Studies No. 60, New York, 1977.

(b) G. Littman and N. Keyfitz, *The Next Hundred Years*, Center for Population Studies, Harvard University, Working Paper No. 101, 27 June 1977.

TABLE 2

Estimated and projected age composition (percentages)

| | 1970 | | | | 2000 | | | | | | | | | | | |
| | | | | | UN medium projection | | | | UN low variant | | | | LK projection | | | |
	Under 15	15–64	65+	Dep. ratios (a)	Under 15	15–64	65+	Dep. ratios (a)	Under 15	15–64	65+	Dep. ratios (a)	Under 15	15–64	65+	Dep. ratios (a)
World total	36.6	57.9	5.5	1.38	32.4	61.3	6.3	1.58	29.9	63.4	6.7	1.73	29.1	64.2	6.7	1.79
More-developed regions	26.7	63.7	9.6	1.75	22.6	65.0	12.4	1.86	20.7	66.4	12.9	1.98	21.6	65.9	12.5	1.93
Less-developed regions	40.9	55.4	3.7	1.24	35.1	60.2	4.7	1.51	32.6	62.5	4.9	1.67	31.3	63.7	5.0	1.75

(a) The dependency ratio used here is the ratio of active persons (15–64 years) to dependents (children under 15 years plus persons aged 65 years and over). Sources as in Table 1.

Notes on Tables 1 and 2. All the projections assume a continued decline in mortality and some decline in fertility. The assumed rates of decline are different for each projection.

(a) UN medium projection. Assumes (i) for developed regions, an expectation of life at birth of 73.4 years and a gross reproduction rate of 1.09 by 1995–2000; (ii) for less-developed regions, an expectation of life at birth of 62.6 years and a gross reproduction rate of 1.75 by 1995–2000.

(b) UN low variant. The assumptions for 1995–2000 are: (i) for more/developed regions, the same expectation of life, but a gross reproduction rate of 0.96; (ii) for less-developed regions, an expectation of life at birth of 60.7 years and a gross reproduction rate of 1.52.

(c) Littman/Keyfitz projection. The detailed assumptions are not stated in the publication. But mortality is assumed to continue to decline and fertility, too, to such an extent that the net replacement rate is 1.0 in 1990–5 for the developed regions and China, and in 2000–5 for all other countries.

above the age of 15 for whom education would need to be provided. In developing countries, primary schooling is often far from universal. Genuinely compulsory primary education, and the extension of secondary education would add greatly to the numbers under 15 years of age to be covered by the educational system. Further, though the proportion of children would fall, the total numbers would continue to increase even with a marked decline in fertility. According to the Harvard projection, which assumes a very substantial fall in the net reproduction rate by 2000–5 in less-developed countries, there would be over 1400 million children under 15 in the year 2000 as compared with just over 1000 millions in 1970.

One final point. Though a substantial reduction in fertility would not prevent a large increase in world population by the year 2000, what happens to fertility in the short run will have important long run consequences. This is especially so for countries which at present contain a large proportion of children and young persons. Take the case of India, with a net reproduction rate of around 1·9 in 1961. If the rate were to fall to 1·0 immediately and continue at that level, the population would increase by 20% in the following 30 years and by about 33% in 100 years, thereafter remaining stationary. But if it took 50 years for the net reproduction rate to fall to 1·0, total numbers would increase by almost 160% before a stationary population was achieved, after 150 years. Rapid population growth and large numbers are certainly not the only factors which impede economic development, and not even the most important factors. Nevertheless, they are obstacles. All the more reason, therefore, for urging that realistic, combined programs of economic development and birth control be implemented as quickly as practicable.

REFERENCES

1. P. G. K. PANIKAR, *Resources not the constraint on health improvement—a case study of Kerala*, paper prepared for the 1978 V1th European Conference on Modern South Asian Studies. See also Registrar General, India, *Sample Registration Bulletin*, **9** (4) October 1975.
2. OFFICE OF THE REGISTRAR GENERAL, *India, Causes of Death 1973: A Survey*, New Delhi. About half the deaths up to five years of age associated with digestive disorders were attributed to gastroenteritis.
3. US DEPARTMENT OF COMMERCE, BUREAU OF THE CENSUS, *World Population: 1977 (Advance Report)*, April 1978.
4. K. S. SRI KANTAN, *The Family Planning Program in the Socio-economic Context*, The Population Council, New York, 1977; R. M. MARU etal., *The Organisation of Family Planning Programs: India, China, Costa Rica, Venezuela, Lebanon*, Smithsonian Institution, Washington, DC, December 1976; PI-CHAO CHEN, *Population and Health Policy in the People's Republic of China*, Smithsonian Institution, Washington, DC, December 1976
5. K. NEWLAND, *Women and Population Growth: Choice beyond Child-bearing*, World Watch Paper 16, Washington DC, December, 1977; and J. SENDEROWITZ, *Women's changing job status: more Theoretic than Reality*, Intercom, April 1978.

SOCIETY TOMORROW

GEORGE ZEIDENSTEIN
The Population Council, New York, NY, USA

WHAT are some of the important facts and factors of today that are likely to affect the society tomorrow? A variety of subjects rush into my consciousness in response to my question:

Economic development and the many ways in which it has affected the lives of people everywhere. This is an important background for several of the more specific facts and factors I shall mention later. In terms of overall economic growth, the performance of the poorer countries of Africa, Asia, and Latin America over the past two and a half decades has no recorded precedent. The same can be said of food production. Health and general living conditions have improved for the average person; this is evident in the rapid drop in mortality rates, which is also probably the key factor in the rapid population growth of this period. This overall record and the spectacular performances of a number of countries were generally unanticipated, even as recently as the early 1960s.

But despite that substantial economic growth, abject poverty remains widespread. More than 700 million people still live in absolute poverty, defined as an income per head of $200 per year or less. This amounts to almost 40% of the developing world's total population. Over 40% of the labor force in the developing world is unemployed or underemployed. Four hundred and fifty million to one billion people suffer from malnutrition. Infant mortality rates are eight times higher in the 57 lowest income countries than in the United States. More than 750 million adults are illiterate and the number is growing. And let us not forget that the differentials between richer and poorer countries are mirrored within countries between richer and poorer classes and, at least equally shocking, between males and females.

Furthermore, the number of poor, underemployed, malnourished, and illiterate people has risen over the years. The extent to which this increase is attributable primarily to the explosive population growth that characterized that period, or to the growth and distribution policies that were followed, can be argued about. Some contend that the proportion of poor has fallen, even though the central fact remains that poverty is massive and that there are more people today than before.

Most of the absolute poor reside in the low income countries and comprise about half their population. However, more than 150 million remain in the middle income nations and account for almost 20% of their total population. These latter countries have generally displayed high rates of economic growth. Their mixed performance in achieving high growth rates amidst continuing abject poverty raises questions about their development processes.

This brief sketching of the results of 25 years of complex development history leads me to an attempt to venture a finer grained listing of the facts and factors of today that are likely to affect the society tomorrow.

Population and its parameters in *fertility* and *mortality* (especially infant mortality)—and in the consequent rates of *population growth* in different parts of the world—the experience with *migration* both within and between countries and with its correlative, *urbanization.*

Energy and *resources* (including as fundamental a resource as oxygen), their distribution and utilization, their renewal and recycling, the political and economic control over them, their pricing.

Ecology and the *quality of human environments,* the impacts upon them of the existing industrial activities of the world and the additional ones bound to come as the poorer countries modernize—the problems of harmonizing the increasing industrial, agricultural, and commercial growth with preservation of environmental quality.

Employment, the extension and improvement of human productivity, the provision of income, and the consequent creation of demand for goods and services.

Modernization and what it is to mean from place to place in the immense and materially poor parts of the world in Africa, Asia, and Latin America, where its processes are now under way—what its impact is to be on values and on social institutions, e.g. on the relations between women and men, within the family and among its members, on the roles and status of women and of children as individuals and as family members and as members of society.

Education and *literacy,* the increasing number of illiterates and the increasing proportions of them who are women.

The *North/South dialogue,* its intensity and seriousness and its possible interactions with a range of development issues included under rubrics like meeting basic human needs and establishing a new international economic order.

Gigantism and *centralization,* as an institutional characteristic of much of what we have come to think of as "modern," and its impacts upon diversity and upon human and societal vulnerability both material and institutional.

Overarching all of these is the astoundingly rapid and pervasive development and spread since the end of the Second World War of *communications technology.* Never in the history of humankind has it been possible for us to know about each other in such detail and to be in direct communication with each other so easily and quickly as it is today. In a series of technological developments that stagger the imagination and that are still so new that their implications for the future well-being of humanity can only be guessed, an elaborate and intricate system of communications instruments have been fashioned and deployed so that the system already penetrates into nearly every place on this planet and into every society, culture, and subculture that resides here. Nearly every one of us is exposed by this system to the others, and nearly all of us are being made aware by this system of how the others are getting on. For perhaps the first time in human history nearly every group of people on earth is aware (or soon will be) of what is possible in the way of material and physical advancement—and has, or is developing, aspirations to be materially and physically better off than before. The central qualitative issues relate to who controls the technological system and how will it be controlled in the next 25 years or so. For example, the number of stationary communcations satellites that can be placed in orbit over the horizon is finite. Who will control? And whose messages will be carried?

Obviously, there is much more in this listing that we can hope to handle in any effective way during a brief set of meetings. Indeed, these matters are among the central ones of our times, the ones that engage the attention of the political leaders of our world. Perhaps the most we can hope to do is begin to articulate with each other some of the concerns we have about these, and other equally important issues in regard to which actions and ideas today are likely to affect the society tomorrow, and to share with each other the information and analyses and judgments that we have. Beyond that, we can plan that the participants in these meetings, who occupy positions of important responsibility in their respective countries, will in turn share their thoughts, concerns, and information about these important issues with others at home because these matters and how they are addressed today are likely to be among the determinants of the society tomorrow.

Although it has been convenient thus far to speak of the society tomorrow, in the singular, a fundamental fact that we must articulate and acknowledge from the outset, in my opinion, is that it is most unlikely that by "tomorrow"—whether we mean by that 10 years from now, 20 years from now, the turn of the century, or some time shortly thereafter—the planet earth will have any single society. Although gigantism appears to characterize many of the institutional, economic, and social developments since the end of the Second World War, it appears that the case is distinctly opposite in regard to the geopolitical organization of our planet. Perhaps the geopolitical cycle is in a different phase than are others that produce institutions whose tendency is toward large size and central control. It was only a short time ago that gigantism characterized the geopolitical scene.

When the United Nations was established in June 1945, the number of member nations was 51 and within 24 months had risen to only 55. Today, a scant 30 plus years later—but following the dissolution of several empires—the number of member nations of the United Nations has risen to 149, an increase of 171%. Most of this increase can be traced to the emergence of new nations from colonial status. As of today, the geopolitical reality that seems dominant in the world is pluralism and diversity rather than the gigantism and centralization that prevailed for hundreds of years during the days of the great empires.

What may appear as the spaceship earth from the moon or a space vehicle somewhere in between the two has quite different characteristics when observed from the surface of the earth itself. Unlike a spaceship, earth is not directed by a single commander (at least not an earthly one); it follows resources and products in ways deemed most efficient or appropriate for the well-being of the planet as a whole. Instead it is divided into many nation-states, each following its own plan determined by and on its own behalf to be in its own best interests (with various direct and indirect influences from the outside to be sure).

The best interests of a particular nation-state are not necessarily in the best interests of the planet as a whole. Moreover, an analogous possibility of disparity and even conflict repeats itself over and over again as we move down the line from the interests of the planet versus those of the nation-states; to the interests of the nation-state versus those of particular areas or groups within it; to the interests of larger communities versus those of the smaller; to the interests of the village versus those of the family; to the interests of the family versus those of its individual members, and here the critically important matters of relative resource utilization as between children (male ones and female ones are not treated the same), women, and men are to be sorted out. In which direction will the wealth flow in a particular society or group within it? These aspects of diversity and contradiction are among the important facts and factors that will affect the society tomorrow.

Projections (as distinguished from predictions) starting now—in July of 1978—suggest that the global pressures of rapid population growth during the remaining years of the 20th century will be somewhat lighter than we had thought earlier. This is because it seems that the ultimate global numbers could be a little smaller and could be achieved rather sooner than was predicted a few years ago. That is to say that if present trends continue, the earth is likely to see its human populations stabilize at a total of about nineplus billion souls in about the year 2100 with the global number at around the turn of the century having been about 6·1 billion. As I mentioned earlier, behavior often contradicts mathematical or other statistical projections. As recently as 1974 it had seemed likely that the earth's population in the year 2000 would number about 6·4 billion and that stabilization could not be seriously expected before about 2100 and would most probably total about 12·3 billion. Why the difference? We do not know in detail. We did not predict the changes that occurred in people's demographic behavior. Nor can we now characterize the causes of those changes in sufficient detail and with confidence. This is not to say that we are entirely ignorant—or even as ignorant as we were a few years ago. Much is being learned day by day regarding people's demographic behavior, not only their fertility behavior but their migration behavior as well. The present calculations and projections reflect the present states of fact and knowledge and they may need to be revised again in a few years from now.

Again, looking at the society tomorrow in terms of what we know today, in many countries of the world what is locally perceived as important from a population point of view is migration and urbanization rather than fertility. As recently as 1976 the responses received by the United Nations Population Division to a questionnaire they had sent out to 156 nations showed that 115 of them consider migration and urbanization as serious problems, but only 49 stated that high fertility imposes severe or substantial constraints. Of course, it must be pointed out that the major portions of the world's population live in a relatively small number of very populous countries most of which do consider population growth a major problem. I speak more specifically of China with a population of about 900 million (with a plus or minus range of 50 million), India with a population of about 635 million, Indonesia with a population of about 145 million, Pakistan with a population of about 75 million, and Bangladesh with a population of about 84 million. On the other hand, two of the most densely populated countries of the world, where growth rates are substantially above world averages, are Nigeria and Brazil, which do not in any official way recognize population growth as a problem for them.

For the society tomorrow—if tomorrow is not significantly further ahead of us than the turn of the century—accommodation of the irreducible population numbers—persons already in being and those who will come into being under even the most optimistic assumptions about effective birth planning during the next 25 years—is as important as continuing to devote ourselves toward limiting population growth. Even rapid, accelerating, and effective attention by and within nation-states to their problems of population growth cannot prevent the substantial growth implied by the sizes of age cohorts coming into their reproductive phases during the 25 years immediately ahead of us. This is not to say that population growth issues do not remain tremendously important and retain a central claim on the world's attention and resources because even differences of several tens of millions in the populations of countries as large as China or India or Indonesia or the like can make major differences in the balance between their resources and their people who use them.

Equally important in a time frame whose outer limit is "tomorrow" are the problems likely to come along with peoples' migratory behavior and its correlative, urban growth. Finally—so far as population parameters are concerned—continued progress or lack of it in the world in extending life expectancy—especially through reduction in rates of infant mortality—is likely to have major impacts upon the society tomorrow. In Africa, for example, only about 850 of every 1000 live births survive beyond the age of one year. In Latin America, the parallel numbers are 925 of every 1000 live births. In South Asia, only about 860 of every 1000 live births survive beyond that age. These numbers are approximate. Astounding as it may seem, the world does not keep careful records about infant or child mortality.

This leads us automatically and directly into the complex of development issues that I mentioned earlier, employment, meeting basic human needs, the new international economic order, the north/south dialogue. I have listed these in what I felt to be a sort of inverse order of generality from the point of view of the individual and the individual family.

Many people believe—and I am among them—that productive employment is probably the single most important factor in determining the material well-being of people in the society tomorrow. Whether we are looking at mortality and morbidity, health and nutritional status, human energy and creativity, we are likely to find that the society that provides opportunities for productive employment to its people is also likely to be the society that has lower mortality and morbidity, better health and nutrition, higher and more productive levels of human energy and creativity.

We can perceive, too, that generation of productive employment may be the keystone of whatever realistic efforts are undertaken to attempt through development efforts and investments to assist people to meet their basic human needs. In this sense, it seems important to distinguish between that concept of meeting basic human needs that sees it as a strategy of aid and the one that sees it as a strategy of development. If it is a strategy of aid, there is an implication that the aid-giving agency or nation attempts to focus its assistance directly to poor people enabling them—with that very assistance—to meet some of their basic human needs. If, on the other hand, the strategy is one of development, then perhaps the aid-giving country or agency focuses its inputs more toward supporting the receiving country's overall development works so long as they are calculated to create and sustain circumstances—primarily, I would argue, those of high and productive employment—under which people will be able to earn the wherewithal to meet their own basic human needs on a continuing basis.

Obviously, my own conviction about how the concept of meeting basic human needs needs to be viewed and administrated programmatically comes through clearly in the way I have stated the difference between the two ways of looking at it.

Closely tied in with the nature of the resolutions that the world works out in relation to development flows of resources, both official and unofficial, and in its understanding of how best to meet basic human needs are the inevitably related aspects of foreign affairs that are very much with us today under the titles of: new international economic order and the north/south dialogue. These resolutions, in turn, will have important effects—both consequential and causal—upon the world's energy situation especially while fossil fuels, principally oil, remain the most important sources of the vast energy requirements of industrialized and industrializing countries.

All this, of course, is much more than we can go into in detail today, or than I am myself capable of going into in more than superficial ways. But, in my opinion, it is most important that in a meeting like this we recognize that along with attention to the concerns as specialists for children and their welfare, we recognize and address the political and social matrixes that regulate the extents to which improvements in children's welfare can be accomplished by the work of concerned experts. The crucial world conflicts that affect us all—the fully grown and the partially grown of humankind—among rich nations and poor ones, industrialized nations and pastoral ones, resource-controlling and resource-using ones are high on the agenda of principal policymakers of the world today. Those of us whose work is more specialized can nevertheless have impacts on the ways in which the major issues are decided. It is most important that in preparing specific proposals for benefiting children we cast them so that they can influence the broader international situation in which they will have to operate in the society tomorrow.

DISCUSSION

IOANNIS PALEOKRASSAS
Ministry of Coordination, Athens, Greece

I SHOULD like to touch on the trends now noticeable in the developed, industrialized societies, which are likely to be transferred to the less-developed countries. Referring to the statement that we have to learn to become more qualitative in our evaluations and less quantitative, we must remember that economists are tempted to rely on counting, which suits our nature and the nature of our science.

We need to set parameters on what we mean when we talk of "tomorrow". In the symposium we are really talking of no more than two generations ahead, the first of these two being very important to us now.

One thing is certain; society is deeply affected by changes in the economic sphere, especially by income increases and changes in the level of wealth index (e.g. GNP).

In the 1950s and part of the 1960s the greater part of the world experienced an economic explosion; rates of economic growth went up, and *per capita* incomes went up much faster in developed countries than in the developing ones. The relationship between population growth and income made a great difference in developing countries, where even though income levels rose, the population growth was so great that the countries generally could only maintain what had been the pattern in the past.

While different growth pictures for different countries are probable it is certain that, in general, growth will be much weaker than in the past. Two of the main factors are:

(1) Increasing scarcity of materials that function in production (e.g. part of the problem in industrialized states is in the last five years petroleum prices rose to such an extent that this pulled down production capacity and, therefore, the rate of growth in industrialized societies began to slow down).
(2) Inflation, which is defined as a "new disease", is a general phenomenon in the developed countries. This new disease ". . . baffles our limited capabilities of diagnosis and treatment."

In general, both the slower rates of growth and inflation will be extorted from the more-developed countries. While *per capita* incomes will rise slightly in some countries, in others, they will not rise at all.

Human biology is slow to react to the changes generated from the economic sphere and a slower rate of growth is an advantage from this point of view. However, social stresses will become more prevalent in the future, due to, for example, unemployment and aging populations, while the change from fast economic growth to a slower one is itself causing stress (i.e. the change in and of itself is stressful).

Barring unforeseen sources of energy, we have to study, in advance, the impending problems of a slower rate of growth.

GEORGE PAPAEVANGELOU
School of Hygiene, Athens, Greece

I should like to stress certain points that emerge from the available population projections and that have to be taken seriously into consideration in planning the future of the child in the world of tomorrow.

All available population projections (United Nations Population Division; Harvard Center for Population Studies; the Population Council) assume a further fall in mortality and a substantial decline in fertility and predict a world population of about six billion by the turn of the century. This is in contrast to similar projections a few years ago, which predicted a population size of about seven billion. I should like to stress that there are certain facts which show that this reduction may have serious effects on the society of the world of tomorrow.

1. It is certain that, despite the decrease of the population growth rate, the size of the present world population will increase by at least 60% by the turn of the century because of the present age structure, especially of the less-developed countries. It is certain that these additional people will create many problems for the society of tomorrow, which have to be anticipated.

2. There is some anticipation of a coming improvement of the dependency ratio because of the impending decrease of the percentage of children under 15 years of age. However, this is not likely to result in an improvement in the standard of living since a great many young persons will be transferred from the labor force to education.

3. Also a decrease in the percentage of children under 15 will not mean an absolute decrease in numbers. Consequently special provisions need to be taken immediately for adequate provision of primary as well as secondary education.

4. The present decline in mortality has been achieved more easily and faster than some decades ago. However, it is still high, and a further decline of mortality is likely to require more effort and to be less fast. Then special efforts are needed for the implementation of public health programs, the organization of primary health care centers, and the general improvement of the educational system. This can be considered as one of the most urgent and effective ways to improve the society of tomorrow for the child.

LEE N. ROBINS
Department of Sociology, Washington University, St. Louis, MO, USA

Sociologists have been notoriously poor at predicting social change. We do very well at identifying which children will have trouble in school and which will have trouble as adults on the basis of family characteristics and their own early behavior, but we do not do well at predicting what the general level of social problems will be in the future. We have been much too conservative in our predictions, assuming a much greater push toward integration among society's values and a much greater tendency to return to equilibrium than actually occurs. People are remarkably able to hold modern and traditional values simultaneously.

We can, however, make a few tentative predictions:

(1) that technology will bring to all societies increasing problems in finding a meaningful role for its adolescents and young adults who have no work experience and who, because of age alone, are bound to be unskilled;

(2) that improved communications will create dissatisfaction and low self-esteem in the youth of developing countries and the disadvantaged youth of developed countries because they will increasingly be able to compare their status with those of other, better-off young people;

(3) that increasing urbanization will lead to increased problems of juvenile crime as more women work away from home and are forced to live in homes that do not allow for adequate visual surveillance of children's play areas.

While these changes will bring new problems, there will also be advantages. Visual teaching techniques such as television make it possible to educate the illiterate. Researchers are only now beginning to develop adequate methods for evaluating the effects of social programs: methods that allow us to make reasonably rapid assessments and separate the effects of the programs from the characteristics of those who participate in them. We are also developing sensible goals for the education of children, recognizing that they must provide success experiences for all children, not just those who fit into one academic mold.

Education programs often use those outcome measures that are relatively easy to handle: measures such as achievement, IQ, or vocabulary tests. But what we hope for in the future is not higher test scores but an improved ability to function in the real world. Measures that can be applied cross-nationality and that are much closer to "real world" measures are the number of days of school attendance and whether children complete whatever minimum level of schooling is agreed on within a particular society as the appropriate required level.

It is doubtful that advice to parents will have much influence on the hard measures such as have been mentioned, though it is worth trying. We are well aware that family competence varies enormously and that parent characteristics profoundly influence children's success, not only in school but in later life. If it were as easy to affect family environments as some studies suggest, we would not expect to see the powerful effects of fathers' histories of school achievement on their sons' school achievement, since fathers rarely are the target group of such programs. Yet our follow-up study comparing school records of parents and children show more correlation between parents' and children's attendance records and high school graduations than between parents' and children's IQ scores, although it has been supposed that IQ is a genetically transmitted trait, while no one has supposed that truancy is a genetic trait.

Before recommending new large scale programs, we need to evaluate them as carefully as possible through small, pilot studies. While there is then no guarantee that programs successful on a small scale will continue to be successful on the large scale, there is every reason to think that programs that *cannot* be proved successful on the small scale will not be good choices for large scale application. In evaluating such programs we would be well advised to use simple and relevant outcome criteria that are easy to obtain. Attendance is such a criterion, since whether a school system is good or bad, it cannot educate children who are not present.

PHILIP RHODES
Regional Postgraduate Institute for Medicine, Newcastle upon Tyne, UK

At the turn of the century a group met to make predictions over 50 years. Apart from a host of other things, they missed radio, television, aeroplanes, and antibiotics. So I am not going to try and talk about a long term look into the future. I also have enormous difficulty in getting any kind of grip on the meaning of the word "society." What I have in mind is a whole group of societies with very different psychosocial and cultural connotations. The philosopher who interests me most today is Professor Karl Popper and his logic of scientific discovery in *The Open Society and its Enemies*. One of the outstanding things that has brought the world into perspective for me is that you start with a problem, you define it, and you try a trial solution. This always goes wrong. Therefore you have to have error elimination to try and put the solution right. This invariably goes wrong too, so you apply a second trial solution and a second error elimination, and you end up with problem three, and so on *ad infinitum*. This means there is no use going for the grandiose utopian solutions to anything and certainly not to the problem of children. On the other hand, it does seem to me worth emphasizing that the main problems for children are poverty, malnutrition, and ultimately the infections that kill them. We can be absolutely sure of the value of trying to get rid of those problems, but what we can not be so sure about is whether one culture should try to impose different sorts of ideas on another. This applies particularly to the psychosocial problems of different cultures, which seem to me to vary enormously.

What I would like to say, as an obstetrician, is that it is the mother who is the environment of the child. She is its physical environment during intrauterinal life. It is she who provides its nutrition. It is she who provides the cultural environment in which the child grows. She is helped or hindered in this by her own education, her physical environment, and her nutrition; but the outstanding problem is the role and status of women in the different cultures. That is not going to change easily, which explains some of the problems of the acceptability of birth control programs.

Another problem is the education of government in social accountancy. This means getting them to understand where you and I feel that the money and the resources ought to go and to act accordingly.

I would finally state that while the human condition *per se* is not remediable, since its problems vary constantly and always will, it is still possible for us to make the lives of some children somewhat better.

GÖRAN STERKY
Department of Pediatrics, Karolinska Institute, Stockholm, Sweden

I have worked both in a developed country—Sweden—and in the developing world—mostly in Africa. When talking of the future I think we should start with something that in Swedish is called *logun,* which means not too much, not too little, but just enough. To me the development of the future really starts with ourselves. From my experiences in the developing world I have learnt a lot that I can apply at home in Sweden, and I think this is true for many others.

We talk a lot internationally of self-reliant development. A fundamental change in my own outlook has been a greater trust in the people around me. This makes for a lot of change in attitudes. It means that it is important for the service society of today to stop and think and not to interfere unless it can offer something much better than the present situation. For example, why do we have to employ people to weigh babies? In Sweden, where almost everyone is literate and has two hands, scales are not expensive and parents themselves can weigh the babies and read the weight. I think we have to be somewhat concerned about the implications of our service society. What is the implication for the future when we take away from people the possibility to take care of each other?

Like many others, I think the GNP is the wrong yardstick, the wrong indicator of economic and social development. I am sure there can be "development" without a rise in the GNP. I accuse social scientists for not developing social indicators that are easy to apply. All the ones we have today are impossible to apply at a community or village level.

I think we have to develop meaningful indicators against which people can measure their social development. A year ago, in collaboration with the WHO family health division, I worked on birthweight distribution as a social indicator. This seemed to correlate with a number of other distributional defects. Birthweight tells something of the past, the present, and the future, and it is operational, so I put it forward as one of the possible quantitative and qualitative indicators that are asked for by Dr. Harfouche*.

Finally, a word about the 'future". A couple of months back there was a paper in the *Lancet* about prevention of diseases, but what impressed me in this paper was a statement that for most of the British population the future is next Friday (pay day). It was impossible for most of the working population of Britain to conceive of the year 2000: the future had to deal with employment next week. So I think that before it finishes, this meeting also should adjust its thinking to next Friday.

Note: Her contribution comes later, but he had read her paper.

SUMMARY OF DISCUSSION

GEORGE ZEIDENSTEIN
The Population Council, New York, NY, USA

MAJOR themes that emerged from our discussions included these:

Diversity. We cannot really conceive of any single society of tomorrow (defining "tomorrow" as the next 25 years or so). Diversity between regions, nation-states, and classes and groups within nation-states characterize the present and are likely to characterize the next quarter century. Embedded in the diversity is gross disparity. Attention has been turned in recent years to this disparity and efforts will be made to relieve it.

International politics. The matrix in which efforts to improve conditions for children will have to be embedded will continue to be that of international political and economic relationships. Questions of political and military power and control over basic resources will inevitably command the attention of decision makers and affect fundamentally the extent to which the welfare of children can be improved.

Economic development. Similarly, the progress of economic development in the world will have profound meaning for the possibilities of improved conditions of childhood. The prospects, assuming continued central importance of free market economies, are for continuing inflationary pressures and slowing rates of economic growth—as measured in classical terms, with main reliance on GNP as an index.

Distribution. Distributional issues will become increasingly important in the face of inflation and slowing rates of economic growth.

Population. Although global numbers of people are likely to be smaller than had been projected earlier (about 6.1 billion at the year 2000 and stabilization at 9 plus billion in about the year 2100 now seem likely), population will grow most and most rapidly in countries that can least afford the growth. Migration and urbanization within countries will continue to create social and economic pressures that will have important effects upon family structure and stability. International migration (much of it illegal) is bound to occur in significant amounts. This, too, will have important effects on family structure and stability.

Communications. The technology will continue to improve and spread, and questions about control over the technology itself, as well as the messages to be conveyed through it, will be increasingly debated. Television will increase its explosive impact on the shaping of the minds of children.

THE FAMILY OF TOMORROW

FAMILY AND SOCIAL VISIBILITY OF THE CHILD IN THE FUTURE

CLIO PRESVELOU

Department of Sociology, Catholic University of Louvain, Belgium

THE FUNDAMENTAL question to which we shall attempt to reply is the following: What kind of society and family will the child of the year 2000 have?

The difficulties and errors of forecasting should not be underestimated. On the basis of available behavioral patterns and of critical appraisal of current trends to be found in a number of societies it is quite possible and even legitimate to imagine various scenarii of the societal and family configurations which will care for the child in the year 2000 and beyond, and attempt to evaluate the advantages and shortcomings of each of them as conceivable loci of the child's socio-psychological environment.

Scenario One: Society and conjugal partners attribute limited importance to children.

This hypothesis is founded on exaggerated individualistic and egoistic values. Living and working environments and schedules as well as social relationships would be subjected to domination (economic, ideological, etc.) of the many by the few. In certain countries and for certain aspects (abortion laws, for example, voted hastily), current social and family legislation tends to outdistance recognized social values. If this trend were to continue and spread it could produce a destabilization of man–woman relationships within and outside the family setting. Furthermore, an Epicurian ideology which already sustains certain forms of conjugal life, encouraging freedom from social conventions and rejecting any type of institutionalization—and consequently all responsibilities and social constraints—could become the reference ideology of those who will be parents in the year 2000.

If these traits were to come together in society, the child who has already become a "rare commodity" in many a technologically advanced society (because of a drastic reduction in the birthrate) could paradoxically become both the object of over-solicitude and overprotection on the part of parents, teachers, and other socializing agents, and be left to himself by the very same social actors and institutions which either in the name of a neo-Marxian principle (according to which the child is alienated by his parents and teachers like the worker is by his employer) or in the name of an American inspired psychoanalytical theory (according to which the child is used as a scapegoat for releasing his parents' sadistic tendencies), claim the right of the child to freely dispose of himself.

Scenario Two: Highly centralized and socially interventionistic societies limit the child's needs for self-expression.

This situation would occur if the delocalized trends already to be found in the social and family policies of several wealthy countries were to be extended further. The interference of the state and of its agencies increases and infiltrates more varied sectors of professional and family life. Not only the definition of social advantages which are promoted but also the choice of criteria for selecting the beneficiaries of these social advantages, are determined exclusively by "experts." Those most directly affected by them, namely families, are not consulted in the planning of social life. If this perspective prevails, it is to be feared that the child will be shaped by elements of the "configurative culture" to use Margaret Mead's expression in *The Generation Gap.* (In a configurative culture the social model that dominates is the behavior of contempories, not that of youth.) This kind of model would be translated to the child by socializing him for utilitarian social roles which directly meet the needs of the society in terms of professional skills, social status, and positions. This would have a negative effect on the aspirations and needs of the child for self-expression and of the parents for a more personal involvement in shaping the child's future.

Scenario Three: Social visibility of the child through reciprocal syncretism and blending of societal, conjugal–parental, and child goals

This is the model which seems, to us, best adapted to a number of countries with differing degrees of economic and technological development. Its effectiveness would require the recognition of values such as individualism, creativity, and freedom from constraints (which are to be found in Scenario One) as well as the acceptance of a certain degree of regulating social relationships, inherent in Scenario Two. To arrive at this result we need a more adequate definition regarding "to whom?" and "for what?" the child is useful; who benefits most from his presence on the emotional and economic levels; we also need to have a better understanding of his specific qualities and of his needs as related to society's. In this manner it is to be hoped that parents, as well as social institutions and services concerned with family well-being, will de-emphasize the current importance which adults attribute to "their" own lives and increase their social conscience about responsibilities in terms of the emotional and financial costs to the child which must be met.

MACROSOCIAL PROCESSES AND CHANGES
IN THE FAMILY

ANTONINA OSTROWSKA

Institute of Philosophy and Sociology, Polish Academy of Sciences, Warsaw, Poland

IN SPITE of the fact that predictions are always formulated in the language of probabilities, the risk of making a false prognosis, or that the prediction will not take into account all relevant factors, discourages many social scientists from making attempts at forecasting. I will follow that prudent policy and in speaking about the connection between macrosocial processes and the family I will not try to create a vision of the family of tomorrow but rather attempt to present "instruments" which may prove useful if you choose to employ them, at your own risk, in a venture of prediction.

The existence of a connection between macrosocial processes in contemporary societies and changes in the family cannot be doubted. Macrosocial processes initiate the changes, provide the framework in which they occur, and determine the directions of their development. The pace of change occurring in the family is proportional to the pace of macrosocial processes.

Every social process can be presented as a certain social change that is either planned or spontaneous. Planned changes are often accompanied by unintended side effects, mostly undesirable. The majority are intended to bring about social progress or improve social conditions. Since the objectives to be achieved are taken for granted, they are not specifically discussed. More space is devoted to the discussion of their negative consequences for various social institutions. Similarly, most of the analytical studies concerning the influence of social change on the family concentrate on such negative influences as social disintegration and pathology. In a sense, it is easier to predict the problems that families will be faced with than to describe their "normal" life.

Robert Blood[1] says that as long as the relations between the families and their environment remain intact, the patterns of family life remain unchanged and the families can function in a "traditional" way. The parents inculcate traditional values in the children and raise them in the accustomed ways. The children adopt the value systems and life patterns of the parents. The elderly enjoy high status in the family structure, they are respected and held up as models for the younger generation. Continuity of social tradition is thereby ensured. Adolescent rebelliousness is rare.

But if the pace of social change increases, the "normal" relation between the generations becomes distorted. The parents appear old fashioned, and their ideas and beliefs are not easily transmitted to or accepted by their children who are growing up in new and different social conditions. Society tends to become stratified into an older generation, clinging to the past, and a younger generation reaching for the future. The younger generation looks on its elders as obsolete and a hindrance to social progress. Their teaching no longer seems relevant. Either conflict ensues or else the generations are so alienated from each other that they cease to have any significant contact. The polarization of the family into contending generations means the loss of control over the young by their elders. The normal processes of family formation may break down. When new families are formed, they may be less stable than usual because of their increased social heterogeneity, uncertain social conditions and inadequate socialization into ways for the performance of normal family functions. Most forms of family disorganization tend to increase: divorce, desertion, marital conflicts. This may be partly a result of the different impact of the changing environment on each of the marriage partners. The fact that the husband and wife are members of the same generation does not guarantee that they will be affected equally by the new social conditions. The wife, for example, may be less exposed to new ideas if she stays at home while her husband goes to work. Thus tension may arise between husband and wife analogous to the split between parents and children.

Most contemporary research on the family has concentrated on the problems of family change in connection with the processes of industrialization and urbanization.

As is well known, industrialization and urbanization are attended by migration, mainly from villages to towns, and transformations in the employment structure, ways of life, and systems of values. New cultural patterns emerge, new aspirations, new behavioral norms. Traditional social ties undergo changes, social control is weakened. The family is a sensitive instrument which monitors all these changes and reacts to them, frequently quite spontaneously but not without going through adaptive disturbances and experiencing disorganization of the family life.

We can mention the following changes within the family, noted in industrial societies: Family size decreases, first, as a result of fewer children, second, due to widespread disintegration of the extended families. Accelerated geographic mobility may also cause temporary separation of the nuclear family members. The structure of the nuclear families tends to evolve in the direction of equalization of the spouses. The gap between the social status of parents and children has lessened, especially for adolescents. In general the power and authority of the father of the family has declined. There is a trend toward a greater unification of the masculine and feminine roles, partly as a result of increasing technical household equipment, partly because of a different perception of the roles and functions of family members. The development of different means of communication has made new patterns, modes of living and norms of behavior more pervasive and uniform, and has accentuated the differences between town and village. Married couples have become less homogeneous with respect to social class or ethnic descent. The analyses of such large scale processes as industrialization and urbanization, and their influence on the family often lack precision because they seem to intermingle with other processes such as vertical and horizontal mobility, modernization processes, cultural diffusion, etc. In fact we are faced with a syndrome of interrelated social and economic phenomena, and it is hard to say which of them cause particular changes. For the prediction of the influence of future social changes on the family, researchers should concentrate on the analysis of different middle range processes and try to assess their combined effect.

But even here some unexpected effects may appear. Slum clearance, for example, is theoretically designed to benefit the families that are moved from overcrowded, dilapidated housing and relocated in new, bigger homes somewhere else. But if the new location is too far away from the old, and if the new housing is more expensive than the old, or the structure and composition of apartments is very different, the new arrangement may be functionally disastrous for some families.

Even small scale changes, undertaken without prior knowledge of the social after effects, may have disastrous results. We can say that, in general, mass processes would proceed more smoothly if they were extended over time and reinforced with a rational social policy that has predicted possible negative after effects and proposed measures for their neutralization or abatement.

But what is the real situation? Do the official policies in different countries employ such protective safeguards for the good of the families in their societies? Politicians often take a "pro-family" stand in the press and other mass media. But to what extent do these declarations reflect any real concern for the "ideal well-being of the families"?

It seems that very often social policy (that is the existing legal instruments, systems of social benefits, and government decisions concerning various social problems) is the resultant of various often incongruous, social needs. Consequently it often happens that one set of needs is overshadowed by another. For example, problems of employment or unemployment may be perceived as having priority over, say social welfare. The family is often used as a responsive and easily manipulated unit. For example, in societies with high unemployment, social policy aims at propagating a family model in which the women stay at home to take care of the children and the elderly or disabled members of the family. The official ideology will exalt this as the ideal family: the warmth and strength of a good home depend on the wife and mother being always there. The reverse happens when it seems necessary to develop a new labor force, as happened from 1947 to 1954 in Poland. This period of accelerated industrialization and reconstruction of the whole country after the war was marked by a demand for full vocational participation by women. Woman was depicted in the first place as a member of a socialist community who must be liberated from the "slavery of the hearth."[2] Plans were made for numerous institutions for child care, but the program changed when it turned out that it was economically impossible to create enough child care centers for all families with both parents working. Another manipulation has been used in contemporary China, where new models of communal living were promoted in order to break down traditional family bonds and reinforce collectivistic attitudes. These new forms facilitated the implementation of a compli-cated demographic policy and more efficient birth control, as well as tighter social control and discipline.

If we were to venture a forecast of what the future family will look like from the macrosocial point of view, we could assume that the existing macrosocial processes will continue unless we can predict what new ones might take their place and what the consequences for the family would be. For higher precisions it seems necessary to identify all the elementary processes and their concomitants which are subsumed under general change. Another factor that has to be predicted is the direction of social policy. This task is not easy since most societies have different ideological foundations. This makes it difficult to predict what families will be taken into account and how their interests will be represented. Finally, it is necessary to observe changes in the systems of values, ways of life and aspirations, since these also affect human behavior and will be reflected in the future patterns of family life.

REFERENCES

1. ROBERT O. BLOOD, Jr., *The Family*, The Free Press, New York, 1972.
2. MAGDALENA SOKOŁOWSKA, Polityka Spoteqna Wobec Rodziny (unpublished paper).

THE HUMAN FAMILY IN A CHANGING WORLD

LEON EISENBERG

Department of Psychiatry, Harvard Medical School, Boston, MA, USA

EACH one of us knows no more than a little corner of the world. Embrace brotherhood and internationalism though we may, our understanding is necessarily parochial. But perhaps sharing the experiences of our separate ways of living may broaden our common horizons. What is it, then, that I, from an American vantage point, can say about today's society that will illuminate tomorrow's?

Let me suggest that America, for much of the world, is a vision of a future it may yet inherit. Note that I said "a vision," not "the vision." For our present is a future other nations may choose to reject in favor of a different pattern of development if they come to understand the good and the bad of it, and what part of the good cannot be had without the bad. In what sense is America a prevision of the world's future? Accidents of geography and history permitted an extraordinary explosion of industrial technology that put us, for the time being at least, well ahead on a time scale which other Western nations seem to be following and which is beginning to be emulated in much of the developing world. What has seemed irresistible to others has been the sumptuous standard of living, represented by such indices as the GNP *per capita,* which high technology has yielded. By now there is growing awareness of some of its environmental and social costs: Pollution, depletion of energy resources, structural unemployment and a permanent underclass, occupational hazards, and the like. What may be less evident to those at a distance and has only just entered the American consciousness—are the ways in which the commanding imperatives of technology have altered our culture, our social relationships, and our very biology.

Let me begin with what may seem the most outlandish of the propositions I have set forth; namely, the impact of sociotechnical change on human biology. This is no contemporary phenomenon. Where human beings live, how many of them there are, and the way they live has always had profound effects on both the evolution of the species and the development of the individual. A few examples may clarify the point. Diseases such as measles and poliomyelitis did not become endemic in human populations until the agricultural revolution permitted human aggregations in numbers sufficient to provide a reservoir for viral recycling[1] and, indeed, such diseases did not begin to exert survival pressures on the species until the last 500 generations of human history.[2] The prevalence of lactose intolerance in human groups varies with food patterns; it is most frequent among peoples who do not utilize milk or its products after weaning. An example of another type of human adaptation is provided by antigens of the Duffy blood group system which, though otherwise innocuous (in contrast to the sickle gene), appear to act as "receptors" for plasmodium vivax malaria at the surface of red cells. The recessive phenotype, Duffy negative, confers resistance to vivax malaria and thus frequencies for the Fy^0 allele approximate 100% among Central African Blacks whereas it approaches zero among Caucasians. So much, then, for the antiquity of a process that continues into the present.

Genotypic change continues into the modern era, as advances in medical care permit the survival to reproductive capacity of persons with such diseases as galactosemia, congenital hypothyroidism, and phenylketonuria. Insofar as the deleterious effects of the double dose of the gene can be largely mitigated or entirely neutralized by medical intervention, no human loss, other than medical costs, is involved.

In the past many parents who knew themselves to be carriers would have foregone child bearing for fear of having an affected infant. The relative security provided by amniocentesis enables such parents to give birth to phenotypically normal children, some of whom will be carriers and may add to the genetic load for future generations.

Nonetheless, since the diseases concerned are fortunately rare, the total net effect on the human gene pool need provide no reason for concern. Moreover, offsetting eugenic effects can be anticipated from public health measures, such as the eradication of malaria which, by eliminating the heterozygote advantage, should lead to the gradual reduction of genes for thalassemia, sicklemia, and G6PD deficiency. The most striking effect of modern society has been to diminish selection pressures. Well over 95% of infants born alive survive to the age of reproduction and post-reproductive mortality has no selective importance. The variance in the number of children born per woman does provide an opportunity for selection by differential fertility, but there is some evidence that birth control is reducing the variation in family size. If we ever did achieve a state in which each couple simply had two children, there would be no room at all left for natural selection. Any subsequent evolutionary changes would be due to mutation and to genetic drift. Mutation may well be on the increase as the result of manmade radiation and the introduction of chemical mutagens, but these represent challenges to the development of effective methods of social control.

The most marked impact of social change has been on the biology of the phenotype rather than the genotype. In all Western nations there has been a secular increase in the mean stature attained by successive generations, reflecting improvements in nutrition and in the control of infection. For most adolescents, taller is better with the exception of the few at the extreme of the distribution who experience social discomfort.[3] I am not aware of any negative biological consequences from attaining close to full genetic potential for height.

The story is more complicated for an even more striking change in the Western world: the secular decrease in the age of onset of puberty, so marked that it now begins some four years earlier than it did a century ago. Although fertility appears later than menarche, because the early cycles are anovulatory, there is a parallel net lowering of the age at which fertility can begin. This sociobiological change (that is, a change in biology that results from socially produced alterations in health conditions) has complex social and biological consequences. For, when the biological phenomenon of early puberty is associated, as it is in the United States, with an increase in the frequency of adolescent sexual activity because of changes in sexual mores, unwanted pregnancy is an all too common side effect, an event which is to the detriment of both infant and mother.[4]

The higher maternal and infant morbidity and mortality associated with adolescent pregnancy can surely be mitigated by the provision of optimal medical care; nonetheless, there will still remain the detrimental social and developmental consequences for the immature mother and for the infant she is poorly prepared to nurture.[5] In the United States in 1976 there were almost 800,000 pregnancies among unmarried women between ages 15 and 19. It is estimated that, had no contraception been used, almost twice as many pregnancies would have resulted; had contraception been used regularly by all of those who did not want children, the number of pregnancies would have been reduced by almost half.[6] Of the pregnancies that did occur, about 1 in 7 terminated in miscarriage and 1 in 4 in legal abortion. Punitive legislation in the United States to deny funds for abortion to mothers unable to afford it will lead both to more unwanted births and to an increase in complications from septic abortion.[7] Clearly, effective public health control measures require (a) better sex education (rarely offered through public schools at present), (b) the provision of contraceptives for those who are sexually active, and (c) the availability of abortion for those who become pregnant and do now want children.

At present birthrates the United States will continue to increase in population until the year 2040 because of the large cohorts still within the fertile period. In this respect, events in Western Europe have outrun us. In both France and the Federal Republic of Germany, birthrates have fallen below replacement values and population decline has begun. By 1985 Scandinavia will be in balance, and by 2000 the European continent will experience a population decline, four decades before the United States. The economic effects of the demographic reversal are already manifest. Over the past 15 years, social security contributions have jumped by 8% per year in Western Europe, about twice the annual economic growth rate.[13] Whether national incentives and sanctions can achieve the means to smooth out the cycles of boom and bust in fertility rates remain a question for the future, but it has become abundantly clear that natal policy is a major issue the world over.

The increase in longevity for women, coupled with the decision to have fewer children and the contraceptive technology to make it possible, has radically transformed women's lives. Two centuries ago, in much of the Western world, not half the children a mother gave birth to survived till age 10, a statistic that still obtains in many parts of the developing world. With decreases in infant and child mortality, many fewer pregnancies became necessary to assure the same family size. Moreover, better social security measures diminished the reliance of elderly parents on the financial support of their children. At one and the same time, the demands of an industrial society required the incorporation of women into the work force and working influenced decisions about preferred family size.

In the United States a social "tipping point" has been reached. That is, the majority of married women are now in the labor force. It is the woman who does not work rather than the one who does who feels the necessity for self-justification. It is a clear extension of human freedom that women now seek, and can more often attain, a wider range of occupational and avocational roles. Community studies on the prevalence of depression in women indicate that the employed wife has fewer depressive symptoms than the housewife, though still more than men.[8] [9] Yet, as women have taken on social roles more like those of men, they have been acquiring self-destructive male behaviors. Because more women now smoke, more will acquire lung cancer, emphysema, and heart disease. Deaths from violence (accidents, suicide, and homicide) may increase as well. Thus women may lose some of their advantage in longevity since violent deaths are the major causes for differential mortality between the sexes from ages 15 to 45. I do not cite these data as an argument for women's place in the home; to the contrary, I note them as cautions against the adaptation of modal male patterns as the prototype for female social roles. Both sexes would profit from a culture which made men more like women rather than the reverse.[10]

An industrial society demands a mobile work force. The consolidation of farming into agrobusiness diminishes the need for agricultural manpower. More and more of our population concentrate in metropolitan areas. Americans seem to be in perpetual motion. One in five families moves every year. On the one hand, this means fresh starts, less parochialism, and more opportunities for young couples to develop free of parental coercion. On the other, it means the loss of support from extended families, fewer ties to the community, and a sense of rootlessness and alienation. Urbanization, of course, is a worldwide phenomenon; its effects are more devastating in the developing world where barrios and favelas of grinding poverty surround cities whose population growth threatens their survival.[11] People move because they despair of satisfaction where they are and they perceive greater opportunity lying elsewhere. The message is clear: without the investment of national resources to improve conditions in the countryside, population movement will continue to the detriment of both rural and urban areas.

I have already mentioned the earlier onset of puberty as a biological phenomenon. Adolescence has been stretched out even further by the delay in the age of transition to full adulthood; that is, the age at which economic independence is attained. This delay has resulted from the progressive lengthening of the formal education demanded by an industrial society. Whereas at the turn of the century, no more than an elite 4% of American 18–21 year olds went onto college, by 1977 almost 50% did. Correspondingly, there has been a steady decrease in the percentage participating full time in the work force. In the word of Professor James Colman:[12] "With every decade, the length of schooling has increased until a thoughtful person must ask whether society can conceive of no other way for youth to come into adulthood".

If personal development were the primary motivation for education, the social investment might nonetheless be well worthwhile, but the major thrust has been for economic gain. Until recently, higher income did accompany a college degree; however, that is no longer so clearly the case.[13] In Italy, France, and other Western European countries—and even in India[14]—university degrees are "fast becoming tickets to nowhere," according to a report from the International Labor Office in Geneva.[15] University students are ambivalent. On the one hand, they protest the irrelevance of their education to their economic future; on the other, they resist efforts to redirect the university curriculum along vocational lines. Rising expectations conjoin with diminished opportunities to create a seed bed for political turmoil among the disaffected young people.

Modern society has come to regard schools as the primary institutions for socializing the young. Schools have been viewed as a means to compensate for the inadequacies of family life, now that centrifugal forces pull the family apart and the young spend increasing amounts of time outside the home. Yet, such evidence as we have continues to point to the decisive effect of the family in determining academic and vocational outcomes, with only a small contribution ascribable to the differences between one school and another.[16] In the most recent study from the city of Warsaw, where housing reconstruction following the devastation of the war had done much to diminish manifest differences between neighborhoods, measures of cognitive ability in children continue to correlate strongly with the educational level of the parents. Schooling has had neither the "leveling" effect feared by elitists nor the "equalizing" effect urged by egalitarians. This does not at all mean that school is inconsequential but rather that its "benefits" may acrue differentially to those who arrive prepared to respond to its academic and social demands and opportunities. Socialization within the family remains a crucial determinant of child development, even though we still have much to learn about the key elements in that process.

As professionals, we have erred in limiting our focus on learning to that fraction of it which occurs in a formal educational setting. For, we have known for long that children who fail to progress at the expected rate in school may demonstrate mastery of a large array of social skills and general information acquired outside the classroom. Furthermore, the separation of productive work from the family setting has restricted the day to day opportunities for learning vocational skills which once were part of family life and remains so throughout much of the developing world. We require a broader view of education than the classroom and a more creative understanding of human development as taking place over the trajectory of a lifetime. Adults should be entitled to an opportunity for work "sabbaticals" for educational purposes; correspondingly, the young will benefit from work interleaved with formal schooling. This need not be a recipe for all; given the wide range of individual difference, very different patterns of learning and doing will be best suited to maximize personal development. What is clearly wrong is the present lock-step which demands an uninterrupted program of schooling for all. For many, work and life experience will enhance the ability to choose, and to profit from, formal education.

Changes in the school curriculum, however, must include more than opportunities for work-study. Today's lower birthrates mean smaller families; today's mobile families mean disrupted family networks. Fewer of those growing up will have had either the opportunity or the responsibility of caring for younger siblings and learning about their needs. In view of the powerful impact of parenting on child development, society must insure that those who will become parents are prepared for parenthood, now that the necessary experiences in child care are no longer provided in the family setting. Thus, nursery schools and day care centers should be attached to junior high and high schools with the older students participating in the care of the young, as well as being taught the principles of child development as an academic subject. This will, at one and the same time, provide direct care for young children in an era where both parents work and enable those who will become parents to develop the skills of parenting.

The evolutionary record makes clear the transcience of species that cannot adapt to ecologic demand. Given our enormous numbers, the unprecedented destructive power of our military technology, and the division of nations into competing camps, only an inclusive concern for the welfare of the family of man will make man fit to survive. What was once a moral injunction has become a biological imperative.

We have been convened to consider the child in the world of the future. I have outlined the sense in which the present state of American society provides a window on that future. "Window" is a faulty metaphor; it suggests that we are mere observers of a drama rather than the playwrights and the actors who will shape its course. Biologic evolution proceeds blindly, unheedful of its consequences until those consequences exert their inexorable control. Until now, social evolution has been no less blind; it has seized upon short term advantage with little regard for long run outcome. But what was once long run has become short term; we have so successfully obeyed the Biblical injunction to be fruitful and multiply that we are now reaching the limits of finite planetary resources. Social evolution must become self-conscious; our children must be helped to understand the constraints that limit humane choices as well as the options for a fully human existence.[17] Either we have a future in which we acknowledge each other as members of a single family, in which human differences become a cause for celebration rather than for oppression, and in which fostering human development over a lifetime is the overriding concern of society—or we will have no future at all.

The choice lies with us.

REFERENCES

1. F. L. Black, Infectious diseases in primitive societies, *Science* 187, 515-518 (1975).
2. J. B. S. Haldane, Natural selection in man, *Acta Genet. Statist. Med.* 6, 321-332 (1956/7).
3. Alan Guttmacher Institute, *11 million Teenagers,* Planned Parenthood Federation of America, New York, 1976.
4. F. F. Furstenberg, The social consequences of teenage parenthood, *Fam. Plan. Persp.* 8, 148-164 (1976).
5. M. Zelnik and J. F. Kantner, Contraceptive patterns and premarital pregnancy among women aged 15-19 in 1976, *Fam. Plan. Persp.* 10, 135-142 (1978).
6. Institute of Medicine, *Legalized Abortion and the Public Health,* National Academy of Sciences, Washington, DC, 1975.
7. J. Kandell, Former French Premier seeks to spur lagging birth rate, *New York Times,* June 6, 1978.
8. G. Brown, M. Bhrolchain and T. O. Harris, Social class and psychiatric disturbance among women in an urban population, *Sociology* 9, 225-259 (1975).
9. L. Radloff, Sex differences in depression: the effects of occupation and marital status, *Sex Roles* 1, 249-265 (1975).
10. L. Eisenberg, La reparatition differentielle des troubles psychiatriques selon le sexe, In E. Sullerot (ed.), *Le Fait Feminin,* Fayard, Paris, 1978, pp. 313-331.
11. F. C. Turner, La estampida hacia las cuidades en Latino America, *Inter Sciencia* 2, 31-41 (1977).
12. J. S. Coleman, Preface to *Youth: Transition to Adulthood,* University of Chicago Press, Chicago, 1974, p. vii.
13. R. B. Freeman, *The Overeducated American,* Academic Press, New York, 1976.
14. W. Borders, Joblessness plagues India's educated elite, *New York Times,* May 28, 1978.
15. M. G. Scully, Youth unemployment stirs international concerns, *Chronicle of Higher Education,* May 22, 1978.
16. C. Jencks, M. Smith, M. Ackland et al., *Inequality: A Reassessment of the Effect of Family and Schooling in America,* Basic Books, New York, 1972.
17. A. Firkowska, A. Ostrowska, M. Sokolowska et al., Cognitive development and social policy, *Science* 200, 1357-1362 (1978).

PROGNOSIS FOR PARENTHOOD

E. James Anthony
Edison Child Development Research Center, Washington University, St. Louis, MO, USA

Last year about one million teenage girls in the United States became mothers, so that last year one million infants at high risk for mortality and morbidity entered a world that was in the main poorly equipped to receive them. The often total disaster resulting in many of these cases is insufficiently stated in these terms since the reproductive casualty, to use Pasamanick's expression,[1] involves not only the children but also the caretakers, among whom there is a substantial incidence of maladjustment. Some of the disturbances found among these premature parents antedate the pregnancies; some are transient and respond to good support systems; but a significant number become chronically maladapted, dropping out of schools, taking to delinquency, succumbing to drugs before being eventually institutionalized. Those with a grosser morbidity are more likely to come from the lower socioeconomic and disadvantaged sections of the general population. Whether disturbed before or after pregnancy, youthfulness constitutes a hazard, and the younger they are the greater is the risk. Hardly out of their own childhood, they are ill prepared for parenthood and poorly defended against the wide range of stresses posed by it on their personalities. In another 21 years, unless population controls begin to function more efficiently, the figure given may be greatly increased. The earlier development of puberty that is taking place in every country will add to the numbers in the vulnerable group.

I want next to consider a series of problems that have been brought about in recent times by the extensive social and cultural changes that have been taking place in this latter part of the 20th century and are likely to be intensified by the year 2000 AD.

THE DEVELOPMENTALLY UNPREPARED PARENT

Parenthood remains the greatest single preserve of the enthusiastic amateurs who resists all attempts, especially in the lower social strata, to professionalize them. Professionalizing the parent also carries its risks since the professionals themselves are often at variance with one another or with previous professionals with regard to what constitutes good parental care or, at least, "good enough" parental care. Another danger in professionalization is that the middle class parent may espouse so many differing views that they become perplexed parents, unable to let instinct or common sense or body chemistry guide them in the management of the young. The two syndromes, therefore, that seem to be on the increase are perplexed parenthood and technological parenthood: the first is torn between the experts while the second is constantly appealing for more and more techniques as their infants fail to thrive on existing ones. Such parents may also ask for programs to modify their parental attitudes and behavior, and the experts have not been slow to construct them. What these programs fail to reach are the well-springs of empathy, of bonding, of attunement, and of identification with the child that leads not only to more sensitive parenting but also to more efficient care and the likelihood (unless genetic or congenital factors obviate it) of more contented and easy babies to manage.

Not only do the tasks of parenthood change with the child's stage of development, but the parents themselves undergo almost ceaseless change as they develop along with their children. Moreover, the parents have already been undertaking a preparation for their parental roles long before the birth of the offspring. The child does not spring fully developed, like Pallas Athene, from the parent, and neither is the parent fully developed as a parent when confronted by the neonate for the first time. Parenthood begins in infancy. For example, the little girl must, in order to develop motherliness, undergo a major developmental switch from the passive position of being given to and of being looked after to the active position of giving and caring for. The switch over results in part from identifications with her mother, with models prevalent in her culture, and is gradually made operational by practice with inanimate dolls and by infants available in the household. This involves not only an acceptance of her femininity but also her ultimate maternal purpose. The feelings are reinforced by appropriate hormonal stimulations at the time of puberty. The father also has a strong role in encouraging the emergence of womanliness in his daughter by responding tenderly to manifestations of it. The psychological origins of fatherliness also have their origins in identifications and the flow of "fellow feeling" between father and son. The father's image established and internalized early in life acts as an internal guide to the masculine transformations in the boy. The wish to be like the father perceptively gives place to the wish to become a father as well as to gain some of the attributes of strength and dependability. The games of childhood in which parental roles are enacted not only provide excellent rehearsals for later parenthood but are also fairly reliable indicators of the strength of the developing fatherliness and motherliness. At adolescence, childhood is extended "beyond identity" to the generative phase of the life cycle,[2] meaning by this the development of new internal and external concerns and competences for guiding the next generation. With these schemata, parenthood becomes a developmental achievement rooted in the individual's own parental experience. A strange, indeterminate law of psychic transmission determines that poor parents make poor parents and that no parents make even poorer parents. Abused children, institutionalized children, neglected children, and rejected children all become developmentally unprepared for parenthood and are mostly influenced by primitive and uncontrolled feelings and fantasies.

THE EXOGAMOUS MARRIAGE

Although quota systems have been hurriedly established or reestablished in developed or wealthy countries with many opportunities, the flow of migrants has been increasing steadily and will undoubtedly continue throughout the rest of this century. Exogamous unions, across social, ethnic, and color boundaries are also on the increase as are the children of such unions. There is no doubt that exogamy puts an additional strain on the stresses inherent in the marital relationship, and for the children it often implies growing up in a somewhat divided cultural milieu with polarities of religion, of language, of habits, of child rearing philosophies, of political attitudes, of eating habits, etc., that create subtle conflicts of loyalty right through a day. The emotional conflicts that dominate the early life of children with their parents are then compounded by psycho-social reactions and add confusion to the developmental experience. The culture facilitates the role of one parent but complicates that of the other, and the children may manipulate the situation to their own advantage or, at adolescence, disown both cultures and take refuge in the adolescent ethos. Such hybrid children tend to become confused and mixed-up adults, leading relatively disjointed lives and liable to suffer from a sense of "rootlessness"—a syndrome that is on the increase and may become a significant problem in another few decades.

SELF-ACTUALIZING VERSUS CHILD-REARING DRIVES

The birth of a child may change the lives of the marital partners even more than their marriage, and many young couples today (and more tomorrow) are showing reluctance at the idea of living a large part of their lives in child-centered homes. They see parenthood as a career as well as a phase of life, and may regard it as an interference with their own idiosyncratic aspirations. Individuation is becoming a psychological end in itself, and is the stated goal in at least one prominent developmental theory. Women especially, having emancipated themselves from centuries of bondage and submissiveness, from endless and inevitable child bearing, from interminable domestic chores, and from the chronic ill-health that come from overprotected living, understandably are seeking more for themselves. The rationalizations that they often give for remaining childless include the specter of overpopulation, loss of faith in the future, and the precarious times that are affecting the whole world. The internal reasons may be different. Many of them are children of divorce, and have not only received poor parenting but have also been traumatized by marital conflict. The girls often see their mothers as having obtained very little for themselves out of life and as being little more than martyrs to their children. One child inquired of her mother: "Why did you grow up to be nothing?" Liberated women themselves are beginning to ask whether they have not exchanged one tyranny for another—the active pursuit of careers (and ulcers and heart attacks) for homemaking and mothering. The conflict is currently intense. The new woman is stigmatized by the other side as child neglecting, emasculating, and selfish, while the traditional woman is demeaned as mindless and masochistic. However, futurologists are inclined to a cyclical viewpoint and are already forecasting that the pleasures of parenthood will again be recaptured and that children will once again lead "normal" home lives as they did in the past.

A new development that is taking place may help to reconcile some of these polarized attitudes. It is a psychological commonplace to think of children as dependent on their parents and to think of parents as active and influential in the development of their passively receptive children. (A similar mechanism operated for centuries in the one-sided conception of the husband–wife relationship.) Today, psychologists are more concerned with mutuality existing between parents and children and with the influence of the child on the parent and his development. The argument is that children bring up their parents as much as the parents bring up their children, and that the relationship is a reciprocal interdependent one with mutual stimulation. The focus has therefore shifted from independence and autonomy to interdependence and mutuality, and it has been suggested that parenthood is in fact a major factor in self-actualization. New movements have consequently come into being that aim at greater unity of mother–father and child from the first few days of the baby's life. As the family regains its stability, so parenthood is regaining its attraction. Where ambivalence and narcissism and resentment toward child bearing persists, the children that are accidentally conceived and not aborted are at high risk for neglect, abuse, and mental disorder. While physical abuse gains the public eye, it is far less prevalent than the syndrome of neglect and ambivalence that is becoming an especially prominent condition as we enter the last two decades of this century.

THE CONTRACEPTIVE COMPLEX

Women's sexuality seems to be on the whole more complex and more closely rooted in biology than men's and the fairly recent disconnection between the sexual act and child bearing with the mechanism of contraception has led to more problems for the women. Many of them become depressed or anxious when contraception is regarded as almost 100% safe; many feel that sexual intercourse is meaningless unless they can conceive, and come may even lose their sexual desire after a while; many feel at their best when pregnant and have their self-esteem gratified by the respect and attention received from their husbands; many crave to have "something alive" inside them and may make mistakes in their management of contraception; many feel guilty about having sex without the risk of pregnancy; and many feel it wrong to "fool around with nature"; many, superstitiously, feel that they have not been cleaned out properly because their menses are scanty when they are on the pill; many wonder whether they are not unfair to their husbands who are unable to impregnate them.[3] There is no doubt that the desire to procreate may be so predominant that at times it may even take precedence over self-preservation, so that a woman will take enormous risks in order to be able to conceive.

THE DEMOCRATIZATION OF PARENTHOOD

Today in many homes in the developed countries and in many elite households in the developing countries, two part-time parents take care of the young children, sometimes with the help of hired help and sometimes with the assistance of the local day-care nursery. Among the poor or less well to do, the grandparents may assume the care of the baby. In many instances the husband may encourage his wife to work, but when she enters an all-absorbing career she may begin to resent the disruption of family life. The woman herself is never completely happy by the surrogate arrangement and feels guilty whenever something goes wrong simply because she is not at home with her baby, even though she may read of evidence that total care by the mother cannot be demonstrated as being better for the child than a few hours of undivided parental attention each day. The biological division of labor is also no longer clearly demarcated in many modern households, and the role functions of mother and father may be even more blurred over the next era. Many working wives today may expect their husbands to share the nurture and care of the child and the housework, and many husbands today appear willing to do so. Although the evidence gathered is not complete as yet, there is some reason to believe that such egalitarian arrangements may have an influence on the child's developing gender identity. Many of us, as clinicians, are seeing more cases of gender disidentity than we did some years ago: this may be in part due to the fashion that is set by some original work in this area, but it could be a problem that could be expected to increase.

ATYPICAL PARENTAL FORMS

In recent times, youth has seemingly become dissatisfied with the families in which they grew up and have lately been experimenting with new arrangements aimed at avoiding or diminishing the commitments of marriage. Presumably arising out of their own unhappy experiences of traditional family life, the nuclear family is regarded by them (and by some psychiatrists today) as the source of all individual unhappiness and disorder.

Various ways of living and raising children have been tried and have culminated in different degrees of success and failure: contract marriages or nonmarital relationships; homosexual marriages; marriage only after the birth of a child; "serial monogamy"; communal living; single parent families; and living in communes that range from the haphazard to the carefully planned and well-organized institution such as the Israeli kibbutz. At times every effort is made to minimize the importance of the biological parents and to inculcate in the children a sense of communal care. Conditions in the kibbutzim are different: biological parenthood is recognized and respected; careful attention is paid to providing adequate mothering, and a good system of surrogate mothers exists. The biological parents spend considerable time with the children each day and give them their undivided attention. These communal forms of living endeavor to recover the advantages of the extended family group. The feasibility and practicality in all these experimental ventures depends very much on the personalities involved. The kibbutz is child-centered and the children are made to feel wanted and accepted by all members of the institution. However, in some of the counter-cultures there is often a gross misunderstanding of the capacities and needs of children, so that neglect and cruelty are often widespread and resembles the treatment of children in urban slums by teenage parents who cannot invest emotionally in their children because of their own intense dependency needs.[4] Ruth Lidz[3] has pointed out the "open marriage" advocated by the O'Neills does not solve critical child-rearing problems. Another problem with the haphazard communes is that they often have a limited time span, and in many cases parents and children move from commune to commune and the children become as disturbed (and as illiterate) as the offspring of migrant workers. In many of the experiments there appears to be a covert attempt to abrogate the responsibilities of parenthood, or at least to share them in large part with others. According to many of these parents, in spite of themselves, the secret of dealing successfully with a child is not to be its parent.

One would expect that in the next 21 years experiments in child rearing will continue and, depending on the amount that the innovators know about basic child development, some of these children will suffer while others will thrive. The new understanding of the family as a unit and the growth of knowledge regarding its function in the basic socialization and enculturation of the new generation may lead to a resurgence of interest in the extended family group as representing one of the most stable and most successful modes of rearing a child. In such a setting, parents will share their nurturing, disciplining, and socializing functions with others in the family group, so that some of the intensities generated in the nuclear form of family will be mitigated.

CONCLUSION

There are still many unanswered riddles, as complicated as those set by the sphinx, and we cannot presume in 1978 to have solved even a few of the questions relating to the factors that make for successful parenting within different settings, except to paraphrase Shakespeare that some are born parents, some achieve parenthood (through the developmental processes described), and some should never have been parents but have parenthood thrust upon them. George Bernard Shaw, the notorious British cynic, used to feel that parenthood was too important to be left to the parents, and, in his play *Back to Methuselah,* he substituted a long incubation period within the egg, with hatching at the end of adolescence. This was well beyond the year 2000 AD. If this wish-fulfilling idea on the part of a childless old man were to come true, the world would certainly be a quieter place to live in, but its inhabitants would be less interesting people. Even in the year 2000 AD, family life will add its own peculiar mixture of human ingredients (sibling rivalry, envy, sexual conflict, aggressiveness, and power struggles) to the human personality.

REFERENCES

1. B. PASAMANICK and H. KNOBLOCH, Retrospective studies on the epidemiology of reproductive casuality: old and new, *Merrill-Palmer Quart. Behav. Dev.* **12,** 7-26 (1966).
2. E. ERIKSON, Growth and crises of the "healthy personality," *Psychological Issues,* **1** (1), monograph Ho. 1, International Universities Press, New York, 1959.
3. R. W. LUDZ, A. RUTLEGE and L. TOURKOW, Patient motivation in selection and acceptance of contraceptives, in *Regulation of Human Fertility* (IK. S. MOGHUSSI and T. EVANS, eds.), Wayne State University Press, Detroit, 1976.
4. J. ROTHSCHILD and S. WOLF, *Children of the Counterculture,* Doubleday & Co., New York, 1976.

SUMMARY OF DISCUSSION

MICHAEL RUTTER

Institute of Psychiatry, University of London, UK

MAJOR social changes are taking place in different parts of the world, in many cases accompanied by unanticipated and undesirable side effects. The changes include a reduction in family size, increased geographical mobility, equalization of power in the family, greater similarity of male and female roles, a growing proportion of single parent families, and changing patterns of family communication. Attempts to improve physical living conditions, as with slum clearance, may inadvertently cause psychosocial problems. Thus poor but cheap housing may be replaced by better but more expensive housing that these families cannot afford. New purpose-built housing may also involve dispersion of families with resulting lack of kin support. Because economic and employment problems are so great and so obvious, there is often a tendency to overlook and give a lower priority to psychosocial needs. The assumption that greater affluence and better living conditions will necessarily have psychosocial benefits has proved mistaken; greater knowledge is required on the nature and meaning of the mechanisms underlying the association between physical living conditions and psychosocial functioning. There is a lack of precision in our delineation of psychosocial priorities. Thus we are agreed that children need loving relationships and stable family bonds, but there is uncertainty as to the political actions needed to facilitate good family relations and a steady home life.

DEMOGRAPHIC CHANGE

There have also been major demographic changes which carry psychosocial implications. Earlier puberty highlights the issue of sexual promiscuity and unwanted pregnancies. The increase of longevity has led to major alterations in population structure, with a much lower ratio of productive workers to dependents. This raises difficult questions with respect to both economic and employment issues. How can healthy older people be helped to continue in useful work without adverse effects on employment opportunities for the young? Contraception has transformed women's lives in many ways. The proportion of married women in the labor force is growing, with implications for both the status of women and the facilities needed for child care in the pre-school years.

INSTITUTIONAL CHANGE

More and more children are having more and more years of schooling. The family remains the main socializing influence, but schools also play an important role in shaping children's behavior and scholastic attainments. Schools have not reduced inequality, but they can do much to improve or worsen psychosocial development. Recent research suggests that the factors associated with pupil success (however measured) reflect the school's characteristics as social organizations. The findings are hopeful insofar as they indicate that the measures needed to bring about improvement are within our control.

SERVICE DELIVERY

Many problems remain in our delivery of services. Families in need often fall between the institutional slots of the available facilities, and all too often service systems are discontinuous and fragmented in their functioning. Serious questions remain: for example, about how the services should be organized, who should run them, how policy makers can be brought in touch with the practical issues of service delivery, and what use should be made of inexperienced or untrained personnel.

CHILDREN'S RESPONSE TO CHANGE

The pace of change, as well as its character, may determine how children respond. However, even in the most devastating forms of deprivation and disadvantage, children differ in their degree and style of adaptation. Some children appear vulnerable to quite mild stresses, whereas others are more resilient. We need to know more about these individual differences and about the nature of possible ameliorating or protective factors.

ROLE OF RESEARCH

It was clear from the whole session that we remain ignorant on many crucial issues and that research is needed to show which of a large variety of good ideas are actually effective in what social circumstances. Social research rarely (if ever) produces absolute "laws" that are independent of social context. Rather, we need to find out more of the general principles involved in optimal psychosocial development, the ways in which these principles are modified by changing conditions and expectations, and how they may be implemented via social policy.

THE OCCUPATIONAL WORLD

WHAT CHANGES CAN BE ANTICIPATED IN THE FIELD OF EMPLOYMENT AND CONDITIONS OF WORK DURING THE NEXT TEN TO FIFTEEN YEARS?

G. D. DE BERNIS

University of Social Sciences, Grenoble, France

CONDITIONS of work and the level of employment of both men and women have direct repercussions on their children's physical, neurological, and psychological state of health (amount of income and amount of food, amount of parental care and attentions or lack of care through fatigue, nervousness and anxiety about returning home, etc). However, it is very difficult to form estimates regarding the future conditions of work and the level of employment, especially in the third world. Any forecasts affecting the third world are always difficult, but in this case we have also to recognize that, to a considerable extent, future events are connected with the evolution of the present crisis and with the nature of issues involved.

If one oversimplifies the situation and refuses to include any of its nuances, one can differentiate two probable futures:

(1) That the outcome of the present crisis is brought about through a new and more coherent organization of the system of capitalist production, dominated by the multinational firms, which impose their economic order upon the world.

(2) That the crisis is resolved by the developing countries themselves imposing a New International Economic Order, which conforms to their developmental requirements.

1. In the first case—order imposed by the multinational firms—present tendencies will continue to develop. Agriculture will continue to decline in the third world with the following consequences:

(a) The continuation of the rural exodus and the acceleration of social instability, a miserable level of urban life accompanied by increasing unemployment.

(b) A reduction in the amount of food *per capita* despite the probable success here and there of some agrobusiness enterprises and the serious risk of famine, due to the destruction of soil. Such precarious food conditions tend to divert the attention of the population from all other problems of health. This is already the case in certain countries of Asia.

Industrial employment can be expected to grow considerably in some third world countries without arresting the progress of unemployment; wages will remain low and housing precarious; the conditions of work in the large multinational firms will be no better than in Europe. This can present greater dangers, due to the low level of general health in the third world. Conditions in other industrial enterprises are likely to be much worse.

Health care—which will increase—may reduce infant mortality, but it will not be able to ensure conditions for the normal development of the children. However, some benefits in public health can be expected from the progressive spread of primary education.

In the advanced capitalist countries the transformation of the productive system caused by the present crisis will maintain a high level of unemployment for a number of years as well as the tendency to reduce the quality of the labor force (although this is in contradiction with the need for the FTN to sell the manufactured products of the developed countries in the markets of the third world).

The length of the working day will probably be considerably reduced but an increase in the intensity of the work done will prevent any reduction in fatigue, with all the consequences that this entails.

2. A resolution of the crisis imposed by a New International Economic Order determined by the third world would not contrast very greatly with the previous scenario, given the delays that would necessarily be incurred in any profound reorganisation of the social and economic structure.

However, the results in the third world, at least, involve:

(a) A halt in the decline of agriculture and a fairly rapid arrest of the rural exodus. This would result in a general improvement in the level of rural life; a return from cultivation for export to cultivation for domestic use, and consequently an improvement in local food consumption; a lessening of the destruction of the soil, and consequently a lessening of the dangers of famine.

(b) In the industrial sector there will probably not be much increase in employment, but—if governments are attentive to the situation and the medical profession is insistant—a relative independence from the constraints of the world market could ameliorate appreciably the conditions of work and prevent industrialization acting to the detriment of the lives of a section of the population. However, this implies a totally new attitude toward the value of the health of the workers and their families, and an active involvement by the state.

In the advanced capitalist countries some aspects of the New International Economic Order could engender a serious economic crisis if the government of these countries, and those responsible for their industrial production, refuse to adapt themselves to the new conditions of international relations. However, the period of crisis could be greatly shortened and finally surmounted if these advanced countries can deliberately orient themselves toward active cooperation with the third world.

THE CHILD AND THE OCCUPATIONAL
WORLD OF TOMORROW

RAYMOND ILLSLEY

Department of Sociology, University of Aberdeen, Scotland, UK

THE LINKS between the economy, the structure and location of occupations, the life styles associated with particular occupations, and the microenvironment of the child are involved and problematic. We have only begun to understand these complex relationships, and our answers will be full of questions.

It is not merely that the structure of occupations differs from country to country, or that the same occupational title denotes different tasks or different life styles in different countries—the child, too, is different, least of all perhaps in his biological nature, but sharply in levels of living, daily experiences, relationships to family and the outside world, and in expectations for the future.

We are talking not about one economy, but about hundreds. The problem is not merely that the direction and pace of change will be different across these economies but that their starting points are different. Two farmers, one in a peasant society and the other in a post-industrial society, not only do different tasks and have sharply different life styles but in the future one may be driven out by mechanization to the industrializing town while the other may be reverting to less-mechanized and more intensive farming.

It is, of course, by no means certain, and in many cases it is quite unlikely that developing countries will travel the 19th century pathway through its various stages to industrialism. But it is clear that occupations cannot be considered outside the economic and cultural contexts in which they occur.

I want to look more generally at some of the mechanisms whereby occupation affects the life of the child.

(1) The first and obvious mechanism is through the effect of *parental* occupation on the family's *level of living*. This itself could mean many things—food, space, clothing, materials. But whether extra money is used for these or other purposes depends, not upon the money itself or the occupation, but upon twin factors of availability and choice. Availability itself depends upon both production and the evenness of distribution of products, whilst choice depends upon consumer preferences. The link between occupation and levels of living is therefore somewhat tenuous, subject to many imponderables, and is mediated through macroeconomic processes and political structures. In theory there is no necessary relationship between occupational tasks and levels of reward. Traditionally, in capitalist societies, the level of reward for a given occupation is determined by the balance of demand and supply—demand for the goods and services produced by an occupation and the supply of available manpower. Postwar years have seen many changes in traditional assumptions and in the operation of the demand and supply

mechanisms. In some countries political systems have emerged which aim deliberately to sever the connection between occupational tasks and rewards, and in still others measures have been adopted to ensure a social reward in the form of redistributive taxation, minimum wages, redundancy, unemployment and sickness benefits, and of essential services provided by the state and available irrespective of occupation and income. In both capitalist and socialist societies that trend seems likely to continue (at least in the absence of major economic disasters), and thus the link between occupation and levels of living to be further attenuated.

(2) A second major influence is likely to be the change in the participation of women in the work force, affecting both the proportion of women in the work force and the nature and status of their occupations. Again, however, the extent and nature of this change will be diverse. In agricultural societies going through a process of industrialization, women who have shared in the domestic economy and whose location of work has kept them in continuous contact with their children and with their wider family, may increasingly be drawn into industrial production as members of a proletarianized work force. This has implications for child care, for the centrality of the family and its associated institutions, and for the stability of marital and family life.

In post-industrial societies, greater participation in the work force is already accompanied by changes in the status and power of the occupations they are able to perform. In such societies women are increasingly engaged in careers rather than a series of jobs. This process is nowhere complete, and everywhere is accompanied by controversy and stress, perhaps providing extra satisfactions but frequently involving the assumption of extra burdens rather than the substitution of one for another. This movement, for which the term "liberation" is misleading if it also involves a double burden, is likely to be a characteristic of the next decades with far-reaching consequences not only for women but also for children. At the most immediate level it is likely to have consequences for the education and socialization of girls who will no longer be preparing for a life of reproduction bounded by the family and with only a minimal preparation for work and for a wider scene of action, but ultimately for full involvement in intellectual, cultural, and political roles additional to their work and careers.

For the woman and the family other consequences can be envisaged. Only in a few places, and in a minority of couples, has the process been pursued to its logical endpoint where it is a matter of negotiation between husband and wife as to which becomes "the chief wage earner", whose career will be sacrificed if family and other factors require partial withdrawal of one partner from work. Examples are beginning to occur increasingly (but still very rarely) where the husband takes the major responsibility for the running of the home and the upbringing of children. If the trend continues and broadens it will signify a major reversal of roles, and for children a different pattern of role models, i.e. boys, too, may grow up with a less sharp distinction between the roles of men and women. A parallel trend, particularly in times of redundancy and unemployment, is for roles to become fluid and alternating; the presence of two incomes may not only shield the family from poverty if one partner becomes unemployed, but allow one or other partner to give up work temporarily to do other things. In this respect there is an interdependence between women's work and the previously discussed factor, levels of living.

We know little about the probable consequences of women's increasing work involvement upon the family. There is inferential evidence for suggesting that it is a major factor (alongside the improved technology of birth control) for the reduction in family size occurring in most advanced societies. There are suggestions, but little evidence, that greater involvement of women outside the home, along with a more equal balance of power, may be associated with the increased frequency of divorce; dependence upon the husband and the family is weakened by wider contacts and the existence of choice. At the least, speculation could be supplemented by research.

There are also a series of practical implications, some of which apply across a range of different societies. Whether the farming mother becomes a factory worker, or the temporary secretary becomes a political leader, traditional arrangements for the care and upbringing of children may no longer be adequate. The substitution of professional child minders, creches, and nurseries for continuous personal mothering emerges, not as an occasional luxury but as an inevitable and necessary consequence to occupational change.

(3) A third major influence mentioned passingly above is the process of industrialization and urbanization. Many countries of the third world have had large cities and population concentrations for many years, nor is it inevitable that in the process of development they will follow the pattern of 19th century Europe. There is, however, plenty of evidence to suggest that empirically development, industrialization, and urbanization are occurring together in third world countries. This entails the migration of families away from rural and village life with its emphasis upon family, kinship, and community life to factory, service, or professional life in the more impersonal and rapidly changing environment of the town.

This raises immediate questions of housing, sanitation, services, schools, clinics, and the necessities of daily living, but these in themselves may have less significance for the child than the breakup of traditional caring arrangements and the adaption of different methods attached to urban life styles. There is nothing new about this problem. It has been occurring and growing decade after decade, and it is responsible already for high rates of morbidity and mortality and of inadequate growth of children, as well as for alienation or revolt in adolescent populations. One major question must be the degree to which these ill consequences may be modified by the spread of birth control usage.

Lest the picture seem one of unrelieved gloom, I should remind my audience that I am looking for problems requiring advance action. For the population as a whole, industrialization may well bring increased wealth and resources capable in the long term of leading to higher levels of living. The problems lie in the transition stage: in the actions of public authorities and in the equality of distribution of the products of industrialization.

At the level of the post-industrial society the situation is currently fluid and unpredictable. The higher productivity of modern technology tends to release workers from highly centralized industrial plants and leaves a greater proportion of the work force unemployed or engaged in the more labor intensive service occupations that are less susceptible to automatic technology. Perhaps the major repercussion is the reduction in centralizing pressures. Already evidence accumulates, not only about the declining inner city, but—more positively—about the conversion of surburbia and exurbia into more self-sufficient small towns, whose existence is heavily based on mutual servicing. Another trend, so far small, is the appearance of an informal economy: barter and the exchange of services, small scale informal enterprises, voluntary periods of part time work. These are sometimes associated with rural living and one certainly more common in communities with close social relationships. I do not wish to exaggerate the significance of these tendencies but merely to note that, unlike earlier periods in this and the past century, they are decentralizing tendencies which may herald a return to more humanized conditions of work and a closer relationship (physically and socially) between home and work.

Fourthly, I must touch on the relationship between occupation and education. The growth of industry and commerce in 19th century Europe was largely responsible for the spread of literacy. The further spread of literacy in today's third world must inevitably arise out of the same industrial needs. Education, however, is rarely socially, culturally, or ideologically neutral, and a major question must relate to the content and meaning of arising educational systems. In the developed world, where mobility is a required feature of modern life—between social classes, between places, between groups—advancing technology may mean frequent changes of occupational tasks. This in turn means a more generalized education centered upon principles rather than upon facts and capable of being converted to many uses.

THE IMPACT OF WOMEN'S WORK ON THE CHILD
IN LATIN AMERICA AND THE CARIBBEAN

TERESA ORREGO DE FIGUEROA

Consultant in Sociology, Santiago, Chile

IT IS not the work of the woman in itself that affects the child's development but the negative conditions imposed by society. The child can win or can lose if the mother works. The quality of her attention to the child is more important than the accumulation of hours dedicated to him. The child is a winner if the mother performs a stimulating economic activity and if appropriate conditions at home and at work enable her to create a positive family relation. The child is a loser if the mother returns home after exhausting, monotonous, and poorly paid work. She then has to perform her domestic work in a state of tension, thus jeopardizing the physical and mental health of the children.

WHY DO WOMEN WORK IN LATIN AMERICA
AND THE CARIBBEAN?

A large majority of women in Latin America and the Caribbean work out of need. Forty-two per cent of the total population is under 15 years of age, living as dependents of adults with restricted economic opportunities, where one out of five members of the active population is out of work. In 1978 the total population of the region was 340 million and in the year 2000 it will reach 597 million. Actually more than 60% of the population is urban, and by the year 2000 no more than 25% will be left in rural areas. Although population growth shows a tendency to decline in several countries, Latin America still has the highest regional birthrate in the world.

The situation of the working mother's child is conditioned by interrelated economic and social factors such as family income, kind of work performed by the mother, working conditions, social security coverage, the presence of adult relatives, the possibility of using domestic or institutionalized support services, the level of education and information of parents, the number of children, nutritional practices, the quality of interfamily relations, the habitat and recreational opportunities.

Considering these factors I will present the situation of preschool children of working mothers in three representative Latin American socioeconomic groups: the urban family in transition, the rural traditional family, and the modern economic sector.

1. The problem for the preschool child of the urban family in transition is critical. Women work out of sheer necessity. Since it is difficult to find a job and there is no flexible working schedule, the woman has to accept any conditions regardless of the consequences that may affect the child. The children are crowded in highly concen-

91

trated housing with indifferent sanitation. Nutrition is inadequate and insufficient. Neighborhood and family solidarity in urban sectors of lower income seem to
operate better among adults than in reference to care of the children. Opportunities
of recreation are nonexistent. Health and education services are infrequent,
inefficient and insufficient. The child of this working mother can grow with serious
mental and physical shortcomings, as these accumulated negative conditions weaken
the mother's attention to him.

2. The rural "traditional" group is rapidly decreasing in Latin America, though
there are large differences between countries. A large proportion of rural families
live in poverty, and the women's role has been mostly circumscribed to the home, her
participation in agricultural production being restricted, sporadic, and seasonal. The
situation is different for those women belonging to Indian communities who work in
the production, processing, and marketing of foods as well as in handicrafts. The
rural household is an extended family with many children and several generations
present. Illiteracy is rampant. The woman works mainly at home, carrying out
various productive tasks with the help of her children and family. Sanitation problems are serious, health services almost nonexistent, and nutrition rather inadequate.

The child in this family, although in socioeconomic conditions comparable to the
poorest urban sector, enjoys the family affection given by a large number of relatives
and has a healthier and more stimulating physical environment.

3. Working women at the top of the urban economic sector are few. They form a
dynamic group comparable to their counterparts in developed countries. The mother
works nearly always for vocation and personal satisfaction. She has the capacity to
select her work and its conditions, adapting it to her family's needs; she has
domestic help and she can pay for preschool and other institutional services if the
child needs them. Parents are educated and informed about birth control, nutrition,
and child rearing; relatives, grandparents, and uncles lend a hand with the children
when needed; the habitat is adequate, recreation varied, and the coverage of social
services is effective. In these conditions the mother's work does not significantly
affect the child's well-being. It is evident that this group is not entitled to
government-supported services. On the contrary, they have a special responsibility
to transmit and share their knowledge about rearing and educating children and to
participate in the improvement of the quality of life of other children in inferior
conditions.

Only 2 out of every 10 middle class families belong to the higher income group.
While the others are informed and educated, labor conditions are more demanding,
and their abilities to pay for support services for the child are more restricted. This
might well result in limitations on their children's psychological and personality
development due to the limited time the mother can spend at home and the lack of
other extended family support, as these middle income groups usually consist of
nuclear families with two or three children and have more restricted help from
relatives. Their children are particularly vulnerable to the influence of TV and the
consumers' society propaganda.

SUPPORT SERVICES

In Latin America and the Caribbean, with the exception of Cuba, support services for working women's children are inadequate in cities and nonexistent in rural areas. During the last decade we have seen an increase in child care centers and preschool children institutions around labor centers, with significant female labor participation, but these give no coverage for women in the informal labor sector.

In this respect it is interesting to follow the remedial action carried out to redress the effects of extreme poverty on children's health like CONPAN and INTA in Chile, and the Instituto de Bienestar of Colombia, among others. More restricted but innovative programs exist in Guayaquil, Ecuador and Lima, Peru. In Mexico a study on the problems of urban poverty is to be started to define needs and to promote and improve facilities for children of working mothers.

HOW MANY WOMEN WORK?

Official labor statistics show that no more than one-fifth of women in Latin America and the Caribbean are in the labor force and that this proportion is decreasing. However, if you are familiar with any country of the region, these figures do not seem realistic.

Labor statistics of working women in Latin America and the Caribbean are not trustworthy because the traditional categories do not register the whole gammut of the women's input to the economy, including such characteristics of women's activities as discontinuity and seasonality. For example, women in the traditional rural sector who produce seasonally, store, process, and market their products in local markets would at best be registered as self-employed small vendors; a category only partially reflecting her performance.

If it is difficult to quantify the number of women who get paid for their work it is certainly harder to analyze the impact of their work on their children. Nevertheless, there are some identifiable features of women in the labor force in Latin America and the Caribbean such as:

— less women work than men in a 1 to 4 ratio;
— women's work is concentrated in urban services: one-third in domestic service and the rest in public and social services; starting in the sixties there is an increase of the women's active population in trade and a decrease in industry;
— women work the same number of hours as men, receive less salary for equal work than men, and their activities are concentrated in the lesser paid categories;
— working women are more educated than men in similar categories and levels of employment;
— the participation of women in the labor force is related to her reproductive and domestic functions. The rate of women's participation in the women's active population reaches its peak at 24 years and thereafter it decreases constantly. Conversely, in the United States and Canada the woman quits around 24 years of age for a period of time of about 10 years, returning to the labor market to stay;
— unmarried, divorced, and separated women work more often than the married ones on a proportion of 1 to 3. Civil status does not affect the labor participation of men;

— women show more occupational mobility than men with periods of absence that coincide with their maternity functions.

CONCLUSIONS

1. Women's work (productive and domestic) has always been related to the objective of their children's well-being, but prevailing conditions in industrial societies have dislocated this function to a point where women's economic activities are perceived as detrimental to the family and the child's development.

2. Woman's work only affects family stability, and therefore the child, when society imposes negative conditions on her participation in the market. Child rearing should be ensured through a redefinition of roles between members of the family, the existence of flexible labor conditions for both sexes, the availability of education and working opportunities, and the promotion of institutional solutions adequate to existing needs.

3. Time for change is now. If existing trends remain unaltered the generation could fail to progress, could perpetuate this situation of need. Generational postponement resulting in prolonged poor living conditions for large groups of population is certainly a dangerous pitfall to be considered in policy making for the children of the year 2000. The next child will be the big loser, for recent findings show that inadequate nutrition in the first months and years will result in poor health, low academic standards, and extreme difficulty to enter and advance in the labor market. Critical conditions in the family can also result in emotional instability and lack of ability to adapt and progress in a highly complex society. This child and his children will have fewer opportunities to break out of the vicious circle of poverty.

4. In Latin America and the Caribbean it is possible to improve social conditions rapidly by a drastic change in approach. Although capital resources are scarce and will remain so, qualified human resources have steadily improved in the last two generations, though the combination of slow economic development and fast population growth has impaired a real participation of this population in improving their children's lives. Women's work has been one of the answers to this objective.

5. The woman in Latin America and the Caribbean has had full access to education and has taken advantage of it when economic conditions have permitted it. Actually women form the fastest growing population in secondary and higher education in the region. Their productive work has become a significant economic input in the maintenance and improvement of the household. However, their opportunities have been lessened by the duality of their roles as viewed by society and by their sense of duty towards their family and their children's well-being.

6. Every planner should consider: first, the extreme urgency of the crisis in child rearing in the Latin American modern urban industrial society; second, the capacity of each social group to contribute to its solution; third, the responsibilities of the public sector, the private sector, and the community. Appropriate programs will succeed to the extent that they are built with the participation of the people in need and that they generate employment compatible with the family's needs and qualifications.

DISCUSSION

HIROSHI AZUMA

Department of Education, University of Tokyo, Japan

IN DISCUSSING the occupational preparation of our children, I want to make two points: first, that humanistic factors will become more and more important in the professions of the future; second, that we should aim at flexible aptitudes and not try to mold children into presently existing occupational patterns.

1. I will briefly discuss the first. In past history, when there was practically unlimited space and natural resources to exploit, man could afford to be aggressive and efficient. But when people had to share limited resources and limited space (as in closed, feudalistic Japan), techniques and systems to prevent and reduce interpersonal and intergroup conflict became of vital importance. In the past, limitations of resources have always been solved by material sciences and technologies, allowing people to retain their belief in efficient production. But to the extent that we are confined to this earth, we have now to expect to reach a saturation point sooner or latter.

For this reason alone, we shall need to have people working on the resolution of human problems rather than on the production of material wealth. It is foreseeable that primary and secondary industries will cease to provide sufficient opportunities of work. Even now, we need much fewer people than 10 years ago to produce the same product. To absorb the potential workers we need to create occupations that serve people in non materialistic ways.

2. As to the second point, I shall refer to our experience in Japan. In 1960 Japan's government made a major effort to improve technical high schools and junior colleges, both in quantity and in quality. The impetus was due to the pressure of middle level engineers and technical supervisors in the locus of production. The leading strategy of this drive was to secure high level expertise by narrow divisions into specializations. Technical high schools usually had more than 20 courses into which students were directed.

During the first few years these schools seemed to succeed, but by the end of the 1960s both the number and quality of applicants had seriously declined. It was not that employment had declined. It was that both the youngsters and their parents were worried about the potential limitations of their future mobility, both vertical and lateral. Today, with very few exceptions, technical high schools have to accept students who belong to the lower and lowest academic strata. This results in a vicious circle; many technical high school graduates now are employed only as a lower labor force in service industries.

The need for technical education itself, nevertheless, is ever growing. Many technical schools of adult education are operating outside the regular school system and without any governmental assistance at over capacity. Electronics students from the best universities attend night school to acquire practical programming skills in computer technology. The specialities of these irregular technical schools cover many branches of engineering plus many other professional skills such as simultaneous interpretership, cooking, photography, accounting, counseling, etc.

One of the factors behind this phenomenon is the rapid development of technologies. The accelerated rate of obsoletion of techniques has made specific technical skills something to be acquired as the need arises rather than something to mold the person into.

Another more important factor is the anticipated shift from a performance production oriented society to a person relationship oriented society. During periods of expansion, performance and production are highly valued. When expansion reaches a limit, human relations within a community becomes more highly valued. Tertiary industry overtakes the secondary industries. Perhaps before the end of this century material expansion by any country will reach its limit. Intra- and international maintenance of human relations will become the major skill required.

The obvious implication is that in preparing our children for the future it will be wrong to try to mold them to the existing patterns of occupations. Flexibility, self-identity, and a humane orientation will be more important than ever before.

D. CARLETON GAJDUSEK
National Institute of Health, Bethesda, MD, USA

The satellite-tracking station of the US National Space Administration at Kwajalein atoll in the center of the Marshall Islands of Micronesia, with its telescopes, radio astronomy, computerized satellite communications, nuclear technology, and jet airstrips, is halfway round the world from Cape Kennedy and is one of the major satellite-tracking and communications centers on the globe. This station alone could employ the entire working force of the Marshall Island, most at a high Western salary level, if Micronesians were trained and educated sufficiently to replace all the imported foreign experts. At present, many Marshallese fly hundreds of kilometers each weekend to and from their homes on Marshall atoll to their workplaces on Kwajalein atoll, but they usually occupy lower-level jobs at the NASA satellite tracking station. There is little likelihood that such a space-tracking center will be abandoned in the next few decades.

On Yap island, in the West Caroline Islands, the 4000 Yapese Micronesians live beside one of the highest manmade towers in the world—the main South Pacific Navigation station sending out microwave signals for all air and sea navigation in this part of the world. The airports for jets and the modern computerized oil port at Palace in the Caroline Islands could employ all the working population of these islands in highly technical jobs if the Micronesians were trained for the work. Instead, the work is done by technicians imported from far afield.

On the Micronesian island of Guam, 35,000 Americans from the United States work mostly at jobs requiring secondary or (often) university education in the tourist hotels, hospitals, port facilities, airports, secondary schools and universities and in the military installations. There are only 35,000 Guamonian islanders, most of whom are already in similar level employment. However, if sufficiently trained and educated, the entire population of the remaining Mariana Islands could replace these immigrant American technologists, and then all Micronesians would be on a high western European or Japanese level economy.

The future occupation for all Micronesians in only a decade or two is clearly in this direction, provided the children and youths are quickly educated to replace the foreign opportunists who have arrived on their islands.

One can conclude, moreover, that up to 30 years ago, a full university level, or at least a post-secondary technical education, would have been appropriate and advantageous for every child of Micronesia in view of the current and anticipated demands there, which today requires the importation of a skilled labor force from halfway round the world, almost equal in size to the total Micronesian working population.

Such a rapid technological invasion of an until recently economically primitive and undernourished region is not unique to Micronesia. It has occurred throughout Southeast Asia and the Pacific as well as in many parts of the Middle East, Africa, and South America.

Today a stationary satellite has already been placed over Indonesia to provide an instantaneous military communication system for the far flung islands of that nation. Already government officers, the army, and American and European oilmen and miners in the jungles and mountain ranges of Sumatra and Borneo can radio and telephone immediately to anywhere in the world with less delay than such communication from Athens; and they can receive international television broadcasts on several channels. An Omega seamaster watch, a walky-talky two-way transisterized radio, a portable battery-operated tape deck, a long-range short-wave radio, a portable television set are all more wanted by the indigenous population than axes, pots, pans, and clothing; and this has been the case for over a decade.

The indigenous people of New Guinea, who were stone age cannibals in their childhood and youth, unfamiliar with the wheel or textiles or ceramics or metal or grain crops, are today coffee planters, owning their own four-wheel-drive Land Rovers and Toyotas for deliveries to coffee factories, often operated by their sons. Elsewhere, their coffee goes to market by small aircraft and helicopter. Their sons drive diesel trailer trucks, fly planes, work in computerized hydroelectric installations, satellite, and microwave radio communications centers, modern hospitals with X-ray units and hematology laboratories, and attend universities by the tens of thousands. They were only three decades ago the most primitive third world economy that existed: stone adze and digging stick agriculturalists in cultures unfamiliar even with tribal organization or the principle of chieftainship or kingship, speaking no written or recorded language. Yet they have entered easily into the world of tomorrow. Radio and satellites, helicopters, jet planes, transistors, and computers are as familiar and as close to them and as much part of their everyday lives as to any American child.

Already in the 1920s, huge gold dredges were flown piecemeal across the jungles and rain-forested ranges of eastern New Guinea to the Bulola Gold Fields, and tons of ore and gold and supplies were brought in and out of the interior by air. The whole highland area was later opened up by air lift, and most New Guinea highlanders have been intimately familiar with airplanes and helicopters, and have travelled in them, before they have seen any other wheeled vehicle. Children go to school by plane, and radio telephone (not telephone lines) is the only means of long distance communication they know. It is the occupational world that will succeed this level of technology for which the New Guinean village child must be educated, from his earliest schooling. He will never use a word of his native language in his school—often not even when chatting with his schoolmaster, who comes from a different language group—or in his place of work.

I suggest that anyone trying to assess the educational needs and occupational future of children in any village, town or city of the world today should first discover where the people, born in that village, town, or city 40 years ago—and their children—are now to be found, and where they have lived and worked during their lifetime. This should include the history of their travels and occupations as sailors or soldiers. Such data will often radically change the planner's view of for whom and for what future occupations he is planning education. As I have indicated, even in the most remote villages of the underdeveloped world, such an analysis may yield surprising results.

Those of us indoctrinated in the modern theories of child development in the faculties of pediatrics, and atuned to the reverence for past cultures and traditions and the need of identity and roots, which has been in vogue in the thinking of the past quarter century, may find some sobering reflections in awareness of the cultures of current day Indonesia and elsewhere in Southeast Asia and the South Pacific.

In the 1940s the emerging Indonesian nation formulated from a group of unwritten dialects of a creole market language and lingua franca, which had spontaneously originated as Bazaar Malay in towns throughout the East Indies as a means of communication between diverse linguistic groups, an artificial synthetic language now called Bahasa Indonesia. This new language, essentially a formalization of Bazaar Malay, was assigned a Roman alphabet, and vocabularies and spellings were formalized and dictionaries and grammars written, and it was adopted as the national language of the future for the nation of over 100,000,000 people who belong to hundreds of distinct ancient languages and cultures. Some of these groups were large, as the 70,000,000 Javanese, who have a language and civilization extending back several thousand years, with over a millennium of written records. All schools turned to educating in this new language beyond the fourth grade, and all newspapers, radio, and all social intercourse switched rapidly to this previously unformalized language from the previously used Dutch of the former colonial rulers and from the local languages of different islands and peoples. A new generation of Indonesians, many no longer speaking the language of their forefathers in their homes or schools, at work, or play, arose. Many children are now even unable to converse in the traditional language of centuries with their grandparents. To compound the wonder, the Indonesians have succeeded in recognizing a major error they had committed in selecting an orthography for their language, based on Dutch spelling, after about a decade of its use. To remedy this, they decided to change the clumsy orthography in academic camera by reassigning several letters to new phonetic representations. Thus, u replaced oe, c replaced tj, j replaced dj, and y replaced j. This, of course, required revising all textbooks and dictionaries in the nation, changing all signs, and altering all maps. This, the Indonesians did in the course of a few further years.

The pessimist looks at all this in horror, rather than seeing optimistically how much a cultural improvisor is man—and he has always been so. The change of language in Singapore to bilingualism in mandarin Chinese and English in the schools, for a largely Hokinese-speaking population of over 2,000,000, has made difficult the school programs for a generation of students; but it is done, and a bilingual nation of Chinese and English speakers capable of coping with the technological future is emerging. I look at this in awe and wonder, and with optimism and joy. I wonder how much future pain and suffering they have avoided by accomplishing this change.

We should remember that before 1066 there was no English language; but that in 100 years a creole based on Norman French and a highly inflected Anglo-Saxon produced our English—a politically determined sudden change which few of us regret.

KARL LÜSCHER
Department of Sociology, University of Konstanz, Federal Republic of Germany

I shall refer to the situation in the Federal Republic of Germany and Switzerland, which are undoubtedly among the world's most wealthy countries.

1. In the microsystem of the immediate environment of the child, the most important change over the last 10-15 years is the change in the role of women. This has included a much greater participation of women in the labor force. One can also observe an upgrading in the work of women at home, expecially in Federal Germany. It is possible that, in the future, the roles of women and men, expecially in the home, may become more similar. I think it very doubtful whether women will adopt the highly competitive career patterns of men or that men may be freed from part of their work and take more responsibility in the home.

2. On the more general level of the community, we must take note of the emergence of alternative forms of living. Many young people (in Federal Germany more than in Switzerland) live in communes in which they try to share in the work of the household. However, one has to be aware that all these communes depend on an ongoing economy of a traditional and highly capitalistic form. It is also still very open whether the commune is an environment in which people want to rear children. Most communes do not have children.

3. A third feature that affects the future of children is the growing importance of support systems. Apart from income subsidies, social security services include institutions such as day care, kindergartens, health clinics, etc. This situation is not without problems, such as the rising cost of the support systems and the fact that those who use them most are quite often people in the upper strata of society. These systems also include a strong professionalization of all the services they provide. This development is not without ambivalence because it can be related with a downgrading of the competence of parental care, which is not considered up to a professional level.

There is another point that is often overlooked. The growing market in products for children has meant that in the highly developed countries the needs of the child are misused as an economic incentive to induce parents to become larger consumers.

4. Germany and (even more) Switzerland have comparatively small problems of

labor shortage because of their heavy employment of foreign workers. But their coming and going has led to severe problems of which the children are the victims. For example the largest foreign community in Germany is the Turks, who are Moslems. But many of the family social services in Germany (and in Switzerland) are funded and administered by the Christian churches. The children of foreign workers also suffer considerable assimilation problems. They are at home in the new country and speak its language, and this, in a sort of way, alienates them from their parents. On the other hand, the parents feel they are losing their children and react accordingly.

5. In considering strategies regarding the amelioration of conditions for children from an economic point of view, we have to be aware that those who take care of children are generally very powerless. They do not form part of the political milieu where the power lies.

One main source of action is to make parents aware of their needs and the needs of their children. Parents may pressure industrial concerns to take much more account of the day to day needs of children for *their fathers* as well as for their mothers. To give an example, in many companies managerial promotion is linked to a move from one city to another. This policy does not take account of the well-documented needs of the men's families.

Another important means of action along this line is to alert the public at large of issues concerning families and children. The German government, for example, is obliged by law to publish family reports every four years. These reports are written by a small group of experts on the basis of their research. The government adds its own—generally more conservative—comments, and the report is then published as a book. These reports have had a great impact on public opinion because, for a certain time, they mean that the family and children become a public issue.

SUMMARY OF DISCUSSION

RAYMOND ILLSLEY

TWO MAJOR questions were posed:

How does the world of work impinge upon the child?
How will changes in the world of work in the next decades change the environment and life of children?

The group recognized two pervading problems in the discussions. On the one hand, we were dealing with many societies, each at a different stage of economic development. We should not necessarily assume that the less-developed societies must follow the process experienced by today's industrial societies but should recognize that they may follow their own industrial pathways. On the other hand, the group was aware of the pitfalls of production and wished to base the discussion upon the experiences of participants in their own and their professional and scientific knowledge rather than utopian views.

The major theme of the discussion centered around the participation of women in the work force, the changing roles, and the potential effect upon the upbringing of children. A simple question, Why do women work?, revealed major differences between developing and developed societies. The point was made, referring initially to Latin American and Caribbean countries, that most women in such societies work because chronic unemployment of males and frequent absence of a male head of household, drives women to work irrespective of the conditions of employment. Even within developing societies, considerable diversity exists. Examples were given of families experiencing the urban transition compared with families living more isolated but more family-supported lives in rural areas. A minority of women in the upper income brackets approximated more to the patterns of work of industrialized societies. In developed societies women worked for two reasons: to maintain or improve expected standards of living (different from subsistence need) and to avoid the social isolation of domestic family life. Depression was a common feature of working class women with young families. The spread of women's participation in work was such that a redefinition of male–female roles in both their domestic and productive roles was beginning to emerge. This would bring about a sharp reversal in role models for children.

The need for support services existed in all types of society though with different degrees of urgency. Services differed in kind ranging from income support, through the provision of day care, creches, nurseries, and kindergartens to the existence of professional support. Conflicting viewpoints were expressed on the desirability of income as opposed to services for parental care.

Disagreement existed on the likely course of the world economy and particularly

101

the likelihood of continued economic growth in industrial societies. Attention was particularly drawn to the present high levels of unemployment, the disadvantaged position of adolescents and of minority groups, the persistence of the class structure, and of unequal rewards. Clear pessimism was expressed about the future economic weakness of third world countries and about the difficulty of combining capital investment with social development affecting the family and the child.

Industrialization, urbanization, and migration had produced traumatic effects in 19th and early 20th century Europe: family disintegration, exploitation, poverty, poor housing and sanitation associated with inadequate child care, malnutrition, infection, and high mortality. Would today's industrialization follow the same unfortunate patterns? The indications were that this process with all its evils was already widespread in developing societies. The urban family in transition needed most help. Migration was identified, however, as a major influence on family life and child upbringing, associated not only with industrialization but with the conditions of employment and styles of life of post-industrial society. This implied study of its effects but also deliberate preparation for migration. The movement of foreign workers into affluent countries presented special problems for family and child. Frequently provision was made only for the migrant male worker. Even if the family and child also migrated they found themselves in temporary, rootless, uncertain conditions. Clear responsibility rested with the affluent societies engaged in this traffic.

Post-industrial societies were experiencing new patterns of education in which the narrow preparation for specific tasks was being superseded in the interests of flexibility by education in general principles. This fitted the rapidity of technological change. It was, moreover, suggested that, in post-industrial service-oriented societies with a large investment in human capital, a more humanistic approach was becoming apparent. The development of personal social services was parelleled by experiments in alternative forms of family and community life and more humanized patterns of work organization.

It was ironic that post-industrial societies were moving away from specialized technical education just at the time that it was being fostered in developing societies. The group was interested in the possible benefits of greater communication between societies which experienced industrial development at different times so that all might profit from such an experience.

REPORT OF WHO/UNICEF WORKSHOP

Presented by J. K. HARFOUCHE
  School of Public Health, Beirut, Lebanon

INNOVATIVE APPROACHES TO MEET THE BASIC NEEDS
OF THE YOUNG CHILD IN DEVELOPING COUNTRIES

Presented by J. K. Harfouche
School of Public Health, Beirut, Lebanon

The young child is transitional as a biological system and highly vulnerable to the stress of adjustment due to his immaturity and special physiological demands. In the developing countries the hazards of stress are compounded by the hostile socioeconomic and sanitary conditions in a rapidly changing environment facing at least three crucial transitions.

(1) A transition in family structure and functions with changes in parental roles and child-rearing patterns.
(2) A demographic transition creating expanding demands for scarce resources.
(3) A transitional society, shifting from a nonspecialized subsistance economy to a specialized exchange economy whereby the constraints of development tend to be most acute.

This is the preliminary report of a joint WHO/UNICEF workshop held in Athens, 28–30 June, 1978, immediately preceding the Symposium on The Child in the World of Tomorrow. A list of the participants is appended.

The special needs of the young child and health problems arising from his unmet needs cannot be handled in isolation from his ecological context: the biological and cultural makeup of his parents, the maternal uterine environment, the dyadic interaction with the parents, the family, the institutions, and political systems in the larger society.

With the complexity of multiple factors interacting within and between the various compartments of the environment, we can never hope to meet the essential needs and combat the problems of the young child by any one single measure at any given age period. Hence, a total attack is required combining various measures (general and direct) strategically tailored to the ecologic context.

The earlier we start in the life cycle of the child to adequately meet his needs and prevent his problems, the less is the cost, and the maximum is the benefit in terms of health, survival, and productivity.

THE BIOLOGICAL MOTHER

The biological mother is the ecological focus of the young child since she provides the environment for the developing embryo, and from the onset of conception they are inextricably intertwined. In the exterogestate phase of the first nine months of life, the mother–child dyad is biologically maintained through breast feeding and psychosocially nurtured by child rearing.

Mothers in rural areas usually have poor body reserves, get the worst part of the family diet, and observe dietary restrictions and taboos during pregnancy and the postnatal period. High rates of general ill health are compounded by excessive pregnancies at short intervals, heavy household chores, work in the fields, and walking long distances to fetch firewood and water.

In the periurban sector the underprivileged mother is often much worse off than her rural counterpart. Being in a nuclear family and an uprooted migrant, she does not get much support from other women in the locality. City life styles have increasingly exposed her to the hazards of "illegitimacy", induced abortion, and a single parent family structure.

On the other hand, mothers belonging to the urban elite are modernized and westernized, enjoy modern household technologies, and convey an image almost identical to the majority of mothers in the developed countries.

PROFILE OF THE YOUNG CHILD

The characteristics of the newborn infant are intergenerationally determined partly by the environmental conditions, which influenced his mother's growth when she was a child, and partly by the contemporary conditions, which characterize the infant's own family circumstances. The intergenerational perpetuation of failure to attain full growth potential due to poverty and chronic malnutrition, is reflected in about 21 million low birthweight babies who are born annually. Unfortunately, most of them are "small for dates", rather than "pre-term", and experience a high risk of death and sublethal damage in the immediate and long term range.

The health problems of any country are concentrated in its young children. In the developing countries about a quarter, or third, or even half, of them die before the age of 5 years, mainly as a result of preventable conditions: malnutrition, gastroenteritis, infection, and unregulated fertility. In addition to these major killers, a heavy toll of unofficially recorded deaths and disabilities occur as a result of natural and manmade disasters, as in Bangladesh, Vietnam, and Lebanon.

Deficiencies in young child stimulation in low income families, limited facilities for preschool education, shortage of toys and play material, high rates of illiteracy and school dropouts—especially among the females—combine to incapacitate the creativity and educability of the young child.

Several indicators point out that the situation of 80% of the underprivileged young children in rural areas and shanty towns is deteriorating, giving rise to what has been termed by UNICEF as the "quiet emergency situation". On the other hand, the levels of health and well-being of the small minority of the urban elite is approaching that of the developed countries.

Mothers and young children continue to be neglected, largely because they are nonvocal and unable to organize themselves in pressure groups to influence high level decision makers in their favor.

The root causes of the deteriorating situation of young children lie in public apathy; inadequate information about the young child, including data on births, deaths, and growth; lack of balanced policies with biological orientation; deficiencies in implementation of social policies; lack of sound models of development; educational and health care systems that are imported from the industrialized countries; effects of the "world food crisis" and of the "international economic system."

SHORTCOMINGS OF DEVELOPMENT MODELS

Shortcomings of adopted development models are of two types: first, a concentration of development plans upon economic growth objectives and the urban–industrial sector; second, the exclusion of demographic objectives and of the integration of women. The first strategy has led to inequitable distribution of income, goods, and services, and has increased the relative disparity between the "haves" and the "have nots" on a national and international scale. The second has maintained the constraints of high birthrates and has failed to benefit from the productivity of 50% of the adult population.

Alternative models that are urgently needed for continued improvement in the levels of living and quality of life must integrate social objectives with economic plans and increase investments in health, nutrition, education, and welfare. High priority should also be given to rural agricultural development, capital-saving and labor intensive policies, the integration of women, and strategies conducive to effective change in fertility behavior leading to small family size.

CONVENTIONAL HEALTH CARE SYSTEMS

The conventional health care systems have doubtful social relevance and are inaccessible to needy population groups, especially mothers and young children. They concentrate on sophisticated technology, curative care in urban hospitals and health facilities, and fragmented services; and they fail to view the total needs of the child in his ecologic context and the mother–child dyadic interaction, particularly in the early neonatal period.

Shortage and maldistribution of doctors and nurses is typical of the developing countries: and their education, whether abroad or locally, does not prepare them to meet the health needs of the community.

In most developing countries the conventional health care systems have failed to meet the essential health needs of the large majority of the population. Complexity and cost put these systems beyond the means of the people, and they are unlikely to be expanded in future to meet these needs. In other words, as John Bryant ably pointed out: "the systems for health care and education of health personnel, with few exceptions, were not designed to meet the needs of these countries."[1]

INNOVATIVE APPROACHES

In this crucial phase of their existence, developing countries are in greater need than ever before of effective and efficient health system models and of innovative approaches in health care delivery designed to achieve "better health for all the people."

Some developing countries (China, Cuba, Tanzania, Venezuela, and others) have already adopted alternative approaches and have succeeded—fully or in part—in making essential health care universally accessible and acceptable to the people at a cost that the country can afford.

Promising innovative health care programs introduced at the national level (and health care actions of more limited range) have provided general principles for the practical "primary health care approach" being promoted by WHO and UNICEF.

The basic principles which determine the success of this approach may be summarized as follows:

1. Clear national health policies and integration of health services systems with other components of development. Primary health care forms an integral part both of the country's health system of which it is the nucleus and of the overall social and economic development of the community.

Health cannot be improved by the health sector alone. An effective health care approach is multisectoral: it attacks the causes of ill health rather than the consequences; and requires the coordinated efforts of all those sectors that can contribute directly or indirectly to the promotion of well-being. This is not only at the central level but also at the intermediate and—above all—the local level, where policies should have their roots.

2. At the local level, high priority is given to: (a) water and improved sanitation; (b) health and nutrition education; (c) maternal and child care, including family planning, nutrition care, and immunization; (d) prevention, early diagnosis, and management of common infections. The components of essential health care are provided as an integrated "package of services" adapted to the local needs; the idea being that the total health effects to be accrued from such a package will be more than the sum total of its individual components; and also their cost will be less due to the use of common infrastructure and resources.

3. Meeting community needs is the basis for the formulation and implementation of any primary health care activity. Communities should be involved from the beginning in identifying their health needs and priorities; in planning national primary health care programs and local health activities, in shaping them around their life styles and patterns, and in participating in carrying them out and evaluating their results.

In communities where material resources are scarce and human resources abound, a community development strategy based on self-reliance is probably the only approach that the community can afford, and it can well turn out to be the most cost effective.

4. The most realistic solution for achieving total population coverage of essential health care is to employ community health workers acting as a team. They can be trained in a short time to perform specific tasks. It is advantageous if they come from the community in which they live and are chosen by it, so that they have its acceptance and support.

The types of such community workers will vary according to the local needs and resources. Hence they may include "bare foot doctors," medical aides, feldshers, practical nurses, general medical practitioners, as well as traditional health practitioners.

Family members are often the main providers of health care. Because of their central position in the family, women (particularly mothers and grandmothers) can contribute significantly to primary health care, especially in ensuring the application of preventive and nutrition measures.

If children are educated to have a good understanding of health, they can be very effective in taking the message to their homes and families as well as by being useful in practical work such as first aid, immunization, basic sanitation, growth monitoring, and nutrition surveys.

Women's organizations, in addition to being important for health promotion in the community, can stimulate the interest of women in other activities likely to enhance the quality of life.

5. A national primary health care policy must insist on simple technology that is appropriate and can be afforded; must encourage its local development; disseminate information about it; and promote its widespread use.

Medicinal drugs are an important component of health technology. It is universally agreed that fewer drugs are necessary than the number at present on the market in most parts of the world. A model list of about 200 essential drugs is now available.

6. The whole health system in a country must be reoriented to support primary health care and to provide training, supervision, technical advice, and referral schemes for the community health workers. Health professionals must perform social and educational functions, in addition to utilizing their technical skills, if they accept the challenge and are willing to become leaders in health.

7. Communication at low cost is essential. Two-wheel (or three-wheel vehicles) are good substitutes for expensive motor cars. Two-way radio schemes and proper utilization of local mass media to promote essential health measures are highly desirable.

8. Finally, human society learns by trial and error and not only by experimentation. Failure may provide a more meaningful learning experience than success. Innovative health care programs and activities need to be constantly monitored and evaluated; by repeatedly going through the process we can overcome our ignorance.

INCREASING COLLABORATION BETWEEN DEVELOPED AND DEVELOPING COUNTRIES

The child is not only the means and goal of development, but also of world peace, justice, and security. Hence the child of today and of tomorrow is the most effective bridge for balanced communication and continued exchange of knowledge, skills, experience, technologies, food, and wealth among the developed and developing countries.

Illustrations of how this exchange can be mutually beneficial are legion, but time and space limitations restrict this challenging topic to a few examples.

(1) The present trend in the developed countries to return to naturalism: such as, the promotion of breast-feeding; the parent-child dyadic interaction; increasing emphasis on the humanitarian approach in the delivery of health care; and recognition of some elements of traditional medicine, including herbal remedies and indigenous birth attendants.

(2) Increasing utilization of problem-solving expertise from the developing countries to complement and supplement technological expertise in the more developed countries.

(3) Exchanging experience in tackling the psychosocial problems of over-development relevant to changes in family structure and functions; to the dual role of women as producer and reproducer; to creches, day care centres, and

child-minding facilities; to adolescence; to old age and protection of the environment.

(4) Promotion of equitable food distribution for the mutual benefit of combating undernutrition in the developing countries and overnutrition in the developed countries.

(5) Financial assistance to deliver essential services to young children, particularly in the 25 least-developed countries whose development plans and child health programs have been severely curtailed by recent increases in prices.

REFERENCES

1. J. BRYANT, *Health and the Developing World,* Russel Sage Foundation, Thraca and London, 1969.

LIST OF PARTICIPANTS

CHUN, Yeong Ja Dr., Department of Nursing, Korea University College of Medicine, Seoul

DA PURIFICAÇAO COSTA ARAUJO, Maria Dr., Direction-genérale de la Santé, Alameda d'Afonso Henriques, Lisbon

CRAVIOTO, Joqaquin Dr., Professor of Pediatrics, Director Cientifico del Instituto Nacional de Ciencias y Tecnologia de la Salud del Niñ-DIF, Mexico 22, DF

GACHUKIA, Eddah Mrs., Kenya Member of Parliament, Educator Child Development, President National Council of Women, Member IYC Commission

ELIOU, Maria Dr., Sociologist, National Centre for Social Research, Athens

LIAROPOULOS, Lycourgos Dr., Health Economist (Consultant), Ministry of Social Services, Athens

MARATOU, Olga Dr., Psychologist, "METERA" Babies' Centre, Athens

THI MINH, Phan Mme., Deputy Director, International Organizations, Foreign Ministry, SR Vietnam

SORGHO, Simeon, Director-General of Management of Upper Volta, Ministry of Rural Development, Upper Volta

MÖNCKEBERG, Fernado Dr., Director, Food and Nutrition Institute, Chile University

MORFI, Pati Mrs., Early Childhood Educator, Nursery School-Kindergarten, Athens

RAJENDRAN, M. M., Joint Secretary, Ministry of Social Welfare, India

RANSOME-KUTI, R. Dr., Director, Basic-Health Services Scheme, Implementation Agency, Lagos

SANGMAHLI, Sman, Deputy Under-Secretary of State for Education, Thailand

SHAZALI, H. Dr., Senior Pediatrician, Wad Medani Civil Hospital, Wad Medani, Sudan

SOYSA, Priyani Dr., Professor of Pediatrics, University of Sri Lanka, Colombo

TRA, le Thu Mme, Vice President of Committee for the Children and Pioneers, S.R. Vietnam

TSITOURA, Stella Dr., Pediatrician, Institute of Child Health, Athens

DIPODILOGO, A. Dr., Pediatrician, Special Staff of the Minister, Coordinator for Peoples Welfare of the Republic of Indonesia

SECRETARIAT

DOXIADIS, S. Dr., Minister of Social Services, Athens

HARFOUCHE, J. K. Dr., Chairman, Department of Public Health Practice, School of Public Health, American University of Beirut, Beirut (WHO Consultant)

McDOUGALL, J. F., Director, IYC Secretariat for Europe, Geneva

MANDL, P. L. Dr., Editor, Assignment Children, UNICEF Office for Europe, Geneva

NAKOU, Sheena Dr., Institute of Child Health, Athens

PETROS-BARVAZIAN, A. Dr., Director, Division of Family Health, WHO, Geneva

WAGNER, M. G. Dr., Consultant, Maternal and Child Health, WHO Regional Office for Europe, Copenhagen

WILLUMSEN, C. Mrs., Administrative Assistant, Maternal and Child Health, WHO, Geneva

The Child and the Family

CHANGING FAMILY ROLES AND RIGHTS

THE CHILD IN THE WORLD OF YESTERDAY

PETER BURKE

Department of History, University of Sussex, Brighton, UK

WHEN, where, how and why our modern attitudes to children arose and developed are fascinating questions which have received a good deal of attention in the last 20 years but I do not propose to discuss them here.[1] I would rather focus on traditional attitudes to children, in particular the attitudes current in preindustrial Western Europe, especially from 1500 to 1800. Not to propose that we imitate this alternative to contemporary Western childhood; still less to denounce it as an example of parental "immaturity"; but to try to explain it.[2] For the study of the child in the world of yesterday has something to tell us about the variety of possible childhoods and also about the constraints that limit this variety. "Child" is a social role, and at different times adults have made very different assumptions about the nature of this role, assumptions that have in turn shaped the experience of childhood in different periods of history. But, of course, concepts of childhood are not freefloating. They are subject not only to biological but also to economic and social constraints. Our own attitudes to children are the product of our society and will not remain appropriate as that society changes. However, attitudes to children are not simply determined by economic and social forces; they are the products of a whole culture. They include assumptions that can outlive their usefulness but can also become conscious and be changed.

To talk about Western Europe between 1500 and 1800 in a few minutes is inevitably to simplify. I shall try to indicate the dominant attitudes and the most important constraints, but you must not think that attitudes to children were uniform. It was precisely because attitudes were not uniform that they were able to change so much in the 18th and 19th centuries.

A discussion of childhood in preindustrial Europe naturally begins with one of the most important facts of life; the high risk of losing it. Infant and child mortality were high. To quote figures for parts of Anjou and Brittany in the 18th century, which were probably fairly typical, of every 100 children born about 25 died before they were one and another 25 before they were ten.[3] What were the consequences of this high deathrate for attitudes to children? It has often been suggested that it discouraged parents from taking small children seriously as individuals and from making an emotional "investment" in them.[4] This point is sometimes made too crudely, but one can at least talk about a fatalistic attitude to the death of children. Parents did not always attend the funeral of a dead child. They might be vague about the number of children they had had or lost. We also find many parents who abandoned their children, legitimate and illegitimate, placing the little bundles outside a foundling hospital or a rich man's door. Many urban parents sent their infants into the country to a wetnurse and apparently failed to inquire after them regularly, although it was well known that mortality was especially high among such nurslings.[5] The nurses had too many children to look after and not enough milk to go around. Deliberate infanticide was not unknown, although we have no means of saying how common it was.

None of these things should surprise us, given that contraception was little known and less practiced before the late 18th century, so that the supply of babies exceeded the demand and parents often produced more children than they could support. Working mothers had to resort to wetnurses. Infant mortality was so common anyway that people did not feel responsible: God gives, God takes away.

What happened to the children who survived? Their training began with swaddling, which was standard practice before 1800 despite the objections of a few intellectuals. Swaddling was defended on medical grounds; whether this defence was a rationalization is difficult to say. It was obviously convenient for mothers and nurses to "park" children in this way while they were busy; and swaddling perhaps symbolizes an attitude to the infant as a being which needs to be restrained and even shaped. Toilet training, on the other hand, was not taken very seriously. Weaning was comparatively late, at about two, but corporal punishment began relatively early, at about the same age. "Break their wills" was advice commonly given to the parents of young children. Some people saw children as little innocents but the norms of socialization implied that child nature was corrupt. Lacking reason, the under-sevens had to be governed by fear. Under-sevens were often compared to animals, and animals, too, were trained by beating.[6]

At about seven the child reached what was called the "age of reason" and came to be regarded as a small, ignorant, inexperienced version of the adult. At this age a boy might take the first steps in a clerical career, receiving the tonsure and the first three minor orders; or take the first steps in a military career, leaving home to become a page in a noble household; or go to school, where the teachers tended to assume that his mind was like that of an adult. Seven year old boys and girls were dressed like miniature adults; thus in the mid 18th century a noble French seven year old was likely to appear in public with a little sword and a powdered wig.

It was at seven that most children began to work. Child labor did not begin with the industrial revolution—it simply became more visible. In preindustrial Europe boys helped their fathers on the farm, herding cattle or scaring the birds from the crops. Girls would be set to spinning or looking after babies. In many places children were sent away from home at about seven, whether to be apprenticed or to enter domestic service. Boys were also in demand as chimney sweeps, because they could wriggle up narrow chimneys, and as pickpockets, because they had small hands and could run fast when necessary. Or they could do less-skilled work; Michiel de Ruyter, later the glory of the Dutch navy, worked a treadmill in a rope works before he ran away to sea.

In short, most children in early modern Europe did not experience childhood as we know it. The protected phase of life came to an end at about seven or even earlier. Child labor provoked some criticisms in this period, but expressions of satisfaction seem just as common. John Evelyn, visiting Amsterdam in 1641, noted, I think with admiration, that "there is hardly a child of four or five years old, but they find some employment for it." Pitt, speaking in the British House of Commons in 1796 about laboring children, stressed "the weight which their support by their labors took off the country."[7]

We shall surely have to admit that Pitt was right. Children formed a high proportion of the population. Under fourteens are now less than a quarter of the population of Europe but the proportion before 1800 was closer to 40%. It would have been difficult to do without the labor of the age group 7–14, all the more because of the lack of inanimate sources of energy. Child labor was a necessity for society as a whole and also for many individual families. Given this necessity, adults simply could not have afforded to see children as needing protection for a long period. The modern attitude to children is a luxury.

In any case, adults did not expect to live long. What we have learned to call the "mid-life crisis," they saw as old age. Montaigne, for example, regarded himself as old at 38, the age at which he retired from active life into his tower.[8] If adult life ended so early it made sense to start it as soon as possible. If adults did not expect to live till their children were over 21, it made sense for them to marry their children off young, or at least to betroth them early. Hence it is not surprising to find that upper class boys and girls were often engaged at six and married at 12 or 14.[9] There was little room for the idea of adolescence as a separate stage of life, although it was recognized that puberty was a dangerous time, and also that men and women in their twenties might enjoy themselves in ways we might consider "childish," throwing snowballs or taking part in blind man's buff. The distinction between childhood and young adulthood was less than it later became.[10]

Did parents love their children or were they indifferent to them? The question may seem an odd one but several historians have argued recently that in preindustrial Europe fathers and even mothers were relatively indifferent to their children, and that the children in turn felt fear or respect rather than love for the parents. As you may well imagine, it is very difficult to find good evidence that will enable us to answer questions about psychohistory, especially collective psychohistory. All I can say is that although it is conceivable that the majority of people in early modern Europe were "affectionless characters" or "authoritarian personalities", I do not think this likely. Such a view rests on an interpretation of cultural conventions (rituals, forms of address, etc.), which I find implausible, and it also involves the somewhat ethnocentric assumption that love cannot exist within an inegalitarian relationship. The quality of the emotional relationships between parents and children was different from today, but it is misleading to describe the difference in terms of the contrast between indifference and love.[11]

Much of this picture of childhood in preindustrial Europe will seem familiar to many of you because children are seen in similar ways in many parts of the world today. Child marriage is still normal in India. Babies are still swaddled in parts of south-east Europe. Child labor is the norm in much of the third world. The Western attitude to childhood is a luxury.

Is it even desirable? Does the modern industrialized West prolong childhood (in the sense of a protected stage in life) too long for children's good and for their happiness? Does it distinguish too sharply between childhood and adulthood? Some people, like Ivan Illich and John Holt, would answer these questions with a resounding "yes", and it is interesting to find that similar ideas about deschooling society were already expressed by British writers in the 17th and 18th centuries. Thomas Tryon (1695) thought it better for children to be "intrusted with the management of business" than "compelled to sit in torment eight hours in a day under the grim and unpleasing aspect of an harsh and ill-natured pedagogue". William Buchan (1759) opposed sending children "too young" to school to be "nailed to a seat seven or eight hours a day.[2] They had a point. Their schools were not altogether like ours, just as their social problems were not altogether like ours; but to reflect for a few minutes about their past may make it easier to plan a future which is not forced into the mold of the present.

REFERENCES

1. The pioneering work in this field is, of course, P. Ariès, *L'Enfant et la Vie Familiale sous l'Ancien Régime*, Paris, 1960, English transl. as *Centuries of Childhood*, London, 1962.
2. L. DE MAUSE (ed.), *The History of Childhood*, 1974; London edn. 1976, 1—54.
3. F. LEBRUN, *La Vie Conjugale sous l'Ancien Régime*, Paris, 1975, p. 139.
4. ARIÈS (New York edn. 1965) pp. 39 f; cf. F. LEBRUN, *Les Hommes et la Mort en Anjou aux 17e et 18e Siècles*, Paris and The Hague, 1971, pp. 422 f, and L. STONE, *The Family, Sex and Marriage in England 1500-1800*, London, 1977, p. 105.
5. R. TREXLER, Infanticide in Florence and The foundlings of Florence, in *History of Childhood Quarterly*, 1, 1973; J.-L. FLANDRIN, *Familles*, Paris, 1976, pp. 176 ff; E. SHORTER, *The Making of the Modern Family*, New York, 1975, ch. 5.
6. D. HUNT, *Parents and Children in History*, New York and London, 1970, pp. 140 ff; cf. Stone, op. it., pp. 159-60.
7. On child labour, J.KUCZYNSKI, *Geschichte der Kinderarbeit in Deutschland*, Berlin, 1958, and J. C. VLEGGEERT, *Kinderarbeid in Nederland*, Assen, 1964.
8. C. GILBERT, When did a man in the Renaissance grow old?, in *Studies in the Renaissance* 14, 7-32 (1967).
9. On child marriage, H. F. M. PEETERS, *Kind en Jeugdige*, Hilversum and Antwerp, 1966, pp. 264 f; I. PINCHBECK and M. HEWITT, *Children in English Society*, London, 1969, 1, ch. 2.
10. Contrast Ariès, op. cit., pp. 29 ff, 62 ff, with PEETERS pp. 258 ff; with N. Z. DAVIS, *Society and Culture in Early Modern France*, London, 1975, pp. 107 ff; and with J. GILLIS, *Youth and History*, New York, 1974, ch. 1.
11. Contrast the approach of Shorter, deMause, and Stone with that of Flandrin.
12. I. ILLICH, *Deschooling Society*, 1971, Harmondsworth edn., 1973, pp. 33 ff; J. HOLT, *Escape from Childhood*, New York, 1974, pp. 6 ff; T. TRYON, *A New Method of Educating Children*, London, 1695, preface; W. BUCHAN, *Domestic Medicine*, Edinburgh, 1759, p.34.

DISCUSSION

B. K. RAMANUJAM

BM Institute of Public Health, New Delhi, India

IN SPITE of the fact that the mortality rate has come down in India, it is still quite high. Under these circumstances it is only natural that parents should develop a fatalistic attitude similar to that found in the 17th and 18 centuries in Europe, described by Dr. Burke. Such an attitude proves to be a very useful coping device. Without it much more grief would be experienced by the parents.

It is significant that the demarcation between the child and the adult world is not very clearly delineated in India. In rural areas, a child is simply not a "child." Because of space limitations, children are continuously interacting with adults and participating in all activities. As soon as he is able to move about, therefore, the child becomes a part of the adult world, and in fact begins to take on responsibilities at a very early age. For example, in rural areas and in the lower socioeconomic groups in the urban world, children have no toys; instead, they improvise their own play material. Since every hand is a useful hand, the value of children attending school regularly becomes questionable to the parents, who are themselves often illiterate; indeed, 60% of the children drop out of school by their 4th grade.

Adoption is not a very common practice in India. If at all, a child may be adopted by his near relatives, but there always remains a hankering for the original home. The same is true in the case of the cottage orphanages, where the prevailing desire of the children to find their real parents once again shows how, in India, there is no real substitute for a family.

Some comments on the changing social scene are perhaps in order. The fact that more women are entering the working force means that the role functions of the parents is in some sense being disturbed. While divorce has not yet attained social sanction, it has been observed that the less educated woman can adapt to her husband's family much more readily than the highly educated woman, who is more easily involved in family conflicts. Generally, even if it is accepted that a working woman is working for the economic benefit of the family, there is still a certain ambivalence in the attitudes of men.

The woman can work as long as she also performs her household functions, but this naturally places a considerable burden upon the women, and thus also upon the families.

In the urban world there seems to be a new uncertainty in the judgements of the adults, and when the adults can no longer communicate their ideas with conviction, this leaves the children confused. While the children and young people of middle class families are not protesting and revolting in the Western sense of the term; and while there is no attempt to get away from their families, the young people would like the adults to be more sensitive to their needs. At the same time, they are angry that their adults cannot provide the necessary leadership as they did in the past.

T. A. BAASHER

WHO Regional Office for the Eastern Mediterranean, Alexandria, Egypt

Despite the fact that through better means of communication the world is physically shrinking, there is still a wide gap, in many respects, between communities in technically advanced countries and in the less-developed countries. The family, as a group unit of society, will naturally reflect these socioeconomic and technological differences, which may be manifested in various ways of life. It is, therefore, not surprising that Mr. Burke's description of childhood in preindustrial Europe may look familiar to many because a similar life situation may still obtain in some less technically advanced parts of the world.

Significantly, because of inherent historical, socioeconomic, technological, and cultural differences, the definition of what constitutes a family may pose certain problems. Contrary to what is generally seen in technically advanced countries, where the family is characteristically small and generally includes a man, his wife, and their children, there are communities where the family is greatly extended and may embrace several generations. These basic differences in family structure seem to lead to differences in functions, in social and legal status, and in human relationships. It is to be remembered that the extended family system traditionally plays a role, similar to a group insurance, which provides psychological, social, and material support within the family setup.

Thus the Western concept of child labor has a very different connotation in such a setting: if the family members work, they work together; if they eat, they eat together; and if they play, they play and they laugh together. There is a very big difference between this sort of cooperation within the family and child labor outside of the family.

When such a system changes, alternatives or substitutes have to be developed to ensure the well-being of the family.

Broadly speaking, there is hardly any society which has not been subjected to change. However, the impact of change and its enduring results on the family and on society at large will be most felt when a new social philosophy, religion, belief, or different means of production have been introduced and a new way of life emerges. Historically, this has been clearly demonstrated in countries of the Middle and Near East as a result of epoch-making events, namely the advent of world religions and the development of the oil industry. Practically every religious doctrine seems to include various references and rules about family relations and duties.

As a code of behavior the Islamic religion, for example, has been generally influential in promoting the role of the family, in regulating the marital relationship, in upholding the place of parenthood, and in securing care and protection of children. Today we take it for granted that every child has the right to live. But there were times when this was not so. In pre-Islamic Arabia, for instance, female children were deliberately killed for fear of poverty and as a safeguard against shame. This ancient practice of deliberate infanticide was effectively given up in resonse to Koranic teaching, when it was seriously and emphatically proclaimed: "Do not kill your children for fear of poverty; we shall provide for them and for you." Furthermore, the child was accorded special recognition when Koranic revelation stated that: "Wealth and children are the adornment of life." Other examples, particularly the influence of religion on mothering, the care of the orphan and the destitute, are of extreme importance in the history of social welfare.

Again, special emphasis was particularly given in Koranic revelation to breast feeding. Importantly, it was specifically indicated: "And mothers shall suckle their children for two whole years, for those who wish to complete suckling." Adherence to such religious regulation in breast feeding has wide implications on the health of the child and on the degree of maternal fertility. The importance of recognizing and abiding by cultural heritage of proven worth and its influence on health has to be weighed against the accelerated rate of socioeconomic change and rapid erosion of useful customs and sound traditions.

In the growing urban centers, on the other hand, there is an increasing changing trend for child delivery in hospitals, where new rearing practices are introduced and a different culture is continuously developing. This needs to be systematically studied in order to promote the family role and enhance child care.

To perform the art of parenthood effectively, the mother needs time, which may not be adequately available, particularly among the low income working group, living a crowded and complex life in rapidly growing cities. More and more it has been realized and increasingly stressed that infant care and child development, especially in the first three years of life, call for a warm, loving relationship with a devoted mother or mother substitute.[1] In settled and closely knit community settings these needs seem to be generally met; however, there are serious and practical problems associated with maternal employment in the heterogeneous social complex of urban life. Clearly, unless special social and legal provisions are made in order to secure the various child needs and to facilitate the role of working mothers, parental care, under adverse conditions of maternal employment may be seriously affected.

With these ideas in mind, it is of central importance that rules and regulations of maternal employment be reconsidered to render them more responsive to the changing needs of the family and, in countries where such social and legal provisions are absent, appropriate national policies have to be formulated.

Internationally, at the Thirty-first World Health Assembly, 1978, the member states, noting with concern the continued decline in breast feeding in many countries, recommended that "the highest priority be given to prevention of malnutrition in pregnant and lactating women, infant and young children and to stimulate permanent multi-sectoral co-ordination of nutrition process and programs by:

(1) supporting and promoting breast-feeding with educational activities to the general public; legislative and social action, to facilitate breast-feeding by working mothers; implementing the necessary promotional and facilitating measures in health services; and regulating inappropriate sales promotion of infant foods that can be used to replace breast milk;

(2) ensuring timely supplementation and appropriate weaning practices and the feeding of young children after weaning with the maximum utilization of

locally available and acceptable foods; carrying on, if necessary, action-merited research to support this approach and the training of personnel for its promotion."[2]

These clearly stated recommendations form extremely useful and timely guidelines for an effective approach and future strategy in the crucial area of infant feeding.

Along with socioeconomic development, parental attitudes and family responsibility in the training of children seem to undergo various changes. Parents as providers of culture and promoters of personality development are bound to be influenced by current assumptions and community values regarding the upbringing of children and their discipline. As pointed out by Mr. Burke, the swaddling and the restrictive approach of preindustrial Western Europe may still be seen among certain traditional families. However, the role of parents under the modern way of life seems to shift gradually to a more relaxed and liberal attitude. Many are still gripped in the middle of change between the two norms of life, between traditionalism and modernism, with their various implications. Such a situation is apt to create certain emotional complications among busy parents who strive hard to uphold community values of a past generation, while the children may take different cues of behavior from their day to day experience, human contacts, and the complex life situation to which they are exposed. Children of today are certainly more knowledgeable than before, and the influence of such powerful media as television are often beyond parental control. Certainly the new media are potent instruments which can be well utilized in child education and amusement. Yet they may have their adverse reactions in learning and emotions. Novel aggressive behavior, for example, may be learnt by children through exposure to aggressive actions shown in television.[3]

The issue of child training and personality development opens up wide areas for consideration. However, it can be concluded that amidst the growing forces of change, the family, most likely, will do well if a middle course is followed in training and disciplinary approaches, building up on proven and useful community values, and being sensitive to the needs of children in a technologically and culturally changing society.

Institutions such as kindergarten, nursery schools, day centres, etc., which have been recently introduced in developing countries, have been generally useful in sharing the family role for the provision of care for children. As a whole, however, they are inadequate in resources and rather custodial in orientation. The needs of the preschool child for stimulation, appropriate facilities for play, safe environmental manipulation, socialization programmes, etc., need no further emphasis here. Nonetheless, many countries need to focus more attention on this important field with a view to developing more relevant future programs, within the context of local conditions and available resources.

Along with the universal movement for educational development, childhood is generally extended, and this puts further responsibility on the family. To enable the family to deal more appropriately with the growing liabilities of care and support for children, it seems important that organized social provisions be made at community and national levels. Children's allowance, better playgrounds, special cultural facilities, summer camps, etc., are but a few examples of what have been developed in this direction.

Another issue which has to be resolved due to the prolonged system of education is the question of socialization. With growing educational facilities it is clear that children and young adults are enjoying better chances for intellectual attainment. However, as educational programs are generally pursued away from the realities of active life, this may create problems of social maturity amongst youth and hence the need for proper utilization of their time in appropriate socialization programs and community activities.

REFERENCES

1. D. A. MURRAY, *Am. J. Orthopsychiatry,* **45**, 773-790 (1975).
2. WHO World Health Assembly, Document A31/71, p. 3, Geneva, 1978.
3. M. B. ROTHENBERG, *JAMA,* **234**, 1043-1046 (1975).

LEON EISENBERG

Department of Psychiatry, Harvard Medical School, Boston, MA, USA

Rather than repeat by agreement that which has already been said, I will confine myself to those issues which are controversial and merit further analysis.

It is, of course, true that when mortality rates for infants and children change as rapidly as they have in the West over the past two centuries, there *are* changes in the *experience* of parenthood as Professor Burke has pointed out. But I do not believe for one moment that parental love for and investment in each child were less 200 years ago—or are less today in the developing man in the industrial world. To accept this unfounded belief is to perpetuate a myth that has been used to justify the colonial mentality; namely, that life is "cheap" for Latin Americans, or Indians, or Africans, and that therefore we need not exercise the same concern for the welfare of their children as we do for our own.

Over that same period, adult mortality rates and with them, longevity, have undergone major improvements. Does that imply that "modern" Westerners love life any more than their 18th century counterparts—or their third world contempories? Suffering and tragedy are not diminished by their frequency. Parents everywhere want happy futures for their children; they differ only in their access to the means to assure that happiness. That is the central point we must keep in mind.

Second, as to the observation by Professor Ramanujam that marital maladjustment is more common among educated women in India; while the observation may be correct, what matters is the meaning ascribed to it. Education opens new horizons and arouses greater expectations than a life of drudgery. Women have been exploited throughout history; there is an honorable tradition of rebellion against that exploitation that is reaching greater proportions today. We should celebrate rather than lament, women's insistence on dignity. There may be no divorce in a society that forbids divorce legally. Does that signify happy marriages—or does it not reflect the persistence of unhappy relationships under duress? A high divorce rate is a measure of how unsatisfactory human relationships are; it is the relationship which we must endeavour to enhance. Broken homes reflect stresses on children, but I suggest to you that they are often a better solution than the formal maintenance of an "intact" but miserable home. It is less the divorce than the poverty of divorced mothers that is likely to impair the development of her children. Adequate social security and the forming of a new and happier relationship are far better guarantees for children than keeping a bad marriage going.

As to Dr. Baasher's important point about religions, religious ideals are, indeed, major forces for the good. However, we cannot overlook the frequency with which *distortions* of these ideals have been used to constrain human development; consider only the "holy" crusades throughout history in which millions of fellow human beings have been destroyed in order to "save" them. Religious hierarchies, no less than professional elites and political oligarchies, have rationalized the subjugation of women and of nonbelievers.

Finally, what needs to be added to this discussion is an explicit recognition of the role of politics and power in determining whether our noble goals for children will be achieved. We have the capacity to produce enough food for children of the world if we, as citizens, can make this a central priority of our governments. That will only occur if we acknowledge our common humanity and abandon our thrust toward obtaining short run personal advantages at the expense of the future of others. The world is small enough today and our capacity to destroy life on earth large enough, that it is rapidly becoming to the advantage of each of us to work for the good of all of us.

PSYCHOSOCIAL ISSUES IN PLANNING FOR THE FUTURE

MICHAEL RUTTER

Institute of Psychiatry, University of London, UK

IN LOOKING ahead to the child in the world of tomorrow there are many issues which should concern us if we are to do all that we should to improve psychosocial development and reduce mental health hazards for the maximum number. In this paper I propose to briefly consider just three aspects: (i) changing family circumstances; (ii) preventive measures available now; and (iii) the psychosocial costs of improved patterns of care.

CHANGING FAMILY CIRCUMSTANCES

During recent years there have been a variety of changes in family circumstances that have serious implications for the upbringing of children. Thus, in many developed countries there are rising rates of divorce and marital breakdown so that increasing numbers of children are growing up in broken homes.[1] The illegitimacy ratio is rising in many parts of the world and the children concerned (often born to very young mothers) are now, in some countries, being less commonly given up for adoption. Many children are being reared in single-parent families with the social and economic disadvantages that this so frequently entails. People are marrying earlier and the proportion of children born to teenagers has increased in many areas in spite of a growth in family planning services. It is difficult to assess the gains and losses involved in all these social changes, but certainly many children face the hazards and stresses of family discord and disruption and many are being reared by young unsupported women living in disadvantageous conditions, who are sometimes illequipped to provide all that is required for good parenting. A surprisingly high proportion of children develop satisfactorily in spite of their unfortunate start to life, but if we are to increase that proportion we must not only reduce the psychosocial traumata, but also strive to increase protective factors and ameliorating influences. Unfortunately, very little attention has been paid so far to these *positive* aspects of development. A shift of emphasis in that direction is required.

A further social change is that in many countries the employment of women is increasing with the result that a large proportion of children experience substitute care during the day. In many cases this is undertaken by kin or friends, but there is also an increasing use of child minders and day care centres. The quality of child care provided is sometimes quite poor,[2] and it is important that we ensure that all varieties of care meet the children's psychsocial as well as physical needs.[3]

Clearly there are many other concerns which stem from patterns of changing family circumstances. These require careful consideration and will be discussed in other sessions of this conference. However, at this point it is necessary to turn attention to some of the many things that we should be doing *now* for children irrespective of what changes occur over the years to come.

PREVENTIVE MEASURES AVAILABLE NOW

There is reasonable agreement on the preventive measures that are already available now to aid psychosocial development and to prevent mental health problems. They have been succinctly summarized by the recent World Health Organization Expert Committee,[4] and its recommednations are closely in line with the steps proposed by the British Child Health Services Committee[5] and the possibilities for prevention suggested by Graham.[6]

First, there is good evidence that chronic physical handicaps (especially those involving organic brain dysfunction) carry with them a substantially increased risk of psychiatric problems. Accordingly, steps to improve the general physical health and well-being of children should lead to accompanying gains in psychosocial functioning. Improvements in maternal and obstetric care, in nutrition, in effective immunization programs, in reduction of accidents, in improved physical and social conditions, in antenatal screening, in the care of the chronically handicapped, and in physical and social conditions generally, may all play a part in this process.

Second, several investigations have shown the mental health hazards associated with unstable and discontinuous patterns of parenting and action should be taken to reduce the chances of this occurring. Thus, in the case of young children whose parents seem unlikely to be able to look after them, early decisions on adoption are needed. Moreover, the provision of alternative forms of child care (as with foster parents or in children's homes) needs to be planned to ensure continuities in parenting.

Third, it has been shown that children's development is influenced by their experiences in day care centers or nursery schools. Improved conditions of adult–child interaction in these facilities should carry with them mental health benefits.

Fourth, children's behavior and development vary systematically according to the social and psychological conditions in the institutions in which they live for either short or long periods of time. Improved conditions in hospitals and other residential institutions, together with a reduction in admissions, should prove beneficial.

Fifth, children who are rejected and unloved are more likely than other children to have mental health problems. A reduction in the number of unwanted births is highly desirable, and family planning should form part of a wider community service that is educational in the broadest sense.

These rather uncontroversial five steps are fairly well based on empirical evidence, and their implementation should be of some value. Nevertheless, it must be said that the *actual* effect of the measures has still to be assessed and, furthermore, even if successful, the actions would have an impact on only a *minority* of cases of mental disorder.

Perhaps, a sixth step should be added, although little is known on how best to undertake it. It is generally agreed that there needs to be an enhanced public awareness of children's needs and of the factors which influence their psychosocial development. Thus people need to appreciate that children learn through play, conversation and experiences; how young children respond to separations and to change; the importance of individual differences in temperamental style; the need for the right balance of emotional support and social control; and the way children are influenced by the emotional climate in the home. It seems reasonable to suppose that steps to increase people's understanding of these aspects of child development would be helpful. Nevertheless, in spite of the occasional encouraging study,[7] evidence is lacking on how best to improve matters, and attempts to improve parenting through educational measures remain almost entirely unevaluated. In this connection it is worth pointing out that it is *not* safe to assume that well-intentioned community mental health education programs are without risk. One such project with respect to adult disorders actually appeared to make things worse.[8]

Of course this brief listing of preventive measures does not exhaust the possible modes of intervention. However, other actions either lack adequate empirical support or little is known on how to achieve the desired objectives. For example, there is abundant evidence that children of mentally ill adults or those reared in discordant and disharmonious families have a substantially increased risk of psychiatric disorder. A reduction in the rate of parental mental disorder or in the amount of family discord would have undoubted benefits—the problem is how to bring about this desirable state of affairs. Or again, there is evidence of the importance of protective influences, which enable children to overcome the effects of stress and disadvantage,[9] but little is known on how to enhance these positive or ameliorating factors. Certainly, it is not that the problems are insoluble; rather it is that there has been little attempt to use research to move from the identification of risk factors to the prevention of disadvantage or the amelioration of stressful conditions. The lesson is clear: research is crucial in the development of effective strategies to prevent psychosocial disorders in childhood.[10]

IMPROVED PATTERNS OF CARE

Let me now turn to the likely psychosocial effects of improved patterns of care. Many children throughout the world are still reared in the most deplorable circumstances, but there is no doubt that in general, there have been major improvements in material standards of care during the last 50 years or so.[11] Thus fewer children are growing up in substandard housing that lacks the basic household amenities; more young people are receiving the benefits of education until a later age; children are generally taller and heavier; and most striking of all, throughout the world there have been dramatic reductions in infantile mortality. No one would pretend that things are satisfactory even in the best-developed countries and, of course, in many parts of the globe children continue to die early in life from the cumulative effects of malnutrition, infectious disease, and abysmal living conditions. Nevertheless, the gains have been great and should not be underestimated. In many respects children's psychosocial development will have been improved by the advances in physical health and in living standards. But have there also been deficits? I suggest that there may have been and that we should learn from these. Let me consider the various areas of improvement in turn.

Material Circumstances

Industrialization has had obvious benefits in terms of making it possible to raise living standards. But the psychosocial costs have been substantial. Especially in developing countries there have been major moves of population from rural areas to large cities. Frequently the father leaves his family behind in the country while he looks for employment. The wife and children may follow later, but in many cases the move to the city has had the effect of disrupting family ties and destroying community cohesion. In addition, the living conditions in some large cities are extremely unsatisfactory with huge numbers living in large insanitary shanty towns on the edge of enormous urban conurbations with inadequate transport, housing, education, health, and welfare services.[12]

Even in well-established industrial nations there is evidence that psychosocial problems are very much commoner in inner city areas than they are in small towns and rural populations.[13] On the other hand, this disadvantage does not apply to all cities, and it is evident that industrialization and urban living need not create such high rates of mental disorder and psychosocial breakdown. It is essential that we identify how cities might be modified in order to bring about mental health benefits. Research is needed to determine how the stresses arise and how they may be avoided.

In many cities, housing problems have been "solved" by the building of tower blocks, which not only increase isolation and interfere with community and kinship ties but also make it more difficult to supervise young children. The evidence is inconclusive on how far such styles of housing have predisposed to mental disorder but they have been associated with considerable feelings of dissatisfaction.[14] Clearly, it is not enough to provide baths, kitchens, and indoor lavatories; we must also consider how far each type of housing meets psychosocial needs.

It might be thought that the increasing affluence of Western societies should have been associated with an overall improvement in psychosocial functioning, but this has not occurred.[15] On the contrary, in many respects things have got worse with a rising crime rate, an increased illegitimacy ratio, and a greater frequency of marital breakdown and family disruption. We have very little understanding of why this has occurred. Certainly, at any one point in time, poverty and poor living conditions tend to be associated with an increased risk of psychosocial disorder. On the other hand, it is all too clear that the naive assumptions that psychosocial benefits would follow from improved living standards were wrong. What is not clear is why. Of course, it may be that the notion that the cross-sectional correlations representing a causal link between poverty and psychosocial disorder was incorrect. However, even if right, it may be that it is not the absolute standard of living conditions which is psychologically important.

Perhaps, instead, it is the degree to which people are "worse off" than they *expect*, or worse off than *other* people, which is important. If this were so, rising expectations, combined with a failure to reduce inequalities, could make things "feel" worse even when in absolute terms standards have risen. Alternatively, it may be that what matters is our control over our circumstances. In this connection it is striking that in Britain the systems of benefits and of taxation have made an increasingly large proportion of the population financially impotent in the sense that the more they earn the more they lose in the way of welfare benefits and tax advantages.[16] The effect is that they can do nothing to improve their circumstances no matter how hard they try—a very dispiriting situation. Whatever the explanation—and the correct explanation is not yet known—what is evident is that improved material living conditions are *not* necessarily linked with psychosocial benefits. The challenge is to ensure that improvements are brought about in ways which are psychologically advantageous as well as materially successful. We are still some way off knowing how to do that effectively.

Education

It is often thought that rising educational standards and the introduction of universal secondary education must be a good thing. Of course, in most respects it is a good thing and a very worthwhile objective. But there may also be disadvantages. In literate societies there are strong associations between severe reading difficulties and disorders of conduct or delinquency. The reasons for the association are ill understood, but it seems likely that part of the explanation lies in the psychologically damaging effect of the experience of educational failure.[17] One by-product of universal education and increased levels of scholastic attainment is the increased number of children who are publically recognized as having failed educationally. The child who is unable to read is unnoticed in a nonliterate society, and his other skills may mean that he is accepted as a competent person. Once literacy is expected, his inability to learn to read is both noticed and taken as a sign of failure. Of course, the solution is *not* to stop providing schools. But it is necessary to ensure that schools are well adapted to cope with large individual differences in ability, that they provide opportunities for success for *all* pupils and that poor scholastic attainment is used as an indication of a need for special help rather than opprobrium combined with a message of inevitable continuing failure.

A second issue with respect to rising educational standards is the consequent increase in employment expectations. If these cannot be fulfilled the high attainments at school may merely constitute an introduction to job dissatisfaction. It is not just a question of the humiliating experience of unemployment but also it is a matter of people developing expectations of certain sorts of work and status, and if these cannot be met the result may be resentment and discouragement.

A third aspect of schooling is the effect on children of spending many of their waking hours in this particular type of institution. There is now good evidence that schools do much to shape children's behavior and that this effect is largely a consequence of the features of the school as a social organization.[18] In short, the social characteristics of a school may either facilititate or impede children's psychological development. The challenge is to ensure that this experience (compulsory in most parts of the world) is to the child's benefit.

Medical Care

The last area of progress to consider is that of improved medical care. The gains in physical health have been great and there can be no doubt that, on balance, so have the psychosocial improvements. However, there are instances in which it seems that some of the medical interventions have involved psychosocial costs. For example, modern methods of intensive care for the newborn have greatly improved the survival rates of very small babies.[9] On the other hand, it seems that the separation of mother and child, which may be involved, can interfere with normal mothering. Infants admitted to special care baby units are more at risk for later child abuse, [20] and it may be that the same procedures which increase the chances of physical survival are those which are most likely to damage mother–child relationships. Of course, this is not inevitable, but if the psychosocial problems are to be avoided it is essential that special care units be devised and run with an eye to the psychological as well as physical risks.

Similar issues arise with respect to the greatly increased use of induction of labour, a lesser increase in instrumental delivery, and the widespread administration of analgesic and anesthetic drugs during the process of delivery.[21] Opinion is divided (and evidence is lacking) on whether the greater use of obstetric intervention involves psychosocial hazards. However, the point is that the evaluation of these new procedures needs to include the psychosocial as well as the physical consequences.

Improved social conditions and the availability of effective drugs has greatly reduced rates of serious infective disease among children in most developed countries. It might be thought that this would have resulted in far fewer hospital admissions, but in fact this has not occurred.[22] Admissions tend to be shorter on the average, but a large number of children continue to have recurrent episodes of hospitalization. Some of these are essential for medical or surgical reasons, but many are admitted largely on social grounds[23] and others could have been dealt with on an outpatient basis if hospital services were organized differently. Recent studies by two separate research groups[24] suggest that recurrent or multiple admissions to hospital significantly increases the risk of later psychiatric disorder. Again, the message is that we need to plan our medical care in terms of psychosocial as well as physical issues.

CONCLUSIONS

In looking to the future it may be thought that we need to know what changes are likely to take place in terms of physical conditions, social circumstances, and family roles and rights. Of course, a knowledge of how current patterns of life will alter would be helpful, but projections into the future based on current trends tend to be a most uncertain guide at best and at worst can prove seriously misleading. This limits the extent to which we can plan efficiently, but our deficiencies as social prophets should not deter us from examining the principles which should guide us in the future nor should it prevent us from identifying the key issues that are likely to be important. These include the psychosocial implications of changing family circumstances, the measures already available to prevent mental health problems, and inadvertent psychosocial deficits that sometimes accompany improved patterns of physical care.

REFERENCES

1. M. RUTTER and N. MADGE, *Cycle of Disadvantage: A Review of Research,* Heinemann, London, 1976.
2. B. MAYALL and P. PETREIR, *Minder, Mother and Child,* Studies in Education (new series) 5. University of London Institute of Education, London, 1977.

3. J. TIZARD, P. MOSS and J. PERRY, *All Our Children: Preschool Services in a Changing Society,* Temple Smith, London, 1976.
4. WORLD HEALTH ORGANIZATION, *Child Mental Health and Psychosocial Development: Report of a WHO Expert Committee,* WHO Technical Report Series 613, Geneva, 1977.
5. S. D. M. COURT, (1977) *Fit for the Future: The Report of the Committee on Child Health Services,* HMSO, London, 1977.
6. P. GRAHAM, Possibilities for prevention, in P. J. Graham, (ed.), *Epidemiological Approaches in Child Psychiatry,* Academic Press, London, 1977.
7. K. J. CULLEN, A six-year controlled trial of prevention of children's behavior disorders, *Journal of Pediatrics* 88, 662-666 (1976).
8. E. CUMMINGS and J. CUMMINGS, *Closed Ranks,* Harvard University Press, Cambridge, MA., 1957.
9. M. RUTTER, Protective factors in children's responses to stress and disadvantage, in M. W. Kent and J. E. Rolf (eds.), *Primary Prevention of Psychopathology,* Vol. 3: *Promoting Social Competence and Coping in Children,* University Press of New England, Hanover, NH, 1978.
10. M. RUTTER, Research and prevention of psychosocial disorders in children, paper presented at the DHSS Social Care Research Seminar, Downing College, July 6-8, 1977, 1978.
11. COURT, op. cit.; RUTTER AND MADGE, op. cit.; WHO, op. cit.
12. WHO, op. cit.
13. M. RUTTER, A. COX, C. TUPLING, M. BERGER and W. YULE, Attainment and adjustment in two geographical areas: I, The prevalence of psychiatric disorder, *British Journal of Psychiatry* 126, 493-509 (1975). N. LAVIC, Urban–rural differences in rates of disorder, *in* P. J. Graham (ed.), *Epidemiological Approaches in Child Psychiatry* Academic Press, London, 1977.
14. RUTTER AND MADGE, op. cit.
15. Ibid.
16. Ibid: LORD DIAMOND, *Royal Commission on the Distribution of Income and Wealth,* Report No. 6 *Lower Incomes,* HMSO, London, 1978.
17. M. RUTTER, J. TIZARD, and K. WHITMORE (eds.), *Education, Health and Behavior,* Longmans, London, 1970.
18. M. RUTTER, B. MAUGHAN, P. MORTIMORE, and J. OUSTON, *15,000 Hours: Secondary School Influences on Children's Development,* Open Books (in press), London, 1979.
19. A. L. STEWART, The survival of low birth weight infants, *British Journal of Hospital Medicine* 18, 182-190 (1977).
20. M. A. LYNCH, Ill health and child abuse, *Lancet* 2, 317-319, (1975).
21. T. CHARD and M. RICHARDS, *Benefits and Hazards of the New Obstetrics,* Clinics in Developmental Medicine, No. 64, SIMP/Heinemann Medical, London, 1977.
22. J. W. B. DOUGLAS, Early hospital admissions and later disturbances of behavior and learning, *Developmental Medicine and Child Neurology* 17, 456-480 (1975).
23. J. WYNNE and D. HULL, Why are children admitted to hospital: *British Medical Journal* 2, 1140-1142 (1977).
24. DOUGLAS, op. cit.; D. QUINTON, and M. RUTTER, Early hospital admissions and later disturbances of behavior: an attempted replication of Douglas' findings, *Developmental Medicine and Child Neurology* 18 , 447-459 (1976).

DISCUSSION

ANNETTE A. YAKER

National Institute of Public Health, Algiers, Algeria

I SHALL rapidly review some characteristic aspects of changing family roles in the developing world based upon what I have studied and experienced in several countries, particularly Algeria.

We have already been reminded several times that the first years of life are decisive for the later development of the child. This crucial period is influenced above all by the family structure, parental attitudes, and educational practices in the social environment.

In most developing countries founded on traditional customs, the social environment is changing so rapidly, so massively, and so profoundly that the development of the infant is markedly affected. Among the most obvious changes are the breaking up of the traditional extended family, modern industrialization and urban life with all its problems of housing, new foods, and a totally new way of life.

Half the population of Algeria is under 16, and almost a quarter (22%) is under the age of 6. More and more of these children are growing up in a greatly disturbed family setting. The young parents in the new nuclear families are quite unprepared for their parental roles. The care and education of young children has traditionally been undertaken by the grandparents. Moreover, the young parents are themselves deeply involved in a process of acculturalization—greatly influenced by the mass media. They are confused as to how to act, yet they tend to demand that their children conform to and perpetuate traditional values. On the other hand, the child is at the core of the acculturalization process, since he is often the first member of the family to know how to read and write. Thus the child faces a strong contradiction between the world of his urban environment and the traditional values enunciated by his parents.

Conflicts arise, and many parents give up and relinquish their responsibilities to the community and the school, forgetting that the social controls exercised by a village community do not exist in an urban setting. Once the child is in the street he is anonymous. The parents also rely upon the school, forgetting that the teacher—loaded down with huge classes, much paper work, and a stringent curriculum—is quite unable to play the role of a father to 100–120 pupils.

The family in the developing world is in search of a new equilibrium. It is seeking to discover its role in a new dimension. In the meantime it is likely that the present disturbing situation will have grave repercussions upon the mental health of numerous children.

CHAIRMAN'S SUMMARY

STIG SJÖLIN

DURING the session it was clearly demonstrated how industrialization and technological development have influenced and are all the time influencing family life. This is true both for highly industrialized countries and for less-developed countries. A basic fact that is rarely recognized or taken into account is that from the family point of view the world cannot and should not be divided into two distinct and well-separated parts— the developed and the developing countries. Instead it must be realized that individual families in both kinds of countries live under very different conditions. Of course hungry and poor families are much more common in developing countries, but hunger and poverty still exist in most of the so-called developed countries, often in large population groups. This should not be forgotten when planning for the future. Neither should it be forgotten that families in all countries are, to a greater or lesser degree, exposed to psychosocial hazards of different kinds. Ignorance and superstition is prevalent not only in the developing countries.

Undoubtedly, industrialization, wherever it has taken place, has brought about enormous changes in family life and structure and in the roles of all family members. Suffice it to mention that an increasing number of families live in large cities, which have not been built to satisfy the needs of families, that fathers nowadays almost always work far from home, that an increasing number of mothers are employed outside their homes, and further that the small nuclear family tending to live in isolation from grandparents and other relatives and neighbors is becoming more and more common. The old belief that eradication of poverty should inevitably lead to an advanced and richer cultural life and to improved mental health, has not proved fully true. On the contrary, there is ample evidence that affluence may and often does create new and serious psychosocial problems, which we have not been able to foresee, nor to prevent or to treat. By research, it would be possible to reveal the cause of these problems and to find solutions to the question of preventions and treatment. In order to avoid a similar development in preindustrialized countries, it must be regarded as urgent to invest money in this kind of research. In doing research of this kind one should bear in mind that under-privileged families often offer excellent child care.

Which are the basic prerequisites for good child care? By what means will it be possible to compensate for the loss of the traditional extended family system? Probably we shall never be able to resist or stop the technological development, but we must try to develop and use technology to the benefit of man. To this end politicians, administrators, and technicians need to learn much more about biology, psychology, and the human being and its reactions to environment and changes in environment. Less haste and more careful testing in pilot studies are means by which disastrous mistakes can be avoided. All the time we must bear in mind that short term profit interests often are of greater importance to the decision makers than the long term well-being of children and families.

After these general observations I feel inclined to bring up some key issues that are closely related to the topic of family roles and rights.

It is easy for me to understand that a married woman in an industrialized society of today cannot devote all her life and time to the care of home, husband, and children. If she did do so, she would as a rule be grossly underoccupied and lose her self-confidence and self-respect, except during the relatively short period when her children are below school age. In order to safeguard her position on the labor market, however, she cannot permit herself to be absent from work outside home for long periods. This means that substitute care of children has become a major family problem in industrialized countries. While in 1930 only about 10% of the married Swedish women aged 15–50 years were economically active outside their homes, this figure has now risen to about 65%. However, the need for day care places for the children of these families is only covered to 30–40%. It is not known how the rest of the children are taken care of, but there is every reason to believe that they are grossly neglected. The politicians seem to regard communal day care as being too expensive, and they also argue, quite illogically, that since day care cannot be offered to all those who need it, day care centers as a system is unfair (to those who cannot obtain it). Most of the politicians do not realize that the quality of the care we give our children and their families determines the future of a country. The less the children in a community are cared for, the more gloomy is the future outlook for that community.

In most countries communal and private day care centers have been the only and insufficient answer to the new family needs of child care outside the home. Personally, I feel convinced that other possibilities should also be considered, mainly because the problems are complex, and it seems most unlikely that all the problems can be solved by one method only. Accumulating evidence seems to show that it is most important for the health and development of a child to be breastfed and cared for by its mother at least during the first six months of life. Even later a child seems to benefit greatly from living continuously in a harmonious family and being allowed to spend a considerable time with its father, mother, and siblings. This does not mean that nursery schools and day care centers are dangerous or useless, only that family life seems to meet some essential needs, which cannot be met to the same degree in other settings or by other means. Institutions can, even if they are of high quality, do no more than complete the resources of the family. The younger the child the truer this statement seems to be. There are reasons to believe that most children under the age of 2–3 years do better in the long run if they are cared for in a good home rather than in a good institution. This leads me to propose that everything should be done to encourage parents to devote much time and company to their preschool children. This can be achieved by different means, but not without the support of politicians and society. Shortening of the working days for parents of young children is one example which can be introduced without any previous pilot studies. Economic support enabling either the father or the mother to stay at home during the child's first year (or years) of life, would certainly serve the same purpose, if only the support is great enough. Under ideal conditions it should not be an economic sacrifice for a family if one of the parents chose to stay at home for a couple of years to care for the children.

Was it significant that the father was not mentioned at all during the session? I hope not, but I cannot get rid of a feeling that the omission of the father was not a pure accident. Anyhow, we have to admit that the father has a role to play in the family and he also has some rights. During the long agricultural era the father lived close to his family and played an important role as a normative example, teacher and supporter. Through industrialization this traditional role was taken away from the father. He spent most of his working days far from home and it was regarded that he had completed his duty when he arrived home late in the evening. Often he became a stranger to his own family. More or less he was expelled from home life. Today it seems that the father is again needed at home, to share with his wife the responsibility of running the house and bringing up the children. This has become necessary particularly in families where the mother works outside the home and no home help is available. In many countries such a situation is the rule rather than the exception. The father, with his often unique experience and knowledge, may further imply an additional stimulus to family comfort and happiness. Even if some fathers do not seem to realize it, it would be rather cruel not to let them enjoy the company of their children. Therefore efforts should be made everywhere to reintroduce the father into the family and to make him an active member of the family team.

Parents are responsible not only for the feeding and dressing of their children but also for their upbringing. Even in countries where future parents attend school for many years, their knowledge of child psychology and upbringing methods are rudimentary. A few parents have a natural gift for the task of upbringing, but many are masters in making mistakes. Most parents would probably be more qualified to handle their children if they had had the opportunity to learn more about children, about their normal development, their reactions to environmental factors of different kinds and about the wide variations between individuals, even siblings. So far little is known about the result of systematic parent education, but there is no reason not to use this instrument in attempts to create optimal growing-up conditions for children. Lax and erratic upbringing and poor emotional relation to parents have a long-lasting untoward effect on a child's personality, and it does not seem too unlikely that such effects could be counteracted by suitable parent education.

This leads me to another issue that was only touched upon during the session. Most parents have a sort of natural ability to avoid the most deleterious mistakes in upbringing, but there is always a small group of unfortunate parents unable to cope with their own problems and the upbringing of their children. These parents need much support and advice to be able to fulfill their parenting. It would seem highly desirable to find methods by which these vulnerable groups could be identified early, long before any damage has been done to the children. Here, more research is needed as well as a closer cooperation between adult psychiatrists, social workers, and the child health centers. It seems likely that early preventive measures would be beneficial, at least in some cases and to some extent.

During the session there was much talk about changing family roles, but almost nothing was said about changing family rights. Was the problem too difficult or too delicate? I think that it is important to assess that all family members have a right to fulfill their individual destiny. Within the family it should never be permitted to oppress or exert undue pressure on other family members. Each individual should be regarded and treated as in independent person. As well as the father's right to play and talk with his children, the mother has the right to an independent professional life. It is more difficult to delineate the child's independence, because the child is always more or less dependent on its parents. When growing the child should be given more and more independence and the parents should learn to regard the child as an individual whose personality and integrity must be respected. Too many parents tend to regard their children as some sort of property. They seem to believe that they own their children. In many countries even the laws seem to have accepted this very old concept. Caning and child abuse are often expressions of this lacking respect for the integrity of children. There is today much talk about the integrity and the rights of adults but too little about the rights and integrity of children.

PARENT/CHILD DYAD

THE PSYCHOBIOLOGICAL SIGNIFICANCE OF INFANCY

LEWIS P. LIPSITT

School of Medicine, Brown University, Providence, RI, USA

How MUCH do we know about the behavior and development of the human newborn, the implications of experience in the first year of life for later development, and the consequences of perinatal risk on the continuing well-being of the child? What do we know, really, about the *significance* of infancy? Precious little, until very recently. But an importantly altered picture of the human infant has begun to emerge.

The neonate arrives in the world with all sensory systems functioning and with a capability far exceeding that suspected just one or two decades ago. Eyes follow objects, certain colors are discriminated and even preferred. Eye contact is made by the infant with the mother even in the first days. The newborn can discriminate the odor of its own mother and chooses to orient more in her direction. The eyes of the newborn function better if the mother has not been heavily drugged at birth. Taste perception is so acute within the first few days of life that the newborn can discriminate stimulus differences as subtle as 5% versus 10% sucrose solution, and shows preference for the sweeter fluid.

The newborn responds with vigorous movements of the head and arms to any stimulus that compromises respiration, and the angry avoidance behavior that the newborn manifests when the nostrils are occluded or the head is restrained serves as a hedonic counterpoint to the avid appetitional behavior which the infant manifests when presented with more pleasant stimulation.

Numerous studies have shown that habituation, or response decrement to the presentation of successive stimuli, occurs within the neonatal period, and this capacity for habituation is correlated with such individual difference parameters as amount of trauma incurred at birth. Similarly, cardiac deceleration in response to specific stimulation, representing a rather sophisticated information-processing capacity, occurs predominantly in infants who are relatively large for gestational age, are not premature, and are born of conditions that are not generally considered hazardous.

The newborn infant is, in fact, capable of learning. Among the paradigms yielding learning effects are those which capitalize upon congenital responses or reflexive behaviors. When such responses are elicited, such as by stroking the baby's cheek (resulting in ipsilateral headturning), and when such responses are reinforced with the presentation of a satisfying event (like putting a nipple in the infant's mouth, allowing the baby to suck), those responses become intensified and tend to occur more frequently in the future when the same stimulus setting is presented. Avoidance conditioning has also been reported in situations where feeding the baby has been accompanied by noxious stimulation, such as undue restraint or respiratory occlusion. In such a situation, the infant will turn from rather than toward the feeding situation on subsequent occasions. Experiences in the earliest days of life may have an enduring impact. This has important implications for the facilitation or discouragement of mother–infant contact early in life. Similarly, the extent to which we appreciate the human neonate as a fully functioning being with rights to health, welfare, and joy affects our adult attitudes towards such institutionalized practices as rooming-in and isolation of the newborn in intensive care units.

Advances in technology associated with the medical care of the newborn have resulted in a marked reduction in neonatal deaths from the beginning of this century (100 deaths per 1000 live births) to the present (20 deaths per 1000). The most recent decade has seen such improvements in the care of high risk infants, including prematures and the small for gestational age baby, that infants who were not viable one decade ago survive routinely today by means of life support systems recently engineered and put into use. The improved survival rate of infants, especially those with birth anomalies that in previous years would have been lethal, has implications for the survivors. While prediction of developmental careers from either early congenital disposition or experiential background has never been an exercise of great precision, the changing conditions of reproduction and development in recent years has increased the difficulty of the task immeasurably. Infants survive today who are virtually unpredictable with regard to their developmental outcomes. Basic research into the genetic and perinatal antecedents of certain basic psychophysiological processes is a need of great urgency.

While unquestionably there will be an increasing number of infants surviving with manifest developmental disabilities, with some of these anomalies (like those of the thalidomide babies) being of immense proportions, some of the recent perinatology advances can reduce the occurrence of certain types of congenital and developmental disorders. It is now possible to assess prenatally certain conditions of fetuses, making it essentially an elective matter as to whether parents will permit themselves to bear, for example, a Down's syndrome child. The chromosomal anomaly associated with Mongolism can be detected through cell examination prior to birth (amniocentesis), whereupon parents may decide whether or not to carry the infant to term. Hopefully, there will be data available on the basis of which parents and their professional helpers can make truly informed decisions.

The recently documented precocity of the newborn has implications, not yet extensively explored, for our understanding of the so-called immature nervous system. Now that it is known that the human neonate has all sensory systems functioning and is capable of learning, some earlier assumptions regarding the structure of the early human nervous system must be questioned. Recent evidence, from animals and humans alike, suggests that the period surrounding birth is actually a time of considerable myelinization, and it is now well established that dendritic development is accelerating rapidly in the weeks and months immediately following birth. While the infant's nervous system may indeed be immature, it is nonetheless *maturing*. The process of maturation may actually be more important than the achievement of maturation. By this is meant that experiences endured in the course of maturation may be precisely those which are most responsible for enduring learning. Languages seem best learned by young people, intelligence does not change *markedly* after the age of six years, and some of the best-preserved memories into adulthood and old age are precisely those from the earliest years of life.

Despite the recent advances, numerous developmental aberrations remain today as much a mystery as they were hundreds of years ago. Crib death, or the sudden infant death syndrome, is one of them. It is believed that approximately 10,000 babies a year in the United States alone die between about two months and four months of age without having manifested any diagnosable problem prior to their deaths. While some of these infants seem, on close examination of perinatal history or through an incisive autopsy, to have had predisposing deficits, most die of as yet undiscovered causes.

Explorations into the mechanisms and processes of psychophysiological development within the first year of life, coupled with intensive explorations of the effects of perinatal hazards on later development and behavior, will probably produce important clues to the causes underlying crib death. It is well known, for example, that many congenital reflexes which the newborn manifests gradually undergo a weakening or waning until by four to six months of age they are no longer present. Some of these, such as the obligatory grasp reflex of the newborn and certain imitative behaviors, are supplanted by more voluntary responses which ultimately serve some of the same functions as the initial grasping reflex. As cortical innervation progresses, subcortical control of reflexes probably becomes subservient to newly learned responses. An area of investigation especially needed now relates to those aspects of first year development in which two processes acting in concert with one another occur, one involving the gradual abatement of infantile reflexes and one relating to the influence of learning in the ontogeny of behaviors, replacing those reflexes. It is a logical and empirical possibility that crib death is due in part either to a premature waning (or other incapacity) of the respiratory occlusion reflex, or failure of the environment to provide the necessary experiential input to enable the infant, by the age of two to four months, to retrieve its respiratory passages for breathing when threatened with occlusion.

Finally, the significance of infancy lies in its importance as a true training period for the exercise of sensory capacities and congenital reflexes. The mutual dependence of experience and neurostructural development suggests that infancy is a period of critical learning experiences from which the young child who traverses the period successfully will emerge capable of defending himself against threats and able to maximize the pleasures of sensation and attachment to others.

EARLY INFANT–PARENT RECIPROCITY

T. Berry Brazelton

Harvard Medical School, Boston, MA, USA

THE CONFUSING demands of a complex, undirected society, coupled with the lack of support (often even negative support) that is provided new parents by our present nuclear family system, leave most parents insecure and at the mercy of tremendous internal and external pressures. They have been told that their infant's outcome is to be shaped by them and their parenting; at the same time, there are few stable cultural values on which they can rely for guidance in setting their course as new parents. Most new parents are separated emotionally from their own parents' standards by the generation gap and all that that implies. Our present generation has actively separated itself from the beliefs and mores of the preceding generation. For example, we can cite the ambivalence with which the press and other media are treating Ben Spock's previously accepted ideas. I am not questioning the need for a change in child-rearing practices, for I certainly endorse many of the revisions (as does Dr. Spock), but I want to show how one more potential prop has been eliminated from the young parents' armamentarium for support. Physicians are not readily available to many young parents and nurse practitioners are not quite filling the gap yet, although I hope and believe that they will be doing so before long. Pediatricians and physicians in family medicine will be pressed toward a primary care paradigm lest they lose the most rewarding and precious asset a physician has: the feedback from maintaining a supportive, interactive relationship with parents as they foster the development of their children.

Our society's backup for parenting often is a negative one. There is virtually no opportunity for most children as they grow up in small, lonely nuclear family settings to experience how their own or other parents go about raising small brothers and sisters. As a result, they come to parenting with little experience of their own.

The childbirth education groups have demonstrated the importance of preparation for childbirth itself. This preparation demonstrates another missed but powerful potential—that of preparing young couples for their roles as parents.

But an infant is not as helpless as he seems, and there are rewards as well as messages from an infant that can guide a new mother and new father as they become faced with their new roles. We have been stuck with one model of child rearing that has long since done its damage and must soon be eradicated. In the 1950s, when I began my work, parents were taught that their infants were lumps of clay, to be molded by their environment—for better or worse. Since this idea was exploited by the process of looking at the outcome of children as if the results were due to parent's mistakes, and since that outcome was evaluated by physicians interested in pathology (psychiatrists, neurologists, and disease-oriented pediatricians), the literature of that era and the popular literature for mothers and fathers available today still is loaded with a pathologic slant. Most of the books for parents are framed with "How to—," "How to be a good parent," "How to avoid problems." Implicit in this approach is that you *may* luck out and do a few things right, but the chances are far greater that you will not. And unless you do everything exactly right, your child will be scarred by his association with you. Everything that goes wrong will be due to your mistakes, and everything that goes right can be chalked up to luck and/or his own strength in the face of an adverse environment. Since most parents feel insecure in their roles, this thinking reinforces their feelings of inadequacy. The end result has been a generation of tensely anxious, burdened young parents. My own children and the teenagers among my patients will all tell you, "The worst thing about our parents is not whether they did or did not discipline me, or whether they did or did not do things right but that they *never* smiled." I am sure that we have put American families under stress with our medical-pathologic model—looking for mistakes and failure—far too long.

I'd like to begin to point to some of the strengths that are inherent in the parent-infant system, including the guidelines that a reciprocal interactional system between a baby and its parents can produce to guide them and to reward each of them, for the infant comes well equipped to signal his needs and his gratitude to his environment. In fact, he can even make choices about what he wants from his parents, and shut out what he *does not* want in such powerful ways that I no longer see him as a passive lump of clay, but as a powerful force for stabilizing and influencing those around him. What I believe we must do is to uncover and expose these infant strengths to parents, to demonstrate the infant's behavior on which they can rely, and to support young parents in their own individualized endeavor to reach out for, attach to, and *enjoy* their new infants. But this is no mean task.

What is the adaptive purpose of prolonged infancy in the human? No other species has as long a period of relative dependency, and I believe that it is important to look for the adaptive advantages in rules of nature, selected over many generations for their survival value. Compared to any other species, the human neonate is relatively helpless in the motor sphere and relatively complex, even precocious, in the sensory sphere. This enforces a kind of motoric dependence and a freedom for acquisition of the many patterns of sensory and affective information that are necessary to the child and adult human for mastering and surviving in a complex world. In other words, the prolonged period of infancy allows for early and affective transmission of all the mores and instrumental techniques evolved by society—and a kind of individuality inherent in each culture with this society that fairly blows your mind as soon as you think of it. I am convinced by my own cross-cultural research that each culture's individual values and expectations are passed on and established in the infants in the first few months of life by the patterns of response and the child-rearing practices to which he is exposed by his parents and other caregivers around him. I even believe that each culture's expectations for its adults are based on an interaction in infancy between the endowment of its infants and the capacity of this endowment to respond to the adult and societal expectations.

What are some of the built-in strengths of the human neonate? A few examples will demonstrate how powerful these are as economical determinants of how he will conserve himself in a new overwhelming world and how he can quickly acquire the information he needs to choose to make his caregivers familiar with him and responsive to him in a way that will latch them on to him at a critical period for them both. Right out of the uterus (a) he can and does turn his head to the human voice repeatedly, and his face alerts as he searches for its source; (b) he will attend to and choose a female vocal pitch over any other;[1] (c) humanoid sounds are not only preferred to pure tones in an equivalent range of pitch but when he is tested with continuous sucking as a response system, he stops sucking briefly after a pure tone, then goes on sucking steadily, whereas to a human tone he stops sucking and then continues in a burst–pause pattern of sucking (as if he were expecting more important information to follow, and as if the pauses in the sucking were designed to allow for attention this further information[2] (d) he will attend to and follow with eyes and full 90°, head turning a picture of a human face, but will not follow a scrambled face, although he will look at it wide-eyed for a long period (in the delivery room and before any care taking has been instituted);[3] (e) he will turn to and prefer milk smells above water or sugar water; (f) he can taste and respond to with altered sucking patterns the difference between human milk and a cow's milk formula designed to exactly produce the contents of breast milk.[4] There are many more such fascinating behavioral patterns that we have captured in a neonatal assessment scale, which after 20 years of work now is available in manual form and on film.[5] The scale examines 26 behavioral and 20 reflex activities of the human neonate as he interacts with an examiner. And we hope and trust that it captures the assets and skills he will bring to the early mother–father–infant interaction. We do have evidence to show that if new mothers (and work in process is designed to show the same thing with fathers)[6] are shown their infants' behavioral responses in the neonatal period, these mothers behave significantly differently from a control group one month later in a feeding situation, and on a scored interview feel and say that their attachment and their self-image as parents are significantly enhanced by having been encouraged to see their babies as individuals, as "people," strong enough to withstand any mistakes they may make due to their inexperience as parents.

In our laboratory at the Children's Hospital Medical Center we have been looking at this early reciprocal interaction between infants and their parents and, more recently, infants and strangers. We start at two weeks and continue with them until 24 weeks in a laboratory situation, designed to film and analyze the ingredients of early reciprocity as it develops between infants and familiar adults. We film the infants in a reclining chair (or baby seat) as the adult comes in to lean over him and enlist his attention in "games" or "play." We first found that as early as we could film it we saw completely different kinds of behavior and attention with a mother and with an attractive object.[7]

With an attractive object, as it was brought into "reach" space (about 12 inches out in front of him), his attention and face became "hooked," his extremities and even his fingers and toes pointed out toward it, making brief swipes out toward it, as he attended with a rapt, fixed expression on his face. When he was satiated, his attention broke off abruptly and he averted his eyes or turned his whole head and body away for a brief period before he came back for a further period of "hooked" attention. Thus, he established a jagged homeostatic curve of attention, and his arms and legs displayed jerky components of reach behavior as they attended to the object—all at a time when a reach could not be achieved successfully.

With his mother, his attention and motor behavior were entirely different; his eyes, his face, his mouth, his extremities all became smooth and cyclic. As he attended, he moved out slightly toward the object with his head, his mouth, his eyes and even with his legs, arms, fingers, and toes. But, almost immediately the approach behavior was followed by smooth, cyclic withdrawal behavior, as if he expected his mother (or father) to come out to him. His attention was cyclic also, and he looked intently at her (his) face, lidded his eyes or turned them slightly to one side, or up and down, still keeping the parent in peripheral view, but alternating between attention and reduced attention, in average cycles of four per minute over a three-minute observation period. This attention–withdrawal cycle within a period of reciprocal interaction looked as if it followed a homeostatic curve of involvement and recovery that was smooth and signaled a period of intense involvement between infant and parent. The parent cycled, too—playing a kind of swan's mating dance, as he or she moved in to pass on information or behavior when the infant was looking, and withdrew slightly to let up in intensity when the infant withdrew.

We have been able to characterize the relative reciprocity and amount of affective, and even cognitive, information that a parent can transmit in such a period by the cyclic quality of the interaction. In parents who are too anxious and are insensitive to their infants' homeostatic needs (for this parallels the demands of the physiologic systems of an immature organism such as is the neonate), the infant necessarily turns off his attention and spends most of the period keeping the tense parent in his peripheral field, checking back from time to time. In failing interactions, the jagged attentional system of the infant resembles a very sparse period of object attention. One can see from some of the failing interactions that the sparseness of message transmission is in direct contrast to a smooth homeostatic curve of attention in an optimal period of reciprocity. Not only does such a cycle allow for long periods of attention without exhausting the immature physiologic systems of the infant, but it provides a rich matrix for choices and change in attention at any moment. These cycles also provide a matrix for adaptability of a very sensitive kind to the few caregivers who must become important to the infants.

What does this kind of reciprocal "set" mean to the infant? It certainly appears to be basic to the healthy development of infant-parent reciprocity. My own feeling is that we are tuning in on the basic homeostatic systems that govern the physiologic processes as well as the attentional ones in the developing infant. If these are "shaped" by his environment in one way, they may press him toward a psychophysiologic adjustment of one kind or another. Certainly when an environment can tune to the baby's needs for such elegant homeostatic controls, the attentional *and* physiologic cycles can be smooth, rich, adjustable. I can easily jump to the kind of tuning up of the CNS cycles that must find regulation as well as input from the environment to proceed toward optional development of motor and cognitive skills. I think we are looking at the precursors of affective development that are so necessary to the child's total development.

For the infant, such a reciprocal system, when it is going well, acts as fuel and information for his ongoing development, entraining the fueling from within that he receives as feedback from learning each new developmental task. Robert White called this latter force a "sense of competence." Both an inner sense of competence and feeling from a gratifying reciprocity with his environment are necessary to the infant's optimal development.

For the parents, the feedback from such a reciprocal system is just as rewarding as it is to the infant and fuels their energy for continuing in such a demanding ongoing relationship as "good" parenting requires. Their awareness of when they are successful must be felt unconsciously when things are going well, and we as supportive experts could and should point out such periods so that they can become consciously aware of their successes as guidelines to their parenting efforts.

Their power in shaping their children to their own requirements might be frightening, but it certainly must be pointed out to them as absolutely necessary for the child's ultimate capacity to grow emotionally and fit into a demanding society. Within such a framework, one could build a matrix for informing parents of the importance of each child's individual needs and individual ways of responding within any situation. These reciprocal needs, as well as the child's individual needs, will change a bit at each stage of development, but basically the reciprocal feedback system can be relied on as a guide for when it is going well, and when it is not, between parents and their small children.

With this kind of reciprocity as the basis for his affective motor and cognitive development, how does this apply to some of our society's new programs? Should we continue to press for early stimulation programs? Yes, *if* these provide a focus around which reciprocal interaction between parents and their babies can form more important affective interaction. *But,* if stimulation with objects or toys intrudes on the interpersonal or is substituted for it, it must be obvious that the infant will lose out on more important learning than he will ever gain by interaction with objects or toys. The possibility for overloading him with too much or inappropriate stimulation can easily be visualized as one thinks about the static, jagged homeostatic curves of his interaction with objects. The possibility that mothers might substitute "learning environments" for themselves makes me shudder.

REFERENCES

1. R. Eisenberg, Auditory behavior in the human neonate—a preliminary report, *J. Speech Hear. Res.* 7, 245 (1964).
2. P. Eimas, E. Signeland and L. Lipsitt, Work in progress.
3. C. Goren, Form perception, innate form preferences, and visually mediated head-turning in the human neonate, paper presented at SRCD Conference, Denver, April, 1975.
4. A. MacFarlane, Personal communication, Oxford University, England, 1975.
5. T. B. Brazelton, *Neonatal Behavioral Assessment Scale,* Clinics in Developmental Medicine, No. 50, Heinemann, London; J. B. Lippincott Company, Philadelphia, 1973.
6. R. D. Parke, Family interaction in the newborn period: some findings, some observations and some unresolved issues, in K. Riegal and U. Meacham, (eds.), *The Developing Individual in a Changing World,* vol. 2, Mouton, The Hague, 1975.
7. T. B. Brazelton, B. Koslowski and M. Main, The origin of reciprocity in the mother-infant interaction, in M. Lewis and L. Rosenblum (eds.), *The Effect of the Infant on its Care Giver,* John Wiley, New York, 1974, vol. 1, pp. 49-76.

DISCUSSION

HIROSHI AZUMA

Department of Education, University of Tokyo, Japan

IN COLLABORATION with American and Japanese colleagues, I have observed the mother–child interaction of male and female children at the age of four (the majority first born) as they interacted with their respective mothers under various game situations. Games were referential communication (mother describes pictures), block sorting (mother teaches child), and free play. The mother–child interactions were videotaped, rated, and analyzed.

It was very impressive to see how wide was the range of the individual differences among mothers. Although there were some cross-cultural differences, the intracultural individual differences were impressive. There was one mother who never showed any attention to her four year old child during the period of 10 minutes free play in the laboratory waiting room. There were mothers who were always dominating and who were critical of any initiative shown by the child. There were mothers who were followers and there were mothers who knew how to enjoy themselves together with the child.

The correlation of the maternal communication with the child at the age of four, with the cognitive performance of the child one or two years later, was also impressive.

To give only a few examples: the following correlations were found with the school readiness test score (Metropolitan in the United States) which we administered at ages 5 and 6 to the same children.

Free play	*Correlation*
Mother accepts the child's proposal	·26
Asks what child wants to do	·20

Referential communication	
Number of descriptors used by the mother	·35
Patient repetition	·27
Presses for successful response	·53

Block sorting	
Accepts imperfect response	·42
Demands verbalization	·44
Lack of direction in maternal approach	·41

Although these individual correlations are modest, the multiple correlations exceed ·7, which match the reliability of the school readiness test, administered with a lapse of one or two years.

This means with certain qualifications that, to a considerable extent, success in the school readiness test is predictable from the observational data of the mother–child interaction in early childhood.

One thing I regret in retrospect is that we could have taken more affective variables—both dependent and independent. If the cognitive development is so much affected by the mother–child interaction, the maternal influence upon affective development should be even more substantial.

Despite my limited data, I have no hesitation in endorsing the developmental significance of parent–infant interaction in very early stages of life.

A GLOBAL OVERVIEW AND IMPLICATIONS FOR HEALTH

ANGELE PETROS-BARVAZIAN

WHO, Geneva, Switzerland

1. PARENT–CHILD DYAD IN A CHANGING WORLD

Health Implications of the Parent–Child Dyad

There is no doubt that the initial health and subsequent development of the child is, to a great extent, shaped by families. Preconceptional factors, conditions arising during pregnancy, childbirth, and events in infancy and childhood, all may influence the health and the ultimate development of the child and the quality of life of the present and future generations. In this process of human development, the parent–child dyad has biological, psychosocial, and economic dimensions. The parent–child dyad, however, should not be viewed in isolation since it forms an integral part of the overall ecological and developmental system.

The importance of the interrelationship between the biological mother and the infant can be well observed by relating the maternal characteristics before and during pregnancy to the outcome of pregnancy. For example, the health of the mother during her own infancy and childhood—her ill health, malnutrition, infection, fatigue, stress, drugs taken during pregnancy and delivery, smoking, closely spaced pregnancies, obstetrical pathology—all can adversely affect the outcome of pregnancy and the immediate health and the future of the newborn child.

The problem of low birthweight (LBW) babies (weighing less than 2500 gm at birth) is a striking example of poor outcome of pregnancy, contributing to high levels of early mortality and long term morbidity. On a global basis it is estimated that out of 125,000,000 births annually, about 21 million are LBW babies.[1]

The majority of these LBW babies are born in under-privileged conditions with poor maternal health, chronic malnutrition, infection, and other intergenerational effects of poverty and underdevelopment (less than one million LBW babies are born in developed areas). Some LBW babies are born after a short gestational period (preterm) but the majority of LBW babies are "small-for-dates," i.e. malnourished babies whose intrauterine growth is retarded with adverse consequences for future health and the quality of life, which are both serious and far reaching. LBW is thus globally a significant problem that calls for urgent action. Improvement of the health and nutrition of potential mothers and pregnant women could help to reduce the high rates of LBW.

From a global point of view, the major health problems of mothers and children and high levels of mortality and morbidity are associated with three interrelated conditions—malnutrition, infection, and ill-timed and closely spaced pregnancies. In underprivileged communities these conditions are compounded by lack (or scarcity) of health and other social services, poor environmental sanitation, poor education, and inequitable distribution of resources.

The health of children is based upon their genetic potential, maternal influences during fetal growth, the quality of nutrition and freedom from common disorders, infections, infestations, and trauma. These factors are in turn dependent upon the parental behavior, their education, cultural habits, and upon the availability of food, water, sanitation, health care facilities, and the willingness and motivation of families to participate in their development and use. The parents (or parent substitutes) have a caring role which they can fulfill most adequately when they are in good health. Thus, in general, family health should be understood to include and mean more than the total (or sum) of the health status of individual family members, because it takes into account the interrelationships and interdependence of the physical, mental, and psychosocial interaction between the family members, determined, in part, by the effective functioning of the family as a biological and social unit within a given sociocultural system.[2]

Since behavior is learned, the mental well-being of the individual child depends upon the emotional stability and cultural beliefs, attitudes, and rearing practices within families or households. Children learn by watching, observing, and then copying behavior, and are likely to behave towards others, both inside and outside the family, in a manner that reflects their home experience. Hence, parental behavior and attitudes are vitally important for the emotional and mental development of the child, and largely determine the response pattern of the child in his or her progressive socialization within the family and outside, such as the school and neighborhood, which themselves act as further socializing forces. Parents need support through health education to better appreciate the importance of their psychosocial impact on their children, as well as the nature of their needs at different developmental periods in the life cycle.

Family Structure and Functions

Evidence from different parts of the world indicates that the family, its function and structure, are being influenced by many changing economic and psychosocial forces. As with other social institutions, the structure and functions of the family have been transformed in the course of history. Patterns of family change in response to these social and economic forces, including forms of production, migration, and religious–ideological movements, which vary considerably in different parts of the world. From a large extended family, or systems of highly interrelated kinship that were mutually supportive and interdependent, we have seen, with the impact of industrialization and urbanization, a significant trend towards small "nuclear families." Although there is no single pattern, in general the family unit is becoming smaller and more remote physically and economically from other kin groups, and is moving, in terms of many of its functions, towards a shorter life span. It should be noted that while we are here discussing the changes from various types of extended to various types of smaller or nuclear families, we are already witnessing in many countries the emergence of single parent families, with women being the head of the household in many cases. And it is in the societies that are passing through a period of transition that families are facing the greatest stress and strain in adjusting traditional child-rearing practices to cope with new life styles.

However, regardless of whether one takes the word family to mean the minimal nucleus of mother and child, isolated in the depths of some huge city, or the interwoven village community, or something between these extremes, the importance of the family for the health and well-being of children and the present and future generations, can hardly be overestimated. As to the future of the family, to quote Dr. Mahler: "I do not share the view of those gloomy prophets who say that, because of high divorce rates, falling birth rates, the dispersion and mobility of families, and changes in moral codes and occupational patterns, the family as an institution will disappear."[3] The family, rather, in spite of changes and pressures, has shown a remarkable evolutionary ability to adapt itself to the changing requirements of the society. Thus, the family—its structure and functions—not only influences the health and disease patterns of the individual, but essentially determines the growth and development in the early years and the individual's social productivity in adult life.

Official global statistics are mostly based on household rather than family characteristics, since these are easier to obtain. In various parts of the world, the household unit comprises two to four generations, or more than one family of the same generation. In industrialized towns nowadays it typically comprises only two generations (parents and children). There is a wide variation in the mean number of family units per household among countries. In some European countries it is less than one, in Costa Rica it is 1.4, and in India 2.6. According to the latest information from the *UN Demographic Year Book,* the average size of a household (number of individuals per household) ranges from 3.1 in the United States and France to 5–6 in the Philippines, Colombia, and Chile, and 8.3 in some African countries. The implications for child development of the type of household or family which constitutes the immediate social environment are obvious.

Family Planning and Patterns of Family Formation

The patterns of family formation, timing, spacing of childbirth, and total number of family size, have important associations with the health of the family as a whole, with striking effect on maternal, infant, and childhood mortality and morbidity as well as on the physical and psychosocial development of the child.

In recent years there has been growing evidence from studies in various parts of the world, that health risks for mothers and children increase in very young and older women, closely spaced pregnancies, and large family size. There is, for example, a higher postneonatal mortality rate for live births when the interval between pregnancies is less than 12 months.

A nationwide survey of high school students shows that educational achievement becomes lower as the size of the family increases, even when income is held constant.[4] The probable explanation for this, particularly in the case of nuclear families, could be that, as family size increases, reduced interaction with parents and siblings adversely affects the verbal development and intelligence of the children.

Thus, planned parenthood, family planning, and availability of fertility regulation methods, including treatment of infertility, if effectively used, can have an important effect on the health of the family, the future family functioning, and improved parent–child interaction.

2. MEASURES FOR SOCIAL SUPPORT

Working Women

The work of women outside the home has been viewed as one of the factors influencing the mother–child dyad. The fact that women work is not new. Women have always worked: in the home, on the farms, and—more recently—in the factories. Historically in agrarian societies, both men and women worked on the land, and sometimes women spent long periods of time away from home on a seasonal basis. Women's participation in industrial work was mainly concentrated in a few industries, particularly the textile and clothing industries. During recent decades, however, there has been an increasing tendency for women to participate in all types of work, and to work farther and farther from home, throughout the year, and for long periods of the day. This is primarily due to changing patterns of production, to increased demands on women to have a cash income, and the need to participate in overall development efforts.

With regard to the dual role of women in production and reproduction, I strongly believe that the role of being a mother is socially no less productive and important than any other productive role. As a matter of fact, it is fulfilling the most essential function within the society. I also believe that, if necessary measures and social support are made available, there is no inherent conflict in this dual role. The key lies in ensuring the free choice of the mother, and how society provides the necessary supportive measures, including legislation, which will enable women to be successful in their complementary dual role. The fact that, nowadays, women are able to plan their families greatly facilitates the successful achievement of their various roles in society.

The element of time in a woman's life and roles—both within traditional and, particularly, modern lifestyles—is of crucial importance in this context. With the involvement of women in highly time-regimented occupational activities, time wasted as a result of contemporary living conditions (e.g. transport complications in big crowded cities), little time is left to spend with children. Development of favorable parent–child interaction is not only influenced by the quantity of parental time but also the quality. Modern lifestyles deprive the parents as well as the child of the fruitful pleasure of interacting and spending time together.Can this be solved? Perhaps the word "solution" is too ambitious, but, certainly, with some imaginative and innovative social measures this could be modified, for example, to allow for flexible and part-time working hours for parents, alternative approaches to child care, community support for day care, etc.

Care of Children Outside their Homes

This subject has been discussed in a recent WHO Expert Committee on Child Mental Health and Psychosocial Development.[5] The committee emphasized that it is not enough for parents to do things *to* their children; they must do things *with* them. Verbal stimulation is provided by talking with the child and not by turning up the volume of the radio. Similarly, it is helpful to provide toys, but children may also need to be encouraged to create their own play opportunities. There is good evidence from numerous studies in a variety of societies that there is a very substantially increased rate of mental health problems in children who are unwanted or who experience rejection, hostility, or serious family discord.

At one time it was thought that even temporary separation for a few hours of a child from his parents created a serious psychosocial hazard. Children do need continuous relationships with a small number of parent figures, but brief separations need not necessarily disrupt these relationships. Good quality day care and a working mother are both compatible with secure parent–child relationships.

As Jack Tizard *et al*. in their book *All Our Children* have pointed out: "There is, for example, widespread agreement that from the age of about three, nearly all children enjoy and benefit from association with other young children, and there is abundant evidence that most of them cope happily with full-time nursery schooling, even without their mothers. Where opinion differs is as to the effects of nursery attendance upon younger children and as to the value of nursery care which lasts throughout a full working day".[6]

Family Life Education

There is no doubt that education of the children for their own health, for the health of the family and the community, and for their roles as future parents, is of utmost importance. "The independence and self-reliance that can be created by the interplay between the individual and those he or she grows up with is especially important with regard to health and disease. Backed by a modicum of sound information, this self-reliance can be a tremendous force for health, and there is no doubt that for purposes of health education the family provides by far the strongest leverage."[3]

In traditional societies the role of parenting, despite some of its possible deficiencies, was learned in the family setting. The girl learned the role of mothering by imitation and by assisting the mother in rearing siblings and attending to the domestic activities. The son, on the other hand, learned the role of fathering by helping his father at home and outside.

In isolated nuclear families the couple have received little or no training in child rearing and are more willing to turn to mass media and the "experts" on how to rear their children. It is difficult, however, for parents to feel at ease with the "experts" advice, since it is often ambiguous and sometimes contradictory.[7]

In many developing countries where young single people form the majority of those migrating to the cities, leaving home often means a break with the cultural and social traditions in courtship, marriage, and reproductive patterns. In traditional cultures, preparation for family life, including sex education and also the responsibilities of child rearing, were often assumed or shared by elders, and governed by a complex system of rites and informal teaching. This is one of the factors in the growing problems of early unplanned reproduction and weakened family ties.

From a global point of view, the number of adolescent parents is significant, and it is interesting to note that this is true both in some developed and developing countries. Moreover, the percentage of live births by young mothers (under 20 years of age) constitutes a considerable proportion of the total births ranging from 6% to 19% in various countries (Table 1).

TABLE 1

Births by young mothers as percentage of all births in selected countries

Country	Year	Total no. of births	Percentage of mothers by age	
			Less than 15 years	15–19 years
Costa Rica	1971	56,338	0·18	17
	1974	56,769	0·30	20
United States	1971	3,555,970	0·33	18
	1974	3,159,958	0·40	19
Guatemala	1971	229,674	0·21	18
Chile	1971	247,970	0·29	15
Malawi (a)	1971	208,179	0·46	13
Australia	1971	276,362	0·06	11
	1973	247,670	0·07	11
Western Malaysia	1971	309,378	0·07	9
	1973	302,867	0·08	9
Philippines (b)	1971	963,749	0·13	8
	1974	1,078,184	0·03	9
Thailand	1971	1,221,228	0·04	8
	1973	1,167,272	0·05	9
Singapore (c)	1971	47,088	0·04	7
	1974	43,268	0·06	7
France (d)	1971	878,647	0·01	6

Source: United Nations 1976 Demographic yearbook, New York, UN, 1976, table 23, pp. 532-579.

(a) Excludes Europeans and Asians.
(b) Data incomplete or of uncertain reliability.
(c) Data tabulated by year of registration rather than occurrence.
(d) Data exclude liveborn infants dying before registration of birth. Excludes births among armed forces outside of country.

In general, the young age pregnancy has serious implications for the well-being of young mothers who may be economically and psychosocially less well equipped than mature women to assume responsibilities for child rearing and parenthood. The problem is more complex when both parents are very young without other family support.

Clearly, therefore, provision should be made within the context of health and educational systems for the promotion of healthy physical and psychosocial development of adolescents with emphasis on health education and preparation for adult and family life, reproductive behavior and child bearing and child rearing. Essential community and social support, particularly in sociocultural systems where family support does not exist, should be developed by active involvement of young families themselves and the community.

Making the Best of Traditional and Scientific Knowledge

As it is widely recognized in all communities, vital events such as birth, death, child bearing, and child rearing practices in families are the ones which are the most affected by cultural beliefs, traditions, and deeply rooted customs.

These have great influence on the health and well-being of children. In this context it is worth noting that not all that belongs to the past is "wrong" and everything modern is "right." The approach should be that of objective, critical appraisal of traditional practices, rather than their indiscriminate rejection as has frequently been the case in the recent past. When traditional child-bearing practices have positive effects they should be actively promoted and preserved.

In many developing rural communities, the problems of children are still dealt with by traditional methods. However, because of industrialization and urbanization, many people no longer rely on traditional practices alone. For example, separation of the mother from the infant has become such a routine process in some settings that, even in maternity wards, the two are expected to lead independent lives, with now well known harmful effects on breast feeding and mother and infant early interaction. If we look back over the last 20 years, the declining trend in breast feeding was thought to be an irreversible trend of urbanization, higher education, work of mothers, etc. Yet, with better understanding of various important biological and psychosocial values of breast feeding, there is a welcome trend in some communities in highly industrialized and developed areas toward a resurgence of breast feeding. It is hoped that appropriate conclusions will be drawn from these experiences for overall promotion of breast feeding.

Self-reliance, Self-care in Parenting

In the past few decades in many developed countries, the advances in knowledge of child development, education, and child rearing have been misinterpreted to the extent that the natural art of child rearing has often become a self-conscious parental behavior, with overdependence on semi-professionals and professionals in matters that do not need the skills and expertise of these various experts.

In some industrialized countries this overdependence on the part of families on professionals and on costly techniques, particularly in child bearing and child rearing, is now being challenged. The recent trend, which emphasizes the role of the individual, the family, and the community for their own health and well-being, self-reliance, and self-care, both in developed and developing areas, is one that will, in my opinion, be further strengthened in the future years to come.

The new perspective of health care through the primary health care[8] approach, emphasizes the crucial importance of the family in health care. Primary health care is essential health care made universally accessible to individuals and families in the community by means acceptable to them, through their full participation, and at a cost that the community and country can afford. It forms an integral part, both of the country's health system of which it is the nucleus, and of the overall social and economic development of the community.

Recent promising experiences of alternative and flexible ways of child care, adapted to sociocultural settings in developing countries that are mainly family and community centred, with necessary guidance and support from community workers and professionals, might increasingly become the approach in the care of children in the world of tomorrow. There would hopefully be an appropriate combination of professional support and self-reliance of the families in the crucial field of child rearing.

Up to the present this important issue has not been thoroughly investigated or properly handled. Viewed in a global perspective it is a high priority problem, both nationally and internationally.

REFERENCES

1. WORLD HEALTH ORGANIZATION, *New Trends and Approaches in the Delivery of Maternal and Child Care,* Sixth report of the WHO Expert Committee on Maternal and Child Health, World Health Organization, Tech. Rep. Ser. No. 600, Geneva, 1976.
2. WORLD HEALTH ORGANIZATION, *Report of Consultation on Family Health, 5–12 November 1973.* World Health Organization, unpublished paper, Geneva, 1973.
3. H. MAHLER, The health of the family, keynote address delivered at the *International Health Conference of the National Council for International Health, Washington, 16 October 1974,* 1974.
4. N. KRETCHMER, The family: a research setting, paper delivered at the Symposium *The Family: Setting Priorities, Washington, D.C., 20 May 1978,* 1978.
5. WORLD HEALTH ORGANIZATION, *Child Mental Health and Psychosocial Development,* Report of a WHO Expert Committee, World Health Organization, Tech. Rep. Ser. No. 613, Geneva, 1977.
6. J. TIZARD, P. MOSS and J. PERRY, *All Our Children: Pre-school Services in a Changing Society,* Temple Smith/New Society, London, 1976.
7. J. K. HARFOUCHE, Background paper for *Joint WHO/UNICEF Workshop "Innovative approaches for meeting the basic needs of the young child in developing countries" Athens,* 28-30 June 1978, World Health Organization, unpublished paper, Geneva, 1978.
8. WORLD HEALTH OANIZATION, *Primary Health Care. A Joint Report by the Director-General of the World Health Organization and the Executive Director of the United Nations Children's Fund,* Geneva, 1978.

DISCUSSION

JOHN TSIANTIS

Aghia Sophia Children's Hospital, Athens, Greece

WORK, such as that of Dr. Brazelton, has given us new insights into child development, with immense implications for preventive action in the field of mental health.

The so-called "cabbage theory" of the mind—prevalent up to a few years ago—is no longer accepted; i.e., that the baby is only interested in pleasure and pain, associated mainly with food, wind, warmth, and wetness, and that, by continued conditioning, he comes to relate his mother with these sensations. We have also rejected the theory that the baby is inherently only concerned with itself, and that it only becomes interested in other persons at the end of some unspecified period.[1]

In fact, the child–parent relationship is a dynamic dyadtriad, each member of which contributes and reinforces each other's behavior in a positive or negative way. Middlemore talked about the nursing couple in 1941,[2] and one wonders which member of this couple starts the behavior by giving clues to the other. Undoubtedly the baby is the more vulnerable of the pair, and the environment (mother and father) must try to adapt delicately and sensitively to the infant's needs.

In examining the relationship between infant and parents it is possible to recognize two kinds of psychological identification. One is the mother's identification with the baby, which precludes separation of the infant from its mother. The other is the infant's identification with the mother. This state of infant–mother unity has been called symbiosis, but it allows, from the start, a possibility of growing independence. The potential for the mother's identification with her baby depends on several factors:

(1) Experimental data suggests that the past experiences of the mother contribute significantly to the modeling of her maternal role. The most important factor is the mother's experience of mothering by her own mother. A mother's inability to gratify her child's needs often stems from the fact that she did not enjoy a relationship with her own mother.

(2) Prevailing child rearing practices play a significant role. In the nuclear family of Western societies there are not enough opportunities for growing children to learn how to care for small children. This is now the case in Greece in the cities, though not in the provinces.

(3) The mother's state during pregnancy is also of importance: the extent to which she welcomed her approaching motherhood, the support, understanding, and help she received from her husband and other relations.

(4) The mother's genetic endowment.

(5) The socioeconomic conditions of the family.

Some of these factors are unchangeable, but several are amenable to intervention.

We know that the baby is, from the beginning, biologically equipped for social communication and object relating. It is no longer seen as the passive recipient of environmental influences. At the same time, the effects of its early environmental influences are of prime importance.

Work done a few years back by Spitz, Bowlby, and Robertson[3] brought out the adverse effects of institutional upbringing on children. As a result we now have the open-door system in children's hospitals (at least in some parts of the world). Work bringing out the importance of early parent–infant interaction could result in similar changes in maternity hospitals, where we know that the usual routine is to separate infants from their mothers at birth. Especially in the Western world, where the family is nuclear, with the resulting lack of support from other family members, and where a lot of emphasis has been put on the medical aspects of giving birth to the child, the mother's normal anxiety about the newborn tends to be seen as abnormal. On the other hand, physicians are now concerned that a more human approach to childbirth, such as that of Leboyer,[4] and a flight from obstetric technology may lead to dangers to mother and child. The evidence for this is conflicting, but, if it is true, we must guard against it, while recognizing what it is that we are losing and what we are gaining.

The same argument applies to incubator babies, whose mothers are sent home and not encouraged to visit or care for them, with the result that the vital bond between mother and baby cannot later be established. This is also the case when young infants require surgical or medical intervention soon after birth, and are consequently separated from their parents.

The maternal role tends to be devalued today. More and more women go out to work for a number of different reasons. I shall not question the reasons, but the important point is that the children are then placed in day care centers or other institutions. The value of these institutions is undoubted, but I would like to question whether *all* children are able to cope with the repeated experiences of loss that this separation involves, and whether they are able to express their sorrow openly. One may easily underestimate the intensity of these recurrent experiences, even among babies cared for in good, ordinary homes. I will not expand on what the quality of day care centers should be, but I would like to add something about the competition that may arise between the institutional caretakers and the natural caretaker (the mother). My point is that sometimes the staff of an institution (hospital, day care center, etc.) may develop personally and socially based defences which prevent them from making effective contact with the babies and their mothers. One can under-stand the staff's problem, which is that they often have to foster normal development under abnormal conditions, involving low staff–baby ratios and an unsuitable physical environment. This may mean that they tend to discourage normal attitudes and behavior, such as the open expression of grief, and that they encourage abnormal ones, such as that parents and babies should not show their feelings.

Bowlby[3] has called the tendency of the child to direct his instinctual responses to a single person "monotropy." In view of the fact that both parents may be working and that day care centers, as we know, usually have changing caretakers, this is a central question, which poses a big dilemma for both parents and health care personnel. I do not think that there are any readymade answers, but we need to be aware of the problem. It is, however, my feeling that parents sometimes give up their children too early and too easily. There are many positive aspects of day care centers and other institutions, but how far are we going to go tomorrow? Will this disturbance of family life interfere with the normal development of the child? What solutions can be proposed? Are we going to have an army of day care personnel? If so, who is going to train them?

I am now going to raise a well known issue that seems often to be undervalued, namely that experience of personal success is essential for satisfactory parenthood. Therefore, when we demonstrate to expectant parents, or infant–parent dyads what they regard as superior and perfect knowledge, we may sometimes increase their sense of inadequacy and failure. All our efforts should therefore be directed toward mobilizing the parents' inner resources and to supporting their self-esteem.

Here I agree very much with Dr. Barvazian's emphasis on the extended family as the basic social unit for child rearing and self health care. In the terms of today and tomorrow, this means that in developing new strategies for optimal child development there should be a continuous link between the family, the community, the professional, and the responsible authorities. Schaffer[6] has criticized attempts to rectify deprivation by adding stimulation or enrichment outside the child's natural environment. The baby cannot develop into a person if there is only a nonhuman environment. Therefore any stimulation programs that are used to substitute parents, or that intrude into the parent–child interaction, must be carefully scrutinized before they are applied. The baby needs human beings—human beings who are imperfect and free of computerized reliability—not machines.

A final point that we as health care personnel should try to convey to parents is that, while becoming a parent is, in a sense, something that happens overnight, in another way it is a role which one has to grow into through experience and through making mistakes. As is well known, the making of mistakes is an essential part of. learning by experience. Approached in this way, parents are likely to be more open to recognize their mistakes and to learn from them than if we allow them to set themselves an impossibly high standard of ideal parenthood.

If we accept that a good and mutually satisfying parent–infant relationship is the basis of later mental health, any work done with the early infant–parent dyad is the most important preventive action we can take for the future well-being of the child. Today's family is tomorrow's child.

REFERENCES

1. J. O. WISDOM, What sort of ego has an infant: a methodological approach, in *Foundations of Child Psychiatry*, (editor E. Miller), Pergamon Press, London, 1968.
2. M. MIDDLEMORE, *The Nursing Couple*, Cassels, London, 1941.
3. R. SPITZ, Hospitalism: an enquiry into the genesis of psychiatric conditions in early childhood, in *Psychoanalytic Study of the Child*, New York, 1945. J. BOWLBY, *A Maternal Care and Mental Health*, WHO, Geneva, 1951. J. ROBERTSON, *Hospitals and Children: A Parent's Eye View*, Gollancz, 1968
4. F. LEBOYER, *Birth Without Violence*, Fontana & Collins, 1977.
5. J. ROBERTSON, Some responses of young children to loss of maternal care, in *Nursing Times*, April 1953.
6. H. R. SCHAFFER, Behavioral synchrony in infancy, in *New Scientist*, April 4, 1974; and Early social behavior and the study of reciprocity in *Bulletin of the British Psychological Society* **27**, 209 (1974).

M. G. WAGNER
WHO, Copenhagen, Denmark

The nuclear family, at least in postindustrial society, is a disaster. We are all familiar with the statistics which support this notion: divorce rates, number of single parent families, etc. But perhaps the best sign is the fact that so many people are insisting that "the family is good"—an insistence which would be unnecessary and superfluous if it indeed, was good. Further indication of the present state of the nuclear family is the fact that there is much talk of family support systems, i.e. they need support to survive.

While the scientists and policy makers are talking about family support systems, the people are doing something about it: they are trying new ways of living together. As one example, over 20% of people in Denmark under 35 years of age are now living in collectives. These collectives are *not* formed on the basis of some principle (political, ecological, etc.) but only on the basis of finding better ways of living. New patterns of parent–child dyads emerge in these collectives. A mother and father who are no longer together as a couple may live in the same collective and share the rearing of their child while leading separate personal and social lives. Adults in the collective who enjoy younger children spend more time with them, while adults who enjoy older children spend more time with them.

Another new way of living together that is being tried increasingly is cohabitation (living together in a stable relationship without marriage). Fifty percent of people in their twenties in Sweden, for example, are cohabiting. Both living collectively and cohabiting have gained popularity only in the last 20 years, and it is likely that the next 10–20 years will see these phenomena spread. These are, however, only two examples of new styles of family life, and the next 20 years will likely see the development of many alternatives to the nuclear family.

In the past we have professionalized health and education so that individuals (and parents) no longer feel adequate to assume responsibility for their own (and their children's) health and education. Very recently, there appears to be a trend to professionalize parenting. Such professionalization is dangerous because of its disabling characteristics—it produces feelings of inadequacy and passivity. This professionalization includes another dangerous phenomenon: the medicalization of natural processes and/or processes which are basically social in nature. Thus, for example, everyone must be born in a hospital, die in a hospital, and soon parents will come to believe that they cannot make any decisions regarding their children without first consulting a doctor.

There are, fortunately, several recent trends which suggest a possibility for reversing this professionalization. First, there is growing interest in self-care—increasing the role that individuals (and parents) play in managing their own lives. This self-care is a reaffirmation of the importance and value of the individual and can lead to increasing self-reliance. A second trend is an increasing awareness among professionals of the importance of giving their knowledge to those they are supposed to serve. A third trend is an increasing realization that in all human services there is a need for community participation, which is of the nature of a *real* partnership between the providers and consumers of the service.

While in the near future we may see a trend toward professionalization of parenting, these three trends may result, in 10 or 20 years, in an increasing balance between the accumulating knowledge of the experts and the accumulated (traditional) knowledge of the culture.

BERNARD E. COHEN

Chaim Sheba Medical Center, Savyon, Israel

In reply to Professor Wagner's remark about communal living, the kibbutzim in Israel developed communal living nearly 70 years ago, and the child was cared for in the "infants' and children's home" by trained nurses. These kibbutzim are now returning to the nuclear family and the infants and children have moved back into their parents' rooms.

ALFRED H. KATZ

School of Public Health, University of California at Los Angeles, CA, USA

Over the last 25 years, and in particular the last dozen years, the United States has seen the growth of an enhanced consumer resistance to professional domination of many aspects of life including physical and mental health care.

In the late 1960s the organization of a number of special research and demonstration projects incorporated and highlighted a specific role of parents in contributing to the education, socialization, and even therapy of children with particular handicaps or deficits. A large number of such projects were conducted in university centers, hospitals, special education centers, and social agencies. Many of their results are summarized and analyzed in two publications of the DHEW in the early seventies: *A Report on Longitudinal Evaluations of Pre-School Programs* by Bronfenbrenner,[1] and *Cognitive and Mental Development in the First Five Years of Life* by Lichtenberg and Norton.[2]

Among the projects I wish to mention are the National Collaborative Infant Project of the United Cerebral Palsy Association, subsidized by the Federal Bureau for Education of the Handicapped, begun in 1971 and continuing to this day. Also, a program for Down's syndrome children at the University of Washington; a number of parent education programs stimulated by the Center for Studies of Child and Family Mental Health of the National Institute of Mental Health, the Portage model project for early childhood education conducted in Wisconsin, projects in Florida and in Nassau County, New York, conducted respectively by Doctors Ira Gordon and Phyllis Levenstein, and the Parents as Educators project of Dr. Earl Schaefer, of North Carolina.[3]

Let me quote from a brief description of the ways parents are involved in the Down's syndrome project at the University of Washington:

"The staff from the first encourage the parents to interact with the infant constantly during his waking hours: to cuddle, to talk to, to hold, and to play with the infant. And, at first, parents are often astounded as they watch the staff doing all of those things. But the staff have found that their enthusiasm about the baby is contagious—parents who had earlier been somehow frightened of this infant with his 'differences' could begin to react to him as they might automatically have reacted to a normal infant . . . .

"Parents are involved from the moment their child is seen by our staff and then throughout his school program. They are trained to use at home many of the exercises and instructional procedures used at school. When their children reach preschool age, they work in the classrooms—they are trained to be observers, data-takers, and teaching assistants. They use many of the data-taking procedures at home so that they and the staff can determine whether the child's behaviors at home and at school are complementing each other, and can then make informed decisions together about his behavioral objectives and program.

"Parents attend staff meetings on days they have worked in school; they have individual and group conferences with their children's teachers at frequent intervals—if necessary, by telephone. . . .

"The parents' activities in the larger community are formidable. Some serve as counselors: they are on call at several Seattle hospitals to visit and talk to parents of newborn Down's syndrome infants almost as soon as the new parents have been told about their child's diagnosis. They lecture to students in various University of Washington departments—education, psychology, social work, and in the School of Medicine. Several have written articles for *Sharing Our Caring,* a nationally distributed journal specifically concerned with Down's syndrome. Finally, in what is surely one of the most appropriate testimonials to 'parents as partners,' several young couples who have moved beyond commuting distance ' . . .have been able, on the basis of their training here, to organize and maintain preschool programs for young handicapped children in communities where previously there had been no educational opportunities for this population'."[4]

Many other instances could be cited if time permitted. The projects I have mentioned varied in a number of ways in the structure of interventions provided. They used different combinations of parent, professional, and paraprofessional effort. In some cases, home teachers were trained who went into the homes, particularly of underprivileged families, and gave instruction to parents on the stimulation of their children. In other cases, parents were brought into the classroom setting to observe teaching methods and to reinforce in the home such observed activities. In others, such as the United Cerebral Palsy projects, parents were brought into the evaluation procedure for young CP children and given a specific role in infant stimulation and exercises in the home. I might say, parenthetically, that, being interested in this type of activity for some years, the most interesting and innovative clinical program that I have personally observed was that organized in Belgrade and Kotor, Yugoslavia, by Professor Cvetko Brajovic, who is at this symposium.

Common to all these varied and important research and demonstration efforts was the *activation* of parents; granting or restoring to them what had hitherto been denied them by professionally monopolistic treatment and education approaches. This was a continuous role with the young child, not only in the provision of emotional support and stimulation of growth through those elements of touching, holding, cuddling, and so on, which are conducive to human bonding, but, quite specifically, in stimulation in the cognitive areas, and in muscular–skeletal development and coordination by means of various techniques. Not only were parents used as interveners, treaters or teachers in this fashion, but they also had an extremely important role to play as observers and recorders of their child's development. Indeed, one of the most impressive aspects of Dr. Brajovic's program is the way parents are involved in record keeping, charting a child's development through diaries and other recording devices, and helping to establish some parameters of expected development at various times for children with particular kinds of central nervous system and other deficits.

The many and varied demonstrations of such programs have shown that IQs on standardized tests can be raised significantly, by some 15 or 20 points, for developmentally disabled children; that significant gains in socialization, the acquisition of language and motor skills, emotional adjustment, social attitudes, and the learning of appropriate social behaviors within the family and toward others can be achieved through conscious, structured interventions by parents and other family members. So it now seems unthinkable to me that any future program for therapeutic and educational work with handicapped children would ignore and not include the vital resource represented by the nuclear family, parents in the first instance, but also quite often including older siblings, grandparents, and other relatives who might be present in the home, and who represent not only a familiar and natural but a continuous therapeutic environment for the child.

From these general developments let us now consider some of the ways in which parents might be systematically involved in home care of their handicapped children, by professional workers and service institutions and agencies. Once there is a commitment to the notion of parent involvement, the great advantages of mutual support or self-help groups to assist parents become apparent. Participation in such groups reinforces the importance of self-care to parents, gives them specific training, opportunities for shared experience about how and why things happen to their children, helps them anticipate developmental problems or crises, and so on. The approach to parent involvement that I am outlining emphasizes the necessity of social support systems for the troubled family. Again, an ancient principle is being rediscovered by professionals in many areas of physical and mental health. Often through a mutual aid group, parents can obtain the vital elements of social support and acceptance, needed in overcoming feelings of stigma, isolation, and disappointment regarding their child. Their ability to define or redefine the child's presenting problem is enhanced, so that it is no longer viewed as simply an affliction but as having positive elements as well. In addition there is a wealth of support to be obtained through the exchange of concrete information regarding management, simple day-to-day problems in which the more experienced group members or those with older children can advise and counsel with newer parents. And, finally, there are advantages that such a form of organization has clearly demonstrated in the area of group action. There is much evidence that group action on the self-help model not only helps individual parents by giving them constructive roles, *vis-à-vis* the child and its problems, but also helps to overcome feelings of helplessness by successful measure of, for example, influencing the policy in a particular school or institution regarding their children. So there is always a dialectic or double element involved in the self-help group activity, whether for parents or others, namely, that of helping the individual or the individual family's coping ability, and that of helping to bring about needed or desirable change of social policy and programs.

What happens to the role of professionals when parents and the organizations that they form are given such an enhanced but natural responsibility in relation to their children? Does this represent a diminution or phasing out of professional expertise? In my opinion, not at all. The role of professionals may shift somewhat, but they are just as necessary in diagnosis, and in the provision of instruction to parents, as they might have been previously when they had major or primary treatment responsibilities in addition to diagnosis. The weight of epidemiological evidence has shown that the lack of social supports and of group interactions is one of the most important factors not only in vulnerability to illness, but also in helping persons in the process of social rehabilitation, and the necessary relearning of social skills and roles to cope with handicap or disability. The educational role of the professional person is important in such a perspective. Professional expertise and resource provision, education, and counseling with the parents or other family members are no less important than previously, but there is some shift of responsibility to the family, with consequent gains in cohesiveness, the sense of shared tasks, and the satisfactions to be derived from an active rather than a passive role, namely, acting on behalf of their child's problem rather than simply being the passive recipients of varied professional services.

It is estimated that for almost every one of the more than 200 diagnostic categories that the World Health Organization uses, some form of self-help organization has been created. These are, of course, especially found in Western societies, but my observations have indicated that they also exist in the East European countries and to some extent in developing societies. Because the studies that I have briefly called attention to in this paper all demonstrate the necessity, in fact, the indispensability of parental involvement in therapy, education, and child socialization, so that the child can develop to the limit of his potential and capacities, it now seems timely to consider the creation of some special organizations in which the views of parents and their involvement in the care of their handicapped children would find a forum that would cut across individual diagnostic categories. There is a great deal to be studied, learned, and organized around the concept of such parent participation. Self-help is an attractive idea, and perhaps what I am now projecting is the notion of "a self-help organization of self-helpers." In other words, a forum for the exchange of experience and stimulation of lay and professional knowledge and research, and for influencing broad public and governmental policies.

REFERENCES

1. U. Bronfenbrenner, *A Report on Longitudinal Evaluation of Pre-School Programs*, 2 vols., Department of Health, Education and Welfare, Washington, DC, Publication No. (OHD) 74-25, 1974.
2. P. Lichtenberg and D. Norton, *Cognitive Mental Development in the First 5 Years of Life*, National Institute of Mental Health, 1973, Department of Health, Education and Welfare, Publication No. (HSM) 73-9135.

3. All these projects are presented and discussed in the volume *Intervention Strategies for High Risk Infants and Young Children* (Tjossem, ed.), Baltimore, MA, University Park Press, 1976.
4. A. H. HAYDEN and N. HARING, Programs for Down's syndrome children, in Tjossem, op cit., pp. 573–607.

CHAIRMAN'S SUMMARY

Lewis P. Lipsitt

> I heard in the night the pigeons
> Stirring within their nest.
> The young pigeon's stir was tender
> Like a child's hand at the breast.
> I said "Oh pigeons, stir not"
> For my breast was touched to tears.
> "Oh pigeons do not stir,
> A childless woman hears."
>
> Frances Cornford

The joys and grief of parenthood, so beautifully set down by the poetess, are as much our concern in this symposium as the behavior, development, and well-being of infants. The persons in the parent–child dyad are inextricably tied up in and bound to one another, not just from the moment of birth, but even before—whether in keen and comfortable anticipation of the birth or in ambivalence or even in dread.

It has become increasingly apparent, in studies of the perinatal precursors of developmental hazards, and of the behavioral and psychophysiological responses of newborns, that the reciprocating interchanges between the parent and the child are of paramount importance to the child, in setting the conditions for subsequent attachments to other persons, in facilitating the child's capacity to endure developmental crises, and perhaps even for avoidance of severe developmental storms such as failure to thrive and crib death.

During the earliest moments of the child's life the parent's commitment to the child is challenged, and the child can assimilate a sense of comfort and community from the parent. The initial greeting and the mutual stimulation provide the opportunity for each to learn what the other is like, and thus what their future will hold. It is a time during which two members of the human species, both of them obligated by biological design or happenstance and by sheer propinquity, must come to grips with one another. The ways in which they accomplish this developmental task, for both of them, will have important influences on later relationships, theirs with one another, and each with others.

This is not to say that the dyad is necessarily about the mother and child and these only. The dyadic relationship can be between the father and child as well, and in the best of all worlds will be. Better, we ought to be talking about triads and symbioses beyond. The shifts in familial relationships when a child is born are in fact many, and the interacting forces at work on the reciprocating behaviors of each member of the family unit are both obvious and subtle. The family unit and its "psychological movement" when a new member is introduced needs more study.

171

Of great relevance to the character, quality, and intensity of the early parent–child dyad is the response repertoire of the *infant*. Numerous developmental scientists, of diverse disciplines and in many locations around the world , have been involved in studies of neonatal behavior over the past 20 years. A contemporary progress report with respect to their findings would have to divulge that the newborn comes into the world with all sensory modalities functioning; that the newborn child is capable of experiencing a wide range of both appetitive and aversive stimulation; and that the infant's mechanisms for conveying to the world his or her pleasure or displeasure with the nurturant or intrusive environment are already in place. In short, the newborn is ready to reciprocate. The environment acts on the infant, and the infant responds; but the responses of the infant are themselves stimuli capable of evoking responses in their caretakers. The baby may behave in such a way, through cuddling, for example, as to promote further cuddling, caressing, and eye contact. In less advantageous conditions the infant may evoke, at best, reactions of ambivalence, and at worst, clear hostility and rejection.

The immense complexities of later human interrelationships should not discourage us from seeking their roots in the earliest reciprocating relationships of the child and its parent. This session is devoted to the celebration of those roots, *and* of the capacity of humans—those who are parents, those who are service workers in the cause of children and childhood, and those who are research observers of all the relevant processes—to come to an enlightened and sympathetic understanding of the most important human relationship: the parent–child dyad.

SPECIAL SESSIONS

CHANGING PARENTAL ROLES

CHILDREN OF FAMILIES
IN NEW SETTINGS

FAMILY SUBSTITUTES

CHILDREN'S RIGHTS AND PARENTAL RIGHTS AND OBLIGATIONS

CHANGING PARENTAL ROLES

Coordinator: EDITH KATZ
Committee of the International Year of the Child, Paris, France

THE SIGNIFICANCE of changing parental roles was considered in this session by way of three main perspectives: EDITH GROTBERG's concern related to changing family structures and parental responsibilities in the United States; ANTONINA OSTROWSKA pointed out some important changes in social policy occasioned by the rise in maternal employment; and ROBERT A. ALDRICH described a specific strategy for coping with the problems of the single parent family.

DR. GROTBERG (Department of Health, Education, and Welfare, Washington, DC, USA) outlined the goals and functions of the family as they relate to parental responsibility. Noting the fact that many changes in family structures have occurred over the centuries and that they have necessarily affected parental responsibilities, the question was posed as to the causes and configurations of such changes. Four primary sources of change in family structures were identified. The first was the broad economic setting which provides changes in occupational roles and thereby contributes to changes in family member functioning. The second was the broad political setting: "The concept of equal rights, equal opportunities, civil rights, children's rights, affirmative actions and participatory governance have been enriched over the past two decades and contribute to greater demand from families and family members to benefit from these concepts." The third concerned change in the broad moral, ethical, and attitudinal settings (where, for example, there is now less respect for outside authority, more tolerance of working women, and child care, etc.). Finally, there are certain pervasive trends such as the steady increase in divorce, decrease in family size, etc., contributing to the present family configurations, which include single career families, dual career families, single parent households, remarried nuclear families, kin families, and new experimental families as well. These configurations necessarily affect the ways in which parents carry out their responsibilities. The strengths and weaknesses of the various family structures were analyzed in these contexts, and it was pointed out that some nontraditional types might be beneficial to the child if certain outside supports, such as economic maintenance, and adequate child care, were provided.

Foster care and child day care were then examined in the context of achieving the goal of parental responsibility. The paper stressed the need for parental involvement and parent participation in program and service policy formulations. For those parents who opt for informal child care arrangements, information must be provided about standards and criteria for the selections of care givers, and assistance given to help them find child care resources in their own communities.

Central to Dr. Grotberg's paper was the insistence that "family structures will continue to change and the future forms are not determinable at the present time. However, change in family structures is not as critical for future concern as is the assurance that parental responsibilities may be carried out regardless of the family structures." The universal goals of such parental responsibility were said to include the following:

(a) To help children become productive individuals capable of autonomy, reciprocal caring and love.
(b) To help each member of the family to achieve quality of life aspirations.
(c) To orient children to the world.
(d) To prepare children for full participation in society, what we commonly call socialization; i.e., the family is an instrument of socialization.
(e) To help children become competent members of society.
(f) To sustain the family institution.
(g) To provide the primary structure for potential socialization of members over the life cycle.
(h) To provide the primary social organization for participation.

Dr. Grotberg concluded that: "the different social policies, programs, and services, the different information needed for families in different family structures and changing family structures, must increasingly be guided by these very goals of parental responsibility. The family must survive and maintain its functions. Supports for families should help families perform and not be replaced. The children of tomorrow deserve this consideration today."

The concern of Dr. Ostrowska (Institute of Philosophy and Sociology, Polish Academy of Sciences, Warsaw, Poland) was also with the significance of the changing roles of parents, but she focused upon the needed changes in social policy arising specifically from the increase in maternal employment. It was admitted that the effect on the child of the complexity of factors resulting from the employment of mothers is not definitely known. However, the most immediate questions are by whom and how should children of working mothers be cared for, at what cost, and paid for by whom?

In Poland, despite the increase in the employment of women, responsibility for the care of children, elderly, and ill members of the family, rests on women. There are insufficient child care resources, and women bear the burden of the dysfunction of the various state and social institutions. This situation was compared and contrasted with policies and practices in other countries.

Maternal leave and family allowances were compared in Poland and elsewhere. In Poland there is unpaid child care leave with full job protection for up to four years. The Polish economy does not yet permit allowances for mothers on child care leave. Only mothers in Poland are entitled to child care leave, and 30–35% of them take an average of one year's leave. This was contrasted with Sweden and other Scandinavian countries, where a policy of sharing the responsibility of child care permits the taking of leave by either parent.

The thesis was also put forward that the quality of parental care might be more significant than the quantity. A study in Warsaw revealed an unexpectedly strong positive effect of the mother's going out to work upon the child's mental capacity. There is evidence that working mothers spend more time with their children than women who do not work, and that in these families the participation of fathers in child rearing also increases. The paper concluded with these recommendations:

(1) Relations between family and work spheres should be made more harmonious. This can be facilitated by improved living conditions.
(2) Family policy should be directed towards a more democratic division of family responsibility for housework and child care.
(3) Child bearing should be encouraged but should not limit women's participation in other spheres of life, neither should it interfere with the realization of other goals such as education, professional advancement, etc.
(4) Social policy should recognize that various new family structures exist. There is no longer a typical family. The values of the decision makers are not always identical with those of the families to whom the policies are directed.
(5) It should be recognized that new social needs have arisen which cannot be entirely satisfied by the family. The collaboration of other institutions is needed but not to the extent of seeking to replace the family.

DR. ROBERT A. ALDRICH (Medical Center, University of Colorado, Denver, CO, USA) began by conceding that: "not long ago, I was told that the family in the third world consisted of a mommy, a daddy, two children, and an anthropologist, whereas in the Western world, the family was said to include a mommy, a daddy, two children, and a psychologist!" However, in view of the fact that what has been regarded as the typical family structure, is everywhere undergoing great modifications, Dr. Aldrich went on to speak of means of coping with the growing phenomenon of single parent families.

The single parent family now forms 16% of all families in the United States of which 90% are headed by women. One strategy for dealing with this problem had been worked out in Denver, Colorado. This is a self-supporting residential complex of 95 units which is inhabited by single parent families who are in a crisis situation. It is managed by a Board of Directors, on which women and men are equally represented.

The complex is located in a pleasant, central residential area, and the children go to local schools. Families stay for up to two years, which was described as a supportive "holding" pattern. An on-site preschool program is included, and immunization and dental care are also available on the premises. A nearby hospital provides medical backup services and gives health counselling to parents.

DR. ALDRICH suggested that this model (which has already been applied in six other areas of the United States) could be replicated in other countries, since it requires little capital investment and has already drawn great interest and been well received when instituted.

Another recommendation put forth by DR. ALDRICH to deal with the low income problems of single parent families was that a guaranteed annual wage should replace the present welfare payments (with their associated investigation and supervision). This should cover all low income families as a way of maintaining the self-esteem of the family, regardless of its structure.

Following these major presentations, a lengthy discussion developed, focusing mainly on case studies of changing family roles in Cyprus, Greece, Iran, Israel, Polynesia, and the United States.

The reports spanned a wide range of possible parental roles: Centering on features of Polynesian child-rearing, PROFESSOR JAMES RITCHIE (School of Social Sciences, University of Waikato, New Zealand) described in some detail how the less intense bonding of shared parenthood could have a very positive effect on the development of the child. Rather than an exclusive parent–child relation, there is a marked strengthening of peer group relations and a greater adaptability of the child within the Polynesian society.

A somewhat less radical intervention into traditional parental roles was considered by MARY E. ROBINSON (National Institute of Mental Health, East Adelphi, MD, USA) in terms of a support system, which is offered to families by the Clinical Infant Development Program of the US National Institute of Mental Health. This is an "innovative preventive intervention program in which a wide range of health and mental health services are offered to constitutionally vulnerable infants and their high risk families. Subjects are drawn from a group of pregnant women who are known to community services as having had previous psychological problems either themselves, or in their child care or rearing. Determinations of mothers' potential care-taking capacities are made on the basis of assessments of their psychological and social functioning during pregnancy. Although a broad spectrum of individualized needs are addressed, the foundation of the program is the provision of general patterns of care based on the needs of all infants.

"The multidimensional approach to working with the family is characterized by a variety of techniques based on principles of learning and psychoanalytic developmental psychology. These include instructing parents in ways to stimulate cognitive development in the infant, and helping parents to understand the effect of their own unconscious experiences as children on their perceptions and emotional facilitation of their own children."

Quite different from advocating shared parenthood, or support systems for parents, MME ASSEFE ASSEFI (Association des Parents et des Educateurs, Teheran, Iran) contended that there is too much outside intervention which prevents parents from remaining properly involved in what should be primarily their own concern: that is, the education of their own children. The reasons for the growing disquietude and delinquency among the young today is none other, she suggested, than the fact the family—*the* primary institution and basis for the proper education of the young—has come to neglect its essential and principal role of providing a discerning and properly integrated education, in harmony with the evolution of society. Parents lose sight of the fact that the personality of the individual is formed within the family by the age of 7. Children are full of creative inspiration and they desire to attain their own identity and place within the society, but when their parents are totally preoccupied with their work and their professions, it is understandable that the children react and revolt. It is because they recognize the gravity of this situation that the National Association of Parents and Educators of Iran have, in the course of 13 years of service and numerous publications, films, and orientation courses, continued to help parents and educators in solving the problems of the education of children.

LIST OF PAPERS PRESENTED

ASSEFE ASSEFI (Association des Parents et des Educateurs, Teheran, Iran): "Le rôle de la Famille dans l'éducation de l'enfant."

THALIA DRAGONAS (Institute of Anthropos, Athens, Greece): "Parental education in Greece."

EDITH H. GROTBERG (Department of Health, Education, and Welfare, Washington, DC, USA): "Changing family structures and parental responsibility."

C. P. MESSIS (Neuropsychiatrist, Cyprus): "Family life and sex education in Cyprus."

DONALD ORR, BETTY SATTERWHITE, CLAIRBOURNE DUNGY, and BARRY PLESS (Department of Pediatrics, University of California at Irvine, USA): "Yesterday's child grows up: implications for tomorrow's family."

ANTONIA OSTROWSKA and MAGDALENA SOKOLOWSKA (Institute of Philosophy and Sociology, Polish Academy of Sciences, Warsaw, Poland): "Changing parental roles and social policy."

MARY E. ROBINSON (National Institute of Mental Health, East Adelphi, MD, USA): "Clinical infant development program."

TOIVO RÖNKA (The Mannerheim League for Child Welfare, Finland): "Developing parent education in normal life and risk situations."

D. SAUVAGE, C. BARTHELEMY-GAULT, A. SAILLANT, and J. LAUGIER (Service de Psychothérapie Enfants, Tours, France): "Psychological aid to parents of children hospitalized during the neonatal period."

GEORGE and VASSE VASSILIOU (Institute of Anthropos, Athens, Greece): "On a systematic dialectic approach to family functioning and malfunctioning."

CHILDREN OF FAMILIES IN NEW SETTINGS

Coordinator: MARIOS RAPHAEL

Graduate School of Industrial Studies, Piraeus, Greece

CONTRIBUTIONS to the discussion ranged from a theoretical and global view of the subject to an empirical approach to specialized topics. The notion of the "supportive environment," the importance of stress and the vulnerability of those suffering from it, as well as problems of children of mothers, who were prison inmates, of children of bicultural families and of day care services for children were discussed. Altogether there was a great variety of contributions, ranging from general issues to specialized topics.

The main discussion, however, was centered around problems of migrant families and their children. It was emphasized that with migration, whatever the cause, voluntary or otherwise, and given the differences in the new settings, millions of people around the world are facing extensive social problems, even if there are some economic advantages.

The migrating populations are counted by the million. They move within and between countries (urbanization and emigration), temporarily or permanently, for reasons as varied as commitment of a parent to an institution, educational studies, seasonal or permanent employment, business interests, missionary fervor, war, or political or religious persecution. Difficulties in dealing with the problems of a migrant population are magnified, not only by forecasts that the phenomenon will continue unabated—and possibly increase—in the future, but also by ignorance and/or indifference on the part of those in a position to take effective action.

The intrafamilial changes and individual problems that are exacted by the new setting depend partly on how the move came about: whether willingly, following a certain amount of deliberation and planning, or forcibly, caused by war or some other major calamity. Although generally such moves are related to work availability, improvement of one's chances, etc., the migrating population is itself far from homogeneous: professionals, businessmen, diplomats, students, differ markedly from refugees, migrant workers, or military dependent families.

In attempting to assess the difficulties of the children of these families, it is important to consider the qualitative and quantitative differences between the old and the new environments, both in what the children themselves experience—directly and via their parents—and what the community and larger society can offer.

Problems in the field of education, culture, health, environment, religion, housing, etc., are acute to these transplanted families and their children, who are faced with difficulties and contradictions in values and behavior, deculturation and enculturation, isolation, alienation, and adaptation. Children particularly are the victims of these situations.

A not untypical situation was mentioned by Professor R. HASSAN (School of Social Sciences, Flinders University, Bedford Park, South Australia). He instanced the plight of foreign workers who become unemployed because the receiving country has closed down factories, etc. The men of such families tend to move in search of work elsewhere, leaving their families behind for a second time. All the old problems of adjustment become intensified, together with some new ones due to the relatively alien environment.

A change of setting means a partial—sometimes a total—substitution of the familiar by the new and unknown. All assumptions, all belief systems, all behavior patterns are suddenly brought into question, and it is not surprising that disorientation, even disorganization, may result.

To mitigate such undesirable effects, PROFESSOR A. RAPOPORT (Department of Architecture, University of Wisconsin at Milwaukee, WI, USA) recommended that the new settings should be made as supportive as possible (i.e. as familiar as possible). In this context, careful studies of traditional and spontaneous settlements can be most valuable. He also recommended that the beneficial aspects of the clustering of people of similar origins should be considered and utilized.

A report on some studies made in Ankara in 1977 was presented by MICHEL MANCIAUX (International Children's Center, Paris, France). These focused on the effects on the children of the emigration of at least one parent (usually the father). A comparison was made between children who emigrated with their parents, children who remained behind with either their mother or grandparents, and children who were sent back at a later period. The aspects studied were health, nutrition, education, and psychosocial factors. Children returning to their home country after having spent some time with their parents abroad were better nourished than those whose parents had never left, but they were subject to more accidents and they were more socially maladjusted.

Children who were left behind when their parent(s) migrated showed poor performance in school—apart from exceptionally gifted children. Children who emigrated with their parents and reached adolescence in the receiving country, experienced greater difficulties in school and showed a higher rate of unemployment than children native there. They were also badly received when they returned to their country of origin. The Ankara symposium therefore recommended that international regulations be instituted to protect the children of migrant families, and that bilateral agreements between the sending and receiving countries should take the fate of the children into consideration.

These recommendations were made more salient when G. D. DE BERNIS (University of Social Sciences, Grenoble, France) reported that in Switzerland babies born to foreign workers are forced to leave the country when three months old. He emphasized that countries which need the labor of foreign workers must reconsider their policies and accept not just individual workers but whole families, who must be granted equal status with the indigenous families. It is the family unit which will continue to absorb—like a buffer—the shocks of transplantation. Consequently every possible care should be taken by governments and private organizations to ease the burden on the family. Education programs should be set up in both the sending and receiving countries to prepare migrants for the changes they are about to meet; to put them in contact with social service organizations and voluntary associations of their own countrymen; to teach them the rudiments of the new language; to inform them as to the conditions of work and remuneration, as well as the conditions of health and medical care and the educational system.

The needs of family members staying behind also need to be considered and M. PAVELLA (Ministry of Agriculture, Athens, Greece) and the MULTINATIONAL WOMEN'S LIBERATION GROUP in Athens indicated that work in this direction had been started in Greece.

The need for more and more day care centers for the children of working mothers was emphasized by M. M. RAJENDRAN (Ministry of Social Welfare, New Delhi, India).

However, day care is not without its problems, as was brought out in a study of day care centers in Belgium, presented by PROFESSOR CLIO PRESVELOU (Department of Sociology, Catholic University of Louvain, Belgium). She said that 162 day nurseries and kindergartens were selected for analysis. Through a structured interview, each center provided information on a number of quantitative aspects dealing with the organization of life in the center. This was followed by an in-depth interview with the head of the centre (or her delegate) to probe the conception and function of the institution towards the child. A third questionnaire was distributed to the parents.

On the basis of over 3,000 valid replies received from parents it appears that daytime child care facilities are used both by Belgian and foreign couples. During its economic take-off, after the Second World War, Belgium encouraged an important movement of immigration in order to fill jobs which national manpower either could not meet or, more often, would not accept, because of the job's low status and pay and the dangers to health (e.g. coal mining).

When defining the mother's social status, according to her husband's occupation and the job she holds at present, it appeared the Belgian mothers belonged to the higher social classes and the migrant mothers to the lower ones (Table 1).

TABLE 1

Distribution of Belgian and alien mothers according to the father's occupation and education

Father's occupation and education	Mother's nationality	
	Belgian	Alien
Inactive	3·9	14·4 ⎫
Unqualified blue collar worker	10·4	26·0 ⎬ 74·1
Qualified blue collar worker	30·2 ⎫	33·7 ⎭
Employee, lower grade of secondary education	13·9 ⎪	8·3
Employee, upper grade of secondary education	16·0 ⎬ 75·0	1·9
Employee, higher education	14·9 ⎭	4·3
Others, (self-employed, liberal professions)	7·6	6·9
No reply	3·1	4·5
Total	100·0	100·0

Though no cases of discrimination against the admission of immigrants' children have been reported either in day nurseries or in kindergartens, the fact remains that there is a *de facto* segregation. This results from the fact that such services are located in certain neighborhoods inhabited mostly by immigrant workers and their families (around or near the railway stations of Belgian cities, for example) or at the periphery of urban centers where families with higher incomes live or which can only be reached by car.

Taking into consideration the fact that nurturance practices followed by immigrant mothers are quite different from those of Belgian mothers, partly because of the cultural distance separating a Moroccan, a Turk, even a Greek or a Portuguese mother from her Belgian counterpart, the relatively low proportion of alien mothers who declared that they changed their children from one daytime center to another because of dissatisfaction shows that mothers of the lower social classes have little choice.

The greater range of options enjoyed by better-off families can also be established by the kind of solution to which families resort in case of an emergency, such as taking care of a sick child (whose admission to a day nursery or kindergarten is prohibited). Belgian mothers depend essentially on their kin in such emergencies. In similar circumstances, the immigrant mother is forced to take time off from her job (and lose her pay) to take care of her sick children: her own kin being unavailable.

To sum up: the analysis of replies from over 3000 respondents, who used the daytime care centers of the sample at the time of the inquiry, reveals a sharp division of the population into two social classes. The first group, representing four-fifths of the "users" who replied to the written interview schedule, is made up of Belgian families. On the basis of the wife's social origin, about 75% of them belong to the lower–middle and middle–middle social classes. A little over half of the mothers hold a qualified job; they are office employees, teachers, nurses, social workers, and the like. Less than a fifth of this group are blue collar workers. The selection of the daytime center does not seem dependent on the distance of the service.

The second group is made up of foreign families who are mostly those of immigrant workers. Three-quarters of the mothers come from the lower social classes. They are cleaning women or blue collar workers. As a result, immigrant mothers are more dependent on extraneous constraints when they come to select a daytime center for their children.

From the in-depth interviews conducted with 37 day nurseries it appears that there is an explicit recognition by the interviewees (generally the heads of centers) of two functions performed by day nurseries. The day care function was spontaneously given as the primary activity in every center. The educational function was presented as complementary to the previous one. The day nursery is a microcosm in itself, where children should be helped, progressively, to develop their intellectual faculties, to become aware of their human and material environment, to reproduce socially accepted behavior, and learn to communicate, exchange, and adjust.

Staff training is generally considered inadequate and of a low intellectual quality. This is due mainly to the low social status of the profession and the low salary. Hence it is very dubious that the educational demand made by parents of higher social milieux is properly met. Parents of the lower social milieux are faced with a twofold constraint. On the one hand, they must accept a social definition of childhood imposed on them by a social class alien to theirs; on the other, being deprived of the chance or ability to express their opinions and desires (partly because of their inability to make verbal statements, partly because of the position of authority that a day nursery run by trained and "expert" personnel takes in their eyes) they have no say in the way their children are taken care of by the center. This double constraint is particularly strong in the case of foreign mothers who make up the biggest part of the lower social classes in our sample.

As an institution established and operated independently of the parents' involvement, responsible to a central administration and hence autonomous from parents' supervision, any day nursery progressively develops a position of superiority toward the parents. The day nursery, by definition, knows better than the parents what is good for their children. Sheltered from open criticism, since it exercises a monopoly for these services, it substitutes its own norms for those of parents'. The institution takes initiatives which parents are supposed to observe and extend in the home:

"Before admission to the day nursery, we explain to parents what is expected of them, that is to say, they are expected to continue at home what has begun at the center, e.g., education in cleanliness.

"Initiative originates from the day nursery. We keep children the whole day and understand better what should be done."

In day nurseries, where a *de facto* segregation of families of the lower social classes occurs, similar comments abound:

"This is a parking lot for babies. It is rare that parents show interest in their child. Perhaps this is due to lack of time. Parents attach great importance to the physical activities (crying, eating) and very little to other activities."

Towards parents of the lower social classes, who are perceived by the staff as indifferent to their children's overall development, day nurseries feel that it is their obligation to counteract the negative effects that the economic, social, and cultural handicaps of parents may produce on their offspring by various techniques and pedagogical methods. It is often forgotten that programs of education imposed from outside the family and from above, as undisputed norms, increase the feeling of inadequacy of parents and reinforce the moralizing character of the institution.

In so far as the day nursery appears to parents as invested with expert knowledge and "know-how", by virtue of which it has a right to invade the sphere of the home in order to "teach parents" how to take care of their children, how to educate them, things will remain unchanged as long as parents are left outside the decision-making process.

To summarize: the tasks ahead are formidable. As is evident from the above reports, they include the identification and bringing to the fore of the problems involved, but the setting of priorities demand that the seemingly contradictory assumptions of some of the proposed solutions be sorted out and evaluated in terms of local circumstances.

Some of the main lines of thought which emerged are:

(1) The immensity of the problem, affecting millions of people in all continents, becomes all the more intensive with increasing geographical mobility.

(2) It is necessary to establish a new infrastructure of social and allied services as well as to elaborate national policies and international cooperation with imagination, foresight, and good planning, to meet the needs created by these problems. A "holistic" approach becomes imperative as the problem cannot be met in a fragmented way, without interdisciplinary and interdepartmental action.

(3) The family remains the basic unit which will take most of the burden of meeting these difficulties when moving to new settings. Every encouragement should be given to the family to enable it to take the proper decisions and action.

(4) Finally, it was felt that, whatever social services are created and whatever economic measures are taken, however good the planning and implementation of these measures, a major element for the happiness and successful establishment of a family in a new setting is the warmth of human communication and contact and the feeling of acceptance that people, already living in a certain setting, will show to the newcomers.

LIST OF PAPERS PRESENTED

DANIELE DIASSITIS (Ecole maternelle Grèco-Française, Athens, Greece): "L'Education biculturelle, est-elle source d'équilibre ou de déséquilibre pour le jeune enfant?"

MULTINATIONAL WOMEN'S LIBERATION GROUP (Athens, Greece): "The family in the cross-cultural setting."

CLIO PRESVELOU (Department of Sociology, Catholic University of Louvain, Belgium): "Communication and exchanges between parents and day nurseries."

C. D. SPINELLIS and E. HATJIS (School of Law University of Athens, Greece): "Children of female inmates."

FAMILY SUBSTITUTES

Coordinators: BARBARA TIZARD

Institute of Education, University of London, UK

ULRICH BECKER

World Council of Churches, Geneva, Switzerland

DISCUSSIONS in the session centered on adoption and other forms of residential care of young children. Day care centers were touched upon, but discussed more fully in other sessions.

ADOPTION

Mention was made of the legal restraints and obligations dealing with adoption in different countries, and DR. HENRY M. SEIDEL (School of Medicine, Johns Hopkins University, Baltimore, MD, USA) presented a careful paper on the rights of all the direct participants in the adoption process: the child, the biological parents, and the adoptive parents. "Our society is no longer fully devoted to the attempt to deny the infant or child his biologic and social past. . . . The right to know one's biologic past may or may not be the vital key to a strong and positive sense of self."

In Western countries the desire for an adopted child greatly exceeds the number of children available for adoption. In Sweden 2000 infants and young children are adopted annually from developing countries said PROFESSOR Y. HOFVANDER (Akademiska Sjukhuset, Uppsala, Sweden), and in Switzerland the adoption of children from Latin America is big business, said DR. N. FRENCK (Pediatrician, Lausanne, Switzerland).

Discussion arose on the problems and "morality" of adopting children from a different culture. PROFESSOR HOFVANDER reported on a follow-up study of 151 adopted children from developing countries. The initial health screening on their arrival showed that only 16% were up to Swedish child health standards, but the catch-up rate was remarkable. With good nutrition and freedom from infection "it may take only a month or two to bring the child up to normal health." Problems of adaptation were not quite so easily solved. "The early problems of adaptation, at least for the older children (aged 3–5), may in part be due to communication difficulties. The child does not understand that the parents do not understand. Attempts to communicate may lead to panic or aggressive reactions and rejection of further contact. The same type of reaction may be seen in Swedish children with late speech development." But after six months or a year at most: "the percentage of children with remaining problems is small, and the problems usually mild." The general conclusion was that interracial adoption presents no special problems if the adoptive parents are well prepared and there is a receptive social environment.

The view was expressed by several speakers that children should be adopted as young as possible. DR. A. A. YAKER (National Institute of Public Health, Algiers, Algeria) advocated that it should be three months or less, saying that in many countries the legal minimum age for adoption is fixed at six months, which means that the infant has to be kept in an institution up to this age, and this is difficult to compensate for afterwards. Other speakers said that the adoption of children above the age of five years was generally "catastrophic." However, BARBARA TIZARD, Coordinator, stated that the anxieties expressed by some speakers about the success of the adoption of older children may be misplaced. "In a recent study of 30 children adopted from institutions between the ages of two and seven years (*Adoption: A Second Chance*, Barbara Tizard, Open Books, London, 1977, I found that parents who adopted children aged 4–7 years were as satisfied as those who had adopted children aged 2–4 years, and that in most cases a close mutual attachment had developed. Although the children's IQs had not, at age 8, increased since leaving the institution, and some of them had personality problems, the difficulties of those children who remained in institutions or who were restored to their natural mothers were considerably greater."

RESIDENTIAL INSTITUTIONS

While adoption was accepted as the best substitute to a good biological family, good foster homes were considered vastly preferable to residential institutions. As LEONARD DAVIS (School of Social Work, Brunel University, Bucks., UK) put it: "Residential establishments reflect a rigidity inconsistent with the present needs of society and this contributes to the long term institutionalization of too many children. A child thrives when he feels that the adults who surround him like being with him; he realizes his potential when at least one adult enjoys a continuous relationship with him, and is able to 'give' beyond the call of duty. Only rarely can the latter be achieved in residential care."

FOSTER HOMES

Several different types of foster homes were described, in particular the SOS Children's Villages, Vienna, which had been started in Austria in 1949 to rescue children who—for some reason or another—could not be adopted, from institutional life. "Everywhere in the world there are women without families of their own, who are widows or alone, but who have strong motherly feelings. Placing this motherliness on the level of social assistance is the goal of the SOS Children'sVillages." DR. H. H. REINPRECHT (SOS Children's Villages, Vienna, Austria) said 135 villages have now been established and the meeting heard reports of their operation in France, Ghana, Greece (starting), and India, as well as in Austria.

Criticism was raised that there were no residential father figures in these villages, and one system was cited by DOROTHY HEEGER in which the Durban Child and Family Welfare Agency in South Africa runs a community, with 11 children to a cottage, with young "house parents." The "mother" is employed by the agency and the "father" works in the community. Another example was given from Puerto Rico, where eight or nine children were adopted by families working in agricultural cooperatives.

A final proviso on foster care was given by DR. A. A. YAKER: "It is absolutely necessary to avoid changing children from one family to another. There are still countries where children are shifted at a certain age from foster mothers for infants to foster mothers for young children, and later to an institution."

MULTIPLE PARENTS

An example of a system that seems to lead to an enviable ease of adaptation in adult life was given to DR. CARLETON GAJDUSEK (National Institute of Health, Bethesda, MD, USA): he said that in many parts of the world where expanded kinship systems prevail, suckling infants of a few months of age have multiple mother figures, and even their nursing may be shared by several kinswomen. "In such populations, children may have several mothers and fathers before they reach school age, and the assemblage of their brothers and sisters includes all their first cousins, adopted and related by blood. Older children and adults are often unable to assign the correct biological parents to their many siblings. This is true in much of Melonesia and Micronesia. This expanded family is further complicated by adoptions in infancy and childhood—both formal and informal—which may involve a third to over half of all prepubertal children, and which makes it difficult, even often impossible, for the child to sort out his so-called 'nuclear family' within the constellation of kinship around him. But adoptions in Melanesian and Micronesian cultures are not the replacing of former parents by new parents, but the gaining of additional parents, who never fully replace the former ones. The new parents are somewhat like godfathers and godmothers in a Christian community, but they often provide residence and full support for the child, and fulfill a role far more like foster parents or adoptive parents in our society. The large extended family, only partly biological, which the child thus acquires is a source of enormous emotional support and security. It is hardly conceivable to these people that a single married couple could have unique responsibility for the rearing and socialization of their child.

"The infants and young children are usually overindulged, by Western standards, rather than deprived of love and affection. Throughout infancy the baby is in the arms of other members of their kinship group, of both sexes, for as many hours as they are in the arms of their biological mothers—and they are rarely not being carried.

"The children and adolescents of these South Pacific island cultures, emotionally secure in their self-assurance, have a remarkable ability to relate warmly to most people, to find love and friendship from foreigners, and to make themselves at home in cultural and linguistic groups remote from their own. This self-confidence in relationships with others has struck voyagers to the South Pacific for centuries. It comes as a surprise to many professionals in child behavior and development in the Western world, who consider some of the practices as forms of behavior which should weaken family ties and disrupt so-called normal family life and social development—and this is obviously not what is occurring in the adult personality development of these Pacific islanders. Many thousands of children from Melanesian cultures, particularly in Papua, New Guinea, who have been born into cultures still in the Stone Age, have already entered in a few decades into the modern technological world as active and understanding participants, with remarkable success. We should be asking what it is in the experiences of an infant and small child in these cultures that has made many of them resilient enough to accept the enormous changes imposed on them, without the emotional collapse which most of us would have expected."

LIST OF PAPERS PRESENTED

CLAUDI CATZARA (SOS Children's Village in Athens, Greece, "Quelques considérations pour une Législation regissant les villages d'enfants SOS et autres institutions similaires en Grèèce."

LEONARD DAVIS (School of Social Work, Brunel University, Bucks., UK): "For those in care there is no Friday."

D. CARLETON GAJDUSEK (National Institute of Health, Bethesda, MD, USA): "Multiple parenthood."

YNGVE HOFVANDER, STIG SJÖLIN, and CLAES SUNDELIN (Akademiska Sjukhuset, Uppsala, Sweden): "Adaptation and development of children adopted from developing countries to Sweden."

JOANNE W. MURPHY (College of Law, Ohio State University, USA): "Consideration of costs and the formulation of child care models."

CALLIOPE PAPIOANNOU (Social Worker, Athens, Greece): "Foster homes: a form of child placement worth reconsideration."

HENRY M. SEIDEL (School of Medicine, Johns Hopkins University, Baltimore, MD, USA): "The changing paradigm in adoption."

CHILDREN'S RIGHTS AND PARENTAL
RIGHTS AND OBLIGATIONS

Coordinator: MIA KELLMER-PRINGLE

National Children's Bureau, London, UK

THIS session was organized as follows: a short introductory statement by the Coordinator, the presentation of six papers by the scheduled participants—three of which are summarized here—and a general discussion accompanied by three other short papers.

In introduction, the Coordinator said that the aim of the whole symposium is to look ahead and see how, perhaps during the next 10 or 20 years, we might succeed in making children's lives happier and healthier; and also see that they are educated. "We are now about to discuss children's rights, and I think it is worth remembering that, in a society where children still go hungry, where children die of malnutrition, where many of them do not have a decent roof over their head, it is premature to talk about their psychosocial rights. There is a sort of hierarchy, as I see it, in terms of needs and rights. Until you are properly fed, until you have a proper physical home, until your parents can take care of you, it is a luxury to talk about the psychological aspects of children's rights. What we should do is to try to look ahead and see—and plan—how all children's rights can become a reality.

In the most developed countries we have the impression that children's rights are met. But that is not so at all. Parental rights are accepted quite without question in almost all countries. There are a few exceptions if there is gross maltreatment, but at the moment the scales are weighted in every country very heavily toward an almost unquestioned assumption that the parents have the right to their 'own' child, in the sense of a belonging, of a chattel. Parental obligations to the child are not stressed enough, and I believe that every right should be matched by an obligation. Children's rights, certainly in Britain, tend to invoke either laughs and giggles, or else people say: 'Oh yes, the kids are going to march on the town hall and take over!' Children's rights in fact are not as yet taken very seriously. But I see it as a very serious topic, and I hope one that will be increasingly paid attention to in the years to come, because children are the largest minority group that has no voice, no vote, very little influence, and—with a few exceptions—very few rights in law."

PROFESSOR TIMOTHY B. DAILEY (Department of Sociology, Clarkson College, New York, NY, USA) said that violence against children is usually talked about as a form of deviant behavior, but he believed that child abuse grew directly out of the basic structure of the modern nuclear family. Why is violence chosen by parents as a way of dealing with their children? First, parents have total responsibility regarding their children. They are held responsible for everything the child does. Second, children tend to be defined as ignorant and incompetent, and therefore have very low status as compared with their parents. The third aspect is that there are no institutionalized alternative ways for reducing conflict when problems are experienced within the family. If one contrasts, for example, the family structure with employer–employee relations, we see there are no unions to bargain for the children, as there are in the case of employees. In a situation of complete authority, anything the child does can be interpreted as rebellion, and the child is powerless to protest effectively. This creates a situation which makes the use of violence possible, as a way to demonstrate authority, especially among parents who have certain kinds of stresses resulting from poverty or from a deprived childhood.

Nowadays, the increasing length of childhood—of the period of dependency—due to longer schooling has also increased the length of the parents' burden of responsibility. This means that, to reduce child abuse, we need to find ways to decrease the authority of the parents. This can be done by increasing the autonomy of the child and giving him greater freedom to participate in the adult world of work. This must involve the modification, perhaps even the abolition of compulsory schooling.

PROFESSOR A. GOLDWORTH (Department of Philosophy, California State University, San Jose, CA, USA) commented: "You consider child abuse is morally wrong, but not child labor." PROFFESSOR DAILEY replied that he was thinking of children being permitted to do things which were not exploitive or physically debilitating but were stimulating and creative, such as running their own radio program.

ANTHY TRIPP (National Institute of Mental Health, Adelphi, MD, USA) opened her paper by quoting André Gide: "What will be said has been said before. But no one was listening so everything needs to be said again." She continued: "I do not think the trouble is that no one was listening but rather that listening and learning and becoming informed is not enough. For ideas to become integrated they need to be sifted through a web of emotions; what appeals to us on an emotional level stays; the other gets discarded as a collection of meaningless facts.

"In ancient Egypt infanticide was common although not legal. In Sparta children were thrown off a cliff if they were in come way deformed because Sparta was geared to raising warriors. Abraham was ready to sacrifice his own child to God. But the misuse of children, whether it was sacrifice or abandonment or excessive use in the labor force, was always attributed to some higher institution, thus leaving the individual free of guilt.[1]

"Our otherwise wise Aristotle said that 'the justice of a father is different towards his children than the ordinary citizen because one can do no injustice to one's own property.'

"In Rome the concept of *patria potestas* gave the father the right to kill, sell, or abandon his children. According to the 1646 Massachusetts 'stubborn child law' a child could be put to death for cursing his parents,and although we have no written record of this happening the spirit of the law is clear enough. The 1601 English poor law provided apprenticeships for poor children, so that they would not become destitute and criminal, and as a result bother the society of adults. The abandonment of children was common in England in the 18th century.

"Formal reform, legal and social, began during the first half of the 19th century. I will mention an incident which happens to have taken place in the United States—it could have happened anywhere. In 1874 a little girl called Mary Allen was violently beaten by her family. This came to the attention of a church lady who could find no institution to which to turn for help. Finally, she turned to the New York Society for Prevention of Cruelty to Animals, arguing that Mary Allen, as a human, belongs to the animal kingdom, and an action began. (It may be of interest to note that even in 1970 the Society for Prevention of Cruelty to Animals received more contributions than the Society of Prevention of Cruelty to Children.) It was not until 1967, in the famous Gault case, that Justice Homes ruled that: 'The bill of rights and the 14th Amendment were not made for adults only,' and some real legal rights of children began to be established in the United States, such as due process and the child's right to go through the usual adult procedures when prosecuted.

"In the Old Testament we learn that 'he that spareth his rod hateth his son' (Proverbs 13: 14), and we have all mumbled with mixed feelings about 'The old woman who lived in a shoe who had so many children she did not know what to do so she gave them some broth without any bread and beat them all soundly and sent them to bed.'

"We hit our children, yet we become nationally 'concerned' with the 'degree' of violence towards children. David Gil (*Violence against Children*), who presents a psychosocial understanding of this very difficult problem, suggests that we sometimes use this concern as a smokescreen to appease our guilt about the greater violence we commit towards them by poverty, unavailable medical care, poor housing, unemployment of their parents, and all other things which have been talked about in this meeting.

"We take children from violent parents but we let judges with no child development knowledge decide about their lives and place them in institutions they have never visited and which are worse than the place they were removed from. The personal prejudices and the idiosyncratic child-rearing beliefs of judges, social workers, etc., when it comes to court decisions, count more than the cultural patterns and attitudes of parents, which we do not even bother to take into consideration.

"We meet and discuss, yet little seems to change.

"I should like to offer observations on three key elements in the process that need to be mobilized if we are to translate theory into action. One deals with our personal psychological, possibly unconscious, attitudes towards children. The second deals with our professional biases and shortcomings. The third deals with the missing link, that vast, available, yet under-utilized resource: the parent.

"1. On the personal level, we are possibly mourning our own childhood, based on the myth, aided by our collective memory, that childhood is the happy lost paradise that we shall never have again; so we take our unconscious regrets out, so to speak, on children, by not meeting their needs. After all they have their precious youth and life ahead of them.

"As we move from the childhood age of dependence to the age of dependence of old age, we frantically try to provide for what is to come. Maybe if we 'remembered' the first age of dependence with less panic, our own old age would not appear so helpless. Maybe if we cared for our children more gently they might be more willing to care for us when they are in the position of power.

"We are a utilitarian society, and since children are 'useless,' cannot contribute to the labor force, have no vote, no political clout, and are not an economic asset our ambivalence about them overcomes our good intentions.

"The attitude of 'do now pay later,' very pronounced in human nature as exemplified by cigarette smoking, makes it hard to seriously take account of the long range effects of our negligence.

"When it comes to children, our divisions along racial, political, religious, and economic lines are more powerful (since they are based on emotion) than our knowledge and information about the significance of childhood.

"The fact that larger numbers of children are now helped to survive makes it easier not to question the quality of these quantities we help survive. Yet interference with nature holds its own responsibilities.

"This list is not meant to be complete; it just tries to concentrate on some unpopular issues to disturb our smugness, particularly at a time when we are possibly feeling that we are doing something particularly innovative and creative.

"2. On the professional level we have, for technical and practical reasons, specialized and compartmentalized our training, our professions, and the services we offer. In the process we split the lives of children into 'psyche and soma'[2] and into the subdivisions health, mental health, nutrition, education, and social needs. But because the holistic approach is imperative, we now find ourselves having to try to put children 'back together again.'

"We also tend to become serious, scientific, supercilious, and condescending, protecting ourselves with knowledge. We are not heard because we speak jargon; we are not effective because we often appeal only to the intellect. When we appeal to feelings, we are often over sentimental and try to shock our audience with extremes.

"We have split, and continue to split, services for children according to their income. But services for poor children are poor services, and often tend to attract poor underpaid staff. We get carried away by ethnicity dictating local solutions, and tend to forget that this may perpetuate the vicious cycle of poverty, helplessness, and lack of opportunity. Overconcentration on high risk children, which are in a way more visible (and guilt producing), lets the great majority of average children fall between the cracks.

"The development of concern about the children has been fueled by the necessity to deal with extremes, such as poverty, child abuse, and so on. So much so, that it often seems that to have services available to a child, it must first be arrested!

"What we need is a balance between universal and selective services, which will not only meet the needs of all children but also improve the quality of services.

"3. The third missing link between theory and practice is the parent. We misuse children not only when we misuse their parents but when we do not use their potential strength as a powerful lobby for change. For all our abstract concern about the anonymous child, I am sure that parents (with all their shortcomings) love and care about their children the most. Between theory and reality, between plan and practice, stand parents. We do not seem to use the consumer of our services in the way other professionals do. Are we bothered about the education of parents on a large scale (as, for example, through television) because knowledge will give them power, and their demands may distort our professional directions? F. D. Roosevelt once said to a delegation: 'OK, you have convinced me; now go out and bring pressure on me.'

"I would suggest that the impact of such pressure will create beneficial results, which will outweigh the initial perturbations in our professions.

"I have talked about three levels of concern; the personal, the professional, and the parent. While recognizing that the road forward will be fixed through structural solutions—such as income redistribution, child social indicators, and a cooperation of the researchers and child development specialists with the politicians—I still feel that there are things that we can each do.

"During the Year of the Child we can:

(a) Formally invite to our local, national, and international meetings, politicians, policy makers, and judges. They were once children, they have children, they are interested in children.

(b) Formally invite parents and, dare I say, children? Dare we say 'this meeting is open (and free) to parents and children'?

(c) Work on establishing an official Children's Day, like Mother's Day and Father's Day: a noncommercial Children's Day when we will close our shops and offices (after all we are willing to close them for dead heroes, saints, and past national victories) and give gifts to our children that are not sold any-where. Give them time, picnics, story readings, listening time, talking time, time to renegotiate their inflexible bed times. Give them responsibilities, praise. It might be an interesting experiment. It will certainly not necessarily, overnight, improve policy, but it will be a small symbolic message to those who make it, and to ourselves, that we honor children as much as adults. If the experiment does not get off the ground; if the stores cannot close; if we spend the day fixing our cars and yards; we need to think twice, because it will show that the problem is more grave than we had suspected.

(d) We can each make children who have a raw deal more visible. We can write about them, talk about them, prepare statistics about individual cases.

"Let us proceed, as the Greek poet says, with 'reason and dream.' Reason has only taken us so far. Why not work on a dream? When we shall have to compromise later (and we shall have to compromise, for reality needs to be respected or it kicks back) we shall still be ahead if the dream was good enough. Saul Alinski was right: 'Maybe it's the dark before the dawn of a beautiful world. We'll see it, when we believe it!'"[3]

REFERENCES

1. KAMMERMAN and KHAN, *Social Services in the United States,* 1976.
2. S. FRAIBURG, *Every Child's Birthright: In Defense of Mothering,* 1977.
3. S. ALINSKI, *Rules for Radicals,* New York, 1972.

CHRISTINE COOPER (Department of Child Health, University of Newcastle upon Tyne, UK) said: "In the past hundred years, Western societies have gradually moved toward recognizing that their children should have rights and should cease to be the chattels of their parents. They do not belong to their parents or to society, but to themselves in the care of their parents.

"In law, society recognizes children's rights in several ways. Compulsory education gives every child the right schooling, and parents are prosecuted if they fail to send a child to school. Parents can also be prosecuted in the Criminal Court for abusing or neglecting a child. In Scandinavia, for the past 12 years, all corporal punishment by parents or anyone else has become an offence, punishable by the Criminal Court, and I look towards a time when all countries bring in similar legislation.

"Doctors, social workers, educators, and others are still reluctant to use these laws. Professionals often condone the abuse and neglect of children by identifying with the parents' problems, by feeling unwilling to break the code of confidentiality, or by reluctance to upset parents and create a crisis in the family. The pediatrician has a particular responsibility to promote optimum child development, and in his close concern with young children, their growth and behavior, their illnesses and injuries, he is especially well placed for recognizing neglect and abuse and doing something to protect the child and help his family. When the doctor ignores the early signs of abuse or neglect, some children will die at their parents' hands and very many more will be permanently damaged—physically, intellectually, emotionally, socially, and morally, by an abusive environment.

"We have to educate professionals as well as the public to report child neglect, ill treatment, and other forms of abuse to a child protection agency. A team should then investigate the child and family to assess their needs and their problems and consider whether court protection for the child is needed. A pediatrician and a social worker are the basic staff in such a team, but other specialists, such as a child psychiatrist, psychologist, public health nurse, teacher, or others, may also be needed. A full psychosocial study of the family, leading to a 'family diagnosis,' is essential at the outset, with reassessment at intervals. Sometimes the family can best be managed by informal advice and practical help, including attention to the mother's health and well-being, and to social problems of the family. Lay helpers can form an important part of such a helping team, encouraging parents and helping with practical tasks.

"If the family does not improve, and if the child's growth and development or health are suffering, there is increasingly felt to be a need to gain control of the child's situation through the civil court because adequate parental care has broken down. The court may order formal supervision of a child at home or it may terminate parental rights. In Britain, at least, this termination of parental rights does not necessarily mean permanent removal of the child from home. After a short period of assessment and good care for the child and of assessment and help for the parents, the child may, in some cases, return home on trial. The crisis produced by the intervention is a useful tool for promoting change in family attitudes and behavior. Parents, at that point, have to face up to the reality of the child's needs that they have been unable to meet. Working through such a crisis, when the parents' inadequacies, anger, and frustration can be brought into the open in a caring atmosphere, can lead to reorientation and amelioration of attitudes. Change for the better at home and the child's improved growth and development may follow. In some cases parental rights can later be restored. If improvement is not maintained at home, placement of the child in a substitute family should be planned on a permanent basis. We have to remember how very damaged some of these parents are by their own childhood, experience and to recognize that, for some of them, their lack of capacity to parent a child properly is incurable and very damaging to the child.

"Not only violence to a child but neglect, rejection, and deprivation of nurture should be recognized as signals of grave family pathology that is harming the child's development and that will leave permanent scars on his personality and sometimes on his body. Western societies have recognized this by their laws on child protection, and the doctor, among others, must become more responsible in initiating action. Parents, in fact, are often relieved when the crisis is over that steps have been taken to help them and to help their child. Most parents love their children and want what is best for them, even if they fail to provide it.

"It is important for pediatricians to educate the legal profession with regard to the parameters of growth and development, which are measured or assessed over time, and about which the court should hear and the court should see the progress charts and photographs of the child.

"Another important step in the legal process is that the parent should be adequately informed about the court procedure, and the doctor as well as the social workers and lawyers should discuss with them exactly what they will need to say in court. The fact that it is a civil and not a criminal court should be stressed to them, and that the child's adequate care is the matter before the court. Handled in this way the court hearing should be part of a therapeutic procedure planned for the family, whether parental rights are terminated or not.

"Three case histories will illustrate several of these points:

"*John,* an 18 month old boy, was seen in a hospital casualty department with a fractured arm. He had had three earlier fractures, all said to have been caused by falls. However, the multiple minor scratches, cuts, and bruises on his face, mouth, and ear, all of different ages, and the remains of a black eye, were sure signs of ill treatment. Help was given to the parents who were both aggressive and mentally subnormal, but legal protection was not sought. This boy was killed by his father a few months later.

"*Frankie,* a 12 month old boy, was admitted to hospital with a fresh black eye, old scratches on the opposite side of his nose, and bruises on both sides of his chin and chest of a few days' duration. The parents said he had bumped himself, but such injuries are usually due to abuse. The finding of unmarried teenage parents, living in squalor and both with records of violent behavior, supported the diagnosis of inflicted injuries. Informal help was offered to the family and as far as is known no more physical injuries have occurred. The abusive environment has continued, however, with indifference, marital discord, hostile critical attitudes to the child, frequent moves and chaotic care, often shared with neighbors, and this was so damaging to the child's development that by six and a half years of age he was an aggressive and very disturbed boy, with poor speech, and unable to learn, and he had to be admitted to a child psychiatric unit. He will be permanently affected psychologically by his damaging environment.

"Finally, the case of *Debbie,* aged 8 months on admission for a minor symptom. The nursing staff noted how seldom the mother visited, and when she did come she seemed to have no interest in the child, or Debbie in her mother. On the psychosocial family study it was revealed how the mother grew up with a violent and drunken father who often beat her. As a teenager she married a violent and drunken man but left him a few weeks later already pregnant. She then cohabited with another violent and drunken youth by whom she conceived Debbie but soon left him. She requested abortion for this pregnancy, which was refused for some reason, and at birth she requested adoption. A week later she changed her mind and took the baby home but became severely depressed and the child had to go to a foster mother at three weeks of age. The mother reclaimed Debbie at five months but admitted she had never liked her. The child was placed again with the same foster parents and parental rights were terminated on the only grounds that the mother and child had a severely negative attitude to each other which was beginning to affect the child's development. The mother's own background and unstable lifestyle also played a part in the court's decision. Adoption should be possible in this case whether or not the mother agrees.

"In Britain, as in most other countries in the Western world, child protection laws are confused. The recent Children Act 1975 does give more protection to children, but three other acts are also involved, and sometimes others as well. There are six ways in which parental rights can be terminated, each with different criteria on which the case will be judged. There are four different kinds of court with different rules of procedure where cases may be heard. A single court, dealing with family problems would probably be better."

During the ensuing discussion, R. VON EULER (Save the Children Federation, Stockholm, Sweden) said that it was not enough to leave the rights of children to their parents or to the legal system—the courts. Children needed their own ombudsman, or spokesman. HELEN ROCHAS (Regional Center for the Development of Education, Fresno, CA, USA) said that a lay therapist system set up in California had been found to work well. Middle-aged couples, who had been loving parents but whose children had now grown up, acted as lay therapists to three or four "abusing families." They became family friends, calling on them on birthdays and festivals and generally keeping in touch. When the "abusing family" had a problem and became stressed ("and that's when parents abuse their children") it called up the lay therapists who were available 24 hours a day. It was found that this informal system worked better than relying on the courts for the protection of children. She then added that she understood that there was very little child abuse in countries with an extended family system; where there are grandparents, aunts, uncles, and godparents who look after the child when its own parents are under stress.

Before closing the meeting, the Coordinator asked: "What are children's rights? As I see it they are sevenfold:

"(1) To be a wanted child; not to be conceived casually and irresponsibly but to have been chosen deliberately.
"(2) To have a permanent loving home and to be given continuous consistent care.
"(3) To be given new experiences to widen his horizons; stimulate language and

intellectual development. Play has an essential role as through it the child explores, imitates, and learns to understand the internal and external world.

"(4) To be given praise and recognition for effort rather than actual achievement: otherwise the slow learner and the handicapped child is additionally deprived of an essential sense of success and achievement.

"(5) To be given a sense of responsibility—like all skills it needs to be practiced and mistakes are inevitable as a part of learning. This includes responsibility for younger children and eventually of being parents. A recent national study in Britain shows that young people themselves would welcome much more preparation for parenthood while still at school.

"(6) To be treated as an individual with a unique personality, assets and weaknesses, and not as a chattel and the parents' personal belonging.

"(7) The right to be heard. A recent study of young people aged 12 to 15 who have grown up in institutional care has shown how well young people are able to express their needs and the shortcomings of the treatment meted out to them. They prepared a charter of rights and listed what should be changed.

"If the above needs are not met by parents, then the crucial issue is how best to complement, supplement, and compensate for what is lacking; or if parental care is actually damaging to the child in a serious way, then to provide substitute family care.

"There are three major principles which would go a long way towards ensuring that these rights are met. First, a national commitment to the well-being of children, especially the youngest age group. If paramountcy were to be accorded to the child's best interests, it would affect the setting of priorities in many areas, including central and local government policy as well as industry and commerce.

"The second principle is to accept parents as full partners with the professionals who plan and staff the services provided for children.

"The third principle lies in the recognition that no single department of local or central government, and no single profession, has 'the key' either to promoting children's all-round development or to providing solutions to disadvantage and handicap. Hence interdepartmental and interdisciplinary cooperation are essential. Community resources, including voluntary workers, self-help organizations and the whole range of voluntary bodies, must be included."

LIST OF PAPERS PRESENTED

CHRISTINE COOPER (Department of Child Health, University of Newcastle upon Tyne, UK): "Children, doctors and the law."

TIMOTHY B. DAILEY (Department of Sociology, Clarkson College, New York, NY, USA): "Power breeds violence."

SANDOR KOMLOSI (Teacher Training College, Pecs, Hungary): "Present-day value system by parents."

THEOLOGOS KOUNTOURIS (Mekanel Technical Co., Athens, Greece): "The effect of the declaration of the rights of the child since it has been signed."

SPIROS A. CHAROCOPOS (Department of Pediatrics, University of Salonika, Greece): "Les droits de l'enfant."

Kɪᴋɪ V. Roe (School of Medicine, University of California at Los Angeles, USA): "Empathy, parental physical punishment and internalisation of values in children."

Aɴᴛʜʏ Tʀɪᴘᴘ (National Institute of Mental Health, Adelphi, MD, USA): "The rights of children, past and present."

Rɪɢᴍᴏʀ ᴠᴏɴ Eᴜʟᴇʀ (Save the Children Federation, Stockholm, Sweden): "The child and violence."

3

The Child and Education

THE PARENTAL ROLE IN EDUCATION

CHAIRMAN'S INTRODUCTION

NORBERTO BOTTANI

THE THEME of the child and education is extremely complex because, in order to foresee the future we need an accurate evaluation of the long past history of the education of children. I am not at all sure that a valid interpretation of this history really exists, but I hope that our discussions may enable us to see some of its lines of development more clearly.

In a panoramic view of the long history of education, two contradictory models appear: the family model and the institutional model.

According to the first model, children's education takes place within the family circle (the extended or nuclear family, or the single parent family), since the family is considered the natural, ordained, and unique setting for this purpose. Consequently everything must be done to assist and sustain the family in its task of educating its children.

According to the second model, the child's education takes place outside the family. In this case, education is considered such an important task that it can only be entrusted to experts, to teachers (and today we would add, to specialists) who alone can ensure its success. It is apparent that the family is quite unable to take on this task. Consequently we justify specialized education that takes the children away from their parents. This model has formed the subject of at least two famous utopias: Plato's *Republic* and Rousseau's *Emile*.

The first model is the subject of our present discussion, and I am most interested to learn more of the kinds of parents who are actively involved in the education of their children. At the same time we must not forget that there are many parents who do not concern themselves at all with their children's education. There is also a considerable scepticism about the role and function of parents in this respect.

It is surprising how many books have recently been published that criticize—sometimes very severely—the part played by parents in the upbringing of their children. These books—many of them novels—open up the hidden life of the family, often revealing the skeletons in the cupboards of supposedly happy *ménages*. We cannot ignore their testimony and I should like to quote from a recent novel, *Corrections,* by an Austrian writer, Thomas Bernhard, which recounts the history of a family: "The family is a tragedy. Our parents create a miserable, stinking world for us [the children], which has no concern for us, which destroys us and desires to overwhelm us. It is essential for these atrocious conditions to be changed so that we may at last be able to say that we could live, at least for a certain time, in our own world."

The point Bernhard wishes to make is that this "tragedy" can be "corrected." Further, that this "correction" can take many different forms. More than 2000 years have passed since the terrible "correction" which Orestes inflicted upon his mother Clytemnestra. Perhaps that symbolic act has served to prevent other such terrible corrections.

SOME VIEWS ON THE CHILD AND EDUCATION

AKIHIRO CHIBA

Education Section, UNESCO, Paris, France

TOMORROW's world lives within today's child, and it is therefore important to review the present status of education of the child in the world. Thanks to intense efforts made by the developing countries, an unprecedented increase in school enrolment was achieved in the 1960s and 1970s. Yet nearly 40% of school age children do not benefit from school education in developing countries. The enrolment of girls lags far behind that of boys. Furthermore, nearly 50% of those enrolled at Grade 1 drop out before reaching Grade 4. In contrast to the industrialized countries, where universal primary education has been taken for granted for more than a decade and where universal secondary education is rapidly being approached, about half of the children in developing countries will not have opportunities to attend primary schools. In order to achieve universal primary education by 1985, the developing countries will have to treble their average enrolment increase attained in the 1960s.

To offer maximum educational opportunities for all the world's children the international community is required to redouble its effort to support the world's least privileged children, deprived of adequate educational opportunity.

Problems of education and children differ from country to country, from one stage of development to another, or from one culture to another. There exists no universally applicable formula to solve the problems. The solution must be sought in each individual context and must be found with the maximum participation of and consultation with all concerned.

To maximize educational opportunities and to create meaningful educational environments, educational authorities are reminded to take into consideration, not only the development of formal education, but also out of school education and informal or incidental learning processes for children. Innovative approaches in the development of education are imperative for preschool or early childhood education. The role of parents and society should be to actively support and enrich these educational processes.

Education of the child should not seek to create a miniature adult of yesterday—perhaps ill fitted for the uncertainty and challenges of the future. It is essential to create young people capable of problem solving, imbued with imagination, creativity, and spontaneity. The role of parents and society should be directed toward facilitating maximum responsible participation of children in living and life tasks.

THE PARENTAL ROLE IN EDUCATION AND CHILD DEVELOPMENT

EDITH H. GROTBERG

Department of Health, Education, and Welfare, Washington, DC, USA

THE PARENTAL role in the education and development of their children is one aspect of family functioning which addresses both the strengths and weaknesses of that functioning and the need for outside support, intervention, and/or policy. This role is of increasing interest in the United States of America and emerges from recent issues in social policy, cumulative research findings, and programmatic experiences. The presentation being made will attempt to: (1) identify some of the issues in social policy; (2) trace and synthesize the various relevant research findings and briefly describe some exemplary programs; and (3) explore implications for the future. The purpose of this format is to clarify the factors contributing to identifying and resolving problems relating to children and their families and to recognize the role of research, development, demonstration, and evaluation, in contributing to identifying and resolving the problems.

ISSUES IN SOCIAL POLICY

One major policy issue in the United States of America concerning parents revolves around the notion of government intervention or, as is stated by some, government intrusion, on the parents and other family members. The issue is about the extent of such intervention and the challenge is to provide services without jeopardizing parental and family rights. There are a number of family-related goals which the government may try to achieve in order to increase the well-being of parents and families, and improve their quality of life without violating the rights and privacy of families. These parent–family related goals are summarized as follows:

(a) To provide services to families and children to increase cohesiveness of the family and to encourage its independence in its child-rearing capacity.
(b) To ensure that alternative care arrangements meet minimum federal and state standards based on research findings of the effects of day time care and on experience in the administration of such programs. These standards include continuity of care, a high ratio of adults to children, cleanliness and nutritional adequacy, safety, health services, and a stimulating environment.
(c) To make it possible for parents to become more involved in the lives of their children.
(d) To help parents understand the process of child growth and development.
(e) To provide assistance that will increase the possibility of the family staying together rather than being separated.

(f) To utilize the strengths of different cultural and ethnic values and different family forms.

The government is challenged to develop social policies leading to the achievement of these goals. One critical role the government can play in achieving these goals is to monitor social changes that affect family functioning and parenting.

MONITORING SOCIAL CHANGE

The conditions of society change, sometimes dramatically and radically, sometimes slowly. Many of these changes affect the family as the basic social institution, and need to be monitored to determine what new policies are necessary to assure the well-being of the family and to help parents in their child-rearing, education, and child development roles. The social changes most directly affecting the family, and particularly families with children, concern broad social changes, changes in the status of women and their work role, and changes in the family structure itself. These changes, because of their importance to parents and their children, require continued monitoring. The changes are:

(1) Large increases in the proportion of women who work, both full and part time:

    (a) increased numbers with children under 6;
    (b) increased numbers with children under 3.

(2) Growing numbers of children living in families headed by women:

    (a) higher divorce ratios;
    (b) higher rates of births out of wedlock.

(3) Attitudes of women regarding their role in society:

    (a) right to work;
    (b) right to child care;
    (c) equality.

(4) Expansion and increasing specialization of the human service occupations.
(5) Continued long term trends toward urbanization and suburbanization.
(6) Greater availability and use of a growing number of birth control techniques as well as a decline in birthrates.

These changes not only must be monitored in terms of their effect on family well-being but also in terms of their impact on the role of the parents in the education and development of their children. In addition to monitoring change, the government plays a critical role in supporting research on the family and on the parental role in the education and development of children.

RESEARCH ON PARENTAL ROLES

In order for the government to formulate policies on what services, what intervention, what supports, and what information are important to help parents in their role in the education and development of their children, the research must be able to answer the following questions:

(1) What is the parental role in the education and development of children?

    (a) What are critical differences in effectiveness?

    (b) What are critical skills?

(2) What kinds of parent involvement in programs for children affect the education and development of children?

    (a) Short term effects?

    (b) Long term effects?

(3) How are parenting skills developed?

    (a) Parent involvement and education programs.

    (b) Exploring childhood: a curriculum for adolescents.

1. Parental Role

Studies that examine the characteristics of parents which are related to the education and early development of children tend to focus on differentials in cognitive and language achievement and emotional development of the children. While a great deal of research has been conducted, Emma E. Werner and Ruth S. Smith,[1] probably summed up the critical factors best in their longitudinal study, *Kauai's Children Come of Age*. A summary of the study and the follow-up data present succinctly the critical role of parents in the education and development of their children.

The entire population of children born on Kauai in 1955 was assessed at birth, at age one, age two, age 10, and age 18. The 1977 book reports on these children at age 18 and incorporates all the previous data presented in the first book, *Children of Kauai*, 1971. The purpose of the assessments was to determine the relationship of birth stress or complications to developmental problems which might take the form of mental retardation, learning disabilities, need for mental health treatment, and, in adolescence, delinquency, crime, drug abuse, sex offenses, and school drop-outs.

The relationship between birth stress and continued developmental and behavior problems was, indeed, established, but with very clear and important qualifications. One of these qualifications was that poverty alone is not a cause of developmental and behavioral problems. Most families in poverty raise their children successfully and cope with the problems associated with birth stress. What is important, however, is a combination of factors, including poverty, which culminate in problems. Thus, if a family is unstable, the mother has little education, and there is poverty, the birth stress will lead to continuous developmental and behavioral probl ms. Poverty, then, adds to the problem; it does not seem to create it.

The second qualification concerns the relationships of parents with their children. When parents are educationally stimulating and emotionally supportive of their children, particularly those who have had birth stress, the subsequent problems associated with birth stress are minimized or eliminated. The nature of educational stimulation and emotional support is defined as follows:

"We rated *educational stimulation* by considering the opportunities provided by the home for enlarging the child's vocabulary, the intellectual interests and activities in the home, the values the family placed on education, the work habits emphasized in the home, the availability of learning supplies, books, and periodicals, and the opportunities for exploring the larger environment (library use, special lessons, recreational activities). To rate *emotional support* we examined the information in the interview on interpersonal relations between parents and child, on kind and amount of reinforcement used, on methods of discipline and ways of expressing approval, on the presence and absence of traumatic experiences, and on opportunities provided for satisfactory identification" (pp. 43–44).

It seems quite clear that educational stimulation and emotional support from parents are the critical factors in differentiating children's education and development.

2a. *Parental Involvement in Programs*

A good deal of research has increasingly focused on parent involvement in programs which are designed to increase the ability of parents to enhance the education and development of their children. Virtually all of the recent and current research relating to parent involvement, however, focus on low income parents and their children. Those few studies, which include middle income and mixed socioeconomic groups, use these groups mainly for comparison purposes. Almost without exception the parent involved is the mother. Few fathers have participated in these programs; those who have are apt to have participated either in decision-making positions or in programs designed to increase the skill of the father for his own development. The programs studied fall into two kinds of parent involvement: (1) the parents are the major focus of training, and (2) the children are the major focus of training.

(1) Programs which are largely parent-oriented training programs include training parents to work in the home with their own children, using television as a media of instruction and training parents through group discussion techniques.

In almost all the studies in which mothers are trained to be tutors of their own children in their homes, the children showed greater immediate gains in intellectual, conceptual, or language development. These findings occur in projects involving home visits only, in preschool projects operated in the home, in preschool plus home-visiting projects, and in projects in which the mothers are trained to work at home with their children but receive few if any home visits. Joyce Lazar and Judith Chapman[2] report that in four studies, parent teaching with or without a preschool component resulted in greater immediate effect on children's language, intellectual or academic achievement than a preschool program only. In one project which was concerned with infants before one year of age, superiority of the experimental group children was not maintained at age two if parent teaching was terminated at one year of age, but it was maintained if parent teaching continued until the child reached age two.

Though relatively few studies have included a follow-up of these home-teaching programs, those which did usually report that gains continued to be apparent. In two projects having only a home visit and which initiated parent teaching after age one, IQ levels remained significantly above or at the initial testing. In two projects involving preschool plus home visits, experimental group children showed beneficial effects without further parent teaching upon entering school and through the middle primary grades.

The few results available on the impact of parent teaching in association with mass media child development efforts suggest that parent encouragement and parent–child activities associated with educational television programs for young children may enhance the cognitive gains made by the children as a result of the television program.[2]

Though difficult, it is possible to engage a sizeable proportion of low income mothers of preschool shildren in groups to discuss concerns about themselves, their communities, and their children. A number of studies have reported that the skill and sensitivity of the group leader or trainer is crucial in getting the attendance of the parents and in subsequently engaging them in active participation in the group. While those parents who attend such groups represent a self-selected population which no doubt differs from the nonattending parents, those who do attend generally express positive feelings about the effect of the group experience on themselves and on the behavior of their children. A number of studies have reported greater success in gaining attendance and participation of mothers when the content of the program was specific, such as language development, rather than sensitivity training or general discussions of child development. Two studies have reported greater immediate gains on the tests utilized for the children when the mothers took part in a structural language curricula than when other types of discussion groups were utilized.[2]

(2) Programs which focus on children with some parent involvement may have the parent component as a secondary or even incidental emphasis. However, among these studies, children in a preschool program tend to show greater immediate mean gains in IQ and achievement when their parents participate in a parent educational component aimed at increasing cognitive development.

Hess[3] found five features which related to the impact of the program on children where parent involvement occured. The more a program concentrated on parents, the more substantial the IQ gains by the children, with one-to-one teacher–pupil relationships being more effective than group teaching situations. Home visits were particularly effective. While no relationship was found between the type of curriculum used by the parents (e.g., verbal interaction vs. sensori-motor) and the magnitude of effects, more-structured activities were more effective than less-structured activities.

2b. *Parent Involvement in Head Start*

Head Start, by law, is required to involve parents in the program. The involvement may be limited to attendance at meetings, membership on a parents' advisory council, or direct participation in the daily program with their children. This range of involvement has been studied to determine the impact of various kinds of involvement on parental satisfaction, development of improved parental skills, and significant changes in the education and development of their children.

In reviewing a number of studies of Head Start programs, Mann *et al.*[4] describe positive impact on parent's satisfaction with the child's educational gains, parent's confidence in understanding and rearing the child, and parent's self-confidence and coping ability. Bissell[5] cites evidence of parallels between the developmental goals of particular models or programs, and the particular changes in parental attitudes. She found increases in maternal verbal communication, maternal praise regulation, child verbal responsiveness, and child success. Mann also reported increases in parental participation in subsequent school programs.[4]

When parents participate in a program which is home based, there are also positive benefits for the family. Evaluations of Home Start found significant differences between Home Start mothers and control mothers in a number of areas: allowing children to help with household tasks, teaching reading and writing to their children, providing books and toys for their children, and reading stories to their children. Improvements were also noted on measures of maternal teaching style and verbal interaction, and in involvement in community organizations.

A review of 67 studies,[4] including parent involvement in Head Start and Home Start programs, leads to these conclusions:

(a) The critical factor appears to be establishing some kind of change in the parent's behavior that will carry over to the parent's interactions with the child and other members of the family. Thus, parent education projects, which emphasize traditional classroom techniques of providing the parent with *information,* do not appear to be as effective in producing gains in the child's development, as do parent training projects which emphasize the development of new parental skills.[6, 7] Modes of parent involvement that attribute a greater sense of importance and responsibility to the parental role appear to be most effective, even though the specific nature of the involvement may differ. White[7] found that, within parent training programs, one curriculum did not seem significantly better than another, and professional teachers and social workers were no more effective in training parents than paraprofessionals. Parent participation, both in decision-making roles and in learner roles, has been found to be associated with gains in child development measures, according to a 1972 study by MIDCO Educational Associates, and the extent of participation was more important than the type of participation.[4] In reviewing findings concerning parent involvement in intervention projects, Bronfenbrenner[6] argues that "a home-based program is effective to the extent that the target of intervention is neither the child nor the parent, but the parent–child system" (p. 34). In line with this, he concludes that the younger the child is when parent intervention is initiated, the more substantial the gains that will accrue; parent intervention delayed until the time the child is school-aged does not appear to produce comparable gains.

(b) An advantage of involving parents in the intervention process is that benefits have shown up in younger siblings of the children actually enrolled in the program. Bronfenbrenner suggests that the effectiveness of this strategy would be magnified if fathers and other family members were involved, although so far most projects have worked exclusively with mothers.[7]

3. *Developing Parenting Skills*

The importance of parenting skill in the education and development of children was recently underscored in a study, *the Persistence of Preschool Effects*.[8] This study examined data from 10 preschool programs which began before 1969 and for which follow-up data were collected over the years up until today. The 10 projects formed a consortium in 1975 to pool their data and have recently issued the *Persistence* report. They found that the preschool programs studied had long term impact even 10–15 years after leaving the program. However, any program that had a goal for parents or involved parents had greater impact on the education and development of their children over time.

No one had expected these findings as recently as two years ago, but they have had the effect of strengthening the argument for expanded preschool programs and increased emphasis on parenting education.

The interest in parenting education has focused not only on present parents but also on prospective parents. A major program for future parents is Education for Parenthood through use of a curriculum, *Exploring Childhood: A Curriculum for Adolescents*. The program, developed for the Administration for Children, Youth, and Families by the Education Development Center, Newton, Massachusetts, has been in operation for several years.

The curriculum would be useful for teenage parents and in centers for parents. It has been used as part of the Head Start program where parents with children under the age of three are involved.

SUMMARY STATEMENT AND IMPLICATIONS
FOR THE FUTURE

The role of the government in formulating policies that affect families should include monitoring social change, assessing the impact of policies on families, supporting research addressing the needs of families, and providing opportunities for parents, present or prospective, to acquire the information and skills needed for the education and development of their children. When parents cannot contribute to the education and development of their children, then the alternative care arrangements must meet standards of high quality and must respect cultural differences.

The research on parenting provides a good deal of knowledge about what characteristics of parents are critical to the education and development of children; what kinds of parental involvement promote the education and development of their children; and what kinds of programs effect changes in parenting behavior and attitudes to enhance the education and development of children.

Parents, in fact, have been discovered as critical to the education and development of their children. The implications of this fact are not readily picked up by many services and professionals, even when the data suggest the need for changes in relationships. Research which helps determine new relationships of families with a variety of services and professionals is already highlighting some ways to improve the relationships.

Finally, parents are not teachers in the same way that certified teachers are. Parents are much more than that. They provide love, security, continuity, and overall concern. The ways they interact with their children, the ways they rear them, however, have important effects on the education and development of their children in childhood and, indeed, over time. To the extent government-supported research helps parents function more effectively, to the extent the government is alert to new problems affecting parents, to the extent the government changes or generates policies to enhance parent functioning, the parental role in the education and development of their children is supported, enhanced, and honored. The parents and children of tomorrow are the beneficiaries.

REFERENCES

1. EMMA E. WERNER and RUTH S. SMITH, *Kauai's Children Come of Age,* The University of Press of Hawaii, Honolulu, 1977. General Mills American Family Report 1976–77, *Raising Children in a Changing Society,* Minneapolis, Minnesota, 1977.
2. JOYCE B. LAZAR and JUDITH CHAPMAN, *A Review of the Present Status and Future Research Needs of Programs to Develop Parenting Skills,* Prepared for the Interagency Panel on Early Childhood Research and Development, Washington, DC, George Washington University, Social Research Group, April 1972.
3. R. D. HESS, Effectiveness of home-based early education programs, paper presented at the meeting of the American Psychological Association, Washington, DC, 1976.
4. A. J. MANN, A. HARRELL and M. HURT, *A Review of Head Start Research Since 1969, An Annotated Bibliography,* Social Research Group, the George Washington University, Washington DC.
5. J. S. BISSELL, The cognitive effects of preschool programs for disadvantaged children, in J. L. Frost (ed.), *Revisiting Early Childhood Education.* Holt, Rinehart and Winston, Inc., New York, 1973.
6. U. BRONFENBRENNER, *A Report on Longitudinal Evaluations of Preschool Programs,* Volume, II, *Is Early Intervention Effective?* (DHEW Publication No. OHD-74-24), Department of HEW, Office of Child Development, Washington DC, 1974.
7. S. H. WHITE, M. C. DAY, P. K. FREEMAN, S. A. HARTMAN and K. P. MESSENGER, *Federal Programs for young children: Review and recommendations,* Vol I-III, U.S. Department of Health, Education and Welfare, Washington DC, 1973.
8. I. LAZAR et al., *The Persistence of Preschool Effects,* DHEW Publications No (OHDS) 78-30130.

DISCUSSION

MICHAEL RUTTER

Institute of Psychiatry, University of London, UK

DR. GROTBERG has provided a useful summary of the parental qualities that influence children's development and of the results of preschool programs in which parents and teachers work together. However, a careful appraisal of the empirical research which constitutes the basis for her conclusions shows that the findings are much more contradictory and uncertain than she implies. The favorable parental qualities she lists are plausible, but our knowledge of how far these are in fact influential is quite limited and does not warrant such firm conclusions.

The effects of most preschool programs have been quite modest and not very persistent. The broad-based approach she advocates is reasonable and likely to be beneficial, but it is misleading to suggest that long-lasting gains of great magnitude can be achieved.

In considering the parental role in education, it is not enough to detail parental assets and limitations. We must also ask why parents behave in the way they do.[1,2] The answer does not lie simply in the information available to them. First, there is the influence of the parents' own childhood experiences. Adults who have suffered a severely disrupted home life during their childhood are more likely to show problems in parenting. The association is not inevitable, however, in that individuals who marry and bear children late and those who marry someone from a more favored background tend to be more successful parents. Second, parents are influenced in their behavior by events in the postnatal period. Thus, forced separation of mother and child may inhibit the development of parent–child relationships. Third, how parents behave toward their children is in part a function of the characteristics of the children themselves. The fourth influence on parenting is the very experience of bringing up children. Several studies have shown that parents respond differently to their second child compared with the way they dealt with their first born. Fifth, and most important, is the wider social environment. Rutter and Quinton[3] found that marital discord and maternal depression were much more common among working class women living in inner city areas; and the particular stresses of child rearing for women of low social status have been well demonstrated by Brown and Harris.[4] It remains unclear why inner city life should provide such strains on families and on parenting, but it is evident that the wider social environment does indeed have an important impact. Parenting must be considered in its social context, and it is essential that we strive to provide people with the living conditions and social circumstances which facilititate good parenting.

REFERENCES

1. M. RUTTER and N. MADGE, *Cycles of Disadvantage*, Heinemann, London (1976).

2. M. RUTTER, Maternal deprivation 1972-1978: new findings, new concepts, new approaches, *Child Development* (in press) (1978).
3. M. RUTTER and D. QUINTON, Psychiatric disorder—ecological factors and concepts of causation, H. McGurk (ed.), *Ecological Factors in Human Development*, North-Holland, Amsterdam (1977).
4. G. W. BROWN and T. HARRIS, *Social Origins of Depression: A Study of Psychiatric Disorder in Women*, Tavistock, London (1978).

PARENTS AND TEACHERS AS EDUCATORS

JACK and BARBARA TIZARD

Institute of Education, University of London, UK

DURING the 1950s and 1960s there was, in most industrial countries, an enormous increase in the amount of preschool provision. Today, France and Belgium in western Europe, and the German Democratic Republic in eastern Europe, probably offer the most comprehensive services. But all other industrial countries have provided much more than in the past, and the American sociologist Sheila Kammerman has predicted that within the next few years governments will be obliged to provide or take responsibility for a nursery service available for all children from the age of three, whose parents choose to avail themselves of it.

The same considerations apply to the under-threes; in France and Belgium, for example, 23% of two year olds are already in *écoles maternelles* and in England and Wales 19% of two year olds receive some sort of day care, almost all of it part time.

In short, the political pressures for early child care and education to become universally available for children whose parents desire this are likely to be comparable in their effects to the pressures which have brought about changes in other social legislation and provision for higher education, for example, for divorce, for family allowances, for equal pay, for abortion, for pensions.

Nurseries, creches, kindergarten, and so on have been established through the education authorities, and in these children are cared for and educated largely by professional staff. Parents bring the children to a center and take them home at the end of the day, but they usually spend little time in the nursery and often know little of what goes on in it.

During the 1960s and 1970s we have become aware that there is something seriously amiss with services, particularly for young children, which largely exclude parents. Thus in 1963, in England, the Plowden Report on children and their primary schools argued that education "will only succeed to the full if it carries parents into partnership." At the time no one in Britain publicly disagreed with this splendid aim, but equally no one spelled out exactly what it would mean to translate it into practice.

The term partnership would certainly seem to imply, at the least, that the parties involved have an *equal status,* and mutually agreed aims, and that they *consult together and inform each other about their activities.* For parents to be partners of teachers *in* the school, radical changes in educational practice would be needed. Equally, if partnership refers to coordinated work in separate spheres, the teacher at school, the parent at home, considerable consultation about aims and methods would be needed. In either case, a *two-way flow* of opinion and information would be a necessary part of the relationship.

At present, such communication as occurs is much more likely to be a one-way flow from the teacher to the parent. It will not normally be a report about what the

221

teacher has been doing, how she has been carrying out her responsibilities, but rather instructions to the parents about what *they* should do—they should send their child to school on time, send him to bed early, talk to him more, play with him more, see that he does his homework, and so on.

Much recent interest in involving parents in education, in fact, arises from the belief that most parents are inadequate: they need to be changed so as to become more like teachers. This "deficit" view of parents underlies most schemes for parent education and home visits; and pressure for parents to help in schools and creches is often because of the assumption that they can learn from watching teachers. The question of what teachers can learn from parents is rarely canvassed. It is convenient for teachers to attribute a child's lack of progress in school to his *parents'* lack of interest, or their failure to stimulate him. There is, however, an alternative, less comfortable inference—that the failure or lack of interest of a child in school reflects rather the failure of the *school* to teach him.

After all, as educators, parents clearly have enormous assets—they are usually intensely concerned for their child's future, they have an intimate knowledge of him, and they are able to give him much more individual attention than he can get in school. If, then, one was able to harness parental energies for education, children would indeed be expected to benefit. That this is possible has been shown in a recent research project of ours concerned with the teaching of reading to seven/eight year old children. This has been carried out in a multiracial area of London, where families are large, both parents are usually at work, and often one or both parents speaks little English. Yet it has been possible to involve over 90% of these families over a period of two years in regularly helping their child to learn to read at home—and the results are very encouraging.

At the start of this project many of these families were seen by the teachers not as a powerful and concerned educational resource but as inadequate and overburdened—as much in need of improvement and education as their children. The teachers complained that the parents "took no interest," did not attend school meetings, spent money on the child unwisely, failed to supervise him closely, kept him up too late watching television, and so on. For their part the parents made criticisms of the school. They said that the children were inadequately supervised, not made to work hard enough, and so on. It was true that parents rarely visited the school and appeared to be uninterested in school activities; and it was also true that children were often held back in their reading because of the lack of suitable books in the school or because teachers failed to hear them read regularly and did not ensure that when a child finished one book he was given another that was interesting and appropriate.

What are the factors which prevent closer communication between teacher and parent? The first stems from the institutional framework of the school. Education takes place within the four walls of the school, and the teacher relates to child and parent only within the school. In this context, both child and parent often behave in limited and uncharacteristic ways. This is particularly true of working class families; but even middle class parents tend to feel inhibitions on entering a school. And the teacher is almost bound to operate with an inaccurate stereotype of the parents; she does not know how families behave in a more natural setting, the ways in which they cope with their environment, what they expect of their children, and what they teach them. Few teachers know who are the significant people in the lives of their children, how their time out of school is spent, what skills and interests they display outside the school context, where their emotional energy is embedded.

Equally, the life of the school is generally hidden from the parent. Except in nurseries, the parent is rarely able to spend time in the classroom to find out what his child is learning and how he functions at school. It is not only the classroom which has closed doors; the parent will also not be able to enter the staffroom. Maintaining social distance between parent and teacher in this way, is, however, bound to create communication problems.

Secondly, even if teachers *inform* parents about what goes on in the school they rarely *explain* it. Yet for parents to understand what the teacher is doing, a massive education program may be needed. This is particularly true at the present time, when teaching methods are constantly changing. Parents may, for example, be totally mystified by the methods used to teach reading and number work to six year olds. And even in nurseries we have found that parents who have spent a lot of time watching or helping the staff, cannot explain, or have quite false ideas of why the play activities are provided. We asked 150 working class parents of children attending nursery school why the school provided various materials. Between a fifth and a half could offer no explanation, or offered explanations very far from the teachers' purposes: for example, it was suggested that sand was provided to remind children of the seaside, water play to teach them the danger of water, a play house (domestic corner) to teach them to keep the house tidy.

Without an understanding of the teacher's goals and methods, parents are bound to feel alienated from the school, and even from their child; they will be quite unable to engage in an educational dialogue with the teacher, help their child at home, or even discuss his school with him.

A third source of difficulty arises when there are major differences in values between the home and the school. These may be manifested in relatively trivial ways, e.g. the decoration and furnishing of the school would often have been very different if chosen by the parents. Other, major differences in educational aims between teachers and parents may be quite implicit. In Britain, for example, nursery and primary teachers tend to value "creativity" and "play"; they are distressed when the "products" of the young child—paper daubed with paint, or pieces of wood nailed precariously together—are received unappreciatively by the parent, who may even be seen to throw them away on the way home. This is not, usually, because the parent lacks interest in his child—a neat row of cross-stitch or a line of carefully traced writing would have been enthusiastically received. It is rather that these "creative" products have a meaning to the teacher which depends on a whole framework of knowledge (e.g. of developmental stages) and values (e.g. appreciation of modern Western art) which the parent may not share.

Similarly, the teachers' attempt to persuade parents to play with their child may founder on the different values and meanings which the parents attach to play. The teacher trained in a Piagetian–Gesellian or perhaps psychoanalytic framework, regards play as a crucial learning experience, whereas the parent is more likely to see it as a way in which the child amuses himself when there is nothing more important to do. This does not mean that the parent may not interact with his child in other useful ways; there are, for example, many alternative methods of developing linguistic and cognitive skills and fostering social relations other than through play.

One reason for the reluctance of teachers to discuss their aims and methods with parents is undoubtedly a suspicion that disagreements of this kind will emerge. So far as "progressive" educational methods are concerned, they are probably right—we have found on interviewing that most parents would like their children to learn to sit down and concentrate, and be taught to read and write at the age of four. It is understandable, therefore, that for this reason primary teachers view parents as a potential threat, and argue that teachers, because of their professional expertise, should decide on educational aims and methods without consultation with parents.

If, however, teachers persist with aims and methods which are alien to parents, it is inevitable that parents will appear indifferent or even hostile to the school. If only to avoid this, therefore, the teacher would do well to know what the parents' values are, and to start at any rate by taking these values into account. The parent who has no desire to play with his child may respond enthusiastically to requests to help him to learn to read and write, or to take him to visit places of interest, or explain the family background and history to him.

It is, in any case, possible that parents might know better than the teacher what is in the best interests of their child. Professionals have made enormous errors in the past—tower blocks in the case of architecture, the widespread use of leucotomy in the case of medicine, and severe beatings for children who fail to understand what they are told in school, are recent examples. Certainly, a partnership between teacher and parents cannot be set up unless the teacher accepts the obligation to systematically inform and consult with the parent.

It must, however, be admitted that there are great difficulties in the way of establishing such a partnership. Many of these difficulties are common to other professional/lay relationships: Professionals tend to regard themselves as having esoteric knowledge beyond the layman's understanding, they tend to be unwilling to share their skills with their clients, and to refuse to recognize that laymen are competent to judge *them* and to comment on the standard of *their* work.

Of course, professionals do have special skills and knowledge, and hence have an important contribution to make in deciding aims and methods. Parents have a great deal to learn from teachers—but, equally, teachers have to work with, and learn, from parents. However, while services are organized centrally, and while professional people are not responsible to their clients, it is difficult indeed to enlist popular involvement in the school, and ludicrous to expect partnership between the parents and the professionals.

Perhaps the most significant developments in services for the young are thus those which have established forms of care and education that involve new power relationships among the "partners," new goals for professionals, and new patterns of communication between parents, teachers, and the general community. In Britain, New Zealand, and some other countries, preschool playgroups have been started, organised, and run by *parents;* and in Britain these provide more preschool places for young children than any other form of placement. Some other countries are also involving parents much more closely in the organization and day to day running of early childhood services. In Yugoslavia, for example, the decentralized and democratic form of government, which gives power and financial control of services to local "interest groups", ensures that parents, citizens, and workers—as well as teachers—decide upon nursery policy and plan the curriculum. In parts of Italy there is what is called *gestione sociale,* democratic self-government of institutions like nursery and creches. In Alberta, Canada, and in Victoria, Australia, the government has made arrangements to fund nurseries once a minimum of about 20 parents have expressed a demand for them. The actual running of the nurseries may be left to the group itself, and if so, subject only to the right of the authorities to prescribe certain standards and to inspect the premises, it is the democratically elected committee of management which appoints the teachers and takes full responsibility for the program and for the running of the institution.

Developments in Australia are of particular interest in that, unlike play group movements in other countries, the voluntary body which has sponsored them has considered the needs of all families with young children in small, geographically circumscribed neighborhoods, and has pressed for services which provide both full day and part time care and education. They have stimulated the setting up of Neighborhood Centres, or Neighborhood Houses: places where families living near one another can meet their many different child care needs in an integrated way. The Neighborhood House accommodates children of different ages and for differing periods of time during the day. Some children come for the whole day, some part time, some only occasionally. The center may function as an advice center, may have a child health clinic attached, may house a toy library, and may take older children of working parents after school and during holidays. Other facilities may be incorporated if there is a demand for them.

Neighborhood Centres are run by the community whose needs they serve. They receive (or rather some have received since the number so far established falls far short of demand) substantial support from the public funds: and the balance of revenue costs is met either by fees or by adult time spent supervising children in the centre.

A service run on these lines would see a central role of professional staff as being to help parents formulate and achieve their own aims for their children. In order to do this the professional staff would have to learn to work with adults and not just with young children; and their training would require them to learn new skills which would enable them to adopt a role different from that which they play today; one which would be wider, and in many ways more exacting, though it would carry with it a quite different type of authority. An essential feature of such an arrangement is that teachers and other professional staff should know about, and be responsive to, the desire and needs of parents; the parents would have, on their side, to learn more about education and about child development.

To introduce services organized somewhat on the lines of the Australian and Canadian ones is likely to prove difficult if not impossible if professionals are resistant to sharing their skills and impatient with ideas that do not fit easily with their own. It might also be thought that it is only articulate, middle class parents who would have the ability and knowledge, as well as the confidence, to be able to formulate adequate goals for the centers their children attend. The experience of those who have actually tried out these new forms of service suggests that these fears are probably groundless. American, Canadian, and Australian experiments, as well as the experience of the vast preschool playgroups association in Britain, and the different, but essentially similar arrangements that have been arrived at in Yugoslavia and in some parts of Italy, all indicate that even poorly educated parents are deeply concerned to do their best for their children, and that where they are given power they are likely to use it responsibly. Indeed, it is only when they have this power that they are likely to be motivated to study how best to use it; and it is only when parents have *real* power that teachers will be obliged to take account of their views. In Britain, the Preschool Playgroups Movement shows the way in which parents themselves have been able to develop an organization which *they* control, in which *they* employ staff, and through which individual parents have benefited by attending training courses that the Preschool Playgroups organization itself has set up and run successfully. And neither in Britain nor in any of the other countries mentioned has this development been an exclusively middle class creation. Furthermore, in the United States at least, and in some parts of Britain today, some of the most dynamic innovations have come from minority group parents—American blacks; and in Britain, West Indian settlers and Asians, for example—who, like the Jews of an earlier generation, have begun to organize their own services, apart from, and sometimes in opposition to, the schools which their children attend.

Like all nursery services, those which are democratically controlled must find ways to ensure that certain children are not excluded from them on racial, religious, or other grounds. In practice, parent-organized groups have been generous in their acceptance of children: if they are not, the public authority, which pays a large part of the costs, can exert economic pressures on them to abandon restrictive administrative policies. Flexibly organized, parentally controlled services for young children must also be able to attract professional staff, paraprofessionals or aides, and volunteers. The best way of recruiting and retaining staff seems to be through a system which enables people to be paid according to the job they do rather than the formal qualifications they bring to it. It should also be possible to lay down common conditions of service in the form of hours and holidays. Furthermore, in the preschool field, at least it should be possible for staff to be able to move from one grade or position to another by acquiring additional qualifications and experience. (At present, in most places, if you want to train as a teacher you have to start from scratch irrespective of prior qualifications and experience in other forms of child care.) The Preschool Playgroups Association, however, has organized training courses that do lead on from one another. These courses are, unfortunately, not recognized by the education system that is responsible for the training of nursery school teachers—but clearly they ought to be.

The power relations between providers and the users of services depend essentially upon who controls the money, who hires and fires the staff, who is responsible for the day to day running of a preschool service and for the admission of children to it, as well as who has the final say in the major policy issues. Perhaps it is these questions rather than those of curriculum that should be receiving most attention from research workers.

DISCUSSION

T. BERRY BRAZELTON

Harvard Medical School, Boston, MA, USA

PEOPLE who care about small children will inevitably be competitive with each other for the child. A mother may abdicate her role to day care centers, the school, etc., but if she has no support from them for her own role as a parent, with a justifiable reason for working, she will become angry, grieved, and competitive for the child. Only if we understand these feelings and help the educators to see that their best role is to support the parent–child dyad can we make the most effective use of all our educational systems.

The kind of grief reaction I am talking about is that, in giving up the child, the mother feels she is no longer the important person to him. She begins to devalue herself and a certain defense system begins to be set up. The first defense is denial: denying that her role is important; the second is projection, projecting onto the other person all the inadequacies she feels, as well as the anger at having to give up this relationship; the third, and most critical, is detachment. If you care about someone and feel he is likely to be damaged by you, you pull farther away.

We see this all the time in day care situations. We have found, for instance, that by four months babies in a good day care center will cycle at a very low ebb through the eight hour day. They go through light periods of sleep and light intense relationships. Then, at the end of the day, when the parent arrives, that low grade cycling ends. The baby goes to pieces and screams at the parent, and after that comes the time when he is ready for intense relationship, but by then—because of these feelings—the mother blames herself and says: "He is angry at me because I haven't been here all the time. I am no good for him." And the day-care person at this point invariably says: "He never cries with me like that," and you can see that the mother is liable to pull farther away from the child. The whole situation increases her detachment instead of building up support for an important dyadic family interaction.

JACK TIZARD

Institute of Education, University of London, UK

We have heard a very eloquent statement by Dr. Brazelton, but quite frankly, I think it is nonsense. I cannot see education as a threat to a child's well-being and development. I think that it is only very well-educated people who see the education of other people as being in some way a threat to their well-being and development. I also think that the whole question of professionalism and what professionals care about is much more complicated than Dr. Brazelton makes out. Professionals care, of course. One of the things we care most about is ourselves, and one of the reasons why in medicine, in education, and in social work, there have been barriers to entry into professions, and barriers between the professionals and the clients is for the self-protection of the professionals rather than because of an enormous concern about the clients.

Another point concerns this grief reaction of parents who give their children up to day care. I do not know what Dr. Brazelton's data are, but we have interviewed four times over a period of four years, 500 parents in London, most of whose children are going to one form of day care or another. They do not at all feel that they have somehow made an enormous emotional sacrifice in order get their children into day care. In fact, the survey literature is quite clear—that many more parents want some form of day care for their children than are given it—and if you know anything about the conditions under which these parents live, it is not surprising. But the reasons they give for wanting their children to go into day care are for the children's benefit, because they believe that, if they get their children to socialize with other children, their children will benefit. Our experience shows that they certainly do not feel an enormous sense of loss; rather, they feel a liberation, because they think they can have a little bit of time to themselves, rather than have the 24 hour care of children on their hands.

The final point relates to the reactions of children to day care centers. There is a certain amount of rather good research data on this, and what I think it shows very clearly is that at good day care institutions children do not have these feelings of grief at separation, particularly if there is proper planning from the outset; indeed, they seem to benefit from it. I think that it is a complete misapprehension to believe that unless a child remains with his parents he is somehow going to suffer. This is quite wrong. It is not supported by the evidence. What the evidence does show very clearly is what you would expect it to show, namely that if a child is in a bad institution, he suffers; but if he is in a good institution, particularly one which is flexible in its policy, then he benefits greatly. This is what common sense would tell us and this is what the *good* research literature tells us as well.

B. K. Ramanujam

BM Institute of Public Health, New Delhi, India

In Ahmedabad there is a great demand for places in day care centers among middle class parents, some of whom demand that their children learn to count to 100 and know the complete alphabet before they enter primary school. I even know of examinations being given in kindergarten, though at 4 or 4½ a child has absolutely no concept of what an examination is. This makes for a very difficult situation and shows that we need to educate the parents as to the purpose of preschool education.

In the school where I work we also have a preschool program in which it is mandatory for the mothers to be present with their children. They come for a program of about an hour and a half to two hours. While the children are spontaneously participating in whatever activities they wish under the supervision of trained teachers, the mothers are talking with a social worker in an informal discussion group about child-rearing problems. This program has been continuing for some 15 years and we find that when these children move into primary school their readiness for learning is much greater.

MARGARET JEFFERY

Clinical Psychologist, Perth, Western Australia

I do not want to jump on the bandwagon of who disagrees with whom, but I must take up a point of Dr. Brazelton's. Although I really do appreciate the value of his work, I think that what he said earlier reveals a complete misunderstanding of what the Women's Movement is all about.

The Women's Movement is not about the denial of motherhood, it is about improving relationships with children. For example, one can not deny the significance of the studies about women's states of depression. Indeed, those who work with children often comment on the lack of joy experienced by women in their children, which is partly due to the 24 hour care of children and the accompanying responsibilities. This is expressed by R. D. Laing, Cooper, Mitchell, and other writers who have studied women's dissatisfaction. I really feel that Dr. Brazelton is looking at the ideal, the dream, what everybody would like to have happen but which does not happen at all.

THE CHANGING ROLE OF PARENTS IN CHILD REARING IN HUNGARY

SANDOR KOMLOSI

Teacher Training College, Pecs, Hungary

I INTEND to show, on the basis of empirical investigations, how the parental attitude to child rearing has changed in Hungary during the past 60 years. Interviews were conducted with parents of present-day pupils asking what they remember of their own upbringing. These 110 interviews reflect the views of families from agricultural areas between the two world wars. At that time much more than half of the population in Hungary was employed in agriculture. Though the sample is small it illustrates the basic conditions.

From the interviews the following picture about child rearing in families 30–60 years ago comes to light. Children were not required to study hard at school. Only a few mothers encouraged their children in their studies and only in 11% of the families did any children proceed further than elementary school. These peasant families did not even let their children study some kind of skilled trade, even if the child wanted very much to do so or showed some talent for it. Instead parents demanded that their children take their places in agricultural labor. The view was that it was not for the family to support the child but that the children should support the family. This was why parents waited so eagerly for their children to finish elementary school, because, from that point on, the children would contribute to the finances of the family.

The child, from a rather early age, was expected to fulfill the duties entrusted to him precisely and responsibly. At the age of 7 or 8 a child was expected to feed the animals, knead dough, bake bread, wash clothes, milk the cows, work in the stable, hoe, hack wood, cut the hay, etc. The struggle for life was so hard that this day after day experience soon developed in the child a strong feeling of responsibility for the family. Thus children gave up any ambition to pursue their individual desires for further studies or learning a skilled trade.

Complete obedience was demanded. Parents demanded respect towards themselves and the acceptance of parental authority. In order to maintain absolute authority a child could not be admitted to be right even if he was right. A child was never allowed to oppose his parents or to dispute with them.

Every activity of the child was controlled. His leisure time was directed and his everyday schedule was designed by the parents. Reading in most families was considered to be a waste of time. Playing was only possible after the child had fulfilled all his duties. Most children did not have any bought toys. Girls especially were strictly controlled to defend them from immorality, bad company, gossip, and rumor. Chastity was most important. Every girl had to be at home well before dark, and if she came home late she was punished.

231

Looking after and taking care of the child was the task of the mother. The parents had no time for discussing problems with their children or encouraging them or even bothering to understand them. Approximately 5% of the children were on good terms with their fathers and 20% were on good terms with their mothers; 75% of the parents were said to be reticent, and there was no intimate, close connection between parents and children. A child could not discuss his problems or even his thoughts with his parents, and was not permitted to express opposing opinions or to dispute anything.

Child rearing was irrational. Parents never explained why children had to do what they had to do, and after having punished a child the parents never told the child why he had been punished. This generation of parents was taciturn, and verbal communication between parents and children hardly existed.

Protection of the child was not an important part of child rearing, since the parents considered it important that the child should become independent as early as possible.

Parents were stingy with praise so as not to spoil their children. The general view of the parents in this respect was that while children should be loved, this emotion should not be noticed by the child.

Parents were careful that they did not overlook any looseness, indiscipline, impertinence, disobedience, or mistakes—these led to immediate punishment. The policy was that parents should be severe, otherwise the children would not be orderly and honest. Parents did not punish out of temper but out of consideration, out of love toward their children. Punishments were severe for both boys and girls. Physical punishment was the most frequent, with whip, strap, towel, stick, hand, etc. Shouting and reproaches were pretty frequent. There were also other kinds of punishments, like kneeling, standing in a corner for a long time, deprivation of food, etc. Deprivation from playing, going outdoors or talking to friends was more rare. Sometimes the mother gave protection to the child against over rigorousness on the part of fathers, taking the risk that she might herself be hurt and hit.

So much for a picture of child-rearing principles and practices before the Second World War.

In 1969 and the following years, 2000 pupils aged 12–14 were interviewed with the help of questionnaires. We inquired about parental attitudes and behaviors in a wide set of everyday situations. Basic patterns of parent behavior were established from the situations described. The children, with different child-rearing experiences, informed us how often their mother or father used different forms of intervention in different situations. We established the following patterns of parent behavior: responsibility, discipline, achievement demands, protectiveness, working companionship, affective punishment, indulgence, expressive rejection, physical punishment, deprivation of privileges, social isolation. Most parents today expect the child to be responsible, i.e. they expect the child to help at home, to be orderly with his clothes and possessions, to help in shopping. The pattern second in frequency today is that parents give reasons and explanations of what the child is expected to do and why the child is punished. Affective reward is also frequent: the child is praised for having done something successfully. Positive features of the child are mentioned before other people—such things have encouraging effects. Support is also important—parents are at hand when the child needs help, they are ready to discuss problems, they defend or console the child.

It is interesting that pupils feel that, compared to the above-mentioned positive parent behavior, punitive behavior occurs rather rarely. Affective punishment is first in order of frequency. Expressive rejection (i.e. shouting at and reproaches) is rather rare. Physical punishment is fortunately almost absent, which marks a great improvement in this respect. The rarest occurrence is the deprivation of privileges and social isolation. A comparison of the frequency of child-rearing activities of fathers and mothers showed that there was no significant difference between mothers and fathers in a total sense. Indeed, it seems that the tasks are shared, which means that fathers undertake a much greater and more active part than they did a few decades ago. A comparison of parents in urban and rural areas shows that in urban areas parents establish more friendly relations with the children, though they control more strictly what the child does with his pocket-money and with his time, and they are less indulgent. In fact, in general, pupils in urban areas receive more up-to-date parental care than those in rural areas.

Parents are more concerned about boys than girls, though this concern is expressed in controlling and punishing them and not so much in an affective relationship with them. Girls receive less punishment and get more warmth and also more indulgence.

The study showed that parents of the intelligentsia interact with and take much more care of their children than parents from any other social group. Also parents of the urban working class establish better relations with their children than agricultural laborers. In fact, agricultural workers are the most conservative in their methods of child rearing. We have found no significant difference between the patterns of behavior of parents when the mother is working outside her home or in the household. However, it should be noted here that in families of working mothers, two-thirds of the most frequently used patterns of parent behavior are of a punitive character.

A quarter of the families investigated were patriarchal in character and another quarter were matriarchal: in these families only the father or the mother made decisions about the child. In the rest of the families both parents made decisions together.

The pupils of today estimate that their parents most frequently exercise direct controls (achievement demands, responsibility, power); less frequently supportive action (sustenance, working companionship, principled discipline, protectiveness, affiliate companionship, affective reward); and least frequently punitive action (physical punishment, expressive rejection, deprivation of privileges, social isolation, affective punishment).

We can conclude that the fundamental social changes that took place in our country after the Second World War have their effects and results in the ways and methods of child rearing in families. The basic and radical changes were the changes of ownership-relations and class relationships, the social collectivization, dominance of state and cooperative properties, and the abolition of exploitation. On such economic–politic grounds the extension of political rights and a large extensive—later intensive—industrialization became possible, that led to a scientific–technical revolution. The gradual transformation of agricultural farms into large agricultural units resulted in the general prevalence of cooperatives.

All these changes brought about significant social mobility: masses of people changed their previous class or social position or occupation, masses of women undertook work outside the family, thus making advances in the process of their emancipation. Industrialization induced a strong process of urbanization: moving into town meant at the same time a change in the way of life of the people. It meant a weakening of traditional bonds, and end of polygeneration families with a general spread of the two-generation nuclear families.

The traditional life of rural areas also underwent great changes. The general standard of living was significantly rising and, parallel to it, the level and content of the needs of the people. The cultural level of the masses was also rising, though not always in equal proportion. The time of schooling of the young became longer, the general state of youth became better, and subcultural differences weakened. Mass communication reached the people. A more rational *Weltanschauung* became general. The mass influence of churches and religion got weaker. Among the efforts consciously forming society, legislative measures propagating the socialistic way of life and cohabitational rules are of great importance (e.g. measures relating to family rights and mutual ruling and responsibility in the family). More democratic relations gained ground in society.

All these changes in the society were accompanied with significant culture shocks. Social shocks were also felt in the family, for we know that all kinds of social changes ultimately affect the family in one way or another. The complex of changes and improvements is still in progress. The conservative authoritarian system of child rearing and parent–child relations, characteristic of the interwar period, has now fallen apart.

Some traces, some remnants still remain that have certain effects on present-day child rearing practices, but a new and more humanistic system of parental behavior is appearing that takes into consideration the desires, wishes, needs, and aspects of the child.

CHAIRMAN'S SUMMARY

NORBERTO BOTTANI

1. Two main models have been mentioned in the organization of the education of the child: the family model and the institutional model. But these categories are too narrow as they take no account of the mutual give and take exercised by the children themselves in their education, or of the influences of other adults who are neither parents nor teachers. One could call this a peer model. It is probable that in the past such a model has played an important part in the education of children, and actually it continues to play an important role; but one must admit that it is so little recognized that no one has thought fit to mention it. Specialists tend to draw back when faced by any disturbing procedure that can not be incorporated in an established institutional framework.

2. There is an insistent repetition that parents have an essential part to play in the success of every phase of education; consequently, the education of the parents themselves needs to be developed. This affirmation is too vague and needs to be better analysed, but in fact none of the discussants suggested how this should be undertaken. As a start it would be as well to be somewhat critical of this declaration, and to ask what has promoted such a pronounced interest in the role of the parents. In addition, it would be important to understand better what parents in fact do and know, before suggesting what it is they should do. Such an analysis should take particular account of the difference in economic, social, and cultural conditions: in short, of the social class differences between the parents.

3. An insistence on the education of parents implies an optimistic conception of the process of conveying information and of the diffusion of knowledge. is it certain that the diffusion of knowledge can change daily behavior? What relation is there between the diffused (or taught) knowledge which is actually utilized? The transfer of knowledge is extremely complex, and the optimism expressed by several speakers seems to me somewhat naive. In addition, it is important to stress that the nature of the origin of knowledge is as important as its content in determining results.

4. The most utilized (or extended) system of education assumes that if enough support is offered to parents the conditions of education will be improved. Consequently, at the same time as asserting the importance of parents, one is acknowledging that they are not capable of undertaking what they are supposed to do by nature, but that they must be assisted.

This poses a contradiction based on two hypotheses which need to be analyzed critically:

— What are the educational norms that the professionals want to inculcate?

— Why don't parents want to do, or know how to do, what the experts desire?

In fact the basic question is the following:

— Are parents educators by nature?

5. Are we prepared to admit that the needs of parents could be validly determined within an education model worked out by a small group? According to Meyer (*L'enfant et la raison d'Etat,* ed. Seuil, Paris) the social and educational policy of the state, through the multiplicity of its services, has resulted in the reduction of areas of social interaction and made parents "unnecessary." It is thus contradictory to insist so strongly on the parental role in education and, at the same time, support a governmental policy which diminishes their importance. This contradiction disappears only if one assumes that the parental role is implicitly defined by the state, which prescribes general norms of behavior and requires that parents adapt their educational behavior in accordance with these norms. Is there a contradiction of this sort? The possibility was not mentioned by anyone.

6. It would also be important to know more about the conditions that have caused a change in the behavior of parents in order to determine what factors have had the most effect. For example, it would be acceptable to proceed to a critical evaluation of the socialist model KOMLOSI provided one did the same for the impact of family policies in the Western world.

7. If it is true that parental behavior is essentially determined by socioeconomic conditions, efforts must be directed to changing and improving the quality of these conditions. Should social manpower policy take precedence over educational policy? This problem was raised only by RUTTER and TIZARD.

8. One must admit that an increased awareness by parents of the consequences of their actions is an important objective, and that the means to attain it is by participation, the involvement of parents, and parents' management of collective projects concerning their children. At present, parents do not have an important role in the educational system, but good intentions are not sufficient to change this situation. It is therefore necessary to consider realistic actions that can lead to a differently organized educational system. Unfortunately there was hardly any elaboration of the suggestion by TIZARD which moved in this direction.

SOCIETY'S ROLE IN EDUCATION

Chairman:
SIR GORDON WOLSTENHOLME
The CIBA Foundation, London, UK

CHAIRMAN'S INTRODUCTION

Sir Gordon Wolstenholme

Discussion of methods and trends in education can always be counted on to provoke dispute. Changes in society, feared or desired, are inevitable matters of controversy—the lifeblood of the media. Bring education and social change together and project our thoughts into the world of tomorrow and we are on a smoke-filled battlefield in which neither friend nor foe can be distinguished.

But perhaps some rules continue to prevail. Dawn will light upon new placements. Humanitarian principles, as so often before, may emerge from conflict and injustice.

I wish to touch on what may seem an odd variety of realities and possibilities—financial investment in education, literacy, telecommunications, family planning—male dominance, the mentally handicapped, and the use of leisure.

Educational programmes of all kinds cost money. The money is an investment in the future. Cost–benefit analyses, if applicable at all, can only be based on long term longitudinal studies not available to the particular generation of investors. Motivation for investment in education therefore rests partly in faith, partly in charity, and substantially in self-interest; in the hope that the achievements and productivity of the next generation will ease the post-earning twilight of the investors' lives. The combination of faith, hope, and charity will ensure the life of the educational plant; how far the plant flourishes and fruits rests upon the proportion of each virtue in any one generation—in any one nation.

A hundred years of compulsory schooling in some countries has not yet spread the opportunity for schooling to the world as a whole. Less than half the children, especially girls, in the poorest countries of the third world receive, or complete, even a primary education. Illiteracy, despite enormous efforts, increases as populations exceed resources. Reading may not be one of the first priorities of life, but no individual can reach a modicum of fulfillment without access to some corner of the treasure-house of knowledge, ideas, and dreams of fellow human beings throughout history.

Money has to be invested. One economical use of it must be to extend to the limit the powers of individual trained teachers through every existing and forthcoming audiovisual aid—including regular educational tele-intercommunication via satellites between one-language regions of the world.

Family planning can be expected to bring about unprecedented changes. Security for the future will no longer take the form of large families of whom only a few survive to adult, earning life. The two or three children of the coming family will be all the more precious, girls as much as boys. Mothers will have much more time to develop careers or skills of their own. Parents may be more ambitious for their few children, more demanding of professional aids from teachers, psychologists, and health workers, and at the same time they are likely to become more responsible and

239

involved in all aspects of their children's physical, mental, and cultural development.

Fewer children and an increased importance of "parenting" do not necessarily imply that the nuclear family will become universal around the world. The creation of new forms of community is an irresistible trend, evolving perhaps into richly supportive extended "families," even if the marriages of any two people become rarer or more transitory. The male partner seems certain to become less dominant, if not markedly inferior. Artificial insemination from pooled semen, stored from generation to generation; sex determination of offspring; even the storage of fertilized human embryos for transplant into "hostess" wombs, have to be taken into serious consideration in any medium term view of the future of human society. The fall in the biological importance of the male may well be followed by a long period of matriarchal dominance in society.

Automation of work must inevitably bring greatly increased hours of leisure. The devil makes work for idle hands, and the human race may well end in self-destruction, but the alternative is wonderfully promising. Communities are likely to take on new meaning; local initiative and responsibility will flourish—or the resulting frustrations will be destructively violent. Decentralization of all but the general economy appears likely to follow. The schools in any one community can be expected to be used day and even night long for learning, sport, and recreations such as drama, dance, and music, for all ages from infancy to healthy old age. All will have a part to play, and generation gaps will disappear. Language and cultural differences, instead of being barriers to communication, are likely to be taken up for the enrichment they can provide. Religious experience will be explored. The landscape can be beautified, new forms of plant food produced, and elaboration of diets made a cultural phenomenon.

The physically and mentally disabled are likely to become proportionately fewer in society, as prenatal diagnosis and intervention become safer and more accurate. Those who are born and survive can expect much greater stimulation and facilitation towards an active involvement in community life.

Vast springs of human imagination, creativity, and concern are likely to be tapped for the first time. After a few generations of spectator sport and television viewing, *participation* should become *the* order of the day. A golden century or two might well ensue. The future is potentially bright—or nonexistent.

SOCIAL POLICIES FOR THE CARE AND EDUCATION OF CHILDREN

KARL LÜSCHER

Department of Sociology, University of Konstanz, Federal Republic of Germany

THE CARE and the education of children, or to use a more technical terminology, the socialization of children, may be seen from two perspectives. Relative to the individual, socialization means all those processes through which the individual in interaction with the environment and with himself develops relatively enduring patterns of behavior, which enable him to take part in social life and to participate in its change. Relative to the collectivity, socialization indicates the differentiated, and, under certain conditions, contradictory, interaction of all those societal institutions that express the economical, political, and cultural conceptions of the task of caring for and educating children. It is this second perspective that is meant when we discuss in one way or another "society's role in education," to use the theme originally suggested to me.

If I prefer to treat the topic under the headline of "social policies for the socialization of children" I do so with the intention of expressing a certain orientation under which I consider it useful to conceptualize the problems involved. Its basic points are rooted in empirical evidence and can be stated as follows:

(a) The care and the education of children is based on an anthropologically given dependency of the young human being for at least the first six to eight years of life.

(b) In view of recent historical developments and foreseeable trends, it seems less and less adequate to strictly separate "education" from other—more care-related—societal actions for children.

(c) Any social action, eg. any institutionalization of this task, is related—explicitly or implicitly—to a notion of the role of the child; in other words, it is related to a certain social knowledge concerning the nature, the needs, and the faculties of the child or of categories of children.

(d) Knowledge—which, of course, is composed of different social cognitions—seems to be the most important vehicle for any deliberate societal action concerning children, although we have to realize that other forces may be much more influential in shaping the life of children.

These basic points suggest the question that I would like to propose as a primary focus of our discussion: How can we—in realistic terms—influence the existing social forces and how can we create new conditions for the efficient and optimal implementation of social policies for children?

Relevant blueprints for general policies concerning children are available in several formats. But, generally speaking, they suffer much too often from a certain neglect of the monetary aspects, which, on the other hand, are doubtless a main concern for all those involved in shaping public policy. It is this harsh, often brutal, reality which I would like us to keep in mind when we consider what is needed and desirable in terms of future public action for children.

It is necessary from a pragmatic point of view to locate the problems which arise in the care and education of children. But what really is a problem? Whatever the answer may be, an appraisal of the situation is essential to its solution. In extreme cases an appraisal of the situation can take the form of a subjective expression, e.g. an autobiographical report. It can also take the form of an "objective" report by specialists who refer to subjectively observable facts and whose analysis takes all different interests and viewpoints into consideration.

Practically all attempts to describe those concrete problems of parents and children requiring societal action fall between these two extremes. A number of categories, resulting from attempts to describe the situation of children, may be distinguished.

1. Individual biographies (highly subjective)
   — autobiographical
   — novelistic, narrative
   — documentary
2. Case studies (isolating typical traits becomes possible through the selection of particular cases)
   — individual cases
   — series of cases
3. Public opinion research (reflects "attitudes")
   — standardized questions
   — open-ended questions
4. General descriptions of the child's situation
   — political commissions
   — official studies by experts
     — group studies
     — individual studies
   — individual monographs
   — reports on social indicators
5. Evaluation studies
   — with respect to types of measures
   — with respect to categories of children
   — action research (researcher participates in the development)
6. International comparisons
7. Historical analyses

In terms of our perspective such assessments can be seen as actual manifestations of the social understanding of the child and of socialization. They represent what can be called an "institutional knowledge" about socialization. Since their focus is on actual problems, such assessments are always rooted (to a certain extent) in conceptions, norms, and values which are taken for granted (sometimes their strength stems from questioning certain of these self-evident truths and facts).

In order for this knowledge to become socially relevant, it has to be disseminated and utilized. This is—in most general terms—the precondition of any social policy for children.

We can define social policy for children, therefore, as all organized efforts pursued in a given society with the intention of changing the living conditions of children. These measures are seen by those who initiate them as a means of improving the general welfare of children as a way to ease and overcome the discrimination suffered by certain groups of children. Whether these measures are viewed as amelioration progress or compensation depends, of course, upon political goals and values.

The organizations responsible for social policies for children may be divided into three categories:

(a) the government at the federal, state, or community level;
(b) non-governmental and voluntary organizations such as churches, charity organizations, and the like;
(c) organizations and committees of parents, inasmuch as they see themselves representing the interests of their children.

If these programs or activities are to be successfully carried out, these agencies and organizations need political influence or a political base. Many observers consider this influence to be very limited in scope.

Any program for children involves first of all costs and does not bring any immediate economic gains. This is an unfavorable precondition for political success. In certain cases one may be able to demonstrate some economic advantages inasmuch as a given measure A involves less costs than a measure B. But there are still expenditures involved. There is no reliable means of calculating the monetary value from investments in the care and the education of children; this is a clear outcome of recent research on this topic. Whoever engages himself or herself for the cause of children stands in a politically weak position.

In order to create better conditions for the dissemination of knowledge on how best to organize socially the care and the education of children and given the absence of a strong economical backing, we have to rely on the strength of arguments based on prevailing conceptions of the child. If one shares the conviction that any conception of socialization (or of educational processes) is determined by social conditions, the obvious conclusion—and it has been stated in such terms—must be that socialization is a process of social reproduction. Consequently, any social policy for children is successful only to the extent that it reinforces existing structures. Society's role in the education of children seems to be to reproduce itself through education. Thus we seem to be caught in a vicious circle.

In the pragmatic perspective of empirical social science it may be useful to depart from the assumption that any concrete action or program concerning the care and the education of children has a tendency to function as a vehicle of reproduction (or to be refused because it promises or threatens not to fulfill this function). At the same time we may say that concrete actions or programs may have the potential to overcome the vicious circle of reproduction if we assume that socialization is ultimately related to evolutionary processes and their historical expression. With this assumption in mind we can conceive of programs for children as possible attempts to improve the living conditions of men in general. They have the character of social experiments in nature.

The task of improving living conditions (and in this way enhancing the potential of human growth) includes several functions typically embedded in social roles. The scientist, for example, is responsible for obtaining valid and reliable knowledge, while the policymaker is concerned with the creation of new and the transformation of already existing institutions. These two roles are the ones usually given primary attention, whereas the institutionalization of the cooperation by children and parents tends to be neglected.

However, there are at least three roles involved in the implementation of any social policy: (a) the "scientist" who attempts a valid assessment of a problem, (b) the "politician" who is concerned with the distribution and redistribution of power and welfare, and (c) the "user" who has a subjective view of the situation. Each role functions within a setting that may be conceived as a complex system. Its processes are partially influenced by immanent forces such as general trends in scientific theory and methodology, bureaucratization, and the application of certain technologies, most of them well known.

A special word seems in place concerning the nature of the relationship between child and caretaker. It is in their interaction with one another that social (or as referred to above) institutionalized knowledge about the child is brought into contact with the subjective understanding of a concrete individual and his (already realized or "intended") biography. In terms of a sociology of knowledge, this means the merger of two kinds of knowledge—institutional and individual.

This process may draw on highly subjective experiences and, consequently, may produce new answers. It has a certain innovative potential and constitutes an essential quality of the process of socialization.

This process throws light on a potential supremacy of parents inasmuch as they are in a unique position to acquire individual knowledge about each of their children. Parents, moreover, may be very close to developing their own conception of the child and they can function, so to speak, as advocates for their child. In this role they may be supplemented or even replaced by other caretakers. But any model of socialization has to take into account this inner circle of privacy.

The cognitions of parents (and other caretakers) are built around the construction of an everyday world involving everyday notions of child rearing and education. Psychologists sometimes refer to these cognitions as "naive theories," a term which expresses a certain connotation of inferiority that does not seem appropriate. Parents' everyday knowledge draws on a large range of intimate experiences and shows a strong practical commitment. Consequently, this knowledge has to be seen as an integral part of all processes of socialization and is crucial to the success of most social policies.

I am aware of arguing on a general level, but even here we are reminded of the complexity of this analysis. Furthermore, to conceive of social policies for the socialization of children as a means of creating social environments allowing for an optimal development of their human potential means influencing the conditions of their daily life. Attempts for its study have to take into account the physical, the social, and the temporal qualities of the child's everyday world plus the capacities of those involved in the activities. This program of study is quite often labeled as research on the ecology of human development. It is related to the systematic evaluation of the possible impact of social programs.

The agenda of such research includes references to historical developments, work on taxonomy of the child's environment, an account of the prevailing power structure, the channels for the dissemination of knowledge, and, finally, reference to concrete problems whether they are those of specific groups or those generated by external changes.

Although there have been promising attempts in this direction, we are still far from deducing a set of comprehensive propositions for actions to be taken in the future. However, what we can do is to engage in a discussion of experiences and, possibly, of pragmatic criteria which seem to reflect them.

Let me close by attempting to formulate five (theoretical and practical) propositions that, however, have to be restricted to the conditions in Western industrial societies:

(1) Given the complexity of the relationship between human growth and the social environment and taking into account the limitations of scientific knowledge and the methodological problems inherent in the observation of real life situations, it seems necessary to pay attention to the knowledge of those who share and shape the everyday life of children. Parents and other caretakers may know more about children in many ways than do social scientists. An appropriate strategy would consist in systematically comparing the meanings that concrete situations have for the caretakers, for the children, if possible for the social scientists. The likelihood that any suggested change will be accepted is greater if it can be accurately and honestly expressed in terms meaningful to all parties involved. This suggestion implies studying the so-called "everyday theories" that parents, caretakers and politicians have about children.
   Conclusion: we should accept the factual relevance of everyday knowledge.

(2) Parents have a unique chance to relate what can be called institutionalized knowledge to the role of the child in a society and in societal substructures with the specific needs of an individual child from the early beginnings of its personal identity. As a result it would be better to design programs reinforcing and supporting the roles of parents rather than to design programs addressing themselves directly to children.
   Conclusion: we should support parents and strengthen their sense of responsibility for their children.

(3) Taking into account the very limited financial resources available for children, it would be better to encourage self-help programs and voluntary activities and to use available funds to support such initiatives rather than to staff governmental agencies at necessarily much higher costs.
   Conclusion: we should encourage voluntary initiatives.

(4) Given the restriction of scientific knowledge and the obvious relevance of everyday knowledge, and given the financial limitations of programs leading to the professionalization of general child care and education, we should try to estimate the possible effects general parental guidance and parental education may have on the self-confidence and motivation of parents and their

willingness to assume greater responsibility for their children. This warning, of course, does not hold for the treatment of serious physical and socio-psychological problems.

    Nevertheless: we should be on the look-out for the possible counter effects of a forced professionalization.

(5) If individual children are to have an optimal chance for individual growth, they will need highly differentiated environments. It seems plausible that the search for such environments would be better aided by social programs which take into account already existing social, cultural, and regional differences. In other words, decentralization seems more appropriate in many cases than centralization. Decentralization may well encourage more personal initiative.

    Conclusion: we should be sensitive to the potentials of decentralization.

Society's role in education can be conceptualized as a process of distribution of behaviors which are seen in a given society as necessary and/or desirable. It is accompanied by processes of production, dissemination, and utilization of different kinds of knowledges or cognitions, concerning these behaviors. These cognitions are held by individuals with respect to their own behavior, by adults who rear and educate children with respect to the fulfillment of this task, and by those who are concerned with the social organization of child care and education.

Because socialization concerns the basic conditions of human life and its potential, any conceptualization of this socialization, both in theory and in practice, is rooted in the fundamental meaning of past and future human existence. Here lies both a strength and a weakness of any argumentation for social policies for the socialization of children. Perhaps our best strategy is to explore more actively the positive aspects, in other words, to discuss socialization not as a burden but as a challenge, which is meaningful for most aspects of personal and social life.

DISCUSSION

ALEXIS DIMARAS

Moraitis High School, Athens, Greece

WE COULD, perhaps, take as a starting point for our discussion Professor Lüscher's conclusion on the needs for decentralization and his "vicious circle" by which society's role in the education of children seems to be to reproduce itself through education. This may be true, and, indeed, it seems to be so in the societies of the so-called "industrialized West". However, this presupposes that there exists a direct relationship between society and the educational system. For, if society can more or less effectively influence its younger members in a number of peripheral ways, it is by systematically gaining control over organized schooling that it can guarantee the perpetuation of its value system. Of course, in this context society has to be considered as a whole, not only (as it is usually expressed) through its ruling class. It is this particular point which links the Greek educational system to our subject, because, as far as I know, it is unique in its isolation from society as a whole.

I am referring to the highly centralized structure of the Greek educational system, whereby everything—from the formulation of a national policy to the details of everyday classroom practice—is laid down by a central agency: the Ministry of Education. As a result of this arrangement, and since for the last 150 years or so there has been no noticeable change in the socioeconomic class which has provided the ruling party, the system has only served the value reproduction pattern of this particular social group. The system, both in its aims and in its means, has evolved only to the extent to which, and in the direction in which this group has changed its own values and has accepted new procedures. Other social groups—often quite considerable in size—have only indirectly and to a small extent been able to influence developments in the way in which their children have been educated.

But the particular problems of the Greek system, burning and frustrating as they may be for us who suffer the immediate consequences of it, fall outside the scope of this symposium. If I have brought them up, it is only because I believe that they have some relevance to future general developments in education. Indeed, we should not forget that, parallel to the tendency toward de-schooling (which seems to be fading out), there is another tendency toward more central control in education. To a very large extent it is due to increased national expenditure on education, and, as the British say; "He who pays the piper, calls the tune."

This trend can be observed even in countries which have long been examples and indeed prototypes of deeply rooted beliefs in decentralization, such as Germany, Great Britain, or the United States. More and more in these countries—and in others as well—the federal or national government has been gaining control over educational matters. It is often indirect and is imposed through the financing of special educational programs, the setting up of national requirements for entrance into institutions of higher education, or the imposition of national examination patterns. But it is, nevertheless, effective in imposing the central authority's values over an increasingly large number of people who have so far felt more or less free to decide for themselves on their children's education. As I have said, the Greeks can testify that this can have the same effects on a large scale as have often been observed under research conditions with a relatively small group of youngsters.

The issue is indeed highly political in the sense in which Professor Eisenberg put it yesterday, and leads to more and more "experts" at the top believing that they know best and acting accordingly. On the other hand, however, as literacy (in the broad meaning of the term—not merely the mastering of the three Rs) rapidly increases in our societies, people become less and less prepared to accept that some one else knows best.

When the solving of problems in education requires the collaboration of a constantly larger number of specialists instead of one all-wise expert it is perhaps characteristic of the culture prevailing at the top that the only other specialist who seems to have been accepted to participate in decision-taking procedures in education is the economist.

What, then, in view of all this is the lesson we could draw out of this session? As I see it, from the Greek point of view, it is, first of all, to accept that "equal opportunities in education" does not mean "equal opportunities to be subjected to a culture and a value system imposed upon the children by some one else." On the contrary, it means that every child should be given the opportunity to develop his or her personality and his or her abilities according to the needs, desires, and expectations of the social group to which he belongs, and at his own pace. To this effect society as a whole and every particular group of it should directly participate—not as a pressure group but as an equal partner—in the decision-making procedure in educational matters.

Finally, we should realize that increased central control in education means the imposition of some one else's culture upon the young generation, that it increases indoctrination, and that it takes away some of the fundamental characteristics that a pluralistic society should have. It is, after all, paradoxical to strongly object to any kind of state interference with our own personalities by way of indoctrination or censorship, and at the same time accept that in what concerns our children there is somewhere a certain gentleman who knows best.

D. V. GLASS*

London School of Economics and Political Science, London, UK

D. Dimaras described the Greek educational system as completely isolated from society as a whole. That is an extreme case. But the imperfect relationship between educational systems and society and its needs obtains generally, both in industrialized countries and in the third world.

Take Western Europe for example. There the concept of "equality of opportunity" in education was not readily accepted until after the Second World War. And even when it was, the measures taken to implement it were often quite inadequate. In

*Died 23 September 1978.

England, universal secondary education began with the tripartite system, based upon an entirely unscientific and unjustifiable assumption regarding different "types" of children. Further, instead of investing maximum priority in genuinely improving secondary education, university expansion became the fashion. But those most likely to profit from that expansion were the middle class children, better prepared culturally and educationally to seize the new opportunities. Hence university expansion has not resulted in equal access of working class and middle class children. Even in Britain, which has an unusually large working class intake, only some 24% of university students are working class in background. And that proportion may well decrease with the fall in prestige and economic return to university degrees.

The situation in the third world is far worse. In those areas which were colonies before the Second World War—and scarcely less with the "internal colonialism" in much of Latin America—the rulers were not generally concerned with mass literacy or mass primary and secondary education. Their interest was far more in training an "intermediate elite" which could serve them as lower grade civil servants, teachers, and white collar workers. The more essential needs of the societies remained unfulfilled. Nor was the indigenous population antagonistic to the resultant educational system. On the contrary, attempts to develop vocational (especially agricultural) training were rejected—understandable, since the most secure and profitable jobs were those for which the colonial educational system provided the training. This system and the pressures for its maintenance has largely continued in the postcolonial era. Indeed, middle class pressures have intensified, so that, in relation to needs far too little is spent on literacy, on primary education, and on ensuring educational parity for girls. In India, for example, in the draft fifth five year plan, the proposed allocation for university education amounted to 23% of the total for education as a whole and 45% of that proposed for primary education. Within the university system, too, middle class pressures have supported degree courses that have little relevance to social needs. Medical graduates, for example, are produced in large numbers on Western models, but do little to meet the needs of the mass of the rural population. It is not surprising that, although the literacy rate has improved, the improvement has been so slow that the absolute number of illiterates is still increasing.

Hence both in industrialized and underdeveloped countries there is a very imperfect relationship between society's needs and the scope and content of existing educational systems. The directions of change required will not be the same in both regions. But in both the necessary change will have to be radical.

J. K. HARFOUCHE

School of Public Health, Beirut, Lebanon

I should like to suggest that the constraints of educational systems, which give rise to unbalanced policies in the developing world, are due to three causes:

(1) *Professionalism*—educational policies are planned by educators alone and exclude parents and children.

(2) *One uniform model* i.e. the same model, is planned and applied to all socioeconomic sectors of the population despite marked differences in needs. Should we stick to such a standard blueprint or should we not modify the standard model according to different ecological contexts?

(3) *Imported models* which are geared not only to obsolete colonialism, but to present-day types of neocolonialism.

JOHN SEELEY

Charles R. Drew Postgraduate Medical School, Los Angeles, CA, USA

There seems to be a widespread, naive illusion that the principle intention of any educational system (let alone, a state-connected one) is to orient the child in a world of reality or to train the child's critical capacity and eventual political autonomy and cooperative competence. Nothing could be further from the truth. The objectives are everywhere:

— to induce serviceability;
— to confuse reality;
— to reduce political consciousness and any tendency to organize and act together;
— to divide and conquer.

BARBARA TIZARD

Institute of Education, University of London, UK

An important decision within any society concerns the proportion of resources to be allocated to education. At the present time, education is under-financed in most countries. For example, in Britain both the status and salary of teachers is very much below that of doctors, and very much less is spent on training teachers than doctors. More money is spent on medical research in Britain in any one year than has been spent throughout the century on research in education. More money, in fact, is spent on research into glue than on educational research. It is therefore not surprising that, although there are gifted teachers, the science of pedogogy is in its infancy. We know very little about the experiences we need to provide in order to allow the maximum potential of children to develop, or the best way to provide an educational service. We want parents to be involved in their children's education, but they need experts to work with them if their hopes for their children are to be attained. This expertise will not be developed until there is a political decision to allocate adequate funds in this area. At present, there is an assumption that many children will fail or attain low standards in literacy, numeracy, athletics, or musical achievement. Yet this need not be the case if our understanding of educational processes could be advanced.

CULTURE–EDUCATION INTERACTION AND THE PROBLEM OF A CHANGING SOCIETY

HIROSHI AZUMA

Department of Education, University of Tokyo, Japan

CRONBACH[1] has pointed out the importance of studying culture education interaction in psychological research, and later he spelled out the concept of aptitude-treatment interaction (ATI), suggesting that optimal educational treatment differs as the pupil's personal traits differ. Expanding the concept of ATI, I should like to consider culture–education interaction, as suggesting the possibility that the effectiveness of an educational practice is influenced by societal and cultural factors.

In 1970 Bruner said that education "crippled the capacity of children in the lowest socioeconomic quarter of the population to participate at full power in society."[2] This was amplified by Illich in his book on de-schooling society.[3] Evidence for this can be found in a study conducted by Nagano.[4]

In Japan there are two kinds of institutions for preschool children. One is *yochien* (kindergarten) and another is *hoiku-sho* (a day care center). Generally speaking, *yochiens* have inherited the spirit of the child-centered education movement. Structured teaching in the cognitive domain is avoided and creative and imitative arts are encouraged. The tendency has been for middle and upper middle class parents to send their children to *yochiens,* whereas working class families send their children to *hoiku-shos.* Unlike *yochiens, hoiku-shos* supplement cognitive development with structured training in order to foster readiness for school. As preschool education has become very popular in recent years, and as job opportunities for educated women expanded, the class differentiation between *yochien* and *hoiku-sho* attendance has lessened.

Most parents choose to enroll their children in a particular form of preschool education on the basis of neighborhood convenience and travel time. Nevertheless, the difference between *yochiens* and *hoiku-shos* in teaching style, training of staff members, and content or textbooks standardized by the government still exist. Most *hoiku-shos* are located in urban working class and rural farm areas, whereas private *yochiens* are densely distributed in middle class residential neighborhoods.

When the nationwide educational achievement test was administered in 1966, Nagano and others sampled about 1000 fifth graders and examined whether their achievement scores were related to the type of their preschool institutions. On the basis of IQ levels the average achievements of *yochien* graduates were found to be better than those of *hoiku-sho* graduates. However, the breakdown of data for working class and middle class families revealed a new aspect. It was found that the achievement of children of working class families who attended *hoiku-shos* was significantly better than those who attended *yochiens,* while the relationship was reversed for children of the middle class families. The average performance of children of the working class who attended *yochiens* was even lower than that of working class children who did not attend any preschool institution. This might lead us to hypothesize that some aspect of *yochien* education, perhaps its middle class orientation, had a certain durable, disturbing effect upon these pupils. These findings warn against hasty uniformalization of education, even within a country known for its racial, educational, and social homogeneity.

The culture–education interaction is observable more strongly when studied cross-nationally. In our survey of maternal control strategies, conducted as a part of a Japan–US cross national study of cognitive socialization,[5] the indices of maternal control strategies were correlated with children's cognitive achievement measures, for each country.

Within each country there were many significant correlations. However, it was very seldom that the signs of substantially high correlations coincided between the two countries. More typically, entries of the corresponding cells were inversely related. The percentage of directive statements made by the mother, for example, was associated positively with better cognitive performance in Japan. In the United States however, the corresponding correlation was significant and *negative*. Since the results were intraculturally stable through replications, such differences are not reducible to errors. Perhaps the directive approach has a different meaning for two cultures. Japanese mothers are in general more flexible in their approach, being ready to compromise, and children know that. A directive order received with such a general background may differ in its function from a similar statement made by more consistent and uncompromising American mothers.

There are many similar examples within our data. I believe that more culture–education interactions will be observed as well-controlled, cross-cultural, process-product researches are widely conducted.

At this time of rapid change within Japan, two cultures coexist in conflict with each other. Within an individual, the newer culture often influences his superficial thoughts, leaving his inner core rooted in traditional mores. This internal cultural conflict tends to be most severe among the progressively educated population, which includes the majority of teachers.

Early in the 1960s, programmed instruction was enthusiastically adopted by Japanese educators. Introduced from the United States almost without time lag, its dissemination occurred as rapidly as it did in the United States. The percentage of teachers involved in the movement was perhaps higher than it was in the United States. Several nationwide journals primarily devoted to programmed instruction were founded and commercially distributed. There were also noncommercial periodicals locally published. Within several years the enthusiasm for programmed instruction significantly diminished. Almost all periodicals were discontinued as teacher enthusiasm and participation was reduced.

I suspect that one of the reasons for this apparent fickleness was the cultural conflict of programmed instruction with the traditional pattern of education in Japan. About 100 years ago when Japan changed from feudalistic to an industrialized capitalistic society, the modern school system was introduced to replace traditional education institutions. Teacher training also followed the occidental pattern. Thus, intellectually, the principles of programmed instruction were very persuasive for our teachers. On a deeper level, however, these principles conflicted with the traditional pedagogical culture of Japan. In the absence of more direct evidence I again make reference to our US–Japan cross-national study.

As a part of our study, Japanese and US mothers were observed as they instructed their children in specific tasks. In spite of large individual differences, significant cross-national variance was found on many observable dimensions resulting in a different teaching style. The most striking and consistent difference was in the use of feedback. When a response of a child is appropriate, a Japanese mother often suggests that he engage in another task, without giving any overt signal that he did well. On the other hand, American mothers tend to give very clear positive or negative feedback often accompanied by affective remarks like: "Oh, I am really proud of you." An opinion survey, also part of our study, shows that compared to responses of American mothers, Japanese mothers show less preference for overt praise and more preference for "quietly watching without telling anything." A recent survey conducted jointly by the Foundation for Child Development and the Japan Centre for Youth Research also confims our findings. American mothers show a much stronger tendency to overtly and directly reward and punish children's behavior when compared to Japanese mothers.

General teaching strategies were also different. American mothers typically partition the task into progressive parts, define the subtask at each stage, give relevant information, and frequently request explicit verbal response. On the other hand, Japanese mothers typically give a global sketch of the task but do not structure much further, leaving children's responses more ambiguous. The task is presented as problem solving for American children but as a guessing game for Japanese children. When reviewing protocol with a Japanese mother I pointed out the apparent inefficiency of Japanese teaching style. She countered: "An efficient method is all right for training a dog, but human children should be given the privilege of ambiguity." Indeed, 300 years ago Basho the poet established the art of *haiku,* and said: "If you tell it all, nothing is left to be appreciated." On hearing this story, an American colleague said: "Now I understand why Japanese children become clever. In the American system, children don't have to think to learn, but, since everything is ambiguous Japanese children have got to think."

The programmed instruction, in its original form, is a highly structured teaching method. It requires that one proceed in small steps, and it asks for an active response at each step and an immediate feedback to each response. Apparently, American—and perhaps occidental—maternal teaching style described above is more consistent with programmed instruction than the Japanese style. In other words, the very features which constitute the strength of programmed instruction conflict with the teaching style prevalent in Japanese homes.

This does not, however, imply a recommendation to stick to the traditional method and philosophy of education.

In the coming years the interaction of different cultures is bound to be accelerated. Our children are bound to live in a community marked by the heterogeneity of cultures. The individual will thus have to internalize not a single, but two or more different cultures which sometimes conflict with each other.

To prepare our children for that age of cultural heterogeneity, the educational culture of the society must become more open and flexible.

On the other hand, however, the cultural background should be carefully studied before implementing a planned educational intervention. The warning is especially applicable to intercultural and international educational cooperation. While there are an increasing number of cross-cultural studies of education, the majority of them have been mono-culturally designed and mono-culturally data-analyzed and interpreted; only the data collection being cross-cultural. I conclude my presentation hoping that genuine cross-cultural educational researches will flourish.

REFERENCES

1. L. J. CRONBACH, The two disciplines of scientific psychology, *Am. Psychol.,* **12,** 671-684 (1957).
2. J. S. BRUNER, *The Relevance of Education,* Norton, New York, 1971
3. I. ILLICH, *Deschooling Society,* Harper & Row, New York, 1970
4. S. NAGANO, *etal.,* Effects of preschool education on academic achievement and personality of primary school children, *Bulletin of The National Institute for Educational Research,* No. 68, 1969.
5. R. D. HESS *et al., The Cognitive Environments of Urban Preschool Children,* Stanford University, 1969.

RELIGION AND THE CHILD

ULRICH BECKER

World Council of Churches, Geneva, Switzerland

FOR MANY people it is certain that the world of tomorrow is a world without any religion. For many others it is just as certain that the world of tomorrow is a world full of religion.

I do not want to enter into this debate for the simple reason that it would then be necessary to explain the main connotations that the world "religion" evokes. There is such a variety of connotations and interpretations that it would be very difficult to reach a general agreement.

I prefer to draw your attention to another aspect of our theme. Already in our present world, in which ideological and societal pluralisms dominate more and more, there are indications that any kind of religious education of children is being called into question. The arguments arise from different philosophical and ideological standpoints, but they all culminate in this often-called "emancipated" point of view that no adult has the right to impose on a child his relationship to religion, to a specific religious praxis, to a church, or to a religious community. Any religious education is said to be, in the end, a form of manipulation or indoctrination, which denies the rights of a child "to develop his abilities, his individual judgement, and his sense of moral and social responsibility. . . ."[1]

Very often, such statements are combined with a strong criticism of the traditional forms and content of religious education, which have often hindered rather than promoted such goals as "emancipation," "self-determination," or "coming of age." To give only one example of such a position, I would like to quote from a German author: "Christian education means suppressing questions, creating taboos, neglecting to examine reality critically, controlling the emotions, obstructing thinking, and educating to produce stereotypes of thought and behavior. Christian education has created authoritarian forms of power for centuries and prevented people from emancipating themselves. . . . Earlier and contemporary authoritarian systems in Germany have benefited from this type of Christian education. They more than hinder the development of a functional democratic society."[2] Therefore this author pleaded for a non-Christian, a non-religious education: an education—to put it more positively—that liberates and sets free (whatever this means in detail).

In the history of pedagogy one can trace back such a plea for a non-religious, anti-authoritarian, humanistic education to Jean-Jacques Rousseau, whose basic assumption was that "all things are good as they proceed from the hands of the Author of all things; all things degenerate in the hands of man."[3]

In order that the child be educated to be as free as possible, and to act as far as possible in accordance with his true nature, Rousseau waits a long time in his work *Emile ou de l'éducation* before he begins to speak to his pupil about religion. "At the

255

age of 15 he still did not know that he had a soul, and perhaps it is still too early at the age of 18 to teach this. For if he learned it earlier than necessary, he would run the risk of never knowing it."[4]

After Rousseau, the desire for an education which is free from an allegedly negative religious influence comes up again and again. But at the same time we must realize that there was no education, there is no education, and there will be no education offered by parents, teachers, or adults which is neutral with regard to values, ideologies, or religions; and that these systems of interpretation of the reality in which our children grow up are a fact and a necessity. A child born in the second half of the 20th century does not come into being as an emancipated or self-determined person, but as somebody who needs to be educated to emancipation and self-determination. In order to reach this goal, specific standards of values must be offered to children by the family, or another group, so that the children can become stabilized and sheltered, and may then find their own standpoint in the course of their development.

Indeed, while many believe that a child does not possess built-in faculties for religious questions or feelings, but acquires such feelings only through imitations and teachings from outside, new concepts of the psychology of development permit us to say that a child has the ability to deal with religious or metaphysical issues by nature, by means of a cognitive activity which stems from the knowledge of a human being about his own existence within a given limit of time. By the age of 5 or 6 a child already begins to ask "from where" and "to where." These questions have nothing to do with explicit religious knowledge, but seem to arise even when a child grows up without any religious education.[5]

So I maintain that the manipulative or indoctrinal character of education does not depend on the question of whether child education is religious or nonreligious, but rather on whether a child is educated in a rigid, binding way, or in a more flexible way, which ensures that a child is free to become an independent human being.

Therefore the question is not one of the possibility or necessity of a specific religious education. For those for whom a religion or a faith in God is an essential element of their own understanding and interpretation of reality, this question is already decided and there is no valid pedagogical objection to it. Rather the main question today is, how can a religious education be achieved which will ensure that a child can really meet the challenges, needs, and problems of the changing world in the course of the child's development.

Of course, religious educators envisage a problem here. They ask themselves whether religious education (and religious communities) does not bear a share of the guilt of creating a disturbed picture of religious faith, such as gives rise to the kind of "enlightened" criticism of religion that I quoted above. Let me quote from an ecumenical theologian: "The forms of faith and piety, as actually lived in our congregations, must be regarded as extremely infantile. Even in their own area of competence—the field of religious learning—the churches are not successful in opening up the growth that is promised. The liberating contents are lost in structures and in a process of mediation that put people again under tutelage. But religion is about motivations, values, aims of life. If growth is hindered for people here, it will very probably fail in other areas of life."[6]

In response to such critical voices it is often emphasized that the Christian's Gospel is actually synonymous with freedom, and that Christian theology and religious pedagogy keep alive the "dangerous memory" of the history of the revolution of freedom. Challenged by modern emancipatory thinking, people have recognized the potential of theological thinking to liberate the unfree human being, so that, ultimately, religious education can declare itself in solidarity with the basic emancipatory concerns of the sciences of education.

I refer here to the Christian tradition which keeps alive the "dangerous memory" of the history of freedom. But, in the end, this is valid for all religious education. There is also a second goal, to which I would like to refer in the words of an American religious educationist: "One of the fundamental dimensions of religious education is its prophetic role. A prophet may or may not predict the future, but he always makes the future. A prophet is one who makes the future come more quickly than would be the case if he did not exist. . . . Religious education by its nature pushes back the frontiers of an individual's or a culture's way of knowing, feeling, and living. Religious education is an activity by which the individual or society is helped to assume the new man, to be propelled more and more into actualizing the pleroma (the spiritual universe). If it is to fulfill its mission, religious education must not so much bring the now into the future as to bring the future into the now. This is true because the educational experience is not one of preparing the learner to live in the future but rather of helping the learner to live the future right now."[7]

Both goals are important for all religious educational work. What these twofold tasks mean with regard to children still needs to be spelled out in detail.

REFERENCES

1. Principle 7, Declaration of the Rights of the Child.
2. DAMM, Plaidoyer eine unchristliche Erziehung (Heading for a nonchristian education), in *Vorgange,* 1969, Vol. 7/8, p. 273.
3. JEAN-JACQUES ROUSSEAU, *Emile ou de l'éducation,* p. 12.
4. Ibid., p. 289.
5. Cf. OERTER, *Moderne Entwicklungs-psychologie,* 1972, p. 284 f.
6. E. LANGE, Sprachschule für die Friheit, in *Chancen des Lernens* (ed. P. Ziegel) 1972, p. 70 f.
7. J. M. LEE (ed.), *The Religious Education We Need,* 1977, p. 1.

SPECIAL SESSIONS

THE MEDIA IN THE
EDUCATION OF THE CHILD

EDUCATION FOR SPECIAL GROUPS

259

THE PRESCHOOL CHILD

CHILDREN OF MIGRANT WORKERS:
A GREEK PROBLEM

THE MEDIA IN THE EDUCATION OF THE CHILD

Coordinator: SIMON NICHOLSON

Oxford Research Unit, The Open University, Oxford, UK

THIS session received papers on the study of film and television in schools; the influence of films on the young child; communications between teachers and pupils; communication between children and the environment; and the values and abuses of the freedom of the press. In addition the Coordinator submitted a commentary on communication during the session.

Most papers stressed the need for the child to develop a critical approach to what he sees, hears and reads. As TARZIE VITTACHI put it, he should be aware that the media is out to put some idea into his head. It may be a good idea, but it is always wise to "let it cool its heels for a little time in the anteroom of your mind before you to let it in."

FILM AND TELEVISION

EILEEN SHARMAN (The Film Study Committee, Brighton, South Australia) presented a paper on "Screen Education" in which she said : "The question of what is screen education can perhaps best be answered briefly and simply as the study of film and television, namely, what appears on the screen, how it gets there, and what is communicated. Screen education can include a study of the history of film, a study of the language of film, by which is meant the way the film communicates by using a variety of shots, a study of techniques covering the use of the camera, and all the skills which contribute to the finished production—music, lighting, colour, dialogue, sound effects, editing—and finally, the most important of all, a study of film and television as a means of communicating something about life.

"In the early sixties there was increasing concern in South Australia about the number of hours children spent watching television. Realizing the educational and social significance of the visual media, the Education Department felt that young people needed help to understand and appreciate film and television. Accordingly, at the beginning of the school year in February 1966, courses of film study—as it was called then—were introduced into 18 metropolitan secondary schools.

"In the 13 years that have passed since then, the number of schools taking the subject has increased from 18 to 186 throughout the state. This, combined with changing attitudes to education, have brought about changes in the school curriculum.

"The Film Study Committee recommended at that time that film study should be placed within the English syllabus. In doing this it recognized that the study of the film is primarily the study of a means of communicating facts, ideas, thoughts, feelings, standards, and attitudes, and that, in this respect too, it is similar to the study of literature. The filmmaker, like the writer, poet, or playright, is a creative artist, and as a result of his imagination and experience the art of the film in its aesthetic sense, can bring us nearer to the true nature of things, particularly of human character and conduct. In this sense it can enrich the student's own experience and open a new window on life in the same way as a good play, television programme, poem, or novel.

"That the film *can* do this, there is no doubt, but that it does not always do so is one of the reasons for screen education.

"However, the passing years brought changes to this literary approach, and several of us on the Film Study Committee felt strongly that the study of film and television should be removed from the English syllabus and become a subject in its own right. Although the visual media can be compared, with advantage, with certain aspects of drama and literature, there are important areas—such as their immediacy, their seeming realism, their conventions, their impact—which are very different and deserve specialized attention. Accordingly, early in 1975 a complete revision of the Film Study Curriculum was begun.

"*Aims.* But what are the aims of the secondary courses? Although the wording is different in the new curriculum, they basically have not changed.

"Television programmes and films—good, bad, and indifferent—are watched by the average adolescent for many hours each week. One of the most important aims of the course is to provide students with the means of developing an intelligent response to what they see, both at home and in the cinema, so that eventually they will develop critical judgment to enable them to understand and fully appreciate what they view. There is no reason why they should not choose and enjoy to watch trivia as long as they understand that it is trivia.

"By introducing the students to a wide variety of television programs, documentaries, feature films, and animated films, both in schools and outside, it is hoped that they will in time be less conservative in their tastes and extend their range of viewing. This should also increase their awareness of the variety of purposes for which the screen media are used. They will gain an understanding of the film and television industries and will explore the implications of a society conditioned by the 'mass media.' Finally, the courses aim at encouraging creative activity in the form of film making and video making by the students themselves. This provides them with an opportunity for dramatic expression in media which are very much part of their world. It also tends to sharpen their critical awareness in their own viewing of the professional screen.

"*Content of courses.* The development of film and television: the word 'development' is used rather than 'history' of film and television as it is felt that the study in this area should not only devote itself to technical changes brought about by inventions but also the gradual development, since 1897, of the new art forms of film and, later, television.

"Purposes of film and television: students examine the different categories of film and television production, explore the filmmaker's intention to see whether he sets out to entertain, inform, record, teach, or persuade, and to discover how far the box office has an influence on the finished production.

"Screen language: screen language includes the study of the whole art of communication by the use of movement, composition within the frame, shot focus, lens, lighting, color, sound, special effects, and pace and rhythm of editing. It includes a study of the conventions of the cinema and the particular style of well-known techniques.

"Form and content: students are helped to understand the ways in which the screen communication is controlled and shaped through selective interpretations of reality—the content—and of the structure and style of presentation—the form. They see a wide range of productions—short entertainment films, documentaries, features, cartoons, and a variety of television programs, which give them the opportunity of analyzing and criticizing the various elements of presentation.

"Film and television in society: here the student considers the influence of the visual media in his life and learns about the highly commercial industries that film and television represent. Many consider this is the most valuable part of the whole course. In studying the screen media as a social institution and its interrelationship with other social institutions in the functioning of society—such as the family, the economy, law and government, education, and beliefs, morals, attitudes, and values, the student is made aware of the vitally important part that film and television play as highly significant social forces in today's world.

"Making models, telling a story using eight simple drawings or cut-out pictures, writing a shooting script, making a collage, choosing mood music to accompany a short silent film, telling a story with sound, painting on clear film, scratching on old film, are just a few examples of the very many worthwhile and practical ways of teaching girls and boys how to communicate with sound and image. Some film making and video making is also attempted, but this always depends on the time and money available.

"*Arrangement of courses.* There is much more to the introduction of screen education than simply arranging a timetable: a screening area, suitably blocked out, and a trained projectionist must be made available several times a week; a room is necessary for editing, slicing, animation, and video work, and somewhere to keep all the equipment safely; a rosta of visits to film and television studios and a program of guest speakers has to be prepared as well as forward planning with arts, photography, science, and music teachers.

"The most important task of all is to provide screen material to illustrate the courses. A computerized booking system has recently been installed in our State Film Library, and multiple copies of a wide range of material can be borrowed on a three day loan turn-around system.

"So much for the bare bones of screen education in South Australia; but what advantages are there to be gained by the student from studying the subject? Children enjoy seeing films and watching television. Here is something they like and can understand. They already know much about the visual media and come to the lesson eager to learn more. Perhaps for the first time many are confronted with a subject which is intrinsically interesting to them. Students who find reading difficult and have, because of this, a limited experience of stories and characterization, now discover that they can add to their knowledge quickly and enjoyably. They find it easy to interpret what they have seen and heard on the screen and join in a discussion on film plot or television technique in a way which they will never do when discussing the style or story of a novel or play. This gives them confidence.

"However, in introducing courses of screen education, care should be taken not to put too much emphasis on 'doing' and not enough on 'thinking.' It is fun to play with equipment and to use a film and a video camera in order to communicate with sound and image, but the primary purpose and value of this practical work with school students is not to make them good filmmakers but to provide them with the means of understanding how they—the viewers—are communicated with, so that they know how they can be manipulated and persuaded by the screen media. The greatest benefit derived from a film and television course is for young people to become aware of the social significance of the visual media in their daily lives and to become critical and discriminating in their use."

TEACHERS AND PUPILS

THALIA DRAGONAS (Institute of Anthropos, Athens, Greece) reported on an analysis of the written opinions of 40 12-year-old schoolchildren and 35 teachers as to what constitutes a good teacher. The children's responses were grouped under the following heads:

Non-domineering discipline. Ninety percent considered this imperative, and the most frequent characteristics were to be able to foster discipline without shouting, hitting, or cursing; to be neither too soft nor too hard; not to oppress; to be fair and just; not to influence the children's opinions; no biases or prejudices. The children should feel free within well set boundaries; should be able to speak up for themselves.

Understanding. Eighty percent considered this very important. The statements were that the teacher should understand; be friendly; be able to follow the child's thoughts and feelings; feel with, come near to, communicate with, and have close contact with the child, and provide support for it.

Discussion. Seventy per cent referred to the value of discussions in class and on personal problems out of class.

Teaching skills. Only 50% specifically mentioned teaching skills as important.

Personal attributes. Only 20% cared if the teacher was young, polite, good, or kind.

To sum up, these 12 year olds want discipline without feeling oppressed; want freedom, but want it structured; want the teacher to communicate with them, showing understanding and providing support. The children seemed realistic. Their concept of a good teacher would not restrict their own autonomy and range of purposeful action.

The teacher's questionnaire was completed by 35 private schoolteachers (male and female) with an average of 12 years' experience. The initial finding was a very strong resistance to the questionnaire, which was originally given to 70 teachers. Even among the half which took it, many were very noncommittal. This can be attributed in part to the fact that Greek private school teachers have recently been through a difficult period of negotiation for more secure tenure, during which they have been under attack from government ministers and parents, so they felt very defensive. When asked about their methods of keeping discipline, most teachers concentrated on traditional and conservative techniques attached to rewards—like good grades. More than half admitted to physical punishment. On the other hand, when asked to comment on the emphasis paid to work handed out by the teacher versus work done on the initiative of the children or on individual versus group work, or on different seating arrangements, the answers given were so "progressive" that they gave rise to a suspicion that "a social desirability element might be present."

When asked to select from a list the characteristics they thought most important in a good teacher; they responded very differently from the children, giving chief place to teaching skills and discussion.

Can the divergence between what the school children desire and what they get be attributed to poor channels of communication? If so, the very fact of informing the teachers of the children's priorities should help to solve the problem. But it seems more likely that better communication will only reveal more clearly the wide discrepancies between the value systems of the students and the school authorities.

THE ENVIRONMENT AND THE FUTURE

ATHENA and LUKIA RIKAKI (The Red Balloon Adventure Playgrounds and Environmental Studies, Athens, Greece) described some of the work they have been doing as part of a research project on new education systems in the Thessaloniki University Philosophical School. They showed a film and said: "We are part of a group of people working on creative games and environmental education. The 'Korais' school is a traditional Greek school where the teachers have agreed to play environmental games with the children. These games start from the most simple things like quickly passing a piece of paper from hand to hand to accustom them to operate constructively in a small space. The children enter a small room and sit down on the floor in a circle—something quite unusual in a Greek school. They start a discussion about the things they see in the neighborhood and try not to interrupt each other without raising their hands. This means they do not communicate according to normal school rules. Then they divide into groups chosen by themselves and proceed to exchange opinions as to what the neighborhood, which they intend to create, should contain. They discuss what are the changes that would make the neighborhood a better place to live in. Then they write down the final decisions of their group so that they can present them to the others. After this they proceed to map out the streets on the floor, the parks, and the different places where they will put buildings. They take off their shoes so that they can step carefully in the tiny spaces of their neighborhood.

"The following week they bring in the constructions that they have made during the week. First they build their own house, then the house they would like to have, then a friend's house. They place these houses where they fit in the neighborhood. They complete whatever does not exist by means of drawings. Then they leave to think about how they should continue, and to bring in new constructions.

"Another group enters. They observe the unfinished neighborhood and make remarks about it. Then they talk about the neighborhood's surroundings, and imagine what could be outside it. They bring in bold colors to paint these surroundings on the walls. This presents several difficulties because they have big surfaces to cover which is something quite new, as up till then no one was ever allowed to paint the walls. At first they draw small things which they know quite well how to draw, until they gradually become used to the new scale. The children can add something to another's work or can work all together in a collective spirit.

"Children from other classes look in with astonishment and ask for something similar for themselves.

"Perhaps the whole exercise does not appear to you very directly related to the subject of 'media in education,' but in fact we make a film of the projects which we can then use to advise and inform other teachers, and we also write up a document which can be used in discussion with parents' groups, etc., and in this way many people become involved in environmental work."

THE PRESS

TARZIE VITTACHI (UN Fund for Population Activities, New York, NY, USA) spoke on the uses and misuses of the printed word in shaping value systems. He said: "We sometimes forget that it is us, the generation of adults, who are in fact the conveyors of ideas and values to the children. The freedom of the press does not belong to the press, it belongs to the people. This is a freedom—a function—that none of us can afford to surrender, especially at a time like this, when the whole world has reached a point of critical change. It cannot be too often repeated that the pace of change is so great, the number of problems reaching the point of critical mass so numerous, that we cannot relegate to anyone else the function of conveying values and ideas to the younger people for whom we are responsible. This means that we, the people, have to scrutinize the press as closely as the press scrutinizes the government of the day.

"I will give an example of what I mean. Some schools in Asia asked me to talk to them about how to read a newspaper. My first course was in New Delhi, and I asked: Will somebody give me a newspaper? Actually I was given a copy of an international magazine. I opened it at random and there was a picture of a mass demonstration somewhere in Africa. I said: 'I bet you that if we read this story we shall find the word "mob" in it.' We read it, and sure enough in the fourth or fifth line the crowd was described as a mob. I turned the pages and found a picture of a demonstration in London against the Vietnam war. I said: 'I bet you we shall not find the word "mob" in this story,' and we did not. I mention this as the kind of trick we journalists play on people. It is the business of a journalist, as a communicator, to lodge ideas in your head. For instance, I will not use adjectives as instruments of prejudice—it is very easy to spot adjectives—but I shall rather use adverbs. And many journalists are very expert at this. For example, if their newspaper is on the side, say of the Shah of Iran, they will write: 'The Shah naturally decided . . .': the word 'naturally' creeps up like a pi-dog into your mind, and stays there. Or one can use verbs. Newspapers that do not like President Carter say that he 'snapped,' which suggests that he is becoming neurotic. Those that like him say he 'declared,' which is full of positive thinking. Words are really deadly weapons.

"In my own home I read the paper and look at television along with my children so that I can pass on to them some of the cunning I have learnt, to help them not to get caught in the traps most people fall into. In fact, when my daughter took her degree she wrote saying: 'I want to thank you for having taught me to read like a detective.' I would like all of you to look at everything you read with the awareness that the person who wrote it was out to put some idea into your mind. It may be a good idea, but let it cool its heels for a little bit in the anteroom of your mind before you let it in.

"We are all media: parents, teachers, preachers, union leaders, professionals, youth groups. You remember the famous phrase: 'The medium is the message.' In Marshall McLuhan's sense we are ourselves the message in our conduct, feelings, and the way we express ourselves and act. To some extent we are also all victims of what is going on in the world because we ourselves have very little power to change anything. But what we can do is to begin to make such nuisances of ourselves in our own society that it becomes unprofitable for the media to perpetuate the stereotypes that now divide the world (north, south, east, west, black, white, etc.).

"During the recent crisis in Zaire I was in London and it amazed me—as an old professional—to find that the main impression coming across was 'Beau Geste strikes again!' The great French Foreign Legion stormed into Kolwesi and rescued three (or four) hundred white people from the barbaric black hordes! The fact that 1800 black people died in this attack was scarcely mentioned, or the fact the whole operation was about protecting access to the uranium deposits for the making of nuclear weapons. This is the kind of dangerous stereotype that I am talking about. The French Foreign Legion were the heroes of the occasion: Gary Cooper and the whole lot of them!

"I turn to a more serious kind of stereotype that we have to watch out for and protect our children from. I asked my Indian colleagues for an explanation of Mrs. Gandhi's defeat at the last election, and they all told me it was because she and her son compelled people to accept vasectomy and sterilization. It is a fact that there was a tremendous backlash, but very often facts are very different from the truth. Suppose you divide India horizontally, so that there are 300 parlimentary seats north of the line and 300 south of it. North of the line, Mrs. Gandhi (who is a north Indian) lost every seat except four. South of that line, she and her allies won every seat except six. How does the story of the backlash from vasectomy explain this voting pattern? If we look a bit further we find that in the south—to mention just one factor—a vast amount of free primary school education had resulted in a whole generation of girls being educated. This has postponed their marriage age and has also made them employable. This, in turn, has enabled their parents to get away from the traditional idea that they must go on having more and more children to have enough boys to earn enough for their own old age—since only boys were employable. Also infant mortality has fallen in the south from about 180 per 1000 to 50 per 1000, so families did not feel that they had to replace children who were bound to die. This was the difference between north and south that was reflected in the election results. There were other differences, of course, but the journalists' presentation was a mere stereotype: the need of a journalist to have a quick black and white explanation. A journalist goes to a country which has just had a *coup d'état* and asks: 'Is this pro-left or pro-right? Is it pro-American or pro-Soviet?' I have been guily of this kind of stupid, superficial explanation myself, so I know how stupid it is, how easy it is, and how dangerous it is.

"Last week the United Nations issued an important report on the state of the world population. It was to be produced one evening on all television channels. But nothing appeared on any of them because Princess Caroline of Monaco was being married on that day. The media say: 'We must give the public what it wants.' This is the last refuge of the pornographer, for it is very easy to corrupt the public taste and then feed it with corruption. The marvelous technology of communications is used in a way which recalls H. G. Wells' statement in 1919 'Man made the aeroplane and the ape got hold of it.'

"But we have reached a point of change. The world is no longer being shaped by events: events are only the symptoms of processes. Population growth, malnutrition, changes in the situation of women, all these are processes not events. For instance, a New York newspaper wrote that the great Sahel drought started in 1971 and went on through 1972, 1973, 1974. Then, in big letters, it said 'Where were you UN?' A good question, but where also was the press? Not one reference to the gathering drought had appeared in all those years. Only after it had become an event, after thousands of people died, was it worth covering. If we begin to think in terms of processes it is possible to act in time to prevent such events taking place."

COMMUNICATION IN THE SYMPOSIUM

After the meeting, the Coordinator contributed the following comments:

"In this session there was an awareness of the 'hidden environment' of the conference. By 'hidden' I mean the fact that many participants were affected, unconsciously rather than consciously:

(a) By the architecture of fixed seating, making the 'lecture' format the only format possible.

(b) By the hidden technology of earphones, filming, taping, fixed microphone stands, xerox, etc., the presence of which limited certain forms of communication.

(c) By the hidden people, e.g. projectionists, editorial assistants, chairpersons, rapporteurs, secretaries, who, by their particular presences, limited certain freedoms.

"When the session moved to sit in an informal circle in the coffee lounge, changes were noticed in peoples' eyes, mouths, words, and their whole mind/body. All aspects of the meeting suddenly flowered and became more alive.

"Children generate this liveliness spontaneously, but as we grow up we lose our abilities to question, to create, to be unpredictable, to cooperate, to be intuitive, to be warm. This was felt particularly during this media session. While we understood that a future built, at least in part, by the children would be a better future, participants of the media session seemed frightened of the greater flexibility that would result.

"The question of how much more frightening is a fixed environment as opposed to a loose one was not actually discussed, though we realized that the conference auditorium was tremendously fixed. The media session was a place where we could have become more aware of this problem, and we could have developed and shared more ideas in a different setting, such as on a mountain, under a gigantic open tent, or in the light of the pure sky and the fresh scent of the sea."

LIST OF PAPERS PRESENTED

THALIA DRAGONAS (Institute of Anthropos, Athens, Greece): "Twelve-year-old students' perception and expectation of the good teacher compared to teachers' attitudes."

MARIA KAVATZA (Association for Protection of the Under-aged, Athens, Greece): "The influence of the movies on the behavior of the under-aged."

CALLIOPE MOUSTAKA (Athens Center of Social Research, Athens, Greece): "Children evaluate their neighborhood."

ATHENA and LUKIA RIKAKI (Red Balloon Adventure Playgrounds and Environmental Studies, Athens, Greece): "Environmental education in schools."

EILEEN SHARMAN (The Film Study Committee, Brighton, South Australia): "Screen education in South Australia."

TARZIE VITTACHI (UN Fund for Population Activities, New York, USA): "The freedom of the press."

EDUCATION FOR SPECIAL GROUPS

Coordinator: JAMES J. GALLAGHER
Department of Education, University of North Carolina at Chapel Hill, NC, USA

THE FUTURE prospects for those children both handicapped and gifted, who are different from the norm, was the concern of this special group meeting. The meeting was divided into four special interest subgroups to encourage communication around topics of common interest.

A common theme throughout the symposium has been the major differences between the developed and developing countries. While they face common problems, cultures differ greatly in the quantity and intensity of the problems and in the particular resources to deal with them. A different set of patterns of service delivery will be needed for the developing countries and that pattern must be determined by the cultural background of the society involved. The developed world can help by providing knowledge and expertise but should not expect their existing models to be accepted or implemented in cultures so clearly different from their own.

The first set of themes reports the future prospects and concerns of those groups discussing the handicapped child and family.

APPROPRIATE ROLES OF PARENTS AND PROFESSIONALS

EDITH H. GROTBERG (*in Chair*) (Department of Health, Education, and Welfare, Washington, DC, USA): One of the desired future accomplishments would be the stabilization of the relationships between parent and professional. A specific call to endorse the position that professionals should have the right to disregard parental wishes if the parent resists treatment for their handicapped child was rejected by the group. The opposition was based upon the parents' right to determine their child's future and the possibility that the professional might be wrong or uncomprehending of the family, particularly when the parents and professional come from different cultural backgrounds.

Another point was that the different factors present in each case are so compelling that any general rule would likely to become an embarrassment. It was much better (the total group agreed) to realize that "professionals and parents are involved in a co-operative task and that the relation is one of interdependence." Therefore we must intensify our efforts to find ways for the professional and parent to work in harmony for the benefit of the child.

It was clear that, although all endorse the general principle of parent participation, the specific operations by which that participation takes place are still vague in the minds of many professionals.

273

However, Dr. C. BRAJOVIC (Department of Psychology, University of Belgrade, Yugoslavia) suggested that, while there has been widespread belief that little can be done to change the fate of handicapped children, early diagnosis and early beginning of therapy through active parent involvement are very important for the effect of rehabilitation. The therapist must teach parents how to apply therapeutic models as well as explain their purpose. He must teach them how to organize the activities of their children and how to respond to specific behavior. Modern achievements in medicine and psychology that are related to the stimulation of cognitive development and to the rehabilitation of handicapped children must be made available to concerned parents. Indeed, the role of the expert is to systematize this knowledge and to present it to parents in a comprehensible way, so that they have means to cope with those disorders which were once considered unchangeable. It was also suggested that since no one profession has all of the wisdom needed to help the child and family, cooperative teams of professionals need to be established who will work in concert to provide the necessary total therapy program for the family of the handicapped child. However, a specific suggestion was made that some linking or coordinating person should be employed to orchestrate the services for individual families.

THE MEDICALLY HANDICAPPED

MIA KELLMER-PRINGLE (in Chair) (National Children's Bureau, London, UK). The importance of early screening and diagnosis followed by appropriate treatment was stressed in all groups. The virtues of intervening early in the development process are obvious, and the main question is how that intervention can best be accomplished in various settings, and where the personnel and fiscal resources will come from to allow it to happen. If at all possible, services should be provided to the family which would allow the handicapped child to remain in the home. The family unit is clearly seen as the better alternative to large institutional settings. The family should be able to participate as much as possible in the screening, diagnosis, remedial and educational processes. The tendency for professionals to take over responsibility for the child and push aside the family should be resisted, and professionals should reexamine their own motivations for such behavior. In fact, there are substantial advantages for the parents of handicapped children in the formation of parent groups. These give emotional support, practical counsel and advice, and provide a better chance for the needs of parents to be heard by the public and professionals. Thought should be given to what kind of incentives should be given to aid most effectively the development of such organizations.

One such incentive would be to make certain that the parents see the gains in the child and the gains in themselves, as well as that others within that community context (so important to parents and children) see the gains in both the child and the parents.

LEARNING DIFFICULTIES

B. K. RAMANUJAM (in Chair) (BM Institute of Public Health, New Delhi, India). There is much that remains to be learned about handicapping conditions and how they unfold longitudinally. We need to investigate better screening methods, particularly for children with learning disability, and better remedial and educational programs. Unless we conduct further research, we condemn ourselves to our current level of professional wisdom, and that level is clearly not high enough. It was stressed that if there is to be meaningful treatment assessment, there is a need to ensure that screening teams are constituted according to local conditions, rather than according to a general and uniform model.

THE GIFTED AND TALENTED

JAMES J. GALLAGHER (in Chair). While a different set of problems and future projections were identified for the gifted and talented, a clear link was found between the gifted and handicapped. Who shall find the new discoveries for prevention, the new models for effective service delivery, and the new concepts for better understanding of the handicapping conditions, if not the future gifted scientists, physicians, and educators? In a strange fashion, then, the fate of the handicapped child of the future is dependent upon the current education of the gifted.

There was a strong consensus that many gifted children are not identified early enough in the educational system, and that failure to identify them can result in greatly reduced efficiency in learning and create special motivational problems for the gifted student. He may well become disinterested or bored with the school program. Attempts to employ existing and new tests (such as new measures of creativity) should be used to identify these children early, as a prelude to some type of appropriate special education procedures.

The group felt that attempts should be made to develop curricula that would provide cross-cultural experiences for the gifted students, many of whom are destined to be business, scientific and political leaders in their societies, and to have to interact with other cultures as part of their natural responsibilities. A special emphasis in such programs should be placed on being able to see the other person's point of view. A specific example that was used would be to ask the student to pretend to be a reporter or historian and write a story from both sides of some major dispute such as French–English in modern Canada; American–English in the Revolutionary War; Greek-Turkish conflicts; Black–White issues in South Africa.

The understanding of the value base from which differing cultures spring was felt to be necessary to encourage national cooperation, if not survival, in the world of the future.

Many children of outstanding talents are viewed as inadequately using their talents, often because of emotional problems and low self-image. Special attention should be paid to a variety of models that could be used for remediation. Some of these would include the development of culturally relevant curricula, and psychotherapy and counseling where necessary. A specific device, commented upon favorably, was the "survival school" especially designed for cultural minorities which allows the children to organize their own educational programs and helps them to develop their own sense of ethnic pride and identity.

Also discussed was the importance of an educational program that stresses the study of morality and values, not for the purposes of indoctrination, but to allow the student to be well grounded in the various philosophical approaches to the use of values and ethics. This is stressed again under the assumption that many of these children will become their nation's leaders and will need a moral perspective to guide their decision making.

RELATION BETWEEN PROFESSIONALS AND POLICYMAKER: PRIESTS AND KINGS

JAMES J. GALLAGHER. Whatever the members of the symposium have been able to agree upon in regard to the desired future of exceptional children, the fate of those children lies in the hands of others who are not present at the symposium. These are the political decision makers who will determine the support or nonsupport of present and future programs. They have the power to allocate or withhold the allocation of those scarce societal resources needed to make those programs operate.

Berle once pointed out that there is always a certain amount of creative tension between the "priests" of the society who control the knowledge of that society and the "king" who controls power and thus the allocation of resources. Each society has some version of these priests and kings. The priests are often disdainful of the king since they know more than he does about certain things, and the king has some contempt for the priests since they are so naive about power and the need to compromise when one is a leader.

In most societies the demographic characteristics of the "kings" are hardly favorable to the support of programs for children. They are mainly:

(1) *Male:* they are often inclined to believe that children are the proper concern of women, not governments.
(2) *Old and getting older:* they worry about this and are more likely to spend research money on cancer and heart disease than on childhood disorders.
(3) *Their own children are grown:* they are less likely to have a child at the age where their own personal experience would help them understand children's problems.
(4) *They are middle class: they do not realize or sympathize with the prob-*lems of poverty or the impact on children through the social disorganization that accompanies poverty.

One major question is how to make the most effective impact on these kings or decision makers. The traditional means of communication for the priests is books and articles. This seems inappropriate as the kings generally communicate through personal contact, where they can use their own well-developed ability to judge the reliability of the messenger.

The formation of parent groups of handicapped children was noted as one device for communicating effectively with political leaders. Such efforts in the United States have brought forth strong political support for programs for handicapped children.

It is clear that the priests cannot content themselves with sitting in their enclaves discussing problems only with each other. If they expect public support for their programs, the price for such support is that they must venture forth into the world of reality and communicate their needs in the language of the kings.

MIA KELLMER-PRINGLE (National Children's Bureau, London, UK): "Present inadequacies and future trends."

MATTI SILLANPAA (School of Public Health, Helsinki, Finland): "International Academy for Handicapped Children."

MULTINATIONAL WOMEN'S LIBERATION GROUP (Athens, Greece): "Creativity in a cross-cultural environment."

JULIETTE VISSARAKIS (Speech therapist, Athens, Greece): "Lutte contre les difficultés de prononciation chez l'enfant par la 'logopédie'."

THE PRESCHOOL CHILD

Coordinator: CONSTANTINE PAPADATOS

School of Medicine, University of Athens, Greece

THE VALUE of day care centers for small children and the need for many more of them was voiced by speakers from Bahrain, Greece, and Indonesia, and examples of efforts to meet these needs within the economy and culture of a developing country were given from Sri Lanka and India.

DR. PRIYANI SOYSA (Faculty of Medicine, University of Sri Lanka, Colombo, Sri Lanka) stated that the Ministry of Health had trained community workers in 800 of the 4000 villages of Sri Lanka. These workers are mostly girls who have finished 12 grades of formal schooling. They are chosen by the local community and paid by the state. They spend one week at a health center and then have on-the-job training in health care, child development, and stimulation with teachers from the Health Education Bureau. Each becomes responsible for 20 families in their village, and they organize play centers for the young children. In all programs of creative play activity the materials used are inexpensive and local, such as eggshells, leaves, and wood shavings. Singing, dancing, and play acting are culturally based and in the local language. The essence of these community programs is their simplicity, from which stems the possibility of duplicating them in the poor socioeconomic setting of Sri Lanka.

M. M. RAJENDRAN (Ministry of Social Welfare, New Delhi, India) described a somewhat similar Indian program, adding that another method was to attach day nurseries to girls' high schools: "so that the older girls can gain some valuable mothering experience."

JOAN LESTOR (House of Commons, London, UK) spoke of the several different types of day care in a developed country, saying: "Although Britain has a central Ministry of Education, each local authority district is responsible for its own education services, and no local authority is compelled by law to provide nursery schools. Therefore the provision varies enormously from area to area, and usually the areas that most need nursery schools do not get them—for obvious reasons. Although the arguments for nursery education have now been widely accepted, it is still regarded as the embroidery of the education system: as something that is not a basic necessity. However, if nursery schools are provided by the local authority, they are free.

"Because of this spasmodic provision and the recognition of many parents of the needs of preschool experience, groups of parents got together and started what has become known as the Preschool Play Group Movement. If your child goes to a play group, you pay something. Sometimes the equipment is not as good as in a good nursery school, but I think this is compensated for by the parents' involvement in running the center. Play groups have now had some government money made available, but the reaction from a number of professional teachers, including the National Union of Teachers, has not been favorable: 'These people are not trained and you should leave the job to us.'

"We also have a third program of day nurseries for working mothers. This is administered by the Ministry of Health and Social Welfare. It is a relatively small program, and by and large you can only get your child into a day nursery if you have very special reasons why you need to go to work. You pay for this care according to your means.

"If your child goes to a nursery school it will be staffed by fully trained teachers, but if your child goes to a day nursery it will be run by young people who have had much less training. This means that the children in greatest need—from single parent or deprived families—are in the care of people who are not as educationally qualified.

"Finally, we have child minding, where women—who usually have children of their own—take someone else's children into their house and look after them. At one time there was tremendous outcry against this. Everybody wanted to clean up and disinfect, to regulate and inspect this service. Then it was realized that child minders meet a real community need, and that this service often suits people very well and tends to be cheaper than state provision.

"One last point: in the last few years there has been some recognition of the stupidity of our division of care for preschool children (between the Ministries of Education and of Health, local authorities, and voluntary organizations) which has produced all sorts of contradictions and anomalies. In parts of London and Birmingham, and in one or two other places, there is now a marrying up of the day care field. This means one gets an establishment—or center—that is open, say, from 8.00 a.m. to 6.00 p.m. and is staffed throughout by trained teachers—by people trained in the care of small children. The children can go for part of the day, if that is the need of the mother or child; they can go for the whole time; or they can go for a nursery school hour or two, if that again is the need. This is the beginning of a recognition that legislation that says there shall be no discrimination and that there shall be equal pay just does not work unless we have proper backup facilities for women who have children, because the responsibility of the children is still left with the woman. However, although we have now won the argument that education is basically about curiosity, and the young child is at its most curious in the preschool years, we still have to convince the politicians that they have to allocate enough money to effectively do something about it."

Day care programs were discussed by a number of speakers. DR. AKIHIRO CHIBA (Education Section, UNESCO, Paris, France) pointed out that day care centers in rural areas and in developing countries usually try to model themselves on middle class urban nursery schools, where the emphasis is very largely upon socialization, which is usually quite irrelevant in village settings. Many parents also press for early training in academic subjects.

MARIAN BARNETT (Department of Education, Carleton University, Ottawa, Canada) described the creative yet educational uses of waste materials in a Canadian village: the children learnt to classify objects by sorting bottle caps and other contributions they brought from home. They also sorted cardboard boxes into small, medium, and large sizes. The children then used these, along with cylinders from toilet rolls and wrapping paper, to build model houses.

A. GEORGOULI (Alexandra Maternity Hospital, Athens, Greece) presented a study showing that the learning ability of a preschool child (as it is going to be tested in the school system) is directly related to socioeconomic factors and to the parents' personalities.

O. FAGERLI (Ministry of Consumer Affairs and Government, Oslo, Norway) displayed a study designed to advise the Norwegian Government on the location of new kindergartens on the basis of local culture and local needs. It was found that children living in homogeneous neighborhoods with a kindergarten close by were better able to concentrate in their play and work than when the kindergarten was outside their familiar local environment. They were also more considerate if the kindergarten did not include children from a different home background (e.g. in a native, working class neighborhood, if there were no children of foreign migrants or from a middle income suburb). Finally they were less hostile than in kindergartens which were both outside the home environment and included children from different backgrounds.

DR. A. NOEL (Service de Médicine Scolaire, Brussels, Belgium) showed how simple but adequate tests for physical fitness can be carried out with the willing cooperation of young children.

Another subject of discussion was the relationship between the preschool child and its mother. Several speakers emphasized that the child under 2 needs a one to one relationship with its mother or a mother substitute. The problem period was between the ages of 2/3 and 5—the period before the child goes to a regular school and when the mother is often occupied with another baby.

H. MORFI and P. SAKELLAROPOLOS (Pati Morfi Nursery School, Athens, Greece) presented a paper entitled "Forms of pathological attachment to the mother and difficulties of adjustment in nursery school." They instanced four forms of parental behavior which inhibited the young child from developing its own individuality. The first was total control over feeding; denying the child any right of choice retards its progress toward independence. The second was restricting the child's physical activity. The third was prolonging the home–school ambivalence by elaborate daily farewells, which augment the child's own anxieties. Fourth was preserving the early childhood phantasy world.

DR. E. N. LIANTONAKIS (State Mental Hospital, Athens, Greece) read a more clinical paper on much the same issue, stating that whatever happens in this critical age will predetermine in many ways the rest of the persons's life. "The harmful end result of parental attitudes of an overdemanding, school-like or didactic type . . . acting either as a causative or as a precipitating agent, is responsible for numerous pathological reactions including the protogenous anxiety-depressive condition."

DR. A. J. VAN BENTUM (Foundation K & O, The Hague, Netherlands) described the work of "K & O" (Child and Parent) which aims at promoting child welfare by offering guidance to parents and other educators. In addition to consultations and distribution of literature, there are frequent group discussions, and parents can borrow books and toys.

Finally the session turned to the care of preschool children in hospital. DR. PRIYANI SOYSA told of the creative play therapy program that she has been operating for five years in a hospital for sick children, with the help of volunteers. It has had such good results that the Ministry of Education has agreed to provide part-time teachers on a permanent basis.

GUNILLA DROSOPOULOU (Aglaia Kyriakou Children's Hospital, Athens, Greece) showed a film made in the Aglaia Kyriakou Children's Hospital in Athens demonstrating the value of play for hospitalized children

DOROTHEA PASSIOS (Miller Children's Hospital Medical Center, Longbeach, CA, USA) described a hospital Child Life Center in the United States. This is a place where children can learn, have fun, and be normal again. The Child Life Staff have opportunities to observe the children and their reactions, and feedback to the hospital staff. Parents are encouraged to participate, and at certain times, brothers and sisters or a very special friend. The therapeutic environment encourages children to be active again, rather than passive receivers of medical treatment. The environment seems to help the parents when they see their child happily involved in normal school and play activity. The staff has opportunities, too, to do informal parent teaching. Children who otherwise might feel very alone or different are brought to the Child Life Center in wheelchairs, beds on carts or in wagons, with IVACs or IVs and catheters. Many exciting things happen there as children interact with each other, like "Hey, he's got a catheter, too!" "We both have the same scars!" Children are encouraged and provided with opportunities to play out their feelings. A very popular area, the play therapy corner, has IVs that run, masks, dolls recovering from surgery, stuffed animals with casts, and a box of syringes and band aids. "You did it to me—now it's my turn to do it to you," one youngster exclaimed as he gave his doll a shot.

It does not take children long, no matter what their age, to realize that the Child Life personnel are nonthreatening. Numerous studies support the fact that skilled psychological management of the hospitalized child has an importance that goes far beyond its obvious humanitarian worth. The calm child not only is an easier patient to manage, but actually responds more favourably to medical treatments.

LIST OF PAPERS PRESENTED

MARIAN BARNETT (Department of Education, Carleton University, Ottawa, Canada): "A home-school community interaction program: improving coping skills of a minority group living in a changing isolated community."

H. SALINI ESHKEVARI (Department of Child Psychiatry, Roosbeh Hospital, Tehran): "Effects of day care centers on the behavior of infants and young children."

ODDVAR FAGERLI (Ministry of Consumer Affairs and Government, Oslo, Norway): "The local environment: kindergarten project."

A. GEORGOULI and M. KOUKOU (Alexandra Maternity Hospital, Athens, Greece): "Verbal learning by preschool children: Family and psychokinetic factors."

E. N. LIANTONAKIS (State Mental Hospital, Athens, Greece): "Parental attitudes of an educative-learning character as a factor of psychological physical disturbances in preschool age."

ELSA MAVRANGO-HARITOU (Lawyer, Athens, Greece): "Crêche d'enfants: leurs fonctionnement et rôle comme substitut de la présence maternelle."

H. MORFI and P. SAKELLAROPOLOS (Pati Morfi Nursery School, Athens, Greece): "Forms of pathological attachment to the mother and difficulties of adjustment in nursery school."

A. NOEL (Service de Médecine Scolaire, Brussels, Belgium): "Préparation psychologique des enfants des classes maternelles à l'examen médical préventif."

DOROTHEA PASSIOS (Miller Children's Hospital Medical Center, Longbeach, CA, USA): "Emotional care of hospitalized children."

PRIYANI SOYSA (Faculty of Medicine, University of Sri Lanka, Colombo, Sri Lanka): "Preschool education in Sri Lanka."

A. J. VAN BENTUM (Foundation K & O, The Hague, Netherlands): "Promoting child welfare by providing support to parents and other educators."

CHILDREN OF MIGRANT WORKERS:
A GREEK PROBLEM

Coordinator: VASSILIS FILIAS

Pantios Higher School of Political Science Athens, Greece

THE COORDINATOR introduced the subject by referring to the process of socialization among the children of emigrant families. He said that in the preschool age, their socialization is significantly influenced by the following basic conditions:

(1) A high percentage of the mothers are illiterate, or have a low standard of education.
(2) Participation of the migrant families in the life of their host country is more or less limited to the working sphere: in other facets of social life their participation is minimal.
(3) Migrant families have often come from preindustrial societies in their own countries to live in highly industrialized societies in an advanced stage of capitalist development.
(4) A high proportion of mothers of migrant children work outside the home in order to accumulate the largest possible amount of family savings in the shortest possible time.

We find that some of the basic consequences of these conditions are:

(1) The migrant families, right from the beginning, feel extremely uncertain about the basic social patterns and rules of behavior which should be transmitted to their young children in the primary stages of socialization.
(2) The time which a migrant working mother can devote to the rearing of her children is much less than in her home land.
(3) The conditions of isolation from the wider environment, plus the state of the *de facto* ghetto in which the migrant families live in the host country, create a feeling of inferiority in the children. This is intensified by the language barrier.

Within this framework the dynamics of the psychological development of the children of migrants would seem, by definition, to be disturbed due to the existence of alienating factors both within the framework of the family and also in their broader surrounding environment.

One of the most severe problems of the children of migrants is that they speak two languages and that they fail to master either of them in depth. This problem could be overcome if child-minding centers were specifically designed for migrant children with simultaneous preschool teaching in both the child's mother tongue and the language of the host country. However, no host country has provided such facilities on a planned scale. Where they do exist they are exceptional. As a rule the child of migrants reaches the age of schooling in a state of linguistic confusion, which expresses itself in a severe underdevelopment of perception patterns.

When the migrant child, under these conditions, reaches the age for making the basic choices which will determine his life vocation, he is already an "outsider." He finds himself in competition with the children of the host country and in this competition he is at a great disadvantage. When these children reach the age when they should be able to enter vocational schools, it is found that there are enormous gaps in their knowledge in all technical and scientific fields. These deficiencies not only hinder them from entering vocational schools but also prevent them from continuing studies in preparation for university.

The big gaps which exist in their education by the time they reach the critical age of 14 to 15, place the adolescent in a dilemma. Either he has to make a tremendous effort to overcome these shortcomings or to seek any sort of odd job that he can find. It is obvious that the second and easier choice is made in the overwhelming number of cases. In this way, another generation of unskilled workers is created to fill vacant jobs which the inhabitants of the host country are not willing to take.

In this second generation of migrant workers, a very high percentage of deviant and anomic behavior is likely to appear as a result of the marginal conditions of work and of life in general for this young population.

Problems exist which can only be solved by a very close collaboration and joint efforts of the governments of both the sending and receiving countries. However, the burden of building a suitable infrastructure must be borne by the receiving countries since they have benefited from the immigration of cheap working labor.

IOANNA MANGANARA (Pantios Higher School of Political Science, Athens, Greece), read a paper examining the education problems of:

(1) children living with their families in the receiving country;
(2) children who have returned to their home countries with or without their parents;
(3) children who have stayed behind in their home countries while their parents (one or both) have migrated.

She said that her comments were not confined to children of Greek parents. In 1974 the estimated number of children of migrant working families in Europe amounted approximately to four million; 1,600,000 were in the age group of 0–6 years; 1,600,000 in the age group 7–16; and 800,000 in the age group 17–21.

1. *Children Living with Their Families*
in the Receiving Country
   Prenatal phase.

Among many other problems, migrant women usually ignore or mistrust the social assistance programs for which they are eligible. This alone may contribute to the high rates of infant mortality and morbidity among migrant families. According to French statistics, the mortality rate for migrant children in France was 42·6% in 1971 and 37% in 1972; while for French children it was 29% and 30% respectively.

The child's first years. Immigrant children's assignments to places in day nurseries are not only limited by a lack of facilities, but also by the opinion that the places which are available should first be offered to indigenous children. As a result, it is quite common for immigrant children to be left all day locked up in a room, given no toys to play with, and never spoken to except when food is brought to them. Often the eldest child will be left with this responsibility.

School-age children. Official statistics show that in most Western European countries only a small percent of immigrant children attend school. One reason for the low attendance figures is that parents often want their children to start earning money as quickly as possible. A second factor has to do with the assignment of the older children to care for the younger ones in the home. Also a basic obstacle which hinders school-age children's integration into the school system of the foreign country is their lack of knowledge of the country's language. There are also many sociocultural factors. Most parents cannot assist their children in adapting to the new culture; more specifically they are unable to help them with their homework. Often the children live and grow up in a very confined space where study is difficult. A further problem is with student–teacher relationships. The teacher, usually with a middle class background, often has a negative view of working class families in general, and especially of migrant working class families.

2. Problems of Children who Return to Their Home Country

Migrant parents often foresee problems for their children in readapting to the higher education system or the labor market of their home country. Therefore they may choose to send a school age child back home. A suggested way of solving some of the problems of readaptation has been the provision of special courses in the receiving countries, preferably integrated with the home country school system. The few programs that have been started in this direction are generally too small, the teachers are not truly bilingual, and they often give extra scholastic work to children who are already heavily involved in overcoming other difficulties.

On the other hand, the sending countries have taken no effective measures to facilitate the reintegration of these children into their own school system by organizing special classes to help them catch up on language deficiencies, etc.

A basic problem encountered by children who return to their home country is an identity crisis, which questions the process of socialization that they have undergone in the host country. The child in this situation feels insecure and socially isolated, with detrimental effects on his school performance.

3. Children who Stay Behind in the Home Country

For the children who stay behind, alienation from the parents is an inevitable consequence of the separation, especially when both parents are employed abroad. These children have low performance at school, possibly due to the fact that they live with grandparents who are often illiterate and cannot help them with their homework. They may also suffer from psychological problems because of separation from their parents. Further, through the grandparents, the child is socialized to traditional values which may impede his adjustment to life later on. In general, the children who stay behind grow up in an intellectually and emotionally deprived environment, with detrimental effect on their mental and psychological development.

To conclude, intra-European migration has an adverse effect upon the life chances of the second generation of the migrants.

DIMITRA MADIANOU (Psychiatric University Clinic, Aginition Hospital, Athens, Greece) then reported on an exploratory study of the sociopsychological impact of out-migration to the Federal Republic of Germany on Greek family members left behind. The study was carried out in 1975 by a multidisciplinary team of the Panhellenic Union for Mental Hygiene. The sample included 39 households drawn from urban Athens and from Drama, an agricultural area in Macedonia. Selection criteria included a father absent for at least two years and not yet returned, and children left behind with either their mother or another adult relative. The conclusions must be considered tentative, since it was a pilot study.

All members of the families left behind were interviewed by a social worker and a psychiatrist. Psychopathological reactions were classified by type; the most important being depression, suicide attempts, neurotic symptoms, behavioral problems, psychosomatic reactions and kinetic disturbances in the children.

Other studies of the influence of the absence of fathers, mothers, or both parents on the lives of children have revealed that children show definite reactions to being separated from their fathers even at 12–18 months of age. However, the source of stress for the children in the present study was not merely separation from their fathers but the fact that all adult members remaining behind had to face substantial readjustment problems.

An important finding was that households, in which both the husband and wife were in favor of the idea of migration, demonstrated significantly less psychopathology among the children left behind. The study demonstrated that underlying and prior conditions may very well be instrumental in determining the effect of migration upon those remaining behind. Among couples who disagreed as to the value of migration there were dramatically high rates of psychic disorder among the children left behind.

It is also clear from this preliminary investigation that relatively sharp differences exist between the urban and rural subsamples. Virtually no psychopathology was found among rural children of migrants, attesting to the flexibility of the extended family and the environmental homogeneity still prevalent in the agricultural parts of Greece. In strong contrast to this, high rates of psychopathological symptoms were exhibited by the urban children of migrants.

ANNA AMIRA (National Center of Social Research, Athens, Greece) spoke of the conditions of Greek migrants in Australia. Greeks who emigrate to settle permanently in another country consider this move not only as a step toward improving their own standard of living but also as a step toward their children's upward mobility. For themselves, they expect more dependable jobs, better pay, and better living conditions. For their children they expect broader educational opportunities, which will enable them to raise their status.

In an effort to monitor this process ANNA AMIRA and PROFESSOR R. T. APPLEYARD of the University of West Australia have for 14 years been following up a group of 130 Greek men and women who migrated to Australia. The follow-up involved three phases: a first contact, just before they left Greece in 1964, focusing on the factors that forced them to emigrate and their expectations of life in Australia; a second contact in 1965–6, focusing on their problems of adjustment; and a third contact in 1976–8, focusing on achievement levels for themselves and their children.

A striking finding of the last contact was the rate of return to Greece. Within a 13 year period 35% of the families of the sample had returned to Greece for permanent settlement, while 75% of those still in Australia intended to return eventually to Greece. Return, and the wish for return, was closely connected with problems in the socialization and education of the children in Australia.

All but two of the 122 children of the survey were growing up in homes where Greek was the main language of communication between the parents. Their playmates were also from Greek households. Consequently the children usually reached primary school with no English language and with Greek social expectations. Therefore they found the traditions of the Anglo-Saxon school and the English language totally alien and incomprehensible. Younger children had some advantage from the first child's exposure, but these younger children often did not clearly understand the parent's Greek language.

Where preschool exposure was possible, the problems were minimal and easily overcome, but preprimary school institutions, especially bilingual ones, were far from abundant.

Sensitive to the needs of migrant children, the Australian government introduced in 1970 a program of child-migrant education. But in 1976 this program was by and large negatively criticized because the need for such a service had been underestimated and not enough teachers and facilities were available.

Inadequate English causes many migrant children to lag behind in the early years of primary school, and this often carries over to the secondary level. Inadequate performance on the part of the migrant child, as well as the administration of intelligence tests not standardized for migrant children, often brands these children as slow learners and effort is abandoned both on the part of the student and teacher.

As a result of these conditions, problems between the student and teacher develop; some of these are summarized below:

(1) The language and culture of migrants is considered inferior by teachers.
(2) The knowledge of another language is not seen as an asset but as a handicap by teachers who are not bilingual themselves.
(3) There is limited contact between the parents and the school; each is alien to the other.
(4) Because parents do not know the system, often do not speak correct English, and are overworked, they are neither able to follow the scholastic development of their children, nor are they able to guide it.
(5) School facilities in high migrant density areas are not satisfactory, and classes are overcrowded.

In spite of these problems, migrant parents have high aspirations for their children and are willing to work hard in order to provide their children with the monetary means that may lead them to success; and in some cases, success is achieved.

MARGARET BAYLEY (Social Worker, Melbourne, South Australia) commented that indeed the situation in Australia for migrant children is far from perfect, but continuous efforts are being made to improve it.

She presented a few facts which offer some encouragement, saying they were by no means being offered as an excuse:

(1) Australia is a multilingual society; educational efforts are continually made to welcome all the languages and cultures represented there.
(2) Special courses are offered to teachers through colleges and universities in order to prepare them to deal with this situation.
(3) Greek as a foreign language is offered in 16 high schools in the state system of South Australia.
(4) Separate schools have been instituted in Melbourne to serve Greek-speaking migrants when 50% to 80% of the students are from this background.
(5) Since April 1977, foreign language assistant teachers have been assigned to Melbourne high schools with high density migrant populations. These assistant teachers are bilingual and have often had to face their own problems of cultural adjustment.
(6) In terms of higher education, at least one college (Wesley College) caters to the problems of Greek migrant students, with 50% of its population from this background. Here, English is taught as a "second language" and Modern Greek is also taught.

Talk of returning to Greece is often heard. In 1974, 12 schoolchildren from Greece were interviewed. All were between 14–16 years, and all said they would go back to Greece to live. In 1978 only one of these 12 had actually returned. Two other families returned to Greece for a short time and then went back to Australia.

PROFESSOR MARIOS NIKOLINAKOS (Department of Economics, Free University of Berlin, Federal Republic of Germany) stated that the previous contributions in this session have thrown some light on the problems concerning migrant children and the impact of migration on their physical, mental, and psychological health. "It is astonishing how these effects are similar in countries that are supposed to be quite different. One might think, for example, that the situation in Australia would be different from that in the United States or western Europe. Considered, however, from the point of view of political economy, the factors under which the migratory phenomenon takes place in all these countries are the same: namely, those factors which determine capital accumulation in a (so-called) free economy.

The following thoughts attempt to formulate some general conclusions or hypotheses in regard to the material presented in the preceding contributions.

It cannot be denied that the situation of migrant children is not voluntary. Immigration countries in general have looked upon migrants as a labor force, not as citizens, and the situation of migrant children can be expressed in terms of labor market economics. Migrant children, often unable even to finish grammer school in the recipient country, much less attend vocational school and learn a skilled occupation, are destined to provide the necessary unskilled labor force for the labor market. It is important to emphasize that this will be the case, irrespective of whether these children remain in the recipient country or return to their home country. After perhaps their fourteenth or fifteenth year of age, the opportunity for these children to regain lost time vanishes for ever.

From a social and political point of view, migrant children who remain illiterate under the conditions described in the previous papers, tend to form a marginal group, with all its sociological and political implications. Psychologically crippled, schizophrenic in their bilinguality, socially unadapted, and isolated, these children do not become nationalized. They do not acquire civil rights, and they are thus excluded from political life in the recipient country. In addition, they may also be excluded from political life in their countries of origin, and they have no direct relation with the political landscape of their home country.

The main features of the present and future labor market can be summarized as follows:

(1) There exists a high rate of unemployment in the highly developed countries, which had until 1974 relatively high immigration rates. This unemployment seems to be of a permanent character due to the need to restructure economies in view of the oil crisis of 1973.
(2) This unemployment has hit unskilled labor[7] to which category almost all migrant workers belong.
(3) Unemployment has struck in particular the young workers in the industrialized countries.
(4) In spite of unemployment, skilled workers will be in demand at least up to 1990 (according to empirical studies).
(5) Also, in spite of unemployment, a demand for foreign workers will continue due to demographic developments such as very low birth rates in the industrialized countries.

The situation existing in Germany is typical of these trends. By 1980 it is expected that about 400,000 young German workers will appear on the labor market. It is also calculated that 265,000 young foreign workers will ask for jobs in the same period. Some of these foreign workers will be Germans coming into Germany from Poland. If the number of unemployed (which amounts to approximately one million) is added to these figures, it means that about 1·6 million new jobs must be created by 1980 if full employment is to prevail.

As migrant children are excluded from the training mechanisms, it is evident that migrant children's fate is that of unemployment.

Programs of integration for these children, which have been announced by almost all receiving countries, seem to be ineffective in the case of second generation migrants. Only by the third generation are the grandchildren of original migrant workers actually free of bilingualism, have no great problems of national or cultural identification, and have grown up within a steady national environment: all factors which contribute to psychical, mental, and bodily health.

LIST OF PAPERS PRESENTED

ANNA AMIRA (National Center of Social Research, Athens, Greece): "The process of mobility among Greek migrants to Australia."

VASSILIS FILIAS (Pantios Higher School of Political Science, Athens, Greece): "Specific aspects of the migrant child abroad."

DIMITRA MADIANOU (Psychiatric University Clinic, Aginition Hospital, Athens, Greece): "The sociopsychological impact of out-migration to Germany on Greek family members left behind."

IOANNA MANGANARA (Pantios Higher School of Political Science, Athens, Greece): "Some problems of European migrant children in the sending and receiving countries."

MARIOS NIKOLINAKOS (Department of Economics, Free University of Berlin, Federal Republic of Germany): "Some issues about migrant children and the future of the labor market in immigration and emigration countries."

4

The Child and Health

MORBIDITY AND MORTALITY TRENDS AND THE NEW ILLNESSES

CHAIRMAN'S INTRODUCTION

John Apley

In opening this discussion I insist on keeping before us the child, alive and kicking—or dead and not kicking. We must not hide the child under a snowstorm of statistics. Of course we need the hard data and the wide-ranging epidemiology of disease and death, and they will be presented by experts. But first let me remind you very briefly, and in the most simplified and vivid way I can, of what can be achieved over a period of some 20 years. It is an impressionistic scenario and it is intensely personal.

The time is 1968–9. The scene is set in Vietnam in the Children's Hospital in what was Saigon. A small medical team of doctors and nurses from Britain is working there with the Vietnamese. The only senior doctor in the team happens to be myself. None of the others have ever seen children dying of diphtheria, measles, or tetanus: here every day we see them dying of these diseases. Few have seen children with active poliomyelitis or lethal malnutrition: here we see them every day. All these and much more were preventable.

The comparison was stark. But it was not so much a comparison between two countries (7000 miles apart) as between two stages of economic and medical progress. The differences reflected 20 years of advancement and countless young lives.

At that time in Vietnam a vicious war was raging, and it made matters worse. Looking into the future today we may wonder how many more wars will the next 20 years see. We may speculate, too, whether there will be a great leap forward in genetic engineering, with the production of "Satan bugs" causing infections to which humans have no resistance.

I prefer to think, or hope, that "Physical disease may prove to be man's friend" if doctors, then nations, unite to conquer infection, malnutrition, and the like, and turn together to conquer other nonmedical afflictions of mankind.

In the next 20 years, how far will medical achievements banish known children's diseases, not only in the technologically advanced countries but all over the world? Will most handicaps—physical and mental—be preventable and prevented? Shall we discover something equivalent to insecticides or antibiotics to help control pysycho-social disorders or, better still, will they too be prevented?

I hope our expert colleagues will tell us what *are* new diseases and how new *is* new. Was the thalidomide tragedy new?—a painting in the National Gallery in London, showing a child with what appears to be thalidomide limb deformities, is by Goya who died 150 years ago. (Incidentally, the thalidomide episode shocked the world into preventing probably many more tragedies due to drugs taken during pregnancy.) I hope we shall hear a great deal about new social and environmental diseases, because to be forewarned is to be forearmed.

In our debate here let us continually ask ourselves what, in 20 years' time, our children, then grown up, will think we have achieved this day.

MORBIDITY AND MORTALITY TRENDS: AN APPRAISAL OF THEIR IMPACT ON THE FUTURE OF CHILDREN AND THEIR LIFE SPAN DEVELOPMENT

ROBERT A. ALDRICH

Medical Center, University of Colorado, Denver, CO, USA

INTRODUCTION

Children of the world have two kinds of future, a future as an individual living his or her life span, and a future as a cohort that is worldwide in distribution. Individual life spans are influenced continuously by both biologic and sociocultural factors, characteristic of the individual and the circumstances surrounding his or her life throughout its course. The worldwide cohort of children varies among nations and the communities within them. Resources for education, health, nutrition, work, shelter, and many other human goals available and accessible to some of this cohort will be favored by the environment or economic situation into which they are born, while others will be faced by very different conditions with much less potential and available resources.

It is quite natural for adult human beings to have expectations for their own children as individuals and particularly for these parents to apply their own cultural values to their offspring in the hope that they will grow to be intelligent, healthy, and successful. In a sense they are raising adults much like themselves. However, there is far less awareness of the world cohort of children among adults of any nation and of the growing interdependence that they (the children) are acquiring as they become the future leadership of the world. The time is at hand when some common goals for the world's children could be agreed upon between nations, even though there are differences in political systems, philosophies, and culture. It is my purpose in this essay to set forth some evidence that another step forward for the world can be achieved if it is based upon human scale and the basic human values that will allow our species to continue to evolve successfully alongside other living things in our planetary environment. In order to illustrate this fundamental relationship in a symbolic way, I use this triangular model showing the interaction between DNA, Man, the species, and environment (Fig. 1).

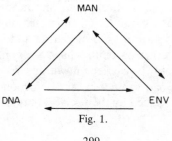

Fig. 1.

299

The central question that I wish to put before you is this: Are we being good ancestors? Is it enough to try only to improve the lives of children as individuals in one's own culture or do we have a far greater responsibility to the world cohort of children who will inherit in a few years that which we have left them?

WORLD POPULATION GROWTH

As our planetary population begins to slow its growth rate, it begins to assume the shape of the familiar sigmoid curve that bacterial or yeast populations follow when growing in media. Speculation that this same curve may turn out to be a feature of man's population growth as well was offered by Jonas Salk in his excellent book, *Survival of the Wisest.*[1]

Evidence that annual world population growth rate is no longer increasing and may actually be declining, comes from estimates that the increase in 1978 will be no higher than the 73 million in 1977. This change in population dynamics is attributed to several factors, depending on the country, social and economic development, family planning, redistribution of income, or combinations of them. It is not my purpose in this paper to do more than point out the evidence and suggest that we do know a great deal about how population has been controlled successfully. Among the general properties of a culture that determines population dynamics is the health of the people. Their levels of nutrition, sanitation, and housing play significant roles in their health. Health over the full human life span is generally a high human value in any culture. Any change in the health of children exerts a considerable influence on the population into which they are born. This in turn leads to additional needs because of increased child survival and a shift in the child–adult population ratio. The remaining parts of this discussion will address the trends in child mortality–morbidity and some of the "new illnesses" that appear to be a product of these trends together with industrialization and urbanization.

Tim Dyson[2] in his recent major analysis of child mortality trends states that:

"Child mortality rates in the developed regions are currently very low, in most cases at or below a level of 1 per 1,000. The predominant causes tend to be accidents and congenital malformations which are difficult to control. However, analysis of child mortality differentials both between and within the developed countries, show that in many instances there is still some room for improvement.

"By contrast, child death rates in many less developed countries are still very high, and the main factors responsible—infectious diseases and malnutrition—are almost entirely preventable through existing knowledge. As a corollary, in developing countries in particular, the childhood mortality rate must be regarded, along with the infant mortality rate, as an important index of public health. Improvements in water supply, sanitation and nutrition should prove particularly effective in reducing child mortality to moderate and low levels. . . .

"Maternal and child health programmes have a very important role to play. But any measures must preferably be carried out within a framework that also includes attacking poor nutrition, bad sanitation, and infectious and other diseases: for specific interventions introduced by themselves, may have an impact below their full potential.

"There is an urgent need for more information on the levels, trends, causes and correlates of mortality at ages one to under five years. In this context, special emphasis must be placed on improving the level of death registration where systems of vital registration exist; where they do not, specific survey methods, expressly developed to measure levels of infant and child mortality have an especially important role to play. Better information is required because health planning with inadequate data can never be fully realistic."

ACCIDENT MORTALITY

In their extraordinarily detailed study of accident mortality among children, H. Marcusson and W. Demisch[3] summarized: "For 50 countries studied the average accident mortality in the age group 1–4 years was 32.7 per 100,000 for boys and 22.8 for girls, dropping to 23.1 for boys and to 10.9 for girls in the age group 5–14 years."

The importance of the accident mortality can be verified by its percentage of the total mortality. In the developing countries it is often less than 10%; in the highly industrialized countries more than 40% for boys and 30% for girls. A medial position is taken by those developing countries where industrialization is progressing and where total mortality has already been reduced. Industrial countries that have succeeded in considerably reducing not only the general mortality rates but also the accident mortality rates, corroborate the thesis that accidents can be reduced in all countries.

In many countries motor vehicle accidents rank first among all fatal accidents; they amount to an unweighted average of 40% of all fatal accidents for both sexes in the 50 countries studied. Northern America, Oceania, and Europe have above average median values, and Asia and Southern America have below average median values. While there are no big differences in the average values between the various age groups, the differences between boys and girls are considerable.

In many countries accidental drowning takes the second place of the fatal accidents, and reaches 23% for boys and 17% for girls aged 1–14 years of all fatal accidents. Fatal accidents met by children must not be accepted as inevitable, and effective preventive measures can lead to improvement.

Accident prevention, however, requires great efforts and should always be a concern of the society as a whole. The causes and effects of accidents are so manifold that an effective prevention of accidents can never be the concern of the health authorities alone. Besides, legislative activities go far beyond the realms of the public health system. Government bodies and social organizations, parents, educationists, physicians—everyone is called upon to do all he can to reduce the number of accidents.

Motor vehicle accidents have to be reduced by all means. Looking after children, road safety drill of children and adults, personal responsibility, discipline, and order are prerequisites for reducing traffic accidents. The cultivation of traffic behavior which begins in creches and kindergartens should be continued at school. Statistics of road accidents show that a great number of accidents met by children were caused by their crossing the road without paying attention to the traffic. These accidents can be substantially reduced by road safety education.

Accidental drowning in the younger age groups can be reduced above all by looking after the children properly. Children often drown in small areas of water near their homes in uncovered wells, cesspools, rain tubs, etc. The elimination or protection of these "artificial death traps" can result in a reduction of the number of children drowned.

To teach swimming in early childhood and to supervize and protect bathing places can help prevent deaths of older children. We have been able to prove that death by drowning could be reduced after compulsory swimming instruction had been introduced.

Better safety measures might also diminish the number of deaths caused by fire.

Measures aimed at the medical treatment of accidents and their sequelae and rehabilitation serve at least to diminish the severity of traumatic lesions and to prevent a fatal outcome. These measures extend from the first aid rendered by laymen to intensive care and specialized treatment. The organizational aspects of providing these activities have to be constantly reviewed and improved.

Finally, accidents do not decrease automatically. Concentrated efforts based on thorough specialized knowledge have been and will be an essential condition for achieving lasting successes in accident prevention. The thesis of the avoidability of accidents, if understood in this connection, has a useful implication.
tion, has a useful implication.

HUMAN LIFE SPAN DEVELOPMENT

A primary assumption that I must expose now is that a humane society requires humane people. We must learn how to raise humane adults in our next hundred years. It is not my generation that will make the difference in that time, nor do I believe that it will be the present child-bearing generation now in their twenties and thirties. It is the offspring that these young people are producing who will determine the nature of our next century. These new citizens will be the ones who should be educated about the full nature of human beings as they live over the trajectory of the life span. They are the population of the future who can create and maintain the new kinds of institutions that should either arise *de novo,* or evolve from those in existence that are capable of change; and they will have in their hands the knowledge and the resources to restore very fundamental elements of society, such as the family.

How do we raise humane adults? How and where do processes of human life span development go astray? Where does the pathology lie? What are the points where intervention is preventative, thus permitting normal processes to continue? These are only a sample of the questions uppermost in my mind today; the remainder of my comments will address some ways by which all of us can start answering these queries.

1. Greatly expanded public education is needed for adults and right on down to the preschool child. We should be presenting what we know about human beings to the young parents of the generation that will make a difference. Those in their twenties and thirties know little about child rearing (or raising adults—as I prefer to call it) except what they themselves have experienced or received secondhand a long time ago. There must be reexamination of parental child-rearing concepts as well as

reeducation of both sexes for parenthood. Life span developments of the male and female are distinctly different, and this ought to be emphasized early in our education for their social, behavioral, and biological implications.

It is quite evident that the complicated new knowledge gained by science can quickly be fed into the organized body of useful knowledge nurturing young minds. I want to emphasize young minds. The same young minds are seeking today to understand man. How do we build bridges between these young minds and those of us who are concerned with the development of human beings? We carry a tremendous burden as well as a challenge in surmounting the difficulties of transmitting knowledge between the generations.

2. We are witnessing today a convergence of major movements of public interests in several important ways. Very specific areas of knowledge are becoming related so that general forms and larger strategies are coming under consideration. Nowhere is this more evident and more exciting than in the life span studies of the fundamental interdependency between human beings, their society, and their habitats or environment.

The impacts of habitat at various times in the life span are known to be both positive and negative in their influences on the processes of growth and development of individual human beings and of families. Serious scientific investigations along these lines are relatively new, but their significance for human beings can hardly be overemphasized.

Synthesis of knowledge regarding the processes of growth and development of individuals is moving at a tremendous rate and bringing together scholars from the social sciences, biomedical sciences, environmental sciences, and humanistic studies in an effort to understand the human trajectory throughout life. We are learning about the effects of inhibiting these processes at critical times, and about opportunities for preventive intervention when sequences are going astray. For example, as health moves closer to the values of "well-being" and "quality of life," medicine is seen by the public as only a modest section of the much larger concept of health.

Above all, we are facing the most basic relationship of all—that between the human species and the planetary ecosystem. There may be an analogy between the discovery of the deoxyribonucleic acid (DNA) code for human beings and a possible discovery of an environmental code for humankind's continuation.

In the face of growing scarcity of planetary resources, the challenge to our institution of higher learning is clear. Sharing of knowledge and concepts between disciplines and professions is one important response. Universities can take leadership in the directions just proposed through providing for students and faculty new ways of working together across disciplines and professions.

I believe that we should reconsider the values we hold before assigning technology to a task. Very often when new technology is developed to a point where it can be put to use, the decision is made to go ahead because it is possible, not because it is a part of the value system of the individuals or community that is directly affected.

There are four Es that should be satisfied before undertaking civic or national projects, because they are part of understanding life span development principles. First of all comes Economics of the project. Is it economically feasible or possible? Second is Engineering: is the project engineered for practical effectiveness and safety? Third, Esthetics is sometimes considered but not always: is the project tasteful, harmonious, and beautiful? Fourth is Ethics: this is the most troublesome. It is usually the one left out and yet it should be given the most thought. Is the project within the values and ethics of a humane society?

The search for the laws of human growth and development seems likely to provide us with clues to the future evolution of human beings and human society.

In view of the complicated nature of this task it is helpful to reread Warren Weaver,[4] who in a profound essay set forth the essential features of "organized complexity" in contrast to "disorganized complexity." The former relates to problems involving a considerable number of variables but showing the distinctive feature of organization, while disorganized complexity, featuring millions or billions of variables, must be handled by statistical mechanics and probability theory, life insurance statistics, the motion of atoms, laws of heredity, and the like. In approaching the solution of problems of organized complexity, Weaver stressed operations analysis, utilizing interdisciplinary teams mixing physical sciences with biomedical and social behavioral sciences. Among the problems he pointed to for analysis by these techniques was the "incredibly complicated story of the biochemistry of the aging organism."

Emboldened by Albert Rosenfeld's essays on the *The Doctor as Biophilosopher*[5] and by Salk's book, *Survival of the Wisest,* my colleagues and I have undertaken to analyze the situations in which human beings live and conduct their affairs in human settlements.

THE LIFE CYCLE MODEL

The human life cycle can be compared to the trajectory of an airplane or a missile. It has a takeoff point and a landing point, with distances in between that are measured in terms of time rather than miles, and which are subject to the characteristics of the individual and the situation in which he or she lives. During the life span there occur a continuous series of critical periods and important life events. The critical periods are usually viewed as stages in the life cycle when a change is taking place at a rapid rate or on a very large scale. Examples of critical periods would be conception (when chromosomes are being sorted out), the generation of form (embryogenesis), birth, puberty, and so forth. At each critical period there are things that can go wrong, and sometimes it is possible to intervene and prevent undesirable events. Life events, on the other hand, can be characterized by infant–mother bonding, the first day at school, the first date, marriage, loss of one's job, the "empty nest," retirement. Dr. Thomas Holmes[6] at the University of Washington has developed a sophisticated scoring system for life events or "life change" as he calls it, which has some capability to predict illness when the scores are too high. His material was developed for application to adults, and so far a comparable investigation has not been completed that will apply to the period of childhood and youth. It is difficult not to be drawn into speculation regarding the relationships that may exist between life events in the adult years and important life events in the years of prematurity.

The life cycle model (Fig. 2) that we have been using can be pictured as a long oval that is three-dimensional. It looks for all the world like an elongated watermelon. On this eliptical model with stripes running from one end to the other are represented organ systems, social processes, and behavioral processes. The purpose of this model

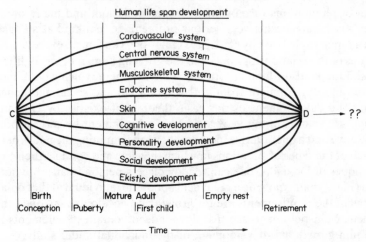

Fig. 2. Life cycle model.

is to portray biomedical organ systems, like the cardiovascular or the central nervous system, alongside social and behavioral processes, like personality development, social development, cognitive development, and so forth. Since all of these must operate in direct relationship to each other if the organism as a whole is to function effectively through the life span, this manner of representing these interdependencies against time has a good deal of practical value.

The critical periods and the life events are depicted on this model by perpendicular lines that cut across the ellipse at appropriate intervals in time. The drawing illustrates the life span model with a selected group of critical periods and life events placed upon it.

The model is flexible enough to be applied to any kind of culture and it is very helpful in separating out the differences in the life span of the male as compared to the female. We have placed special emphasis on four aspects of each critical period—lifestyle, genetics, education, and environment. This particular approach assists greatly in identifying things that can go wrong at each critical period and what possible remedies are available to prevent them from going wrong. Here, basically, we are able to synthesize the mainstream of anthropological and biomedical thinking which is the history of man and the life cycle of man with unavoidable questions arising about the future of the species.

EKISTIC DEVELOPMENT

Human beings have always devised their own human settlements as far back in time as we are able to go. Very ancient settlements had to be on a human scale so that they met the limitations of human beings of the time. With the arrival of technical inventions leading to the high technology of today, human settlements have left behind some of these basic human values and the human scale to which man as a species was able to adapt. The modern metropolis exceeds the capability of human beings to adapt in an almost limitless variety of ways. Noise, vehicular traffic, air pollution, limitations of movement, water pollution, and many other features of today's cities are posing very serious problems to mankind at all ages.

In a remarkable book by C. A. DOXIADIS [7] one can find an exceedingly illuminating analysis of the relationships between the growing human being at different stages of life and the kinds of human settlement environment which would, indeed, prosper growth and development from both a biological and social and behavioral standpoint. The development of the basic theories of ekistics by Doxiadis across the human life span is in my view a singular achievement because it provides both a qualitative and a quantitative methodology for examining the needs of human beings in each of the types of situations in which they live and conduct their lives. Using the techniques of Doxiadis, one can readily place a person in any one of the 15 ekistic units (Fig. 3) and, knowing a great deal about the individual at that point in his or her life (what the requirements are for growth and development), one can analyze that particular ekistic unit to see if it does indeed contain the elements necessary for optimum growth and development of the individual under study.

In studying an individual such as a 13 year old male at the onset of puberty, it would be apparent that the second ekistic unit, a room in a house, is not going to provide the sorts of things that a boy at this age requires, while it might be quite adequate for a newborn baby. Therefore one needs to examine each ekistic unit from 1 to 15 in terms of the individual under study and hopefully arrive at an appropriate type of situation for that particular individual.

In each of the 15 ekistic units one observes five elements (Fig. 4). These are nature, man, society, shells, and networks. From these five elements it is possible to make a synthesis of the situation and draw some conclusions that connect the particular individual (or group of individuals) under study with a specific ekistic unit.

COMMUNITY SCALE		i	ii	iii	I	II	III	IV	V	VI	VII	VIII	IX	X	XI	XII
		1	2	3	4	5	6	7	8	9	10	11	12	13	14	15
EKISTIC UNITS		ANTHROPOS	ROOM	HOUSE	HOUSE GROUP	SMALL NEIGHBORHOOD	NEIGHBORHOOD	SMALL POLIS	POLIS	SMALL METROPOLIS	METROPOLIS	SMALL MEGALOPOLIS	MEGALOPOLIS	SMALL EPEROPOLIS	EPEROPOLIS	ECUMENOPOLIS
	NATURE															
ELEMENTS	ANTHROPOS															
	SOCIETY															
	SHELLS															
	NETWORKS															
SYNTHESIS: HUMAN SETTLEMENTS																

Fig. 3. Ekistic units.

The helpful matrix developed by the scholars at the Athens Center of Ekistics depicts in a visual manner the relationship between an individual at a particular point in the life cycle and each ekistic unit. The volume, *Anthropopolis—A City for Human Development,* provides scores of illustrations of these relationships.

My major point here is that a synthesis of the life cycle with the principles of ekistics (ekistic development) offer a very good method for studying man holistically within the environmental circumstances in which he finds himself. It draws conceptually form Warren Weaver's[4] exposition of "organized complexity" and, in my opinion, provides an enormous area for both qualitative and quantitative research enlisting the minds and vigor of a very much wider constellation of disciplines than we customarily encounter in the study of human development. This is necessary if man is to continue to survive as a species and to evolve as a species and a society. He must take his dual role seriously, for he is both guinea pig and research director on this planet. Man is not infinitely adaptable as René Jules Dubos has so eloquently described. We must return to human scale and values that prosper human development as man moves ahead toward the future.

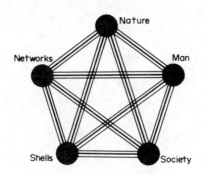

Fig. 4.

REFERENCES

1. J. SALK, *Survival of the Wisest,* Harper & Row, 1973. *Interchange,* May 1978, a publication of the Population Reference Bureau Inc, Washington, DC.
2. T. DYSON, *World Health Statistics Report,* Vol. 30, No. 4, pp. 282–311 (1977).
3. H. MARCUSSON and W. DEMISCH, *World Health Statistics Report,* Vol. 30, No. 1, pp. 57–92 (1977).
4. W. WEAVER, Science and complexity, *American Scientist,* October 6, 1948, pp. 536–544.
5. A. ROSENFELD, *The Doctor as Biophilosopher, Modern Medicine,* New York Times Media Co., 1975.
6. T. HOLMES and M. MASUDA, Life change and illness susceptibility, *Separation and Depression,* AAAS, pp. 161–186 (1973).
7. C. A. DIOXIADIS, *Anthropopolis: City for Human Development,* Athens Publishing Center, 1974.

NEW MODELS FOR NEW PSYCHOLOGICAL ILLNESSES IN A NEW AGE

E. James Anthony

Edison Child Development Research Center, Washington University, St. Louis, MO, USA

THE CONCEPT OF METABLETICS

Metabletics, a term coined by the Dutch psychologist van den Berg[1] is in many respects closely bound up with the concept of ekistics. The first has to do with the phenomenon of change, and the second with the relation of interchange to outer structure. Metabletics is on the way to becoming a little science on its own, and it concerns itself with all aspects of change in relation to development, environment, the changes brought about gradually over time, and changes precipated by catastrophe; from the changes effected by the individual on his own behalf to changes to which he is compelled to submit passively.

Metabletics has a special relevance to the realm of psychological illness. Psychohistorians have commented on the changes and manifestation of psychopathology over the past centuries and have attempted to correlate these with new changes that are rapidly overwhelming the world and generating a state of "future shock." It has been noted, for example, that the psychopathology observed by Freud and his followers in the early part of this century in Vienna has almost disappeared from the psychology of today and that the dramatic outpourings recorded by Freud and Brauer in a series of hysterical young women have been replaced by chronic, monotonously manifested disorders of the total personality in which people, as it were, become their defences. As a technical outcome to this development, the cathartic procedure gave place to a monotonous preassociative process: certainly, in the area of psychoanalysis, the Appolonian approach has largely replaced the Dionysian.

Metabletics recognizes that the individual changes over time and yet, in some mysterious fashion, remains the same; that illness changes over time, and yet may remain recognizably the same; that the world changes technologically over time, sometimes gradually and sometimes rapidly, but that the individual accommodates himself to change and adapts himself to new circumstances unless his inner and outer resources fail and he "breaks down."

The extent to which we contrive to create new models of illness for the world today depends to what extent, as individual clinicians, we are more impressed by constancy than by change. Therapists, like their colleagues in other disciplines, are prone to be reactionary or revolutionary; to maintain their techniques because of a belief in inner constancy or to modify or change their techniques in response to changing demands, changing theories, changing psychopathology, and changing models of change itself.

In a total model, combining illness, prevention, and intervention, to deal with new developments, it was important to include the dimension of change. Before looking at such a comprehensive model, we should take a hurried look at the psychological illnesses that are beginning to emerge out of today's world and to find their way to our clinics and we would anticipate that the clinics in the year 2000 will see many of them and will have needed to have revised their diagnostic classifications of disease even further.

NEW MODELS FOR NEW ILLNESSES

I must confess to a weakness for model making that has persisted throughout my life from as far back as the nursery. Whenever things went right or wrong, in play or in work, I tried to understand the structure and process involved and to represent it schematically. (It was said of the psychologist, Kurt Lewin, that he could only explain himself by resorting to circles and arrows. Freud was another schematizer.) All behavioral science models, even those that can be quantified, are at best only conceptual devices that enable us to isolate certain elements from the complexities of objective reality so that the interactions and implications can be more readily perceived and analyzed. Inevitably, phenomena are oversimplified and the relevance of the model to reality is often sacrificed to its logical elegance.

I will start with a basic assumption: the world of tomorrow, containing the child of tomorrow, will be in a state of transition undergoing a transitional process, and the model I have in mind is a model of this transitional process. It would endeavour to describe simultaneously several inextricably intercorrelated processes in transitional societies: the formation of individual personality and sense of identity and selfness; the transmission and learning of social roles and culturally determined patterns of feeling, seeing, believing, acting, and aspiring; the methods of managing anxiety and conflict generated by inconsistencies within the processes; the interaction between the disintegrating and integrating forces operating in the society; and the ways in which these stimulate or inhibit the emergence of a stable identity.

The model starts with the process of socialization that constitutes the essential link between the individual and society and involves the taking in of cultural concepts, values, and norms by the individual. As this occurs, the personality is formed. It is clear that this part of the model is a simplified form of the one devised by Freud and extended into social theory by Talcott Parsons.[2] The model contains the ingredients with which we began this presentation and we may schematize thus:

(1) Change leads to transition and brings about shifts from traditional through transitional through modern societies.
(2) Transition brings about novelty to which the individual or society may react with resistance and withdrawal or with curiosity and exploration.
(3) Novelties begin to accumulate and conduce to increasing complexity, heterogeneity, and differentiation.
(4) Complexity may become overwhelming and create conflict.
(5) Conflict may be resolved with stable identity formation or remain unresolved with identity confusion and diffusion.
(6) Stable identity formation enhances the sense of constancy and continuity in the presence of change.

In traditional societies, the so-called "paradigmatic figures," i.e., the models on whom the child patterns his attitudes and behavior take the form of a dominant male, usually the father, outwardly directed toward mastery of the environment and an inwardly oriented nurturing and protecting mother, but in the transitional society the role differences may be diminished or obliterated, conflict is increased, and there is a continuous dynamic tension with regard to identifications; the child may strive to be like his father, like his mother, or develop the courage, as Tillich puts it,[3] to be both himself and a part of the group to which he belongs.

The transitional world of tomorrow will be by definition more inconsistent, unstable, incongruous, and ambiguous; the child will experience more conflict and more confusion and the environment will be more difficult to understand. The transitional societies are more in a state of flux, more mobile, more prone to fragmentation, and less given to altruism and support. Each subgroup within the transitional world tends to pursue its own ends. On the other hand, the children in the transitional process seem more liable to become conscious of themselves as individuals. As individuals, they resent traditional authorities but are very likely to submit to authoritarianism when offered by a new charismatic leader. The nature of any particular transitional society limits the extent and rate of social change so that there is no single design to encompass the total transitional process. About three-quarters of the world will be in a state of transition by the year 2000. This is a conjecture based on current rates of progress.

In order to understand the impact of transitional societies on the developing child it is important to understand that they are inherently precarious, erratic, unstable, and changeable. This will allow us to predict from the transitional model to the new psychological and psychosocial illnesses that may harass children of tomorrow.

The transitional model is only part of a more total model, the components of which I have previously tried to construct independently of one another. In order to explain more clearly brain dysfunction (the existence of which is still open to doubt), I tried to construct a comprehensive model containing developmental, representational, and interactional aspects involving brain with body, brain with mind, self with body, self with people, and self with things.[4] Over time a sophisticated body of knowledge accrues around each of these, and they are interconnected by means of language that also provides the model with associations, with content, with meaning, and with a dimension of time, so that the child learns to postpone gratification when he masters words such as today, tomorrow, now, and soon. In this context, the child with minimal brain dysfunction can be shown to be more than his pathology and more than the extent to which he copes with his pathology. He is not just a cluster of symptoms or a set of provisional hypotheses. When looked at psychodynamically and psychodevelopmentally, he is seen to be not only capable of constructing a reality for himself but also able to apprehend his own experience, to observe what goes on in his own mind, to feel and to know what he feels, to strive and to know that he strives, to know and to know that he knows. In relation to the family, I attempted to construct a model again with both longitudinal and cross-sectional properties[5] that brought together dynamic, transactional, and developmental facets in a comprehensive approach. This developmental–transactional portrayal of family life took into account that a family was also a micro society in transition with its membership functioning on different psychosexual, psychosocial, and psychocognitive levels, all out of phase with one another. Family life is further confused by the fact that every member is at a different stage of linguistic development and that there is no basic family language, like Esperanto, that serves all its members, irrespective of age and sex. This leads to a great deal of incomprehensibility in ordinary family living that is more or less taken for granted by the children and rarely considered by the parents. To explain differences in the casualty rate within the same family, I then constructed the risk–vulnerability model,[6] which was a quantifiable model, and attempted to summate the amount of risk to which each individual is exposed in his life space and lifetime and his degree of resilience and competence to withstand these risks. The model was effective in explaining the different incidents of psychological illness in children at high genetic risk for psychosis.

This holistic model takes in the culture, the particular society, the family, the individual, his personality, his mind, and his brain. My only defense for its convoluted quality is the undeniable fact that the transitional world of tomorrow will be far more complicated than even the one in which we live today.

NEW PSYCHOLOGICAL ILLNESSES IN A NEW AGE

Always remembering that models are simplifying, let us take a predictive look at what change may do to the developing child of the future.

If the model operates successfully for the child, we should see him develop a good sense of identity, an interest in novelty, a curiosity about the world and its people, a capacity to understand the present and future in terms of the past, a tolerance for change, a propensity for turning inward, and an ability to withstand and master conflict and turn it to his own advantage.

If the model is not operating successfully, the developing child becomes at risk, and the more vulnerable ones in this group will begin to demonstrate transitional psychopathology.

Let me try and summarize the Protean aspects of transitional psychopathology.

In a transitional world, as Mannheim[7] pointed out, the power of technology steps in increasingly and converts "the walled horizon of the medieval city into the limitless world" in order to bring home quick profits, caring nothing for the wasted landscapes that they leave in their wake, which include the destruction of tribal customs, semi-starvation, tuberculosis, and soil erosion. The small, self-regulating groups, characteristic of traditional societies, disappear as the population grows and space becomes limited. In traditional societies, from time immemorial, the limited size allowed everyone to understand what is required of him and what was expected from the group. In direct everyday contacts with other group members, each could discover for himself the causes of success or failure and seek collective remedies when things went wrong. The agora of the Greek city and the market place of the medieval town, where the church, the guild hall, and the market stalls were close to one another, enabled the citizen to take in the whole orbit of his world at a glance. The differentiation of human activities and growth of the corresponding social types happened along the lines of gradually expanding cooperation. Everybody knew his function since he could clearly see how the village supplied the town and the town the village. In the transitional society the nature of an integrated social pattern more or less disappeared. The last traces of organic cohesion soon fade, and the principles of common living, functional interdependence, and clarity of common purpose are destroyed. The failure of coordination, the disintegration of controls, the antagonisms between groups, lead inevitably to a disintegration of personality and interpersonal bonds.

The vulnerable ones gradually develop what Durkheim[8] called *anomie* or sense of rootlessness and anarchy; alienation from society as a whole and from the self so that a sense of estrangement persists; paranoid attitudes that tend readily to blame everyone else for the misfortunes to which one is exposed. Dysphoria is manifested in affects that are out of control and liable to inexplicable elations and depressions, and a whole host of characteristic reactions that include outer-directedness, materialism, passivity, resistance to further change, identity confusion, crises of helplessness and hopelessness, and increasing resort to drugs of all kinds. There is often a flight into impersonalization and emotional shallowness. The victims begin to live in an anthill instead of a brotherhood. Those who master this predicament will be strengthened in their personalities, will be personal in their relationships, will be deeper in their consciousness and self awareness, and, above all, constant and consistent and continuous in their identities.

CONCLUSION

All this is of course conjecture, but we have been invited to conjecture, and intelligent guesses about the future may prepare us for work of prevention should this become necessary.

The next step from the transitional world is the modern world, which has its own problems, its own difficulties, and is less confused, disorganized, and chaotic. The child of the 21st century may reach a new level of consciousness, a new harmony between the outer and the inner life, as asked for by Socrates in his famous prayer.[9]

Conjecture is partly science and partly subjective. If we are optimistic, with a Rousseau-esque belief in the perfectibility of man, we shall look forward to the evolution of the new child of the future as a confident and competent little human being. If, on the other hand, we are negative and pessimistic, we shall base our predictions on the fact that everything has been tried and no one way has shown itself as perceptably better than another. We shall then anticipate that nothing much better can be expected than what we have today, and that new illnesses will be added to older ones and add immeasureably to the problems of treatment.

Will we discover new treatments for new illnesses or will we fall back on revisions of the therapeutic armamentarium used by the ancient Greeks? I remember being struck by the use made by the pediatrician–psychoanalyst Winnicott[10] of the "healing" dream which took place during therapy and marked the arrival of the patient at a new stage in his emotional development. I thought this was new, only to discover that at Epidaurus, where the Asclepian cult was localized, the patient was expected to dream a "healing" dream that would reveal the course of treatment, the mode of treatment, and lead eventually to recovery. In one of the case histories that have come down to us, Ambrosia of Athens, blind in one eye, came somewhat unbelievingly for treatment. She laughed at the idea that cures could be obtained by merely seeing a dream. However, she herself had a dream in which the god stood by her and said that he would cure her, but that in payment he would ask her to dedicate to the temple a silver pig as a memorial of her ignorance. After saying this, he cut the diseased eyeball and poured in some drug. When morning came, she walked out with perfect 20/20 vision!

In the face of all this conjecture, there is a part inside me that begins to wonder whether the new models are not simply elaborations of old Hippocratic models, new psychological illnesses, not merely manifestations that have appeared before over and over again during periods of historical crisis, new interventions nothing better than a rehash of ancient psychological prescriptions, and the new child of tomorrow a replication of the Greek boy of long ago. This is very much in keeping with some modern speculations[11] that there is a circular family pattern common to many societies which was first noted in Homeric times, was intensified during the Athenian civilization, and is reflected in Greek mythology and tragedy. Slater attributes "the glory that was Greece" in large part to maternal ambivalence and the narcissism that it engendered, but he does concede that narcissism in any society can only be regarded as a contributory not a sufficient condition for cultural achievement; not even if we add the further concept of a shame culture (as opposed to guilt culture). There was no doubt that in 5th century Athens sex segregation was carried to great extreme and may have interfered with further development. Such a segregation does breed fear and mistrust between the sexes, and leads to subordination and delegation of one or the other. As Margaret Mead has observed, "To the extent that either sex is disadvantaged, the whole culture is poorer, and the sex that, superficially, inherits the earth, inherits only a very partial legacy."[12] She attributes the decline of many civilizations to the too rigid adherence to the insights and gift of one's sex. Another ancient pattern that is coming around again is the mother–child household which McClelland has noted that "homosexuality, poorly developed super egos . . . . and high frequency of personal crimes."[13] becomes prevalent. Yet powerful fathers may also have a dampening effect on achievement drives, leaving us to conclude that psychopathology is full of such contradictions.

One of the hopes that a child psychiatrist may entertain about the future world and its children is bound up with the pessimistic notion that the course of history tends to circularity. In this future world he would hope that the family and its dynamics would be understood and treated as a whole; that life crises would be seen as debilitating for some and stimulating for others, and that careful monitoring of early experiences of adoption, hospitalization, parent loss, serious illness, or divorce may help us to develop sophisticated instruments to differentiate the resilient from the incompetent. Well localized and accessible centers for preventive psychiatry, together with new skills developed in the preventive field, may help families face the multiplying psychosocial hazards that will threaten at all times to overwhelm them. By focusing on the family, we may counteract that fundamental structural flaw in the ancient Greek family that has reappeared so frequently in various civilizations: the father is effective only outside the home but, within it, the thin patriarchal veneer tends to collapse and the child experiences paternal inadequacy. We have Clytemnestra in Euripides saying: "Husband, do your man's work and leave the home to me."

In the face of all these vicissitudes of the time and the seeming inevitability of history repeating itself, will we, in fact, develop new insights, new preventions, and new interventions that will give us, perhaps for the first time, a psychosocially well-balanced family with children who take the Oedipus problems in their stride and without the torments that have haunted us for so long? In the words of the Sophoclean Jocasta:

As to your mother's marriage bed,—don't fear it.
Before this, in dreams too, as well as oracles,
Many a man has lain with his own mother.
But he to whom such things are nothing bears
His life most easily.

As a child psychiatrist of the year 1978, I would wish the child of tomorrow, of the year 2000, the life that he bears most easily.

REFERENCES

1. J. H. VAN DEN BERG, *The Changing Nature of Man,* Norton, New York, 1961.
2. T. PARSONS, *Social Structure and Personality,* The Free Press, New York, 1964.
3. P. J. TILLICH, *Courage To Be,* Yale University Press, New Haven, 1952.
4. E. J. ANTHONY, A psychodynamic model for minimal brain dysfunction, in *Minimal Brain Dysfunction* (ed. F. de la Cruz, B. H. Fox, R. H. Roberts), *Ann, NY Acad. Sci.* **205,** 1973.
5. E. J. ANTHONY, A working model for family studies, in *The Impace of Disease and Death* in the Yearbook of the IACPAP *The Child in His Family,* vol. 2 (ed. E.J. Anthony and C. Koupernik) John Wiley, New York, 1973.
6. E. J. ANTHONY A risk–vulnerability intervention model, in *Children at Psychiatric Risk* in the Yearbook of the IACPAP *The Child in His Family,* vol. 3, John Wiley, New York, 1974.
7. K. MANNHEIM, *Freedom, Power and Democratic Planning,* Oxford University Press, New York, 1950.
8. E. DURKHEIM, *Suicide: A Study in Sociology,* The Free Press of Glencoe, Chicago, 1951.
9. SOCRATES, *Phaedrus,* 279B.
10. D. W. WINNICOTT, Hate in the countertransference, in *Collected Papers,* Tavistock, London, 1958.
11. P. E. SLATER, *The Glory of Here,* Beacon Press, Boston, 1968.
12. M. MEAD, *Male and Female,* Menton, New York, 1955.
13. D. C. MCCLELLAND, *The Achieving Society,* van Nostrand, Princeton, 1961.

THE ROLE OF HEREDITARY FACTORS
IN GENERAL PATHOLOGY IN CHILDHOOD

Yu. E. Veltichev and A. M. Kapustyan

Pediatric Institute of Scientific Research, Moscow, USSR

THE ADVANCE in medical genetics of the recent decades has rendered a significant influence on pediatrics. A majority of hereditary diseases in man have been recognized in childhood years and, no less important, a hereditary predisposition has been established in numerous chronic diseases.

Due to this influence, notions have changed markedly on general pathology in childhood which has common features with and at the same time differs from general pathology in adults.

The conventional view was that pediatrics is general medicine shifted to the childhood age group, but the latest developments in physiology, genetics, and medical chemistry suggest that such a definition fails to take into account specific traits and pathology in the growing person, which actually never occur in the adult.

We can identify three basic differences between pediatrics and adult medicine:

(1) Disturbances of growth and harmonious development, which demand the special attention of pediatricians, are not present in adult pathology.

(2) The development of a specific defense system of humoral and cellular immunity, determined by genetic factors but induced by contact with the micro- and macro-world. Total or partial immune system defects are also specific to pediatric pathology.

(3) Any deviations in the early development of functional and social adaptation occurring at any level— molecular, organic, systemic, and those of overall personality—may result in severe pathology in the child.

Many, if not the majority of adult diseases are also found in children. However, pecularities of individual and age-related responsiveness give special features to their clinical manifestation and course, which significantly complicate differential diagnosis and require highly individualistic theurapeutic policy.

Thus, pediatrics needs to be interpreted not only as "general" medicine but also as a special field of biological sciences which deals with the health of a human being during its growth.

The setting up of a well-balanced system of pediatric health care in the USSR has made it possible to solve a number of important problems in a short space of time and has resulted in the radical improvement of sanitary conditions, the elimination of a number of infectious diseases in children, and a reduction in child mortality. However, the appearance of new trends influencing child health needs to be borne in mind. In the first place, there has been a relative (and absolute) increase in the incidence of hereditary and congenital diseases. An increase has also been observed in respiratory viral infection morbidity and growing pathogenicity of a number of agents—*Staphylococcus, Escherichia coli, Salmonella,* and *Meningococcus.*

There has been an increased tendency to sensitization in children associated with numerous factors: early artificial feeding, vaccination effects, antibiotic drug abuse, wide domestic usage of chemicals, environmental pollution, etc.

The interrelation between these factors results in a tendency for acute diseases to become chronic (pathologic process chronization), which is particularly manifest in respiratory and renal abnormalities. Totally or partially genetically determined factors have serious effects on such specific functions of the young organism as physical and mental development, biological and social adaptation, and immunity system development. It has been reported that hereditary defects today affect the rates of growth and harmonious development of approximately 6% of children. Of that 6%, 0·5–1% of the newborn have conditions in which genome and chromosome mutations are implicated, 0·5–1% are born with abnormalities induced by gene mutation, and approximately 4–5% of newborn children show developmental defects of a polygenic nature or diseases of polygenic inheritance.

The increased occurrence of congenital anomalies, noted in a number of world countries, determined the development of population teratology as a speciality exploring the epidemiological aspect of deviations from normal gestational development. This is important primarily for controlling the mutagenic effects of environmental factors.

Following the elaboration of chromosome-staining methods and the application of fluorescence techniques, it has been shown that in spontaneous abortions in the first trimester, chromosomal abnormalities are found in 61% of cases and, if occurring later, 55% which exceeds the rates obtained previously using conventional methods of research.

Genetic mutations are among the factors affecting growth and development of the child and are responsible for both the congenital anomalies and a large group of hereditary metabolic diseases.

Four classes of metabolic defects provide the biochemical basis of hereditary diseases:

(1) Abnormal synthesis of structural proteins, mainly of autosomal dominant inheritance.
(2) Genetically determined changes in the structure and function of enzyme proteins, or enzymopathies, mainly of autosomal recessive inheritance.
(3) Hereditary abnormalities in defense protein synthesis and maturation of immunocompetent organs.
(4) Hereditary pathology in membrane transport.

The most severe disturbances in physical and mental growth and development are related to hereditary enzymopathy.

Nowadays, mass neonatal screening for hereditary metabolic diseases is conducted in many countries.

Besides controlling the genetic structure of human populations, which is of the utmost importance, such examinations help to detect hereditary metabolic errors at the preclinical stage, when dietary treatment and appropriate medication can ensure complete prevention from gross invalidism and severe cerebral degeneration. Mass screening programs for phenylketonuria and mucoviscidosis are implemented in Moscow, frequency rates being 1 in 15,000 and 1 in 6000 respectively.

Genetic factors have an essential impact on immunity system development, determining both its normal formation and its multiple abnormalities.

Hereditary immune deficiency states are now better understood. Still the occurrence of serious hereditary abnormalities of immunity is relatively small, and children with partially impaired immune status comprise a far greater portion of the population, with increased susceptibility to infectious diseases and probably their chronization. Such hypoimmune states seem to have multifactorial genesis.

Adequate genetic control of immune response intensity explains both the persistent inflammatory process and the development of septic states with normal values of T & B lymphocyte function, though a similar situation may also be observed in neutrophil functional deficiency.

Polygenic inheritance is the basis of a delayed immunologic "start," i.e. a significant lag in the development of the child's immune systems, manifested by his low humoral resistance to infections.

It should be noted that pharmaceuticals at the pediatricians' disposal include only a limited group of immune response stimulants, among them levamisol, artificial polyelectrolytes such as polyacryl acid, poly-4-vinylpyridine, and synthetic RNA. Reports have been made of the immunostimulating effect of immunoglobulin molecule products (F_{ab} fragments) nucleic acids, isolated from sensitized lymphocytes, transfer factor, and other lymphocytic factors.

In the pathology of the biological functional and social adaptation of a child, great importance is to be attached to hereditary factors. Delayed development of extremely important functional systems (maintaining homeostasis, nutrition, energy supply, discriminate behavioral activity, etc.), is also to a large degree associated with hereditary factors. In certain cases, lagging development of functional systems is caused by a monogenic disease, though the majority of hereditary diseases produce not only functional immaturity but also disturbances in growth and development.

A feature of a number of diseases is tissue dysplasia or hypoplasia, which implies a discrepancy between morphologic maturity of tissue and chronologic age of the child.

A still more obvious interrelation is observed between congenital insufficiency of the thymus, which controls the cellular immunity development (T-lymphocytes), and physical retardation with intact embryonal, hypoplastic tissue structures, which are normally eliminated through the active functioning of lymphoid T-cells.

Threshold polygenic variations cause hereditary enzyme polymorphism, which appears to be a flexible system of adaptation to changing environmental conditions. It is known that, together with stable protein systems whose mutations are detrimental, a group of human enzyme proteins has been found, characterized by marked variations in physical–chemical traits even within a particular family.

Regarding general theory of adaptation, consideration should be given to the possible significance of hereditary protein polymorphism as a factor in resistance to a disease.

Preliminary data show that manifestations of incomplete hereditary polymorphism of enzyme protein (in this case, variant enzyme homozygosis) or the appearance of new abnormal variants, restrict the possibility of functional adaptation.

Specific protein structure can be revealed by fractioning enzymes by gel electrophoresis or electrofocusing. Changes in normal variants of the composition of structural defense proteins and enzymes may determine numerous diatheses.

The establishment of molecular–genetic roots of predisposition to diseases acquires special importance when one considers that numerous chronic diseases in adults can be traced back to childhood years. Early detection of genetic predisposition markers in children will make it possible to change the regime and diet at the appropriate time, and to correctly approach occupational orientation so as to avoid the development of a disease at a mature age.

Thus, hereditary factors play an enormous role in childhood pathology by significantly influencing those functions and characteristics that are vital in a growing person: development, immunity, and adaptation.

DISCUSSION

KATHERINE ELLIOTT
The CIBA Foundation, London, UK

I FEEL increasingly aware of at least two very different sets of interests within this symposium, and it seems to me that we are hearing much more about one of them—the interests of our so-called developed societies as opposed to the societies of the third world. I want to offer a thought or two about the future for both of these voices and perhaps try to reconcile them a little more, at least in the field of health.

I come from the Ciba Foundation where, some years ago, we discussed the future of the family in an effort to see how its shape might change once conception could be a totally separate act from sexual intercourse. It was not until almost the end of the meeting that Dr. Ralph Hendricks came out with the suggestion that everyone was avoiding: that it was becoming perfectly possible, biologically and technologically, for men to be made redundant and for women to run the world. This, he proposed, was a deep-seated fear in the minds of many men, and it was behind much of our discussion. Obviously, we all much prefer having two sexes. It makes life much more fun. But with reproductive biology moving as fast as it is, with artificial insemination, embryo transfer, the frozen storage of eggs, sperm, and fertilized embryos already happening; likewise parthenogenesis, cloning, predetermination of sex and all kinds of complicated genetic engineering all on the horizon, Huxley's Brave New World could indeed be just around the corner, and that may be why there is so much anxiety manifest here about parenting, bonding, and the like.[1]

To turn to the other quieter voice that speaks at this symposium for the much greater number of children in the third world (85% as opposed to 15%), their health needs are urgent for their sheer survival. 1973 was Human Rights Year as 1979 is to be the Year of the Child. It was in 1973 that the Ciba Foundation decided that in a world where men walked on the moon and had devised the means to blow up the universe, it was time to think seriously about what needed to be done to provide for all children, wherever they happen to be born, a minimum of at least four essential birthrights in health. The ones we chose were safe water to drink; enough of the right kinds of food to prevent malnutrition; protection against communicable diseases where protection is possible; and knowledge about and access to the means of controlling fertility.

It was immediately clear that to bring these birthrights to every child there would have to be in every community, however small, at least one or two people who knew enough to keep the feces out of the drinking water; who knew how to encourage breast feeding and to make the most of locally available foodstuffs; who could make sure that everyone got immunized or otherwise protected against communicable diseases; and who spread the idea of contraception along with the kind of simple maternal and child care which would ensure that most of the babies born into that

321

community would survive. Such "health agents," or agents of change, could also become referral points for the sick; treating simple illnesses themselves, and acting as essential bridges between the ordinary people and the conventional health and social services. This kind of infrastructure would make the efforts of the small number of professional physicians so much more effective, because everyone would eventually become involved in a new style of health and development service program which made proper use of the biggest resource for the future which the world possesses—the people themselves.

This was in 1973, and it is all beginning to happen, but much too slowly. This year, WHO and UNICEF join forces in a primary health care program which may, if we are very lucky indeed, meet the call for primary health care for all by the year 2000. To make even this minimum provision for the health of tomorrow's children, we, the professionals, have to act and to act fast. We have to use all our imagination and all our ingenuity to create such a worldwide web of care and concern for the health of mothers and children everywhere, that the politicians and the bureaucrats—the holders of power and the keepers of the purse strings, the final decision makers—are clearly, firmly, and properly guided and supported in making the effort that is needed to provide a healthier and better life for the underprivileged millions.

We, the professionals, need also to set a good example ourselves, sharing our knowledge and our expertise, and being at the same time ready to listen to ordinary people who have their own wisdom, which has, after all, kept the human race going through so many so-called civilizations.

If Professor Jelliffe were here he would certainly have already mentioned the "doula." She is the woman of experience who advises, helps, and supports the new mother as she begins to breast feed for the first time. Unfortunately, doulas are seldom available in our modern nuclear style of society, and the professionals who supervise the birth process are often sadly lacking in knowledge about the art of successful breast feeding. Professor Sir John Butterfield, who also was unable to come to the symposium, very much wanted me to mention the work of Dr. Margaret Whichelow[2] on food energy intake in relation to successful lactation. It seems that young mothers nowadays are not advised about eating well and regularly in order to keep up their supply of breast milk. We need Dr. Whichelow's data to influence those who deal with education and with policy, but it is surely no great surprise to discover that a well fed mother makes more milk—any farmer knows this. There are, however, very many societies where the mother comes last of all in the sharing of the scarce supply of food.

Breast feeding from the mother's angle was the subject of another Ciba Foundation symposium, which followed one we held about "Acute Diarrhoea in Childhood," so often the sad result of the decline in breast feeding throughout the world and which is most lethal among the most poor. To end, I wanted to mention here in Athens the picture on the jacket of the book on breast feeding, which shows Hera suckling Herakles, whom she had adopted. There is no biological law which says that a woman may suckle only the child to whom she has given birth. Perhaps, with the need for more sharing of children and of parenting, the future will bring along more sharing of breast milk. This, indeed, may be one way for young women to combine working outside their homes and breast feeding—they can share with a friend in similar circumstances but with different working hours. Sharing happens all the time in tribal societies, and it is interesting that it is now beginning to happen among the intellectual elite in the West.

I submit that the privilege of being breast fed is something to which every child is entitled (except in the most special circumstances), so that every child may be given the best beginning to life according to our present knowledge. If we believe this to be true, then we have to insist on socioeconomic development taking place in a way which safeguards the nutrition of women of child-bearing age and of young children. We have to demonstrate the paramount importance of this policy for the healthy development of the Child in the World of Tomorrow; for the small girls of today are the mothers of tomorrow, and we have to persist until we have won out over this fundamental issue. I hope that we will not go away from this symposium without making this message clear to the world.

REFERENCES

1.   On July 25, 1978 (i.e. after the symposium), the first "test tube" baby was born in Britain by Caesarian section at 37 weeks. Louise weighed between 2.26 and 2.27 kg (5 and 6 lb) and is normal, breast-fed, and doing well. The two scientists involved in the fertilization and implanting of the egg are Dr. G. R. G. Edwards and Patrick Steptoe.
2.   MARGARET WHICHELOW, cf. Archives of Diseases in Childhood, 50, (1975); also Proceedings of the Nutrition Society, 35, 64–65A (1975).

HEALTH CARE: WHOSE RESPONSIBILITY?

Chairman:
JOHN APLEY
　　Bristol Royal Hospital for Sick Children, Bristol, UK

WHOSE RESPONSIBILITY?

THOMAS MCKEOWN

Department of Social Medicine, University of Birmingham, UK

IT IS only in the last few decades that a serious attempt has been made to assess the influences on which health depends. This inquiry has led to the conclusion that the transformation of man's health since the 18th century was due mainly to nonpersonal measures, and it has been suggested that the same influences may be important for the solution of the residual health problems of developed countries.

In general, the predominant influences leading to the advance in health were improvement in nutrition, better hygiene (particularly in respect of water and food), and modification of reproductive behavior which limited numbers. With the decline of the infections and the transition from poverty to affluence, health problems have changed, and in developed countries behavioral influences (related to diet, exercise, smoking, and the like) are now probably more significant than nutritional and environmental ones.

This interpretation of the determinants of human health has at least three major implications: it suggests directives for medical research; it underlines the need for increased attention to nonpersonal influences on health; and it has a bearing on personal health services, particularly the significance of behavior and the relation between acute and chronic care. In the present context we shall be concerned only with the last two of these three issues, and in particular with the respective responsibilities of society, the individual, and the health professions.

SOCIETY

It is evident that society has a dual obligation, to make provision for the care of the sick and to take such steps as are possible to preserve health. In doing so it must attempt to arrive at a reasonable balance between these activities and between the demands of the present and the needs of the future. Understandably, in the health field a high priority is given to the immediate problems, particularly those of patients with acute illnesses, and to some extent this is at the expense of preventive measures and of patients with chronic diseases. Whether this balance of effort is reasonable turns to a considerable extent on the results of treatment after disease has recurred; if intervention is likely to be effective we can afford to wait, but if it is not, much attention must be given to the alternative approach. Both experience of the infections and the theoretical grounds referred to above suggest that emphasis on preventive measures is needed, particularly in respect of food policies, control of the environment, and modification of behavior.

Two objections are often raised to attempts to modify behavior: that they would be an unreasonable intrusion on individual rights, and that they are unlikely to be effective. On the first point, an important distinction needs to be made between outlawing an action and creating an environment which makes it less likely. For example, there would be objections in most countries to a general prohibition of smoking; it is quite another matter to prevent advertising of tobacco, to prohibit its sale to children, to make it expensive, and to restrict its use in public places. The elimination of smoking can also be pursued in many subtler ways, designed to make it unacceptable to public opinion. The same approach is needed to other aspects of personal behavior which are known to be important to health. It is not suggested that we should be required to limit consumption of alcohol, sugar, and dairy products, and to avoid self-prescribed drugs and some of the physician-prescribed variety, beneficial as all these measures would undoubtedly be for our health. But it is not inconsistent with respect for personal freedom to seek to create an environment which encourages people to do what is good for them and to avoid what is bad. It seems particularly reprehensible to do the reverse.

The conclusion that personal habits cannot be modified is I think mistaken and arises largely from the application of too short a time scale; we do not detect movement when we are close to it. The most impressive evidence of variation in habits is the remarkable change in reproductive behavior which has spread through society in, roughly, a hundred years. And in the much shorter post-war period there are signs of limitation of smoking, increase of exercise, and changes in diet. Although the modification of habits may be slower than we should like, there is no reason to doubt that it occurs and can be encouraged by appropriate action from society.

In respect of nutrition there are the different problems of deficient food for some people and excessive or ill-balanced diets for others. Both can be influenced by food policies, e.g. in the form of the food supplements and subsidies used during the Second World War, whose success was reflected in health indices in spite of deterioration of some other features of living conditions. The effects were marked in mothers and children. Having regard for the importance of food and to health, the aim of public policy should be to put essential constituents within the reach of everyone, and to provide inducements for people to prefer foods that are beneficial to those that are harmful. Of course these aims cannot be expected to exclude all other considerations, such as international agreements and the solvency of farmers who have been encouraged to produce meat and dairy products rather than grains. Nevertheless, in future evaluations of agricultural and related economic policies, the health implications should be given a primary place.

THE INDIVIDUAL

From the conclusion that in technologically advanced countries personal behavior is the predominant determinant of health, it follows that responsibility for its maintenance now rests largely with the individual. This is not the message which has been conveyed to the public hitherto. Many references to the right to health, e.g. by the World Health Organization, suggest that it is a commodity which can and should be provided by society; and the medical emphasis on the importance of early detection of disease carries the implication that when discovered it can be treated effectively.

I think there is little doubt that public attitudes have been influenced in the past by the belief that health is preserved essentially by treatment of the sick. The adolescent who begins to smoke does not consider whether chronic bronchitis and cancer of the lung can be cured, but many parents would be concerned about setting their children a bad example by smoking if they were aware of the intractable character of the diseases to which it leads. Parents will often do for their children what they will not do for themselves, and already there are mothers, possibly many, who have stopped or curtailed smoking during pregnancy because of its harmful effects on the fetus.

There are numerous ways in which the message of individual responsibility for health can be conveyed, and no doubt one of the most effective would be to harness public provision of medical care to personal actions in relation to health. This possibility was discussed by Morrison who asked: "I wonder how much longer we can go on talking about a right to health without some balancing talk about the individual's responsibility to keep health."[1] And in his thoughtful examination of these matters in the United States, Kass wrote: "Even leaving aside questions of justice, and looking only at the pursuit of health, one has reason to fear that the new insurance plan, whichever one it turns out to be, may actually contribute to a worsening rather than an improvement in our nation's health, especially if there is no balancing program to encourage individual responsibility for healthy maintenance."[2]

He refers to the possibility of building both negative and positive inducements into insurance plans by measures such as refusing or reducing benefits for chronic respiratory care to persons who continue to smoke. Whether such methods will prove acceptable is an open question; what is hardly in doubt is that further substantial advances in health will depend largely on personal decisions about ways of life.

THE HEALTH PROFESSIONS

When considering the extent of medical responsibilities it is important to distinguish clearly between the role of the practicing doctor and the role of medicine as an institution. With a few exceptions (e.g. occupational health) the doctor who treats sick people cannot be expected to be concerned from day to day with nonpersonal influences (although an understanding of their significance to health seems no less relevant to his work than a knowledge of the chemistry of the drugs he uses). But there are compelling reasons why medicine as an institution should be involved. In the first place it seems essential to have some professional organization which deals comprehensively with health matters, and indeed some of the difficulties of the past were due to medicine's equivocal position in relation to the larger role. Secondly, while environmental measures (for example) are now largely in the hands of non-medical specialists, it is desirable to preserve and extend the medical interest, since the scope of inquiry is greatly enlarged when it starts from a knowledge of disease problems as well as of environmental planning, and many examples could be cited to support the conclusion that medical participation is needed for investigation of environmental influences on health, if not always for their day-to-day control. It is for these reasons that the institution of medicine should be concerned with nonpersonal influence and that some medically qualified people should be trained as consultants in environmental medicine.

The role of medicine in relation to behavior is, if anything even more significant. In pursuit of the objectives of preventing sickness and premature death, the doctor can often do more for his patients, particularly young patients, by influencing their behavior (not least by his example) than by any treatment that can be offered.

Finally, I must refer briefly to the role of medicine in relation to that of other health professions. This issue has been obscured to some extent by identification of the institution of medicine with clinical practice. From acceptance of the wider interpretation of the institutional role, it follows that it should be concerned with the activities of all the related professions and with the training arrangements needed for them. It is not, of course, suggested that medicine should be considered responsible for the training of nurses, psychologists, medical social workers, biochemists, and many others. But as these people have to work together to provide a comprehensive service covering a vast range of activities, it is most desirable that there should be some focus for consideration of their common problems and interests. It is this focus that the institution of medicine should provide.

REFERENCES

1. R. S. MORRISON, Rights and responsibilities: redressing the uneasy balance, *The Hastings Center Report*, **4** (2), 4 (April 1974).
2. L. S. KASS, Regarding the end of medicine and the pursuit of health, *The Public Interest*, **40**, 42 (Summer, 1975).

WHO PROVIDES HEALTH CARE FOR CHILDREN?

ROBERT J. HAGGERTY

School of Public Health, Harvard University, Boston, MA, USA

IN MOST of the world, children have been born, raised, and cared for when ill by their mothers, with advice and assistance from grandmothers, lay midwives, and only occasionally from medicine men. For less than a century have technical and scientific advances been applied to child health care. But so rapid has been the rise of modern medicine that in most developed countries today the popular view is that children have all of their health care, including behavior, guided by professionals from birth; indeed, often even before conception. In spite of the idealized popular image of the doctor (with or without other members of the health team) providing for all the health care needs of children, the reality is quite different. Mothers still provide the majority of health care to children, even in areas with an abundance of medical resources.

A few years ago we carried out a series of studies of child health services in Rochester, New York— a city with close to a million people and very well endowed with health care personnel. Among a random sample of families with children, mothers were asked to keep a diary for a month recording all illnesses, and what they did about them.[1] As is well known, children have a large number of acute illnesses—an average of 8–10 per year, mainly mild respiratory or acute self-limited febrile in nature. But some action was felt necessary by the mothers for most of these illnesses, and the action was taken by the mother alone in 90% of all illness episodes (Table 1). The short answer to who takes care of most children's illness is clearly mothers.

It is somewhat surprising, therefore, with all of this care already being provided by mothers, to see the movement that is growing in the United States for self-care. It is almost as if many people feel that all decision making has been taken from them and they are desperately seeking to regain control over their lives, forgetting that, for children, care within the family without professional help is the norm.

There are several streams leading to the present resurgence in self-care. First we have a long history of self-help in the United States, some generated by the needs of the frontier which was often without formal medical care. A second stream is the current women's movement which has often been more concerned with self-care for themselves[2] than their children, yet nevertheless has fostered a resistance against medical authority, with a result that there are a proliferation of self-care medical books on the market now including a new one arranged with a branching decision tree model for children's illnesses.[3] It extends the extremely popular Spock book on child care to include more on treatment of illness. A third stream is the general consumer movement with its concern over the depersonalization and technocratic professionalism which has included medicine as one of its targets. Finally, there is the recognition of the importance of personal lifestyle and health habits as probably the largest factor in producing health. While smoking, drinking, exercise, stress-coping abilities, etc., are in part governed by societal forces, they are also clearly personal habits under the control of the individual.

All of these forces have led to what I perceive as a major revolution in health care, especially for children and young families: a greater interest in self-care, directed at achieving more autonomy from professions. Courses for lay persons in medical decision making may still be an upper middle class phenomena, but they are symbolic of the desire that families and children wish to play a greater role in health care, especially for the preventive issues.

I might point out the practical implications. In our Rochester Study, where 90% of all children's illnesses were cared for by the mother, it was still estimated that at least half of all the illnesses brought to the doctor were minor and self-limited and that with only a little more knowledge and self-confidence most mothers could have managed without a doctor's help. The potential for reduction by half of all illness visits to medical services by more self-help has enormous potential for cost savings in an era when cost controls are unfortunately the first priority in many countries. It also has potential effects on reducing visits to pediatricians who, with lower birth rates, are beginning to be less than fully busy.

The careful empirical studies necessary to know how to foster affective self-help are only now beginning to be made. The Lewis' study of child initiated care in a Los

TABLE 1

Actions reported on days with a complaint or symptom; 11,625 complaint days (6249 adult complaint days; 5376 child complaint days), Rochester Metropolitan Area, 1969

Part of question No. 3	Adults				Children			
	Mother	Father	Other adults	All adults	Youngest child	Second youngest	Other children	All children
Total days with a complaint reported	3622	2020	607	6249	2488	1446	1443	5377
Perceived need?								
Yes	82.9%	80.4	87.2	82.6	86.9	86.7	81.9	85.5
No	17.1%	19.6	12.8	17.4	13.1	13.3	18.1	14.5
	100.0	100.0	100.0	100.0	100.0	100.0	100.0	100.0
Action possible?								
Yes	92.2%	92.3	97.7	92.8	97.8	96.5	95.9	97.0
No	7.8%	7.7	2.3	7.2	2.2	3.5	4.1	3.0
	100.0	100.0	100.0	100.0	100.0	100.0	100.0	100.0
Type of action								
Self decision* (medications, home remedies)	94.0%	92.2	91.6	93.2	92.7	93.7	91.1	92.6
Semiprofess.†	0.1%	.3	—	.2	—	.1	.5	.2
Dentist visit	0.4%	1.1	.6	.6	.3	.3	.6	.4
Doctor visit	4.5%	6.4	7.8	6.0	7.0	5.9	7.7	6.8
	100.0	100.0	100.0	100.0	100.0	100.0	100.0	100.0

*Most of these decisions concerned taking medications, either for over-the-counter medications or, following doctor's instructions, for prescribed medications. About 30% of these decisions also mentioned home remedies, mostly bedrest, soaking, and heating pads.
†Of the 16 semiprofessional consultations, 9 were given by nurses, 3 by pharmacists, 2 by chiropractors, and one each by a chiropodist and a physical therapist.

Angeles grade school[4] shows how difficult it is to change the way first grade children use medical care. After 2 years of education on how to care for themselves, children changed the way they used health services very little. Among these children, their ego strength or self-image seemed to be more important in their ability to care for themselves than specific knowledge.

In a study of asthmatic children, however, education about how to care for attacks resulted in marked decrease in symptoms and use of hospital emergency rooms as compared to a control group.

There is a bright and important future for increasing the competence of parents and children in providing some of their own medical care and especially in developing healthy life styles.

But, like any therapy, this movement has potentially undesirable side effects. In addition to the obvious one of poor or wrong care, there is the danger of blaming the victims and absolving society of any responsibility for ensuring that all children receive care, an issue to which I shall return.

There is also the unfortunate implication that more self-help would be especially useful for the poor because it would substitute for medical services that we in the United States have found difficult to deliver to the poor. Self-help should not be used as a cheap way of providing services only for the poor. At the moment this does not seem to be a danger since most of the interest is among the intellectual upper middle class.

A second major change in recent years in who provides child health care is the vast expansion of professionals other than the physician who are involved. Fifty years ago 1 of every 2 health workers was a doctor—today it is less than 1 in 10. In pediatrics most attention has been placed on pediatric nurse practitioners, but a number of other child health professionals have also appeared in large numbers in recent years—especially psychologists and counsellors of various types.

Like the self-help movement, the use of nonphysicians in expanded roles has a long history. Lay midwives, public health nurses, settlement house workers, etc., have met health needs of many children in the past. What is new is the increase in formal training programs, licensing, and in some instances independent practice for these groups.

The profound implications that stem from both the self care and the physician extender movements is that the doctor now must share the responsibility for health services for children with others. This has understandably produced tension within medicine. People vary in their desire for self-care and use of nonphysicians even for minor ills. Many still want a well-trained compassionate doctor to provide these services. Doctors are also needed as research leaders, for the importance of evaluating the efficacy of these new approaches remain largely limited to physicians. Other professions and the public have generally been more willing than doctors to accept as proven what one's own limited experience suggests is successful. This is not to say that physicians have been all that scientific in their demand for evidence of efficacy, but only relatively more so. There is great need for careful evaluation of new programs. Who cares for the health needs of children has thus become more a shared responsibility—shared between the physician and parents—the child and nonphysicians, and generally I believe that is a healthy state.

Now let me turn to the other side of the coin—whose responsibility should it be to organize health services to ensure that all children receive the benefits of health care? After my rather enthusiastic espousal of self-care in the first section, I should now make clear that I am not so nihilistic about what modern medicine has to offer that I would neglect organizing medical services for all. In fact medical care has had an undeserved bad press lately. I would not deny that the major reason for the decline in childhood mortality has been from social advances—better food, housing, and sanitation. But medicine should never have claimed so much credit for these advances.

My own view of what medicine can do is perhaps more limited, but no less important. It should:

(1) provide for easy access to the universal comfort-caring functions that everyone has a right to when they are ill;

(2) at the same time medicine should be able to recognize and treat those relatively few diseases for which medicine does good: e.g. bacterial meningitis;

(3) it should offer counsel and efficacious technological services for children with chronic but nonfatal diseases, e.g. asthma or emotional disturbances;

(4) it should provide high quality technical care with compassion for very serious and often fatal diseases, e.g. leukemia;

(5) medicine should be involved in ensuring, if not actually delivering, preventive services of proven value to all children.

Even the most libertarian philosopher would not deny to children the right to equity in access to the range of services I outlined, even if the family did not seek them (although he would feel differently about adults). Most of our societies, no matter what their political philosophies, have placed high priority on children's health services. I am ashamed that in the United States we have a longer way to go than many in ensuring that all children have access to care which combines effective high technology with humaneness.

The question is, How to organize services to achieve this goal? It seems to those of us from the Western democracies that the more authoritarian regimes can more easily achieve this goal. Cuba, the Soviet Union, and China give examples of well-organized, population-based health services that seem to reach all children. The ingredients for success include some political entity setting a policy that all children will receive services; that services be organized on a defined population basis in order to know what children live where; that there be a system of outreach to seek and find all children in the defined area and either offer services directly or inform, direct, and monitor their use of services elsewhere.

There are those in the United States who worry about the potential intrusiveness of such a system into what has traditionally been a very private, family responsibility. The discussion earlier in this paper, about the movement toward self-help, might seem antithetical to this part where I espouse more responsibility by the state. But I believe that the two goals of more self-help, while at the same time ensuring that all children are in some health care system, can be compatible. One way to keep the intrusiveness to a minimum is appropriate training for health workers. The goal of public health, or community health, nurses and doctors should be to see that all children in their defined area are in some reputable service, but not to impose their own personal views on child rearing or their own services for curative medicine on families.

Two other ways to protect against intrusion and yet ensure access to care are (1) have the public health services separate from the clinical services, and (2) have both public health and clinical services accountable to those that they serve through such vehicles as community health councils made up of the parents and older children whom the health professionals serve.

In the United States we have not yet worked out an appropriate balance. When children with parental abuse are reported in the papers there is an outcry for more intrusion: "How can you let this happen?" "Take the children away from such parents" are heard. Yet when Professor Kempe suggests[5] that a public health nurse visit the home of all newborns to determine the risk of child abuse and initiate intervention, there is an equally shrill outcry from the other philosophical point of view that this is an unwarranted intrusion into the sanctity of the home. When it is found on school entry that 30% of children are not immunized, there is shock and calls for more vigorous immunization programs. Yet when it is suggested that all children receive a unique identification number at birth with unification of medical records and follow-up of those with incomplete immunizations, there is an uproar that this is an invasion of privacy. Clearly we need an information system that tells us who does not get care and a system of service to provide it, at the same time keeping intrusion into family privacy at a minimum.

What some countries seem to have worked out, either through social reinforcement on a neighborhood level (as in China) or by more centralized means (eastern Europe), remains a major unsolved problem in the United States. Until it is resolved we shall not be able to ensure access and equity of use of health services there.

Meeting in Greece we would be remiss if we did not acknowledge that ancient Greece was the first civilization to give power to the intellect of its people as distinct from a very small elite of priests or despotic rulers. "The exercise of vital powers along lines of excellence in a life affording them scope"[6] is an old Greek definition of happiness. In Greece at the height of Athens the individual, for the first time in history, achieved importance and men were encouraged to think for themselves. "Know thyself" and "nothing in excess" were put forward as the formula for healthy life. In this setting physicians for the first time were freed from magic and advised to study nature.

How appropriate and symbolic to emphasize here the current reemphasis on self help and personal efforts to achieve health through wise living, at the same time to recognize the responsibility of the state to ensure equality of access to health care for all.

REFERENCES

1. K. J. ROGHMANN and R. J. HAGGERTY, The diary as a research instrument in the study of health and illness behavior, *Medical Care* **10** 143 (1972) (also see R. J. Haggerty, K. J. Roghmann and I. V. Pless, *Child Health and the Community*, Wiley Interscience, New York, 1975).
2. BOSTON WOMEN'S HEALTH BOOK COLLECTIVE, *Our Bodies Ourselves,* a book by and for Women, Simon & Schuster, New York, 1976.
3. R. PANTEL, J. FRIES and D. VICKERY, *Taking Care of Your Child,* Addison-Wesley, Massachusetts, 1977.

4. C. E. LEWIS, M. A. LEWIS, A. LARIMER and B. B. PALMER, Child initiated care: the use of school nursing services by children in an "adult free" system, *Pediatrics* **60** 499 (1977).
5. H. KEMPE, Family Intervention, *Pediatrics* **56** 693 (1975).
6. E. HAMILTON, *The Greek Way,* p. 35, W. W. Norton & Co., New York, 1942.

DISCUSSION

IHSAN DOGRAMACI

Haceteppe University, Ankara, Turkey

DR. APLEY, in his introductory remarks, told us of his experience in Vietnam in 1968 when he saw children dying of diphtheria, measles, tetanus, and actie polio. He said that he and his group of young doctors were astounded by this situation. I am afraid, however, that the situation is not brighter today in many parts of the world. In certain of the underprivileged areas of the world, 80–85% of the population has no access to any kind of health services. Children still die from these same diseases.

Dr. Aldrich told us that infant mortality in the United States was generally 15·8‰ although it was 26‰ in certain minority groups. He also told us that in Mississippi this rate was exactly double in the black population what it was in the white: 34‰ and 17‰, respectively. Let us look at the situation in the rest of the world: infant mortality is 200‰ or higher in certain developing countries, which means 20 times as high as in some developed areas. In preschool children aged 1–5, the difference can be up to 40 times. Indeed, the mortality rate is 15–20‰ in the developing world, whereas it is only 0·5–1·5‰ in the developed regions.

The greatest portion of underprivileged children in developing areas live in rural areas. At the beginning of this decade, 75% of 1910 million people lived in rural areas. With all due respect to Dr. Salk's sigmoid curve as described by Dr. Aldrich, the population will grow faster in developing areas than in the developed ones, so the outlook is not good. Today it is known that in about 50% of the rural areas of the developing countries there is either no water at all or no safe water. We also know that diarrhoea is the main cause of death in many developing countries. To combat diarrhoea and the resulting malnutrition, we have to supply all areas with water—and clean water.

The situation in the urban population is also not very bright: 18–20% of the population of developing countries live in cities, and this proportion is increasing rapidly. There is a strong movement toward the towns, and in certain Latin American countries the population of urban dwellers is already up to 45%. They live in shanty towns and under most unhygienic conditions.

In the developing areas there is maternal malnutrition, there is protein energy malnutrition and there is vitamin A deficiency and blindness. Bronchiolitis and pneumonia are the second cause of death in many countries. The reason why these last two are killers in developing countries is because the child is malnourished and cannot resist such infections. I wish to underline Dr. Aldrich's statement to the effect that we have to do something about the situation for the children of the future if we want to deserve to be called "good ancestors."

Now let us come to the search for an answer to the topic of this session: Whose responsibility is health care?

337

On November 29, 1959, the United Nations General Assembly adopted the Declaration of Rights of the Child. In each of the 10 principles there is some implication for the health of the child. Principle No. 1 states that the health of the child, physically, intellectually, morally, spiritually, and socially, shall be assured irrespective of race, color, sex, language, religion, political beliefs, and economic situation of the family.

The constitutions of most countries require provision of health to the citizens. Therefore, the answer to the question Whose responsibility? must be that the individual, the family, professional personnel, and voluntary societies have their roles, but in the developing societies it is the *government* that must provide public health education, clean water, and an infrastructure for primary health care.

T. A. BAASHER
WHO Regional Office for the Eastern Mediterranean, Alexandria, Eygpt

In the introductory part of his presentation, McKeown described in historical perspective the determinant of health and emphasized the importance of nonpersonal factors in the transformation of health and in solving some of the long-standing medical problems in affluent societies.

Haggerty, on the other hand, based on his experience in the United States, dealt with the growing movement for self-care and its future effects on child and family health.

Both indicated the thrust of social development in the health field and the changing focus of responsibility. These conclusions are drawn from experience in technically advanced countries and obviously lead to the pertinent question: How far are they applicable to the health situation in underprivileged countries and in what way can they influence the future development of health care and shape the focus of responsibility?

I will make an attempt to address myself to the four main issues covered by these two speakers, namely:

(1) nonpersonal factors and health;
(2) society and the organization of health care;
(3) self-care and individual responsibility;
(4) professional responsibility and health care.

1. NONPERSONAL FACTORS AND HEALTH

The importance of nonpersonal factors as a major determinant in health care seems to be well demonstrated by the sharp contrast in the current situation between developed and developing countries. Significantly, glaring differences are mostly seen in the field of child health, and the main contributing factors are related to poor hygienic conditions, shortage of food supply, and inadequacy of provision of health care.

The differences are clearly reflected in the high rate of infant mortality and child morbidity in developing countries. It is estimated, for instance, that of 120 million or so births a year in the world more than 80% take place in developing countries. However, the infant mortality varies from approximately 9 or 10 in developed countries to 200 per thousand in developing countries. On average the infant mortality in developing countries is 10 to 20 times that in developed countries.[1]

To demonstrate this further, it has been reported that out of 11 million children born every year in countries of WHO Eastern Mediterranean Region (EMR), one and a half million die before the age of one year and a further half a million between one and five years. General analysis of available data shows that diarrhoeal diseases are the causes of 30–45% of the total deaths under five years of age.

As has been repeatedly indicated (and similar to the conclusions outlined by McKeown), the main underlying determinant factors of the high mortality under the age of five are infection, malnutrition, and poor hygienic conditions.

To identify the causes and assign responsibility for dealing with the overriding nonpersonal factors in health constitute, no doubt, a major step along the difficult road of finding the proper solution. However, one has also to examine the complexity of the increasing needs and the overwhelming constraints which beset general efforts for meeting these needs. In this respect let us take the example of the provision of a safe water supply which is a major determinant factor in the maintenance of health, particularly in the health of children. On reviewing the progress made in countries of WHO EMR, it is reported[2] that, while in 1970, 56% of urban population had access to piped water supply through house connections, only 52% had similar facilities in 1975, a drop showing that the services were not keeping pace with the population increase. Similarly, in 1970, while 19% of the rural population had reasonable access to safe water, in 1975 the percentage had decreased to 16%.

Another area of sharp contrast between developed and developing countries, and which is of central importance in the maintenance of health, is food production and the state of child nutrition. In 1977 it was reported by the Organization for Economic Cooperation and Development that over the last six years food production failed to match up to population growth in no less than 50 countries and declined significantly on a *per capita* basis in Africa. Insufficiency of food production, together with a host of psychosocial factors, have seriously led to a state of malnutrition among millions of children with well known deleterious effects on physical and mental development and on resistance against infections.

The differences in health conditions between developed and developing countries can be explained (as indicated by McKeown) by differences in the predominant influences, mainly by nutritional state and hygienic conditions. If these determinants of health are viewed in their proper perspective, the future strategy for approaching health problems in developing countries should be directed along a wide base, ensuring an adequate supply of food with appropriate distribution, provision of safe water, establishment of an effective system of environmental sanitation, development of immunization programmes, and health education aiming at proper personal hygiene and appropriate child care.

2. SOCIETY AND THE ORGANIZATION
OF HEALTH CARE

It is clear from the above that health care should be viewed as an end product of a chain of activities with varying inputs and different responsibilities invested at the level of the individual as well as at the levels of society at large. This implies that health care is more than the mere provision of services for dealing with medical problems and should therefore be conceived as an integral part of the overall social development.

Contrary to this, the overall social aspects of health have been neglected in the past and the provision of medical services has been conceived as the role of society. As an outcome of this, more attention has been given to the development of curative facilities with increasing tendencies toward specialization.

Even in poor countries, where resources are very limited, the image of health care has been seen as the building up of highly technical medical services. Under such circumstances it is not uncommon to observe super-specialized medical centres which are out of tune with the body of facilities, and which only meet a rather small part of the health needs of children.

Importantly, with growing self-awareness in developing countries, it has been increasingly recognized that the conventional model of health care, which is clinically oriented and hospital based, has often fallen short of meeting national needs. There are several developing countries where the health coverage is not more than 20%. Naturally, among communities where there are no organized health services, mothers and relatives are primarily responsible for the health care of their children. In countries where the health services are deficient, auxiliary workers often provide limited care for children with physical illnesses. Behavioral disturbances, on the other hand, are generally looked after within the family set-up, and according to cultural practices and societal customs and beliefs.[3]

In recent years, and in order to make health accessible to all people, the concept of primary health care has been developed. In essence primary health care resolves around the measures and activities undertaken at the first level of contact with individuals and the community. A basic element in this type of health care is involvement and sharing of responsibility by the community. Furthermore, primary health care is considered an essential component of the overall development at the community level, and its activities are closely integrated and coordinated with those of other sectors in the society. Though the scope and range of primary health care may differ from country to country according to the recognized area of responsibility given to the health sector, and from community to community according to health needs and priority, this approach has opened up new possibilities for the extension of health care and mobilization of social resources.

Along with the development of primary health care and the provision of the necessary health coverage, more and more emphasis has been recently laid on the concept of appropriate technology. It has been increasingly realized that despite the enormous growth of health technology, there is a wide gap between this and its application at a community level. To bridge this gap, health technologies must be made simple, cheap, acceptable, and easily understood by the community in order to be effectively and appropriately used.

Oral hydration can be cited as an example. Recent efforts for the development of simple, easily administered, cheap, and readily available ingredients for oral hydration has made it possible for it to be widely used at the community level, and this has saved the lives of children who otherwise would have succumbed to the common diarrhoeal diseases.

3. SELF-CARE AND INDIVIDUAL RESPONSIBILITY

While the right to health has been given due emphasis in recent years and has been embodied in the Declaration of Human Rights and in some national constitutions, individual responsibility in health care has not been given the wide attention it deserves.

Several diseases can be prevented if bad personal habits, such as overeating, much drinking, smoking, and abuse of drugs, etc., can be given up. On the other hand, maintenance of health calls for an appropriate behavioral style of life by fostering a harmonious family relationship, keeping a proper diet, attending to one's health, exercising regularly, and so forth. Obviously there is a wide range of activities that can be undertaken at the individual, family, and community levels.

Though initial efforts for improving the knowledge, skill, and attitudes of children regarding diseases are promising (such as bronchial asthma as pointed out by Haggerty), it is clear that the field of self-care has not been adequately explored and, in many countries, individual responsibility has not been appropriately enhanced.

In general there are certain barriers that have to be removed and difficult obstacles to be overcome. Lack of knowledge regarding good living; harmful knowledge through advertisement and the media; rapid social change and its adverse effects on useful cultural practice, such as breast feeding; a high illiteracy rate among children of the rural populations of developing countries, etc., may run counter to the development of appropriate health knowledge.

It is true that changing people's habits may not be that easy. However, one would like to support McKeown's views that changes in human behavior, including bad habits, have to be measured against a time scale. Furthermore, the modification of behavior has to be considered within the context of personal factors as well as the interacting social, psychological, and physical forces in the society. It is envisaged, for example, that changes in the reproductive behavior among the rural population of the developing world will be a rather slow process. In other words, the habit of unregulated fertility should be considered along the continuum of historical differences in socioeconomic development and the inherent cultural background of underprivileged communities. In approaching such issues it is, therefore, important that the historical evolution of societies and the various variables determining personal behavior should be taken into consideration.

How do we see the child in the world of tomorrow with respect to self-care and individual responsibility? It seems that there can be a general agreement that—given an optimum opportunity to know what constitutes good health; how to protect oneself against preventable diseases; what to do in case of illness; and how to develop an appropriate style of behavior, the child in the world of tomorrow will play a more central role in self-care and will enjoy a better life: though I repeat that this needs time and a continuous sharing of knowledge.

In many countries the education of children in health technology is rather limited and generally deficient. From Haggerty's observations it can be concluded that in the United States there is "a greater interest in self-care." The same may be true for other countries. However, it seems that more concerted efforts are needed in planning, programming, philosophy, and strategy of self-care. This should be considered as a long term operational activity, starting in early childhood, and continuing along with other educational programs.

4. PROFESSIONAL RESPONSIBILITY AND HEALTH CARE

Clearly the growing emphasis and current interest in self-care, self-help, and the extension of health coverage imply a changing movement in the delivery of health care. Both Haggerty and McKeown have described the changing responsibility of the health professional and the possibilities of their future role.

However, as has been indicated previously, health care is not the responsibility of the health professional sector alone but of the society as a whole. Because of this, the health professionals have to be trained to share information experience, thinking and responsibility with others outside the medical field (namely with politicians, community leaders, and other professionals). The health system, too, has to be evaluated and appropriately adapted to the new needs and changes. Medical education has often been developed in isolation from the community which the health professionals are striving to serve, and medical training is generally confined to super-specialized teaching hospitals, which are out of harmony with the peripheral services where the health need is most felt.

There is no doubt that in the majority of the developing countries the super-specialized hospital complex has created an anomalous situation, which has to be resolved. In essence there is a growing need for striking a balance between hospital services and specialized medicine, on the one hand, and community care, on the other. Information is dismally lacking regarding recipients of medical care, and questions—such as Who consults the health professionals and for what? What is the quality of health care? and What are the deficiencies, and whose responsibility are they?—remain inadequately answered.

In certain communities in developing countries, medical problems are divided into treatment of disease and others. The former mainly denotes surgical and major physical illness, and the latter, social and behavioral problems for which traditional healers are often consulted. Despite the general growth of modern medicine, there are certain problems, such as developmental and behavioral problems of children, where the professional responsibility is not clearly defined. The policy for dealing with mental retardation, for instance, varies greatly from country to country. In some countries it is treated as a purely medical condition; in other more attention is given to the educational and social aspects of this problem. In brief, there are certain health problems where the responsibility is ill-defined and health care suffers from lack of a proper framework and a defective organizational set-up.

The sharp contrast between developed and developing countries with regard to health professionals is rather significant in the delivery of health care. It has to be realized that in many countries there are very few pediatricians, and the category of the pediatric nurse practitioner (as described by Haggerty) is non existent in the majority of countries. Therefore if the health professionals are accepting the responsibility for community health and community care, it is of central importance that alternative and innovative approaches be developed in order to meet the preventive, curative, and restorative needs of children.

One of the approaches is the delegation of responsibility of health care to auxiliary and community workers. In this respect it may be worthwhile to note that, in a country like the Sudan, with 16 million population, where there is a mere handful of pediatricians, it was only possible to enable maternity and child health care to penetrate into remote areas by training village midwives.

Now with the burgeoning movement in primary health care, the role of the health professional must be more clearly defined. The differences between countries have also to be noted. For while, in some countries, primary health care is the responsibility of the medical professionals, in others it is that of auxiliary health personnel or the nonmedical community worker.

Obviously, in the light of changes in the health field, educational institutions have to be more responsive to these new developments, and training programs have to be sensitive to community needs.

More and more countries are becoming aware of the importance of coordination and the need for sharing responsibility in the planning and programming of medical education and the development of health services. A lot of effort is still needed to ensure that an effective and practical model of functional unity between the supplier of health workers (training institutions), the provider of health care (health system), and the user (community) can be developed.

REFERENCES

1. V. DJUKANOVIC and E. P. MACH, *Alternative Approaches to Meeting Basic Health Needs in Developing Countries,* WHO, Geneva, 1975.
2. *World Health Statistics Report,* Vol. 29, No. 10, 1976, WHO, Geneva.
3. T. A. BAASHER and H. H. IBRAHIM, Childhood psychiatric disorders in the Sudan, *Afr. J. Psychiat.* **1** 67–78 (1976).

M. G. WAGNER
WHO, Copenhagen, Denmark

A HUNDRED YEARS AGO

Medical care began to be "organized" for the first time in history about 100 years ago. This "organization" resulted in several important consequences: (1) the breakdown of the informal network of local health providers (what we are now calling primary health care); (2) increasing emphasis on science and decreasing emphasis on experience and common sense; (3) perhaps most importantly, a shift of responsibility for one's health from the individual (and in the case of children, the family) to the health care establishment.

TEN YEARS AGO

Approximately 10 years ago there was a growing realization that something was wrong with health care. Contributing to this growing realization were several factors:

(1) the traditional health indices such as infant mortality were no longer improving in consistent ways and seemed less and less correlated with health care. Examples of these inconsistencies included the fact that the United States was ranked seventeenth in the world in infant mortality, and also the fact that in some of the most developed countries there began to be a trend for a higher infant mortality in urban areas than in rural areas (a reversal). (2) It was shown that with regard to a number of "traditional illnesses," such as tuberculosis, the improvement in morbidity and mortality over time was not a function of improved health care or of improved medical technology. (3) A growing prevalence of health problems such as chronic diseases and psychosocial problems which are not very amenable to traditional health care systems. Also an increasing awareness of the tendency to medicalize what are basically social problems. (4) Recognition that the emphasis on high technology in health care had certain undesirable results including: a weak primary health care system and a strong secondary and tertiary health system; increasing iatrogenesis; increasing cost of health care with no evident improvement in level of health. (5) Gradual realization that health is not an end but a means. In evaluating health care it became apparent that what was lacking was "output indicators" or new "health indices." The search for these indices has led inevitably to the realization that the only valid, final index is patient satisfaction or happiness and that health care (and socioeconomic development in general) is only one means to this end.

TODAY

This growing realization that something is wrong with health care has led to the necessity of reevaluating our health care systems. So today we find rapidly increasing interest in health care research and a willingness to consider alternatives and innovations in health care. This will, in turn, produce the trend in health care in the future.

FUTURE

The trends in child health care in the future, as I see them, are natural outgrowths of the various realizations just reviewed.

1. An increasing emphasis on primary health care for children. We lost primary health care and now we are trying to find it. Many questions remain with regard to primary health care for children: Who should provide this care (pediatricians, family physicians, nurse practitioners, others?) but it appears that there is a trend toward increasing flexibility in providing this primary health care; What should this primary health care include? (for example, it appears that there is a trend for increasing integration of preventive and curative primary health care). Part and parcel of this increasing emphasis on primary health care is an increasing questioning of the appropriateness of secondary and tertiary health care. Thus, for example, there is a question "What is the hospital for?" Is the hospital the best place to be born, to be sick, to die? I think there will be an increasing trend for less hospitalization and more outpatient and home care in the future.

2. Increasing integration of health, social, and educational services. We cut children up into pieces and now we are trying to put them together again. This increasing

integration will take place mainly at the primary care level but to some extent at the secondary and tertiary level. The logical result of such attempts at integration are already seen in a few countries, where there is a trend to a local neighborhood, one-door office where families can seek health, social, and educational advice and services.

3. Increasing emphasis on nontraditional approaches. We have already seen many examples of this nontraditional approach, including the "free" health clinics for adolescents and the youth advisory services. The predominant difference between traditional services and nontraditional services is that the former are organized by and for the providers while the latter are organized by the consumer (or with the active cooperation of them) and for the consumers. Thus, we do not tell them what they need, they tell us what they need and in what way it should be provided for them.

4. An increasing role of the individual and family in their own health care. We took the responsibility for their health away from them and now we will give it back. This trend has many profound ramifications: there will be changes in the doctor–patient relationship from professional dominance to a dialogue. We do not tell them what to do any longer, but we give them all of the facts and they decide. And if we judge their decision is poor (noncompliance) we do not blame the victim but ask what we, the providers, are doing wrong. We not only give them facts but also skills. Thus we not only teach the diabetic how to give his own insulin injection but we can teach many other skills especially in chronic diseases, such as taking one's own blood pressure and monitoring one's own medication.

5. An increasing attention to the psychological problems of children and the psychosocial consequences of health care. The newer health problems of children, particularly in industrialized society, are more and more psychosocial in nature—drug abuse, unwanted adolescent pregnancy, etc. There is an urgent need to study these problems and create appropriate services. In going about this, however, we must be careful not to medicalize what is basically a social problem. Perhaps one of the best examples of this tendency to medicalize a problem is the case of child abuse. We must also be careful to evaluate the psychosocial consequences of our own health care. Many of the characteristics of current health care services, perhaps most especially the high technology, can have psychosocial consequences of which we are only beginning to be aware. Perhaps one of the best examples of this is the high technology of neonatology and intensive care units for newborn infants and the resultant problem of infant–mother bonding. This will perhaps gradually lead to more appropriate levels of technology and more consideration of the psychosocial and human elements in health care.

CHILD NUTRITION

THE ECONOMIC DIMENSIONS OF
MALNUTRITION IN YOUNG CHILDREN*

Marcelo Selowsky

Development Economics Department, the World Bank, Washington DC, USA

INTRODUCTION

One billion people, half the population of the developing world, are suffering from calorie deficient diets. Four hundred million of them are children below age 10. What are the economic consequences of this? How can economists help to identify policy options to solve the problem?

The involvement of economists has come through various fronts. First, an increasing disenchantment in the development literature concerning the use of gross national product (GNP) as an indicator of welfare in comparisons across countries and over time.[1] It results from the interest in the distributive dimensions of economic well-being as well as a consensus for the need of a wider definition of welfare. Health, low mortality, and education have become indicators of welfare in their own right in the interpretation of economic performance.

The second front is the search by economists for wider definitions of capital (physical and human) capable of explaining the sources of growth of countries as well as the distribution of income between individuals. To the extent that malnutrition affects the economic productivity of the individual, nutritional status becomes part of that definition of capital.

THE MAGNITUDE OF THE PROBLEM

The Global Picture

Ideally, one would like to define child malnutrition in terms of its consequences and not in terms of the amount of food consumed by the individual. Mortality, health status, and indices of psychological achievements are some indicators of these consequences. In practice, however, it is difficult to define precisely underachievement in some of these categories and to be able to trace them to malnutrition. Although this has been done for particular case studies and communities, the data is not available to provide a global picture of malnutrition on the basis of indices of nutrition-related achievements.

If one has to settle for an index of food or nutrient for the purpose of measuring malnutrition, the best indicator is calorie consumption. Calorie deficits usually signal deficits in the intake of proteins and other nutrients; this is particularly true if one accepts the hypothesis that in these cases, part of the protein is used as energy. There is empirical evidence showing that it is only in very few cases that individuals suffer

*Views expressed herein are those of the author and do not necessarily reflect those of the World Bank.

349

from a protein deficit when their calorie consumption approaches their energy requirement.

The number of people with a calorie deficit in a country can be estimated from household food consumption surveys, of enough detail to provide *per capita* calorie consumption data for the household. In the absence of this data, the alternative is to allocate the known total consumption figure—derived from national aggregates—across income groups in the population. This requires information on the distribution of income and some assumptions on the relationship between increases in calorie consumption and increases in the *per capita* income of households. This was the method used by my colleague, Shlomo Reutlinger, and me in an early attempt to derive an estimate of the distribution of the world calorie deficit.[2]

Table 1 presents these estimates. The first two columns show the number of people with calorie intake below physiological requirements; the last two columns show the cereal equivalent of that caloric deficit (on a yearly basis).

At the world level two factors are striking: first, the large number of people with deficit, 55% of the population of the developing world. They are concentrated in the poorest countries and in the lowest income groups within countries. Second, how small the deficit is, is expressed as a fraction of the world production of cereals. The fact that this deficit is only 2% of the world's cereal production contradicts the widely held view that malnutrition is the result of an imbalance between world population and world food supplies. At the global level, *malnutrition is the result of the unequal distribution of world income and not the result of an insufficient availability of food. It is clearly a poverty problem and not a food problem.*[3]

The argument holding at the global level also applies to particular regions, the Middle East, and Latin America in particular. Approximately 35% of their population have calorie deficit yet this deficit amounts to less than 3% of the total cereal consumption. People consuming more than one-third of their requirements amount

TABLE 1

Afflicted population and size of the calorie deficit, 1975(a)

Region	Population with consumption below calorie requirements		Cereal equivalent of the aggregate calorie deficit(b)	
	Million people	% population	Tons per year (millions)	As a % of total cereal consumption(c)
Latin America	112	36	2·2	2·9
Asia	707	63	18·4	9·4
Middle East	61	33	1·6	2·6
Africa	193	61	5·2	14·7
Total	1073	55	27·4	7·5
As a fraction of the world cereal production				2·0

(a) From Reutlinger and Selowsky,[2] (op. cit.), Projection C.
(b) It is assumed a metric tonne of cereals has 3·5 million calories.
(c) This consumption figure includes cereals used in animal feeding.

to 8·9 and 32·5% of the total population in the case of the Middle East and Latin America, respectively.

To a lesser degree, the distributive dimension is also important for the other regions. Within these regions, malnutrition is concentrated in the poorest 20 or 30% of the population. In the case of Asia, the *per capita* calorie deficit in the poorest quintile is twice the *per capita* deficit in the next two richest quintiles of the population.

The Incidence of Calorie Malnutrition in Young Children

Whatever the method used to estimate calorie consumption, we can derive information only on the mean *per capita* calorie intake of the household. Sample surveys do not provide information on the distribution of food within the family and it is not even clear if this possibility is technically feasible. It is therefore impossible, from the usual food surveys, to derive the extent of calorie deficiency in children as distinct from that in adults.

An alternative is to assume that when the *per capita* calorie intake of the family is below the (weighted) *per capita* requirement for the household, both children and adults experience a calorie deficit. Given this assumption a difference in the global incidence of malnutrition between children and adults (i.e. the fraction of the total number of children that are malnourished relative to the one for adults) can only be the result of "undernourished households" having a larger number of children than the typical household. This does happen to be the case.

The empirical evidence shows that calorie intake is closely related to *per capita* income and that malnutrition characterizes the poorest segments of the population. Since the poorest income groups have a substantially larger family size (and number of children) the share of children that are malnourished becomes larger than the share of adults. It is this distributive dimension of malnutrition—the association between malnutrition and poverty—that gives origin to a larger incidence of malnutrition among children.

By using this simplified method we have derived the incidence of calorie malnutrition in young children in two regions—Asia and Latin America. The results are shown in Table 2. The figures clearly show a higher incidence of malnutrition among children. In Asia, 69·2% of children below age 10 experience calorie deficits; the figure for individuals above age 10 is equal to 60·1%. For Latin America the difference in the incidence is much stronger: 55·4% of children suffer calorie deficit whereas only 27·4% of the rest of the population is undernourished.

The difference in the incidence of malnutrition between children and adults depends on two factors: (a) how strong is the (inverse) relation between the number of young children per household and the *per capita* income of the family; and (b) how small is the size of the malnourished population as a fraction of the total population. The smaller this fraction, i.e. the more important is the distributive dimension of malnutrition, the larger will be the incidence of malnutrition among children relative to that in adults.

The economic justifications for improving children's nutrition can be classified into three types: (a) the ones based on the notion that children's nutrition is a "public good" or an "externality" to the rest of society, i.e., the rest of society derives a

TABLE 2

Number (in millions) of children and adults with calorie deficit
(Figures in parentheses show the percentage with respect to the row total(a))

Age group	Asia, 1975			Latin America, 1975		
	With calorie deficit	Without calorie deficit	Total	With calorie deficit	Without calorie deficit	Total
Children (ages 0–9)	232 (69·2)	103	335	51·6 (55·4)	41·4	93·0
Adults (over age 9)	475 (60·1)	315	790	60·4 (27·4)	159·6	220·0
Total	707 (62·8)	418	1125	112·0 (35·8)	201	313·0

(a) The figures are described by using the estimates of undernourished individuals in each income group (as estimated by Reutlinger and Selowskyz) together with the mean fraction of children per household figure specific to each of those income groups.

consumption benefit from eliminating malnutrition. Under this notion, the existence of malnutrition implies a distorted or nonPareto optimal allocation of present economic resources; (b) the ones based on the "resource savings" effect of better children's nutrition. If particular social objectives to which governments are already committed (infant mortality rates, incidence of infectious diseases, minimum standards of literacy in children, etc.,) are the product of nutrition plus other policy manipulatable causal factors, better nutrition can, at the margin, be a cheaper intervention than these other interventions in achieving those objectives; and (c) the ones based on the notion that better infant nutrition can increase the future productivity of the individual, i.e., the "human capital" argument.

THE NEED FOR SPECIFIC INTERVENTIONS

Perspectives for the Future

Will the normal course of future events eliminate calorie malnutrition in the poorest segments of the population of developing countries? The answer depends on the future income growth of the malnourished groups, their preference toward consuming calorie intensive foods (i.e. the calorie–income elasticity defined as the percentage change in *per capita* calorie consumption resulting from a 1% increase in *per capita* income) and the future changes in the relative price of the main staples, basically cereals.

At constant food prices the increase in *per capita* calorie consumption can be expressed as the product of the *per capita* income growth and the calorie–income elasticity. Annual *per capita* income growth in the lowest income groups in India and Bangladesh (which accounts for two-thirds of the global number of people with calorie deficit) is not expected to exceed 1·5% per year. Growing empirical evidence shows that the calorie–income elasticity is substantially lower than 1·00, even for the poorest income groups. Values around 0·5 are consistent with almost all evidence to date.

On the basis of the above two figures, it will take 30 years before the poorest 20% of the population of these countries—presently experiencing a deficit of 450 calories per day—will reach the required level of calorie consumption. During this period, marginally deficient and nondeficient income groups will also increase their consumption and may reach levels substantially higher than requirements. Thus, it could well be that during part of that period, malnutrition in the poorest groups will coexist with a calorie surplus at a country level.

This probable future situation in Asia will resemble the present situation of Latin America, where the poorest 20% of the population has a *per capita* daily calorie deficit of at least 200 calories, while at the regional level, total calorie consumption exceeds requirements by at least 70%. It is clear that the "market solution"—to wait for the regular income growth in the malnourished groups to close their calorie gap—is not an acceptable solution.

An alternative and widely suggested solution—to rely on accelerated food production—while acceptable, is, unfortunately, not feasible. Given the purchasing power of the poorest groups, accelerated food production over and above the rate at which food demand is expanding will tend to lower food prices. Lower consumer prices can be consistent with constant or increasing cost to food producers only if governments would be willing to finance the difference with general subsidies. In most cases this is not a feasible solution from a fiscal point of view. The solution can only rest on target-oriented food programs, concentrated in the most needy segments of the population. For countries having a calorie surplus at the aggregate level—as in Latin America—the problem could be solved by reshuffling food availabilities from the groups with calorie surplus to those in deficit.

The future situation of young children belonging to low income groups will not be much better. Since malnutrition will be more concentrated (i.e. in the poorest 10% instead of the poorest 20% of the population) and given the relation between family size and income, malnutrition will be much more of a "children problem" than at present.

Why does the future look less bright for the representative child in the poorest income groups than it does for the representative adult? First, the scattered empirical evidence does not show significantly higher calorie–income elasticities for children than for adults. Second, to the extent development in general (and urbanization in particular) will increase women's participation in the labor force, infant nutrition could deteriorate due to further declines in breast feeding. If the additional food for the infant, purchased out of the additional earnings of the female now participating in the labor force, does not compensate for the losses in breast milk consumption, the net effect is a deterioration in the infant's nutritional status.[4] Higher incomes of the household due to the mother's participation in the labor force could be consistent with a deterioration in the level of nutrition of the child.

Other factors associated with urbanization—and urbanization will be a distinctive feature of the future—will have an adverse effect on young children. Other competing expenditures (transportation, clothing, housing) become more important in urban areas, affecting the share of income spent on food. Relative prices of food tend to rise. New commodities such as entertainment and fashion become available to be consumed basically by adults. The result is that the share of income spent on food for children can decline.

The above considerations suggest that in the future the problem will not be solved with the desired speed without specific nutrition intervention programs.

General Programs and Target-oriented Programs

Interventions to increase calorie consumption in malnourished children range from general food subsidies at one extreme (i.e., subsidies on the imports of cereals), to specific programs for poor children at the other (i.e., breakfast in specific schools).

In order to reach children in the poorest group, the first type of program subsidizes all types of consumers—rich and poor, adults and children. The program has what might be called a large "leakage." The second clearly has less leakage, only to the extent that some food is diverted to the adults in the family as a result of the breakfast program. However, target programs can be very expensive administratively; but general food subsidies can be concentrated in foods consumed by low income groups and particularly by children.

The above becomes clearer if we divide the cost of a program, whose objective is to increase children's food consumption by one dollar, into (a) the cost of the intra-family leakage, equivalent to the subsidy on adults' consumption in poor families that is necessary in order to achieve the objective; (b) the income group leakage, the subsidy received by nontarget families; and (c) the administrative costs of the program.

We can call general programs those where (b) becomes an important part of the fiscal cost of the program, i.e., nontarget groups must be subsidized in order to reach target families. Typical programs are general food production subsidies, or subsidies on food imports, ration shops, or schemes for all the population, etc. Target-oriented programs are those where this component of the cost is relatively smaller: food stamps or ration shops with free or subsidized rations for preselected families, take-home and on-site feeding programs for children in specific schools and health centers are some examples.[5]

What is the effectiveness of these programs in increasing children's food consumption? How much of a program's food simply replaces old consumption? How much of the intended food for children is diverted to adults? What are the magnitudes of these replacements and diversions that make these programs better, equal, or worse than an income transfer to the family equivalent to the value of the food?

A well known principle in economic theory is that consumers receiving any transfer in kind will attempt to convert the transfer into income. This reestablishes the control of the consumer on the composition of his expenditure. Any transfer of a food commodity in excess of what the household voluntarily is willing to consume will be sold to households with different food preferences or households not reached by the program. If the resale price is similar to the cost of the food to the government, the household has received an income transfer equivalent to the fiscal cost of the program. In this case, and without exception, food programs will simply have an effect equal to an equivalent income transfer.

The effectiveness of income transfers in increasing the consumption of food by children is proportional to the marginal propensity to spend on children's food. The effect on calories will depend on the calorie content of that additional food. A parameter that captures both elements is the calorie–income elasticity of children's consumption; if that elasticity is 0·5, any food program equivalent to a *per capita* income transfer of 10% will increase the calorie intake of children by 5%.

Several food programs operate like an income transfer even without the need of reselling the concessionary food. Programs that transfer free or subsidized food in magnitudes smaller (or inframarginal amounts) than the amount previously consumed by the family will replace initial levels of consumption and release purchasing power of a value equal to the subsidy. This is also true when several foods are involved in the program and the amount of each food being distributed is smaller than the amount previously being consumed. In these circumstances the program does not generate a substitution among foods, which is the condition for the program to act like an income transfer. We believe these characteristics hold for most of the ration shops and take-home programs presently being implemented in most countries.

Under the same circumstances, a site-feeding program for children (i.e., breakfast and lunches in schools) can have an effect on children's consumption—no larger than an equivalent income transfer. It will be true if the amount of each type of food being consumed on site is smaller than the amount of that food previously consumed by the child at home. In this case, the site food will partly replace the food eaten at home without changing the marginal rates of substitution among foods.

A food stamp program, providing stamps of a smaller value than the initial (preprogram) food consumption level of the family, will also be equivalent to an income transfer; this will be true without the need for reselling the stamps. The income transfer is equal to the concessionary component of the stamps, the difference between the value of the stamps, and the price charged for them. Most of the food stamp programs provide stamps of a smaller value than the initial level of food consumption: the effectiveness of these programs have been equal to equivalent income transfers.

What happens if programs do change the composition of food consumption? How do we then predict the change in calorie consumption? When substitution takes place, the increment in the consumption of a particular food (that is being subsidized or provided by the program) can induce a decline in the consumption of other foods, i.e., foods that are substitutes. If that substitution is strong and the foods being substituted account for an important share of the initial calorie consumption, the net effect on calorie intake could be negative. Information on this subsitution is extremely scanty even at the level of aggregate household consumption. For children it is absent. Thus, we can only speculate about the effectiveness of programs where these substitutions are present. It will become clear that many of the present nutrition interventions fall into this category.

Milk price subsidies or free distribution (take-home programs) of milk in amounts substantially above the previous consumption of the household are typical cases. If resale is not possible, these policies will induce a substitution among food commodities. Assume children were consuming two basic foods—cereals and milk. The effect of those programs will be (a) to increase children's consumption of milk and (b) to increase or decrease children's consumption of cereals, depending if milk and cereals are complements or substitutes, respectively. If milk and cereals are substitutes (the decline in milk's implicit price decreases children's cereal consumption), total calorie consumption could decline if, as it is usually the case, most of the calories are derived from cereals. It can be shown that, in this case, even a small degree of substitution between the two foods could induce a negative effect on caloric intake. Milk subsidies and free distribution of milk programs are popular programs at present. Perhaps they were basically conceived with the objective of increasing the consumption of "high quality" proteins. However, if calories are the major nutritional problem, a reevaluation of milk programs along the lines described earlier becomes of prime importance.

The problem of predicting this substitution becomes even more difficult when a program introduces a food previously not being consumed by children. In this case, the notion of an inframarginal or noninframarginal program loses its meaning: any amount of the food being distributed could affect negatively the consumption of calories.

When a program distributes an inframarginal amount of a food previously being consumed, the released purchasing power is used to expand the consumption of all food commodities, by both adults and children. If the new food being introduced by the program can only be consumed by children (specific baby foods), or is fed directly to children (milk programs in schools when children were not previously consuming milk), the only mechanism by which the rest of the family can also benefit from the transfer is by withdrawing some other food from the child in question. Substitution takes place automatically. The net effect on calorie consumption will again depend on the caloric content of the food being distributed relative to the caloric content of the foods whose consumption is being displaced.

These above considerations do apply to many nutritional interventions being carried out today. Milk programs, to be consumed in schools and health centers, are being implemented in environments where milk was not being previously consumed at home.

To conclude, a final point becomes important: if most of the food programs being implemented today do act like an income transfer, should we not simply—in the absence of having more cost effective programs—replace them by equivalent income transfers? Very possibly direct income transfer programs are cheaper administratively.

We believe this to be a dangerous line of thinking. Politically it is much easier to justify food programs—even if they do not have a food effect better than an income transfer—than direct income transfers. It is difficult to conceive a political scenario in which food programs could be easily replaced by income transfers of equivalent values.

REFERENCES

1. H. CHENERY et al., *Redistribution With Growth*, Oxford University Press.
2. S. REUTLINGER and M. SELOWSKY, *Malnutrition and Poverty: Magnitude and Policy Options*, World Bank Staff Occasional Paper No. 23, Johns Hopkins Press, 1976.
3. For a more extensive discussion of this issue see S. REUTLINGER, Malnutrition: a poverty or a food problem, *World Development*, Vol. 5, 1977.
4. For specific estimates of this effect for Calcutta, see REUTLINGER and SELOWSKY, op. cit., pp. 35–38.
5. For an excellent survey on the present experiences in supplementary feeding in different countries, see S. MAXWELL, *Food Aid and Supplementary Feeding: Impact and Policy Implications*, Institute of Development Studies, University of Sussex, November 1977.

EFFECTS OF EARLY MALNUTRITION
AND STIMULI DEPRIVATION
ON MENTAL DEVELOPMENT

JOAQUIN CRAVIOTO

Instituto Nacional de Ciencias y Technología de la Salud del Niño, Mexico City, Mexico

NUTRITION, good or poor, is an integral aspect of the total context of our social and cultural reality. At the community level, malnutrition is a manmade disorder, characteristic of the lower economic segments of society; particularly of the preindustrial societies, where the social system (consciously or unconsciously) creates malnourished individuals generation after generation through a series of social mechanisms, among which limited access to goods and services, limited social mobility, and restricted experiential opportunities at crucial points in life play a major role.

From the health point of view, nutritional problems, although affecting large masses of the population, are particularly prevalent in the so-called "vulnerable groups" of small infants and children, and pregnant and lactating mothers; due principally to the sociocultural characteristics of these groups plus their increased physiological requirements for nutrients.

Vega-Franco[1] (with calculations based on the probability of being alive from year to year, the probability of being employed, and the actual wages earned) has estimated that the economic loss suffered by Mexico due to deaths in preschool children caused by malnutrition is of the order of 4820 million Mexican pesos. The implications of this economic loss in a developing country are obvious.

Kardonsky et al.[2] found evidence of reduced mental functioning in Chilean preschool children hospitalized for severe malnutrition in the first year of life. When these infants were reexamined at 3–4 years of age their mean IQ was 73. These authors have reported a marked increase in performance level for the period 5–6 years. Taking weight deficit as a criterion of the time in life at which malnutrition was apparent, those children whose malnutrition occurred earlier, and whose recovery was more rapid, tended to present less marked IQ deficits. Reduced exploratory activity was a constant feature of the behavior in these malnourished infants. This finding is in agreement with all the published descriptions of behavior carried out in malnourished children and probably constitutes the single most common behavioral feature. The condition becomes so marked in the severely malnourished child that renewal of interest in his surroundings is considered by clinicians as one of the most reliable signs of improvement. "The child who smiles is well on the way to recovery."

It would, of course, be ingenuous to view the observed apathy as the simple and direct result of malnutrition. If one uses Wilson's[3] attempt to distinguish four categories of apathy (primarily physiological, primarily psychological, apathy at the community level, and apathy as a characteristic of a regional culture), the apathy of the protein–calorie deficient child can most profitably be viewed as a mixed type.

Nutritional deprivation *per se* can and does contribute to apathy and unresponsiveness, as in the case of experimental animals fed on low protein, high carbohydrate diets. However, when noted clinically, such behavior is never separable from possible sequelae to emotional deprivation and loss which may be produced by the separation which accompanies hospitalization. It has been repeatedly stated that, in most communities where malnutrition is highly prevalent, the mother–child relationship prior to weaning is very close, and frequently includes the mother taking the nursling with her wherever she goes. This fact, when considered together with the observations made by Geber and Dean[4] that recovery is more rapid among infants whose mothers show the greatest interest and solicitude, has been interpreted as suggesting that separation from the mother may make an important contribution to the behavioral disturbance. In any event, the behavior of the malnourished infant strikingly resembles that described by Bowlby[5] in the 15–20 month old healthy child who has been abruptly separated from his mother by hospitalization.

Recently, we have made a comparison of the levels of competence in two intersensory integration tasks, kinesthetic–visual and auditory–visual, analyzing data obtained longitudinally in survivors of early severe malnutrition and control children drawn from the same birth cohort being followed up from birth onwards.

One control group was made up of children matched case by case with the survivors of malnutrition, for sex, gestational age, season of birth, body size at birth, and mental performance at one month of age. Socioeconomic conditions included *per capita* income; percentage of total expenditure on food; sanitary facilities present in the home; family structure and size; birth order; literacy, body weight, and height of both parents. All these were strictly similar for control children and survivors.

Since the scores in home stimulation were significantly lower in the survivors of severe malnutrition right from the beginning of their lives, a second control group was made up with children from the same birth cohort having similar socioeconomic characteristics, and matched with the survivors, case by case, for total scores on the inventory of home stimulation.

The data clearly showed that survivors of early severe malnutrition exhibit a marked developmental lag in kinesthetic–visual competence. This lag, in a mechanism basic for learning to write, is greater than the lag which could be expected as an effect of the low level of stimulation present in the homes of the malnourished children before and after the episode of severe malnutrition.

The data of previous studies on kinesthetic–visual intersensory integration are thus in agreement with our data from the longitudinal study in the sense that the antecedent of severe malnutrition, independently of the characteristics of the stimulation available at home, is *per se* strongly associated with the levels of competence in the kinesthetic–visual task. Since the quality and quantity of the stimulation available at home also showed a significant correlation with the intersensory task, the developmental lag observed in survivors of malnutrition appears to be the result of the effects of earlier malnutrition in association with certain microenvironmental factors related to child care.

The findings in relation to auditory–visual integration give a totally different picture. When the difference in home stimulation between survivors of severe malnutrition and control children was cancelled out, the performance of the survivors was at the same level as was observed in the control children with low scores in stimulation. The disappearance of the developmental lag in the survivors points to a strong association between stimulation available in the home and competence in auditory–visual integration, and to a lack of association between a previous history of severe malnutrition and auditory–visual competence.

Winick et al.[6] have shown that a remarkable amount of recovery can occur in the mental performance and physical growth of previously malnourished children if a stimulated environment is introduced before 3 years of age. To attempt an answer to the question of how early should stimulation be increased in order to obtain better development in survivors of malnutrition, Winick undertook a second study with children adopted after age 3 but before age 5 years. The results demonstrated that the malnourished group, in regard to both IQ and achievement, performed below the expected norms. A comparison of the data in the two studies demonstrates a reduced IQ and school achievement of roughly equal magnitude in all three groups of children adopted after age 3. Again, however, the IQ and achievements, even in the malnourished group, exceed what we would expect if they were returned to their original environment. Thus, environmental enrichment at any time up to age 5 would seem to improve the learning ability of previously malnourished children. If the environment is "enriched" by adoption before age 3, almost complete recovery can occur.

In the presence of a syndrome such as protein–energy malnutrition, whose ultimate link in the chain of events leading to tissue deficiency of nutrients, is the insufficient intake of adequate foods, it becomes essential to consider the meaning of food and feeding along at least three dimensions.

The first one is the physiological dimension, which has as a unit of measurement the nutrient or the joule and whose function it is to provide chemical substances to the organism for purposes of growth, maintenance, and metabolic regulation.

The second dimension of food may be considered as psychophysical. Its unit of measurement would be the foodstuff which, though its organoleptic characteristics, would provide the organism with a variety of stimuli (texture, color, aroma, taste, temperature, etc.). In this context, a foodstuff presented at the table as two different kitchen preparations having the same nutrient and energy content would, in fact, behave as if two different foods were offered to the individual.

Finally, the third food dimension may be considered as psychosocial in nature. Its unit of measurement would be the mealtime. The functions of food along this line are, on the one hand, to aid in symbol formation through the value family and society attach to food, such as a form of reward or punishment, as an experience attached to a gratifying person, or as an identifying characteristic of an ethnic or subcultural group. On the other hand, the meal time provides opportunities to demonstrate, clarify, and practice role and status at the family and at the community level. Who is waited on? Who sits at the place of honor at the table? Who receives the best part of a dish? Who moderates conversation at the table? These are some examples of the way in which this food dimension is expressed.

It seems easy to visualize that food deprivation in young children represents not only a shortage of nutrients necessary for the increase in mass, but also a deprivation of sensory stimuli and of social experiences.

In spite of the multiple roles of food it is surprising that little attention is given to these aspects in the rehabilitation of malnourished children. Moreover, most of the data suggesting long term mental developmental lags in individuals who suffered early malnutrition, have been obtained in studies in which remediation was directed almost exclusively to the nutritional and health needs of the children, and not to the social environment which contributed to the development of the malnutrition and lower levels of intellectual functioning in the first place.

In attempting to define a causal linkage between insufficient dietary intake and subnormal mental functioning, at least two possibilities should be considered. The first one would postulate that nutrient deficiency affects the intellect by directly modifying the growth and biochemical maturation of the brain.

In favor of this explanation are the reports from investigators in Chile, Mexico, and Uganda, who have found a reduction in brain size and cell number in children who died from severe malnutrition.[7]

The second hypothesis considers that malnutrition in children does not need to produce structural lesions of the central nervous sytem to affect intellectual competence, behavior and learning. Three possible indirect mechanisms are postulated:

(1) *Loss of learning time.* Since the child was less responsive to his environment when malnourished, at the very least he had less time in which to learn, and had lost a certain number of months of experience. On the simplest basis, therefore, he would be expected to show some developmental lags.

(2) *Interference with learning during critical periods of development.* Learning is by no means simply a cumulative process. A considerable body of evidence exists which indicates that interference with the learning process at specific times during its course may result in disturbances in function that are both profound and of long term significance. Such disturbances are not merely a function of the length of time the organism is deprived of the opportunities for learning. Rather, what appears to be important is the correlation of the experiential opportunity with a given stage of development, the so-called critical periods of learning. It is possible that exposure to malnutrition at particular ages may in fact interfere with development at critical points in the child's growth course and so provide either abnormalities in the sequential emergence of competence, or an undesirable redirection of the developmental course.

(3) *Motivation and personality changes.* It should be recognized that the mother's response to the infant is to a considerable degree a function of the child's own characteristics of reactivity. One of the first effects of malnutrition is a reduction in the child's responsiveness to stimulation and the emergence of various degrees of apathy. Apathetic behavior in its turn can function to reduce the value of the child as a stimulus and to diminish the adult's responsiveness to him.

Thus, apathy can provoke apathy and so contribute to a cumulative pattern of reduced adult–child interaction. If this occurs, it can have consequences for stimulation, for learning, for maturation, and for interpersonal relations; the end result being significant backwardness in performance on later, more complex, learning tasks. It has been shown that experimental animals subjected to stimuli deprivation have a significant reduction in number and size of cells in the cerebral cortex.[8]

EARLY SEVERE MALNUTRITION AND RISK OF SCHOOL FAILURE

Apart from whether or not insufficient nutrient intake *per se* can cause mental subnormality, it is evident that children who have survived the severe forms of malnutrition show alterations in intellectual performance and learning ability which clearly place them at a higher risk of failure to profit from school exposure.

Given the high correlations between kinesthetic–visual integration and learning to write, and between auditory–visual integration and learning to read, it is not difficult to visualize the handicap that children retarded in their neurointegrative organization will have in the acquisition of these basic academic skills. The child who lags in the performance of basic mechanisms related to fundamental skills such as reading and writing will be illprepared for the learning tasks required of him when he enters school. If he is behind when he enters, he may never have an opportunity to match the performance of his mates. If the initial impression he gives is of a child who cannot fully benefit from the learning experiences provided by the school, the behavior of his teachers toward him will reflect their expectations of his lower performance, thus reinforcing the probability of inadequate performance.

Recently, Richardson *et al.* have examined the scholastic achievement of school age children who suffered severe malnutrition in early life.[9] Efficiency in reading, writing, and arithmetic abilities, as well as the teacher's evaluation of school performance, was lower in survivors of malnutrition and in their siblings when compared to that of peers attending the same school grade. Teachers judged the survivors of malnutrition as lower in school performance level with poor ability in the school tasks and giving a higher frequency of school problems. The school grade attained by the survivors of malnutrition was below the grade attained by both siblings and school mates of the same chronological age.

It is apparent from all that has been said that children who survived a severe episode of chronic malnutrition are at a higher risk of failure to profit from the cumulative knowledge available to their socioeconomic group. Survival from severe malnutrition may be the event that starts a developmental path characterized by psychological defective functioning, school failure, and subsequent subnormal adaptive functioning.

At familial and societal levels, the ultimate result of this chain of events is what, in an ecological sense, could be called a "spiral" effect. A low level of adaptive functioning, lack of modern knowledge, social custom, infection, or environmental insufficiency of foodstuffs can produce malnutrition, which gives rise to a large pool of survivors who come to function in suboptimal ways. Such survivors themselves risk being the victims of their poor socioeconomic environment and less effective than otherwise would be the case. In turn they will choose mates with similar characteristics and may rear children under conditions and in a fashion fatally programmed to produce a new generation of malnourished individuals.

The review of the available evidence leaves no doubts about the strong association between the antecedent of malnutrition in infancy and subsequent lower performance during the school years. Nonetheless, the fact that malnutrition does not occur in a vacuum and that many of the circumstances which lead to or accompany malnutrition are in themselves capable of influencing mental development and learning make it imperative not only to define malnutrition in terms of the degree of impairment of biological functioning (physical growth, cognitive development, communication skills, school performance, resistance to disease, work performance, etc.) associated with different degrees of nutritional deficit at different ages, but also to quantitate the synergistic and/or antagonistic effect of the nonnutritional factors almost always present in malnourished populations such as stimuli deprivation, increased morbidity, poor mother–child interaction, etc, at different periods of the child's age and at different degrees of deficiency.

Since early development is characterized by the changing nature and organization of mental abilities, and the notion of a unitary intelligence factor may not be meaningful until age 5,[10] it could be speculated that among the specific mental abilities some might be influenced by certain specific environmental or host factors, while other abilities would be influenced by other specific factors. This speculation seems to be in accordance with findings that suggest that early performance in tests of specific abilities may be better predictors of IQ at latter ages than tests that are aggregates of various specific abilities. Along this same line would be the reports showing better prediction of mental performance in early infancy by socioeconomic indicators than by mental scales[11] and the studies of Pedersen and Wender[12] who found significant associations between early social behavior and certain forms of cognitive and perceptual abilities; e.g., children who at 2½ years of age were categorized as more contact oriented and showed more attention-seeking behavior, had significantly higher verbal intellectual functioning four years later.

The importance of sorting out specific mental abilities as a function of the environmental (macro and micro) factors that would exert a more powerful influence on them, is obvious from both the practical and the theoretical viewpoints. It is of primary importance to recognize with John Dobbing[13] that perhaps no single disadvantage plays a major part in lowering human achievement, and that the human may have a great capacity to compensate for one disadvantage by advantage in other direction.

If intelligence is operationally defined as the process through which individuals acquire the tools of the culture to which they would like to belong, in order to know and to manipulate the environment for their humanistic advantage, one primary task of pediatrics is undoubtedly the scientific study of child development, behavior, and learning, across the gradient of disadvantage, with emphasis on the quantitative assessment of the effects of environment (malnutrition among them) on biological functioning of the individual.

REFERENCES

1. L. VEGA-FRANCO, Ecología de la Desnutrición y su Repercusión Socioeconómica en México in *Nutrición y Pediatría* (A. Cuellar, ed.), Soc. Méx. de Pediat. México, DF, 1972.
2. V. KARDONSKY, M. ALVARADO, O. UNDURRAGA, A. MANTEROLA, and T. SEGURE, Desarrollo Intelectual y Físico en el Niño Desnutrido, unpublished manuscript, Santiago, University of Chile, Department of Psychology, 1971.
3. A. T. M. WILSON, Fostering nutritional change: some points from social research, *Proceedings of the Sixth International Congress of Nutrition* (Mills and Passmore, eds.), Livingstone, Edinburgh, 1964.
4. M. GEBER and R. F. A. DEAN, The psychological changes C accompanying kwashiorkor, *Curier* 6 3 (1956).
5. J. BOWLBY, Separation anxiety, *Int. J. psychoanaly.* 41 89 (1960).
6. M. WINICK, Malnutrition and brain development, *J. Pediat.* 74 667 (1969).
7. R. E. BROWN, Decreased brain weight in malnutrition and its implications, *East Afr. Med. J.* 42 584 (1965). K. AMBROSIUS, E. Comportamiento del Peso de Algunos Organos en Niños con Desnutrición de Tercer Grado, *Boletín Médico Hospital Infantil de México* 18 47 (1961).
8. M. R. ROSENWEIG, D. KRECH, E. L. BENNET, and J. F. ZOLLMAN, Variations in environmental complexity and brain measures, *J. Comp. Physiol. Psychol.* 55 1092 (1962).

9. S. A. RICHARDSON, H. G. BIRCH and M. E. HERTZIG, School performance of children who were severely malnourished in infancy, *Am. J. Mental Def.* **77** 623 (1973).
10. N. BAYLEY, Value and limitation of infant testing, *Children* **5,** 129 (1958). R. B. McCALL, P. S. HOGARTY, and N. HULBURT, Transitions in infant sensory motor development and the prediction of childhood IQ, *Am. Psychol.* **27** 728 (1972).
11. S. H. BROMAN, P. L. NICHOLS, and W. A. KENNEDY, *Preschool IQ: Prenatal and Early Developmental Correlates,* Wiley, New York, 1975.
12. F. A. PEDERSEN and P. H. WENDER, Early social correlates of cognitive functioning in six-year old boys, *Child Developm.* **39** 185 (1968).
13. J. DOBBING, Vulnerable periods in brain growth and somatic growth, in *The Biology of Human Fetal Growth* (D. F. Roberts and A. M. Thomson, eds.), Taylor & Francis, London, 1976, p. 137.

A GLOBAL VIEW OF NUTRITION IN PREGNANCY

FRANK FALKNER

Fels Research Institute, Wright State University, Yellow Springs, OH, USA

GROWTH starts at conception. A newborn full term infant is 40 weeks old, hence the critical importance of materno-fetal nutrition.

There are certain critical periods for growth in the human; for the all-important brain, probably the last trimester of fetal growth until 18 months. If growth and development has been diminished below normal levels during such critical periods, catch-up growth will not occur and the growth failure will be irreversible.

Genetic factors have nearly always been considered to be the major influence upon fetal growth, and hence birth size, due to the maternal–placental–fetal nutrition system functioning so that the fetus is much favored and protected, even if at maternal expense.

One brief example will present the inaccuracy of such a simplistic view and emphasize the number of important variables involved.

Twin growth may be studied to determine the relative importance of genetic and environmental influence on growth and development including that of the fetus. Since environment in the shape of maternal–placental–fetal nutrition presumably has an influence upon fetal and early postnatal growth, many substances and agents may be transferred from one twin's placental part to the other's in the case of monozygous (genetically identical) twins with monochorionic placentas. It has been suggested that the placental tissue mass supplying each twin, denoting a capacity to supply nutrients, could be regarded subsequently as a monument for this factor. We have shown that the wet and dry weights of placentas, or placental parts, were significantly correlated with the corresponding twins' birthweights, and that this was so for all twins and placentation.

At this stage it is profitable to consider the growth and development of one twin pair, exemplifying the nutritional and multifactorial nature of prenatal influences upon growth.

The monozygous male twins whose progress is shown in Fig. 1 were born near term.

Routine study of the placenta revealed that there was a marked difference in mass between the placenta part supplying one twin and that part supplying the other. The first born twin (A) weighed 1460 g at birth and the second born (B) 2806 g. The corresponding placenta part supplying twin A weighed 258·5 g (wet), 37·40 g (dry) and measured 20 × 7·5 × 2·0 cm; twin B's placenta part weighed 551·0 g (wet), 85·90 g (dry), and measured 30 × 15·5 × 2 cm. The above measures are highly related to the birthweights of the twins.

Both were full term infants of nearly 40 weeks gestation, yet one is a small-for-date infant—"premature" (PTI) by an old definition. Since both are genetically identical it is interesting to follow their postnatal growth pattern.

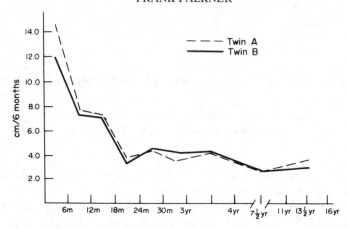

Fig. 1. Six-monthly increments in length (in centimeters).

Anthropometrically, the within-pair weight difference was reduced in the first 9 months and was lowest of all at 12 months. Although the within-pair subcutaneous tissue measurement difference remained more or less constant, at one year twin A was slightly above twin B for the only time. After one year the within-pair difference relative to total body size remained about the same: at 11 years there was a 5·1 kg difference, and at 16 years, 8·0 kg.

Length and stature growth patterns are illuminating. In the first 9 months twin A's rate of growth exhibited marked catch-up, and he grew significantly faster in length than twin B, as if to try and make up the birth length deficit of 7·0 cm.

Figure 1 shows this, and also illustrates the fact that since that time the twins continued to grow in length at approximately the same rate—at least until 16 years of age. The smaller twin did not experience sufficient catch-up growth to reach his brother's height curve. With only two measurements, at ages 11 and 16, since 4 years of age, the adolescent growth spurt and its onset is of course obscured. There are, however, acceptable observations that twin A is somewhat advanced over twin B in puberty status, and it is interesting that twin A's velocity curve for height rose above twin B's, albeit by a small amount in the 11 year to 16 year period. Thus, whatever their actual individual ages for the onset of puberty and their peak height velocities, their difference in size remains notable at 16 years.

There is no essential difference in their IQ scores, and their overall achievement in school has been the same for both while in separate classes.

Head circumference measurements exhibit the pattern of growth expected from an infant of low birthweight (ILB)—namely, very rapid growth compared to a full term infant with normal size limits reached in the early months. Twin A was 4·0 cm smaller in this measure than twin B at birth, yet by 9 months he became (even if slightly) larger. From then on he has maintained a head circumference very similar to that of his twin. Other anthropometric measures follow, in general, the overall body size indications already presented.

By 2½ years the twins should have been virtually free of perinatal influences and onto their genetic growth curves. Is there (at 16 years when their adolescent growth spurt is approaching its end) now an irreversible difference in their length and size due to the factors already described? Presumably twin A is following the growth pattern of a SFDI, and the illustration of this pair is contributory because we can hold the genetic growth factor constant between the two.

Cruise[1] showed that both PTI and SFDI grew much faster than FTI in the first 9 months, and that given good neonatal care, PTI continued catch-up growth and had reached the size of FTI by three years of age. SFDI, however, did not continue catch-up and had not achieved FTI size by three years. Since intrauterine growth retardation, perhaps due to prenatal fetal malnutrition, is thought to be associated with SFDI, the above example would tend to support this view. However, recently Brandt[2] has demonstrated that two subdivisions of SFDI can exist—those who do catch up and those who do not. The prenatal influences and their evaluation may assume great importance relative to the outcome of growth and development for SFDI.

In fact it seems to be a comparatively uncommon situation for MZ twins to have grossly differing birthweights. Babson and Phillips[3] found in such situations that, as in the case of the twin pair just described, the much smaller twin at birth does not exhibit sufficient catch-up to achieve the size of his larger twin. Buckler and Robinson[4], however, followed a pair of MZ–MC twins, the smaller twin having a birthweight 45% less than that of her larger twin. Rapid catch-up of the smaller twin occurred and continued, and by 10 years both twins were similar in size and mental ability. It is interesting to note that the MC placenta part supplying the smaller twin was 87% of the weight of the larger twin's part. The corresponding percentage of the smaller twin's placental part in the twins described earlier in this text was 46%—the smaller twin's birth weight being 52% of the larger twin. This might indicate that placental function, perhaps indicated by placental mass, could be related to differing growth outcome for MZ twins; it is also possible that there is a "critical level" of size for a placenta or placenta part below which growth deficit occurs which may be irreversible. Buckler and Robinson's twin pair also supports the view mentioned earlier that SFDI may be divisible into two subgroups. One of this pair clearly exhibited sufficient and prolonged catch-up.

The reason time has been spent upon presenting the growth and development of these twins is that one can hold the genetic factor similar for markedly different growth in two individuals and provide a model for studying intrauterine growth retardation in single fetuses, concentrating upon the maternal–placental–fetal nutritional system of malnourished mothers. The whole basis of any discussion on maternal–fetal nutrition is outcome. Does an individual fetus die, survive intact, or survive damaged? Does the subsequent newly born infant become a healthy adult?

A very great number of variables affect the outcome issue, and nearly all these interact with each other. Maternal–fetal nutrition is one of the variables of great importance.

Thanks to colleagues in WHO, I am able to present the following rather shaking appropriate vital statistics to you. In 1976 it was estimated that there were 21 million infants born in the world of low birthweight (under 2500 g). Of these, 20 million were born in the developing countries. Not only is that startling but, whereas in the developed world, one-third of all infants of low birthweight are small for dates (and two-thirds prematurely born), the percentage of small-for-dates in the developing world rises to 75%. If maternal malnutrition is a major factor in intrauterine growth retardation, the lesson is clear that a major difference lies between the developing and developed world—the nutritional status of the pregnant woman.

In a rich country this is reversible, and I am grateful to Dr. Jeffry Pomerance and his team at the University of California at Los Angeles for the following data on the economics involved.

In a 2½ year period at one hospital in California, 75 infants were born weighing 1000 g or less. Thirty (40%) survived and 70% of these were judged to be "normal," neurologically and developmentally, when between 1 and 3 years of age.

The adjusted mean individual cost, excluding physicians' fees, for the 30 survivors was $450 a day, with a mean total cost of $40,287. For those 70% of the survivors who were later judged to be "normal," the total cost was a staggering $88,058. The cost for the 47 infants who died was $825 a day, an average total of $14,236 for each.

One cannot in any sensible way relate these costs to the emotional benefits and life projection of these tiny infants, but the figures bring home the staggering costs involved when a society is presented with a newly born infant weighing 1000 g or less. The society must then judge whether such costs are justifiable—if, indeed, economically possible.

Surely it would be far more profitable and beneficial for the child of tomorrow if we were to attack vigorously the problems of maternal malnutrition, so as to minimize the occurrence of infants of less than 1000 g.

REFERENCES

1. M. O. CRUISE, A longitudinal study of the growth of low birth weight infants, *Pediatrics* **51** 620-628 (1973).
2. I. BRANDT, Growth dynamics of low birth weight infants with emphasis on the perinatal period, in *Human Growth*, Vol. II (F. Falkner and J. M. Tanner, eds.), Plenum, New York, 1978.
3. S. G. BABSON and D. S. PHILLIPS, Growth and development of twins dissimilar in size at birth, *New England J. Med.* **289** 937 (1973).
4. J. M. H. BUCKLER and A. ROBINSON, Matched development of a pair of monozygous twins of grossly different size at birth, *Arch. Dis. Childh.* **49** 472-476 (1974).

DISCUSSION

Artemis P. Simopoulos

National Institute of Health, Bethesda, MD, USA

Data on animals and humans indicate that the consequences of malnutrition in early infancy are more severe in babies born at low weight than in those of normal weight. There is also evidence that infants malnourished *in utero*, even if adequately nourished thereafter, still show certain stigmata of their intrauterine experience when they reach adulthood. In animals, for example, a derangement of nitrogen metabolism in adult life has been shown to follow fetal malnutrition. Studies in Formosa suggest that children in poor families who were undernourished in early life excrete more nitrogen than children from more affluent backgrounds.

There is evidence suggesting that behavioral abnormalities may be more common in older children and adults who suffered from malnutrition *in utero* than in those whose mothers were adequately nourished.

Furthermore, there is epidemiologic evidence implicating the nutritional status of the mother in fetal growth. In affluent societies there is no correspondence between maternal size and birth weight, but in developing countries (where maternal height tends to reflect previous nutrition) there is a direct correlation between maternal height and infant weight at birth. The smaller the mother the smaller her infant. Several studies have indicated that this direct correlation has a nutritional rather than a genetic basis, thus nutrition appears to affect more than one generation.

The title of Dr. Selowsky's paper is The Economics of Child Nutrition, but he covered only the concept of undernutrition. To me malnutrition is both under-nutrition and overnutrition, and I would like to make a few comments on that.

Between 30 and 40% of the people of the United States are considered overweight and obese. Obesity is associated with diabetes, hypertension, and cardiovascular diseases. Cardiovascular disease is the major cause of death in the United States. Epidemiologic studies indicate that one-third of all infants who were above the tenth percentile for weight during the first six months of life were obese at ages 7–8. Additional studies also indicate that obese children become obese adults. We must think of nutrition as a pediatric antecedent to adult disease. The child in the world of tomorrow therefore should neither be undernourished nor overnourished.

Medical science does not particularly lend itself to accurate prediction, and nutrition is only one of the factors determining health status. However, nutritional considerations should enter into all development programs, so that the impact of development and economic programs on the nutritional status of the population will be precisely defined and countries (or governments) should be actively encouraged to develop nutrition policies. Nutrition policies should precede food policies.

The "bottom line" goals of nutrition policy, of course, relate to the health status of the population. Nutrition research, nutrition education, regulation of food safety, nutrition manpower training, delivery of nutrition services, and monitoring and surveillance of nutritional adequacy are all important only in so far as they:

(1) reduce the incidence of nutrition-related diseases and conditions;
(2) maintain the health of the general population;
(3) result in a better-informed public.

M. M. RAJENDRAN
Ministry of Social Welfare, New Delhi, India

The number of children below 6 in India is more than 125 million, and the infant mortality rate is as high as 12.2 per 1000. Deaths among children under 5 account for 40% of all deaths compared with less than 7% in most developed countries. More than 50% of the people live below the poverty line and, even after spending 80% of their income on food, they do not get a balanced diet. Children, being the most vulnerable, are the worst sufferers of poverty and malnutrition, and it has been identified that malnutrition is the single most important factor in child morbidity and mortality. A survey by the National Nutrition Monitoring Bureau of India has shown that the bodyweight of three quarters of our preschool children is less than normal, and that 40% require nutrition intervention. Because of the acute poverty, the malnutrition is of the calorie–protein type. It is undeniable that combating malnutrition is a high priority task in developing countries such as India.

What are the factors affecting the nutritional status of the child? Apart from general health, the following are important:

(1) Overall economic development, coupled with a proper income distribution policy, must secure that the benefits of development reach all, including the poorest.
(2) Agricultural development must be oriented so that the benefits of the "green revolution" reach the small and marginal farmers instead of stopping at the well to do ones, as at present.
(3) A properly balanced agricultural production program must maintain local and regional balances between food and cash crops.
(4) Safe drinking water must be available in adequate quantity.
(5) Functional literacy of women must be promoted, particularly among the young mothers.
(6) Vocational training for women must be encouraged to impart and to upgrade skills, so that they are equipped to supplement their income, which is generally used to buy the food for the family.

In dealing with the problems of malnutrition and child health the following policy considerations should also be borne in mind:

(1) A commitment by the government at the highest level to the care of children and their proper development can be very helpful. In India there is a national policy for children.
(2) It is necessary to sensitize decision makers to the special needs of children so that adequate resources—financial and physical—are made available.

(3) As resource constraints will exist for a long time in developing countries, it is necessary to identify priority areas for investment. In introducing child care projects, priority should be given to the most backward and neglected areas when it is not possible to cover the whole country.

(4) The coordination of public services in such backward areas can have a synergetic effect, and the demonstrable result of a few experimental programs can persuade other people to go in for more of them.

(5) As malnutrition is mainly due to poverty, supplementary nutrition is necessary as an intervening strategy. But this should be coupled with the necessary health support and with the education of women in health and nutrition.

As a result of experience gathered in India in nutrition intervention strategies, a model has been evolved for the simultaneous delivery of a package of basic early childhood services. The Integrated Child Development Services (ICDS) program includes supplementary nutrition, immunization, health check-ups, referral services, safe drinking water supply, and preschool education for children between 3 and 6. The mothers are given pre- and postnatal care, immunization, supplementary nutrition, and education in health and nutrition. Other women are also given health and nutrition education.

The programs is implemented at the grass-roots level through an anganwadi—a child care center—in charge of an anganwadi worker. This is a woman selected from the local community who is given training for 4 months. The evolution of the anganwadi as a grass-roots level institution, serving as the focal point for all public services for mothers and children, has proved a great step forward in the strategy for the efficient delivery of public services. Even services for which the anganwadi worker is not directly responsible, are delivered through the center to facilitate coordination.

The scheme was initiated in 1975 with 33 projects covering a population of roughly three million. It is now being expanded to 100 projects covering a population of about 10 million.

In view of resource constraints the program has been started in the most backward rural areas and in the urban slums. The response to the program has been very encouraging, and monitoring is carried out by a built-in evaluation and monitoring system. This scheme is the first major attempt to deliver an integrated package of services to children, and it has been shown that the model has proved to be effective.

M. PAVELLA
International Federation for Home Economics

The International Federation for Home Economics is a non-governmental world organization with special concern for problems involving children. It believes that the family setting remains the best place for a child to grow up in a balanced way. It is aware that if the family is to play its proper role, parents and future parents must be provided with the right education to prepare them for responsible parenthood.

The IFHE considers that a primary factor in the harmonious development of children is proper nourishment, based on local resources and local eating habits, and providing every individual child with the vital ration of the various foodstuffs needed for physical and psychological growth. This involves an educational problem. This is a problem of basic learning which can enable women—in particular—to evaluate and select foodstuffs in accordance with their family's needs. Such education could well form part of a more general consumer educational program to help people acquire a basic knowledge of good nutrition so as to appreciate the difference between what foods are necessary and what are not, as well as the quality–price criterion.

The IFHE feels that the child's health depends on health education involving simple rules. It also believes that birth control could contribute to better health among mothers and children, though it is not concerned with the actual methods used.

Further, the IFHE is concerned with the setting in which the child is growing up, both materially and psychologically, as regards the home and the members of the family. In particular, it feels that the quality of communication among members of the family should be improved by teaching the various individuals how to achieve a better dialogue and a greater sharing of their thoughts. Adults must be ready to listen to their children. Nothing can replace love— that "vitamin of growth" to use Professor Henyer's expression.

While not ignoring extreme cases involving handicaps, illtreatment, violence, delinquency, drugs, prostitution, desertion (partial or total), the IFHE believes that a better understanding of the child's situation within his home setting, regardless of individual cases, would enable preventive action to be taken through education. In this respect, coordination between home economics teachers and the staffs of all other educational and welfare departments could lead to substantial results in assisting the fulfilments of all children regardless of their social condition.

Finally, the IFHE, while concentrating its efforts on improving the quality of family life, is not indifferent to the problems involved in the child's socialization and integration into the various groups and communities within which he will be pursuing his development.

The essential task appears to be to define the child's rights more clearly in order to protect him against himself, against his family if necessary, and against the society to which he belongs, if such protection is required. This forms part of the more general problem of human rights, the Universal Declaration of which was drawn up exactly 30 years ago.

In conclusion, although the IFHE feels that young children should be encouraged to develop their skills by engaging in manual forms of education, the fact remains that in many countries larger numbers of children are exploited and forced to work beyond their physical capacities. This exploitation of young children seems to the IFHE as much a scandal as their prostitution by adults.

Only peaceful home surroundings, endowed with adequate resources, properly managed and used to ensure the well-being of each member of the family, can provide a real solution to children's problems. Such a situation—regardless of the type of civilization—cannot be attained without a better sharing of the world's resources in a new economic order.

Children remain the best investment for the future. It is up to adults throughout the world, especially those with political power, to take decisions that will not endanger this human capital.

JÖRN ELFVING
School Health Service, Helsinki, Finland

It may be even more important than saving the lives of these "small-for-dates" babies to ensure that the lives saved are worth living. As things are now, the baby who dies today of malnutrition or diarrhoea may have a happier fate than one who lives and, at the turn of the century, has no decent home, no job, and a bitter struggle to maintain the life we saved. I believe that the most important task mankind faces today (and tomorrow) is to see to it that the baby to whom it cannot offer a life worth living is not even conceived.

CLAUDIO SEPULVEDA
UN Asian and Pacific Development Institute, Bangkok, Thailand

Expectations of a better situation for children in the world of tomorrow, beyond individual successes and in a socially meaningful way, depend to a very large extent on the priorities for resources allocation chosen by societies, countries, and governments.

In Asian countries the total government expenditure represents, on average, only 15% of the country's GNP. In addition, the disposal of this 15% is very largely to purposes which do not have any influence on the improvement of the situation of children. Only Sri Lanka and New Zealand, among the Asian countries, allocate more resources per head to health than to defense. In Iran only $US8 per head are devoted to health whereas $US300 per head are devoted to defense. On an average less than 1–2% of the GNP in Asian countries is devoted to public expenditure on health care, which amounts to less than $US1–2 per head per year. The amount spent on children's health is of course far less than the general average.

As long as this priority pattern remains unchanged there is little hope for a better childhood in the world of tomorrow.

SPECIAL SESSIONS

NEW CONCEPTS OF CHILD CARE

PRENATAL FACTORS IN CHILD HEALTH

SCREENING

NEW ILLNESSES

NEW CONCEPTS OF CHILD CARE

Coordinator: M. G. WAGNER
WHO, Copenhagen, Denmark

THIS session's discussion can be divided into three sections:

1. HOW HEALTH IS VIEWED CAN INFLUENCE HEALTH CARE

(a) We need to synthesize: to "put man together again rather than take him apart" (ROBERT A. ALDRICH, Medical Center, University of Colorado, Denver, CO, USA) and to consider the total human life-span as a unity.

(b) Health is a continuum from a condition of total well-being to death. While we have measures of the illness–death half of the continuum, we have no measures of the well-being half.

(c) Health is basically a concern about the quality of life, and health care is an educational process. People learn how and when to break down, how to be ill, and how to get help from the external networks (family and society) and the internal network (oneself).

2. HOW HEALTH CARE IS VIEWED CAN INFLUENCE
THE TYPE OF CARE GIVEN

The power methods used by health providers (in particular medical practitioners) affects the quality of care given to their patients. DR. A. F. SINGLETON (Martin Luther King General Hospital, Los Angeles, CA, USA) reported on a study of the use of power by physicians in clinical care situations in America. The methods were classified as threats, opinion, information, reference-comparison, reward. "Results indicate that most subjects use information giving as the primary power method (67%). As alternative methods, they use threats (16%) or reward (13%). They rarely use comparison (4%), a method which is predicted to have the most persistently positive effects on others."

How the health provider views self-care is important. Health is not an end but a means to happiness and self-fulfillment. There is a danger that self-care can be used by the medical profession to train patients to use the present system better. For example, ANGELA KIOSSOGLOU (Biologist, Athens, Greece) stated: "I have experienced the psychological consequences of being suddenly anesthetized as my baby's head appeared "for the sake of the doctor" and only being given the baby when she no longer seemed mine. I have also been reprimanded by a doctor for being acquainted with the medical literature on matters concerning my own body."

379

3. TYPES OF HEALTH CARE APPROACHES

(a) Parent groups. These were described by DR. ALFRED H. KATZ (School of Public Health, University of California at Los Angeles, CA, USA) in his paper "Self-help roles of the family in health care", reproduced on pp. 165–9.

(b) Less hospitalization for emotional problems: advocated by DR. M. EVANGELAKIS (School of Medicine, University of Miami, FL, USA), who described the functions of a day treatment program as:

To provide a period of intensive treatment which might noticeably alter the emotional crisis who may not need 24 hour inpatient care and treatment.

To provide a period of intensive treatment which might noticeablely alter the pattern of dependence upon various medical inpatient and outpatient psychiatric facilities.

To provide day psychiatric treatment and education for the emotionally disturbed children and adolescents under the supervision of the child psychiatrist who operates on an interdisciplinary team basis.

To provide a treatment modality in the form of a milieu as an effective therapeutic tool in the modification of symptomatic or abnormal behavior.

To provide a well-rounded special elementary and junior high school program and curriculum for the patients.

To provide ongoing casework, parental counselling and family therapy for the parents of the child and adolescent.

To serve as a bridge for children and adolescents in transition from the residential treatment to the community outpatient clinics for treatment or complete discharge.

To maintain the children's ties with the family and the community. The day treatment program could counter the regressive pattern that is usually associated with becoming a psychiatric inpatient.

To develop liaison services with the community agencies for the provision of the best possible psychiatric, psychosocial, and psychoeducational treatment of the child who requires the service of day treatment program.

To develop channels of public relations to acquaint the community with the day treatment modality as a concept and not as a place.

Day treatment versus day care. The day treatment concept is active and treatment oriented, geared to the needs of emotionally disturbed and/or mentally ill children and adolescents, and is far removed from the custodial or "baby sitting approach." The primary distinction between "treatment" and "care" involves the concept of change. Treatment implies potential for change and optimism about resources, whereas care, at best, means maintaining a certain level of functioning and, at worst, a condition of hopeless stagnation.

Day treatment versus outpatient treatment. Outpatient treatment, particularly for the moderately or severely disturbed child is not enough (1–5 hours per week). The "outpatient" disturbed child is often forced to remain at home and unnecessarily drain and exhaust all parental energies. Often younger siblings are neglected because of the demands of the disturbed child.

Day treatment versus inpatient treatment. Limitations of inpatient treatment include rising costs, the shortage of highly trained personnel, demands for treatment and for cures, and criticism of delivery of services, located at a considerable distance from the child's home. The child loses positive aspects of family life when removed from the family and becomes accustomed to an institutional environment; the family becomes reorganized and its members regroup and can no longer accept the mentally ill child back into the household.

With day treatment, the drawbacks of residential programs which occur when there are many workers on several shifts can be avoided, since it is possible for the children to relate to one constant group of workers rather than to several groups on changing shifts. Other advantages are found in that the bedtime and night patterns of the children do not need to be interrupted, and the children can maintain their roots at home which, in many cases, proves quite therapeutic.

Our own experience points to the number of children who can benefit by day treatment and whose relapses are often better controlled than by readmission to the residential program. Also, we believe that day treatment is much less expensive than keeping the patient in the hospital for a long time. Moreover, it frees beds for children who need them. Long term hospitalization often is a retreat from normal living. The day treatment challenges patient, family, and staff to close community ties and thus may be considered as performing a preventive function.

We believe that two-thirds of inpatients, in both adult and children-adolescent residential psychiatric settings, can be responsibly treated in well structured and directed day treatment programs.

LIST OF PAPERS PRESENTED

S. Nousia-Arvanitakis (University of Kansas Medical Center, USA): "The child with cystic fibrosis: new concepts of multidisciplinary and cooperative health care programs."

Leonard J. Duhl (College of Environmental Design, University of California at Berkeley, CA, (USA): "The future of health services for children," (see pp. 459–61)

M. Evangelakis (School of Medicine, University of Miami, FL, USA): "Day treatment as an alternative to children's and adolescents' outpatient and residential psychiatric treatment."

Holger Hulton (National Board of Health, Helsinki, Finland): "Child health care in Finland."

Alfred H. Katz (School of Public Health, University of California at Los Angeles, CA, USA): "Self-help roles of the family in health care."

P. O. Petterson (University Hospital, Uppsala, Sweden): "Child health services today and tomorrow."

A. F. Singleton (Martin Luther King General Hospital, Los Angeles, CA, USA): "Power usage in clinical settings: a preliminary study."

PRENATAL FACTORS IN CHILD HEALTH

Coordinator: PHILIP RHODES

Regional Postgraduate Institute of Medicine, Newcastle upon Tyne, UK

THE GENERAL outline suggested that the session should focus on "what will be happening to children of the world in the next 10–15 years; that it should define "desirable developments to be encouraged"; and that it should pinpoint "undesirable tendencies to be avoided."

The long term philosophy which grips medicine and health care at the moment is that of the greatest good of the greatest number. The proposition is perhaps arguable at a philosophical level, but it imbues the humanitarian spirit of medicine and health care. It was the basis of this conference, and it directed our thoughts at this session.

Not all children start life with equal advantages and handicaps. The session sought to explore these *differences*.

Variations in culture are probable determinants of family size, and so of population increase or decrease. They also affect educability in different patterns of reproduction. Religions play their part, too, as well as economic status.

Large families and increasing populations tend to make it difficult to improve living standards and nutrition. This led to a consideration of the various forms of family limitation and of how acceptable they have been; emphasizing the contribution of smaller families to the health of mothers and their babies and to rising economic status. This may require education in the uses of technology to increase agricultural and industrial productivity, but family limitation increases educability and reduces strain on formal educational services.

If numbers of women needing prenatal care can be reduced the problem becomes simpler. Nevertheless, there will for many years be a need to get some form of care to millions of women in many countries, where it will not be possible to have all looked after by highly qualified Western type doctors. Who then is to look after childbearing women in pregnancy and labour? This requires a look at the use of health care professionals of all standards of attainment in giving prenatal care. How should they be trained? How can they be recruited? What facilities should be afforded them for the task?

Education, a long term process, is the key to changing reproductive attitudes for the better life for future children. Such education must work within the various cultures and understand them to gain reasonable effectiveness. It seems obvious that the first thing to do is to get prenatal care of some kind to as many women as possible. This is a very large task, but it is needed badly, at almost any level, in many parts of the world. It should allow for health education to be brought to bear on those susceptible to its influence—the mothers. It is through them that the welfare of children can be improved. The special session therefore considered some of the factors, in culture and economics and family limitation, on the production of babies

383

with physical attributes that give potential for development on apparently desirable lines.

VARIATIONS IN REPRODUCTION WITH
ECONOMIC STATUS

Patterns of reproduction vary in different countries, in different socioeconomic classes, in the educated and uneducated, in rural and urban communities. Moreover, economics affect the level of nutrition with effects on the stature of women, the size of the pelvis, difficulties in labor, birth trauma, and the size of the baby at birth, and so its subsequent development.

Some of these aspects were brought out by DR. A. SIMOPOULOS (National Institute of Health, Bethesda, MD, USA) in her paper on "Nutritional requirements in pregnancy." She stated that there is increasing information supporting the hypothesis that maternal nutrition affects the materno-fetal nutrient supply, and that fetal growth retardation is accompanied by suboptimal immune response to some infectious agents. It is becoming evident that the nutritional status of lactating mothers may affect breast milk output and infant growth, at least during the first 3–6 months of age. Requirements for most nutrients vary with body size, and the requirements per unit of bodyweight are greater during periods of rapid growth and during pregnancy and lactation than they are for maintenance.

The requirement for a nutrient is the minimum intake that will maintain normal function. Nutritional requirements differ among individuals and, from time to time, for a given individual. These requirements differ with age, sex, body size, physiological state, and genetic make-up. Some are further influenced by how active a person is and by the environment in which he lives.

For years we have known that birthweights were lower in developing countries than in more advanced areas of the world. We have also known that birthweight among poor people in the United States is lower than among the rich.

The increase in birthweight in Japan over the past two decades lends support to a nutritional explanation. Although many changes in addition to improvement in nutrition have occurred in Japan during this period, certainly the genetic or racial factor has remained the same. Furthermore, it has been shown that second generation Japanese in the United States are on an average several inches taller than their parents. This difference can be explained at least in part by the different diet consumed by the mothers during pregnancy. If malnutrition of the mother makes a significant contribution to low birthweight, then adequate feeding during pregnancy should increase birthweight and diminish fetal mortality. Improved maternal feeding does have this effect.

There are two other strong epidemiologic arguments for the important role of maternal nutrition in fetal growth.

The first piece of epidemiologic evidence implicating the nutritional status of the mother in fetal growth is the relation between maternal size and birthweight. In affluent societies there is no correspondence between these two variables. In developing countries, however, where maternal height reflects previous nutrition, there is a direct correlation between maternal height and infant weight at birth. The smaller the mother, the smaller her infant. Several studies have indicated that this direct correlation has a nutritional rather than a genetic basis. The second is that birthweight correlates with increase in maternal weight. Within limits, the more the mother gains during pregnancy the larger the baby. The optimal amount of weight gain has not been determined and will no doubt vary depending on the mother's previous nutritional status. At present, the committee on maternal nutrition of the National Academy of Sciences recommends an average weight gain of 11.0 kg for previously well-nourished women. This is quite different from the practices of the past when women were told to keep their weight gain to less than 5.0 kg or to gain no weight at all, or actually to reduce.

In summary it seems clear that fetal growth is to some degree responsive to maternal nutritional status. Although maternal reserves can be utilized for fetal growth, adequate nutrition must be supplied during pregnancy. In chronically malnourished populations this is particularly true since the depleted mother has little if any nutritional reserve for the fetus to draw upon. We do not as yet know how much of the low birthweight in our own poor can be ascribed to inadequate maternal nutrition.

The Coordinator noted that the recommended weight gain of 11·0 kg did not make much sense. A satisfactory gain could range from 4 to 16 kg.

DR. R. B. McGUCKEN (Wesley Guild Hospital, Lagos, Nigeria) opened his paper by saying: "The theme of this conference is 'the child in the world of tomorrow.' But do we realize that for many children born today in the developing countries the world of tomorrow will never dawn? I will present some information on the serious problems encountered in the neonatal period in a unit situated in the tropical rain forest belt of Western Nigeria. I will also suggest some ways in which, at relatively low cost, the outlook for these children may be substantially improved. The study, which covers a two year period, concerns babies born in the maternity department of the hospital or admitted from a surrounding area of some 200 square miles. The neonatal unit was run on simple lines, with mothers invariably admitted together with their baby. Nine hundred and twenty-two babies were admitted, 82% having been born outside a maternity center: 411 babies had significant infection and 366 weighed 2 kg or less on admission: 101 babies had diarrhoea and 67 tetanus. Soft tissue infections, serious conjunctivitis, and umbilical sepsis accounted for another important proportion of the infections."

"Two hundred and twenty-seven babies died, a mortality rate of 23·5%: 78 died essentially because of their prematurity, the remaining causes of death can be grouped under the heading of infections. Thus in very general terms infection and low birthweight were the principal problems facing these newborn infants. Factors contributing to low birthweight included poor availability or inadequate use of antenatal facilities, maternal infection, particularly with malaria, and—in this particular series—a high incidence of twinning.

"The survival of very low birthweight infants often depends on sophisticated care, involving expensive equipment and highly trained staff, the provision of which is not practicable in the rural areas of developing countries. Efforts must, therefore, be directed at prevention, and in this connection the provision of antenatal care is of prime importance. When this is available in the villages from trained midwives who are locally resident, health education efforts (explaining the importance of antenatal and neonatal care) can be carried out more naturally; the progress of pregnancy can be clinically assessed: iron and vitamin supplements can be given and anti-malarial therapy can be prescribed throughout pregnancy. The result of such a program will be a reduction in the incidence of low birthweight babies.

"Infections play a major role in morbidity and mortality. The two conditions with the highest individual mortality rates were tetanus and umbilical sepsis. Both were the result of poor hygiene at delivery and improper cord care subsequently. Improved midwifery services and local delivery rooms attached to each village clinic can reduce the incidence of such infections in the immediate neonatal period.

"Acute diarrhoeal disease was frequently encountered and was often related to the introduction of artificial feeds, which are almost invariably contaminated in the course of preparation. The importance of natural feeding with breast milk must be emphasized, and the advertising of artificial feeds is to be deprecated. Many of the other infections, such as skin sepsis, conjunctivitis, and soft tissue infections would become much less frequent with attention to simple hygiene.

"Improved survival of low birthweight infants in the neonatal period is of little value if there is a high mortality rate after discharge from the hospital. A prospective study of 50 of the low birthweight infants in this series showed a mortality rate of 18% in the first 12 months of life, and 43% of the survivors had failed to reach the tenth centile for weight.

"In conclusion, therefore, a practical solution to the problem of the neonate in a developing country lies not only in improved neonatal services, but also in improved antenatal care and in health education for the mothers."

DR. G. D. DE BERNIS (University of Social Sciences, Grenoble, France) raised the problem of miscarriages in early pregnancy among working women, saying that this risk is particularly great among women working long hours in a standing position or in an uncomfortable position or carrying heavy weights. Very few studies have been made of these accidents because, first, they usually happen within the first three months of the pregnancy. This means that, even in countries where a declaration of pregnancy must be made to the social security offices, the accident often occurs before the declaration is made. Second, when a woman goes to a hospital with a miscarriage, she is very seldom asked to state the socioeconomic cause of the accident. So there is no chance to establish a relationship between the miscarriage and the working conditions of the woman. However, the problem is a real one, and quite serious in the already industrialized countries. It is also likely to become more important in the developing countries as industry expands. Wages are low and conditions tend to be less good than in the developed world. Moreover, the general health level of the population is lower. This makes it important for us to realize that the quality of births and the life of children tomorrow can be improved by the systematic organization of an occupational health service, and careful attention to the working conditions of women.

THE DELIVERY OF PRENATAL CARE

DR. MARY L. HICKMAN (Central Valley Regional Medical Center, Fresno, CA, USA) said that ideally, all children born in the world of tomorrow should be free of preventable handicaps. Research studies from numerous countries and many disciplines indicate that utilization of the rapidly expanding knowledge in genetics, medical technology, nutrition, and child development would enable society to prevent 30–50% of the developmental disabilities. Included in this category are mental retardation, cerebral palsy, epilepsy, and other neurological handicapping conditions.

An effective plan must provide preventive treatment and educational services during three critical periods: preconception, throughout pregnancy and delivery, and during infancy and childhood. A prevention program as outlined above is attainable in only a few developed countries. This means we face the dilemma of providing costly obstetric and newborn intensive care to a few while 70% of mothers in developing countries deliver at home without adequate nursing or medical assistance. Obviously prevention services in third world countries must concentrate on priorities and basic medical care.

How does one convince the pediatricians of the necessity or provide the financial resources to improve the socioeconomic status of a given population? It is unfortunate that governments in many developed countries will fund 30 years of institutional care of handicapped children at an annual cost of $18,000, but are unwilling to pay the comparatively small cost of good prenatal care that would have prevented the handicap.

Even greater philosophical problems arise when we contemplate use of anmiocentesis and abortion. If this procedure becomes freely available to all by the year 2000, what will be the implications of selecting children by sex preference? Might the male–female ratio be distorted with far-reaching social changes? In countries where religious belief is strong, the already available medical technology is useless if it is not acceptable to parents. Ultimately one has to answer the question: Does human life begin at the time of conception or after the twenty-second week, the time after which for example, termination of pregnancy is illegal in America?

Lastly, how does one persuade individuals to assume responsibility for their own health and that of their children. Even though adequate education regarding prevention techniques should be made available, attempts at healthy living may be thwarted by a culture oriented to pleasure and high consumption of media-advertised products.

THE PSYCHOLOGY OF PREGNANT WOMEN

This is an important field, for the psychology of the mother determines much of family life, her approach to childbirth, and the physical, psychological and social development of her children.

DR. P. ALLISON (National Institute of Mental Health, Adelphi, MD, USA) said: "It is well known that a mother's relationship with her baby antedates the time of delivery. Beyond the usual influences of personal history, important maternal orientations towards an infant are activated during the course of pregnancy. Biological changes precipitate essential psychological processes which unfold dynamically. It is this state of psychic disequilibrium that we must examine if we are to understand the nature of the maturational task of parenthood during the period of normal pregnancy.

"During times of crisis, including the crisis of pregnancy, familiar patterns have to be changed and we are more vulnerable to fears of the unknown, and irrational. Anxiety emerges during periods of psychological growth such as when a pregnant woman is in the midst of working through her new mothering identity and confronting conflicting feelings regarding her own mother and family.

"Our basic question is what are the processes during pregnancy which contribute to maturational progression and what processes contribute to regression to earlier developmental states? Further, is it possible to delineate factors which may lead to optimal development during pregnancy? There is general agreement in the literature that narcissism increases during pregnancy making all women more vulnerable to regressive psychopathology.

"In contemporary obstetrics, the biological phenomena of conception, pregnancy, and childbirth are dealt with scientifically and matter-of-factly. While we welcome this openness and directness, we deplore the usual exclusive focus on physical management alone. We wonder what factors have contributed to the relative neglect of the emotional aspects of pregnancy in the usual professional care of pregnant women. Given the reciprocal nature of the mother's and infant's maturational progression, we contend that it is essential for those responsible for the care of pregnant women to encourage the mother to express, rather than suppress and deny her understandable apprehensions about her relationships, her pregnancy, childbirth, and motherhood. Unrealistic idealization of pregnancy and insistence on the part of obstetrical professionals on seeing this time as a period of psychological bliss and fulfillment only adds to the crisis. Moreover, we agree with Caplan that during the crisis of pregnancy, preventive intervention has a much greater effect in terms of influencing the attitudes of the participants in the family drama than it would have during periods of stability of emotional functioning.

"Psychoanalytic researchers frequently formulate the changing psychological tasks of pregnancy as a process of incorporation, differentiation, and separation. First, the woman must accept or incorporate the fetus in her body; then differentiate its being in her, yet actually not being herself; and finally prepare to separate from the fetus.

"The more or less orderly progression of changing psychological themes during pregnancy are the following: during the first trimester the woman is usually thinking mostly of what is happening to her, since the baby has not yet demanded attention as a separate being. Towards the end of this trimester the woman becomes concerned with her relationship to her own mother. During this inward, regressive phase, she begins one of the key tasks of pregnancy: the formation of a personally relevant and unique mothering identity, separate from that of her own mother. The feelings of love, hate, frustration, satisfaction, dependency, and rebellion that are part of every mother–child relationship must be worked through anew. The complexity of this task and the conflict associated with it are usually guilt and anxiety-provoking.

"The second trimester is characterized as a period of quiet with time of quickening viewed as the pivotal event. By moving, the fetus establishes itself as an individual who is differentiated from the mother and who will soon be born. Under normal circumstances, the attention of the mother turns to what is best for the baby, even at the expense of her own self-interest.

"During the third trimester, reality issues emerge in much sharper focus than earlier in pregnancy. The mother begins to be troubled more explicitly about whether or not she will have a healthy baby; she deals with realistic as well as unrealistic fears about delivery; and the anticipation of actual mothering becomes a tangible focus for understandable apprehensions.

"In assessing the psychological aspects of pregnancy, which need to be resolved if this normal developmental crisis is to lead to a new appropriate equilibrium, we reiterate our thesis that pregnancy is a prime time for preventive intervention. We emphasize the need to realize that pregnant women are more prone to form trans-ferential attachments; the societal emphasis on the rational and technical rather than the psychological aspects of life; the lack of an extended family in today's mobile society and the need for supportive relationships; and the necessity of interrupting intergenerational transmission of psychic disturbance."

DR. COHEN (Chaim Sheba Medical Center, Savyon, Israel) commented that an Israeli study showed that 80% of women have serious emotional disturbances during pregnancy. One nagging problem is the sex of the child. Many women continue to have children to have one of a different sex. Is it ethical to tell the mother the sex of her child at an early stage? In Germany, when the sex was made known, abortions followed for 29 females and one male. In the United States amniocentesis is only used for high risk women (advanced maternal age) or those having some previous genetically related disease, etc. Its use is considered unethical for sex determination alone.

DR. P. O. ELFSTRAND (Pediatrician, Stockholm, Sweden) told of a campaign undertaken to inform pregnant women of the dangers of smoking. It has been known for 20 years that a pregnant woman who smokes 20 cigarettes a day will have a baby with a birthweight 200–300g lighter than a non smoking mother. This is not a premature baby but a small-for-date one. A slightly increased perinatal mortality is also well known to occur, which may be due to the small-for-date child. If the mother is a heavy smoker, nicotine in the breast milk can induce symptoms in the child. Colley, among others, has shown that parents' smoking can cause increased infec-tions such as bronchitis and pneumonias in small children. It is also well known that smoke can induce asthma. One thousand three hundred pregnant women were interviewed in Sweden: 45% were smokers. After information almost half the smokers reduced or stopped smoking; 14% continued, but with guilty feelings; 40% did not react at all. Six months later the interviews were repeated: 77% who had stopped smoking during pregnancy started or increased again after delivery. It was therefore necessary to repeat warnings about breast-feeding dangers.

PROFESSOR Y. HOFVANDER (Akademiska Sjukhuset, Uppsala, Sweden) added that smoking has probably more bad effects on small children than low birthweight, and has certainly increased the upper respiratory mortality rate.

Finally, DR. A. J. WARD (Henry Horner Children's Center, Chicago, IL, USA) presented a paper indicating that early infantile autism is a developmental deviation, rather than a solely psychogenic disorder, with an etiology rooted in a pregnancy that is characterized by ongoing interpersonal stress between the mother and father, which the mother feels helpless to resolve. It is further hypothesized that this background of helpless interpersonal stress generates an analogue of Selye's Generalized Adaptation Syndrome (GAS) in the pregnant women. It is further hypothesized that this anologue generates elevated levels of serum cholesterol or similar stress byproducts, which are transmitted through the placental barrier to the fetus and have a delaying or deviating effect upon the laying down of the central nervous system of the fetus.

Thus, it is hypothesized that the characteristic of early childhood autism of (1) lack of development of object relationships since birth (2) lack of the use of speech for communication and (3) maintenance of sameness via stereotypic behavior are all indications of deviant central nervous system development and functioning, which slows the cognitive and affective development of the infant, and thus interferes with the normal development of maternal–infant attachment bonding.

The above hypothesis leads to the following recommendations:

(1) Change the emphasis in study of early childhood autism from a view of it as a psychiatric disorder to a developmental deviation.
(2) Put an emphasis upon early detection and intervention of those family situations that display a potential for the syndrome of "helpless maternal interpersonal stress."
(3) Encourage research on the chemical effects of stress byproducts upon fetal development, using current research on the effects of smoking, alcohol, and addictive drugs as a model.
(4) Encourage research on the relationship between cognitive and affective development in young infants, with a special emphasis upon the delaying or distorting effect of subtle neurological dysfunction.

LIST OF PAPERS PRESENTED

PATRICIA ALLISON and ANTHY TRIPP (National Institute of Mental Health, Adelphi, MD, USA): "Psychological processes of pregnancy."

G. D. DE BERNIS (University of Social Sciences, Grenoble, France): "Miscarriages among working women."

P. O. ELFSTRAND (Pediatrician, Stockholm, Sweden): "An anti-smoking program for mother and child health care centers in Sweden."

P. A. GEORGAKOPOULOS (Marika Eliadi Maternity Hospital, Athens, Greece): "The dangers of intravaginal drugs in pregnancy."

Mary L. Hickman (Central Valley Regional Medical Center, Fresno, CA, USA): "To be well born in the world of tomorrow."

R. B. McGucken (Wesley Guild Hospital, Lagos, Nigeria): "Morbidity and mortality in a neonatal unit in Nigeria."

G. C. Pangalos, C. S. Bartsocas and C. J. Papadatos (Department of Pediatrics, University of Athens, Greece): "Chromosome mapping and the prevention of hereditary diseases."

Artemis P. Simopoulos (National Institute of Health, Education, and Welfare, Bethesda, MD, USA): "Nutritional requirements in pregnancy."

H. Symeonidou-Alatopoulou (National Center of Sociological Research, Athens, Greece): "An account of factors affecting fertility in Greece."

Sheila Wallis and Christine Parkinson (Queen Charlotte's Maternity Hospital, London, UK): "Environmental assessment and the abilities of small-for-date children."

Alan J. Ward (Henry Horner Children's Center, Chicago, IL, USA): "The prenatal antecedents of autism."

SCREENING

Coordinator: MICHEL MANCIAUX

International Children's Center, Paris, France

IN HIS introductory remarks, the Coordinator reminded the meeting of the classical definition of screening given by the WHO in 1966, which was confined to screening for diseases. This "disease-oriented" approach is still prevalent. Only two of the ten papers presented for this session dealt with developmental screening.

The Coordinator also stressed the need not to restrict the discussion of screening to the developed countries. Some screening procedures may be applicable for children of the developing world provided they are directed toward priority health problems and are simple enough to be the responsibility of community health workers.

Finally, he pointed out the difference between mass screening and selective screening for at risk individuals or groups, selected on the basis of epidemiological surveys.

MEDICAL SCREENING VERSUS DEVELOPMENTAL ASSESSMENT

Two main contributors (EDITH H. GROTBERG and T. BERRY BRAZELTON) introduced some very important points: the necessary enlargement of the concept of screening to developmental screening (it is better to say developmental assessment); the differences between screening for diseases and screening for health; the subtle danger of labeling children through screening procedures; that it is worthless to screen children if there is nothing to offer them in terms of care; that screening can be harmful if it is performed in a clinical, pathological, or negative way.

EDITH H. GROTBERG (Department of Health, Education, and Welfare, Washington, DC, USA) said: "Medical screening is a sophisticated concept; such screening is usually simple, quick, capable of 'pass or fail' interpretation; it is applied once to each subject to minimize noncooperation, and lends itself to evaluation in terms of sensitivity, specificity, and repeatability. Developmental assessment of psychological functions, on the other hand, is a clinical procedure to which 'pass or fail' interpretation should not be applied; repeated examinations are essential, and it is not amenable to detailed quantitative evaluation. The essentially clinical nature of developmental assessment must never be overlooked; screening cannot be a 'one-shot' attempt on a parameter that is developmental.

"The problem of combining these two approaches, as seems desirable, is that the screening procedure is largely in the hands of the medical and health professions. It is rare to see psychologists, specialists in developmental and learning disabilities, other

393

behavioral scientists, and environmentalists among screening teams. To the extent the medical model of disease–wellness shapes screening, the developmental assessment is relegated to secondary or referral status. It is important to change some basic notions about health and development. Development is not a disease which yields a judgment of present or absent. We are basically concerned with the concept of competence: how well has a child met and how well does he or she now meet the expectations implicitly and explicitly set by his/her society for an individual of his/her age group. Disease is an obstacle to development. Wellness enhances the opportunities for development.

"Developmental assessment is more consistent with preventive approaches to health problems and it needs to be continuous. Medical screening can detect disease and malfunctioning."

T. BERRY BRAZELTON (Harvard Medical School, Boston, MA, USA) asked: "Screening for what? Screening for labelling is destructive for both parent and child, but screening for intervention has a different goal. But assessment must include the present status of the child and of the parent as well as the 'coping systems' which they demonstrate during the assessment, and which will affect the child's recovery and future development. An assessment must include the total child (its personality, temperament, etc.) as well as the target developmental defects. For the assessment to be used as part of an intervention, it must not just be static but an analysis of the child as a total individual, and of the environment as a potential for recovery."

SCREENING FOR HANDICAPS

Papers were presented on screening for handicaps, dealing with blindness, color perception, deafness, and epilepsy.

John X. KOLIOPOULOS (National Ophthalmic Center, Athens, Greece) said: "Vision is by far the most important of our senses, and the one that helps us to adapt in the environment and to establish the 'I/you' relationships. Therefore, one of our most important and serious tasks is to detect and treat children with potential visual handicaps as early as possible."

DR. BRAJOVIC (Department of Psychology, University of Belgrade, Yugoslavia) said that their 18 years of research had shown a direct correlation between the degree of auditory impairment and the level of development of verbal communication. Deaf children should therefore be classified as early as possible according to the degree of their hearing impairment and rehabilitation started immediately. An interdisciplinary approach both in the diagnosis and therapy of deaf children can help them to develop better phonation and articulation as well as the development of phonetic structures.

Dr. Stores (Park Hospital for Children, Oxford, UK) described four studies carried out in a search for high risk factors in schoolchildren handicapped by epilepsy. He said that measurements of reading retardation, inattentiveness of various types, dependency, and other aspects of disturbed behavior in epileptic schoolchildren suggest that male sex and the presence of a persistent left temporal lobe spike discharge are consistently associated with these problems. He suggested that preventive or remedial measures can be introduced at an early age in order to minimize the adverse social effects of recurrent seizures.

In the following discussion, the emphasis was put on cost–benefit studies and on the necessity for integrating the screening procedure with the full range of health services. What should be said to the parents of screened children—mainly in the sense of positive advice—was also considered.

SCREENING FOR DISEASE

Papers were then given on screening for metabolic diseases: PKU, hypothyroidism, G-6-PD deficiency—of great interest in some African countries—and of screening for the risk of degenerative diseases: high blood pressure and obesity. The necessity of using a carefully designed schedule and up-to-date standards was emphasized.

Dr. Cohen (Chaim Sheba Medical Center, Savyon, Israel) said: "Until 1960 phenylketonuria was unknown amongst Jews and had not been considered as a cause of mental retardation. When we found our first cases amongst Yemenite Jews in 1960 we decided to look at the incidence in institutions for the retarded and found some 3% affected. Case finding at this stage was on the basis of family search after an affected retarded individual had been found. When Guthrie published his screening procedure in 1961 we began to look into the possibilities of using this to screen all newborn babies. In 1964, with the assistance of a research grant from the Children's Bureau of the Department of Health, Education, and Welfare in Washington, we started a pilot project for three years and were thus able to show the screening procedure was feasible and viable, and the total cost of screening including treatment of the cases so found was found to be about $1·00 per infant tested. As a result we were able to 'sell' this scheme to our Ministry of Health who have subsequently been responsible for maintaining our screening and treatment program.

"At the outset we used the generally accepted criteria for requesting repeat specimens, viz. a Guthrie test of 6 mg% or over at the first test, and later over 4 mg%. Some three years later, however, we decided to change our criteria and repeat all the blood spots where there was any growth at all (even between 2–4 mg%) so that an 'internal standard' was used. Naturally this produced more false positives but, as you will see in the second column of Table 1, there is also a marked increase in the number of cases of mild persistent hyperphenylalaninemia that are now more frequent than the cases of 'classical' PKU. You will also notice that, having screened over 700,000 babies (our birth rate is approximately 66,000–75,000 cases per year), we now have fairly steady incidence rates and an average overall incidence rate of 1 in 15,000 but the 'at-risk' group of non-Ashkenazi Jews have an incidence of about 1 in 10,000, which is comparable with most other places in the world. As we know the approximate ethnic make-up of our population, we are able to work out incidence rates for each ethnic group so that our Yemenite Jews have an incidence of 1 in 5000–6000 whereas the North African Jews (Morocco, Libya, Algeria, etc.) are closer to 1 in 30,000.

TABLE 1
Summary of phenylketonuria screening program among newborn in Israel 1964–77

	1964–67	1967–77	Total
Total number of live births	197,225	813,683	1,010,918
Infants screened	118,535	587,406	697,941
Screening coverage	56%	72%	69%
PKU casés	7	44 (11)a	51
Frequency of PKU	1:15802	1:13,350	1:13,685
Frequency in communities other than Ashkenazi	1:11,000 (approx.)	1:9345 (approx.)	1:9580 (approx.)
Presumptive positives	42	649	691
Frequency of presumptive positives	1:2663	1:579	1:693
Mild persistent HPAs	2	68b	70

(a) 11 of these were "atypical."
(b) Until 1975.

"We have also tested for G-6-PD deficiency. This is technically easy, giving reliable results, and we have continued with it for one or two of our maternity hospitals. Our pediatricians, however, were not convinced of the need for it, and because of the high incidence of this deficiency in certain of our ethnic groups (e.g. Jews from Kurdistan where it is over 50%) they felt that it would cause too much anxiety amongst the parents, so that they declined the offer.

"Finally, we have started screening for hypothyroidism, and Dvr. Y. Zack and his colleagues have done more than 20,000 tests so far. Using the T4 and TSH levels on the same dried blood spots collected for the Guthrie test, they have discovered five cases of hypothyroidism—one of these being a panhypopituitarism. This would suggest that this procedure is likely to be even more productive than the PKU screening, particularly as the treatment is much easier."

DR. DARILLIS (University Pediatric Clinic, Aghia Sophia Hospital, Athens, Greece) described a research project in the north of Greece where measurements were made of the amount of lead in the blood and urine of 207 infants of 7–15 months in environments with different levels of pollution. A difference of $0.01 < p < 0.05$ was found between the amount of lead in those who lived in the country and in the industrial towns.

Following DR. CASSIMOS' paper on obesity among Greek primary schoolchildren, the Coordinator said that perhaps we should be screening for the at risk factors which promote obesity rather than calculating the number of obese children. This had to do with developmental screening. The problems of the value, and the acceptance of "preventive measures" for at risk individuals led to a discussion on an evaluation of the whole screening procedure as a public health practice.

DEVELOPMENTAL SCREENING

CAROL MILLER (Central School of Speech and Drama, London, UK) said that wherever developmental screening takes place, the examiner must be aware of the need to include an assessment of the child's speech and language. If communication is to develop normally, the following areas must be looked into:

Hearing: tests appropriate to the child's age and level of development are essential.

Perception: this includes attention control and concentration, the ability to listen, to discriminate between sounds and to memorize them. The integration of vision and hearing must also be considered.

Symbolic play: the young child's understanding of the world about him is reflected in his play. He should be observed for the use made of materials and the general organization of himself and others. The play will reflect "inner language."

Nonverbal communication: uses of gesture, eye contact, and body language are important. The child may rely on these too much and have all of his needs interpreted without the use of speech.

The child's own use of expression must be examined. Use of words may begin after the first birthday and the child then begins to put words together. As he gets older, the clarity of his speech should be examined. Is he able to express ideas clearly using phrases and sentences? Can he make all the sounds of his language? Is his voice of normal quality? Is he generally fluent, without too many hesitations and repititions?

The mouth must be examined. The shape and structure of the articulators must be checked together with their functional movements for both feeding and speaking.

The child's environment must be considered. A child can only learn a language if it is spoken around him, and the possibility of understimulation must not be forgotten.

Finally, the parents' feelings must be noted. If they are worried about their child's speech, then detailed assessment is necessary. It is only in this way that their fears can be allayed. It is not sufficient to send them away, saying that their child will "grow out of" his speech problem. Their anxieties are real and it is important that they are well advised. If speech therapy is not available, they must be given practical suggestions for helping the child themselves.

CHRISTINE COOPER (Department of Child Health, University of Newcastle upon Tyne, UK) spoke in more general terms of developmental screening but with special reference to the parent–child relationship, which, she said, was often not sufficiently taken into account. She referred to a diagram (Fig. 1) which she had found helpful, saying that the majority of children have "good enough" parents, to use Winnicott's

THE CONTINUUM OF PARENTING CAPACITY

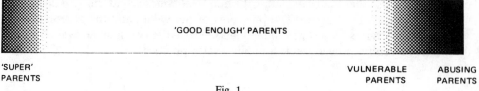

'GOOD ENOUGH' PARENTS

'SUPER'   VULNERABLE   ABUSING
PARENTS   PARENTS   PARENTS

Fig. 1.

term, who bring up their children with success and enjoyment. "By success we mean promoting to the full the child's innate potential. Towards one end of the scale are the vulnerable parents, in whom various forms of stress exists which makes them prone to have serious problems managing their children and the children to have distorted growth and development. With a heavy burden of multiple stresses most parents could probably become vulnerable, and our efforts as professional or lay helpers should always be to help parents move away from the vulnerable end of the scale. At the extreme of this end of the continuum are the abusing parents whose capacity to parent a particular child, or sometimes all their children, has broken down, sometimes temporarily, sometimes permanently.

"At the opposite extreme of the continuum are parents who have an abundance of nurturing skills and, even when faced with a difficult or handicapped child or when stressed themselves, they manage to provide good care and promote the child's innate developmental potential. Such parents make superb foster parents, or adopters for difficult children.

"When we see a baby or young child with his parents, and especially with his mother, we can observe the degree of reciprocity between them and we note a number of feelings in the mother, some of which are listed in Table 2.

TABLE 2
The "good enough" mother shows:

Interest	Also at times:
Delight	Uncertainty
Concern	Anxiety
Tenderness	Fatigue
Affection	Frustration
Pride	Weeping
Preoccupation	
Adaptability	
Confidence	

"On the left of the table are some of the positive feelings we can observe and most mothers show plenty of these. On the right of the table are other emotions, which we can call negative or painful, which we also see from time to time in most normal mother–infant pairs. We have to learn to recognize when the negative feelings predominate and find the cause of the mother's distress. Often this stems from her own psychological make-up and immaturity and from unresolved problems of her own childhood, especially emotionally depriving experiences. Marital stress and other family problems may also be a factor or a number of social difficulties such as poverty, overcrowding, alcohol and drugs abuse, gambling, or other evils. Sometimes the mother's difficulties have subtle and complex origins which are not easy to discover, especially in families in comfortable circumstances.

"Sympathetic discussions with an experienced doctor or social worker will usually uncover the basic causes of stress and lead to appropriate measures to help the family. In a few cases, even with prolonged help, mother and infant cannot adapt to each other, and alternative care for the child must be found. This should not be for more than a few weeks in the case of an infant, if the mother is to resume its care. Sometimes a mother or family need help to relinquish a child for adoption when their personal, family, or environmental problems are overwhelming and not capable of resolution.

"Fatigue and isolation from the wider family or supporting friends is frequently a cause of maternal stress in the early weeks of the infant's life in Western societies with social mobility. Premature parenthood is another cause of problems in urban societies where the needs of the immature parents conflict with those of their young child or children.

"Whenever possible, observations should be extended to the father and the role he plays with the mother and with the child. His feelings should be noted in the same way, and where possible his protective role and his pride in the growing family should be promoted. The need for him to encourage and support his wife should be stressed in subtle ways.

"Observations of mother and child during a feeding situation is very productive and helps us understand the ebb and flow of feeling between the two. This is not surprising since food is the most basic need of the child, without which it will not survive. The mother, subconsciously or consciously aware of the importance of feeding, usually shows her greatest nurturing care during the feeding sequences, which normally include some toileting and play as well.

"Observe the frequency and quality of the mother's holding and watching her child, how and how often she makes eye-to-eye contact, smiles at, talks to, and plays with the baby to initiate action or respond to it. Record the frequency of cuddling, kissing, rocking, fondling, grooming, and responding to the child's signals. Assess the degree of liveliness, reciprocity, and pleasure in the interactions. Observe how the mother exerts control.

"The innate capacity of the infant to respond to maternal care from the moment of birth is being increasingly understood, and there is no better way of promoting bonding between parents and infant than alerting them to the skills an infant shows even from the moment it is born. Vision and 'following' can be shown to them then, and listening by the baby within a few days. To know that she is so important to her infant enhances the mother's self-esteem and adaptive ability, and by the second week the baby will 'know' her by her face, voice, smell, and probably by the way she holds and moves him. She has already become the expert for her child, and the smooth sequence of his development is interrupted and slowed down if others care for him often in his early life. The baby will adapt to the father as well, and to one or two other close family members, but when he is handled or cared for by many different people, his sensitive being becomes confused and early learning processes, especially communication and language development, are delayed.

"Finally, we must learn to translate the intuition we have about parents and families into words and records to help health and welfare workers understand and foster the delicate relationships which grow and develop between parents and young children. Unobtrusive observation, sensitive understanding, and practical encouragement and help is needed. The worker should be sympathetic to the mother's enhanced emotions and feelings, positive in his or her remarks about the infant, and should remain outside the mother–baby unit, promoting and encouraging the mother's developing skills and adaption to her child."

Although developmental screening was only the subject of two papers, it led to a very wide exchange of views. Its possible application in the context of MCH activities within the basic health services of developing countries was reviewed by R. RANSOME-KUTI (Basic Health Services Scheme, Lagos, Nigeria), who said they had to rely in Nigeria on the use of local personnel for screening, which meant they had to be cautious in the use of elaborate technology. The means used must be easily understood and interpreted as well as simple to transport and set up in rural areas. For example, they used weighing scales which were not heavy, and they detected anemia by using a simple colormeter. Sickle cell anemia was screened by the presentation of symptoms. They did not screen for G-6-PD deficiency because usually those infants would show signs of jaundice during the first week of life. In this case they were automatically tested to see if they had the deficiency.

ANNETTE A. YAKER (National Institute of Public Health, Algiers, Algeria) raised two other points with regard to developmental screening in the developing countries. First, the importance and need for genetic counseling in countries and regions where there is a high rate of marriages among close relatives (consanguinity); second, the danger of training personnel to carry out developmental assessment unless the local health system can provide immediate specialized care and treatment, immediate psychological support and educational help, and adequate follow-up services.

The dynamics of developmental assessment were stressed by several other speakers, leading to the need for complete and repeated examinations to assess both the harmony and the progress of the developmental process.

It was generally agreed that the word "assessment" was more meaningful than "screening", which still had a negative, disease-oriented connotation, with a yes or no response.

In conclusion, the Coordinator emphasized the role of parents not only as passive, information sources but as active observers of the child's development. The future of screening was defined as trying to identify causative factors and to determine at risk individuals or groups through the use of sound and feasible indicators. Screening should be integrated into the normal range of health services, and also extend its field toward the positive aspect of the assessment of the normal growth and development of children.

C. Brajovic (Department of Psychology, University of Belgrade, Yugoslavia): "The future of the deaf child."

CH. Cassinos *et al.* (University Pediatric Clinic, Aghia Sophia Hospital, Athens, Greece): "Blood pressure levels in normal Greek children and adolescents," and "The problem of obesity in Greece."

Bernard E. Cohen (Chaim Sheba Medical Center, Savyon, Israel): "Newborn screening in Israel."

Christine Cooper (Department of Child Health, University of Newcastle upon Tyne, UK): "Assessing parentship skills in early childhood."

E. E. Darillis (University Pediatric Clinic, Aghia Sophia Hospital, Athens, Greece): "Taux de plomb aux enfants du Nord Grèce et relation avec l'environnement."

Edith H. Grotberg (Department of Health, Education, and Welfare, Washington DC, USA): "Medical screening versus developmental assessment."

J. X. Koliopoulos (National Ophthalmic Center, Athens, Greece): "Better vision—better life."

Carol Miller (Central School of Speech and Drama, London, UK): "Screening for speech and language problems."

Gregory Stores (Park Hospital for Children, Oxford, UK): "The identification of children with epilepsy at special risk of educational and other environmental problems."

NEW ILLNESSES

Coordinator: C. Eric Stroud

King's College Hospital Medical School, University of London, UK

THE GROUP decided that the papers that had been prepared did not represent the scope of the subject of the session, so they were presented very briefly, leaving more time for discussion.

The group further decided that the title "New Illnesses" was too restrictive, because while some diseases, such as those due to radiation, pollution, social environment, commercial activity, and genetic diseases, as well as iatrogenic disease, were not new, they were nevertheless diseases in which new influences created by the modern world have led to an alteration in their prevalence, incidence, and modes of presentation, as well as an alteration in the types of research, identification, therapy, and prevention which may be required.

After long discussion the following categories were agreed as being the main headings under which the subject should be discussed.

RADIATION

The major danger to children appears to come from industrial radiation, e.g. atomic power stations, either by explosion or by leakage, with chronic radiation exposure. Some such disaster seems almost inevitable, and it is hoped that adequate monitoring is taking place. Concern was also expressed about the cumulative effects of radiation over generations, the dangers of which may not be appreciated at present because of inadequate knowledge. Another source of danger, perhaps minor, is medical radiation, the effects of which are appreciated by radiologists but perhaps not by generalists.

IATROGENIC DISEASES

A number of groups were defined under this heading:

1. *Polypharmacy and new drugs.* Of special concern are the use of drugs in early pregnancy. Tests on animal models do not represent complete protection.

2. *Congenital abnormalities.* Increasing therapeutic success on the part of doctors has led to children surviving with abnormalities which hitherto were fatal. The long term survival of these children places a firm responsibility on pediatricians to monitor their progress, identify any abnormality, and ensure that the child's true potential is achieved. Of special importance are the newborn babies successfully treated in neonatal units. Here care should be taken not to overlook the damage which can be caused to them by interference with the process of mothering. In the Western world

403

many abnormal deliveries or ill neonates can be predicted before labor by history taking or by investigation and measurement. No mother should be separated from her baby, and it is to be hoped that all mothers with a risk of giving birth to a baby requiring intensive care will be delivered in a unit with full intensive care facilities on site.

Some genetically determined diseases, previously almost intractable in the homozygous state, are now responding to treatment, and consideration regarding medical care and genetic counseling will have to be given to parents in cases such as thalassaemia, sickle cell anemia, etc.

3. *Long term technical procedures*. Probably the largest group of iatrogenic diseases is that covered by necessary therapeutic and investigational attention paid by doctors to mothers and children. A film shown by GINETTE RAIMBAULT (Hôpital des Enfants Malades, Paris, France) was extremely impressive in demonstrating the potential for dangerous psychological consequences of long term technical procedures. The babies were obviously disturbed by the interference with their ability to communicate well or react to their environment. It was a superb illustration of the way in which modern medical technology may create new psychological and organic illnesses in children who of necessity have to receive "high technology care." From this film and subsequent discussion, a certain number of irrefutable points emerged:

— Parents must understand the need for and the nature of the therapeutic and investigative procedures.
— Research is needed (along the lines of the work done by DR. RAIMBAULT and PROF. BERRY BRAZELTON) into the effects on small children of admission to hospital investigation and therapy.
— The neonatal period is an exceptionally sensitive time, and no mother should be separated from her baby then, unless there is an imperative clinical reason.
— At risk pregnancies should, if possible, be identified before delivery and special arrangements made for them.

DISEASES INDUCED BY COMMERCIAL AND INDUSTRIAL PROCESSES

Radiation and pollution (e.g. lead, mercury) are obvious dangers. But of more immediate concern is the organic chemical industry, and especially such products as insecticides which cannot be reliably declared safe by pre-marketing trials. Their effect on pregnant women should be closely studied.

For the future, the biggest commercial danger in a worldwide sense is the processing and marketing of cows' milk as a replacement food for breast milk. The so-called "new" milks have been modified to remove certain dangers (e.g. hypernatraemia), and this may lead to a false impression of safety. The spread of bottle feeding in Western society can lead to its enhanced status in the developing countries. This alone is a strong indication for all developed countries to have programs in obstetric, pediatric, and community medicine for the encouragement of breast feeding.

Many investigations have shown increased admissions to hospitals, increased use of drugs, and increased death rates amongst bottle-fed babies, so that the cost to the community of bottle feeding is more than the cost of the purchase (or importation) of the milk.

A recent study by L. and D. GRECO (Faculty of Medicine, University of Naples, Italy) was cited: "In less than 15 years breast-feeding practices have fallen among the Naples population from almost the totality of children to a small minority. This sudden and dramatic interruption of one of the oldest forms of human behavior has led to new morbidity patterns. In 1974 all newborn children were contacted in two typical areas (over 400 infants) and were followed up by regular visits until 1977 (almost three visits a year per child). The results revealed that only 12–14% of the babies were breast fed for three months, and less than 2% were breast fed at six months. Incidence of diseases—gastroenteritis, respiratory diseases, and anemia—were two to three times higher in bottle- and mixed-fed babies than in those who were breast fed for two months. The percentage of better-educated mothers who breast fed was higher, and the fall off in breast feeding less than among the socially deprived." These findings were corroborated by similar studies carried out in England by H. B. VALMAN (Northwich Park Hospital, Harrow, UK).

A move to bottle feeding in the developing countries could have disastrous results. Apart from the costs to poor countries and the deaths of children from malnutrition and gastroenteritis, there may be possible immunological and evolutionary effects. The modification of cows' milk has not made it "safe" in the Western world, because whatever modification is attempted the protein and fat are of necessity of nonhuman origin. Cows' milk feeding has been shown to be related to certain diseases such as eczema, asthma, and allergies, but we must not overlook the possible dangers to our evolution as a species from feeding our own young on the milk of a different species, which has been developed over hundreds of thousands of years as a result of evolutionary forces on a different animal.

Pollution by heavy metals (lead, mercury, etc.) is a known danger, but of particular concern is the growth of the organic chemical industry whose products cannot efficiently be tested against a human population of children. These dangers are well illustrated by the Dioxine tragedy in north Italy but they may not always be seen so dramatically, particularly as regards effects on the fetus. This danger threatens to spread, along with industry, to developing countries, whose population, being less well informed, may welcome industrial development without adequate safeguards.

EFFECTS OF THE NEW SOCIAL ENVIRONMENT

The development of new types of cities with large inner-city areas and new methods of transport has given rise to many new disease situations. In particular, as pointed out by PROFESSOR GROSSMAN (School of Medicine, University of Southern California, Los Angeles, CA, USA), motor-car accidents account for an enormous number of deaths and handicaps in childhood, yet there is little activity on the part of most countries to control this epidemic. Many palliative steps will have to be taken before prevention becomes effective; for instance, in Canada the death rate amongst adolescents from motor-cycle accidents alone is greater than the death rate among adolescents from all causes in Great Britain. In Great Britain the wearing of crash helmets is compulsory.

Any condition which can be shown to prevent a child from developing the potential with which he was endowed at conception should be considered as a disease. It is now abundantly clear that in developed and developing countries the damaging effects of inner city living need elucidation. Particular attention should also be paid to education and employment.

A disease which seems to be inadequately monitored is nonaccidental injury in childhood (or child abuse). So much is now known about the epidemiology in terms of etiology and diagnosis that more attention should now be paid to research and services for prevention by timely intervention. The "at risk" nature of families in this connection is known for certain cultural groups, yet no attempt is made for early identification of "at risk" situations and for provision of appropriate preventive services.

AT RISK INFANTS

In particular, attempts must be made to define and control those aspects of medical care which are known to be etiological. The early minutes, days, and weeks of life are therefore the time when the creation of good mother–father–child relationships must be encouraged and not damaged. This will certainly require research and new designs for action, not only individual actions on the part of medical and social professionals, but also alteration of the structure of health services, to ensure the existence of truly caring services rather than the automatism which is so widespread today. Doctors will certainly have to alter their roles somewhat. Pediatricians in the Western world, faced with less organic disease, will have the time to learn about and therefore support good parenting practice. Obstetricians will have to become more aware of the sensitive nature of mother's feelings and anxieties, and to accept (in the developed countries) that complicated deliveries should not take place in units without adequate facilities to give modern intensive neonatal care in a compassionate environment.

In the developing countries, the work of DR. J. CRAVIOTO must be applied, so that not only are mothers well nourished in pregnancy but they are also helped to communicate with their children in a manner to facilitate normal child development and to ensure the proper nutrition of the child.

No doubt new discoveries in Western world medicine will produce enormous changes in identifying diseases, and particularly in identifying individuals who are likely to develop diseases, some of which may be preventable by manipulation of the environment. Thus development of the knowledge of HLA genes will lead to more successful development of transplantation medicine: and control of genetic disease will lead to the need for developing counseling services. Most important, however, is the need to improve the identification of "at risk" groups in society. Modern medical and social care and surveillance are expensive, and growing more so. The hope was therefore expressed that there would be a wide acceptance of the view that it is part of the duty of medical and social workers—with the help of the government—to identify "at risk" groups and to make certain that help is received by them in a useful manner. At the same time, of course, proper health services must be available for all.

To achieve these goals it is essential to identify priorities to make sure that the order of priorities is determined by the needs of the local population; not by the degree of interest or technical challenge it represents to doctors and other professionals. The efficiency of services should always be monitored. For example, it should be obligatory for perinatal mortality statistics to be published every year by any service or unit which provides facilities for childbirth.

In conclusion, the group regarded intellectual and alimentary malnutrition as the major problems facing children in the modern world, and the major need was to identify the "at risk" situations and the "at risk" individuals and groups and to make sure that they are given help.

LIST OF PAPERS PRESENTED

G. N. CHRISTODOULOU, A. GARGOULAS, A. PAPALOUKAS and A. MARINOPOULOS (Department of Psychiatry, University of Athens, Greece): "Psychosocial factors in children's primary peptic ulcers."

L. and D. GRECO (Faculty of Medicine, University of Naples, Italy): "Breast feeding and morbidity in an urban community of southern Italy."

A. M. GROSSMAN (School of Medicine, University of Southern California, Los Angeles, CA, USA): "Mobilopathy: the obscure plague of the twentieth century."

A. G. KAFATOS et al. (Department of Epidemiology and Public Health, University of Miami, FA, USA): "Risk factor status of myocardial infarction (MI) and nonMI subjects and their children in Greece."

GINETTE RAIMBAULT (Hôpital des Enfants Malades, Paris, France): "Les enfants en réanimation digestif."

MICHAEL SALMON (Stoke Mandeville Hospital, Aylesbury, Bucks., UK): "Lesions of the anterior hypothalamus and their possible role in the catabolism of lipids."

H. B. VALMAN, E. C. COLES and S. COTTER (Northwich Park Hospital, Harrow, UK): "Incidence of breast feeding in Harrow in 1977."

5

The Child and the Environment

THE MICRO- AND MESO-ENVIRONMENT
OF THE CHILD

THE MINI- AND MICRO-ENVIRONMENT
OF THE CHILD

R. S. LOURIE

School of Medicine, George Washington University, Washington DC, USA

THE LARGE complex of sciences concerned with both the child and the environment, are preparing, usually separately, for the future, but, as we shall see, they should be inevitably interlocked. When Churchill said "Man shapes the environment and then the environment shapes man" he was not thinking of children. Children do not shape their environments. It is therefore heartening to find new branches of the environmental sciences such as environmental psychology, environmental design, and socioenvironmental studies among many others becoming concerned with child development. Ekistics, the science of human settlements, born here in Athens, pulls these all together. It starts with man, including the beginnings of man in his earliest development. It then deals with the interface of the human with society, nature, shells (or the home of man), and the networks involved in man's survival and functioning. How these components relate to the child was conceptualized by Constantinos Doxiadis, the founder of ekistics, in a landmark book titled *Anthropopolis: The City for Human Development*.[1]

The goal of pediatrics, of child development and all their related sciences, is to have a live child functioning as well as possible. Then the environmental forces take over to fit "the father of the man," the child, to be part of the culture in which we will live. As we look to the child in the world of tomorrow, we see that cultures all over the world are changing rapidly. To put the role and importance of the environment in relation to the child in this perspective, when humans or anthropos (as the Greeks called them to bypass calling them men) first appeared on this earth in the present form, it was the result of change. To summarize this we can no longer ask Which came first, the chicken or the egg? It had to be the egg because the chicken cannot change while the egg can, particularly in its earliest phases of development. But through natural selection the changes, the mutations created by "chance or necessity,"[2] which allowed anthropos to survive, progress to an advanced condition and then become perpetuated, took literally millions of years. In turn anthropos had produced changes in the earth and the environment, which are taking place so rapidly that they are challenging us as responsible humans to deal with them. However, the basic structure of the human cannot change as fast. Rapid physical adaptions cannot be expected if we look at the history of how many millennia were necessary to evolve appropriate changes in body structure. For example, the human male evolved into a usually larger, stronger, and more active person than the female in order to be the hunter and the fighter, the provider, and the protector. Technology and industrialization are changing the needs for those male roles in many parts of the world, but male structure can be expected to take at least thousands of years to change.

413

We see the impact of environmental changes on the human's ability to function most dramatically in the developing countries. In Africa many men from the bush villages go to work in the cities or the mines, and the women grow the food and protect as well as raise the children alone. At the same time, from biblical reports onward, and currently on an accelerated rate in the industrial parts of the world, men have taken a more active part in bringing up the children. Sexual patterns are changing over the world. The young African, brought up with sexual freedom as normal, when he is exposed to Western religions, finds sex is sinful outside of marriage. At the same time Western youth are moving to sexual freedom with changes in sex role expectations.

NATURE

As we look ahead to the world of tomorrow we see technologies accelerating the changing of not only roles but also of many other expectations. Let us look at these changes in the context of the child and the mini- and micro-environment and also look at these in terms of the five ekistic elements (nature, anthropos, society, shells, networks). Starting with nature: as nature becomes better controlled and less harsh, anthropos has to spend less energy in providing for the survival of its young. As disease is conquered and more children who would have died under earlier conditions are kept alive, there is less need to have large families to ensure that there will be enough manpower to take care of the parents and to carry on the life of the state. This is the long range hope of solving the threatening population explosion. These are changes that take place more rapidly in the developed countries, and inevitably and, unfortunately much more slowly and to different degrees, in the slower developing parts of the world. In terms of the environmental factors involving the process of conquering nature, the first mini-environment of the child is the womb. Here the old concept of the womb providing the most protected and safest mini-environment available in the human life cycle has been considerably modified with the increasing body of information about mutations, genetic distortions, metabolic, nutritional, and toxic conditions, etc. Increasingly ingenious techniques are being explored which make possible the diagnosis and treatment of these first mini-environmental hazards. These phenomena plus Liley's delightful review of "The foetus as a personality,"[3] reinforces the concept that, like the ancient Chinese, we must view the baby as nine months old at birth.

When we look back at the old folklore and mythology about the many experiences of the pregnant woman that influence what happens to the unborn baby in its first mini-environment, we realize a cyclic phenomenon in human patterns of thinking. Yesterday's superstition is today's science, and today's science becomes tomorrow's superstition. This latter is illustrated by what has happened as a result of new findings about the mini-environment of the infant after it is born. When René Spitz after the Second World War reported on the destructive effect on infant development of sterile, impersonal, depriving mini-environments for babies in institutions,[4] a shock wave hit the social services in the United States. Almost all the states passed laws forbidding babies to be brought up in institutions. Thus science created the myth that all institutions were detrimental to infants and young children. It is only in the last

10–15 years that properly staffed and programmed group care settings for infants have been found to be much better than inadequate foster homes.

In learning how to pervert one of nature's laws, the survival of the fittest, we find another cyclic pattern that has involved the mini-environment of the newborn infant. Our eagerness to apply new knowledge and techniques can lead to excessive zeal in applying it with a disregard of what we know about developmental needs of infants. The new subspeciality of neonatology has developed mini-environments for newborns which can keep those alive who used to die, such as the very premature, birth injured, metabolically deficient, congenitally handicapped, etc. The talented and valiant techniques to keep such babies alive often center around increasingly complex mini-environments: incubators. Caryl Larue Jones, my human factor engineering colleague at the NIMH, has demonstrated that while the baby is kept alive and overcoming handicaps, new mini-environmental hazards are being introduced which can impede other developmental areas As she describes it:[5]

"The intent of an incubator or infant oxygen tent is to provide oxygen, but the baby is not only deprived of essential mothering, he is subjected to destructive levels of noise for weeks or months: 70 or 80 decibels sound pressure level at 125 Hz; the sound of an overhead jet aircraft, with improved models no less than 48 decibels. It is sufficient to place the baby at risk for later hearing impairments. The deprivations to other senses and to human contact place the infant at risk in other areas of development."

Modern medical technology has created the sterile newborn nursery in the obstetrical units of modern hospitals. These have also saved babies' lives but at the cost of providing a mini-environment which is delaying two of the first steps in development. The separation from the mother delays bonding which Kennell and Klaus[6] have demonstrated should begin by direct mother–newborn physical contact immediately after birth. The establishment of biorhythms is delayed.

In intensive care units as well as newborn nurseries, the infants need to be under constant surveillance. The overhead fluorescent lights in these units are always on with no variation day or night. Infants need alternating cycles of lightness/or darkness to aid in their development, to help regularize the baby's biorhythms. Harvard pediatrician T. Berry Brazelton, in working with neonates who did not gain weight, had gowns placed over their cribs at night to provide some degree of darkness, and the babies began to gain weight.

A word here about a very different aspect of nature in the meso-environment of the child as it reaches stages in which it begins to reach outside of its family. The child should have the opportunity to know what the earth is like and capable of. When Adam and Eve left the Garden of Eden and began the science of agriculture, I am sure that their children, Seth, Abel, and Cain, came to know how to live by learning from and controlling nature. We lose this opportunity for children to get to know nature on these terms by the current way in which we structure our cities. In this context, the ekistics approach is to make green areas within walking distance of all homes, and to make these green areas continuous throughout the city.

NETWORKS

Turning to networks: in the child's mini-environment these are chiefly concerning the patterns of relationships within its own family and extended family, and they overlap with our later considerations about societal influences. However, networks such as transport and energy networks make survival and pleasurable needs more available in the developed countries. In the meso-environment technological advances in transportation systems and communication networks have impinged on the world of the developing child. Automobile accidents involving children increase as our cities become clogged with cars. Pollution from car exhaust is suspected of contributing to lead poisoning. In the world of tomorrow can we look again at putting our major thoroughfares underground and plan for safe traffic free streets in residential areas as has been suggested in the *City for Human Development*?[1] As radio and television become part of the young child's experience they also invade the mini-environment.

SOCIETY

When we look at the child in relation to the ekistic element, society, the developmental goal is to help a small, helpless, mindless being to become a member of the society with the society's value systems, patterns of survival, and "civilizing" of impulses necessary for belonging to it. The process begins in the most intimate environment and is most apparent in those societies in which survival needs are at a premium. For example, the rural African infant carried on its mother's or sister's back or on a crib board becomes part of all that goes on in the mini- and meso-environment. Talking in global terms, this infant is imprinted in the tasks that lead to enhancement of survival intelligence and expectations. The more protected middle class baby, if allowed to explore its earliest environment first hand, is encouraged to develop with an emphasis on a very different level of learning, such as imagination, curiosity, the encouragement of questions, etc., i.e., with a greater premium on cognitive development and the value of formal learning to build up a capacity to deal with a more complex world.

Every society takes ultimate responsibility for the environment for the development and care of the child but each in its own way. There are wide differences between those in which the child becomes the responsibility of every member of the community and those which take responsibility for the child only when the parents fail to. However, when the younger child, usually by age six, is ready to move outside the family and become a member of its peer group and neighborhood in the meso-environment, society takes the responsibility almost universally to provide the setting in which the peer groups form, the boys with the boys and the girls with the girls. Here there is an explosion of study and planning, involving environmental psychologists, environmental designers, educators, architects and social and behavioral scientists, and more lately pediatricians, as to the best form this first "human crucible" (Jones) should take. How space is used to enhance play (better called the work of children in solving problems), formal learning and physical development, begins to appear in the literature of all these disciplines. Examples are the Wittmans' study of the "Psychosocial Use of Space"[7] and Proshansky, Ittleson and Rivlin's books, *Environmental Psychology: Man and his Physical Setting*[8] and *Environment and Behavior*[9]. These meso-environments (which incidently are reaching younger and younger children as day care programs for preschoolers, toddlers, and even infants proliferate) are the settings in which society indoctrinates young children with society's value systems.

In the world of today, particularly in the Western world, we seem to have lost one of society's most significant values in the education of our children, the importance of the work ethic as a foundation stone of societal progress. As civilizations advance the child becomes less and less an integral part of the family's work. School and play increasingly becomes the child's work when it enters the meso-environment. Here again a significant societal advance has closed out what was valuable when child labor laws were passed because children were exploited and their development stunted. The end result is a significant segment of our young who grow up only too often seeing "labor" as something to be avoided, to be done for them and certainly not to be enjoyed when they become citizens of the macro-environment or the larger community. There is a movement in our intellectual youth who seek the fundamental values of work they missed as children in which they go to work with their hands in the labor market before or after they finish college. In the world of tomorrow as the child emerges into the meso-environment we should plan to make paid, limited work part of the responsibility for its own immediate surroundings an integral part of the child's expectations of what the world outside the mini-environment of the family requires.

SHELLS

When we consider the shells, or the house, as the major mini-environment in which the child develops, here, just as all the ekistic components overlap with each other, there is considerable overlapping between society and shells. As the homes of man have become more complex and crowded in our cities, society has become concerned with their impact on human health and safety. Thus a variety of public health and sanitary codes, building codes, life safety codes, and ordinances and regulations and guidelines and policy manuals have proliferated. In the process the developmental needs of the child tend to be forgotten. Prime examples are the highrise apartment houses. For the young child who is able to walk, particularly as a toddler and preschooler, it becomes important to explore and learn from the meso-environment outside its own family's rooms. At the same time the child is in a stage in which it is concerned with fears of separation or loss of significant, close people, or with fears about bodily harm. Studies have shown that, when its mother is above the second story of the house, the child cannot have good eye contact with her. Above the fourth floor it is a great strain to make any contact. It is reported that tensions in mothers increase as they live higher above the ground, but there also is a hazard in resolution of these fears in the child. In the infamous Pruitt–Igoe highrise housing project in St. Louis it was reported that the urine smell and blood stains in the elevators came mostly from young children who could not make it to their home toilets in time or to their source of bandages. We only too often find a lack of confidence in children's body integrity and controls when they grow up under such conditions.

In the world of tomorrow we need to find how to build the house of man to provide the mini-environment of the child to enhance optimal development. Survival tasks and intelligence are learned early in the one room for the family in the primitive village and in the favellos, barrios, and shanty towns which grow on the edge of the cities. To optimize intellectual development, the lessons learned about folkways and in the kitchen should be put together with what we know about appropriately stimulating the child who grows up in the city.

ANTHROPOS

In consideration of the final ekistic element, anthropos, it is evident that we have been talking in all these examples about man's earliest development in relation to all the other elements involving the environment in which anthropos functions. What is missing in terms of our mission in this survey is the collaboration between those of us who plan, administer, and build the environment and those of us who are concerned with the proper development of the child who we are preparing to take over the world from us.

Those of us in the health, behavioral, and social sciences have a responsibility to share with the environmental scientists, and especially with the ekisticians, what we know about the child's development, particularly its needs, as the basis for planning the environment of tomorrow. For example, among the tasks of normal personality development which could challenge the planners are:

(1) to integrate the senses which are not synthesized at birth so that the individual can know and deal with the environment;
(2) to be able to relate, to know how to be close to and part of another person;
(3) to have the proper physical equipment to thrive, function in, and participate in the environment and society;
(4) to learn how to regulate and control innate feelings, needs, and urges;
(5) to learn what is reality and how to deal with it;
(6) to develop the capacity to think, acquire knowledge, remember, and exercise curiosity and imagination to the child's normal capacity;
(7) to develop useful and functioning abilities to cope and for mastery;
(8) to have the help in dealing appropriately with the expected anxieties and fears which are part of growing up.

In the world of tomorrow—as cultures and societies become more complex with the aid of new technology, as the fantasies of today about the future become facts, as star wars will take place in space instead of on earth—if we are to prevent human wastage in development, we must plan together with the creators of the environment. In this we must think always about where the human beginnings are, above all in the earliest years of life. But in this process let us not forget the lessons of yesterday. If we do, in the words of Cassius: "The fault, dear Brutus, is not in our stars, but in ourselves, that we are underlings."

REFERENCES

1. C. A. DOXIADIS, *Anthropopolis: The City for Human Development*. Norton, New York, 1974.
2. J. MONOD, *Chance and Necessity*, Random House, New York, 1972.
3. A. W. LILEY, The foetus as a personality, *Aust. NZ J. of Psychiatry* **6** 99 (1972).

4. R. SPITZ, Hospitalism: an inquiry into the genesis of psychiatric conditions in early childhood, *Psychoanalytic Study of the Child* **1** 53 (1945).
5. C. L. JONES, Animate/inanimate design relationships in infant factor engineering, *Proceedings of the Human Factor Society, San Francisco, California, 1977,* pp. 472–476.
6. M. H. KLAUS and J. H. KENNELL, *Maternal-infant bonding,* Mosby, St. Louis, 1976.
7. M. WITTMAN and F. D. WITTMANN, the psychosocial use of space: crucial issues in physical environment, social space, and mental health as part of planning for integrated human services, paper presented at the Annual American Orthopsychiatric Association, New York, NY, April 14, 1977.
8. H. M. PROSHANSKY, W. H. ITTLESON and L. G. RIVLIN (Eds.), *Environmental Psychology: Man and His Physical Setting,* Holt, Rinehart & Winston, New York, 1970.
9. W. H. ITTLESON, H. M. PROSHANSKY, L. G. RIVLIN and G. H. WINKEL, *An Introduction to Environmental Psychology,* Holt, Rinehart & Winston, New York, 1974.

THE CHILD AND CHANGING
HUMAN SETTLEMENTS

EARL FINBAR MURPHY

College of Law, Ohio State University, OH, USA

MANY of us in the modern city see ourselves as victims of historical accident. We may be victims but we are not victims of any accident.

At the beginning of the present century the novelist of sciences, H. G. Wells, was asked by a magazine to anticipate the future, and he did so in a series of articles. I will only focus on his comments relating to the city of the future, that is the city we live in today.

Wells pointed out that the city he lived in had very serious problems. It was an impacted city, overly concentrated, because it was dependent upon direct energy sources. He said that the problems of that city would be solved by two innovations: the provision of electricity in energy cascades, and the extensive use of the automobile. Those two technical developments would enable the city to spread out into the country and to realize the dream of St. Thomas Moore in his *Utopia*. All of humanity would live in the city, and at the same time would live in a green countryside. He went on to say that the families would bring with them to the country all the amenities of the city. Wells already knew of the film and the phonograph, but he said there would be new inventions that would make images and sounds available in the home which previously could only be seen or heard in the threatre or concert hall.

About the time of the First World War, we find American writers and theorists also talking about the dispersed city as the ideal of the future. Many architects and planners, such as Stanley McMichael in Cleveland, published books of ideal city plans. As we page through these books we see that their sketches foreshadow many of our problems today. We can see the source of urban sprawl and every indication that the center of the city had to be emptied out as the countryside filled up.

In 1933 the American government changed very radically, and a great many young people went to the national capital. One thing we know about young people is that they do everything they can to realize the dreams of their old professors. This is exactly what these young people did. They organized a series of housing and home finance agencies which proceeded to make it possible for the middle class in America to realize a version of the Garden City dreams of Ebenezer Howard and to live in suburban detached villas. Certainly these people had no intention of destroying the old center city, but that was to be an indirect consequence of their action.

After the Second World War, people in the United States moved to the suburbs in large numbers as the result of the federal home financing programs and the federally funded highway and municipal infrastructure programs. The centers of the cities were left with the elderly, the poor, the isolated, and the disadvantaged young.

America slid into what Margaret Mead called "a pit of deterioration, corruption, apathy, indifference, and outright brutality toward the weak, the sick, the young, and the poor."

The end result of this situation can be seen in a publication of the US Chamber of Commerce. It argues that the best national policy toward the city would be to allow its obsolescence and further deterioration to continue until the blank rottonness of the central city and the growth of the suburbs produce a cross-point on some entrepreneurial chart. At this moment, they say, speculating investors will start reassembling vacant center city blocks for reinvestment purposes. Perhaps this is right. But meanwhile we have to admit that a heavy burden will be imposed on those who live in the rotting and segregated city.

C. A. Doxiadis used to say that one of the chief crimes of planners of the modern city was that they plan as though they had declared war upon the vulnerable: the children, the elderly, the handicapped. Of course the most significant of these victims are the children, because they are the bearers of the future, and to declare war upon children is to declare war upon our future. C. Northcote Parkinson has said that the city as a center of human activity requires affection. How long has it been since Americans felt affection for their city? The course of the modern segregated American city makes affection very hard to form, and harder still to maintain.

Segregation in the United States has grown far beyond the conditions of race and income. We now have ordinances being passed forbidding the presence of children in entire towns: these are the "golden age" communities. They contain the people whom Margaret Mead has called the traitors to the role of grandparents. Will these laws be constitutional, upheld, and enforced? I think not. But the fact that they are wanted is a very serious social matter.

Planning for integration is what we need, and this means the physical rearrangement of the city: the physical rearrangement of the networks, of the shells, of the resources of the city. We cannot thrust this responsibility upon the schools or upon any other single institution. We are where we are not by accident but as a result of intent and of planning. If we are to change the situation we too must plan, we too must integrate the city and redirect growth toward the center.

But why should this be to the benefit of those of us adults who live in the pleasantly isolated "Alsatias" of suburbia? I assert that it is because in the future there can be no isolated "Alsatias." Everyone must flourish together or we shall find ourselves confronting a social turmoil to keep down those who have been isolated in the center city and to protect those who have gone out into the suburbs.

I suppose the most foolish statement that Henry Ford ever made—and he made several—was: "We shall avoid the problems of the city by leaving it." We have not avoided the problems of the city but, like carriers of plague, we have spread the problems across the green country environment.

A HOME FIT FOR A CHILD

P. PSOMOPOULOS

Athens Center of Ekistics, Athens, Greece

LISTENING to the various presentations and discussions in this conference on children and their relations to parents or family and their substitutes, education, health, nutrition, and many other important issues, one has the impression that a lot is being done for the children of the world. But very little that I have learned from the conference has dealt with the spatial dimensions of the problems discussed. And there is no doubt that all these phenomena have a spatial expression. For example, I heard about abuse of children and I do not know how much this abuse was related to bad spatial arrangements rather than to the innate hostility of the parents.

The majority of human settlements at present—old and new (particularly new), large and small, in rich or poor countries—are designed and built with complete disregard of children.

Whatever structure or space in human settlements that children are exposed to—even those specially addressed to them, such as schools, kindergartens, and playgrounds—are designed and built on the basis of the limited, and at times even harmful concepts, that grown-ups have about children's needs and aspirations.

Think for a moment of a city in which children have disappeared, of a city in which there are no human beings between 0 and 13 years of age. What changes in the physical structures do you think we would have to make in a human settlement without children? Primary schools? The buildings could as well be used for illiterate adults. Children's hospitals? We could use the pediatricians just as well for grown-ups, and the number of hospitals, their structure and distribution, would not change. Playgrounds? Adults would welcome such recreational areas. What else? The road system would not change because roads are not accessible to children anyway. The houses would not change because there is nothing scaled for children in present-day houses. No libraries, museums, shops, or parks would change because nothing is built, in physical terms, especially for children. Everything is for the adult. Children are regarded as appendages to adults (and to healthy adults in their physical prime).

How much of what we do today is not only not helping children but is actually prohibiting children from performing? Children have to be considered among the disabled members of society because they suffer the same frustrations that any other disabled person feels within the city. Think of buses and tell me how easy it is for a child to get on a bus. How different is this from the problem of a crippled person? Problems in settlements arise from two fundamental mistakes: The first is that we consider that anything that is technically feasible is socially desirable. And the second, that society feels that once it has told people what they should do it can ignore the real ability of people to grasp messages. Think of the green and red traffic lights. Everyone in the city (and every child) is supposed to know what these mean and to obey them even when they are absentminded. If you are absentminded you can be killed and nobody will pray for you. Think of the financial and economic aspects of such actions. I will give you another example. When you are in an airplane you see a light saying, "Please fasten your seat belt". Then somebody on the loudspeaker says, "Would you kindly fasten your seat belt." Then a young lady comes to you and says, "You didn't fasten your seat belt." Finally, the captain comes and says, "Please fasten it because we can't leave." There, because of economic interests, the staff is concerned to tell you three or four times in various ways because they understand that you may be reluctant to obey or you may be absentminded.

Turning now to the future, I have first to state that the needs for houses in the future will be enormous. We have to provide dwellings for an additional three billion people by the year 2000 and many existing houses are in terrible condition, so the total number to be built is really enormous. But statistics are misleading and there are such differences in the types of houses in various countries that I shall take another dimension which might give us a better estimate of the total need. I take the room. The room is a space where people can fulfill almost all their basic, biological, physiological needs, and many of their psychological needs. And the room is a space which is connected to the rest of the family or the building, and to the rest of the community. It cannot be independent.

Now what do I mean by room? I mean not only a space where you can have a bed and other furniture, but also a bathroom, a water closet, and storage space. Think of what we have in hotels. It is space for individuals. When we want to give comfort to people who can afford to pay, we give them this minimum space. The same should be considered as a minimum for everybody. It does not exist now but it will be one of the patterns of the future, and, as we want to develop the individuality of children and have them as independent as possible, we have to have a room for every child as well as for every adult.

How can we make these rooms adjusted to children on the basis of the different needs occurring at each age of the child? The rooms should be very flexible. Technology allows us to have mobile walls, so that there can be a connection with the parent's room and later a separation from the parent's room. The room should have the possibility to open to the environment in a way that can be appreciated by the child. What children do you know who live in a normal house and can see out of the window before the age of 6 or 7? The room should simultaneously afford maximum possible access and maximum possible privacy. It seems that 9 square meters for the room itself is the minimum (or 18 square meters including the other facilities) and probably the most luxurious rooms will be around 32 square meters (or 46 including the facilities).

At present we have four billion people and around two billion rooms because there is an average of two or three persons per room. Therefore, four to five billion rooms are needed by the end of the century. Of course, we cannot afford to develop all rooms of the type I described, but we can combine bathrooms, we can combine cooking areas, and we can combine other things. But the independent room should remain as our standard.

I am not going to talk about the wider community because I promised to stick to this specific scale. But let us think for a moment of a city in which all people would have a role in the decision-making process and thus the needs of all people would be more fully met. This model city would have no cars, no nasty people, and no other dangers around. It would be a city where steps and entryways and roads are designed to be used by all people: small people and old people and not only the strong, healthy adults. In such a city, children would be free to go wherever they liked and to explore life.

As they grow, children gradually expand their kinetic fields from the room to the house and then to broader areas. They seldom, however, go beyond the limits of a certain area, which is usually equivalent to a neighborhood. Study of this scale of human settlement is thus most relevant for defining and solving problems related to the child in the city. Some communities of this scale offer the child a great variety of experiences and a full spectrum of the facets of life; others are just dormitories where nothing happens.

A final word about architects. During this symposium, some people have said, "architects are doing horrible things." Architects are idiots and they do whatever clients ask them to do. If they did not, they would not survive long. Of course, the main role of the architect and planner is to find alternative solutions, to define the repercussions, and to tell the client—whether he is a private individual or a politician—what are the likely consequences of his decisions. Clearly that is something very few do. But the decisions rest with the client, so do not blame the architects. Blame yourselves for having done what you have done with the city.

THE HOME RANGE OF THE CHILD

Amos Rapoport

Department of Architecture, University of Wisconsin at Milwaukee, WI, USA

These comments attempt to relate the environment to human (and child) behavior, i.e. to relate behavior to spatial organization.

We have heard several times that education takes place in two places: the family (parents) and the school (professional). But this leaves out other important components, one of which is the built environment, which, in itself, is a teaching and enculturizing medium. It is in the environment that people learn behavior, roles, etc. Another teaching setting is other children in the environment and their activities. These are related, i.e. one needs a certain environment both for actual teaching and for children to move around in, to explore, to meet other children, and to experience the activities of other people.

The outcome is that the "home range" of children (i.e. the spatial extent of regular movement and activities) is of the utmost importance to the development of the child.

This home range varies with age, as C. A. Doxiadis has pointed out, starting with birth and expanding over the years to a variable maximum. Then, as old age draws on, shrinking back again. The home range varies with sex, with culture and class, etc., so that cities contain home ranges that vary from a few blocks to vast areas.

This raises the question as to whether children *per se* are a valid group, or does one not need to be more specific? (This is a general question: e.g., Are the elderly a valid group for planning, or the urban poor, etc.?) Children's ranges, the permitted or prohibited use of the environmental setting, vary, and we must conclude that we need to consider the problem cross-culturally.

The home range is also influenced by the character of the environment, and this is especially so for children. In other words the environment has a higher salience or criticality for the children.

The home range does not occur in a vacuum. It involves other people, other children, other purposes, and activity systems, which are all culturally specific. When we talk of activity systems it becomes difficult even to define "dwelling" because activities take place in different parts of the house settlement system.

Activity systems happen in settings which are appropriate, i.e., they fit specific activity patterns. For example, in Taiwan two subcultures can be found. In one the children play in the street with whatever children they meet there. In the other they only play with invited children in the house or courtyard. Another type of example occurs in Hong Kong and parts of the United States, where all adults in the environment (not just the parents) exercise control over the children. When the physical design inhibits this social control, delinquency can increase drastically. We can

therefore conclude that environments need to be supportive of the behavior conso-
nant of each local culture.

The house settlement system is an especially important environment for the child,
and even most adults spend the greater part of their lives in this localized setting
rather than in the metropolis or megalopolis *per se.* Such micro- and meso-environments are much more constant and invariant than the macro-environment. This
means that traditional settlements, which have changed little over the years, are very
relevant for learning what good micro-environments can be, and how well they can
work for special groups, including children. Mobility is easier in such setting, so that
the home range of the children can be larger and richer than in an amorphous city or
suburban areas. Traditional settlements also offer more perceptual complexity with
cognitive clarity, more multisensory stimuli, more exposure to activities, etc.

How do we judge if such traditional settlements really are better, and what does
this mean for the future?

The idea of constancy and change can be applied both to behavior and to future
environments. We have heard a good deal about change, unknown futures, the need
for flexibility, etc., and I have also stressed the need to look at things cross-culturally.
Yet, at the same time, we need to consider constancy and invariance, because in the
interplay between constancy and change a knowledge of the constants reduces the
area of variability.

To plan and design future environments, one must have some knowledge of
requirements, and here I may propose a somewhat heretical approach. In the world
of the future we need to consider not only the aspects of constancy in the physical
environment, but also in behavior patterns. Increasingly discussions arise about the
possible existence of behavioral baselines, related to the physical and social environments in which homo sapiens has evolved over millions of years. One cannot
assume that environmental change is something that is automatically appropriate
and acceptable. It may be maladaptive.

Suppose we took behavior and human needs as the datum to evaluate the validity
of physical environments? This would mean that we would have to use a behavioral
baseline and traditional life-styles as decisive for the design of the environment.

Too often it is taken as given that there will be great changes in the future to which
the people are supposed to adapt. It may be wiser to consider environments that can
be adapted to the constant needs of the people—including the special needs of the
children.

DISCUSSION

WILLIAM MICHELSON

Department of Sociology, University of Toronto, Canada

THE PREVIOUS speakers have raised your consciousness in admirable fashion. In my opinion they have made clear the importance of considering the person–environment relationship for those who are not allowed to help themselves (i.e. children). I hardly want to disagree, or diminish your raised consciousness.

But if we are looking to the future we must ask what we might do with our raised consciousness. I do not have a crystal ball, but I do suggest that if we do not attend to the discontinuities which have emerged to constitute the present, future troubles are predictable. We should now be preparing for a future of attentiveness to dilemmas now in view.

I am currently involved in an interdisciplinary, policy-oriented research and demonstration program at the University of Toronto (Canada) called "The Child in the City." This program has identified for its efforts five aspects of recent change in urban society with implications for children which require pursuit: (1) changes in physical environment (e.g. larger buildings and projects, new forms of development); (2) changes in the structure of families and child rearing; (3) increased cultural diversity; (4) changes in the passage between childhood and adulthood (particularly respecting the work and sex); and (5) the legal basis and structural interrelationships of the child, the family, and the state (including the delivery of social and health services). In work soon to be published, we have looked closely at the dynamics of the child in the city in all these areas.[1] Some of the points emerging from our work on the urban physical environment may usefully supplement the statements by the main speakers and help channel your raised consciousness.

1. Talking about environment for children is just as complex as talking about environment for adults. Children come in greatly differing stages of development, and the land use needs they have in the conduct of everyday life are highly diverse and at various levels of scale. The well-meaning adult who creates the world's best playground but only that is neglecting several developmental stages and many other everyday needs. And we mostly do not create the world's best of anything. Teenagers are consistently neglected in most places.

2. In order to create works in the environment which benefit children, we must have not only good intentions but an understanding of how goals are to be reached. There are roughly three kinds of ways environments impinge on children:

(a) Environments may occasionally have a direct impact (e.g. airborne pollution, traffic safety, etc.).

(b) More commonly, environments provide or restrict spatial opportunity for children to do something, provided motivation and other necessary functional and percentual aspects are suitable (e.g. playing, learning).

(c) Environments provide or restrict support for parents to act in desired ways with their children (e.g. socialization).

All three of these alternative causal models must not only be recognized, but also their substance must be paid more attention in design.

3. For example, when we think of parents' needs, such as for day care, we must recognize that day care has locational aspects which, if optimized, can give mother (or father) and children more time together with less stress.

4. With respect to spatial opportunity, we must recognize that we must go beyond simple functional possibility when we plan for children's activities and consider such vital dimensions as belonging, control, learning, competence and interest, as the basis for full use of and proprietory attitudes towards facilities.

5. Even when viewing the occasional direct effects of the environment, we must recognize that standards and tolerances for children vary from those of the adults for which most are set. For example, we looked at auto accident statistics and discovered, to our dismay, that in our area many more children are injured and killed by automobiles when they are passengers than when they are out in or near streets. But we do not typically equip our cars or enforce the use of seat belts designed to accommodate children.

6. But even when we do set standards with children in mind, they are largely viewed only on an aggregate basis. We do not monitor how our facilities are distributed with respect to where children of various ages live. We must become more aware of how far a child of a given age can be expected to travel for any given activity, the common barriers to activity, and the importance of suitable public transportation for older children. In Toronto, our "Child in the City Programme" is planning (in cooperation with geography teachers in the schools) for a systematic survey of land uses relevant to children, and access to them, to be analyzed in relation to the distribution of children. The work will be done by an army of our young people, themselves, as a self-help contribution to the International Year of the Child.

7. Finally, I must note that my colleagues in the World Society for Ekistics long since gave the world an exemplary form—the ekistics grid—for observing reality, which, after all, is interdisciplinary. The challenge that faces us now is in operationalizing that form so that we take action that recognizes complexity and applies the multiplicity of perspectives to solve concrete problems. But interdisciplinarity is a necessary though not a sufficient means to an end. To work it must be addressed to well-defined problems, and there must be commitments made to solving problems. If we wish the environmental problems of our children to be solved, we must engage the commitment of those that matter and then make available to them a sufficiently organized interdisciplinary machine which accepts and then works with the complexity of the real world situation facing us.

REFERENCES

1. WILLIAM MICHELSON, SAUL V. LEVINE, and ELLEN MICHELSON (Eds.), *The Child in the City: Today and Tomorrow,* University of Toronto (in press) and WILLIAM MICHELSON, SAUL V. LEVINE, ANNA-ROSE SPINA, and STAFF, *The Child in the City: Changes and Challenges,* University of Toronto Press (in press).

ROBERT A. ALDRICH

Medical Center, University of Colorado, Denver, CO, USA

I would like to touch on some aspects of the increase in worldwide radiation which is one of the things we can predict for the future and certainly an environmental problem.

First, there is the industry engaged in mining uranium. The miners themselves develop cancer of the lung in about 17–20 years. They are not children, but they bring the dust home with them, so their homes also become contaminated. There is a significant risk here.

Second, uranium tailings have been used in several places as building materials. One city, not far from where I live, has large areas that are radioactive. The cement blocks have uranium tailings in them, so have the driveways and the land fill. Very sophisticated studies are now being done to trace the occurrence of congenital malformations and other genetic damage to people living in these areas. This is an example of gross carelessness, to put it in the most polite way.

A third environmental contaminant are the nuclear power plants which are being built and operated in many parts of the world. There have been a great number of leaks and misfunctions, and these can be very dangerous because some of the plants release plutonium. My most recent information—10 days ago— is that so far no one has been able to demonstrate a safe threshold for plutonium: it is so toxic.

There are some other aspects of nuclear power plants that need to be considered. We have witnessed in more than one country the use of a "peaceful" nuclear power plant for the production of nuclear weapons. This is a relatively simple thing to do, and we can expect many other countries to have nuclear weapons produced from nuclear power plants.

Another issue concerns land use. If land is contaminated by a leak from a nuclear power plant, this land is probably not safe to use for very many years—maybe thousands of years. Recently, the US Supreme Court upheld an Act referring to the liability of nuclear plant operators for damage to land. The highest level of liability is around $580 million. One only has to look at quite a small city to realize that the actual value of the land that might be despoiled is far greater than that.

We witnessed recently the disintegration of a nuclear-powered satellite when it returned to earth. There is some hazard from that source. But more important are the enormous stockpiles of nuclear weapons which are held in many places in the world. If you ask schoolchildren what they think about these things, you will hear the word "fear." Many children have a good deal of anxiety and fear about nuclear weaponry.

Finally, there is the fact that nuclear power plants usually have an active life span of about 30 years. After this, they have to be closed down and guarded as a radioactive hulk for thousands of years before they lose their radioactivity. Trying to guard something with high security for just five years boggles the mind, so trying to guard something effectively for thousands of years does not look very easy.

My reason for presenting this unpleasant subject is that it is a reality; a reality that may significantly limit the areas of land that are habitable, to say nothing of the direct dangers of genetic damage to future generations. Are we really being good ancestors?

JOAQUIN CRAVIOTO
Instituto Nacional de Ciencias y Technología de la Salud
del Niño, Mexico City, Mexico

A child from the country came into the city, escaped from his elders, and went into the street. Across the road he saw another child and tried to go over to talk with him. But of course the rush of traffic made this impossible. So he called out: "How did you get across?" "I didn't. I was born on this side."

I think this summarizes one view of the city not built for children. As long as we regard children as pre-stages of adulthood, we will go on planning rooms and homes and communities and cities for adults only. What we need is to define the specific goals and objectives of each phase in the life of a child in positive terms. At present these are only defined in terms of the adult: for example, 75% of the brain weight of the adult is attained by the age of 2. By 3 the child should be able to run at one half the speed of a normal 40 year old adult. And so forth. We are always considering the child as a pre-adult, but we need to realize that children have rights in themselves and their own specific satisfactions and gratifications at each stage of their development.

I now turn to a different matter. Once upon a time pregnancy and motherhood were just parts of growing up. Fortunately both have now become acts of volition, but we still face another problem. This is that at the same time that a physical child is being developed in the uterus, another child of fantasy is being developed in the mind of the mother. This child had sex even before its conception. (Would you like your child to be a boy or a girl?) It has color of skin, hair, and eyes. It has intelligence and may even have a planned life, including the university it will attend. When the real infant is born the mother is confronted with two children—a physical baby and the child of her fantasy. The likeness or discordance between the two can be the start of an acceptance or rejection of the real child.

My final point is that we should not discard behavior or environments just because they are old. To give one example: the extended family is beginning to disappear in developing countries. But let us turn for a moment to some animal experiments. DR. FRANKOVA in Prague described the normal behavioral changes produced by malnutrition in rats—malnutrition right from the uterine stage of development. He then put a spinster rat (adult female) into the cage of one group of malnourished rats. As a result, 90% of the undesirable behavior produced by malnutrition was eliminated. In other words, the introduction of an aunt into the family meant more resources for more individual stimulation.

My plea, therefore, is that we should examine traditional behavior very closely, because by looking at the past we may find a better way to look into the future.

IMPLICATIONS FOR THE CHILD OF CHANGING CONDITIONS IN HUMAN SETTLEMENTS

Chairman:
FELIPE HERRARA
Programa de Estudos Conjuntos de Intergração de
America Latina, Rio de Janeiro, Brazil

CHAIRMAN'S INTRODUCTION

Felipe Herrera

I SHOULD like to make three points. First, human settlements are themselves a result of changing economic, social, political, technological, and cultural conditions. We can only understand the movement from tribal societies to village cultures and from village cultures to urban civilizations by studying these changes. It is changes in these conditions that have determined the present realities of metropolis and megalopolis, and that will determine the future ecumenopolis.

Second, human settlements have acquired their own life, with what we could call their own "internal laws." It is the interaction of human settlements with the changes in economic, social, political, technological, and cultural conditions that generates development. This is a genuine dialectic reality.

Third, The Child of Tomorrow is going to be much more affected than us by the present rapid changes in the environment and the new condition of human settlements. This is why it is a "must" in this symposium to consider the future of the environment.

THE CHILD IN A MOVING, QUARTERNARY-ORIENTED SOCIETY

JEAN GOTTMANN

School of Geography, University of Oxford, UK

HUMAN settlements are changing fast, and the lives of children in them will not acquire stable forms for a long period to come. It may be hazardous to forecast changes and characteristics in future settlements on the basis of presently observed trends; however, two modern trends are likely to continue developing in the foreseeable future and modifying the structure and modes of life in human settlements. These trends are, first, the more migratory character of urban life and work, and, second, the increasing evolution of the labour force towards the nonmanual, quarternary occupations. Both these trends require that children be prepared for the new type of settlements, and settlements could be designed with some of the child's need in mind. Indeed, the child is already affected, and will increasingly be affected in daily routine and problems, by these two trends.

The migratory character of modern society is well known and multifaceted. Human settlements are inhabited by rather unsettled populations. In the future a high percentage will often be moving their residence. More will make trips to work (daily or otherwise recurrent) involving substantial distances. Commuting already affects tens of millions; tomorrow it will likely be the way of life of hundreds of millions of workers: how much time will they spend with their children? The child is likely to be separated from his father, possibly from both parents, for long periods during the day, the week, perhaps the year. This, of course, used to be common in the past in the more aristocratic level of society. The future may well bring such new separation of the generations to much wider strata of mankind. Where, by whom, and how will these children be brought up?

Another aspect of migratory movement, which already affects many million families in relatively privileged sectors of society, is the oscillation between different places during the week and during the year, due to the spreading custom of spending recreational periods (weekends, longer holidays) away from the main residence. In the past, for millennia, most people were locked into one place most of their lives—the place where the work had to be done producing the goods or services expected from the worker. Now such obligations are restricted to a certain decreasing number of days and hours; a relatively liberated individual and his family can and do spend much of the rest of their time away from the place connected with work. Massive migrations during summer holidays are and will remain collective rituals. Children are increasingly spending their time in a multiplicity of environments, often away from the main home. They begin to realize the possibility and, indeed, the advantages of having a plurality of homes. If this is still the privilege of a minority it is an aspiration of the mass and will certainly become more common.

The child's education must be less rooted in belonging to one place, one settlement. If education continues to teach the necessity of belonging to one place, while real life develops on a network with much movement and transhumance, the child may be upset and unbalanced in later life. But education could adapt to the great revolution which has just begun, unlocking people from a single permanent location in space.

The spatial unsettlement of masses of people has also made long range migrations easier, in which a home is left to move to another home, sometimes far away. It is often mentioned that, on average one out of five American households moves its home every year. It is less often realized that the rapid rate of urbanization throughout the world also means that large populations move to new places, in urban areas, all the time. International and intercontinental migrations have taken on in the last 50 years unheard of dimensions. Although such trends will evolve in different and unequal ways in the various parts of the world, it can hardly be doubted that long range migrations will, on the whole, continue and probably increase the numbers of persons so displaced in the foreseeable future. The implications for the children will be a need to adapt to successive, different environments. This may be easier to achieve in terms of the physical components of the environment (such as living quarters, recreational facilities) than in terms of the human qualitative components: the schools, the companions at play, the community of friends of the same age. The human components may change even for children in families that do not move but stay in the same place because of the moving in and out of the local neighborhood and community by others. The fluidity of the environment deeply affects children; it often worries the parents more than the child, but the adults' attitude reacts also in the long run on the latter. It would seem that this sort of fluidity could be compensated for by family ties, a greater acceptance of a pluralistic world to live in from an early age, an education system adapted to the new environments. Such needs have seldom been realized, however, to this day. The theoretical approach endeavoring to isolate the child until a certain age in a set, rather enclosed, somewhat artificial environment prevails. Does it really give the child the hoped for stability, and a stronger base on which to operate later on in a fluid world?

In that future, more fluid and more diversified world, another unavoidable trend will be the gradual quantitative shift within the occupational structure of the workforce towards nonmanual, whitecollar occupations, towards work requiring greater and specialized skill especially in the quarternary sector of economic activity. Increasingly, instead of handling materials, people will operate complex and remote controls; direct other people; gather, distribute, process, and assess information. The amount of bits of information produced in all fields and to be taken into account for daily work in all specialities will continue to swell. Human responsibility and interpreting skill cannot be delegated to robots. Professional training skill cannot be delegated to robots. Professional training will increasingly prepare people to handle abstract materials with special methods and complex equipment.

The danger is to prepare children mainly to service robots and to live and work in a manner assuming a predominantly artificial and largely abstract environment. The previously mentioned migratory trend, liberating the individual in terms of his moorings in space and time, giving more options in the use of both time and space opportunities, may compensate the "abstractionist" trend in the nature of work. The new opportunity must, however, be used to such ends in deliberate and systematic fashion. Outdoor recreation, do-it-yourself games, and the like, are steps in a good direction but they are not sufficient. A deeper evolution of education and of the child's environment is clearly desirable to compensate more efficiently for the possible consequences of the abstract and theoretical tendencies recently noticeable in professional training.

Human settlements have been increasingly planned as zoned systems, separating residential sections, business districts, industrial zones, etc. This is probably an inheritance from the past which is not any longer necessary or helpful. A more diversified and liberal mix of land uses may better fit the needs of tomorrow and particularly prepare the child better to face the complexity, diversity and fluidity of the forthcoming structure of society, employment, and settlement. As the child spends the early part of life exploring a real world, new to him though made by adults for their own concerns (and for usually outdated purposes), he would hardly benefit by being given an image of a homogeneous, orderly, sedate, enclosed environment. It is our belief that the future requires a more open, diversified, moving picture to be impressed on the child. Is the task of education in forthcoming years to prepare for a more monistic or a more pluralistic world? Present indicators point to a good deal of pluralism. Learning to integrate a diversity of elements for one's own purposes will be needed by the child.

In this connection it may be essential to remember that modern schooling often emphasizes mathematical abstraction, the need for knowing methods rather than materials, the theories of the unity of fields, and of the universe rather than their diversity. Perhaps during the early age (before the methodology to be learned after the age of 15) we ought to compensate by an emphasis in the school, in the home, and on the street, on the variety of the world, of things and of options. Learning to choose becomes an increasingly essential ability as well as learning to coordinate.

In the concluding session of the Convention at the Massachusetts Institute of Technology in March 1976 that commemorated the centennial of the invention of the telephone, the novelist and physicist, Arthur Clarke, described the possibilities held in store for the 21st century by the promise of communications technology. Most individuals, he said, would then apparently be able to spend all their life in one place, in the same building if they so chose, just processing information provided to them from any other place. What a prospect of a perfectly settled life, in stabilized settlements, serviced mainly by robots. One could thus visualize a static unmovable future. But is this man's and woman's choice? Is this the aim to which mankind aspires? Whether you consider mankind's past, present, or the child's normal impulses to look beyond his immediate horizon, the answer is "No." The impulse is for dynamism and novelty.

C. A. Doxiadis, the Athens School he founded, and the World Society for Ekistics, have contributed a great deal to help society at large understand its own dynamism and the fruits thereof: the dynamic city. A basic implication calls for preparing the children for a world of change, dynamism, diversity, wide open choices. I trust that we realize this and that we can explain it to the parents and teachers whose responsibility it is to orient the children. This is a momentous and difficult task for which I have no simple set of instructions to offer. The only obvious conclusion seems an urgent need to revise and modify many of the established ideas on education and prepare for a pluralistic and open vision of the future.

SOME OBSERVATIONS FROM ASIA

RIAZ HASSAN

School of Social Sciences, Flinders University,
Bedford Park, South Australia

SOCIAL and cultural patterns play a determinate role in shaping the form and conditions of human settlements. But what is even more significant is the role of human settlements in reproducing the social and cultural patterns which define their form and conditions. The main concern of this paper is the latter proposition.

The comments which constitute this paper are based primarily on my research on the relationship between the environment and human behavior. This research was carried out in Singapore from 1970 to 1975.[1]

Until 1960, the settlement pattern in Singapore was markedly shaped by colonialism and mercantile capitalism. The ubiquitous classes of merchants and laborers created a settlement pattern which was characterized by multifunctional shop–houses built along long and relatively narrow streets. The ground floor of the shop–house was used for business and commerce and the upper floor was used primarily for residential purposes. And as the population of Singapore grew under the influx of immigration, the living accommodation of the shop–house was further subdivided to accommodate more people.

The streets were ethnically and linguistically homogeneous and socially integrated by the common social position and shared culture of their residents, which gave them the characteristic features of micro-urban neighborhoods. By and large the family and the neighborhood played a crucial role in socializing children into the occupations of their parents. This pattern continued until about 1960.

In 1959, soon after assuming power, the Government of the People's Action Party embarked on a plan to attract industrial and financial capital, mostly from the United States, England, Western Europe, and Australia, for economic and social development of the country. As part of this plan the government initiated massive urban redevelopment and public housing programs. Within two decades these programs have altered the form and conditions of human settlement in Singapore. The majority of Singapore's population now resides in the highrise, high density blocks of flats in the public housing estates that have been planned as self-sufficient new towns, except for employment.

THE IMPLICATION FOR THE CHILD OF THE NEW SETTLEMENT PATTERNS

In the last 16 years, 200,000 families have resettled in the public housing. For these families, rehousing in the new environment has involved changes in spatial and social organization. Between 1969 and 1976 a series of studies on the sociological consequences of rehousing (especially on the low income families) were carried out by me and my students in the Department of Sociology, University of Singapore. One of the problems investigated by several of these studies was the impact of relocation on the child and the family.

In our studies one particular feature of housing, namely crowding, was of special interest, because studies elsewhere have found it to have a serious impact on certain aspects of family functioning and organization. In one study, based on data collected from 121 families residing in a 12-storey one-room block of flats, it was observed that children who came from larger families (with more than six members) tended to play outside more frequently than children who came from smaller families (with less than five members). Generally, though, both in the case of large as well as small families, the majority of the children played inside the home. This was true in the case of all children between the ages of 1 and 10. In the case of children between the age of 6 and 10 years, 57% played inside the flat and 64% of the younger children between the ages of 1 and 5 years played inside the flat.

The parents of the larger families with children of 6 years and above were then asked whether they were aware of where their children were playing when they played outside the flat and in what activities they were engaged. Generally they had some idea, but most of them said that they were not absolutely sure; in fact, given the choice, they would have liked their children to play inside the flat, as the outside was "full of bad elements," which would teach their children undesirable things. Studies carried out elsewhere of the implications of such situations suggest that under conditions of higher internal density (crowding) there is less parental surveillance and control over children.

Let us assume that in the case of children who came from larger families the tendency to play "outside" most of the time did result in reduced parental control over children. In extreme cases, one should then expect children coming from larger families to exhibit a greater tendency towards socially deviant behavior such as juvenile delinquency. We attempted to ascertain, in the context of Singapore, whether or not such a relationship in fact existed. This was done by comparing the floor area per person for 90 juvenile delinquents who came from public flats with the overall floor area per person for all public housing flats.

The comparison showed that the juvenile delinquent cases came from the flats that have considerably smaller floor area per person compared with all public-housing flats. The smaller floor areas were also found to be related to poverty. Though it is possible that poverty could have a potentially confounding influence, it seems reasonable to assume that overcrowding is one of the contributing factors in causing juvenile delinquency because of the decline in parental supervision and control.

These findings are further supported by another case study of 15 large and 15 small families residing in one-room public flats. One of the objectives of this study was to ascertain the effect of internal density on children.[2]

In this study it was found that internal density is perceived as the factor that forced children out of their flats to play. Children from 11 of the 15 large families (with more than six members) generally played outside most of the time, whereas children from only three of the 15 small families (with five or less members) played outside most of the time. All mothers (respondents in the study) whose children played outside preferred their children to play inside. The interior was considered safer and more secure because it ensured that the children would not get involved in fights or mix with bad company. In short, the outside environment was perceived by the respondents as undesirable and dangerous for children. However, the lack of space for children to play inside the flats left little choice for the mothers except to allow their children to play outside.

Of the respondents whose children played outside, nine knew what their children were doing because the study block consisted of only three stories; consequently mothers could keep an eye on their children. They pointed out, however, that if they were staying in a highrise block of flats this supervision would not be possible, as from higher stories it would be difficult to see their children and recognize them visually. Five respondents reported that they had only a very vague idea of the activities of the children when they were playing outside. It was observed, however, that for safety reasons only those children who were more than 10 years of age were allowed to play downstairs in the playground. Younger children mostly played in the corridor where their mothers could supervise them.

The children from the smaller families generally played inside the flat. In fact, some parents had erected barriers at the doorsteps to prevent their children from going out. The practice of confining the children inside could, of course, have serious sociopsychological consequences, since it deprives them of experience in the physical world, and this could stultify their sensory development.

In this study it was found that internal crowding was a constant hindrance to children's studying. Lack of privacy, frequent movements of other family members, demands by the mother for their help, and noise from the surrounding area were some of the distractions which prevented children from concentrating on their studies. Similar findings have been reported in another sociological study of a school located in a HDB estate. As a result, it was found that most of the children from the large families (11 out of 15) fared very badly in school. Some of them had to repeat a year once or twice and, in cases where they did well in the first year of schooling, their performance declined in later years.

Equally revealing aspects of this study were the manner in which mothers justified their children's poor school results. Mothers, especially from the larger families, tended to perceive their children as "stupid" and comments like "my children cannot talk intelligently" were made frequently in front of the children. The mothers were found to be often ashamed of their children's poor scholastic achievements, and they had very low aspirations for their future. They thought that, since their children were stupid, there was little that could be done, and therefore they expected the children to go to work in order to supplement the family income, or else earn enough to look after themselves independently. The mothers had no conception of the influence of social factors (poverty, malnutrition, etc.) or of the physical factors (such as housing).

The perception of mothers (that children are stupid) is internalized by the children, who then come to regard themselves as "backward." In these circumstances it is not surprising that there tends to be high dropout rates among children, one of the consequences of which is that their chances of social mobility are effectively blocked.

The findings show that conditions of high internal density in flats occupied by the lower socioeconomic groups tend to weaken parental surveillance over children and adversely affect children's academic achievement. These and other related ill effects of crowding, however, can be minimized to a great extent by the availability of modern medical and social welfare services, and through the development of social infrastructures such as urban community development programs to facilitate children's as well as their families' adaptation to their environment. However, notwithstanding their limitations, these findings also indicate the need for alternative housing design for the low income groups more congruent with their life-styles and, therefore, more conducive to reducing some of the problematic aspects of living in a high density environment.

NEW SETTLEMENT FORMS AS A LEARNING ENVIRONMENT

The studies to which I have alluded in the last section involved a great deal of time in the field in order to collect the sociological and ethnographic data. During the fieldwork it became very obvious that the new environment was also a very significant learning environment. It shaped certain patterns of social interaction and attitudes, and reinforced others. A further examination of this problem is beyond the scope of this paper. But certain observations, though speculative in nature, are worth recording.

During casual conversations with children in the study areas, I noticed that they were very conscious of the hugeness of the buildings which surrounded them and of the one in which they themselves lived. The building size and form appeared to have an intimidating effect on the children. The parents frequently told their children to be careful, for a fall from the building would mean serious and fatal injuries. Such exhortations about these dangers, combined with the size of the buildings, evoked a fear of the environment and perhaps served as an early learning experience of the meaning of danger and fear.

The new settlement pattern also served as a learning environment in other important respects. For example, children are exposed to the impersonality and superficiality of the social contacts among neighbors and friends; extreme routinization of social life; social transactions in which material wealth plays an important role; the housing bureaucracy and the family environment characterized by instrumental value orientations.

By and large, the interaction among neighbors is characterized by an ideology of "noninvolvement" and avoidance of meaningful social contacts. As a result, social interaction among the residents tends to be superficial, impersonal, and instrumental. The children are socialized in this environment and are discouraged from having close associations with other children in the block. In their remarks about the problem of raising children, parents very often implied that the neighborhood was full of "bad elements" and if only they (parents) could prevent their children from mixing around with bad company, they would have no problem with their children. But what constitutes bad company is never explicitly defined, and their instructions to their children are usually vague and very general, such as "avoid playing with other children." One could, therefore, argue that the children's learning of the "norm of impersonality" begins at a very early age and is reinforced both by their parents and the environment of the new public housing estates.

Children are often involved in buying sundry goods for their families or for their own consumption. These transactions constitute some of their very first exposures to market transactions involving the use of money. Through these exchanges (as well as through observing their parents' market behavior) the children acquire an awareness of the market exchange which is mediated through money. They also begin to develop a certain orientation towards money and its handling in that money becomes a desired and valued object and its acquisition a highly desirable social goal.

The means to acquire money are subtly imparted by the way parents acquire it. Children learn very quickly that money is earned and that, to earn money, their fathers (and often mothers as well) have to work. Parents send their children to school but only in order to equip them with marketable skills or a certificate. Education in this social context acquires purely an instrumental value and, through its emphasis on the memory-recall system of learning and frequent examinations, the school system reinforces this orientation.

Children also learn the significance and necessity of following rules and regulations of the outside world. This learning takes place when they see their parents (and other people) paying the rental and other rates regularly at the local offices of the housing board. They also come to know of regulations when parents talk about not being able to make any alteration in the flat because of the housing board regulations, or through the maintenance services rendered periodically by the housing board employees. Observance of the rules pertaining to maintenance of the flat, payment of rental and rates, etc., by their parents exposes the child to the rules and regulations which it is necessary for them to observe.

This exposure, combined with the children's experience in school where they are also required to observe the school rules and regulations, constitutes their first major experiences with bureaucratic organization, and the children learn that the best way to deal with these bureaucratic organizations is to mechanically and passively observe their rules and regulations. At home, children must also submit to parental wishes and observance of their expectations. The codes of observance and obedience which the child begins to learn at home in the formative years is reinforced by their exposure to the school system and housing bureaucracies.

The above observations are but a partial description of the importance of the new residential environment in the socialization process of the child. I have suggested that the new environment plays a significant role in socializing the child to some important concepts and codes of behavior such as danger, fear, norm of impersonality, code of obedience and observance, and the meaning of work and money. All of these I would further suggest play a central role in the reproduction of the society of which they are a part.

The new settlement pattern has been shaped by the overall strategy for economic development of the Republic. This strategy involved restructuring the spatial, industrial, and social patterns in order to make Singapore more attractive for multinational and other foreign and local capital investment. I have suggested that the new environment (i.e. public housing) can also be viewed as a learning environment for the child, and that the conditions and the form of the environment introduce the child at a very early age to an instrumental value orientation.

REFERENCES

1. The major findings of this research have been published in my book, *Families in Flats,* Singapore University Press, 1977.
2. LOH ENG JUAN, Sociological consequences of internal density on personal and family relations, Honours Thesis, University of Singapore, 1974.

PLANNING FOR CHILDREN IN NEW COMMUNITIES

Suzanne Keller

Department of Sociology, Princeton University, NJ, USA

This paper directly addresses the problem raised at the start of the symposium by Dr. Spyros Doxiadis of the crucial importance of implementation, that is of the translation of ideas into action, without which our ideas remain sterile.

It also seeks to emphasize the fact that to anticipate the world of tomorrow is not simply to watch it unfold, but it is to actively create it.

It is new communities which try (with often rather little success) to do just that—to create for, rather than wait for, the future; and as we are likely to have more innovative communities in the future, we should take a closer look at them by drawing on an in-depth post-construction evaluation of a planned community for a projected population of 10,000, which the author explored during the first five years of its life.[1] The community, located in the state of New Jersey, USA, is the first planned unit development in that state, where a mix of townhouses and condominiums on 715 acres now serves some 12,000 residents.

As is typical of those who move to such communities in the United States, Western Europe, and perhaps elsewhere, the residents consisted largely of upwardly mobile young couples seeking the proverbial house and garden for their growing families.

The objective of the study was to assess the fit between physical design and behavior, and to note what is satisfactory and unsatisfactory about the built environment for different types of users. The more long range aims of this and similar studies are to increase our understanding of how to design desirable living environments and how to improve our skills in doing so, thereby avoiding some of the more blatant planning failures of recent years.

Of the more than 300 lengthy interviews with individual residents, 80 involved children who were interviewed without an adult being present. They ranged in age from 11 to 17 years but clustered in the 13–14 year category.[2]

In this brief paper I will summarize some highlights of these interviews, and then compare the findings with those of other studies with a view to deriving some general lessons for planners.

It has often been noted that pre-teenagers and adolescents are among the more disgruntled and least satisfied residents of new communities. This is due not only to the generally stressful nature of this particular stage of life, but also because new communities are so often oriented primarily to young adults and very young children, leaving the older child relatively neglected and deprived. The reasons for this are as yet obscure, but each study adds another piece of the puzzle. Let me therefore start by summarizing the main findings and then go on to consider their implications.

Starting with the move itself, adults are not always aware of how wrenching it can be for a child of 8 or 10 to leave behind close friends and a familiar environment. But it clearly is. One half of these youngsters, for example, said that leaving friends behind was the hardest part of the move and another one-fifth cited the loss of a familiar environment. Despite this rupture, however, the move was seen as a rather positive experience for the large majority (85%) who thought that their lives had changed for the better in terms of more activities, new friends, and more freedom. And since, at that age, most readily made friends in the new community, they began to feel part of it within a fairly short time. In contrast to their parents, moreover, they turned out to be far less spaceocentric, the large majority (nine-tenths) drawing on the entire community for their social contacts. Their parents, on the other hand, confined their friendships very close to home, one-half to the street and one-third to the quad in which they lived.

The youngsters also appreciated the community for its openness and safety but they voiced strong complaints on other grounds. The lack of transportation facilities, not enough recreation, and inadequate shopping all loomed large in their minds, with the girls more dissatisfied with shopping and recreation, while the boys stressed the absence of adequate space for various athletic activities.

Both boys and girls complained about the absence of public transportation to get them to desired athletic, cultural, and social events outside the community. Many had come from urban settings that had public transportation and a great many activities with in easy reach and to which they could get under their own steam. In the present community they could walk and bicycle to various sites, which they did to some degree, but this proved inadequate for great distances; or if they had to carry along cumbersome equipment; or in inclement weather. On all those occasions, either mother, the chauffeur, was called upon, not without some resentment, or they simply did without—again, not without some resentment.

One facility which was keenly missed was a teen center of their own at which they could gather away from the watchful eyes of the adults. Given the skewed age distribution of the new community population heavily weighted with young couples and toddlers, adolescents cannot count on the critical mass necessary for their social life which seems to require both anonymity and visibility for maximum success. All in all then, not being very numerous in the first generation, older children and adolescents tend to get shortchanged in a number of respects important to them.

TABLE 1

Teenagers' perception of how others feel about them

Feelings of:	Strongly positive (%)	Anti-teen [a] (%)
Your own parents about you	79	2
Your own parents about other teens	42	9
Other parents about teens	19	13
Adults in general about teens	10	23
Other teens about you	31	3
Children about teens	36	7
Teachers about teens	33	10
Police about teens	11	30
Store owners about teens	5	55

(a) Anti-teen includes strong and average dislike.

In appraising this unfinished community basically designed for other age groups, they stress feelings of relative deprivation both in regard to special facilities of interest and in regard to community support. High on the list of grievances is the lack of enough things to do in the community, a sense of being cut off from other communities, and their not having a place of their own.

One fascinating question asked the youngsters to rank the groups shown in Table 1 by how they feel towards teenagers.

The only group that the teenagers perceived as being very favorably disposed towards them were their own parents. And even there we see a sharp drop in their perception of how their parents respond to other teens. Adults in general are seen as less positive still; and police and shopkeepers are perceived as actively hostile.

A parallel question asked the youngsters to state their own feelings towards each of the same groups (Table 2).

TABLE 2
How teenagers feel about others

How do you feel about:	Strongly pro (%)	Dislike (a) (%)
Your own parents	85	1
Other parents	27	8
Adults in general	16	11
Other teens	35	6
Children	30	9
Teachers	35	7
Police	19	16
Store owners	5	20

(a) Dislike includes strong and average dislike.

The teenagers obviously respond in kind. They are highly positive about their own parents but far less approving of other adults, the shopkeepers, and the police. A sex difference may be noted here, with the girls perceiving the shopkeepers as most hostile, the boys the police.

Of further interest to planners is the focus of most youthful complaints on design aspects of the community, including its impact on their social and recreational life. The adults are seen as reluctant and often hostile compatriots who tend to monopolize the desirable spaces for their own benefits. Hence the persistent refrain of the young that there is nothing to do and no place to go and no one who cares about them. Their complaints are particularly pronounced in bad weather and in the evening hours since the community was basically designed for daytime and good weather.

Ironically, all that open space for which the parents left the crowded city is experienced by their children as too confining by its lack of activities, variety, and excitement. By contrast, the cities left behind in retrospect emerge as havens of freedom and mobility.

These findings are not confined to this one community. They are corroborated by a number of other studies both within and outside the American setting.

For example, in their careful comparison of 36 communities, of which 17 were new communities, Burby and Weiss[3] found that, as regards the younger children, although child play areas are the most ubiquitous feature of new communities, most children did not use them. They preferred to play in their own or a neighbor's yard or in the streets and parking areas. Similar preferences were evident in the community I monitored.

As for youngsters aged 14 and older, the majority were not satisfied with the organizational activities and programs; did not feel that there were enough good places to get together with friends; and did not rate their teen centers very favorably. We also noted a discrepency between the parents who generally rated such facilities highly and the youngsters who did not.

In this connection, there is Richard Dattner's observation to the effect that although children are "the most deeply affected group of users of play facilities, they are at present least able to influence the design of their environment."[4] As for parents, although they obviously have a great interest in successful play facilities and will "go through great lengths to provide a good environment," the problem is that either they, too, are not consulted or they seek to satisfy their own personal needs in the name of providing for the children. In his view, the group that has the greatest influence of all are the city officials with money and decision-making power who are also, however, "least affected by the results."

Then there is the study of a British housing estate in a working class area[5] which also noted that the children "were exposed to constant repressions and frustrations and the working of a system which was inconsistent and capricious." The result was "marked hostility" to the adults and to the environment.

A comparative study of a Swedish and an American suburb[6] found complaints similar in tone and context to those we have reviewed in the New Jersey community. Youth complained that activities were too supervised, too hard to get to in the evenings, and the environment too unstimulating. Lack of transportation was also mentioned, as was monotony and boredom.[7]

Finally, noting that new towns are boring to children, C. A. Doxiadis cites a German study that found that "children gauge their freedom not by the extent of open areas around them, but by the liberty they have to be among people and things that excite them and fire their imaginations."[8]

There is thus cumulative evidence that the designed environment leaves much to be desired for children and youths in planned communities. Access is one problem, inadequate public transportation, and recreational and cultural activities are others. A lack of participation in the design is yet a third.

I agree with Dattner's observation that every environment is a learning experience, even a poorly designed one.[9] In his view, the lessons learned in all too many planned environments by the young residents are negative ones. He mentions among the specific lessons, the idea that the young do not matter as individuals but only as a category, thereby being forced to yield their individuality to uniformity and standardization. In addition, the young learn that they can have no constructive effect on the fixed and immobile environment because they seem to be able to change it "only in a destructive way"[10] and all too often they learn that the adultmade world is dull, ugly, dangerous, and "empty of sensuous satisfactions."

What, then, are some of the criteria to keep in mind when planning for children and teenagers?

(1) providing a place of their own—away from adult supervision and interference;
(2) play, sport, and recreational facilities that are appropriate to their needs, ages, and interests;
(3) ready access to desired facilities and services and public transportation to get around under their own steam and to go outside of the community
(4) facilities and services specifically geared to them and not having to be shared with younger children; especially
(5) shopping, movies, and other diversions geared to their pocketbooks;
(6) individual attention; not being reduced to a single uniform category called ten year olds or teenagers;
(7) respect from adults; a feeling of being wanted; a positive attitude toward them in the community generally;
(8) participation in design decisions affecting them.

None of these are beyond reach, though some may involve certain costs, but so does the abuse or neglect of inappropriate facilities. The potential rewards are considerable too—improved morale, creativity, and a vital connectedness of children to the world they live in.

What greater indictment can there be than the often observed phenomenon that children will prefer dangerous streets and unsightly junkyards to the formal play equipment provided for them? The architect C. T. Sorenson, who designed the first playgrounds around this idea, noted that children were immediately at ease amidst the "junk," whereas the adults seldom saw anything more than chaos and danger. The ease of the children stemmed not from their indifference to their environment but from their unique response to it. They created "their own kind of order based on criteria quite different from those of adults."[11] It is this order that planners must come to understand and respect.

REFERENCES

1. See SUZANNE KELLER, *Twin Rivers, Study of a Planned Community,* NSF Grant G1 41 311, 1976, 550 pp.
2. Specifically, 19% were 11–12 years old; 41%, 13–14 years old; 20%, 15 years old, and 21%, 16 years and older.
3. RAYMOND J. BURBY, III, and SHIRLEY F. WEISS, *New Communities USA,* D. C. Heath & Co., Lexington, MA, USA, 1976, pp. 232 ff.
4. RICHARD DATTNER, *Design for Play,* van Nostrand, 1969, p. 4.
5. L. E. WHITE, The outdoor play of children living in flats: an enquiry into the use of courtyards as playgrounds, in HAROLD M. PROSHANSKY, W. H. ITTELSON, and L. G. RIVLIN (Eds.), *Environmental Psychology,* Holt, Rinehart & Winston, 1970, pp. 235–258.
6. DAVID POPENOE, *The Suburban Environment,* University of Chicago Press, 1977.
7. Ibid., pp. 135, 158. By contrast no such boredom was found among the Swedish youngsters who seemed to be content with the community and what it had to offer. Possibly the ready accessibility of Stockholm and the existence of adequate recreational facilities, including a teen center, accounts for this.
8. C. A. DOXIADIS, *Anthropopolis, City for Human Development,* Athens Publishing Center, 1974, p. 92.
9. DATTNER, op. cit., p. 37.
10. Ibid, p. 7.
11. Ibid, p. 53.

DISCUSSION

GERALD DIX

Department of Civic Design, University of Liverpool, UK

THERE are three main elements in our theme today: children, settlements, future.

Most of the children in tomorrow's world will be in what we somewhat euphemistically call the developing countries. What changes can we reasonably expect and work for in these areas to improve the lot of children and of society?

We must relate plans and action to resources. We must determine what our priorities are to be, as they did in Singapore, for we cannot do all things at once. This may well involve some determination of standards. Health is most important. A clean water supply and drainage should be top priority. To use a medical analogy, we should have preventive medicine to minimize the need for surgery. Even in shanty towns, potable water and drainage should be our aim.

Panaghis Psomopoulos has spoken of housing, and the need for rooms. We need simple shelter suited to the demands of the local climate; a house base for a family that is safe from risk and disease. If the people are to have the necessary security of tenure, many landownership problems will have to be overcome. Incentives should be provided for good development as well as controls to stop bad building.

Irrigation to grow food brings us again to water supplies. Put water on most deserts and they will produce food. The food must then be distributed and roads must be built. Agricultural improvements that do not involve mass mechanization can slow down the rush to the cities, but we must accept that it cannot be stopped.

In many new settlements the type of dwelling as well as the process of migration from the rural areas breaks up extended families, which have served as a kind of in-built social service system. Professor Butterfield has emphasized the importance of grandparents, and in most countries the maternal grandmother is very important in establishing health behavior. High density apartment blocks, of the kind Professor Hassan has analyzed, often crowd young families together in circumstances where they have little to do but become unsettled, unhappy, and politically volatile. The substitution of urban subsistence for rural subsistence is no gain to anyone and a loss to most. It becomes a grouping together in fear rather than in strength.

If we create healthy conditions, more children will live to school age. We shall have to consider the physical implications of school locations to minimize transport costs and to provide space for recreation. The education field provides an opportunity for the constructive use of high technology in the developing countries. Transistors and electronic technology, which I suggest will make a bigger impact on the world than atomic power, make possible the quick, cheap distribution of teaching for school-children farmers and workers. It may be standardized—and Mr. Dimaras may object to this—but, even so, it can prove most valuable.

These and other requirements point to the kind of nucleated systems of settlements that C. A. Doxiadis advocated, each with readily accessible community facilities and convenient part-time work available for mothers, so that they can remain close to their children. It also points to a reexamination of old ways of building, using traditional materials, such as Hassan Fathy has set down. He, among others, has shown that good design—functionally and aesthetically—need cost no more than bad. Improved communications will be needed. Above all, development of confidence between government and people. But, make no mistake about it, however much consultation and participation there may be, the job of a government is to govern—whilst taking account of people's needs, interests, and aspirations. It requires giving priority to health measures, food, and shelter. If the children of tomorrow are healthier (partly by being better fed) and wealthier, they will themselves have fewer children, and the future will be brighter for them.

There is no reason why this should not be so. The places—villages, towns, nations—where the challenge is greatest are places where the opportunity is greatest if we have the courage to grasp the nettle while yet we may. As C. A. Doxiadis told us: "If we try we may fail, but also we may succeed. If we do not try, we can only fail."

DEMETRIUS IATRIDIS
Department of Social Planning, Boston College, Boston, MA, USA

Market forces and public policies of distribution are dynamic underlying common denominators that determine conditions in human settlements, increase social inequities, and have a negative impact on lower income families and their children. Market functions of supply and demand and the profit motivation are dominant forces in determining modern urbanization patterns, such as slums, suburbia, high densities, public transportation, separation of residence and workplace, public services and facilities, life-styles, segregation, affluence, and deprivation. The slums and the suburbs may differ vastly in terms of spatial arrangement, geographic location, facilities, and aesthetic form. But they are both outcomes of urbanization under free market forces. Distributive public policies (of income, wealth, services, facilities)—the center piece of social planning—are public interventions concerned with social inequities produced by the market on human settlement patterns, and are designed to change their impact. In this sense, distribution policies should be concerned with the rights of all population groups (particularly lower income groups) and with institutions for social interaction. The production, for example, of 4–5 billion rooms for this planet's residential needs (estimated by Panaghis Psomopoulos) is fundamentally a market concern. But, equally if not more essential from the viewpoint of policy distribution, is who will actually use these rooms, where, and how, at what private and public cost?

All three papers reflect this fundamental dialectic in various forms and degrees.

Professor JEAN GOTTMANN identified two modern trends likely to affect both the pattern of human settlements and family and child behavior: the migratory character of modern society and the increasing revolution in the labor market. Both trends are postulated on a market-based environment and on free enterprise dynamics. Both trends, he suggests, are likely to create an even more migratory and less-settled mode of life. But, I assume that, even in this more mobile society, lower income families and their children will continue to be trapped in ghettos and be relatively immobile, socially and geographically, if market forces prevail and distributive public policies are ineffectual.

PROFESSOR RIAZ HASSAN, who described settlement patterns in Singapore, attributed the dramatic changes in their structure to market forces in the context of economic development. For example, when pre-1960 colonialism and merchantile capitalism was replaced by post-1960 policies to attract investment from market-based nations for socioeconomic development, there was a shift from shop–houses built along narrow streets to highrise apartment blocks, separated some distance from the industrial areas. Singapore's economic strategy to attract multinational foreign and local capital investment had a negative impact on the life-style of its lower income group due to the lack of effective public policies of the distribution of social services.

PROFESSOR SUZANNE KELLER described experiences gained in planning a small, new community in the United States for young, middle class couples. Several of the reasons why this did not fulfill some of the good intentions of the planners seem to have been due to the same socioeconomic parameters of social order, equity, and distribution policies concerning institutions involved in social integration and participation.

At the opening of this symposium, the President of Greece underscored the essence of our theme when he suggested that poverty is the number one enemy of children. Certainly in market-based nations like Greece, poverty cannot be reduced without effective public policies of redistribution.

Urban patterns which permit the wealthier classes to preserve their exclusive residential areas at a physical distance from poorer areas have their roots in market functions, reinforced by nondistributive public policies. The suburban ghetto is the product of a partnership between institutions, investors and home owners. It is the product of a middle and upper class movement, fortified by urban decay, stimulated by speculative profit and government spending, and tolerated by public distribution policies. The forced transportation of children to schools outside their residential areas (in both slums and suburbia) is a reflection of the effect of free enterprise market forces unconstrained by public distribution policies. Ownership of the means of production influences prices, incomes, residential location (including access of children to community facilities). The methods of resource allocation, through the use of prices, influence the ability of poor families to provide for their children, and the locus of power limits the participation of poor families in the decision making that affects their community life.

Let me close by recommending that the redistribution of public services becomes a conscious policy instrument to promote social equity and an adequate standard of living for all. However, I am not optimistic that distribution policies can significantly change the effect of market forces on the patterns of human settlements in the near future. The ideology incorporated in the social institutions of market-based nations will have to undergo considerable evolution before effective redistribution policies can be implemented. Urban planners, social and behavioral scientists, educators, and all professionals in the field of health-care face a formidable challenge to facilitate and speed up this evolutionary process.

MELY G. TAN
Indonesian Institute of Sciences, Jakarta, Indonesia

I should like to comment on the paper by Suzanne Keller. This paper and other presentations since the beginning of the symposium have clearly indicated to me that an environment of affluence does not guarantee that the child will grow up healthy and mentally stable. The results of her study of the new community in New Jersey have shown that the children in this community feel bored, alienated, and, as a result, often resort to acts of vandalism and other asocial activities. It is clear that these environments, which are located in the industrialized countries, have grave problems.

Nonetheless, the reality is that two-thirds to three-quarters of the children of the world live in the developing countries, in underprivileged, subhuman environments, in absolute ignorance, in abject poverty, riddled with disease. I submit that if the attention given to these children is proportionately as little as has been given to them at this symposium, the environment of over two-thirds of the children of the world will be the same tomorrow as it is today: bleak, harsh, subhuman.

In this connection, I would like to quote from a paper presented by Dr. Soedjat-moko at the National Committee of UNICEF in Brussels, April, 1978:

"In the final analysis it is the quality, the health, the intelligence, the skills, the capacity for cooperation and organization in adulthood, of the children in the poor two-thirds of the world; their aspirations, their values, their hopes, but also their frustrations, their despair and their anger, which will shape our nations, and the common future of humankind, in what is most likely going to be a crowded, hungry, and competitive world. These may well have a greater impact than any of the projections which the futurologists of today are capable of making us believe."

ANASTASE DIAMANTIDIS
UN Environment Program, Geneva, Switzerland

Our present technological society has shown a great degree of irresponsibility and instability towards the destiny and future of our children, whose growth and development and real chance to live a better life in a stable and safe world have so often been sacrificed in the name of short term economic growth and so-called progress.

However, we have increasingly become aware of the disastrous effects of our actions and have initiated a process of recuperation, control and preservation of our environment, and a readjustment of our attitudes and behavior towards our only "one earth" and our responsibility to ensure that the basic human needs and quality of life of future generations are met with a minimum burden on the finite resources of the earth's ecosystems. We have finally understood, but have still to prove in the practical sense our good will, that a proper management of human activities in the environment is the only way in which a sound and sustainable development can be ensured to meet all people's basic needs and aspirations; for it is undeniably true that development pursued without due regard to the ecological realities on which it depends, is ultimately self-defeating.

In December 1972 the United Nations General Assembly created the United Nations Environment Program to coordinate and give common objectives to many environmental activities undertaken within and outside the United Nations system.

UNEP is primarily concerned with all aspects of the environment, including protection and preservation of its resources, maintenance of its quality from the physical, biological, social, and cultural perspectives, and the control of all human activities which impinge upon this quality and make a decisive impact on its well-being.

All the work of UNEP is favorable to the child. By its mandate UNEP focuses more than other institutions on the long term effects of development in order to ensure the preservation of a decent world for children, the so-called future generations. The social sciences have already established the importance of environmental factors in the growth and development of the child.

The environment program has encouraged and stimulated the development of activities that have a direct bearing on the education, health, social, and spiritual well being of children, especially in the areas of water, human settlements, and environmental education. For example, current UNEP programs in water emphasize the promotion of the integrated approach in water supply schemes to blend with the general improvement of life. This relates especially to women and children, who are the most affected in rural areas. Whenever feasible, water supply and water development projects should be geared to contribute to the control of water-related diseases such as schistosomiasis, malaria, guinea-worm, and some enteric problems. UNEP supports projects which emphasize this principle and which encourage community involvement through information dissemination, and education, so as to ensure that the community accepts these projects as their own and participates in their implementation.

In the area of human settlements, one of the major concerns in UNEP is the provision of a proper habitat within which children can grow healthily and safely. A number of demonstration projects for an environmentally sound improvement of marginal settlements have been successfully carried out in Indonesia and the Philippines.

Considerable advances have taken place in the conceptual and methodological approaches to innovative programs of education for children which take into account the child's environment and make use of his ideas and initiatives focusing on experiential learning by doing. In this respect UNEP has continued to support new and exciting developments in environmental science education for the young age groups.

THE FUTURE OF HEALTH SERVICES FOR CHILDREN

LEONARD J. DUHL

College of Environmental Design, University of California
at Berkeley, CA, USA

MANY of us who are especially concerned with the health of children have come out of the fields of medicine and the allied health professions. We have been preoccupied over the years with providing services where there may have been no previous health or medical service. We have moved from the provision of emergency medical care, clinical service, maternal and child health programs, and well-baby clinics to some recent attention to preventive health services. We have worked hard to make possible specialized treatment programs for children with special health and medical problems. In other words, we have moved from finding ways to provide basic services to finding ways to prevent health problems, to finding ways to treat special problems.

But we have done all this only within the narrow context of the health and medical care institutions as they are now. Only recently have we begun to reach out to expand the meaning of health, to make health services more thoughtful and caring (and less damaging), to realize that the issues of health cannot be separated from the larger and broader issues of personal growth and development, and of the physical, social, and spiritual environments in which we and our children live.

The dilemma which we in health and medicine face is whether, indeed, the subject of health is one that can be adequately dealt with by the health professions. We have to face the crucial question now as to whether health is a true concern of health and medical workers, or whether, as recent critics have charged, the health care establishment is more interested in protecting and perpetuating its institutional self than it is in providing a healthier world.

We must become more aware that we cannot separate our care for children from their surroundings, their context. Increasingly we are becoming concerned with family and community as an aspect of health. We have begun to hear some talk of the networks required in every culture to preserve, educate, and integrate the child. We know that family networks and community networks tend either to reinforce or to fragment the child's life resulting in, on the one hand, a healthy child, and on the other, a child who has become an ostensible "patient" in a situation of difficulty.

If we are to face up to the ecological context in which the child lives, grows, and develops, we must be aware of the relationship between the complex environment of the world in our time and the process of normal growth and development. Our world is disconnected, discontinuous, disorganized, and dehumanizing. Because of this, normal development becomes difficult even in the best of local settings, and a very painful one in those settings where poverty, racial, or ethnic stigmas, and general lack of resources are the order.

Even though we are becoming aware of these issues, we really know so little. We know little about the norms of growth and development. We have strong ideas about

459

the biological nature of the developmental processes and we have acted as if individual development can be separated from that of the family, the tribe, the colony, or community. Despite all our work in anthropology we know little about the many varieties of cultural and group adaptations. We have not related individual and group development (even the little we know) to aspects such as climate, rural or urban setting, geography, native or technological architecture, and a host of other impinging factors.

Yet if these areas are areas of guesswork, we know even less about what happens when normal development is blocked and intervention of some sort is clearly indicated. We have concerned ourselves primarily with the kinds of intervention familiar to us as part of the medical and health professions, yet I have a feeling that there are many other levels of intervention both possible and important to health.

Basically, what we have done is separate treatment from healing. Treatment is the more immediate intervention that perhaps can halt some major or minor deviation from growth and development, but healing to me means returning an individual to the healthy growth and development cycle which is potentially his or hers.

Thus we must look carefully at medical and health care, realizing that, while it may be doing a necessary task, it is only a small part of the job, and healing must attempt to deal with a larger complex of issues. What we are really facing is a question of context.

The issues we face may not be health issues at all but issues that involve political, social, ethical, philosophical, even spiritual answers. What kind of world do we want? What kind of lives do we want for ourselves and our children? Do we want to live and be alive, or just survive? Or will we become preoccupied with questions of illness, death, dying?

We might also have to realistically face a very basic question when we attempt to design future environments for our children: Are children all that important to us? Often the answer seems to be "No." There are many arguments today against having children. We have found ways to keep children outside of the processes of real life because we are not clever enough to find a place or a function for them. And we hold many values that do not seem to reinforce or maximize healthy development.

Health, then is a larger issue than the rational organization of health services and health professions. The future health of our children is linked to the future health of our societies.

The question of what kind of world we want and what kind of lives we want can only be answered by some understanding of how we perceive the world, how we organize that perception, and what our view of reality itself is.

We need some vision of the whole before we can begin to comprehend or make change in any of its parts, such as the health care system.

I find some hope in being here, in Athens, where for many years we wrestled with the idea of ekistics, the pulling together of an understanding of the totality of the environment. Many people here today who are concerned with specific issues of health have taken steps across the boundaries of health care issues into politics, planning, physical design, problems of urbanization, and social welfare. We are becoming more aware that it is the very structure and philosophy of our communities, our networks, our tribes, and families that will determine the health of our children and the design of health services for them.

It is no accident, for instance, that groups with coherent world and life views, such as religious groups of various kinds, often produce healthier people with longer life expectancies and a greater sense of well-being and self-respect because of their common outlook and goals.

In conclusion, I would like to make simple proposals. I would like to ask that whatever we do in our nations and our societies, whether it is in dealing with the environment and its pollution, or in business, or in politics, in whatever field we presume to take action, we first ask: What will be the effect on individual and social health? I would like to see a kind of family/child health impact statement required of all social decisions. If we build a gigantic dam in Asia or Africa, or plan a cardiac clinic in Montana, or a sports stadium or a school or a park, we must first ask: What will be the effects on health?

Second, I would ask those of us who are working in the health fields to perform two functions: (1) do the best we can at the jobs we have been given to do, however narrow they seem; and (2) expand our concern, our horizons, to the point where we begin to raise critical questions about how the larger environment impinges on a child's development or on our ability to deal with their illnesses.

Finally, I ask that whenever we treat illness or disease we remember what we have learned from the healers of past times—the shamans, if you will: that we are treating not only an isolated case, but that we must also return the patient to a contextual situation that will lead to further development and growth. The shaman performed this task of contextualizing, or networking, by involving the community in the healing process through rituals of eating, dancing, and singing, in order to reintegrate the community in which the patient was caused to suffer.

That reintegration of community may be as important to health as the specific treatment interventions we know so well how to manage—it may be more important, finally. The future of health services for both children and adults may lie more in these directions than in anything we can do in planning more buildings, equipment, management schemes, or financing procedures. We need to begin thinking about how we can make whole.

DISCUSSION

J. K. HARFOUCHE

School of Public Health, Beirut, Lebanon

I WISH to emphasize the need for the participation of children and of women in the design and implementation of plans and action programs that affect their immediate environment and self-care. Inequitable distribution includes the lack of representation of these nonvocal groups. This symposium should have had direct "inputs" from mothers and children. In Asia, children are supposed to be seen but not heard. That has been the case here. The youngest participant has been at least 25 years removed from the age of the youngest child. Kahlil Gibran in *The Prophet* said:

> Your children are not your children.
> They are the sons and daughters of Life's longing for itself.
> They come through but not from you,
> And though they are with you yet they belong not to you.

If the children do not share in shaping their own future, indeed, the future will be gloomy.

MIA KELLMER-PRINGLE

National Children's Bureau, London, UK

Sharing power with women: I do not agree with Professor Lourie that it will take thousands of years to change manmade structures. The transistor and radio enable new understanding and attitudes to spread much more rapidly. Women's influence in planning and running services will, I hope, replace competitiveness and aggression with caring and cooperation—attitudes that women value and practice daily in their home-making and child-rearing roles. Our manmade world has created much of which we are ashamed—I feel sure women could not do worse.

Sharing power with children: I can give three concrete examples of allowing children and youth to be fully participating partners. First, in building a playground on wasteground, 12–16 year olds gained a sense of achievement. When it was vandalized, they accepted that fighting the rival gang was useless; instead they rebuilt the playground. Second, the same age group wanted to set up their own "club and activity centre" but, as they felt they were discriminated against, they decided the club should exclude white youth. Although this violated anti-racial discrimination laws, the authorities turned a blind eye in the hope that events would force the youngsters to change this rule. This came to pass when one 16 year old black boy brought his white girl friend. This incident caused the group to see that the rule worked against their own best interests and, incidentally, to learn greater racial tolerance at first hand. Third, another project gave young people (aged 12–16) who

463

were growing up in residential care, the opportunity to state their views on what was wrong with the care they were receiving, and also to make proposals on how it could be improved. The results were excellent, practical, and *not* costly. The National Children's Bureau conducted and then published this work in a book entitled *Who Cares? Young People in Care Speak Out*. In six months the book has had to be reprinted because of the great interest which it has aroused.

SPECIAL SESSIONS

HOMES AND COMMUNITIES

ACCESSIBILITY OF FACILITIES TO CHILDREN

BALANCING SAFETY WITH ADVENTURE

HOMES AND COMMUNITIES

Coordinator: GERALD DIX

Department of Civic Design, University of Liverpool, UK

THE COORDINATOR opened the session by stating that the words "homes" and "dwellings" were not synonymous, any more than communities were just collections of buildings. "Houses, of a size, construction and layout for healthy living became homes when families adopted them and adapted them, when they became a base to come home to!"

Communities can be of different sizes, but to be a community each must be provided with a range of facilities appropriate to its size and situation. In all communities one would expect to find, in addition to dwellings, employment of appropriate kinds, social facilities, and places of association. The range of types of employment would be related to the location and size of the settlement—generally larger settlements include a wider range of kinds of employment—but even in primarily residential communities there should be some employment conveniently located for working mothers with young children, and to provide essential services. Social facilities that affect the lives of children (including schools and clinics) must be readily accessible for those who use them: older children may be expected to travel further to school, etc., than the very young. But it is the informal, less organized meeting facilities which are probably even more important to children and parents: opportunities for meeting at the shopping center or market and in small open spaces of appropriate scale. These are essential in communities of all sizes.

It is important that design, in the architectural sense, should not be neglected, and that buildings should be appropriate in size and scale for their use: all being related to the human being. The human—anthropos—is our automatic measure of size and duration: human height and human generations can be instructively used as scales.

Toward the end of his life especially, C. A. DOXIADIS was deeply concerned with ecological influences on settlements—on homes and communities—and vice versa, and we would be wise to heed his warnings and consider his proposals carefully, if tomorrow's children are to enjoy a reasonable environment in their homes and communities.

DR. ROBERT A. ALDRICH (Medical Center, University of Colorado, Denver, CO, USA) talked about the accessibility of health care in communities and the increasing specialization of the medical profession. In many places of the United States home visits by general practitioners were a thing of the past. Individuals who need care have to know what specialist to consult. This creates problems. He then offered some community oriented predictions for the future:

"(1) We shall see small-scale clinics decentralized or located in residential neighborhoods instead of being centralized in large hospitals.

"(2) Neighborhood schools will provide preventive medical education. (By being near the neighborhood clinic they will easily be visited by the health professionals.)

"(3) There will be neighborhood birthing centers where mothers can give birth in familiar surroundings without disrupting her relations with her family circle and network of connections.

"(4) Day care centers will be connected to the birthing centers so that there can be a fluidity of personnel and services.

"(5) In the city I live in we have a very large Spanish-speaking population and there are a number of excellent Mexican origin 'corandera' healers, who are so much better than many of my psychiatric colleagues that some of them are now working full time in our mental health clinics. They are very cooperative and know a whole field of healing that none of us have had a chance to learn."

DR. MIA KELLMER-PRINGLE (National Children's Bureau, London, UK) commented on the need for playspaces for children and cautioned against the use of television as a form of child minding. The passivity which watching television induces seemed to her more dangerous than the content of the programs: "You can't discuss with TV, you can't argue. It doesn't stimulate independence." She also referred to the National Child Development study in the UK which had followed through, since birth, all the children born in the UK during one week in 1958. They were seen again at the ages of 7, 11, 16, and (now) 20. An enormous amount of material has been collected on their physical, emotional, educational, and social life, and it has been found that, of all aspects studied, overcrowding and the lack of amenities has had a statistically significant effect on their attainment and behavior after allowances have been made for all other factors: "so it isn't just a luxury to ask for adequate space for children to grow in." In the cities of developed countries today huge areas are given over to car parks but often no space at all is provided for children's play. Fortunately a new law in the UK requires all new housing developments to make provision for play areas: "recognizing that play isn't just a waste of time but a way of development and learning." A lot could be done in existing communities by better use of existing buildings. Schools and universities are empty for large parts of the day and for long holidays, but people are very unwilling to throw these facilities open for community use.

DR. KELLMER-PRINGLE also described the family advice centers which had been set up in very deprived city areas. "We simply took a house or flat as run-down as any of the others, put a community worker in it and had an open door." First the small children ventured in, then their parents followed, and the community worker was able to help the people to become involved in their own planning and to make their wishes known to the officials and those in authority. They found that natural leaders emerged from the people of the community, who went out and found lonely old people or children who were being abused, and brought the families into the center and began to help them. "This kind of grass roots development can be done at relatively little cost."

PROFESSOR MUNTANOLA I THORNBERG (Department of Architecture, University of Barcelona, Spain) considered that environmental education was essential to avoid the three dangers of psychological stress, sociological resignation, and psychosocial deprivation. He found it hard to divide problems between the micro and meso scales of environment: all were present generally and locally.

Time did not permit DR. SEPULVEDA (UN Asian and Pacific Development Institute, Bangkok, Thailand) to discuss his paper, which dealt with a study of the situation of children in 12 Asian countries, but he was able amply to demonstrate that the biggest problem facing the Asian child of tomorrow was that of survival. Also national development policies have been of no help to children, and he saw little hope of any abrupt change in the future. The anguish of survival could only be overcome by a radical reallocation of resources on an international scale.

PROFESSOR FIAWOO (Department of Sociology, University of Ghana, Accra, Ghana) had studied 4500 children in rural communities in Ghana. He emphasized the importance of rural areas in national development planning, since the height and weight of the urban child is definitely greater than that of his rural counterpart. "Poor sanitation, unwholesome water-supply, malnutrition, insect infestation, large family size, economic poverty and sometimes inflexible tradition are well-known barriers of optimum physical growth."

DR. KATHERINE ELLIOTT (The CIBA Foundation, London, UK) recounted two relevant ideas she had received from MRS. TARA ALI BAIG, President of the International Union of Child Welfare:

(1) The Minister of Education in India is planning to make primary school education much more relevant to community development and is looking for simple means of training in appropriate technologies that can stimulate the children toward improving their communities and give them the idea that they can do things for themselves.

(2) For 1979: "For every child a tree." She hopes to get every child to plant a tree in every country. The tree will grow with the child and interest the whole family. It will also sow the idea of restoration and environmental reclamation.

PROFESSOR ILLSLEY (Department of Sociology, University of Aberdeen, Scotland, UK) reminded the meeting that many cities in the developed world had problems that should not be overlooked. He saw little chance for change for the better in Glasgow over the next two decades. He said that you can see in its physical structure residues of the mistakes of the last century and the gross errors of the past decade. "You can see the decline of its traditional industries and the failure to replace them by anything else. You can see the growth of ethnic conflict. It is to cities like Glasgow (and there are hundreds like it) that we must devote ourselves. The problem is not just of money but of its political structure, its economic structure, and its value system. We do not start with a green field. We have to work with an existing situation, cluttered with many residues of the past, and we have very limited abilities to handle those industrial and group relationships which could correct what has gone wrong."

Other speakers emphasized the contrasts to be found in countries, such as Indonesia and India, where the *per capita* income is very low and children grow up in an environment that combines the bullock cart and the jet plane; where there are highly sophisticated elites and almost stone age cultures; where there is open heart surgery and the witch doctor.

Dr. CHUN (College of Medicine, University of Korea, Seoul, Korea) told of a Community Development Movement concerned with the amelioration of the environment which was also attempting the important task of spiritual revival of the people. When people had little hope and felt exploited or neglected it was difficult to maintain an environmental program at an effective level. This could only be achieved if viable social units helped actively in the determination of the goals.

This approach was strengthened by two examples from UNICEF's work in Egypt. J. F. McDOUGALL (International Year of the Child Secretariat, Geneva, Switzerland), described how UNICEF had worked with the government of Egypt to set up services for mothers and children in the new villages built on reclaimed land, opened up by the construction of the Aswan Dam. The population of the villages was a very mixed group of landless laborers and people evacuated from the canal zone. UNICEF found that it was extremely difficult to get any participation from the people in these amorphous communities. However, when they continued their work in a second set of old villages, into which electricity from the Aswan Dam had just been introduced, the situation was very different. Here there was a structured society with traditional leadership. The people knew their own needs and were prepared to participate in meeting them.

JOHN BAYLEY (Victoria Town and Country Planning Board, Melbourne, South Australia) pointed out that it was easy to underestimate the resistance people had to change and the fears generated by even the most benevolent of unexpected change. He gave an example from Australia in which desired and desirable planning changes were set back many years because too precipitate action had been taken. Several speakers had stressed the need to start with small beginnings, and he quoted a saying of C. A. Doxiadis: "What the world needs is people with a vision of the city of the future who can build a room tomorrow morning."

The meeting closed with KATHERINE ELLIOTT saying that it is strange that so many international and voluntary agencies—with so much goodwill, expertise, and funds—have achieved so little. She wondered whether it was because they were located in such pleasant places. Maybe, if their offices were in Calcutta, for example, and if the officials had to take the bodies of the children who had died overnight off the doorstep before they could get inside in the morning to start their work, it might be that they would take swifter action to remedy matters.

LIST OF PAPERS PRESENTED

JOHN BAYLEY (Victoria Town and Country Planning Board, Melbourne, South Australia): "Priorities for action in the human environment."

KATHERINE ELLIOTT (The CIBA Foundation, London, UK), "Three encouraging ideas from India."

K. K. FIAWOO (Department of Sociology, University of Ghana, Accra, Ghana): "Aspects of the young child's physical and social environment in Ghana."

CALLIOPE MOUSTAKA (Education Counsellor, Athens, Greece): "Children evaluate their neighborhood."

C. SEPULVEDA (UN Asian and Pacific Development Institute, Bangkok, Thailand): "Child perspectives in Asian development."

J. MUNTANOLA I THORNBERG (Department of Architecture, University of Barcelona, Spain): "Towards an environmental childhood: guidelines for the environmental education of tomorrow."

ACCESSIBILITY OF FACILITIES TO CHILDREN

Coordinator: WILLIAM MICHELSON
Department of Sociology, University of Toronto, Canada

THE PARTICIPANTS in this session agreed to explore the kinds of facilities children need now and in the near future. They also agreed to pursue the access children have to them, while noting barriers to sufficient (or equal) opportunity, which have to be overcome. The results of research projects were reported from a number of countries, including Norway, Iran, Switzerland, Canada, Indonesia, and Greece.

The major facilities considered particularly important for children (in addition to play facilities attached to schools and universities) were public parks, sports grounds, playgrounds, and gymnasia; libraries, cultural centers, and craft activities; cycle paths and just plain space. It was emphasized that those activities requiring specialized spaces and facilities cannot occur unless provided for by the community. Traffic hazards were noted by many as particularly crucial barriers to most forms of activity by children. Speakers also pinpointed socioeconomic, regional, and sex disparities in accessibility of facilities.

The tone of the session was set by MAGNA and TORE RAUNDALEN (Institute of Psychology, University of Bergen, Norway) who reported the findings of several large scale surveys of children's reactions to their environment in that country. Many of these children were very fearful, particularly of traffic accidents on the route to school and of violence from other children in the school playgrounds. While they expressed desires for several facilities lacking in their environment, what they desired most of all was a greater concern for their needs by adults: "doing something together with us," "having time to help us."

The popularity of children's libraries was brought out in a film showed by F. MOEZI MAGHADAM (Institute for the Intellectual Development of Children and Young Adults, Teheran, Iran). This institute was founded 13 years ago with a staff of four. This has now expanded to over 1500 staff in 150 cultural centers. There are many mobile libraries which tour the rural areas. Last year, more than 11,600,000 visits were made to the centers by children from 5 to 16 (boys and girls) to read or borrow books; watch films, film strips, and plays; sing or play musical instruments; paint or do graphic work on their own wall newspaper; write poems, articles, scripts; act, photograph, record, and direct their own films and plays. The children are now even getting involved in the administration of these cultural centers.

From Greece, KATHERINE THANOPOULOU (Greek Library Association, Athens, Greece) reported that the Greek Library Association will open a model children's library in Athens in November, and that a campaign has been launched to establish children's libraries throughout Greece.

There were a number of presentations from Greek researchers, mostly made without previous knowledge of the work of each other. All of these suggested that Greek children face many severe challenges. TONY EVANGELOPOULOU (Early Childhood and Elementary Education Center, Athens, Greece), for example, presented pictures painted by 300 elementary schoolchildren showing what the child would like to have in his neighborhood and school that is now missing. It is generally considered that the neighborhood and school form the microworld in which the child develops his social nature. Most of the children depicted their schools as barren, cold, underequipped, and authoritarian. They cried out for more space for playgrounds, more space for sidewalks, more space for parks, more space for "green."

DR. JANNIS PAPADOPOULOS and his colleagues (Evangelismos Medical Center, Athens, Greece) presented comparative statistics and standards on active play and sports facilities, as well as on safety, from quite a number of cities in Europe. These comparative figures showed that Greek cities are greatly undersupplied with such facilities as playgrounds, sports grounds, swimming baths, green space, cycle paths, etc. In some cases comparative figures or standards were not available in Greece for things on which information was readily available elsewhere.

Successful independent action to improve the lot of Greek children was reported by A. and L. RIKAKI (Red Balloon Adventure Playgrounds and Environmental Studies, Athens, Greece), who had pioneered various kinds of adventure playgrounds in Athens and Thessalonika. Instances of the success of similar playgrounds were reported from Toronto, Copenhagen, and London.

There was a consensus on the part of participants that all those concerned with the accessibility of facilities for Greek children should be encouraged in their pressure for official standards and public action to recognize and meet the everyday needs of children. Several speakers reported the value of citizens organizing to bring about at least initial results independent of official support. It had taken this symposium for the Greek participants to become aware of one another and, on the initiative of ANGELA KIOSSOGLOU (Biologist, Athens, Greece) they decided to meet again as an independent group to advance their mutual interests. They also agreed to seek to enlist the cooperation of others with similar concerns for the everyday environmental welfare of children.

LIST OF PAPERS PRESENTED

JEAN-GILLES BOULA (Faculty of Educational Sciences, University of Geneva, Switzerland): "Projections for the future by children of 5–10."

Marie Eliou (National Center of Social Research, Athens, Greece): "La distribution des chances scolaires en Grèce."

Tony Evangelopoulou (Early Childhood and Elementary Education Center, Athens, Greece) with Yannis Pannayiotopoulos and Soula Pannayiotopoulou Private Psychiatrists, Athens, Greece): "The child draws his future."

F. Moezi Maghadam (Institute for the Intellectual Development of Children and Young Adults, Teheran, Iran): "How can the child participate in social development?"

E. C. Utami Munandar (Faculty of Psychology, University of Indonesia, Jakarta, Indonesia): "Are educators fostering creativity in children?"

J. S. Papadopoulos, M. Yannakou, and H. Asitopoulou (Evangelismos Medical Center, Athens, Greece): "Possibilities of self-action and interdependence of the child in the Greek cities of tomorrow."

Magna Raundalen and Tore Raundalen (Institute of Psychology, University of Bergen, Norway): "Interviews with 4000 Norwegian girls and boys about their daily life and the future."

Athina Rikaki (Red Balloon Adventure Playgrounds and Environmental Studies, Athens, Greece): "Red balloon adventure playgrounds."

BALANCING SAFETY WITH ADVENTURE

Coordinator: Amos Rapoport

Department of Architecture, University of Wisconsin at Milwaukee, WI, USA

The Coordinator opened the discussion by saying that: "All living things, all humans, and—above all—all young humans, engage in exploratory behavior. It is this exploratory behavior that leads to mastery over the environment, learning, self-confidence, etc., as several psychological models have demonstrated (e.g., Erikson's life stages or Witkin's growth of field independence). It is thus important that the home range of the child should be an area for active movement controlled by children. One can refer to Held's work with kittens, Piaget's sensori-motor development studies, the greater and less dimensions of mental maps, etc. In this connection one can reiterate the point made earlier about the advantages to the child of traditional settlements and small towns which offer more extensive home ranges and greater mobility. It is noticeable that children who live in such settlements draw more extensive and richer mental maps than those who live in large cities. Finally, Terence Lee's work on the journey to school is significant. He found that journeys under the control of the child result in less anxiety, aggressiveness, depression, and greater popularity with other children than journeys by bus over which the child has no control. The reason was that, in the former, the child maintains his lines of communication and hence acquires the ability to construct cognitive schemata. This suggests that we are dealing with perceived qualities of the environment—perceived threats and perceived safety—as seen by children, parents, caretakers, and institutions. The child's ability to use the environment is thus a two stage process: first parents, caretakers, institutions allow or prohibit activities on the basis of their perceptions; then the child's perceptions come into play in the sense of their identification of desirable, undesirable, dangerous, etc., and their actual ability to perceive in terms of maturation and experience.

In considering safety and adventure, we are dealing with perceived positive and negative qualities. The first include perceived hazards or threats, such as crime, "bad" people or neighborhoods, distance, weather, topography, traffic, drugs, etc. Many or most of these are subjectively defined and evaluated, i.e., they are culturally variable. This means that danger—and attractiveness—of environmental settings must be approached cross-culturally. In fact what is perceived as dangerous may be reversed. For a child from the desert or the mountains, the city is dangerous; for a child from the city the desert and mountains are hazardous.

DANGER ON THE ROADS

Diana Firth (Transport and Road Research Laboratory, Berks., UK) presented a paper showing that the child pedestrian is the road user at most risk. Figure 1 shows

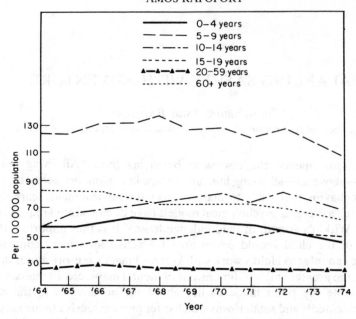

Fig. 1. Pedestrians killed or seriously injured per 100,000 population: 1964–1974 (by age).

the graph for great Britain of pedestrians killed or seriously injured between 1964 and 1974 with respect to age. In most other countries the picture is very similar. Table 1 shows how close the sites of the accidents were to the home of the child. There was an age but no sex effect here.

TABLE 1
Distance from home by age (percentage of accidents)

	All	0–4 years	5–9 years	10–14 years
Less than 100 yds (90 m)	35	56	36	19
100 yds to ¼ mile (400 m)	25	17	27	24
Over ¼ mile to ½ mile (0.8 km)	19	12	19	23
Over ½ mile to 1 mile (1.2 km)	8	5	8	12
Over 1 mile	13	10	10	22

Less than one-half of the children were alone at the time of the accident, and over one-third of the preschool victims were in the charge of an adult.

Regarding the activities of the child, 2 out of 5 children said they had stopped at the kerb before crossing, and 4 out of 5 were said to have been running across the road when the accident occurred.

In general it has been shown that children's knowledge of traffic signs is poor and, as might be expected, they become confused at complex traffic signals, not knowing which lights are relevant for them. Children's knowledge of safe behavior varies with the situation but their knowledge of simple road procedures is relatively good: 80% of children in one study mentioned that one had to look before crossing.

Table 2 shows the percentage response to a question on when should you cross. Less than 50% of the youngest group were correct, that is when the green man is showing and cars have stopped. Twenty percent thought that the flashing green man signal meant you could cross, but in fact this is the signal for not starting to cross although you may continue if you are already on the crossing.

TABLE 2

Percentage response to question:"When should you cross?" (Pelican crossing)

	7–8	8–9	9–10	10–11
Green man	47	75	70	77
Flashing green man	7	3	15	20
Traffic lights	13	3	3	0
When cars stop	10	13	3	3
No cars coming	13	3	3	0
Don't know	17	3	6	0
Totals	107	100	100	100
Base Nos.	30	32	33	30

The "green cross" code was launched in May 1971 with a large scale publicity campaign. This resulted in an 11% reduction in child casualties. The code has since been emphasized as a teaching guide for parents, teachers, and road safety workers to make best use of. The result is that most children in the UK know of the code. Knowing the green cross code is of course not to understand it or even carry out its instructions when crossing roads. Publications, leaflets, and pictorial learning aids, aimed at both adults and children, are used to emphasize its importance. In addition, television advertising is being regularly used in an attempt to make pedestrians more aware of road safety problems. A recent survey showed that only 37% of schools included road safety in the normal school curriculum, although in many other countries road safety education is compulsory.

Improvements in town planning and the introduction of pedestrian segregated areas have been shown to be most effective in reducing the casualty rate of pedestrians. These efforts are, however, long term, and the major part of our road environment will remain unchanged for some time to come.

With the increasing number of vehicles on roads it is difficult to prevent casualty figures from rising year to year. However, child casualties have been slightly reduced in the UK over the last 10 years, and although it is impossible to attribute the overall reduction to specific measures, this paper has attempted to show some of the ways in which it has been achieved.

V. I. VAN DER DOES (International Federation for Pedestrians, The Hague, Netherlands) supported this paper, saying that "The latest statistics I could lay hands on are from Tübingen University in West Germany, published in June of this year. These show that in the Bundesrepublik 44% of the 0–5 years old who died did so from road traffic accidents, 70% of the 5–10 years of age, and 66% of the 10–15 years old. Half of these were pedestrians. Road traffic is killer number one among certain age groups. Most child road accidents happen on their way to or from school and during play near to their home. However, to grow up into a healthy well-balanced youngster, a child has to play".

In 1960 PROFESSOR SANDELS of the Institute for Child Development Psychology at the University of Stockholm, Sweden began her research on the causes of child road accidents. She found that a child under eight cannot yet cope with road traffic for many reasons. He is too small to look over cars and so cannot have an insight in the situation—he looks against the cars. He is impulsive and his age does not permit him to combine various actions. His impressions of what he sees make place quickly for new ones—they do not yet "stick" in his mind. A young child has difficulty in establishing the correct location of a sound, as tests have proved. He reacts slower to movement from the side (i.e. turning traffic at crossings). As the child of 8–9 years of age cannot yet assess speed correctly or relate it to time and distance, the fact that a car which is overtaking—although it is further away—has more speed and will reach him sooner than the car which is overtaken, is not yet understood.

These and many other causes make it necessary to adapt the environment—the road to school, the surrounding of the street he lives in—to the child. Parked cars are a fine place for play (e.g. hide and seek) and one of the worst causes of child road accidents.

With the very best education and best brochures, a young child cannot be adapted to today's road traffic as he cannot yet put into practice what he is taught. However, right from the beginning, his parents must teach him the right way to behave in traffic, and, first of all, give him a good example. Also they must plead with the authorities for protective measures.

The precedence given to motorized traffic today is often maintained under the slogan "We have no money for adapting or improving the residential area or the hazardous street." No attention is paid to the sky-high financial consequences of road accidents. These can be calculated in all kind of ways: there are direct and indirect costs which are caused by a road accident: hospital costs and expenses arising from, for instance, the repeated operations necessary on children with leg prothesis which have to be changed constantly; legal costs; and costs of movement due to invalidity; costs of retraining; and the loss to the society caused by an early death.

ACCIDENT PREVENTION

LARS H. GUSTAFSSON (Joint Committee for the Prevention of Accidents of Children, Uppsala, Sweden) said that in Sweden, during the last 15 year period the number of accidental deaths per 100,000 children has fallen from 25 to 12: a 50% decrease. All types of accidents have decreased in frequency. Even the deaths from traffic accidents have decreased despite the greatly increased traffic intensity. This development is a result of a number of collaborative activities and it is possible to distinguish the following steps:

1. In 1954 two pediatricians joined with the Swedish Red Cross and the Swedish Save the Children Federation to form the Joint Committee for the Prevention of Childhood Accidents. The committee has since been extended by the addition of representatives of a number of official and professional bodies, national safety organizations, and major women's organizations.

2. Intensive information directed towards parents followed the usual methods, but now we know that pamphlets and booklets have just a marginal effect, if any at all. We have learnt that the most efficacious control of children's environmental risks is the direct knowledge of the parents and of the children themselves.

3. In 1973 leglislation was introduced requiring safety arrangements in the homes. Regulations were drawn up for residential construction concerning the safety of windows, staircases, balconies, storage places for medicines and chemical preparations, stoves and other hot external surfaces, electrical outlets, and so forth. Further measures are necessary, especially with regard to the external environment, including regulations for the planning of streets and major roads and for the design and positioning of playgrounds and bicycle areas. Active legislation has now been generally accepted as a means to grant all children a minimum safety standard level in their homes and playing areas.

4. In 1977 a special State Commission for Investigation on Childhood Accidents was set up by the Parliament. One task is to find the appropriate way of setting up a central official body dealing with children's environment in a broad, comprehensive way to reinforce the work of the Joint Committee. Another task is to test new methods of local prevention.

5. In cooperation between the State Commission and the Chief Medical Officers for Child Health in Uppsala, we are now trying to develop an alternative strategy for the accident prevention work of the child health centers. The idea is to activate parents and children themselves into taking more responsibility for their own environment. We have trained a number of parents and even teenagers to become what we call "ombudsman for the children's environment." That means a special kind of safety supervisor. They are working as independent committees in their own housing areas but in close cooperation with the child health centers. We are providing them with accident reports from the hospital and with our basic knowledge of preventive strategy.

MICHEL MANCIAUX (International Children's Center, Paris, France) added that accidents represent one of the major problems of today's pediatricians as well as a great threat to all children in the world of tomorrow, in both the developing and the developed countries of the world. In most nations of the third world, accidents come second or third among the causes of child mortality after the age of 2. Yet accidents are a problem whose importance is almost everywhere badly underestimated. In most countries—developed as well as developing—nobody seems to care. Among the constraints considered by the people who are building our environment (who are designing the framework of our lives), weight, size, cost, and aesthetics far outweigh considerations of safety. In any device affecting our daily life, safety is very often the most neglected aspect and the last to be taken into consideration.

With young children, parents are often aware of the risks but do not know how to avoid them. With older children they often tend to overestimate the physiological abilities of their child to cope, for example, with the traffic situation.

It is not possible, indeed not desirable, to try to remove all possibilities of accidents from the child's environment. The risks may be worthwhile and positive, provided they are known—even calculated—and provided the child is prepared to experiment in risky situations with a good chance of overcoming the difficulties. On the other hand, unmanageable risks should be removed from children's lives.

EXPLORING THE ENVIRONMENT

The final paper followed MICHEL MANCIAUX's lead. It was presented by ROGER A. HART (Environmental Psychology Program, City University of New York, NY USA). He said that it is important to distinguish "danger" from risk or unpredictability; "safety" from security. To remove risk or uncertainty completely would deny adventure; but we must do all we can to remove "danger" from children's everyday lives. "Danger" is undoubtedly a culture bound notion. However, certain elements and situations in the environment are universally dangerous: they defy learning through experimentation by infants and young children because they are beyond their physical or perceptual abilities. Other parts of the environment are simply "unpredictable" to children; they await experimentation and learning. It is valuable, then, to think of children facing an "unpredictable" world; one full of risks, which it is necessary for them to engage with if they are to develop competence and go on further to explore an ever-expanding world. Our job, as social scientists and child and environmental professionals, is to consider how to guarantee children in the future accessibility to an environment without danger but one which provides unpredictably (or risk) which is the basis of "adventure." This demands that we think of two sides of the issue: the degree of safety in the environment and the quality of the child's learning situation. Too often, approaches to child safety consider only the environmental side of the issue, showing little concern with the child as an active learner, striving for competence and adventure in the environment.[1]

Figure 1 is a schematic representation of the major forces influencing the outward expansion of children's exploration of the physical world. It draws considerably from the writing of John Bowlby[2] on the attachment behavior of children and their caretakers, and from my earlier conceptualizations on this subject.[3] The diagram emphasizes that, in thinking of a child's environmental exploration, it is necessary to think of the child as part of an interactive system made up of child and "caretaker(s)." In many societies the traditional caretaker has been a child's mother, but as countries become more industrially developed, women's roles and family structures have changed, and more women find employment outside the home, leaving child care more and more to be shared with other persons. The term "caretaker" represents all of these persons and institutions.

Children want to learn how to engage competently with the environment. They want to know how to climb steps, cross streams, and play in the road. At the same time, they have no desire to get hurt, and they grade the challenges in the environment which they set up for themselves; setting each challenge just a little beyond their existing experience with the phenomena. It is for this reason that a single tree can often satisfy the same child's climbing aspirations for many years.

Exploration is the outward vector in Figure 1. It expresses the urge found in all healthy children to move out from their home base to explore the environment in order (it is hypothesized) to learn about it and about themselves.[4] "Adventure" involves the search for new and challenging experiences, and serious restriction of exploration will deny a child the ability to develop into a competent, happy individual, and is to be avoided at all costs. Bowlby has distinguished two dynamically interacting forces which guarantee the renewal of contact between an exploring child and his or her caretaker: attachment behavior, exhibited by the child, and maternal caretaking, practiced usually by the mother.

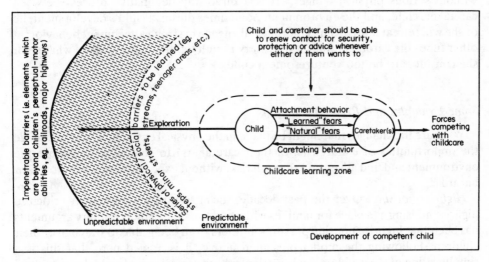

Fig. 1. A schematic representation of the balance of safety and adventure in child development.

Attachment Behavior

Attachment behavior begins with an infant's proximity-maintaining behavior in the form of crying when mother leaves the room. This begins between six and nine months according to Bowlby. Over the next two to three years a child gradually makes excursions away from the mother and occasionally goes out of sight. It has been found that children will explore more readily if their mother is present, which becomes particularly marked when mother and child are in a strange (i.e. unfamiliar) place. After three years of age children become much better able to accept their mother's temporary absence and to engage in play with other children. Children in their fourth year of life are increasingly able to accept surrogate attachment figures, such as a school teacher. There remain conditions, however. First, the substitute must be a familiar person, preferably known through the child's mother. Secondly, the child needs to have a healthy personality and not be easily alarmed. Finally, a child needs to know where the primary caretaker is, and he or she needs to feel confident that contact can be resumed at short notice in an emergency. In this way children are gradually able to reduce their degree of attachment to their caretakers; but even at six or seven years of age a child often attempts to hold a parent's hand and resents it if they refuse. Throughout the latency of a normal child, attachment behavior continues as a dominant strand of life.

Caretaking Behavior

Maternal caretaking is defined by Bowlby as "any behavior of a parent, a predictable outcome of which is that the young are brought either into the nest, or close to the mother, or both" (p. 291).

Together, the child and his or her maternal caretaker, work as a learning system to experiment with and evaluate the child's ability to explore new places and situations without serious physical danger.[5] It is a three-way negotiative process between caretaker, child, and the environment. Sometimes during a child's development, he or she will retreat more from exploring and engage in strong attachment behavior; at other times the caretaker finds it necessary to pull tightly on the reins of what he or she considers to be too venturesome a child.[2]

Some Examples and Recommendations

What are the changes that might be made in the physical environment to maximize the opportunities of children (with their caretakers) to competently explore the environment and find adventure through risk, without exposing themselves to major hazards?

Highrise housing. Over the past decade, social scientists have heavily criticized highrise housing as a place for families with children. One of their primary arguments has been that highrise housing prevents mothers from being able to watch over their children. Following the model presented above, it is argued here that this is a simplification of the problem: highrise denies both caretaker and child the opportunity to see, hear, or otherwise recontact each other at will. If a child is playing outside of a highrise tower, the "childcare learning zone" is broken and no negotiative learning can occur. This results in an "all or nothing" approach to child care for those low income families who commonly live in highrise housing: either the parents relinquish care and let their children play outside anywhere they wish, or they take the overprotective route of keeping them inside the apartment all of the time.

Although certain countries have stopped providing public housing in highrise for families with children,[6] the problem remains in many countries throughout the world and is even growing in many of the third world nations.

The suburbs. A central rationale for the suburbs, both from the point of view of planners and parents who have moved to them, has been that they provide an ideal environment for children. The argument was that they offered a safer, cleaner, and healthier environment than cities. An often unstated argument was that they also offered social homogeneity, removal from the poor, and, hence, less mobile classes of people. So powerful has this image been that most city parents' images of an ideal play environment for their children are based on suburban examples. But suburbs are probably not the ideal environment for children they have been claimed to be as in attempting to create a safe environment the suburbs have at the same time often created an extremely boring environment. Opportunities for interest and adventure are destroyed by the creation of a manicured physical landscape and a homogeneous social environment.[3] The use of motor vehicles to find greater diversity beyond the suburb does not solve the problem for the children, but only compounds it by making children even more dependent on adults. This dependence is not in keeping with the model presented here, that free exploration and learning by the child are central to the development of his or her competence.

Traffic-segregated housing development. With much enthusiasm, numerous postwar new towns embarked upon plans for segregating traffic and people. It had been hoped that this would liberate people, particularly children, to freely explore and utilize the landscape without the danger and nuisance of traffic. While these systems have apparently met with some success, British research has revealed a pattern of children's play behavior which illustrates the value of understanding the human ecology of settlements.[7] It has been found that children in traffic-segregated housing areas commonly chose to play in the access roads and parking areas rather than in the courtyards and play places which were planned for them. Children want to be where there is activity.[8] This is a clear demonstration of the dangers of thinking of single "solutions." It is necessary to look comprehensively at interacting human-environment systems.

Adventure playgrounds. Adventure playgrounds proponents in Europe and North America argue that opportunities for adventure are missing from many children's environments and are particularly absent from the traditionally designed concrete and steel playgrounds.[9] However, strong resistance to these very exciting self-built and ever-changing play settings has come from many parents and institutions because of their fears of accidents to children, particularly in the insurance bound United States.[10] Nevertheless, recent data shows that fewer serious accidents occur in these playgrounds than in traditional ones.[11] In looking for explanations one simply has to turn to a model of children's environmental exploration presented above. If children have the chance to experience risk, or uncertainty, as in the adventure playgrounds, they will learn to grade environmental challenges for themselves. If they are unsure or need help, they have the option of turning to the "playleader," the formal caretaker in this setting, who is there as a support for a child's expanding explorations and experiments in competence. In contrast, a traditional playground offers very little room for manipulation or modification and a child's self-imposed graded challenges. A child quickly becomes bored and seeks further excitement in such pranks as tying chains up to make swings higher, climbing the steel scaffolds of slides, etc. Such dramatic experimentation in concrete and steel playgrounds is dangerous. The mistake has been made of thinking of safety as lying in the environment rather than in the behavioral transaction between the environment and children.

Is Danger to Children Increasing as a Problem?

During the symposium on the "City for Human Development" organized by the World Society for Ekistics in Athens, 1973, C. A. DOXIADIS[12] presented his ideas for guaranteeing the safety of children in cities. He argued for a series of spaces fitted to the age of the child which gradually expand as the child develops. RENÉ DUBOS responded to this suggestion critically, arguing that children have a higher degree of behavioral adaptability to external dangers than DOXIADIS credited them with.[13] As support for his arguments he noted: "On the Navajo reservation, preschool children tend sheep and goats almost in solitude; in New York City they play games in crowded streets, unconcerned with automobile traffic. Most of the children who grew up among the countless hazards of the small family farm, or of the Lower East Side in New York, developed into well adjusted adults and many have become highly successful in various walks of life" (p. 254).

PROFESSOR DUBOS was correct in challenging the mechanistic approach of suiting the environment to human behavior and arguing for the more dynamic stance of human adaptation. However, some dangers defy the learning abilities of young children. These must be identified and removed. But, in doing so, we must not seek to remove all risk and uncertainty from the environment, for such an environment would deny all interest and adventure to children.

I conclude with four recommendations for change:

(1) Those hazards which cannot be safely learned by children should be identified and removed from children's lives.

(2) Parents and planners should leave opportunities for children to explore and find and create their own environment rather than attempt to provide special places and equipment to meet all children's needs.

(3) Environmental planning and design should be based upon an understanding of human ecology.

(4) Environmental planning and design of local areas should always involve the participation of residents to the maximum degree possible.

REFERENCES

1. S. SANDELS, *A Report on Children in Traffic.* Skandia Insurance Co. Ltd., Sweden, 1971.
2. J. BOWLBY, *Attachment and Loss,* Vol. I & II. Basic Books, New York, 1969.
3. R. A. HART, The genesis of landscaping, in *Landscape Architecture,* October, 1974, Special Issue: "Children Know Best".
4. D. W. FISKE and S. R. MADDI (eds.), *Functions of Varied Experience,* Dorsey Press, Homewood, Illinois, 1961.
    H. FOWLER, *Curiosity and Exploratory Behavior,* Macmillan, New York, 1965.
    R. A. HART, *Children's Experience of Place: A Developmental Study,* Irvington, New York, 1978.
5. M. MEAD, Neighbors and human needs, *Ekistics,* February, 1966.
6. *Childhood City Newsletter,* No. 8.
7. DEPARTMENT OF THE ENVIRONMENT, *Children at Play,* HMSO, London, 1973.
8. J. JACOBS, The use of sidewalks: assimilating children, *The Death and Life of Great American Cities,* Random House, New York, 1961.
    A. BENGTSSON, *Environmental Planning for Children's Play,* Praeger, New York, 1970.
9. HURTWOOD, LADY ALLEN of, *Planning for Play,* Thames & Hudson, London, 1968.
    R. MOORE, Anarchy zone, *Landscape Architecture,* October, 1974 Special Issue: "Children Know Best."
10. C. COOPER, *The Adventure Playground,* Center for Planning and Development Research, University of California, Beserkly, 1970.
11. A. HOLMES and P. MASSIE, *Children's Play: A Study of Needs and Opportunities,* Michael Joseph, London, 1970.
    R. OWNE, *Insurance: A Survey of Insurance Aspects of Playground Management,* National Playing Fields Association, London (no date).
12. C. DOZIADIS (ed.), *Anthropopolis: City for Human Development,* Athens Publishing Center, Athens, Greece, 1974.
13. DOXIADIS, op. cit., p. 254.

LIST OF PAPERS PRESENTED

DIANA E. FIRTH (Transport and Road Research Laboratory, Berks., HK): "The child in the road environment."

LARS H. GUSTAFSSON (Joint Committee for the Prevention of Accidents of Children, Uppsala, Sweden): "Childhood accidents today and tomorrow: what can we learn from Swedish experience?"

ROGER A. HART (Environmental Psychology Program, City University of New York, NY, USA): "Children's exploration of tomorrow's environments."

V. I. VAN DER DOES (International Federation of Pedestrians, The Hague, Netherlands): "Why do we use the word epidemiology when discussing road accidents?"

6

The Child and the State

THE STRATEGY OF LEARNING FROM MISTAKES AND INFLUENCING DECISION MAKERS

AUBREY KAGAN

Laboratory for Clinical Stress Research, Stockholm, Sweden

LEARNING

It is normal to learn from mistakes. We have difficulty in learning any other way. But mistakes are often made without learning from them. This is expensive and we cannot afford it. The population is still increasing, resources are diminishing, and distribution of good things is such that 33% of the population remain at or below subsistence level whatever is done. It is more important than ever to make fewer mistakes and to learn from them quickly.

Rapid changes in fundamental aspects of family life—such as reproduction, rearing and educating children, the role of parents to each other and to the children, and the role of women in work—are being made with little more than expediency or conflicting philosophies as a guide. At such a time, fundamental mistakes are likely to be made and lessons need to be learnt before much harm is done.

So how do we learn? Are we failing seriously? What can we do to improve the future?

The usual human learning procedure is to take some action in response to an innate or acquired drive, identify the error in the action, make a correction, see if the error is changed, repeat the process until the correct action has been found. This procedure works very well providing the signal of error is clear and closely follows the action. But it must not be too drastic and the consequences must not be lethal. With this procedure, we learn profoundly important actions that may be quite simple or very complex. For example, the baby teaches the mother how to respond to it by crying when she acts wrongly and smiling when she acts correctly. Babies teach themselves how to grasp objects and the young child learns how to walk. In these examples the drive is innate. Learning to speak, play a musical instrument, or think logically or in terms of mathematics, are all combined innate and acquired drives in which the learning process is again by trial, feedback of error, and repetition of the process. The child's understanding of the rules of behavior within its own society follows the same pattern.

At one end of its range of application we share this pattern of learning with animals. But we go beyond this. The same pattern of learning is the basis of the scientific method. In the latter, the process differs only in that the object of the learning process and the methods of testing for error are often acquired, and logical developments are deliberately designed for the purpose.

For example, the objective of preventing children from dying of measles by applying a procedure developed in a laboratory was tested and found to be successful by applying it to a large number of children in a randomized controlled trial. Most of the errors had been worked out in the laboratory prior to exposing the children to what might otherwise have been risky. But the relatively small scale trial allowed the method to be applied on a large scale with greater efficiency and less risk.

As another example we may take the successful randomized controlled trial to show the effect of summer sessions of broad but intensive "educational, artistic, and recreational experience" on subsequent staying at school and entering college.[1]

Another trial showed that a method of teaching designed to "remedy disorders in culturally disadvantaged youth" worked well in the school in which it was developed but not when it was applied elsewhere.[2]

We may look for the impact of this process of learning on the children of the world during the third quarter of this century. In the developed countries birthrate has been reduced (in some too much perhaps) whilst in the developing countries it has changed very little. On the other hand, despite the billion extra mouths to feed, food *per capita* has not decreased in the developing countries (in 47 countries there was an increase in calories *per capita*). Further, in the developing countries due to diminished perinatal and childhood mortality, life expectation has increased from 40 to 50 years. Technically there have been marked successes in birth control, nutrition, and infectious disease control. Administratively there have been marked successes in infectious disease control in all countries, some improvement in nutrition, sucess in birth control in developed countries, but to a much lesser extent in developing countries. There seems to have been very little progress, either technically or administratively, in family care, education, or social interaction.

Examination of the literature shows that advances, e.g. in health and nutrition, are closely associated with learning from mistakes. On the other hand, whilst little has been learnt from mistakes in the fields of family care and education, there have been many changes. In a world in which the rate of social change and social expectation have both increased markedly, changes in family care and relationships and in education have been to the fore.

In spite of the ideas of Bowlby and Spitz, now nearly a quarter of a century old, we have no hard facts on what care a child needs or the best ways to provide it. In spite of the many different types of education practiced and the innumerable so-called experiments, we do not know what is best for what purpose for which child. There are opposing schools of equal plausibility and unproven value in all these fields. In spite of plenty of mistakes we have learnt very little from them.

OVERCOMING TECHNICAL DIFFICULTIES

There are technical and psychosocial reasons for this neglect and there are psychosocial reasons for nonacceptance of technically satisfactory methods of proven worth.

Technical difficulties that arise when there is a long interval between cause and effect can be overcome by the randomized controlled trial.

The pseudo-ethical objections to a randomized controlled trial must give way to the logical and humane conclusion that—when you do not know whether an action will do more harm than good, and when you do not know who it will benefit and who it will harm, and when you do know that it will cost the people concerned a lot—it is unethical to not carry out a trial.

Difficulties due to the large variety of hypothesized approaches and the wide range of differing situations in which they are to be practiced can be overcome by making observations on a small scale in many places. The world is rich in diversity and numbers of people. Instead of grumbling about this we should take advantage of it for the collective benefit.

The technical difficulty due to our inability to infer, without special mathematics, what is likely to happen when three or more partly independant factors are interacting (Forrester's definition of a complex situation) would be overcome if a systems approach could be applied. In the absence of an applicable systems approach, a more clumsy method depends on continuous monitoring for good or bad effects. That is to say that after improving an approach as a result of its initial evaluation on a small scale, there should be a continuous monitoring on a sample basis of its application on a large scale. Unexpected ill effects or effect of changing social conditions will be detected at an early stage.

The technical difficulty of applying the systems approach is due to the need to have good information on the quantitative relationships of the many different factors affecting the outcome as well as a good idea of what makes the whole system work. Such information is not usually available and is generally expensive to obtain. But in all randomized controlled trials the various factors will be interacting even if the study design neutralizes their effect on the outcome. For very little extra cost the quantitative relationships can be determined within the context of such trials. Collectively they might provide the necessary data at little cost.

Hypotheses of a fundamental and general nature—how the system works—may also be tested for little extra cost, in some places, within the framework of randomized controlled evaluations. Applied and basic research can be combined to the benefit of both.

OVERCOMING PSYCHOSOCIAL DIFFICULTIES

Psychosocial obstacles to evaluation and application of evaluated methods are due to subjective threat to needs. The needs can be thought of as survival, love and belonging, status and self-esteem, self-expression. It is important to remember that we are concerned here only with the belief that need is threatened. It is, of course, important for other reasons to know if the need is really threatened, but here we are only concerned with the belief. Further, we are concerned with such subjective threats at many different levels. It is clear that parents can feel threatened by the same action in all or any of the above respects. But it is not so generally appreciated that the same action may threaten the survival, belonging, status or self-expression needs of the child's peer group, its teachers, the medical profession, commune leaders, international representatives. All these are human and all feel these needs but in different ways. It follows from this that there may often be conflict in felt needs. What satisfies the commune (e.g. a particular form of education) may threaten the parents, teachers, or children.

Furthermore it is seldom that there are clear cut priority rules accepted by society, and these are fewest when they are needed most.

That these considerations can be powerful restraints on proper action is well exemplified in all aspects of childhood from conception to adolescence, even when the good effects of an action are well established, e.g. breast feeding (where the baby's health and the mother's status may be in conflict) or in family planning (where community survival and parental security may appear to be in conflict).

When the beneficial effects of an approach are in doubt, e.g. mother substitutes for toddlers, then each of the interests concerned with the action will substitute their own value system for reality and the group with the strongest voice will have its way.

Small groups living at or below subsistence level have a subjective fear of any change as a threat to survival. This is not surprising because most change in their experience will have been harmful, and though they have little to lose they are likely to lose all. Such groups are by necessity traditionalists but tradition prevents them from getting out of their present rut. The way to overcome such difficulties, which are very real for a large proportion of the world population, must be to provide them with a safety net when any new approach is being tried out. We make sure that when a child is learning to walk that it will come to little harm when it falls. We would not leave it on the edge of a precipice. But that is analogous to what has been done when a new method of farming (single crop) or infant feeding (dried milk) is introduced to a developing society. Thus as a general principle we may say that whenever new actions are being tried out by a group of people, a safety net or insurance against grave danger must be provided either by the community itself, if it can afford it, or collectively from other communities if it cannot.

A difficulty of psychosocial origin, fundamental to the nonrecognition of mistakes, is that people often do not want to know them and are therefore reluctant to support any evaluation of their actions.

I think that most of us have experienced this. It is common even amongst the most scientific of the scientific. In the medical and scientific fields we can overcome the threat to "status" by knowing that evaluation is not made to condemn us but to better understanding. We make acceptance of evaluation, as a sign of status. Administrators, and particularly politicians, have greater difficulty because disclosures really threaten their security. The only way to get over this is for all to accept that mistakes are bound to happen and all to admire the administrator, and vote for the politician, who makes a point of looking for them.

The technical and psychosocial difficulties that I have mentioned have been overcome on occasion in social sciences and practice, particularly in recent years. Some of the work already mentioned, the work presented at this symposium by Cravioto and his colleagues in Mexico, the work of McKay and his colleagues in Colombia on evaluating the effect on "cognitive ability in undernourished children" of a combination of nutrition health and education at different ages,[3] and our own small contribution on day care in Sweden, and quite a few other studies all go to show that learning from mistakes is a practical approach to complex social problems. The future depends on a more frequent application of this approach and this depends on its acceptance at all levels of the community. The following principles will promote this approach:

(1) There should be no action without evaluation.
(2) The local, national, or world community should provide the costs for evalua-

tion and for a "safety net" for those who might need it as a result of evaluating procedures.

(3) What is shown to be harmful or useful for one community should be available knowledge for all.

(4) Evaluation should be seen by all concerned as a means to get what is wanted with minimum risk. It should also be seen as a means of reaching a reasonable compromise agreement when needs conflict.

Avoidance of evaluation should be seen for what it is—a threat to the future and support for the charlatan. The best way to secure acceptance of learning from mistakes in the social field is to show that it works. I believe that this is best done by planning and carrying out evaluative studies with the knowledge and assistance of all concerned—parents, teachers, health advisers, commune leaders, and to some extent children themselves. All concerned should be informed of the results and given opportunity to question and discuss them. In this way satisfaction is maximized, threat minimized, and acceptable compromise solutions can often be found.

The process of learning from mistakes is a natural one and understood, even when not applied, by most people. Society has removed authoritative and traditional guides to social action. Now it must provide the means whereby people can produce their own.

REFERENCES

1. J. YINGER, K. IKEDA, and F. LAYCOCK, Middle Start: Supportive interventions for higher education among students of disadvantaged background, Final Report, Project No. 5-0703 Oberlin College, Ohio., Dept. of Psychology, 1970.
2. S. FESBACH, A training, demonstration and research programme for the remediation of learning disorders in culturally disordered youth, Fernold School, Department of Psychology, UCLA 1970.
3. H. McKAY, L. SINISTERRA, A. McKAY, H. GOMEZ, and P. LLOREDA, Improving cognitive ability in chronically deprived children. *Science* **200**, 270-278.

THE LAW AND A BETTER ENVIRONMENT FOR GROWING UP

RICK J. CARLSON

Commonweal Inc., Bolinas, CA, USA

THE USUAL LITANY

The subject is the child and the state. The things which come to mind are problems of delinquency and anti-social behavior (including discussions of the appropriateness of adult status for the child), the various laws and programs to protect children until maturation, and a cluster of welfare and social service programs. These and other state-sponsored programs are supposed to enrich the lives of the young as well as afford them protection against the rigors of the world until they can cope by themselves. All of this makes sense; it is the usual litany. But is it enough?

Recently I was reading an article in *Time* referring to the development of a large industrial complex in the heart of a Brazilian forest. The article sketched out the environmental ravages, especially water contamination, soil and wind erosion, and the destruction of a number of habitats for some rare animal and bird species. The point of the article was that each of the particular blunders, such as water contamination, for example, could be dealt with, at least to some degree, by existing laws, but there were no laws to prevent the loss of the whole forest. We may be in much the same situation with children today. We have been successful in identifying particular dangers to the child and then in fashioning particular protections. But in our emphasis on particular threats, dangers, and stresses, we may be close to losing the whole forest. What if the quality of life for children has deteriorated substantially even as we have been successful in dealing with particular threats? To turn this around and put it hypothetically, is it possible that the quality of life and the well-being of the young in our world has declined, due to the total stress imposed upon them by an increasingly artificial environment, itself a product of rapid and recent technical growth and development? This is a crucial question, and in my reading of the literature on children, one not yet addressed, much less clearly formulated.

THE COMMONWEAL RESEARCH PROJECT

Commonweal, a center for health and human ecology in Bolinas, California, has begun to address this question through a modest but vigorous research program. yield to no one in our capacity to wildly speculate. This paper is a concise summary of our work thus far.

We approach the subject through four stages of conceptual and empirical development. In the first stage we are arraying the evidence for and against a decline in the quality of life for young people by looking at a number of biological and social indicators. At the second stage we are trying to identify those environmental conditions and factors which may be associated with the declines which we identify at stage one. Our intent at stage three is to introduce two concepts: first, the notion of "total stress" and, second, the idea of synergistic interactions. And at the fourth and final stage we return to the hypothesis and speculate that the evidence may show a "biosocial decline," which we argue is associated with uncontrolled technological development, or better put, the result of insufficient attention to ecological considerations in technological development. We hope to have a complete report on our work by this fall. For now this paper serves as an overview.

STAGE I. THE INDICATORS

During the years since the Second World War there has been an increase in chronic degenerative disease in the United States far greater than the aging of the population accounts for. As Arthur J. Vander wrote for a *Scientific American* publication:

> "No one doubts that the decrease in infectious diseases has been due to environmental alteration. . . . [Yet] the assumption is frequently made that, with the "conquest" of serious infectious diseases, people are simply living to be old enough to succumb to the chronic degenerative diseases. However, this assumption rests on another: that these modern killers strike only the aged, and are inexorable concomitants of aging. But such is not the case. The incidence of these diseases has been steadily rising in the young age groups as well; moreover, many societies have much lower incidences of the disease within the same age group. . . . Many factors in our environment increase our susceptibility to what might better be called "diseases of industrialized societies" rather than "diseases of aging."

In the single decade 1958–67, the proportion of Americans reporting one or more chronic conditions increased by over 7% from 41·4% to 49·1%[1] Heart conditions, high blood pressure, arthritis, rheumatism, digestive disorders, vascular lesions of the central nervous system, visual impairments, and orthopedic impairments increased, with a few minor exceptions, in all age categories.[2]

There was an increase of over 5% in the proportion of children under 17 reporting chronic conditions during that decade (from 18·8 to 24·6%) and there was a similar increase among 17–24 year olds (39 to 44·4%).[3] A closer look at 3000 New York children 11–12 years old revealed that 40% had at least one risk factor for coronary heart disease. The details give a sombre picture of urban American childhood. Twenty percent of the children had used alcohol that week; 20% did not exercise much; 18% had cholesterol levels equivalent to those of middle-aged men in Japan; and 10% were regular smokers. Of all American children aged 1–5, 30–40% are below standard for healthy hemoglobin levels. A low hemoglobin level is one of the major indicators of malnutrition.

During the same 10 years (1958–67), in which the federal study cited above gives us a window on the increase in chronic disease among children, arrests of children under 14 for acts of severe violence—murder, nonnegligent manslaughter, aggravated assault, forcible rape and robbery—increased from 38·2 per 100,000 to 123 per 100,000. There was a fivefold increase in arrests for these crimes during the 15 years 1952–67.[5]

During this same period, there was an enormous increase in reports of children with learning disabilities and such behavioral disorders as hyperactivity. Between 50% and 80% of children in juvenile halls and other penal institutions have learning problems—a very substantial proportion have specific learning disabilities. There is also ample clinical evidence that a high proportion of these children have health problems. So while we cannot fully document the following statement, it seems clear that during the 15 year period 1952–67 there was a marked increase in the proportion of American children whose bodies and minds would not serve them properly. Some of these children became so accustomed at failing to achieve their positive intentions that they turned to acts of violence and destruction, in which success—even for those with a host of physiological, perceptual, motor, and mental control problems—is reasonably well assured.

During much of that same 15 year period, the divorce rate increased sharply, increasing from 2·1 to 4·0 per 1000 between 1958 and 1972.[6] This divorce rate approached the record high of 4·3 reached at the end of the Second World War—but this time there was no vast demobilization to explain the increase.

Similarly, illegitimacy rates tripled during the post Second World War period.[7]

If one examines more closely the data on arrests of children for violent crimes, the divorce rate, and the illegitimacy rate, it is very striking that the rate increases are without exception the highest for the youngest group in the population, and decrease uniformly with increasing age.

Thus the increase in arrests for children under 14 was fivefold, for 15–17 year olds threefold, for 18–24 year olds twofold, and for over 25 year olds less than twofold.

Similarly, the increase in divorces was sharpest among the youngest couples, up between 67% and 70% for 20–29 year olds in the six years 1963–9.[8] And mothers 15–17 years of age showed a 49% increase in illegitimacy in the nine years 1966–75, with rates for older mothers declining in proportion to age.[9]

The above suggests that the trend among young children—exposed early to steadily increasing levels of environmental stress—is toward increasing social disintegration. The largest part of thie increase is evident in escalating homicide and suicide rates. Homicides, suicides, and deaths due to violent crime have increased at more dramatic rates for young people during the past 20 years than in the population as a whole. In fact, while deathrates have declined for all other age categories, mortality has been rising sharply within the 15–24 year old age group. Within the 12 month period between July 1976 and July 1977 alone, there was a 9·1% increase in the number of deaths for this age group.[10] In 1965 there were 6·8 homicides per 100,000 persons aged 15–24 years old. By 1975 there were 13·9 deaths per 100,000 persons. This represents a 104% rate of increase in deaths due to homicide. Among 25–34 year olds, during the same period, there was also a sharp increase in homicides, 55% higher in 1975 than in 1965.[11]

The increase in homicides among young people is accompanied by rises in the four other major crimes of violence, as is clearly shown in Table 1.[12]

While criminal activity has increased generally in the population since 1960, violent crimes have doubled for 18–24 year olds since 1960, more than doubled for 15–17 year olds, and tripled in the youngest age category—the 11–14 year olds.[13]

TABLE 1
Urban police arrests of suspected offenders for crimes of violence by age of suspects: 1960–74
(Rate per 100,000 urban population)

Year	Total, all ages	11–14 years old	15–17 years old	18–24 years old	25 years old and over
1960	144·1	70·3	273·0	357·6	111·3
1961	150·5	69·1	287·5	386·5	114·1
1962	144·0	76·3	272·4	360·9	109·6
1963	145·3	73·7	272·9	356·9	108·0
1964	151·6	79·1	279·9	368·5	111·8
1965	162·8	99·3	323·0	379·9	115·7
1966	176·2	110·9	362·4	400·5	123·7
1967	189·2	122·9	408·3	436·1	127·3
1968	200·0	146·0	437·3	473·3	125·4
1969	215·9	153·1	476·5	526·0	130·6
1970	232·1	163·9	523·5	550·3	140·0
1971	261·0	180·3	574·6	599·4	150·3
1972	270·6	194·9	601·2	634·3	163·0
1973	262·6	186·7	595·3	607·7	158·0
1974	291·5	195·3	674·7	703·4	169·4

Note: Crimes of violence comprise murder and nonnegligent manslaughter, forcible rape, robbery, and aggravated assault.

Source: National Commission on the Causes and Prevention of Violence, Staff Report, *Crimes of Violence*, Vol. II, 1969; US Department of Justice, Federal Bureau of Investigation, *Uniform Crime Reports for the United States,* annual issues, 1960–74.

Suicide is now the third most common cause of death among teenagers. Since 1950 the number of suicides has more than doubled for boys between the ages of 10 and 14. The rate for girls, although lower, has also increased, and the annual rate of suicides among 15–19 year olds is estimated to have tripled since 1950.[14] This means that "between the ages of 15 and 19, suicide is the cause of half as many deaths as all purely medical causes combined."[15] Suicide rates go up and down, characteristically following economic trends, but the increase in suicides among the young at present is particularly striking.

Professor Richard Seiden, of the University of California School of Public Health at Berkeley, who has made an in-depth study of suicide among the young and its correlation with our changing technology, asserts that "We are currently facing an epidemic of violent deaths in our youthful population."[16]

During this same period of substantial increases in chronic disease, violent crime, increased divorce, illegitimacy, homocide, suicide, and accidental death among the young, the average scores on the Scholastic Aptitude Tests for College Admissions went into an unprecedented and precipitous decline. The scores declined on the verbal SAT from 478 to 429; on the math SAT from 502 to 470, with scores over 700 declining by half in the seven year from 1969 to 1976, and scores over 600 declining by a third during this same period.[17]

STAGE II. ENVIRONMENTAL STRESSORS

The indicators are striking. Nonetheless, at this time we cannot prove indisputable associations between some of these indicators and anything more than a handful of environmental conditions. Consequently our work thus far has focused on deriving a list of potential environmental stressors which may be implicated. The following is an outline of those stressors:

I. Unintentionally contaminating by-products of technology
   A. Industrial practices
      (1) Chemical pollution
         (a) Industrial wastes, PCBs, PBBs
         (b) Petrochemicals
         (c) Pesticides
         (d) Particulate matter
      (2) Air pollution
      (3) Water pollution
      (4) Ionizing and nonionizing radiation
         (a) Nuclear pollution
         (b) Electromagnetic (microwave) pollution
         (c) X-ray stress
      (5) Toxic heavy metals
      (6) Ozone depletion
      (7) Noise pollution
      (8) Resource extraction, e.g. strip mining
      (9) Non-biodegradeable junk
   B. Agricultural practices
      (1) Pesticides and petrochemical fertilizers
      (2) Soil management, e.g. leaching of minerals, depletion of humus content, erosion
      (3) Large scale single crop farming
      (4) Hybridizing
      (5) Livestock management, e.g. crowding, feeding practices
      (6) Food processing and distribution, e.g. decline in nutritive value, contamination
   C. Global ecological transformation
      (1) Change in weather patterns/thermal pollution
      (2) Deforestation and desertification
      (3) Changing oxygen and carbon dioxide ratio
II. Individual lifestyle impacts
   A. Nutritional stress
      (1) Hunger
      (2) Unbalanced diet
         (a) Vitamin, mineral, and protein deficiencies
         (b) Excessive consumption of sugar, salt, fats, caffeine, empty calories
         (c) Over- and undereating
      (3) Food additives, e.g. coloring, preservatives, synthetics
      (4) Prenatal nutrition
   B. Destructive lifestyles
      (1) Addictions
         (a) Alcohol

      (b) Legal and illegal drugs
      (c) Tobacco
      (d) Caffeine
    (2) Lack of exercise
    (3) Over- and understimulation
    (4) Toxic cosmetics
    (5) Television
III. Sociocultural stresses
  A. Poverty
  B. Interpersonal and familial tension
  C. Overpopulation and crowding
  D. Work-related stress
    (1) Under- and overemployment
    (2) Dehumanizing work
    (3) Job pressures
    (4) Occupational toxins
  E. Apocalyptic stress, e.g. fear of species extinction or ecological disintegration

STAGE III. THE CONCEPTS OF TOTAL STRESS AND SYNERGY

To this point, the propositions offered in this paper are not necessarily very controversial. In other words, inquiries into the effects of a specific environmental condition on the human organism are quite acceptable; the literature is full of putative associations. It is our belief, however, that this one-by-one approach is inadequate. If the kind of deterioration which we speculate is taking place is occurring, we may not have the time to wait for a one-by-one assessment of stressors. Consequently, for reasons of urgency as much as anything else, we believe that the concept of "total stress" must be introduced to enrich the debate. At the level of the human organism, stress is experienced altogether and at once, irrespective of the number and nature of the stressors. To use a simple-minded illustration, a person who eats a piece of bacon and at the same time drinks a glass of white wine creates in his or her stomach a nitrosamine through the synergistic interaction of the two chemicals (along with chemicals in the body). In like manner our hunch is that the human organism does not process stressors one at a time through some clever evolutionary means to separate out their effects. Rather, stressors impinge on an individual at all times and at once; hence the organism is in a determined and potentially deadly dance with stress at all times. Hence it is our contention that it is possible to crudely quantify the *total* amount of stress impinging on an individual; and we further argue that a synergistic understanding of the impact of stress suggests that the overall impact of the stress is greater than the sum of the impacts of the individual stressors themselves.

If this approach makes sense the policy implications are staggering. For example, most regulatory policies dealing with stressors are based on a kind of "parts per million" approach, whereby assessments are made of the toxic effects of a given stressor on the human organism (or animal subject). Then, based on this evidence, a level is established for the introduction of that chemical or contaminant into the environment. This approach has at least two major flaws. First it assumes that the human organism is biologically consistent whereas all the emerging evidence argues in favor of biochemical uniqueness—one person's stress may be another's nurturance; and, second, it entirely ignores the concepts of "total stress and synergy" which we believe to be so important. If in fact the organism experiences accumulative and compounding effects of stress, a parts per million approach will always result in trying to catch up. Hence we argue that future regulatory policy should recognize that stress is not only cumulative but potentially "exponential." Consequently, the introduction of each new product, service, or chemical, should be assessed in terms of its additive and synergistic impact on the human organism. This approach also suggests that all existing technology assessment techniques are deficient to the extent to which they fail to recognize the interactions among stressors. These are just a few of the policy implications which emerge from our work thus far; there are obviously others.

STAGE IV. THE BIOSOCIAL DECLINE HYPOTHESIS

In Jonas Salk's book *the Survival of the Wisest,* he argues that an array of biological evidence suggests that a species reaches a critical point in its evolution when its choices, conscious or otherwise, will either plunge it into decline or allow it to recoup and move on to its next evolutionary rung. For the human species he suggests that we are at such a point; we are poised to make choices which will move us out of the current epoch which he calls Epoch A, into a new and more conscious epoch, Epoch B. The evidence we have been accumulating at Commonweal has been developed with this point of view. We are not disinterested researchers. We believe that as a species we are experiencing a deterioration of our world, and in the quality of our lives. With Salk, we think we are poised at an epocal transition. Accordingly, the choices we make in the near future are crucial. If the evidence we have arrayed thus far makes any sense, even if only impressionistically, a fundamental challenge is posed to the assumptions upon which our society (particularly in the United States) is grounded. In the epoch in which we live, we have assumed that growth is an unvarnished good and that widespread technological development and diffusion is sound, rational, and plausible. Our work and the work of many others challenges that assumption. But the major problem with many of the arguments about the limits to growth is that they have lacked probative evidence. What we have been trying to do is to produce evidence about the quality of life of young people so the challenge can be more resoundingly made. It is clear that much of what we have done thus far is rashly speculative. But we really have no choice since the kind of questions we are asking have simply not been asked. We are swimming in an uncertain sea, one which many scientists argue is too vast and murky to yield useful and dependable results. We disagree.

REFERENCES

1. NATIONAL CENTER FOR HEALTH STATISTICS (NCHS), *Vital and Health Statistics,* Series 10.
2. C. ERHARDT, *Mortality and Morbidity in the United States,* Harvard University, Press, 1974.
3. Ibid., table 4.6.
4. DEPARTMENT OF HEALTH, EDUCATION, AND WELFARE (HEW), *Subcommittee Report on Health and Environment,* September 1977.

5. *Social Indicators, 1973,* Statistics Policy Division, table 2/13.
6. HEW, *Facts of Life and Death,* Public Health Statistics, 1974.
7. Ibid.
8. NCHS, Series 21, No. 22.
9. *JAMA* **109** (1) (Jan. 2, 1975).
10. *Vital Statistics Reports, 1977.*
11. *Vital Health Statistics, 1956–77.*
12. *Social Indicators, 1977,* p. 250.
13. *Social Indicators, 1976,* p. 250.
14. PUBLIC AFFAIRS REPORT, *Bulletin of the Institute of Governmental Studies, University of California at Berkeley* **15** (4) 3 (August 1974).
15. Task Force Report on Pediatric Education by Subcommittee on Manpower Funding and Non-Pediatric Providers, 1974.
16. From April 1978 Interview with Professor Richard Seiden, School of Public Health, UC, Berkeley.
17. From *Educational Testing Services, 1956-1972.*

THE SOCIALIZATION OF CHILDREN IN THE PROCESS OF TRAINING FOR THE MANAGEMENT AND ORGANIZATION OF SOCIAL LIFE

CONSTANTINE SCHIFIRNET

Research Center for Youth Problems, Bucharest, Romania

1. SOCIALIZATION is one of the basic requirements of the child after a certain age.[1] Fundamentally, it is a training to enable him to understand and to participate in the organization and management of social life. This training must take place without hindering the normal development of the child or impeding his biophysical evolution.

2. Social experience is assimilated in a number of different ways dependent on the social group and the environment in which the child lives.[2] Each stage of his growth is characterized by certain learning abilities, related to his biological, psychological, and cultural development.

Once the child has started school, the area of his understanding and socialization widens and it becomes possible to organize his activities in different ways. In response to the need for socialization, society sets up frameworks within which the future citizen can develop a social behavior related to the aims, ideals, and nature of that particular society.

3. In the perspective of the evolution of contemporary society, induction into the social life of the country is an essential component of the child's development.

The increasing complexity of social life, the increasing participation of the populace in the processes of organization and management and the manifestations of initiative have caused a transformation of the means of preparing the individual (especially in the socialist societies).

Beforehand, initiation to social life was undertaken when the young people approached maturity, and the passage of this examination was an indispensable condition of their entry into adult life. Today, the idea grows continually stronger that the process of direct participation in management should penetrate all age groups. In effect, the traditional system had not recognized any special roles or status in society for children, and they were practically deprived of rights and liberties.

Modern society now accords the child a clearly defined position and seeks to create optimum conditions for the expression of his personality, both at his present age (with its especial needs and aspirations) and as a future citizen, participating fully in social life. However, the conditions differ from one country to another, and one social system to another, according to the social and historic traditions, and philosophic and political concepts, which shape their systems of education and training of children.

In working out a program of political education for children, it is essential to take

507

cognisance of the child's needs, capacities, and potentialities, and to create a harmonious union between his personal aspirations and the country's present and future social needs. It is this balance that provides the means to realize the objective of training children for the management of social life.

4. The program of work of the organization of Pioneers completes the education carried out in the schools. By offering the children their first practical experience of social life, work in the Pioneers deepens the process of social education.[3]

In the Pioneers, the child is not just a passive recipient of social norms and demands, he is actively involved in the life of the group. Within the framework of the organization, the child follows the principles of cooperation and mutual aid in the same way as any responsible adult.

The children are involved in a complex of interpersonal relations which, in general, resemble the system of social relations in society at large, thus foreshadowing their future human relationships. There is a close fellowship between the individual child and the group to which he belongs. Relations between the different groups contribute to the assimilation of social experience, but the development of useful civic activity is acquired through learning the technique of working as a group. By cooperation and collaboration the child widens his experience of life. Yet this concern cannot be separated from the general framework of social relations. Directly or indirectly, this influences not only interpersonal relations but the interpretation and the objectives of the social education given to the child. This is why every organization designed for children—especially political ones—imparts the objectives of the political forces on which they are dependent.[4]

The socialization of children through the intermediary of the organization rests equally on the principles of organizing and of carrying on their own activities. Self-management does not come of itself; it is the outcome of a process which acquires new values at each stage in the growth of the child. Education must intervene to shape habits of self-management. In this context, the educator has the important role of using tact and sympathy to give the child an understanding of the principles of organization, of social life, and the practice of management. This means that the educator must be able to relate, justly and clearly, those activities in which the child is guided by adults and those in which he is self-motivated. When we consider that all children can assimilate knowledge in any sphere at no matter what stage of development,[5] it is not too much to affirm that—by an open system of education—the characteristic principles and habits of social behavior as a future adult can be crystallized during the period of infancy.

5. The organization of the Pioneers of the Socialist Republic of Romania is a proof of the concept that children represent the future of the nation, as is stressed in the program of the Romanian Communist Party. The all-round education of children and their professional, political, moral, and cultural training, as well as their physical development, is the highly responsible duty of the whole society. All important decisions, all programs of development and of education adopted by the political representatives of Romania, have the welfare of the child in view, both now, as a child, and in the future, as a beneficiary of present actions. All political, social, and educational projects aim at the creation of better conditions which can assure a happy life for children (the absence of all material cares, free education, intellectual and cultural development, satisfaction in varied kinds of creative abilities, social

assistance, and free medical care) as well as a secure future through the possibility of the genuine practice of basic human rights.

Children are shaped by a complex system which comprises the school, the family, and other educational institutions, so that they come to understand their present reality and their future. Social and political education takes an important place in this training. For it, we use a large range of procedures, means and methods. Among them, a decisive role is played by children's organizations— such as the Pioneers— which are able to give reality to the educational objectives of Romanian society. Life in these children's organizations aims at the formation of a creative personality with initiative, capable of action, and of the assumption of responsibilities. At the same time the child is assured of a moral and political development with a correct orientation to the world of human values.

The program of work in the Pioneers assigns different social roles to the children in accordance with their social status in the group, thus creating a framework within which they experience rights and duties as members of a society. Membership of the Pioneers is preceded by membership of children between 4 and 7 in the organization "Soimii Patriei." Here, using methods related to this age group, preschool children and those of the first grade are introduced into group life and become aware of social realities.

The social roles played by the children in the Pioneers contribute to the active integration of the individual in society and prepare the children for the roles that will come to them in adult life. Childhood experiences cannot possibly prepare the individual for all the roles he will later have to play; nevertheless, they have the effect of setting the child in situations in which he has to train his capabilities and his inclinations for management and organization and to assimilate the country's culture and social principles. In this way he is enabled to acquire the "human"[6] qualities of a future adult.

The training of a citizen capable of organizing and leading can be carried out just as well in a children's organization as by the traditional means of school teaching. The child acquires the rights which result from being a member of a children's organization.[7] The statutes of the Pioneers contain clauses expressing the special needs and aspirations of children as well as the general objectives of Romanian society.

The child who becomes a Pioneer has the right to elect and be elected to the management bodies of the organization, thus playing the role of a full citizen. This has a theoretical and practical consequence of considerable importance: the child is considered as a full member of society, able to exercise his rights in proportion to his capabilities and to the limits of his knowledge. The old notion that childhood only represents a period of transition to the status of an adult is thus abolished.

Bearing in mind the differences between the stages of childhood, the statute of the organization of Pioneers divides the rights and duties of its members into two phases: 7–10 years and 10–14 years.[7]

The children are familiarized with democratic precepts and put them into practice by participating in the management of their own organization of Pioneers and assuring rights and liberties (freedom of speech, opinion and initiative, and participation in discussing and adopting decisions).

One of the fundamental objectives of the Pioneers is to train children in the process of management so that they may become future organizers and directors of social life. Participation in the life of an organization has a strong influence on the children, especially in their self-education and self-training to develop their own personality.

As members of the Councils of Pioneers Organizations, the children participate together with adults in the debating and working out of decisions related to the management and working programs of the organizations. The principle of collective work and management at all levels of activity is basic to the process of training children in self-management.

On the initiative of President Ceausescu, annual forums of Pioneers are organized where children discuss and take decisions upon their own problems. These constitute active schools for the assimilation and initiation of management and for the development of democracy in the organization of the Pioneers.

The Pioneers are organized in groups, detachments, and units, controlled by leading bodies consisting solely of Pioneers. The program of work is in accordance with the statutes of the organization, and is differentiated according to the age, abilities, and interests of the children. At the level of the groups and detachments, the specific activities are organized by the children acting as organizers, directors, executives, and appraisers. The children discuss and decide upon their own action. They undertake actual roles in social life (in enterprises and on agricultural holdings). They do not just mime them but gain practical experience as an effective training for later life.

The questions raised by the children in their annual forums are made known to society in various ways. The most important is the direct participation of the pioneers in the "Front of the Socialist Union", which represents all the political, civic, and popular organizations of Romania. By this means, the Pioneers are able to make known the questions raised by the children and to work for their solution in a well-defined legal framework.

REFERENCES

1. R. COUSINET, *La vie sociale des enfants, Essai de sociologie enfantine,* Editions de Scarabee, 1959, p. 12.
2. P. A. OSTERRIETH, *Introducere in psihologia copilului* (Introduction to the psychology of the child), Bucharest, 1976, p. 26.
3. V. RADULIAN, Directii si perspective in activitatea organizatiei pionierilor din RSR in *Bazele psihopedagogice ale activitatii pionieresti,* Political Publishing House, Bucharest, 1970, p. 12.
4. C. ROIG and F. BILLON-GRAND, *La socialisation politique des enfants,* Librairie Armand Colir, Paris, 1968.
5. J. BRUNER, *Process of Education,* Harvard University Press, 1960.
6. A. GESELL, *Le jeune enfant dans la civilisation moderne,* P.U.F., Paris, 1967.
7. *Virstele pionieriei,* Political Publishing House, Bucharest, 1977, p. 231.

THE SCHOOL AS AN INSTRUMENT
OF POLITICAL SOCIALIZATION

IOANNIS METAXAS

Faculty of Law, University of Athens, Greece

THE SCHOOL plays a decisive role in the process of political socialization. But, despite its undoubted importance, it does not act alone. It works alongside the family, society, and the mass media. Besides, the school is a more or less formal institution established to enable the older generation to transmit more or less fundamental information to the younger generation. Thus it is primarily an agent of general socialization, not of specifically political socialization. Indeed, in most cases, an overt political role is officially excluded.

I have said that the school's task is to transmit "fundamental information." What is this? In reality it is a basic minimum of social, cultural, and technical instruction, with the aim of "facilitating" the integration of individuals into the life of their society by giving them, not specific knowledge, but a general awareness of potentialities. By this I mean whatever is considered necessary for subsequent specific studies.

In addition to the acquisition of basic information, the school also provides an apprenticeship in the social roles—otherwise called structured behavior—which can help individuals to become active participants in their given social system. In further-ance of its scheme of structural identification, the school is characterized by a system of teaching which is more or less daily imparted by persons whose background in their specialities is more or less uniform, and on the basis of a curriculum that is more or less common to all schools.

Later, I shall touch on the role of the teachers and of the curriculum in the process of political socialization, but here I must stress the fact that teaching in schools is a daily occurrence which means that it has an enduring influence. With this I would like to draw attention to the regular repetitions in the functioning of this institution, justified on both social and economic grounds.

These prefatory remarks are perhaps sufficient to introduce certain essential aspects of the role of the school in the process of political socialization. In this paper, I will limit these to:

(1) The role of the teachers.
(2) The influence of the curriculum.
(3) The role of the "life in school."

THE ROLE OF THE TEACHERS IN POLITICAL SOCIALIZATION

We know that in the process of political socialization it is the role of the father to establish the first "pattern" of authority. Is the role of the teacher any different? At first sight it might seem that the schoolteacher simply extends the "pattern" of authority set by the family. However, there are certain specific differences. The teacher, not being linked to his pupils by a parental tie, represents a model of authority which cannot be called into question by an appeal to affection. This is because the role of a teacher is, in a way, disassociated from his personality. This means that the pupil has to learn to make a distinction between a statutory position and the person who occupies it. The child's father is a somewhat confused "pattern" of authority in which his personality outweighs his position. The teacher is a clearer "pattern" of authority since his position outweighs his personality.

Certainly the pupil is unable to explain that he is aware that his teacher's "position outweighs his personality," and that this is the reason why he obeys his teacher. But he senses that he must obey his teacher more than his father, which means that he understands that the teacher derives his authority from some outside source which is less disputable than the family. This includes an understanding that, while he may have an affection for his teacher, he may not display it because this is "not done." This relationship enables the pupil to cross an important threshold and to pass from a particular relationship (the family) to a more general one (the teacher) and from there to society at large.

What I have said so far only concerns the role of the teacher in general political socialization, not in relation to any particular brand of political opinion. But we shall now examine this aspect.

To recognize what kind of political or social values are being imparted by school-teachers, one must remember that teachers cannot help transmitting a culture that is, in effect, the result of the political socialization they themselves received. This may mean that they only disseminate a former social ideology. Despite the fact that this established ideology has two categories of values—conformist and conflicting—as the recruitment of schoolteachers is usually in the hands of the state, their ideology cannot be very different from that of the ruling regime. For example, in the United States, teachers never fail to extol the virtues of democracy, a two-party system, free enterprise, etc., while generally refusing to discuss social and ethnic conflicts, etc. Thus, in the case of the United States, the role of the teacher in the process of political socialization is essentially conformist. The position is much the same in France, though less pronounced.

In the framework of the secondary schools, where the teachers have greater liberty and the students greater maturity, questions of social conflict can be raised. But we must distinguish between rural and urban environments in this respect, and also take into consideration the different social origins of the teachers themselves, etc. Such so-called "external" conditions exert considerable influence on the direction and style of their teaching.

I have said that, in principle, the role of the teacher is to assure the continuation of the existing political culture. While this is true in general, we must distinguish between those countries (developed and developing) which have more or less "stable" governments and those which are in a process of transition. In the latter, it is probable that the culture transmitted by the schoolteachers is different from the traditional culture. This does not necessarily mean that the two must be in conflict. In most cases it only means that a new conforming culture is temporarily at odds with an old conforming culture.

In certain countries in which the geopolitical and technological conditions impede communication, the role of the village teacher is not confined to the framework of the school. He occupies a relatively elevated social position in the framework of village life. He has a certain prestige and is the representative of a cultural "ideal." In such cases, he not only takes part in political socialization but is often "used" by governments to ensure that the official ideology is implanted and conserved.

THE ROLE OF THE CURRICULUM IN POLITICAL SOCIALIZATION

I move to another aspect of the school: the role played by the curriculum in the process of political socialization. In this context it is useful to distinguish between:

(a) general political education;
(b) civic education;
(c) political "indoctrination."

General political education is based on matters that are not specifically political. That is to say, certain matters have a direct or indirect effect on political attitudes. For example, the teaching of history can effectively ensure that nationalist (or other) ideas are progressively imprinted on the personality of the young people. The glorification of the past in history textbooks may induce "traditional," "patriotic," or "ethnocentric" behavior with consequences for internal and international politics.

Civic education, where it is taught, is intended to inculcate those civic values and basic political attitudes which characterize a "good citizen." In addition, in some cases, civic education seeks to encourage participation of the people in political life. It is always interesting to learn in which cases and for what reasons such encouragement is given or not given. A certain manner of writing, talking, or otherwise expressing oneself can aid or impede such participation. Some countries, which have cast off former autocratic regimes, now encourage the active participation of their citizens in political life, and the school curriculum is oriented in this direction.

Political "indoctrination" seeks to orient the people toward a particular political ideology, which is more or less the official, or legal, ideology of the country. While political indoctrination is not completely absent from the so-called free countries,[1] it is incontestably prevalent in the autocratic regimes. In these countries the aim is to create a more or less standardized political behavior: to create "safe" people. The school has to contribute toward this end, even in the least political subjects, as, for example, physics, which is sometimes represented as due to the genius of a single nationality. We find books claiming specific national achievements, especially in the technological realm. In certain circumstances these have gone so far as to declare that national socialist physics was the only authentic science of physics.

In some countries the textbooks, both in primary and secondary schools, use more drawings and photographs than writing of an informational character. These representations have three characteristics:

(a) an immediate reaction: not inviting criticism;
(b) an optical tangibility: making the object an evident reality;
(c) an emotional esthetic: making an appeal to sensationalism.

One can find many school texts full of pictures of battles, flags, heroic personages, etc. The same effect can be achieved, not only from pictures and photographs but by cartoons and slogans which call for immediate acceptance and interiorization. Some of these slogans are not themselves directly political, but their indirect political effect is obvious. Examples are not hard to find.

However, political socialization via political indoctrination is not always efficacious. In certain autocratic countries one finds that the daily "political brain washing" renders some of the youth indifferent to messages from the authorities. At the same time, these young people become potentially more responsive to books and journals which speak a less monotonous language. The Greek youth under the dictatorship of the colonels (1967–74) offered a striking example. The monotonous cultural messages of the regime induced a radical opposition among the young people in high schools and universities. At the same time, sales of foreign newspapers practically tripled.

The school program in civic education, political education, or political indoctrination, is conditioned by two other factors which need to be taken into consideration, especially in the developing countries.

(a) the level of development;
(b) relations between the socialization taught in the schools and the socialization experienced in the family home.

Concerning the level of development, one must distinguish between the periods of colonization and independence. Under colonization there is an absence of civic socialization and political education; during the period which precedes decolonization, there is an indirectly political attempt to diffuse tranquillizing doctrines; during the transitory phase "toward development," school programs are more or less polemic. This helps to build up a national consciousness, though it does not exclude the risks of a prolonged aggressiveness. Some countries have followed a middle way: while giving verbal affirmation to a certain ethnocentricity, they issue textbooks which express a more balanced and rational point of view. To find which system gives the best results, one needs to make careful local studies.

It is interesting to note that in those developed countries with an authoritarian political structure, the school programs of political indoctrination do not have an exclusive influence. I have mentioned the purchase of foreign books, whose reflection of cosmopolitan opinion can have the effect of indirectly opposing the political indoctrination of the schools. There is also the relation between what is taught in the school and what is practiced in the family circle. If the political socialization in both is similar, no conflict arises. But if they are different a cultural discontinuity,[2] or "traumatic disjunction," is experienced. An interesting study was made in France by L. Wylie. It showed that while the civic and political education in the schools presented the government as composed of sincere, disinterested people, a quite different picture was presented in the home.[3] There, a feeling of distrust for all politicians was expressed, which directly opposed the school approach. Whereas the schoolteaching relied on general, theoretic arguments, the parents recounted actual political, economic, and financial scandals which destroyed the positive images built up in the school. A study of the discontinuity between the political socialization of school and family in the autocratic regimes should be interesting. It is probable that there, too, the daytime political indoctrination of the school is ridiculed in the evening family circle.

THE ROLE OF THE LIFE IN SCHOOL ON POLITICAL SOCIALIZATION

By the life in school we mean all collective activities, ceremonial, pedagogic, and social, as well as all symbolic demonstrations to which the young people are exposed, either constantly or intermittently.

The more or less ceremonial forms of collective activity are the cultural, patriotic, and national festivities, such as celebrations of historic events, parades before the authorities, folk dances, etc. These activities are an efficacious means of socialization, especially when they conform to the two principles of "group dynamics":

(a) synergetic sentiment (the "we feeling");
(b) a message with emotional potential.

The "we felling" is induced when young people act as a group. It gives a sort of legitimacy to their common action. Indeed, a unanimous "we feeling" can exert such a strong social control over a group that it is almost impossible for anyone to escape from it without great difficulty.

The second principle—the emotional potential—is present in all national fetes and ceremonies. Celebrations of historic battles, especially victories over a more powerful enemy which demonstrate "the triumph of justice," induce an active identification with the events celebrated. We can call this identification the process by which an individual apprehends an event through his personal participation in its celebration. Theatrical performances in which the roles are played by the pupils are also examples of active identification. Further, taking part in a heroic play gives rise to far less critical evaluation than reading about the same event in a textbook.

Another aspect of life in school is the attitude displayed toward certain posters, photographs, portraits, landscapes, etc. In some schools, photographs or portraits of the founder or of the head of state are constantly in front of the pupils. Even if the position and importance of the personage is not discussed, this constant view of the picture causes it to be "interiorized." The carefully retouched and discretely smiling face gives the young people a feeling of protection as well as of power. National historic heroes have an even stronger influence that living rulers, because their position in the past reinforces their legendary character, while at the same time removing the possibility of those criticisms that can be associated with a living person. Even beautiful landscapes, which have no apparent political content, can induce a nostalgic feeling leading to a sort of patriotic aestheticism. Such feelings are very efficacious in building support for national and regional plans. To certain emigrants, a picture of a local landscape creates a bond which gives meaning to the more abstract idea of a mother country.

In some cases a "political community"[4] is kept alive by the free distribution to schools of books, flags, cockades, or historical and cultural documents. For example, after the Second World War some countries were literally bombarded by a mass of documents from foreign countries destined for the schoolchildren. These dealt with the principles, values, and merits of the victorious country. They represented a political socialization oriented toward the creation of a homogeneous political climate which would ensure the long term stabilization of a certain political approach. Both the outside and the inside of the booklets were characterized by representations that were both eye catching and simple—even simplistic. The red and blue colors used for "us" and the gray and black used for "the others" were significant.

REFERENCES

1. R. MILIBAND, *The State in Capitalist Society,* Basic Books, 1969, pp. 245–261.
2. P. W. MUSGRAVE, *The Sociology of Education,* 1965, p. 227.
3. L. WYLIE, *Village in the Vaucluse,* Harvard University Press, 1959, p. 207.
4. D. EASTON, *Systems Analysis of Political Life, John Wiley,* 1964, pp. 166–177.

DISCUSSION

P-D. BALSVIK

Provincial Medical Service, Krokelvdalen, Norway

THE POLITICAL orientation of parents belonging to the ruling class is transmitted to their children. Thus, corrupt regimes will not change unless a revolutionary change takes place.

FELIPE HERRERA

Programa de Estudos Conjuntos de Integração de America Latina, Rio de Janeiro, Brazil

I should like to make three comments: (1) I do not agree that the church is necessarily an element of conservative thinking. In Latin America during this last decade, the Catholic Church has become a vital element for social change. (2) In connection with authoritarian governments and the political orientation of the child, we have to make a distinction between those governments who have a clear philosophical orientation, and convey this approach to all the community, and other technocratic governments which are apparently nonpolitical. These blame the former politicians for the present problems of their country, but while doing so, they are pursuing their own politics, generally in the line of avoiding the workings of a democratic system. (3) I think that the political orientation of the children is at present received to a minimal degree in schools. The child's knowledge of the external sociopolitical world is mainly received through the mass media (television, radio, etc.).

NIKOS FAKIOLAS

Ministry of Social Services, Athens, Greece

It is important I think to keep in mind the question of how to establish equal preventive health programs and how to improve health care and education for all children, irrespective of their social or cultural origins. Medical scientists and other health care professionals must try not only to provide health care, but must provide equal health care to all. If a new injection or drug is discovered, or a new and useful technique is introduced, it is a major responsibility to ensure that every person who needs it, gets it, before we re-direct our concerns to another drug or technique.

The parallel contribution, which we could make as social scientists, would be to

517

specify how an appropriate re-allocation, and re-distribution of such basic health resources could best be made available within a community, a society, or a group of societies; and we must consider how we could best continue to play a substantial and optimistic role. After a new health care program has been introduced to a society, for example, it could be useful to meet in order to discuss schemes and techniques for new health and social developments, as well as discuss their implications.

CHAIRMAN'S SUMMARY

Joan Lestor

ONE OF the points that came across very clearly to me was that we learn from mistakes. When we look at the conditions in areas of the third world I hope that their countries represented here are looking for solutions to their problems; and that they will learn from the mistakes that America and many other countries in the West have made. Because if they do not learn from some of those mistakes, much of what we have had presented to us at this conference will be wasted in our search for a better future for the children of tomorrow.

There have been many knocks at politicians and administrators at this conference and I will take them up as I am one of the few politicians here. But I must just remind you that, at the end of the day, the decisions that are taken both in the West and in the third world are going to be political decisions and economic decisions. Therefore, if some of the arguments and some of the propositions that have been put forward here are to be brought to fruition, you have got to get at the politicians and you have got to get at the administrators. I am sorry that more of these were not represented here, because what we have been talking about today will end up in their hands, and if pressure is not put on them to make those decisions and allocate resources in the right way, then the responsibility is as much yours as indeed it is ours.

We were talking about learning from mistakes, and one of the things that has always worried me is that all politicians have really to rely on the views of the experts, of the researchers, of the authorities. When these make mistakes we politicians then have either—if we are honest—to say that we were wrong because we have done what they have said, or—if we are dishonest—to stick to our guns, as, let's face it, many professional people also do, because all of us are reluctant to admit that we were wrong.

I have learnt something else here today. Just before coming here I was handed a letter from my own Home Office. Some of us have taken up the question of children in prison, because it is now the policy in Britain that if a mother goes to prison, if it is humanly possible, she shall have her young child with her up to the age of 5. I have questioned the conditions under which these children live, as have one or two of my colleagues. In the letter the point had been taken about our worry and our concern about the effect of prison life on these children, but we were reminded that many of these children were very young (under the age of 3) and therefore they were unlikely to be affected by the prison surroundings. Well, I have learned here that that is wrong, and I shall go back and make that point very strongly indeed.

I am also concerned about children, who, in my view, have their rights almost totally eroded when they go into the care of the local authority or some other institution. Who speaks for them? They, to my mind, constitute a very grave problem. I am relieved at the way in which attitudes to children who are adopted

519

have changed. Until recently the researchers and the professionals said: "Never tell the child its origins; keep quiet about them." Now, happily, I believe it is accepted that the children have the right to know who their biological parents were. They did not begin to live at the moment they were adopted.

One could go on with other examples, but I think we can conclude that when considering children's rights and the role of politics and the state in regard to children we must all of us work together. It must be a partnership; not one side blaming the other or ensuring that we simply must avoid losing face at all costs.

The point has also been raised in discussion about the rights of ethnic minorities, and I think most countries—my own, the United States and also some in the third world—face a very real problem in the way in which ethnic minorities are exploited for political reasons. This is related to a question, which is a political question: how we run our country. That is to say, to what extent do we allow ethnic minorities to be exploited on the grounds that people have freedom and rights to say what they wish about one another. I do not believe that, and I hope that most people do not believe it either; because if we are going to have a society which takes into account a better world for the children of tomorrow, we have to talk about all our children—the majority of our children and the minorities of our children.

We have to recognize that we must apply all that we know now to meet the challenge of changing conditions. We must be prepared to lose face, but in losing face (as Aubrey Kagan told us) we may also gain more respect as well as a better understanding of the problems of tomorrow.

CONCLUDING SESSION

HENRY R. LABOUISSE
UNICEF, Geneva, Switzerland

As AN old friend of Greece, who has a deep affection for this country, there is an event that I recall with particular pleasure: after the General Assembly of the United Nations proclaimed 1979 as the International Year of the Child and designated UNICEF as the "lead agency" for the year, the first official communication I received was from the Greek Government. Early in 1977 I was informed in a letter from the Minister George Rallis that his country was eager to take positive action in relation to the International Year of the Child and that plans were being made for an international seminar in Athens. The symposium has now taken place. Many of its participants have spent a large part of their lives in the service of children or in related work aimed at improving the quality of life in the diverse societies of our world. I am grateful that they should have come here to share some of their knowledge and experience with each other and with all of us. From the beginning, my greatest concern regarding IYC has been that it should not turn into simply an occasion for declarations of good intentions soon forgotten, and for a series of empty and costly ceremonies. I feel that you have set the right tone by making this a truly working reunion between highly qualified participants, each of them deeply committed towards building a better world for the children of tomorrow.

As you well know, the Year of the Child is for *all* children, in all countries, rich and poor: unfortunately, there are children in desperate need of help even in the most affluent societies. The list of problems affecting children in the industrialized world is, indeed, very long. It goes from inadequate education and nutrition to violence, the use of drugs, the abuse of the young, and to many special problems affecting the children of minorities, of migrants, the handicapped, the orphans, and many others. But, of course, the most colossal and shameful deprivations are suffered by children in the developing countries where three-quarters of the world's children live. Eighty percent of them are without health care, adequate sanitation, and access to clean water. Malnutrition and hunger are still their daily lot, and unless drastic measures are taken, less than half of those children will ever complete even primary education.

This dramatic situation was emphasized at the meeting of representatives from developing countries which took place under the auspices of UNICEF and WHO, during the week preceding your symposium. The report on that workshop, drafted by an old friend whom I greatly admire, Dr. Harfouche of Lebanon, describes in striking terms the condition of children in the developing world and some innovative approaches toward improving it. I feel very strongly that a special emphasis of the Year of the Child should be on helping the children who are most deprived and that there should be an increased cooperation between affluent and poor countries to save the generations to come from the same miseries.

I do not need to tell this audience how vast is the task to be done. It will require the combined efforts of all governments, of many national and international agencies and—most important—the active participation of the deprived populations themselves in innovative community programs of self-help. Big as the task is, I profoundly believe that it can be accomplished and that a very significant advance can be made toward meeting the essential needs of all children by the year 2000.

We have evidence, for example, that a large number of developing countries—as a result of their own aspirations and stimulated by IYC—will be setting higher targets in fairly specific terms toward improving as soon as possible the condition of their children. We also have some evidence that significant increases in external assistance will be forthcoming in the years ahead.

In the 37 years of its existence, the United Nations Children's Fund has focused its efforts on assisting programs benefiting children and also on acting as the children's advocate in the field of development. For us, in a sense, every year has been, and will be, the Year of the Child. But our resources are limited and we well know that, by necessity, the part we play is not very large.

I should like, in conclusion, to recall in very simple terms what I conceive to be the objectives of the Year of the Child:

— it is an invitation to all governments to review the situation of their children and to develop a greater awareness, at all levels of their nation, of their children's needs;

— it is an encouragement to governments to draft plans and set realistic goals for the improvement of services benefiting children;

— it is a recommendation for starting the execution of those plans, hopefully with the aid of increased resources.

We should like the accent to be put on action—a review of legislation, the launching of new services, more experimental projects at the grass roots level—and more assistance from affluent countries to the children of the developing world. This is the reason why it was decided to put the emphasis on national action rather than on a worldwide conference.

You, of this symposium, in discussing many fundamental aspects of the task before us, have magnificently contributed toward launching the Year on its proper tracks and helping it to have its desired impact. I congratulate you once again—and, on behalf of the Children of Tomorrow I thank you with all my heart.

MARCELO SELOWSKY
Development Economics Department, the World Bank, Washington DC, USA

IT IS not easy to summarize a symposium like this, and perhaps we should not attempt to—it is hard to find a meeting with more difficult terms of reference, since we have three elements interacting: the future—and it is very difficult to predict the future; the interdisciplinary nature of the problem; and the variety of countries involved. I do have, however, some "on the spot" reactions that I should like to convey with the help of some examples.

First, it is crucial when addressing an issue like this, to separate our views as individuals with certain ideals, from our views as professionals who must advise in a particular context. As professionals we have to take certain constraints as given and try to make the best of the situation. This does not mean that we are not in favor of change, but that, as professionals, we sometimes must accept certain trends as given.

Let me give an example: some views were of the opinion that before making statements about improving the status of children we had first to reach a concensus on the type of society we want children to live in, in the future. I am afraid that a lot of children live, and will live, in societies where few social developments will take place in the future. We do have to be prepared to say something about children in these societies; in other words, we have to be prepared to identify policy options in a world of constraints.

Some of these basic trends—or "givens," that will characterize future societies have been mentioned here. It is useful to summarize them: in the richer countries we expect changes in the institutions of union and marriage; children leaving home earlier; smaller numbers of children per family; children living in environments where adults are becoming the majority; an increased exposure to information, domestically and internationally; a strong increase in the cost of schooling and housing and an increased pressure for recreational space. Rich countries also continue to have a problem of minority groups, and evidence shows that the relative position of minority groups has not improved as much as we would have liked.

I now turn to trends in developing countries—and 80% of the children live in developing countries. A high population growth in the low income groups will most likely prevail through the next couple of decades. Indeed, our estimates show that the number of malnourished children will not decline—percentage-wise they will, but not in absolute numbers. Our evidence also shows that it will be difficult, at least in most market economies, to expect strong changes in the distribution of income and that mortality and infectious diseases will prevail in large sections of the population.

Given these trends, how do we identify policy interventions specifically geared to improve children's well being? Such an identification requires two stages of interdisciplinary concensus, (1) What specific dimensions of children's welfare we want to change and what indicators do we use to measure this change? (2) What is the optimal mix of policy interventions influencing these indicators?

All of this sounds perhaps too academic. Let me again use some examples: assume, that on the first stage, we agree that the welfare implications of children's malnutrition is our first concern. Can we reach a concensus on how to measure malnutrition? Should we measure it by the amount of food or calorie intake, or by height or weight?

Or should we measure it in terms of its effect on indices of psychological achievement? As an economist I cannot answer these questions: physicians and psychologists have to provide the information on the psychological and medical effects of a 100 or 300 per day caloric deficit so other scientists can take calories as the point of intervention. But still—even within the medical field—there is big debate concerning physiological calorie requirement, even for individuals of the same age, weight, and living in the same climate.

Having reached a consensus on the indicator we want to change, the mix of policy variables to be chosen will depend, first, on the net effect of these variables on the indicator and, second, on the cost of changing that policy variable. These are perhaps one of the most fertile areas of interdisciplinary collaboration.

Let me again illustrate this with an example. Assume our objective is to improve, in a particular context, the performance of children in a battery of achievement tests. We want a research methodology able to separate the net effect of different variables on those scores. One of the best studies of this kind, and I was surprised not to hear it mentioned here, is the International Study of Educational Achievement. This study attempted to explain achievement scores in 19 countries in terms of a series of variables: quality of teachers, reading material, home environment, family background, etc. This allows the identification of the effect of each variable and a choice of policy interventions based on the relative cost of each intervention.

The above illustrates the fact that we do have a methodology to identify the optimal degree of intervention in each policy variable. I felt somehow disappointed when, in the first sessions, a heated debate presented the relative merits of home environment relative to compensatory education almost as a conflict. I see this in terms of a trade off rather than a conflict. There is an optimal mix of the two interventions and it will depend on the particular society we are talking about and on the relative cost of these interventions.

In this short presentation I have tried to spell out some kind of scientific language that could be conducive to greater interdisciplinary collaboration. This is fundamental for a better understanding of the complex issues posed by this conference.

TARZIE VITTACHI
UN FUnd for Population Activities, New York, NY, USA

THE WORLD of tomorrow is an invisible reality. Today's need is how to make the invisible visible. Action for change must be made now, and thinking for change must begin now. This is the responsibility of all of us—teachers, doctors, trade and professional associations, medics.

Did we achieve this at the symposium? Yes and No. A beginning of an urgent process was made, but did we devise "a window into the future" as Dr. Spyros Doxiadis wanted, or was it a mirror of the past? Perhaps it was a bit of both, because wisdom is the ability to see the future retrospectively.

Do we leave with even a rudimentary program for action as Dr. Doxiadis hoped? If so, is it any different from what we brought here? On the positive side of the balance sheet, we have:

(a) The fact that the conference was held at all.
(b) The great Athenian synoptic view and inspiration offered us by the President of Greece and Dr. Spyros Doxiadis.
(c) The general recognition that the present is in a state of rapid transition. The pace of change has accelerated; but trend is not destiny.
(d) The appreciation (shown by Psomopoulos, Aldrich, Duhl, Carlson, and others) of the need to consider the design for tomorrow as a process and to consider the environment as a whole so as to make a world fit for a child to live in.
(e) The realization (inspired mostly by Cravioto) that poverty is not a problem of the poor world alone, but an urgent problem for all.
(f) The recognition that food and nutrition, health, and population problems are primarily a question of distribution.

On the negative side, the questions I have are:

(a) Did we give sufficient attention to the "inner environment," to the content of change? The values which must influence and determine the nature of that change were neglected, probably because values smack of philosophy, and—even in Athens—philosophy is suspect. We need to change from competition to cooperation, from aggression to consideration, from independence to interdependence, from rights to obligations, from expansionism to conservation, from quantity to quality.
(b) We have succeeded in talking for five and a half days about the world of tomorrow with scarcely a mention of the $400 billion—more than a billion a day—being spent on armaments: a reality which makes any future at all a very doubtful proposition.
(c) We have failed to recognize in any positive way that, if the world survives to 2000, the order of magnitude of population, cities, and countries will be very different from what is familiar today. This means a radical change of institutions in a progressively distorted world.
(d) Too many of the talks looked at children as pathological subjects or as empty sacks to be stuffed with "education." The possibility that education should be

a process of drawing out the sense of continuum within a child was not considered at all. We have not been considering sufficiently the pathology of the world—our present world—in which tomorrow's children are being raised.

(e) We should have spoken here as parents rather than as experts. We are experts at solving other people's problems. The relationship between experts and their own children would make a fascinating study.

(f) The bleak lack of interest on the part of the international press.

On balance, I would not have missed this symposium for anything, and my hope is that we may be able to meet again next year as a smaller group and consider what action we can take immediately—as parents, as professionals, as power points in politics, and administration—to bring about those changes which will make tomorrow's world fit for a child to live in.

LEON EISENBERG
Department of Psychiatry, Harvard Medical School, Boston, MA, USA

ATHENS is a particularly appropriate locus for a symposium on the child as the major ideas of Western science were philosophically anticipated by the philosophers Thales, Anaxamander, and Anaximines, and the basic ideas of philosophy are to be found in the works of Socrates, Plato, and Aristotle. I would call to mind a particular comment (which I think I have approximately correct) that Aristotle made in his book on *Politics*: namely, that laws should not demand of men behavior they cannot attain, any more than standards of height should exceed human stature. I think the goals we have to set have to be in keeping with the nature of man.

We also respect the ideas of Athenian democracy, which flowered because it was expected that every citizen would participate to some extent in government. Government was not to be left to the politicians. Though some were to rule the state, they were to be advised by the citizens. We also remember that the Athenian democracy failed, and failed for at least two reasons. First, that it depended upon the large underclass of slaves, and no society can so succeed; second, that the Athenians themselves, as they attained affluence, began to disregard their responsibility for the welfare of the state. The relevance of this to the theme of the conference is, as several people have pointed out, that politics underlie the control and allocation of resources which determine the future of children. Everything we have said here has to be couched in terms that deal with the reality of politics.

At times, this symposium became a battle of tongues. The problem was not translation between languages, but difficulty with people using the same words within their own language to mean different things. Let me take up a few of those words.

Statistics: there will be no hope for the children of the world and no way of planning facilities unless we get accurate estimates of numbers and needs and unless we use numbers to evaluate proposals. Mere numeration can ignore individual human reality, but without numbers we cannot devise programs to help people.

Research: is research an excuse for inaction? ("We don't know enough; therefore, let's not do anything.") Or is research a guide for action? Unless one has data, having a good heart is really not enough. It is not necessary to do research to determine that hungry children should be fed. On the other hand, it is a serious and difficult question, when resources are limited, to determine what is a minimally adequate diet and how to make sure that food gets to the children who need it and is not bled off in a variety of other ways. Major errors in policy have been made by the lack of scientific knowledge on the part of the people who intended to help children. One of the worst disasters in South America was fostered by INCAP because it gave out dehydrated food for infants without thinking about the contaminated water it would be mixed with. It was not an American drug company that made that mistake. You have to know what you are doing, and for that you need accurate information. If we do not examine what has been done, we are condemned to repeat the errors of the past.

Expert: are experts a self-perpetuating elite or do they have special knowledge which is useful? Opposed to the expert is the "common man" or "woman." Some speakers have tended to celebrate the wisdom of the common man or woman. But common men and women, in parts of the world where information is limited, may deny their children what the children should have (and what they would want their children to have if they understood). I would suggest to you that, while the experts are not to be trusted all the way down the line, let us not make the mistake of romanticizing common wisdom. Sometimes that wisdom is there; sometimes it is not. Experts are best regarded as navigators of ships. You entrust them with the job of guiding you through the shoals, but the people decide where they want the ship to go. The matter of control should rest with people in a democratic way, but experts can help the people to achieve the goals they seek.

Parents: there were complaints that not enough parents were represented here, but as a parent and a grandparent, I am insulted in being considered as not having been represented. Parents, however, face a very serious problem. That is, parental care in a traditional hunter-gatherer neolithic society is totally adequate for survival in that society today, but the old ways do not work when social changes place demands which are incompatible with the old ways. It is our job as experts to help people who are going through rapid transitions to learn as much as possible, so that they can then decide for themselves how to adjust to a changing world. We should not make the mistake of sentimentalizing or romanticizing everything that goes on in the third world. There are countries whose resources are usurped by a small power elite, and there are parts of the third world where ethnic hatred is even more marked than in the developed world. There is an enormous difference between Tanzania and Zambia; between Costa Rica and Uruguay; between the People's Republic of China and Taiwan; between Cuba and Haiti—so let us not agglomerate such very different societies under one general title.

Having acknowledged, as we have throughout this meeting, many problems of infant and child mortality and malnutrition, what priorities can we set forth? The developing nations workshop listed a number of priorities which I will paraphrase.

(1) Recognition of the mother as the primary health care provider. Dr. Haggerty's data from the United States showed that most health care is provided by the mother even in a country where there are plenty of doctors around. In the third world, care is provided by the mother or there is no care at all. We must help mothers to become more effective through better health care education and by giving mothers the elementary resources for supplying care to their children. It is not enough to know that a child with diarrhoea needs rehydration if there are no means with which to rehydrate the child.

(2) Health care in the developing world can only be based on the training of indigenous primary health care workers. The worst thing that could happen to the third world would be to imitate the pattern of the United States, just when we are coming to realize the misfortunes associated with that pattern of overdependence on superspecialization. Primary health care is the scheme of the future. It has been developed with enormous skill in China, in Tanzania, and in several other countries. However, it is often opposed in developing countries by the professional elites within those countries. I have had some colleagues try to help an African country plan a health care education system based on primary health care workers, only to find that the local doctors want to duplicate more of themselves, and the local leaders want to squander their

health resources upon a large hospital in the capital city (which of course will take care of them and their own children should they get sick).

Maternal and child care services must include family planning. And I would like to end this résumé with a point that was made not quite in these terms in the summary of the third world workshop (p. 105): improving the conditions of women and expanding their participation for full decision making in the society is at the centre of defending children's rights. They cannot be defended without defending women's rights.

Now what about the other side of the coin? What of the developed or the industrial world? I will make only two points. Several speakers have pointed out that affluence is no guarantee of healthy personality development and indeed it is not. My first suggestion is to challenge children and adolescents in affluent societies by giving them the opportunity to join the human crusade against disease, poverty, and ignorance in their countries and in other countries. Only if children have a super-personal goal—something that matters beyond their own personal gain—can they become fully human.

What we need is what the American philosopher William James called "the moral equivalent of war ." He pointed out that in time of war, nations rally and unite in their effort. A war against poverty—a moral war— could indeed bring about that sense of union.

My second suggestion is that the developed world can make research contributions to the clarification of issues. Professor Rutter has been doing work on the quality of schooling that affects outcome. His studies in London show that, at least with respect to the behavior of delinquent adolescents, the school environment makes a decisive difference.

It turns out that what matters are the personal relationships, leadership, organization, concern, and factors like that, and not how many years of schooling the teachers have had, or the physical quality of the building *per se.*

We need to know more about the optimal conditions for early development. We have heard a bit about the excellent research of Dr. Barbara Tizard. Professor Jack Tizard has contributed enormously to understanding the problems of the handicapped child, which transcend national boundaries. Finally, Joaquin Cravioto has given us an example of research in a developing nation that is of benefit to all of us.

I will end with a call for optimism. I do not mean the optimism that things will work out for the best in the best of all possible worlds, automatically and on their own. They don't and they won't. I mean an optimism that identifies problems clearly, in order to overcome them, an optimism based on the belief that mankind, in the world of Protagoras, is the measure of all things; that man sets himself only such problems as he can solve; and that ordinary men and women, the world over, have the energy and the genius to create a world of justice and equity.

There is an old Chinese folktale of which Mao Tse Tung was fond. It is the story of a foolish old man in his seventies who was seen every day going to the top of the mountain and digging away with a small spade. When his neighbors asked the foolish old man what he was doing, he said "I am levelling the mountain because it shuts off the sun from the valley." People laughed at him as an absurd person, but he said: "After me, my sons and their sons and their grandsons will dig at this mountain, and some day there will be no mountain blocking the sun from the people." It is that kind of optimism that I refer to.

Let me conclude with a favorite quotation of mine, this time not from a Greek philosopher but from the Rabinical scholar, Hillel, who posed three question:

(1) If I am not for myself, who will be for me?
(2) If I am for myself alone, what am I?
(3) If not now, when?

His words remind us that if we are to improve our human condition we must act for ourselves and not wait for others; that if we are to achieve full humanity, we must regard others as not less than ourselves; that, life being brief at best (and today altogether uncertain), we must act now or there will be no tomorrow. This is a heavy charge, indeed, but one that is an inescapable part of being human.

LIST OF PARTICIPANTS QUOTED IN TEXT

ALDRICH, Robert A., Medical Center, University of Colorado, Denver, CO, USA

ALLISON, Patricia, National Institute of Mental Health, Adelphi, MD, USA

AMIRA, Anna, National Center of Social Research, Athens, Greece

ANTHONY, E. James, Edison Child Development Research Center, Washington University, St. Louis, MO, USA

APLEY, John, Bristol Royal Hospital for Sick Children, Bristol, UK

ASSEFI, Assefe, Association des Parents et des Educateurs, Teheran, Iran

AZUMA, Hiroshi, Department of Education, University of Tokyo, Japan

BAASHER, T. A., WHO Regional Office for the Eastern Mediterranean, Alexandria, Egypt

BALSVIK, P-D., Provincial Medical Service, Krokelvdalen, Norway

BARNETT, Marian, Department of Education, Carleton University, Ottawa, Canada

BAYLEY, John, Victoria Town and Country Planning Board, Melbourne, South Australia

BAYLEY, Margaret, Social Worker, Melbourne, South Australia

BECKER, Ulrich, World Council of Churches, Geneva, Switzerland

BOTTANI, Norberto, Center for Educational Research and Innovation, OECD, Paris, France

BRAJOVIC, C., Department of Psychology, University of Belgrade, Yugoslavia

BRAZELTON, T. Berry, Harvard Medical School, Boston, MA, USA

BURKE, Peter, Department of History, University of Sussex, Brighton, UK

CARLSON, Rick J., Commonweal Inc., Bolinas, CA, USA

CHIBA, Akihiro, Education Section, UNESCO, Paris, France

CHUN, Yeong Ja, College of Medicine, Korea University, Seoul, Korea

COHEN, Bernard E., Chaim Sheba Medical Center, Savyon, Israel

COOPER, Christine, Department of Child Health, University of Newcastle upon Tyne, UK

CRAVIOTO, Joaquin, Instituto Nacional de Ciencias y Technología de la Salud del Niño, Mexico City, Mexico

DAILEY, Timothy B., Department of Sociology, Clarkson College, New York, NY, USA

DARILLIS, E. E., University Pediatric Clinic, Aghia Sophia Hospital, Athens, Greece

DAVIS, Leonard, School of Social Work, Brunel University, Bucks., UK

DE BERNIS, G. D., University of Social Sciences, Grenoble, France

DE FIGUEROA, Teresa Orrego, Consultant in Sociology, Santiago, Chile

DIAMANTIDIS, Anastase, UN Environment Program, Geneva, Switzerland

DIMARAS, Alexis, Moraitis High School, Athens, Greece

DIX, Gerald, Department of Civic Design, University of Liverpool, UK

HERRERA, Felipe, Programa de Estudos Conjuntos de Intergração de America Latina, Rio de Janeiro, Brazil

HICKMAN, Mary L., Central Valley Regional Medical Center, Fresno, CA, USA

HOFVANDER, Yngve, Akademiska Sjukhuset, Uppsala, Sweden

IATRIDIS, Demitrius, Department of Social Planning, Boston College, MA, USA

ILLSLEY, Raymond, Department of Sociology, University of Aberdeen, Scotland, UK

JEFFERY, Margaret, Clinical Psychologist, Perth, Western Australia

KAGAN, Aubrey, Laboratory for Clinical Stress Research, Stockholm, Sweden

KAPUSTYAN, A. M., Pediatric Institute of Scientific Research, Moscow, USSR

KATZ, Alfred H., School of Public Health, University of California at Los Angeles, CA, USA

KATZ, Edith, Committee of the International Year of the Child, Paris, France

KELLER, Suzanne, Department of Sociology, Princeton University, NJ, USA

KELLMER-PRINGLE, Mia, National Children's Bureau, London, UK

KIOSSOGLOU, Angela, Biologist, Athens, Greece

KOLIOPOULOS, John X., National Ophthalmic Center, Athens, Greece

KOMLOSI, Sandor, Teacher Training College, Pecs, Hungary

LABOUISSE, Henry R., UNICEF, Geneva, Switzerland

LESTOR, Joan, House of Commons, London, UK

LIANTONAKIS, E. N., State Mental Hospital, Athens, Greece

LIPSITT, Lewis P., School of Medicine, Brown University, Providence, RI, USA

LOURIE, R. S., School of Medicine, George Washington University, Washington DC, USA

LÜSCHER, Karl, Department of Sociology, University of Konstanz, Federal Republic of Germany

MADIANOU, Dimitra, Psychiatric University Clinic, Aginition Hospital, Athens, Greece

MAGHADAM, F. Moezi, Institute for the Intellectual Development of Children and Young Adults, Teheran, Iran

MANCIAUX, Michel, International Children's Center, Paris, France

MANGANARA, Ioanna, Pantios Higher School of Political Science, Athens, Greece

McDOUGALL, J. F., International Year of the Child Secretariat, Geneva, Switzerland

McGUCKEN, R. B., Wesley Guild Hospital, Lagos, Nigeria

McKEOWN, Thomas, Department of Social Medicine, University of Birmingham, UK

MEAD, Margaret, American Museum of Natural History, New York, NY, USA (died 14 November 1978)

METAXAS, Ioannis, Faculty of Law, University of Athens, Greece

MICHELSON, William, Department of Sociology, University of Toronto, Canada

MILLER, Carol, Central School of Speech and Drama, London, UK

MORFI, H., Pati Morfi Nursery School, Athens, Greece

MULTINATIONAL WOMEN'S LIBERATION GROUP, Athens, Greece

MURPHY, Earl Finbar, College of Law, Ohio State University, OH, USA

NICHOLSON, Simon, Oxford Research Unit, The Open University, Oxford, UK

NIKOLINAKOS, Marios, Department of Economics, Free University of Berlin, Federal Republic of Germany

NOEL, A., Service de Médecine Scolaire, Brussels, Belgium

OSTROWSKA, Antonina, Institute of Philosophy and Sociology, Polish Academy of Sciences, Warsaw, Poland

PALEOKRASSAS, Ioannis, Ministry of Coordination, Athens, Greece

PAPADATOS, Constantine, School of Medicine, University of Athens, Greece

PAPADOPOULOS, J. S., Evangelismos Medical Center, Athens, Greece

PAPAEVANGELOU, George, School of Hygiene, Athens, Greece

PASSIOS, Dorothea, Miller Children's Hospital Medical Center, Longbeach, CA, USA

PAVELLA, M., Ministry of Agriculture, Athens, Greece

PETROS-BARVAZIAN, Angele, WHO, Geneva, Switzerland

PRESVELOU, Clio, Department of Sociology, Catholic University of Louvain, Belgium

PSOMOPOULOS, P., Athens Center of Ekistics, Greece

RAIMBAULT, Ginette, Hôpital des Enfants Malades, Paris, France

RAJENDRAN, M. M., Ministry of Social Welfare, New Delhi, India

RAMANUJAM, B. K., BM Institute of Public Health, New Delhi, India

RANSOME-KUTI, R., Basic Health Services Scheme, Lagos, Nigeria

RAPHAEL, Marios, Graduate School of Industrial Studies, Piraeus, Greece

RAPOPORT, Amos, Department of Architecture, University of Wisconsin at Milwaukee, WI, USA

RAUNDALEN, M., Institute of Psychology, University of Bergen, Norway

RAUNDALEN, T., Institute of Psychology, University of Bergen, Norway

REINPRECHT, Hans Heinz, SOS Children's Villages, Vienna, Austria

RHODES, Philip, Regional Postgraduate Institute for Medicine, Newcastle upon Tyne, UK

RIKAKI, Athena, Red Balloon Adventure Playgrounds and Environmental Studies, Athens, Greece

RIKAKI, Lukia, Red Balloon Adventure Playgrounds and Environmental Studies, Athens, Greece

RITCHIE, James, School of Social Sciences, University of Waikato, New Zealand

ROBINS, Lee N., Department of Sociology, Washington University, St. Louis, MO, USA

ROBINSON, Mary E., National Institute of Mental Health, East Adelphi, MD, USA

ROCHAS, Helen, Regional Center for the Development of Education, Fresno, CA, USA

RUTTER, Michael, Institute of Psychiatry, University of London, UK

SAKELLAROPOLOS, P., Pati Morfi Nursery School, Athens, Greece

SCHIFIRNET, Constantine, Research Center for Youth Problems, Bucharest, Romania

SEELEY, John, Charles R. Drew Postgraduate Medical School, Los Angeles, CA, USA

SEIDEL, Henry M., School of Medicine, Johns Hopkins University, Baltimore, MD, USA

SELOWSKY, Marcelo, Development Economics Department, the World Bank, Washington DC, USA

SEPULVEDA, Claudio, UN Asian and Pacific Development Institute, Bangkok, Thailand

SHARMAN, Eileen, The Film Study Committee, Brighton, South Australia

SIMOPOULOS, Artemis P., National Institute of Health, Bethesda, MD, USA

SINGLETON, A. F., Martin Luther King General Hospital, Los Angeles, CA, USA

SJÖLIN, Stig, Department of Pediatrics, University of Uppsala, Sweden

SOYSA, Priyani, Faculty of Medicine, University of Sri Lanka, Colombo, Sri Lanka

STAPLETON, Thomas, School of Medicine, University of Sydney, Australia

STERKY, Göran, Department of Pediatrics, Karolinska Institute, Stockholm, Sweden

STORES, Gregory, Park Hospital for Children, Oxford, UK

STROUD, C. Eric, King's College Hospital Medical School, University of London, UK

TAN, Mely G., Indonesian Institute of Sciences, Jakarta, Indonesia

THANOPOULOU, Katherine, Greek Library Association, Athens, Greece

THORNBERG, J. Muntanola i, Department of Architecture, University of Barcelona, Spain

TIZARD, Barbara, Institute of Education, University of London, UK

TIZARD, Jack, Institute of Education, University of London, UK

TRIPP, Anthy, National Institute of Mental Health, Adelphi, MD, USA

TSATSOS, Constantine, President of the Hellenic Republic

TSIANTIS, John, Aghia Sophia Children's Hospital, Athens, Greece

VALMAN, H. B., Northwich Park Hospital, Harrow, UK

VAN BENTUM, A. J., Foundation K & O, The Hague, Netherlands

VAN DER DOES, V. I., International Federation for Pedestrians, The Hague, Netherlands

VELTICHEV, Yu. E., Pediatric Institute for Scientific Research, Moscow, USSR

VITTACHI, Tarzie, UN Fund for Population Activities, New York, USA

VON EULER, Rigmor, Swedish Save the Children Federation, Stockholm, Sweden

WAGNER, M. G., WHO, Copenhagen, Denmark

WARD, Alan J., Henry Horner Children's Center, Chicago, IL, USA

WOLSTENHOLME, Sir Gordon, The CIBA Foundation, London, UK

YAKER, Annette A., National Institute of Public Health, Algiers, Algeria

ZEIDENSTEIN, George, The Population Council, New York, NY, USA

INDEX